AUSTRIA

M. Hertlein/MICHELIN

"Land of mountains, land on the river,
Land of fields, land of cathedrals,
Land of hammers, rich in outlook!
You are the native home of great sons,
A people uniquely gifted for the beautiful,
Much applauded Austria."
Austrian National Anthem
(Translation of original text by Paula von Preradović)

Executive Editorial Director David Brabis
Chief Editor Cynthia Clayton Ochterbeck

THE GREEN GUIDE AUSTRIA

Editor Gwen Cannon
Principal Writer Andrea Schulte-Peevers
Production Coordinator Allison Michelle Simpson
Cartography Alain Baldet, Andre Prevault, Peter Wrenn
Photo Editor Lydia Strong
Proofreader Connor Morrison
Layout & Design Tim Schulz, Frank Ladd
Cover Design Laurent Muller, Ute Weber

Contact Us: The Green Guide
Michelin Maps and Guides
One Parkway South
Greenville, SC 29615
USA
☎ 1-800-423-0485
www.michelintravel.com
michelin.guides@us.michelin.com

Michelin Maps and Guides
Hannay House
39 Clarendon House
Watford, Herts WD17 1JA
☎ (01923) 205 240
travelpubsales@uk.michelin.com

Special Sales: For information regarding bulk sales,
customized editions and premium sales,
please contact our Customer Service
Departments:
USA   1-800-423-0485
UK   (01923) 205 240
Canada 1-800-361-8236

Note to the reader
While every effort is made to ensure that all information printed in this guide is correct and up-to-date, Michelin Maps and Guides (Michelin Tyre PLC, Michelin North America, Inc.) accepts no liability for any direct, indirect or consequential losses howsoever caused so far as such can be excluded by law.

One Team …
A Commitment to Quality

There's just one reason our team is dedicated to producing quality travel publications—you, our reader. We want you to get the maximum benefit from your trip—and from your money. In today's multiple-choice world of travel, the options are many, perhaps overwhelming.

In our guidebooks, we try to minimize the guesswork involved with travel. We scout out the attractions, prioritize them with star ratings, and describe what you'll discover when you visit them.

To help you orient yourself, we provide colorful and detailed, but easy-to-follow maps. Floor plans of some of the cathedrals and museums help you plan your tour.

Throughout the guides, we offer practical information, touring tips and suggestions for finding the best views, good places for a break and the most interesting shops.

Lodging and dining are always a big part of travel, so we compile a selection of hotels and restaurants that we think convey the feel of the destination, and organize them by geographic area and price. We also highlight shopping, recreational and entertainment venues, especially the popular spots.

If you're short on time, driving tours are included so you can hit the highlights and quickly absorb the best of the region.

For those who love to experience a destination on foot, we add walking tours, often with a map. And we list other companies who offer boat, bus or guided walking tours of the area, some with culinary, historical or other themes.

In short, we test and retest, check and recheck to make sure that our guidebooks are truly just that: a personalized guide to help you make the most of your visit. After all, we want you to enjoy traveling as much as we do.

The Michelin Green Guide Team

PLANNING YOUR TRIP

INTRODUCTION TO AUSTRIA

SYMBOLS

🔣 **Tips to help improve your experience**
🔣 **Details to consider**
🔣 **Entry Fees**
🔣 **Walking tours**
🔣 **Closed to the public**
🕐 **Hours of operation**
🕐 **Periods of closure**

CONTENTS

DISCOVERING AUSTRIA

5

HOW TO USE THIS GUIDE

Orientation

To help you grasp the "lay of the land" quickly and easily, so you'll feel confident and comfortable finding your way around the region, we offer the following tools in this guide:

- Detailed table of contents for an overview of what you'll find in the guide, and how it is organized.
- Map of Austria at the front to the guide, with the principal sights highlighted for easy reference.
- Detailed maps for major cities and villages, including driving tour maps and larger-scale maps for walking tours.
- Map of Regional Driving Tours.

Practicalities

At the front of the guide, you'll see a section called "Planning Your Trip" that contains information about planning your trip, the best time to go, different ways of getting to the region and getting around, basic facts and tips for making the most of your visit. You'll find driving and themed tours, and suggestions for outdoor fun. There's also a calendar of popular annual events. Information on shopping, sightseeing, kids' activities and sports and recreational opportunities is also included.

LODGINGS

We've made a selection of hotels and arranged them within the cities, categorized by price category to fit all budgets (see the Legend at the back of the guide for an explanation of the price categories). For the most part, we selected accommodations based on their unique regional quality, their typical Austrian feel, as it were. So, unless the individual hotel or bed & breakfast embodies local ambience, it's rare that we include chain properties, which normally have their own imprint. If you want a more comprehensive selection of Austrian accommodations, see the red-cover *Michelin Guide Osterreich*.

RESTAURANTS

We thought you'd like to know the popular eating spots in the country. So we selected restaurants that capture the Austrian experience—those that have a unique regional flavor and local atmosphere. We're not rating the quality of the food per se. As we did with the hotels, we selected restaurants for many towns and villages, categorized by price to appeal to all wallets. If you want a more comprehensive selection of dining recommendations in the region, see the red-cover *Michelin Guide Osterreich*.

Attractions

Principal Sights are arranged alphabetically. Within each Principal Sight, attractions for each town, village, or geographical area (such as the Kaunertal Valley) are divided into local Sights or Walking Tours, nearby Excursions to sights outside the town, or detailed Driving Tours—suggested itineraries for seeing several attractions around a major town. Contact information, admission charges and hours of operation are given for the majority of attractions. Unless otherwise noted, admission prices shown are for a single adult only. Discounts for seniors, students, teachers, etc. may be available; be sure to ask. If no admission charge is shown, entrance to the attraction is free.

If you're pressed for time, we recommend you visit the three- and two-star sights first: the stars are your guide.

STAR RATINGS

Michelin has used stars as a rating tool for more than 100 years:

★★★	Highly recommended
★★	Recommended
★	Interesting

SYMBOLS IN THE TEXT

Besides the stars, other symbols in the text indicate tourist information ⓘ; wheelchair access ♿; on-site eating facilities ✗; camping facilities △; on-site parking Ⓟ; sights of interest to children Kids; and beaches ◠.

See the box appearing on the Contents page for other symbols used in the text.

See the Maps explanation below for symbols appearing on the maps.

Throughout the guide you will find peach-coloured text boxes or sidebars containing anecdotal or background information. Green-coloured boxes contain information to help you save time or money.

Maps

All maps in this guide are oriented north, unless otherwise indicated by a directional arrow. See the map Legend at the back of the guide for an explanation of other map symbols. A complete list of the maps found in the guide appears at the back of this book.

Addresses, phone numbers, opening hours and prices published in this guide are accurate at press time. We welcome corrections and suggestions that may assist us in preparing the next edition. Please send your comments to:

Michelin Maps and Guides
Hannay House
39 Clarendon Road
Watford, Herts WD17 1JA
UK
travelpubsales@uk.michelin.com
www.michelin.co.uk

Michelin Maps and Guides
Editorial Department
P.O. Box 19001
Greenville, SC   29602-9001
USA
michelin.guides@us.michelin.com
www.michelintravel.com

Principal sights

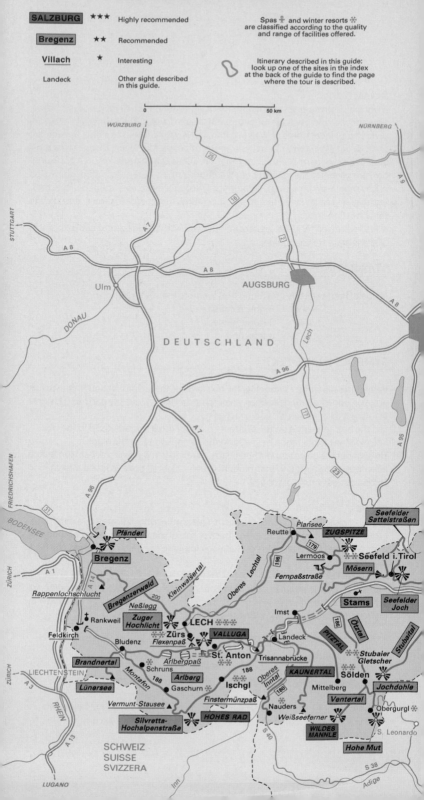

SALZBURG ★★★ Highly recommended

Bregenz ★★ Recommended

Villach ★ Interesting

Landeck — Other sight described in this guide.

Spas ⚓ and winter resorts ❋ are classified according to the quality and range of facilities offered.

Itinerary described in this guide: look up one of the sites in the index at the back of the guide to find the page where the tour is described.

0   50 km

WÜRZBURG   NÜRNBERG

STUTTGART

Ulm

AUGSBURG

DONAU

D E U T S C H L A N D

FRIEDRICHSHAFEN

BODENSEE

ZÜRICH

Rappenlochschlucht

Pfänder

Bregenz

Bregenzerwald

Neßlegg

Zuger Hochlicht

Feldkirch

Rankweil

Bludenz

Zürs

Flexenpaß

LECH ❋❋❋

VALLUGA

Reutte

Plansee

ZUGSPITZE

Seefelder Sattelstraßen

Lermoos

Fernpaßstraße

Seefeld i. Tirol

Mösern

Stams

Seefelder Joch

Imst

Landeck

Ötztal

PITZTAL

Stubaital

LIECHTENSTEIN

ZÜRICH

Brandnertal

Lünersee

Montafon

Schruns

Arlbergpaß

Gaschurn

Arlberg

St. Anton

Ischgl

Trisannabrücke

Finstermünzpaß

Oberes Inntal

Nauders

KAUNERTAL

Mittelberg

Weißseeferner

Stubaier Gletscher

Sölden

Jochdohle

Ventertal

Obergurgl

Vermunt-Stausee

Silvretta-Hochalpenstraße

HOHES RAD

WILDES MANNLE

Hohe Mut

S. Leonardo

SCHWEIZ SUISSE SVIZZERA

LUGANO

RHEIN

Inn

Adige

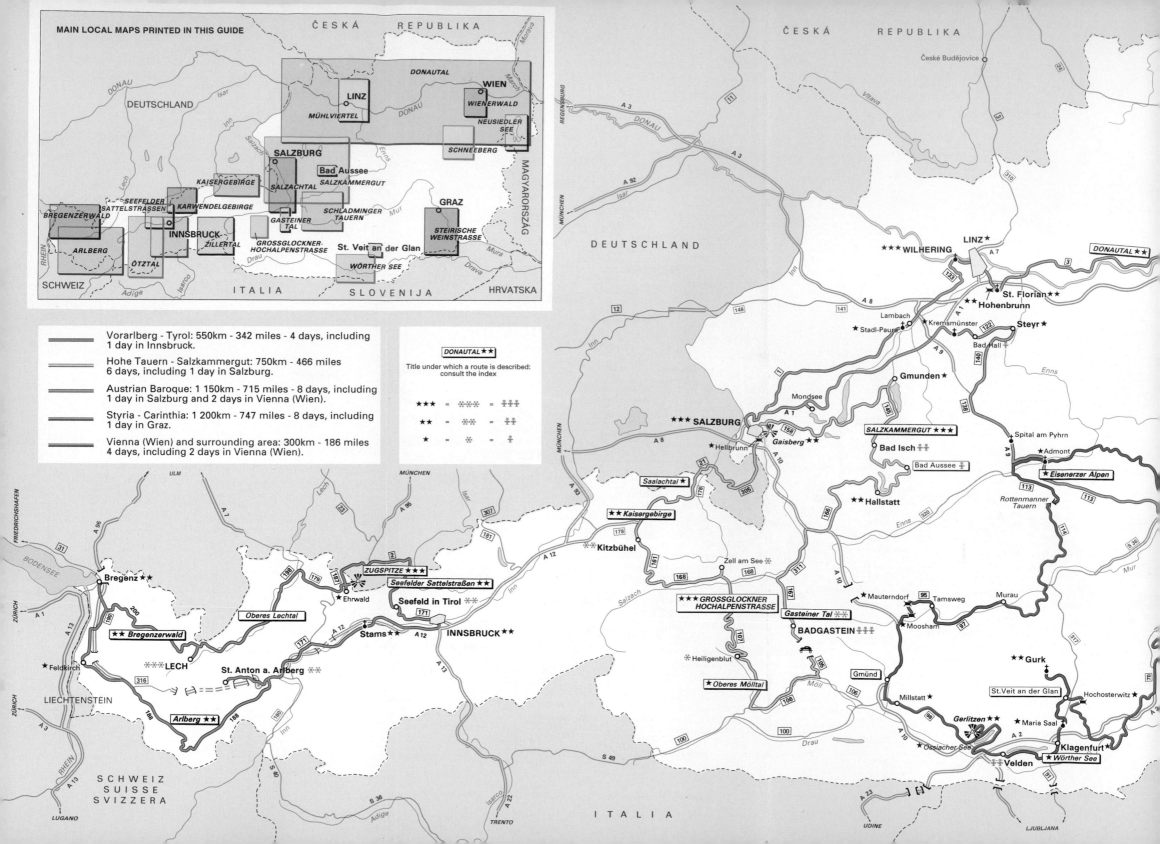

MAIN LOCAL MAPS PRINTED IN THIS GUIDE

Vorarlberg - Tyrol: 550km - 342 miles - 4 days, including 1 day in Innsbruck.

Hohe Tauern - Salzkammergut: 750km - 466 miles 6 days, including 1 day in Salzburg.

Austrian Baroque: 1 150km - 715 miles - 8 days, including 1 day in Salzburg and 2 days in Vienna (Wien).

Styria - Carinthia: 1 200km - 747 miles - 8 days, including 1 day in Graz.

Vienna (Wien) and surrounding area: 300km - 186 miles 4 days, including 2 days in Vienna (Wien).

DONAUTAL ★★

Title under which a route is described: consult the index

★★★ = ✳✳✳ = ‡‡‡
★★ = ✳✳ = ‡‡
★ = ✳ = ‡

Driving tours

*Salzburg old town and
Hohensalzburg*
G. Simeone/ DIAE

ZÜRICH-KOSMOS

WHEN AND WHERE TO GO

Seasons

Austria, two-thirds of which is covered by mountains, is justly popular for its ski resorts in **winter**, with slopes suitable for everyone from beginners to expert skiers. The fun in the snow kicks off in the Arlberg pass region around Lech and St. Anton in the far western corner of the country. This segues into the Tyrol, the most popular area, whose profile was raised considerably by the Winter Olympic Games held in Innsbruck in 1964 and 1976. The Salzburg region is also well developed for skiing, with major resorts such as the Sportwelt Amadé. Styria offers a variety of opportunities in the ski resorts of the Dachstein-Tauern and Schladming areas.

In **spring** it is still possible to ski at the higher altitudes, with longer days being a welcome bonus. The season is also enlivened by carnival processions.

Summer is the time for enjoying Austria's mountain scenery to the full and for making the most of its rich cultural scene. Welcoming Carinthia, with its warm-water lakes, attracts swimmers, water-skiing enthusiasts and anglers. Colder, but more romantic, are the picturesque lakes of the Salzkammergut. Mountaineers will be drawn by the glaciers of the Ötztal or the Hohe Tauern, or the slopes of the Karwendel, the Kaisergebirge, the Dachstein or the Gesäuse.

Fall, with the sun shining and a nip in the air, sheds a particularly beautiful light on the old stone buildings in the towns. This is a good season to discover the wealth of Austria's museums. The wooded valleys of Styria and Carinthia are a pleasure to explore on foot. A journey through the vineyards of the Burgenland or Lower Austria, or along the Danube beneath the Wachau, is unforgettable at this time of year, which is also marked in Vienna by the reopening of the theatrical and musical seasons (1 September and October respectively).

Driving Tours

See Driving Tours map on pp 12–15.

Österrich Werbung

KNOW BEFORE YOU GO

Useful Web Sites

(*Unless noted, websites listed here are in English.*)

www.austria.info
The official website maintained by the Austrian National Tourist Office is an excellent pre-trip planning tool with information about the regions, eating and drinking, accommodation, history, famous people and other topics.

www.austria.org
Excellent general website maintained by the Austrian Press and Information Service of the Austrian Embassy in Washington, DC. Includes travel information as well as a link to Facts & Figures, a comprehensive snapshot of Austria today.

www.austria.gv.at.
This Austrian federal government website is a portal to the country's political landscape with links to all ministries. Learn about Austrian current affairs and policy stance on such issues as security, bioethics and data protection.

www.tiscover.com
Another useful vacation planner, this site has detailed information on all provinces and allows you to book hotels, packages and cars. Also has a route planner and details about road closures, current traffic, weather reports and other useful data.

www.lawine.at
Go here for up to date information about snow conditions, avalance warning and other snow-related information (in German only).

www.aeiou.at
This encyclopedia-style database has 14 000 entries on history, culture, geography, politics and other topics; a music archive that allows you to download and listen to original works; as well as image, video and photo librareis. Partly in English.

Tourist Offices

The Austrian national tourist office offers information on a whole range of special deals for tourists and other practical details of interest to holiday-makers in Austria.

AUSTRIAN NATIONAL TOURIST OFFICES

Australia
1st Floor, 36 Carrington Street, Sydney, NSW 2000,
☎ (2) 9299 3621.

Canada
2 Bloor Street West, #400, Toronto, ON M4W 3E2,
☎ 416-967-3381.
anto-tor@sympatico.ca

Ireland
Merrion Hall, Strand Road, Sandymount,
PO Box 2506, Dublin,
☎ (01) 283 0488.

UK
9011 Richmond Bldgs, London W1D 3HF,
☎ (020) 7318 1651,
info@anto.co.uk.

USA
120 W 45th St, 9th Fl, New York, NY 10036,
☎ 212-944-68 80,
travel@austria.info

TOURIST OFFICES OF THE AUSTRIAN PROVINCES

Vienna
Wiener Tourismusband, Obere Augartenstraße 40,
A-1025 Wien,
☎ 01/21 11 40,

Fax 01/2 16 84 92,
www.wien.info.

Burgenland
Burgenland-Tourismus,
Schloss Esterházy,
A-7000 Eisenstadt,
☎ 0 26 82/63 38 40,
Fax 0 26 82/6 33 84 20,
www.burgenland.info.

Carinthia
Kärnten Information,
Casinoplatz 1,
A-9220 Velden,
☎ 0 463/30 00,
Fax 0 42 74/5 21 00 50,
www.kaernten.at.

Lower Austria
Niederösterreich Werbung,
Fischhof 3/3,
A-1010 Wien,
☎ 01/5 36 10 62 00,
Fax 01/5 36 10 60 60,
www.niederoesterreich.at.

Salzburg *(province)*
SalzburgerLand Tourismus GmbH,
Wiener Bundesstraße 23,
A-5300 Hallwang
☎ 06 62/66 88 44,
Fax 06 62/66 88 70,
www.salzburgerland.com.

Styria
Steirische Tourismus GmbH,
St.-Peter-Hauptstraße 243,
A-8042 Graz,
☎ 03 16/4 00 30,
Fax 03 16/40 03 30,
www.steiermark.com.

Tyrol
Tirol Info,
Maria-Theresien-Straße 55,
A-6010 Innsbruck,
☎ 05 12/72 72,
Fax 05 12/7 27 27,
www.tirol.at.

Upper Austria
Oberösterreich Tourismus Infor
mation,
Freistädter Straße 119
A-4041 Linz,

☎ 07 32/22 10 22,
Fax 07 32/7 27 77 01,
www.oberoesterreich.at.

Vorarlberg
Vorarlberg Tourismus,
Bahnhofstraße 14,
A-6901 Bregenz,
☎ 0 55 74/42 52 50,
Fax 0 55 74/42 52 55,
www.vorarlberg-tourism.at.

LOCAL TOURIST INFORMATION CENTRES

These are indicated by the symbol
🛈 on the town plans in this guide.
Addresses and telephone numbers
are given in the Admission times and
charges section. Further addresses
and details can be obtained from the
national or regional tourist offices.

International Visitors

AUSTRIAN EMBASSIES

United Kingdom   Embassy
18 Belgrave Mews West
London SW1X 8HU
☎ (020) 73 44 32 50
www.aussenministerium.at/london

Ireland   Embassy
15 Ailesbury Court
93 Ailesbury Road
Dublin 4
☎ (01) 269 4577

USA   Embassy
3524 International Court NW
Washington DC 20008
☎ 202-895-6700
austrianembassy@washington.nu

Australia   Embassy
12 Talbot Street
Forrest, Canberra ACT 2603
(Postal address: PO Box 3375,
Manuka, ACT 2603)
☎ (02) 6295 1533
www.austriaemb.org.au

Embassies and Consulates

Australia   **Embassy**
Mattiellistraße 2-4,
A-1040 Wien,
☎ 01/50 67 40
www.australian-embassy.at

Ireland   **Embassy**
Rotenturmstraße 16-18, 5th Fl,
A-1010 Vienna,
☎ 01/7 15 42 46
vienna@dfa.ie

UK   **Embassy**
Jauresgasse 12,
A-1030 Wien,
☎ 01/71 61 30.
www.britishembassy.at.

USA   **Embassy**
Boltzmanngasse 16,
A-1090 Wien,
☎ 01/31 33 90,
www.usembassy.at.

DOCUMENTS

Most citizens of the European Union only need their national identity card or **passport** to enter Austria. Citizens of Australia, Canada, New Zealand, the USA and Israel need a valid passport but no visa for tourist stays up to 3 months. Citizens from most other countries need to apply for a visa at the **Austrian Embassy** in their home country. Austria is part of the Schengen Agreement for holders of visas to other Schengen countries.

CUSTOMS

No duty is charged on items brought into the country for their personal use. If arriving from a non-EU country, you may bring the following amounts into Austria duty-free: 200 cigarettes or 50 cigars or 250g loose tobacco; 2 liters of wine and 1 liter of liquor; 50g of perfume and 0.25L of eau de toilette; and additional items up to €175 in value. Contact your country's customs office for duty-free restrictions and other regulations about what you may bring back home. UK Revenue & Customs,

for instance, produces a helpful guide downloadable for free at *www.hmce. gov.uk* (link to Travel Information). The US Customs & Border Protection has a similar publication called *Know Before You Go* available at *www.cbp.gov.*

HEALTH

Citizen of the EU should obtain a European Health Insurance Card (EHIC) from their local health authority, which entitles them to receive low-cost or free emergency health care while in Austria. It does not cover emergency repatriation.
Non-EU residents should check that their private health insurance policy covers them for travel abroad, and if necessary take out supplementary medical insurance with specific overseas coverage. All prescription drugs should be clearly labeled, and we recommend that you carry a copy of the prescription with you.

Accessibility

Regional tourist offices provide information about traveling in Austria as a disabled person. Some have put together handy guides of which the following are available online: Tirol Without Barriers (*www.ohnehandicap. tirol.at*), Upper Austria's Ferien ohne Handicap (*www.oberoesterreich. at/nohandicap, in German only*) and Vienna for Visitors with Disabilities (*http://info.wien.at, link to 'Specials'*). For barrier-free farm holidays, consult Urlaub am Bauernhof (*www. farmholidays.com*). Austrian rail, the Österreichische Bundesbahnen (ÖBB), operates a hotline (☎ 05/17 17) offering trip-planning assistance for the mobility-impaired. Many of the sights described in this guide are accessible to people with special needs. Those marked with the symbol ♿ offer access for wheelchairs. However, it is always best to phone ahead for details.

GETTING THERE

By Air

Airlines providing scheduled flights to Austria include: **Austrian Airlines** (*www.aua.com*), **Aer Lingus** (www.airlingus.ie), **British Airways** *(www.britishairways.com)*, **British Midland** (*www.flybmi.com*), **First Choice Airways** *(www.firstchoice.co.uk)*, **easyJet** (*www.easyjet.com*), **Lauda Air** (*www.laudaair.com*), **Lufthansa** (www.lufthansa.com), **Niki** (*www.flyniki.com*), and **Ryanair** (*www.ryanair.com*). Most flights land at Vienna, although there's also service to Graz, Linz, Salzburg and Innsbruck.
From overseas, the only direct flights are operated by Austrian Airlines and land at Vienna. Your options widen if you fly to another major European hub, such as London or Frankfurt, and catch a connecting flight there. Munich airport in Germany and Zürich airport in Switzerland are convenient if you're bound for destinations in western Austria.

By Rail

Austria is well served by rail from destinations throughout Europe. Coming from the UK, the easiest way is to catch the **Eurostar** (*www.eurostar.com*) from London-Waterloo to Paris Nord, change to Paris Est and there board the one direct daily train bound for Salzburg and Vienna-Westbahnhof. The trip takes about 15hr 30min and 19hr 30min, respectively.
A good source for tickets and information is **Rail Europe** (*www.raileurope.co.uk*). The Web site maintained by **Österreichische Bundesbahnen** (Austrian rail; *www.oebb.at*) has comprehensive timetable information and other details as well.

ÖBB Vorteilscard

If you're planning extensive rail travel within Austria, this rail card (€99) may save you a bundle. For the period of one year, it entitles the holder to reductions of 45% (50% for tickets bought online or from vending machines) on standard fares within the ÖBB network and most private lines. For trips outside Austria, the discount is 25%. Holders also qualify for cheaper rates in sleeper cars, free bicycle transportation and assorted other benefits. The card is also available for people under 26 (€20) and seniors (€27). It is sold at Austrian railway stations and travel agencies with ticket sales facilities and some mainline stations abroad. For further details call ☎ 05/17 17 or check www.oebb.at.

Steam engines and tourist trains

Steam engines and tourist trains operate in many regions year round, but predominantly during the summer season. These offer a pleasant and relaxing way of discovering some of Austria's most beautiful natural regions. Further information is available from Erlebnis Bahn & Schiff Österreich (www.erlebnis-bahn-schiff.at).

By Car

Austria is linked to its neighboring countries by fast and well-maintained highways. Coming from the UK, you can be just about anywhere Austria in about 10 to 12 hours, depending on where you arrive on the Continent. Besides the Eurotunnel linking Folkestone with Coquelles near Calais (France), there is ferry service from Dover to Calais, from Hull and Rosyth (near Edinburgh) to Zeebrugge (Belgium), from Harwich to Hook van Holland (Netherlands) and from Newcastle to Amsterdam. All border crossings are open 24hr.
Michelin offers a free and handy online route planning service at: *www.viamichelin.com*, which calculates distance, time and gasoline use.

Motorail train services, where you load your car (and yourself) onto a train, operate between Vienna and Villach (372km/231mi), Vienna and Salzburg (317km/197mi), Vienna and Innsbruck (572km/355mi), Vienna and Feldkirch (731km/454mi), Graz and Feldkirch (607km/377mi) and Villach and Feldkirch (466km/290mi) and Vienna and Lienz (476km/296mi). In summer, motorail services also operate to/from Italy, Slovenia, Croatia and Germany. An hourly motorail shuttle also runs through the **Tauern tunnel** (Böckstein-Mallnitz, 8km/5mi). For further details, including fares, contact Österreichische Bundesbahnen (Austrian rail; 05/17 17, *www. oebb.at*).

Driving in Austria

DOCUMENTS

It is necessary to have a valid driving license (preferably an international driving licence), and third party insurance cover is compulsory. Carrying the International Green Card from insurance companies may be helpful.

ROAD REGULATIONS

- Traffic in Austria drives on the right and the minimum driving age is 18.
- Driving with the lights on at all times is now compulsory, as is the wearing of seat belts and the carrying of a first aid kit and emergency triangle.
- Children under the age of 12 and less than 1.5m/4ft 11in tall must travel in appropriate and approved booster seats.
- The blood alcohol limit is 0.5ml/g.
- The use of cell (mobile) telephones inside a moving vehicle is only permitted if you have a hands-free set.
- Motorcyclists must wear a helmet.

Speed Limits

Unless signposted otherwise, speed limits are 130kph/80mph on autobahns/highways, 100kph/62mph on country roads, and 50kph/31mph in built-up areas. Private cars towing a load in excess of 750kg/1 650lb must not exceed 100kph/62mph on autobahns/highways, 80kph/50mph on country roads and 50kph/31mph in built-up areas.

BREAKDOWN SERVICE

This is provided *(charge for non-members)* by two Austrian automobile clubs:
- **ÖAMTC** Österreichischer Automobil-, Motorrad- und Touring Club, Schubertring 1-3, A-1010 Wien, ☎ 01/71 19 90, www.oeamtc.at, breakdown number ☎ 120.
- **ARBÖ** Auto-, Motor- und Rad-fahrer-bund Österreich, Mariahilfer Straße 180, A-1150 Wien, ☎ 01/89 12 10, www.arboe.at, breakdown number ☎ 123.

ROAD TOLLS (MAUTGEBÜHREN)

Since 1 January 1997, tolls have been levied on autobahns, dual carriageways and urban highways in Austria. Drivers must buy a toll disc (vignette, or "Mautpickerl") and display it behind their windshield. Vignettes are available for 10 days (€7.60), 2 months (€21.80) and one year (€72.60). Vignettes can be bought from Austrian motoring associations (ARBÖ, ÖAMTC), larger petrol stations, post offices and tobacconists' and at the border crossing points.
Vehicles weighing more than 3.5 tons must be equipped with a so-called GO-Box, a small electronic device that registers the kilometers you've driven every time you pass by a toll gantry and deducts the appropriate amount from the pre-paid credit stored in the GO-Box. Drivers must mount the device on the inside of their car's windshield. Boxes are available for €5 from gas stations mostly located along autobahns. Charges start at €0.13 per kilometer and depend on the number of axles. For full details, consult www. go-maut.at.

Additional Tolls

These are levied on certain stretches of road not covered by the vignette:

◆ **Arlberg-Schnellstraße**
(information line ☎ 0 54 46/20 66 67; car toll €8.50);

◆ **Brenner-Autobahn**
(☎ 05 12/52 01 20; total stretch €8; *www.autobrennero.it*);

◆ **Dachsteinstraße**
(☎ 0 36 87/8 18 33; €8);

◆ **Felbertauernstraße**
(☎ 0 48 52/6 33 30; €10; *www. felbertauernstrasse.at*);

◆ **Gerlos Alpenstraße** (☎ 0 65 64/72 61; €7; *www.gerlosstrasse.at*)

◆ **Grossglockner-Hochalpenstraße** (☎ 0 65 46/6 50; €26; *www.grossglockner.at*);

◆ **Karawankentunnel**
(☎ 0 42 53/26 60; €6.50);

◆ **Maltatal-Hochalmstraße**
(☎ 0 47 33/2 20 15; €15.50);

◆ **Nockalmstraße** (☎ 0 47 36/2 65; €13; *www.nockalmstrasse.at*);

◆ **Pyhrn-Autobahn** (☎ 03 16/6 07 30; total stretch €12);

◆ **Silvretta-Hochalpenstraße** (☎ 0 55 58/8 31 50; €10.90);

◆ **Tauernautobahn** (☎ 06 62/62 05 11; total stretch €9.50);

◆ **Timmelsjoch-Hochalpenstraße** (☎ 05 12/58 19 70; €13; *www. timmelsjoch-hochalpenstraße.at*);

◆ **Villacher Alpenstraße**
(☎ 0 6 62/8 73 67 30; €13; *www.villacher-alpenstrasse.at*).

For some of these tollroads monthly or annual passes are available.

ROUTE PLANNING

The **Michelin map 730** (scale 1:400 000) covers the entire country and gives details of likely road closures in winter. For online route planning, go to www.viamichelin.com. The hikers' maps published by Freytag and Berndt are useful for more detailed exploration.

TRAFFIC REPORTS

These are given on the hour, after the news bulletin, on radio station Ö3. Information on traffic and road conditions is also available on the ÖAMTC's recorded message service ☎ 01/1 75 20.

CAR RENTAL

Car-rental firms:

◆ **Avis**: ☎ 08 00/08 00 87 57 (toll-free), www.avis.at

◆ **Europcar**: ☎ 01/8 66 16 33, www.europcar.co.at

◆ **Hertz**: ☎ 01/7 95 32, www.hertz.com

◆ **Sixt**: ☎ 0 08 00/11 11 74 98 (toll-free), www.e-sixt.at

DRIVING IN WINTER

In snowy conditions winter tires should be fitted, or chains if conditions are particularly severe. The ÖAMTC and ARBÖ have snow chain rental outlets in every Austrian province.

Winter closures – In winter the passes and tollroads listed in the charts below are closed.

Winter Pass and Tollroad Closures			
Pass	**Linking**	**Tollroad**	**Toll point**
Bielerhöhe	Partenen – Galtür	Breitlahner Schlegeis-Stausee	Ginzling/ Mayrhofen
Furkajoch	Laterns – Damüls	Maltatal-Hochalmstraße	Fallerhütte – Kölnbreinsperre
Grossglockner-Hochalpenstraße	Ferleiten – Heiligenblut	Silvretta-Hochalpenstraße	Galtür – Partenen
Hahntennjoch	Boden – Imst	Sölden-Rettenbachstraße	Ötztaler Gletscher
Sölker Pass	Gröbming – Murau	Timmelsjochstraße	Gurgl
Timmelsjoch	Obergurgl – St. Leonhard im Passeier Tal		

Name of pass	Altitude (meters)	Route	Michelin map 730 fold no	★ = road barred; 🚐 = not recommended
Seefelder Sattel (1)	1 180	Innsbruck – Mittenwald	16	★
Rottenmanner Tauern	1 265	Oberes Murtal – Ennstal	22	🚐
Aflenzer Seeberg	1 254	Mariazell – Aflenz	23	🚐
Präbichl	1 227	Ennstal – Leoben	23	🚐
Bielerhöhe	2 036	Silvrettastraße	28	★
Hochtannbergpass	1 679	Reutte – Dornbirn	28	🚐
Timmelsjoch (2)	2 474	Ötztal – Italy	29	★
Gerlospass (3)	1 507	Zell am Ziller – Zell am See	29	★
Hochtor	2 505	Grossglockner – Hochalpenstraße	31	★
Kartitsch-Sattel	1 529	Kötschach – Sillian	32	🚐
Radstädter Tauernpass (4)	1 739	Radstadt – St. Michael Im Lungau	32	🚐
Katschberg (5)	1 641	St. Michael im Lungau – Spittal an der Drau	33	🚐
Turracher Höhe	1 793	Murtal – Carinthian lakes	34	🚐
Loibltunnel	1 067	Klagenfurt – Slovenia	35	🚐
Gaberl-Sattel (5)	1 551	Direct link: Oberes Murtal – Graz	36	★★

(1) Easy access to Seefeld when heading from Mittenwald to Innsbruck.
(2) Access for caravans less than 3.4m/ 11ft high along the Ötztal as far as Untergurgl.
(3) Easy access to the Gerlos pass and to Gerlos heading east-west.
(4) We recommend taking the A 10 motorway
(5) Inaccessible in winter; not recommended in summer.

CARAVANS

Some mountain roads have gradients steeper than 20% (1 in 5), as well as very narrow stretches. Steep gradients are indicated on Michelin map 730, which also gives dates of likely road closures in winter. Certain stretches of road, such as the approach roads to the Tauerntunnel, may be unsuitable for caravans because of heavy traffic. The table above indicates the most difficult stretches on the various access routes across the Alps (east to west).

WHERE TO STAY AND EAT

Where to Stay

HOTELS

Austria offers a great variety of hotel accommodation, with facilities for families, cyclists, tennis players, riders and golf players. Lists of hotels can be obtained from the Austrian national tourist office or from local and regional tourist information centers (addresses listed on p 19). The *Michelin Guide Europe* (for Vienna, Innsbruck and Salzburg) and The *Michelin Guide Deutschland* (for Salzburg and Bregenz) are revised annually and give a selection of hotels and restaurants based on inspectors' reports.

FARM HOLIDAYS

These are popular in the Tyrol in particular, and they can often be combined with some sort of course (embroidery, sculpture, riding etc). Themed holiday accommodation on offer includes organic farms and healthy farm holidays. Details available from the Austrian National Tourist Office or from the Austrian farm holiday association Urlaub am Bauernhof in Österreich (Gabelsberger Straße 19, A-5020 Salzburg, ☎ 06 62/88 02 02, Fax 06 62/88 02 023, Web site: *www. farmholidays.com*).

CAMPING AND CARAVANING

Autria has about 500 campsites, many of which are open year round. Lists are available from the Austrian National Tourist Office and from regional and local tourist information centres. Alternatively, contact the following Austrian associations: Camping- und Caravaningclub Austria (CCA), Mariahilfer Straße 180, A-1150 Wien, ☎ 01/89 12 12 22, www.campsite. at/cca; and Österreichischer Camping- club (ÖCC), Schubertring 1-3, A-1010 Wien, ☎ 01/7 13 61 51, www.camp- ingclub.at. Another excellent online resource with a searchable campsite database and information about campsites, toll-charges, alpine passes and more (in English) is Camping in Austria at *www.camping.at*.

YOUTH HOSTELS

Austria has about 100 youth hostels affiliated with Hostelling Interna-

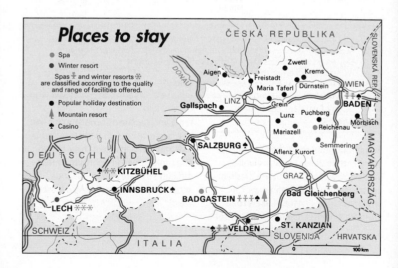

Places to stay

tional. Staying here requires an HI membership card from your home country. Non-members need to buy a Gästekarte (guest card) for €3.50 euro per night from any hostel. After six nights, it automatically counts as an HI membership card. For addresses check with the Austrian youth hostel association (Österreichischer Jugendherbergsverband, Schottenring 28, A-1010 Wien, ☎ 01/5 33 53 53, www.oejhv.or.at).

"SCHLANK & SCHÖN IN ÖSTERREICH"

Health, beauty treatments, stress management and relaxation are the goals of the "Schlank & Schön" ("Slim and Beautiful") organization. The catalogue is available from the Austrian National Tourist Office or directly from "Schlank & Schön in Österreich" (Hauptstraße 203, A-9210 Pörtschach, ☎ 0 42 72/36 20 40, www.schlankundschoen.at).

MAP OF PLACES TO STAY

The map of places to stay below shows the principal Austrian vacation resorts (spas, winter sports and mountain resorts).

Where to Eat

Specific restaurants in major cities are mentioned in the Address Books within the *Discovering Austria* section. Traditional Austrian cuisine is hearty, stick-to-the-ribs fare, with dishes usually revolving around some cut of meat, potatoes, boiled vegetables and gravy. Many Austrians eat their main meal at lunchtime, which is served between noon and 2.30pm.

A full meal consists of three courses, often starting with a clear, flavor-packed soup. Frittatensuppe, laced with thin strips of seasoned pancake, and Leberknödelsuppe with liver dumplings, are both typical culinary overtures. The best known main course is the Wiener Schnitzel, a thin slice of breaded veal panfried to a crispy, golden tan and served with a slice of lemon. Other classic dishes commonly found on menus are Tafelspitz (boiled beef paired with an apple-horseradish sauce); Schweinebraten (sliced roast pork); Zwiebelrostbraten (roast beef slices doused in fried onion slices); and Backhendl (fried breaded chicken). Some dishes also reflect influences from the cuisines of neighboring countries, especially Hungary. Peppers stuffed with rice and beef (*gefüllte Paprika*) and Gulasch, a paprika-spiced beef stew, fall into this category. If fish makes it onto menus, it's usually Zander (pike-perch), Forelle (trout) or Karpfen (carp).

Austrians truly excel when it comes to desserts. Delicious temptations include Apfelstrudel (apple strudel), filled with apples and raisins, sprinkled with powdered sugar and served either hot or cold; and Palatschinken, a pancake stuffed with apricot jam or curd cheese.

Restaurants tend to be rather formal places with crisp table linen and attentive service. For a more casual atmosphere, head to a Gasthof or a Gasthaus, which are traditional inns with a homely, authentic ambience. In wine regions, the place to go for atmosphere is a Heurige, an earthy wine tavern where food is usually presented buffet-style. Austria's famous Kaffeehäuser (cafés) also serve hot meals, while places called Café-Konditorei are best for sampling Austria's delicious cakes and pastries. Celebrated staples here include Sachertorte, a chocolate cake with apricot-jam stuffing, and Linzer Torte, which blends almond pastry with red currant jam.

Wine and beer are the most common beverages of choice. Grüner Veltliner is the most common wine variety, although Riesling and Weissburgunder (pinot blanc) are also popular libations. Famous beer labels are Gösser from Graz, Stiegl from Salzburg and Ottakringer and Gold Fassl from Vienna. Many Austrians like to finish their meals with a Schnaps, a potent spirit usually flavored with fruit.

WHAT TO DO AND SEE

Outdoor Fun

THE GREAT OUTDOORS

National parks

Austria's six national parks let you appreciate nature at its unspoiled best: rare flora and fauna, magnificent scenery, trails off beaten track and other charms await. For an overview, see www.nationalparksaustria.at.

Nationalpark Hohe Tauern (Carinthia, Salzburg province, Tyrol)

The park authorities offer excursions, slide shows and other events such as "children's days" or Alpine hikes. Web site: *www.hohetauern.at*.

- ◆ Regionalverband Nationalpark Hohe Tauern, A-5722 Niedernsill, ☎ 0 65 48/84 170;
- ◆ Nationalparkverwaltung Kärnten, A-9843 Grosskirchheim, ☎ 0 48 25/61 61 14;
- ◆ Nationalparkverwaltung Tirol, A-9971 Matrei in Osttirol, ☎ 0 48 75/51 610.

Nationalpark Neusiedler See-Seewinkel (Burgenland)

This is the only nature reserve of the steppes in central Europe. It offers

Reed banks by the Neusiedler See

H.W. Partaj/ BILDAGENTUR BUENOS DIAS

guided excursions, tours in horse-drawn carts, on horse-back or by bicycle. A must for keen bird-watchers.

- ◆ Nationalpark Informationszentrum, A-7142 Illmitz, ☎ 0 21 75/3 44 20; *www.nationalpark-neusiedlersee-seewinkel.at*.

Nationalpark Nockberge (Carinthia)

This national park lies between the Lieser Valley and the Turracher Höhe range and is characterized by its gently undulating hills of crystalline rock ("Nocken").

- ◆ Nationalparkverwaltung, A-9565 Ebene Reichenau 22, ☎ 0 42 75/66 50; *www.nationalparknockberge.at*.

Nationalpark Kalkalpen (Upper Austria)

This park in the Pyhrn-Eisenwurzen region extends as far as the High Alps. It runs a varied program for walkers of all levels of experience and fitness.

- ◆ Nationalparkverwaltung, A-4591 Molln, ☎ 07584 3651; *www.kalkalpen.at*.

Nationalpark Thayatal (Lower Austria)

This cross-border park is managed in cooperation with the Czech Republic. The Thaya Valley cuts deeply into the ancient rock of the mountains, forming a breach.

- ◆ Nationalparkverwaltung, A-2082 Hardegg, ☎ 029 49/7 00 50, *www.np-thayatal.at*.

Nationalpark Donau-Auen (Lower Austria)

This park stretches from just east of Vienna to the Slovakian border and is home to a tremendous variety of flora and fauna, earning it the nickname of "Central Europe's rainforest." Its unique features can be discovered on foot or by boat.

- ◆ Nationalparkverwaltung, Schloss Orth, A-2304 Orth an der Donau,

☎ 0 22 12/34 50; *www.don-auauen.at*.

Nationalpark Gesäuse

Rocky cliffs, shaggy meadows, thick forest and the gushing Enns River characterize the country's youngest national park in Styria in central Austria. Its boasts 50 types of wild orchid and serves as the breeding ground of 60 bird species.

◆ Nationalparkverwaltung, A-8911 Admont; ☎ 0 36 13/2 11 60 20; *www.nationalpark.co.at*

Nature parks

The 40 Austrian nature parks are also conservation areas and cluster mostly in eastern Austria, especially Styria, Lower Austria and Burgenland. For details contact **Verband der Naturparke Österreichs** (Alberstraße 10, A-8010 Graz, ☎ 03 16/31 88 48 99, *www.naturparke.at*.

BIRD-WATCHING

◆ **Burgenland**: Neusiedler See; Seewinkel/Lange Lacke; veterinary care centre for storks and other birdlife at Parndorf (A-7111).
◆ **Carinthia**: Eagle observation point from the castle ruins at Landskron; bird reserve on Gros-

sedlinger Lake (near Wolfsberg); Völkermarkter reservoir.
◆ **Lower Austria**: Danube, March and Thaya river plains; Thaya Valley near Hardegg.
◆ **Salzburg (province)**: Pinzgau (between the Gastein and Habach valleys); Zeller See (south shore of the lake).
◆ **Styria**: Mur reservoir (southern Styria).
◆ **Upper Austria**: Danube plain in the Linz Valley; Schmiding bird reserve.

ANGLING

On the whole, two fishing permits are required: one valid for the whole province and the other a local, private one from the owner of the stretch of water. For details, contact **Verband der Österreichischen Arbeiter-Fischerei-Vereine**, A-1080 Wien, Lenaugasse 14, ☎ 01/4 03 21 76; *www.fischerei.or.at*.

WATER SPORTS AND BOATING

Austria boasts no fewer than 1 000 lakes, including 200 in Carinthia alone and several with drinking-quality water. For information on water temperature: ☎ 01/15 28 (recorded

Ossiacher See

R. Chéret/MICHELIN

Walking in the Dachstein range

message May-Oct) or ☎ 01/89 12 17 (ARBÖ information service).

From mid May to the end of September, there are regular passenger boat or ferry services on some of the larger lakes, such as the Achensee, the Attersee, Lake Constance, the Hallstätter See, the Ossiacher See, the Traunsee, the Wörthersee and the Wolfgangsee. In almost all cases, it is possible to row, sail, surf, water ski or quite simply swim in Austria's lakes. Further information on these possibilities is provided by the tourist offices of the lakeside communities.

Boat trips on the Danube

From early April to the end of October, a number of companies offer boat trips on the Danube, including:

- **DDSG Blue Danube Schiffahrt** Friedrichstraße 7, A-1010 Wien, ☎ 01/5 88 80; *www.ddsg-blue-danube.at.*
- **Donauschiffahrt Ardagger** A-3321 Ardagger 155, ☎ 0 74 79/6 46 40, *www.tiscover.com/donauschiffahrt.*
- **Donauschiffahrt Wurm & Köck** Untere Donaulände 1, A-4020 Linz, ☎ 07 32/78 36 07, *www.donauschiffahrt.at.*

RAFTING & CANOEING

Rafting is permitted from 1 May to 31 October but is not allowed in the Hohe Tauern national park. Rivers on which it is possible to go rafting are:

- in **Carinthia**, the Gail, Gurk, Isel, Lieser and Möll;
- in **Lower Austria**, the Enns, March, Salza and Thaya;
- in the province of **Salzburg**, the Enns, Lammer, Mur, Saalach and Salzach;
- in **Styria**, the Enns and Salza;
- in the **Tyrol**, the Gerolsbach, Inn, Isel, Ötztaler and Tiroler Ache, Sanna and Ziller;
- in **Upper Austria**, the Enns, Steyr and Traun.

The Web site of the Austrian National Tourist Office has links to numerous outfitters. Altenatively contact the regional tourist offices or the Austrian canoe association, **Österreichischer Kanuverband**, Giesereistraße 8, A-5280 Braunau, ☎ 0 77 22/8 16 00, *www.okv.at.*

HANG-GLIDING AND PARAGLIDING

Venues for hang-gliding and paragliding include:

- **Carinthia** – Bad Kleinkirchheim, Katschberg, Seeboden;
- **Salzburg** – Dorfgastein, Golling-Werfenweng, Mattsee, Salzburg;
- **Styria** – Graz, Gröbming, Ramsau am Dachstein;
- **Tyrol** – Galtür, Hall, Kössen, Lienz, Neustift im Stubaital, Niederau, Seefeld;
- **Upper Austria** – Hinterstoder, Leonstein, Linz, Spital am Pyhrn, Weyregg;
- **Vorarlberg** – limited to certain summits and following prescribed routes only.

Further details, contact **Österreichischer Aero-Club**, Prinz-Eugen-Straße 12, A-1040 Wien, ☏ 01/5 05 10 28; www.aeroclub.at.

GOLF

The popularity of golf in Austria has steadily increased in recent years and the country now boasts 128 golf courses in all provinces. For details contact the Austrian golfing association **Österreichischer Golf-Verband**, Prinz-Eugen-Straße 12, A-1040 Wien, ☏ 01/5 05 32 45, www.golf.at.

CYCLING & MOUNTAIN BIKING

Austria has over 10 000km/6 200mi of cycle paths to offer sightseers on two wheels. One of the most popular is the **Donauradweg**, a cycle path following the Danube from Passau to Hainburg (305km/190mi). The Austrian National Tourist Office publishes a brochure called Radtouren in Österreich with detailed route descriptions and lodging information about select long-distance cycle routes. it can be ordered from **Radtouren in Österreich,** c/o Oberösterreich Tourismus Information, Freistädter Straße 119, A-4041 Linz, ☏ 0732/22 10 22. Or check the organization's Web site at www.radtouren.at.

Mountain bikers are well taken care of as well in Austria with some 17 000km/10 625mi of well-marked routes throughout the Alpine regions. For further details, contact Mountain-bike Holidays, Glemmerstraße 21,

A-5751 Maishofen, ☏ 0 65 42/8 04 80 22; www.bike-holidays.com.

Cycles can be transported by rail, or hired from some 50 Austrian railway stations. Check with the tourist office for details or consult the Web site of Austrian Rail (ÖBB, www.oebb.at), which has a section called Bahn & Bike (in German only).

HIKING

With a network of about 50 000km /31 100mi of waymarked trails, Austria is a hiker's paradise. Ten long-distance trails (Weitwanderwege) make it possible to explore the entire country on foot, if such is your wish. Three long-distance European long-distance trails also cut across Austria.

Many villages who promote nature tourism have formed an association called "Österreichische Wanderdörfer" (Austrian hiking villages), Unterwollaniger Straße 53, A-9500 Villach, ☏ 0 42 42/25 75 31, www.wanderdoerfer.at. This association publishes a quarterly newsletter as well as an annual catalog (both free) with route descriptions and lodging and dining recommendations. It is also available from the Austrian National Tourist Office..

Walking in the mountains

Austria boasts about 680 mountain peaks over 3 000m/10 000ft and 528 carefully managed mountain huts, offering mountain enthusiasts a wide variety of possibilities for walking and climbing routes of every imaginable degree of difficulty. Many of these are managed by the **Österreichischer Alpenverein**, Wilhelm-Greil-Straße 15, A-6010 Innsbruck, ☏ 0512/5 95 47 17; www.alpenverein.at.

For safety reasons, it is essential to plan the route of any mountain excursions very carefully in advance, to ensure that you have the right equipment and to match the route to your level of fitness.

Mountain safety

The mountains, while spectacular to behold, conceal very real dangers, which can catch both inexperienced

WINTER SPORTS RESORTS(1)	Michelin map 730 fold #	Altitude above sea-level of the resort in metres	Cable-cars	Chair-lifts and ski tows	total length in km of ski slopes	distance (in km) covered by cross-country ski runs	Skating rink	Indoor swimming pool	Horse-drawn sleigh rides	Summer Skiing
Aflenz-Kurort St	23	765 - 1 180		8	20	18	x	1		
Altenmarkt/Zauchensee S	20	856-2 130	3	24	150	150		5		
Badgastein/Sportgastein S	33	1 083-2 686	6	25	175	31	x	10		
Berwang T	16	1 336-1 740		14	40	15	x	4		
Brand V	27	1 050-1 920		9	30	36	x	6		
Brixen im Thale/Westendorf T	18	800-1 827	1	12	32	18		1		
Dorfgastein S	33	835-2 033	3	19	80	20		1		
Ehrwald T	16	1 000-3 000	3	18	25	50	x	7		
Ellmau T	18	820-1 550	1	12	35	10	x	2		
Filzmoos S	20	1 057-1 645	1	15	32	34		6		
Flachau/Flachauwinkl S	20	925-1 980	7	45	60	150	x	6		
Fulpmes/Schlick 2000 T	30	960-2 260	2	7	20	15	x	8		
Galtür T	28	1 584-2 297		11	40	45	x	2		
Gargellen V	27	1 430-2 300	4	9	33			3		
Gaschurn/Partenen V	27	1 000-2 370		27	100	30	x	6		
Gerlos T	31	1 250-2 300	2	26	70	25		9		
Gosau O	20	766-1 800	3	35	65	45		2		
Großarl S	34	920-2 033	3	21	80	15		4		
Heiligenblut K	32	1301-2 902	1	11	55	14	x	5		
Hermagor/Sonnenalpe/ Naßfeld K	33	600-2 004	4	22	101	100	x	3		
Hofgastein (Bad) S	33	870-2 300	3	21	175	37	x	10		
Innsbruck/Igls T	30	575-2 256	5	7	25	25	x	15		
Ischgl T	28	1 377-2 872	5	36	200	48	x	11		
Kaprun S	32	800-3 029	5	22	50	15	x	10	x	⛷
Kaunertal T	29	1273-3 160		8	25	15	x	2		⛷
Kirchberg in Tirol T	18	860-1 995	1	17	44	30	x	7	x	
Kitzbühel T	18	800-2 000	4	24	158	48	x	12	x	
Kleinarl S	33	1 014-1 980		11	120	20		2	x	
Kleinkirchheim (Bad) K	34	1 100-2 055	3	29	85	16	x	16	x	
Kleinwalsertal/Hirschegg Mittelberg Riezlern V	15	1 088-2 080	2	33	80	44	x	30	x	
Kössen T	18	600-1 700	1	10	25	83		1	x	
Kühtai T	29	2 020-2 520		10	40	15		3		
Lech/Oberlech V	28	1 450-2 444	5	29	110	19	x	15	x	
Lermoos T	16	1 004-2 250		19	29	61	x	10	x	
Leutasch T	16	1 130-1 605		4	9	150	x	8	x	
Lienz T	32	673-2 250	1	11	55	23	x	3		
Lofer S	19	639-1 747	2	12	30	50	x	6	x	

WINTER SPORTS RESORTS(1)	Michelin map 730 fold #	Altitude above sea-level of the resort in metres	Cable-cars	Chair-lifts and ski tows	total length in km of ski slopes	distance (in km) covered by cross-country ski runs	Skating rink	Indoor swimming pool	Horse-drawn sleigh rides	Summer Skiing
Mallnitz K	33	1 200-2 650	1	11	36	28	x	1	x	
Maria Alm S	19	800-2 000	2	33	70	30		8	x	
Mariazell St	23	785-1 267	1	6	11	70	x	1	x	
Matrei in Osttirol T	32	1 100-2 400		6	29	29	x	2	x	
Mayrhofen T	31	630-2 250	3	20	90	10	x	13	x	
Mitterndorf (Bad) St	21	812-1 965		21	25	95	x	1	x	
Mühlbach am Hochkönig S	20	853-1 826	1	22	160	12	x	2	x	
Nauders T	28	1 400-2 750	1	15	65	40	x	6	x	
Neukirchen am Grossvenediger S	31	856-2 150	2	13	30	35	x	3	x	
Neustift/Hochstubal T	30	1 000 3 250	4	26	68	124	x	17	x	☃
Obergurgl/Hochgurgl T	29	1 930-3 080	1	21	110	17	x	14		
Obertauern S	33	1 740-2 335	1	25	120	17		10	x	
Partenen V	28	1 100-2 370	5	27	100	30	x	6	x	
Radstadt S	20	856-1 677		10	17	150	x	3	x	
Ramsau am Dachstein St	21	1 100-2 700	1	20	40	155		5	x	☃
Rauris S	32	950-2 200	1	9	25	43		4	x	
Saalbach-Hinterglemm S	19	1 003-2 100	9	50	180	10	x	20	x	
Saalfelden S	19	744-1 550		5	14	80	x	2	x	
St. Anton am Arlberg/St. Christoph T	28	1 304-2 810	4	37	260	19	x	8	x	
St. Gallenkirch/Gortipohl V	27	900-2 370	4	24	100	30		3		
St. Jakob in Defereggen T	31	1 389-2 520	1	8	35	26	x	2	x	
St. Johann im Pongau/Alpendorf S	20	650-1 850	2	26	19	25	x	5	x	
St. Johann in Tirol T	19	663-1 700	2	16	60	114	x	6	x	
St. Michael im Lungau S	34	1 075-2 360		11	60	65	x	7	x	
Schladming St	21	750-1 894	1	23	25	10	x	1	x	
Schruns/Tschagguns V	27	700-2 380	3	10	40	13	x	5	x	
Seefeld in Tirol T	16	1 200-2 100	3	18	25	170	x	32	x	
Semmering N	24	1 000-1 339		5	12	18	x	6	x	
Serfaus T	28	1 427-2 700	2	17	80	42	x	14	x	
Sölden/Hochsölden T	29	1 377-3 250	3	30	101	6	x	6		
Tauplitz/Tauplitzalm St	21	900-2 000		18	25	80		2	x	
Turrach/Turracherhöhe K/St	34	1 763-2 200		11	30	25	x	3	x	
Tuxertal/Lanersbach T	30	1 300-3 250	4	29	126	23	x	11	x	☃
Wagrain S	20	900-2 014	6	42	150	35	x	3	x	
Werfenweng S	20	1 000-1 836		12	25	38		2	x	
Wildschönau T	18	828-1 903	2	25	42	30		4	x	
Zell am See S	19	758-1 969	6	27	70	40	x	15	x	
Zürs V	28	1 720-2 450	5	29	110	4		3		

(1) The letter following the name of the resort denotes the Land in which it is situated: B Burgenland, N Niederösterreich, S Salzburg, T Tirol, K Kärnten, O Oberösterreich, St Steiermark, V Vorarlberg

and experienced hikers alike unawares. Avalanches, rock-falls, sudden weather changes, heavy mists, unstable terrain, the icy water of mountain streams and lakes, loss of orientation, mistaken judgement of distances – all these represent potential danger to mountaineers, skiers and hikers. Mists and storms are difficult to anticipate and can manifest themselves unexpectedly even in high summer. At high altitudes, the snow cover remains into early July and snow banks often make north-facing slopes impassable. Never to set off alone or without having communicated your planned route and estimated time of return to a third party.

Lightning

In rocky countryside the arrival of lightning is often heralded by an electrostatic charge in the air (and one's hair). During storms you should not seek shelter on narrow ridges, or under overhanging rocks, just inside the entrance to caves or in clefts in the rock. You should also avoid standing under isolated trees or near metal objects (such as fences). Crampons and ice-axes should not be carried on your person. If possible, you should put at least 15m/49ft between yourself and any outcrop (such as a tree or a rock) and remain in a crouched position with your knees well drawn up to your chest and any exposed areas of skin (such as your hands) not touching any rock. During storms, the car is an excellent refuge, as it acts as a Faraday cage (electrostatic screen).

MOUNTAIN CLIMBING

Mountain guides and climbing schools are to be found in the following areas:
- **Carinthia**: Ferlach, Gmünd, Grosskirchheim, Heiligenblut, Kolbnitz, Kötschach-Mauthen, Spittal an der Drau, Villach;
- **Lower Austria**: Gloggnitz, Puchberg am Schneeberg;
- **Salzburg**: Filzmoos, Kaprun, Maria Alm, Mauterndorf, Neukirchen, Salzburg;
- **Styria**: Bad Aussee, Graz, Ramsau am Dachstein, Schladming;
- **Tyrol**: Ehrwald, Ellmau, Fulpmes, Galtür, Going, Innsbruck, Kufstein, Landeck, Lanersbach, Mayrhofen, Nauders, Obergurgl, St. Anton, St. Johann, Sölden;
- **Upper Austria**: Ebensee, Gosau am Dachstein, Grünau im Almtal, Gschwandt, Hallstatt, Hinterstoder, Linz, Mondsee, Spital am Pyhrn, Windischgarsten;
- **Vorarlberg**: Bartholomäberg, Brand, Lech, Mittelberg, Vandans.

Further information is available from **Verband Alpiner Vereine Österreichs**, Bäckerstraße 16, A-1010 Wien, ☎ 01/5 12 54 88, *www.vavoe.at*, an umbrella organization for a dozen Alpine hiking organizations, including the Österreichischer Alpenverein (◐ *see Walking in the Mountains*).

WINTER SPORTS

Here are some statistics on winter sports facilities in Austria:
- 22 000km/13 700mi of ski slopes
- 147 cable-cars
- 2 708 ski tows
- 512 chair-lifts
- 16 000km/9 900mi of cross-country ski tracks
- 900 resorts with cross-country ski runs
- 292 resorts with snow-board runs
- 500 ski schools with 8 300 ski instructors
- 50 children's ski schools
- 500 natural toboggan runs
- 1 500 curling rinks
- 14 000km/8 700mi of snow-cleared winter hiking trails

Austria has numerous famous ski areas equipped with excellent infrastructure. Web sites are listed throughout this book or contact the regional or local tourist offices for details.

Year-round skiing is possible at the following resorts:
- in **Carinthia**, Mölltaler Gletscher;
- in **Salzburg**, Kaprun/Kitzsteinhorn;
- in **Styria**, Ramsau/Dachstein;
- in the **Tyrol**, Hintertux/Tuxer Gletscher, Kaunertal, Stubaier

Gletscher, Ötztal/Rettenbach-und Tiefenbachferner, Pitztal/Mittel-bergferner.

For the most current, snow and weather reports as well as avalanche warnings, see *www.lawine.at*)

All the resorts shown in the above table have ski schools.

SPAS

Austria has a wide selection of spa resorts equipped for the most varied treatment. In the skiing season many of these spa resorts (such as Badg-astein) keep their thermal baths open.

Sulphur springs – These are used mainly to remedy ailments of the joints, muscles, the nervous system and skin troubles at resorts such as Baden whose thermal beach draws many Viennese and, in the Salzkam-mergut, at Bad Ischl and Bad Goisern.

Salt springs – Waters impregnated with sodium chloride (salt) from natu-ral springs or "mother-waters", the residues of the refining of industrial salt, are exploited alongside the salt mInes themselves. They are used in douches and baths and are good for gynecological and infantile diseases, and for inhaling, when they clear the bronchial tubes. To this group may be added the bicarbonate bearing waters, like those of Bad Gleichenberg in Styria, which are also recommended for drinking to treat the stomach, intestines and kidneys.

Iodized springs

These are invaluable for curing meta-bolic and circulatory disorders, and for vision and glandular troubles. They are particularly well represented by Bad Hall in Upper Austria. In addition to the true mineral springs, some hot springs such as those at Badgastein also have radioactive properties.

The Austrian national tourist office issues a brochure entitled *Von Körper, Geist und Seele empfohlen* listing establishments offering various treat-ments (spa, thermal baths, Kneipp etc) with a brief description of each health centre. Regional tourist offices can provide specialised lists of spa resorts in their area.

Further details can also be obtained from the Österreichischer Heilbäder-und Kurorteverband, Josefsplatz 6, A-1010 Wien, ☎ 01/512 19 04, Fax 01/512 86 39.

Activities for Children 🇰Kids

In this guide, sights of particular interest to children are indicated with a KIDS symbol Kids. Some attractions may offer discount fees for children.

Calendar of Events

Below is a selection of Austria's most popular events. Most take place annually, although precise may vary slightly. 🕐 For details, contact the local or regional tourist offices. For additional events, see the Address Book sections under Graz, Innsbruck, Klagenfurt, Linz, Salzburg, St. Pölten and Wien/Vienna.

TRADITIONAL FOLK FESTIVALS

JANUARY

6 Jan: **Bad Gastein** — *Perchtenlauf:* carnival procession (every 4 years, next time 2010)

FEBRUARY

Imst — *Bubenfasnacht:* carnival procession (every 4 years, next time 2010)

Imst — *Schleicherlaufen:* carnival procession (every 4 years, next time 2008)

Telfs — *Schleicherlaufen:* carnival procession (every 4 years, next time 2009)

MAY & JUNE

1st May weekend: **Zell im Zillertal** — *Gauderfest:* centuries-old beer festival with folk music and other events, ☎ 0 52 82/22 81

H. Kautzky/ VIENNASLIDE

Schleicherlaufen at Telfs

Whit Monday: **Freistritz an der Gail** (west of Villach) — *Gailtaler Kufenstechen:* a joust using a barrel as target, followed by dancing

Corpus Christi (2nd Thur after Whitsun): **Bischofshofen** — Procession with floral poles *(Prangstangen)*

Corpus Christi: **Brixental in Tirol** — Procession on horseback

Corpus Christi: **Gmunden** — Procession

Corpus Christi: **Deutschlandsberg** — Procession and carpet of flowers

Corpus Christi: **Hallstatt, Traunkirchen** — Processions on the lake

24 June: **Zederhaus** — *Prangstangentragen:* flower-decorated poles up to 8m/26ft long are carried to the church in a procession and left there until Assumption Day (Aug 15)

AUGUST

early Aug: **Krakaudorf** Murau (15 August) — "Samson" processions

SEPTEMBER - DECEMBER

late Sep, early Oct: **Burgenland and Lower Austria** — Wine harvest: processions, wine fountains, fireworks

late Nov-Christmas: **Nationwide** — Advent and Christmas markets

5 Dec: **Bad Mitterndorf** — *Nikolospiel:* street festival in honour of St Nicholas

27 Dec-15 Jan: **Thaur** (northeast of Innsbruck) — Christmas nativity scenes are on display in people's houses, some of which are open to the public

PASSION PLAYS

late May: **Erl** (northeast of Kufstein) — Every 6 years (next time 2008)

May-Oct: **Thiersee** — Every 6 years (next time 2011)

FESTIVALS

(& *see also the Address Book sections under Graz, Innsbruck, Klagenfurt, Linz, Salburg, St. Pölten and Wien/Vienna*)

MARCH-APRIL

Graz — Diagonale: Austrian film festival

Salzburg — Easter Festival

MAY-SEPTEMBER

May-Jun: **Vienna** — Vienna Festival

May-Sep: **Millstatt** — International Music Festival

Jun-Jul: **Innsbruck** — Tanzsommer: summer dance festival

Jun-Jul: **Krems und Wachau** — Danube festival, with a wide range of theatre, dance, music, arts etc, ☎ 0 22 36/21 2 12, *www.donaufestival.at*

Jun-Aug: **Wiesen** — Open-air festivals (reggae, alternative rock, jazz, rock, reggae-Afro-Latin), ☎ 0 26 26/8 16 48

Jul-Aug: **Ossiach/Villach** — Carinthian Summer Festival

Jul-Aug: **Klagenfurt** — Musikforum Viktring

Jul-Aug: **Innsbruck** — Festival of ancient music, Schloss Ambras concerts

Jul-Aug: **Petronell** — Art Carnuntum: world theatre festival, ☎ 0 21 63/34 00

Jul-Aug: **Vienna** — Musikalischer KlangBogen

mid-Jul-late Aug: **Mörbisch** — Operetta festival (by Neusiedler See)

late Jul-end Aug: **Bregenz** — Lakeside festival

late Jul-end Aug: **Salzburg** — Salzburg Festival

SEPTEMBER

Linz — Festival Ars Electronica

St. Anton am Arlberg — Film festival ("mountains, people, adventure"), ☎ 0 54 46/22 690

1st week: **Mondsee** — Mondsee festival of chamber music and literature, ☎ 0 62 32/35 44

2nd week: **Eisenstadt** — International Haydn Festival in Schloss Esterházy, ☎ 0 26 82/6 18 66

Sep-Oct: **Linz** — International Bruckner Festival

Sep-Oct: **St. Pölten** — Musica Sacra

OCTOBER

Graz and its surroundings — Steirischer herbst: Styrian autumn festival

Shopping

LOCAL CRAFTS

Those looking for good quality souvenirs in memory of their holiday should visit the **Heimatwerk**, an official outlet for the work of local artisans. Burgenland – China (Stoob), basket-weaving (Piringsdorf and Weiden am See), jade jewelery and serpentine marble (Bernstein).

◆ **Carinthia** – *Kärntner Heimatwerk*, Herrengasse 2, A-9020 Klagenfurt, ☎ 04 63/55 5 75. Costumes, ceramics, carved wooden boxes; wrought iron (Friesach).

◆ **Salzburg** – *Salzburger Heimatwerk*, Residenzplatz 9, A-5010 Salzburg, ☎ 06 62/84 41 19. Pewter, china, regional costumes.

◆ **Styria** – *Steirisches Heimatwerk*, Paulustorgasse 4, A-8010 Graz, ☎ 03 16/82 71 06. Printed linens, jewellery (Bad Aussee), carved wooden masks (Mitterndorf), painted pottery (Gams), *Loden* cloth (Ramsau and Mandling).

◆ **Tyrol** – *Tiroler Heimatwerk*, Meraner Straße 2-4, A-6020 Innsbruck, ☎ 0 51 25/58 23 20. Wooden Christmas cribs, tablecloths and embroidered fabrics, wrought-iron; majolica (Schwaz), cut and engraved glassware (Kufstein and Kramsach).

◆ **Upper Austria** – *Oberösterreichisches Heimatwerk*, Landstraße 31, A-4020 Linz, ☎ 07 32/78 45 62. Painted glassware and painted wooden boxes: handwoven linen (Haslach); leatherwork, candles (Braunau); wrought iron, steel-engravings (Steyr); china (Gmunden); headdresses and silver jewellery (Bad Ischl).

◆ **Vienna** – Petit point, Augarten porcelain, embroidered blouses. Viennese bronze and enamel.

◆ **Vorarlberg** – *Vorarlberger Heimatwerk*, Montfortstraße 4, A-6900 Bregenz, ☎ 0 55 74/4 23 25. Wooden articles, painted glassware, hand weaving; embroidery (Schwarzenberg and Lustenau); candles (Schruns).

Sightseeing

As admission times and charges are liable to change, the information in this guide should only be used as a guideline. Prices listed apply to individual adults, but discounts for children, seniors, groups and families are almost always available.

At the end of the introductory paragraph for each destination we list the telephone number, address and Web site of the local tourist office whose staff can help with tours, lodging, etc.

Churches do not permit sightseeing visits during services and are usually closed between noon and 2pm. Admission times are given if the interior is of special interest. It is customary to make a donation, especially if accompanied by a church caretaker.

DISCOUNTS

The following cities and regions offer special discount tickets covering a range of leisure and cultural activities, as well as transport: Innsbruck, Carinthia, Linz, Salzburg, Salzburg region and Vienna.

Books

The Austrians: A Thousand Year Odyssey by Gordon Brook-Shephard
A Brief Survey of Austrian History by Richard Rickett
Contemporary Austria and the Legacy of the Third Reich by Robert Knight
Chronicle and Works (volume 2) *Haydn at Esterházy 1776-1790* by HO Robbins Landon
Fin de Siècle Vienna by Carl E Schorske
Mountain Walking in Austria by Cecil Davies
Music and Musicians in Vienna by R Rickett
The Fall of the House of Habsburg by Edward Crankshaw
The Habsburg Monarchy 1618-1815 by Charles Ingrao
The Habsburg Monarchy 1765-1918 by Robin Oakey
Vienna, the Image of a Culture in Decline by Edward Crankshaw

LITERATURE

Aichinger, Ilse: *Die größere Hoffnung*
Bachmann, Ingeborg: *Malina, Die gestundete Zeit*
Bernhard, Thomas: *Das Kalkwerk (The Limeworks), Die Berühmten (The Famous), Holzfällen (Woodcutters), Heldenplatz (Heroes' Square)*

Freud, Sigmund: *Die Traumdeutung (The Interpretation of Dreams), Das Unbehagen in der Kultur (Civilization and its Discontents)*
Frischmuth, Barbara: *Die Schrift des Freundes*
Grillparzer, Franz: *Das Goldene Vliess (The Golden Fleece), König Ottokars Glück und Ende (King Ottocar, His Rise and Fall), Ein Bruderzwist in Habsburg (Family Strife in Habsburg)*
Handke, Peter: *Die Angst des Tormanns beim Elfmeter (The Goalie's Anxiety at the Penalty Kick), Die linkshändige Frau (The Left-Handed Woman), Publikumsbeschimpfung (Offending the Audience), Wunschloses Unglück (A Sorrow Beyond Dreams)*
Hofmannsthal, Hugo von: *Jedermann (Everyman), Das Salzburger Grosse Welttheater, Der Rosenkavalier* **(libretto)**, *Chandos-Brief* **(essay)**, *Cristinas Heimreise (Christina's Journey Home), Der Turm (The Tower)*
Musil, Robert von: *Der Mann ohne Eigenschaften (The Man without Qualities), Die Verwirrungen des Zöglings Törless*
Rilke, Rainer Maria: *Sonette an Orpheus (Sonnets to Orpheus), Duineser Elegien (Duino Elegies)*
Roth, Joseph: *Radetzkymarsch (Radetzky March), Kapuzinergruft (The Capuchin Tomb)*
Schnitzler, Arthur: *Liebelei (Playing with Love), Reigen (Merry-Go-Round), Leutnant Gustl (None But the Brave), Der Weg ins Freie (The Road to the Open)*
Stifter, Adalbert: *Der Nachsommer (Indian Summer), Bunte Steine (Colourful Stones)*
Zweig, Stefan: *Schachnovelle, Sternstunden der Menschheit (The Tide of Fortune), Ungeduld des Herzen (Beware of Pity)*

BASIC INFORMATION

BUSINESS HOURS

Most shops are open Mon-Fri 9am-6pm and Sat 9am-1pm (to 5pm in Vienna and other bigger cities). Shops in tourist areas often remain open longer (Mon-Fri until 9pm, Sat until 6pm, in some stations and airports daily until 11pm).

MAJOR HOLIDAYS

1 January (New Year), 6 January (Epiphany), Easter Monday, 1 May (Labour Day), Ascension Day, Whit Monday, Corpus Christi, 15 August (Assumption of the Virgin Mary), 26 October (Austrian National Holiday), 1 November (All Saints' Day), 8 December (Immaculate Conception), 25 and 26 December (Christmas).

MAIL

Post offices (where currency can also be changed) are generally open Mon-Fri 8am-noon and 2-6pm. Cash-desks close at 5pm. A small number of post offices open on Sat 8am-noon. In major cities, one or two post offices may keep longer hours or even stay open 24hr, including at weekends. Stamps are also sold at *Tabaktrafiken* (tobacconists).

Letters addressed to a destination in Austria should indicate the international abbreviation "A" in front of the post code.

Sending a postcard or letter up to 20g costs 55¢ to an address within Austria or Europe and €1.25 to anywhere else.

MONEY

Along with 11 other European countries, Austria introduced the euro as its official currency in January 1999 and put it into circulation in January 2002. One Euro is divided into 100 cents. Euros come in seven notes (five, 10, 20, 50, 100, 200 and 500 euros) and eight coins (one and two euro coins and one, two, five, 10, 20 and 50 cent coins).

Travelers' checks and foreign currency can be changed into Euros at banks, bureaux de change, and in some travel agencies and hotels. Major credit cards such as Visa and MasterCard are generally accepted throughout Austria, although you should always check before making your purchases. Banks are generally open 8am-12.30pm and 1.30-3pm on Mon, Tues, Wed and Fri, and 8am-12.30pm and 1.30-5.30pm on Thur.

TELEPHONES

The international dialling code for Austria is 43, so to call from abroad dial +43, then the local code (minus the first zero), then the correspondent's number.

To call abroad from Austria, dial 00, then the appropriate international dialling code (Australia: 61, Canada: 1, Eire: 353, New Zealand: 64, UK: 44, USA: 1), then the local code (minus the first zero, if applicable), then the correspondent's number.

Telephone cards (*Telefon-Wertkarte*) for pay phones are on sale at post offices, Tabaktrafiken and hotels.

Emergency Telephone Numbers
+ Fire: 122
+ Police: 133
+ Ambulance: 144
+ Breakdown service: 120 or 123

TIPPING

Tipping is customary in Austria, especially in restaurants, cafes and bars where you should tip about 10% or round up the bill. Rather than leave money on the table, hand over the tip at the time of payment. Taxi drivers, hairdressers, room cleaning staff, bellhops and other service personnel also appreciate a small tip.

Traunkirchen in the Salzkammergut
G. Simeone/ DIAF

NATURE

Topography

At the heart of the Alps, Austria covers an area of 84 000km²/32 430sq mi, stretching for 580km/360mi from Switzerland to Hungary. For a distance of 2 600km/1 600mi it shares a border with Germany, the Czech and Slovak republics, Hungary, Slovenia, Italy, Switzerland and Liechtenstein.

The River Danube, which acts as a catchment for virtually all the rivers of Austria, flows west-east for 360km/224mi across the Danube plateau, a vast upland region abutting the Bohemian mountains to the north and encompassing the mountainous Wachau region. This is the historical heart of Austria. Two thirds of the country is covered by the Alpine chain. To the east, Austria runs into the Puszta, or Hungarian plain.

ALPINE COUNTRY

The Austrian Alps are divided from north to south into three chains: the Northern Limestone Alps, the High or Central Alps, and the Southern Limestone Alps, separated from each other by the valleys of the Inn, the Salzach and the Enns in the north; and the Drava and the Mur in the south.

The Northern Limestone Alps

These overflow into Bavaria and extend - west to east - into the massifs of Rätikon, Lechtal, Karwendel, Kaisergebirge, Steinernes Meer, Tennengebirge, Dachstein, the Alps of Ennstal, Eisenerz, Hochschwab and Schneeberg. The highest point is the Parseierspitze at 3 038m/9 967ft .

Transverse valleys

The Northern Limestone Alps are divided into distinct massifs by transverse valleys, along which the Lech, Ache (the Alz in Bavaria), Saalach and Enns rivers flow towards the Danube plateau. As a result, it's not particularly difficult for drivers to cross or go around these massifs.

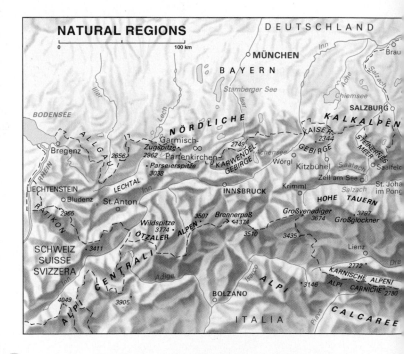

Karst plateaux

East of the Ache, the Dachstein, the Hochschwab and the Raxalpe rise sharply to more than 2 000m/6 500ft. Due to the porous nature of the limestone, these mountains are like stony deserts, scored here and there with narrow furrows. Here, the flow of the water is almost entirely subterranean, which has resulted in the formation of numerous caves, including the famous ones in the Dachstein.

Long river valleys

The Northern Limestone Alps are bounded to the south by a deep cleft, separating them from the High Alps. This cleft is divided into valleys, each with its own river, the Inn, the Salzach and the Enns. This major break in the landscape makes it possible to drive along the chain for its entire length.

The High or Central Alps

The High Alps, mostly of crystalline rock, appear as a succession of ridges topped by glaciers, comprising (west to east): the Ötztal Alps, the Hohe Tauern and the Niedere Tauern. For more than 250km/150mi the crestline rarely drops below 3 000m/10 000ft. The Brenner pass, the medieval route to Venice, links the valleys of the Inn and the Adige. The Grossglockner Hochalpenstraße and the Felbertauern tunnel make it possible to cross the imposing massif of the Hohe Tauern. To the south of the High Alps, the furrows of the Drava, Mur and Mürz rivers form the natural link between Vienna and northern Italy.

The Southern Limestone Alps

The Carnic Alps and the Karawanken are Austrian on their northern slopes only. Under the terms of the St-Germain-en-

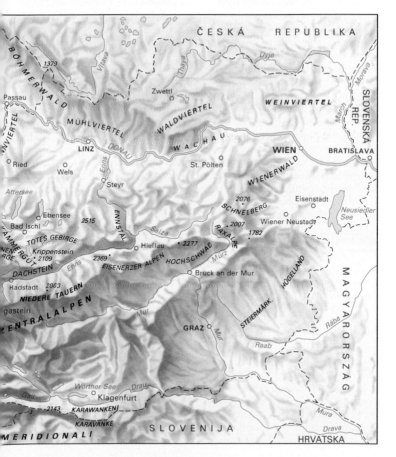

Laye Peace Treaty in 1919, the southern part of the Tyrol was ceded to Italy and the Julian Alps to then-Yugoslavia.

ALPINE GLACIERS

About 10 000 years ago, immensely thick Alpine glaciers advanced northwards, extending over the Bavarian plateau almost as far as modern Munich.

The glaciers substantially remodeled the relief of the Alpine valleys. They scooped out natural amphitheaters known as cirques (like the one closing off the Brandnertal), scoured valleys into a U-shaped section (like the steep-sided Saalach Valley north of Saalfelden), and created hanging valleys (such as the one above the Achensee). These funnel-shaped basins with their steep cliffs often feature spectacular waterfalls .

Glaciers tended not to follow the existing continuous slope of a valley but to carve out a series of well-defined steps (as evident in the Karawanken), creating natural sites for modern hydroelectric plants. The reservoirs often lie amid breathtaking mountain scenery, as in the case of the impressive Glockner-Kaprun installation.

Carrying along a mass of rocky debris, which when deposited is known as a moraine, the glaciers added an extra, complex layer to the landscape of the pre-alpine plateau. The semi-circular moraines created natural dams behind which water accumulated to form the lakes of the Bavarian plateau and of the northern Salzkammergut.

MOUNTAIN CLIMATES

In contrast to weather in the valleys, the mountain climate varies considerably according to altitude, geography or exposure to sunshine.

Winds

In the late morning warm, expanded air creeps up from the valley and causes cloud formations around the summits. Due to this weather phenomenon, viewpoint atop the mountains are best visited early to mid-morning. Around 5pm the cold mountain breezes sweep back down into the valley, creating a sudden plunge in temperature.

The Föhn

This warm fall wind is most strongly felt north of the Alps, in the Alpine valleys of the Rhine, the Inn (especially in the Ötztal) and the Salzach. It is caused by the passage of a deep depression along the north slope of the Alps. Having shed its moisture on the Italian slope of the range, where storms and rain are frequent, the air drawn in by the depression spills over the crestline. Warmed by compression as it loses altitude, it is transformed into a dry, warm wind that creates wonderfully clear skies.

In the mountains everyone is on the alert. Torrents are in spate, avalanches rumble and the risk of fire is great. Locals live in such a state of nervous exhaustion that, for example, examinations are sometimes suspended in Innsbruck schools. The Föhn is even said to be submitted as a mitigating circumstance in criminal trials.

Flora

In mountain areas the pattern of vegetation is not only influenced by soil type and climate but also strongly linked to altitude and aspect. Tree species in particular tend to succeed one another in clearly defined vertical stages, though this staging is much modified by human influences as well as by the orientation of the particular slope. Northern, ie south-facing, sunny slopes offer the best growing conditions and have therefore been the most subject to deforestation. Southern, ie north-facing, slopes by contrast have tended to keep their trees, which flourish in the prevailing wetter and more shady conditions. This pattern is seen at its best in valleys running east-west.

In most parts of the Alps, farming is practiced up to about 1 500m/5 000ft. Above here is a belt of conifer forest that gives way to alpine pastures at around 2 200m/7 000ft. Above 3 000m/10 000ft bare rock prevails, only occasionally relieved by mosses and lichens.

Edelweiss
Leontopodium alpinum
July to September

Stemless Trumpet Gentian
Gentiana acaulis
May to August

Alpine Sea Holly
Eryngium alpinum
July and August

Martagon Lily
Lilium martagon
June to August

Orange Lily
Lilium bulbiferum
June and July

Alpenrose
Rhododendron ferrugineum
July and August

TREES

The following conifers dominate the Alpine forests.

Spruce (Fichte)

This is the typical tree of north-facing slopes. It has a pointed outline, drooping branches, reddish bark and sharp needles.

Larch (Lärche)

The only European conifer to lose its needles in winter, the larch is prevalent on south-facing slopes. Its delicate light-green foliage casts a relatively light shade, allowing grass and herbs to grow underneath. The small cones are carried upright on the twigs.

Austrian pine (Schwarzkiefer)

The medium-high Austrian pine has a dense crown, dark green foliage and a pale and darkly fissured bark. Its needles grow in pairs. It is undemanding in terms of soil and climate and frequently used in reclamation work in difficult conditions (eg on thin limestone soils).

M. Janvier/ MICHELIN

Austrian Pine

Stone pine (Zirbel)

This pine has upward-curving branches that make it look like a candelabrum. It grows right up to the tree line, often twisted into fantastic shapes by the wind. Its bluish-green needles grow in clusters of five. The dense wood of this pine is much appreciated by woodcarvers and makers of rustic furniture.

ALPINE FLORA

The name "Alpine" is normally used to describe plants growing above the tree line. Because of the short growing season (June to August) they tend to flower early and be resistant to drought (woolly leaf surfaces, thick leaves for water storage). Flowering plants found in the Austrian Alps include the Alpine Rose, Gentian, Primrose, Globe Flower and Cyclamen, Martagon Lily, Alpine Aster, Carline Thistle and on the edges of the snow-fields Soldanellae. Rocky areas are home to Edelweiss, Saxifraga, Alpine Poppy and Glacier Crowfoot.

Fauna

Austria has a rich and varied animal life. The shores of the Neusiedler See are a paradise for 250 species of waterfowl and waders (👉 *see illustration under entry*), including kingfishers, river terns, spoonbills and herons. Storks are also regular visitors here. On the lakes of the Salzkammergut and Upper Austria, swans add a fairy-tale element to the scene.

The Danube is home to 60 of the 80 species of fish to be found in Austria, including eels, perch and catfish.

Various kinds of deer, wild boar, badgers and foxes make their home in Austria's forests, while the fields and woodlands are a playground for rabbits and hares.

ALPINE FAUNA

Visitors never fail to succumb to the charms of Austria's cutest Alpine resident, the grey-brown **marmot**. Unfortunately, being of a somewhat shy disposition, it only rarely grants lucky ramblers a public audience. The **blue hare** is another cautious creature.

Herds of nimble **chamois** are to be seen principally in the Limestone Alps. **Alpine ibex**, equally agile and also very strong, live above the tree line. Red deer are common throughout Austria.

Typical Alpine bird life includes the snow-partridge, the Alpine jackdaw, the griffon vulture and the capercaillie. On the whole, and especially during the mating season, these birds are more likely to be heard than seen. King of them all, however, is surely the **golden eagle**, a truly majestic bird with a wingspan of 2m/7ft, which sadly rather seldom makes an appearance.

HISTORY

Time Line

The main events since the rise of the Habsburgs.

THE HABSBURGS

1273-1291 — **Rudolf I**, founder of the Habsburg dynasty, is elected by the German princes to succeed the Babenbergs, defeats Ottokar and divides Austria and Styria between his sons.

1335 — Carinthia and Carniola are annexed to the Habsburg territory.

1358-1365 — Reign of **Rudolf IV.** The Tyrol is annexed to Austria (1363).

1440-1493 — **Friedrich III,** Duke of Styria, inaugurates a policy of political succession and intermarriage which raises the Habsburgs to the highest rank in the west. His son Maximilian is the first to benefit from this.

EXPANSION OF THE HABSBURG EMPIRE

1493-1519 — By his marriage to the daughter of Charles the Bold, **Maximilian I**, Emperor of the Holy Roman Empire, gains possession of most of the Burgundian states. He marries his eldest son, Philip the Handsome, to the Infanta of Spain. Their son, Charles V, inherits the whole of their possessions.

1519-1556 — Reign of **Emperor Charles V.** Vienna is besieged by the Turks (1529).

1556 — Abdication of Charles V and partition of the Empire. Charles' brother, Ferdinand I, becomes Emperor and head of the Austrian branch of the House of Habsburg. He founds the Austrian Monarchy and also reigns over Bohemia and Hungary. Charles' son, Philip II, is given Spain and Portugal, Sicily, Naples and northern Italy, the Low Countries and Burgundy.

1618-1648 — Thirty Years War begins as a religious conflict and ends up as a Europe-wide power struggle.

CONSOLIDATION OF THE AUSTRIAN EMPIRE

1657-1705 — Reign of Leopold I. Vienna is again besieged by the Turks (1683). The Hungarian monarchy falls to the Habsburgs (1687).

18C — Throughout this century, Austrian policy is overshadowed by three great problems: the Succession to the Empire; the territorial threat from the Turks, the Piedmontese and the French; the unified administration of very different countries.

1713 — To ensure his daughter's succession to the imperial crown in the absence of male heirs, Charles VI sacrifices territorial rights to the great European countries and promulgates

ROGER VIOLLET

Maria Theresia

the Pragmatic Sanction. When the king dies, Maria Theresia has to defy its signatories in order to keep her empire. War of the Austrian Succession (1740-48). Seven Years War (1756-63).

1740-1790 — Reign of **Maria Theresia** (1740-65). With the help of able ministers, she becomes popular for her financial and administrative reforms. Reign of **Joseph II** (1765-90) who, in the authoritarian manner of enlightened despotism, continues the reorganization begun by his mother.

1781 — Abolition of serfdom.

1786 — Secularization: Dissolution of 738 houses of contemplative orders under Joseph II.

1792-1835 — Reign of **Franz II**. In 1805 Austria receives the territory of the archbishops of Salzburg as compensation for the losses of territory suffered under the Treaty of Pressburg. Franz II renounces the title of Holy Roman Emperor and adopts that of **Franz I**, Emperor of Austria in 1806.

1809 — Austrian policy, particularly foreign policy, is directed by Chancellor **Metternich** who seeks revenge against France. Andreas Hofer leads the Tyrolean rebellion against the Franco-Bavarian alliance.

TROUBLE AND DOWNFALL OF THE MONARCHY

1814-1815 — **Congress of Vienna** redraws the map of Europe. Austria recovers Lombardy and Venetia, lost in wars with France, and takes a leading position in the Germanic Confederation of which Metternich is the mastermind.

1848-49 — March Revolution in Vienna. Fall of Metternich, Hungarian rebellion is suppressed with the help of Russia.

1848-1916 — Reign of **Franz Joseph.**

1866 — War between Austria and Prussia. Austria is defeated, gives up on intervening in German politics and looks towards the Balkans.

1867 — Creation of the dual Austro-Hungarian monarchy, with common foreign, defence and economic policies.

1914 — Outbreak of the First World War (1914-18), triggered by the assassination of Crown Prince Franz Ferdinand at Sarajevo in Bosnia and Austria's subsequent attack on Serbia.

1916-1918 — Reign of **Karl I**. Collapse of the Austro-Hungarian monarchy after defeat in the First World War.

THE REPUBLIC

1919 — The Treaty of St Germain-en-Laye re-draws national border, ceding South Tyrol to Italy. Following a plebiscite (1920) southern Carinthia remains in Austria and is not be ceded to then-Yugoslavia. Women are given the vote.

1920 — Federal constitution passes.

1933 — Chancellor **Engelbert Dollfuß** inaugurates an authoritarian regime, hostile both to the Social Democrats and to the Nazis.

1934 — Social Democratic Party banned. Suppression of Nazi putsch. Assassination of Dollfuß. His successor seeks to avoid war with Germany at all costs.

1938 — Hitler annexes Austria to the German Reich. Austrians approve the annexation **(Anschluß)** in a referendum.

1939-45 — Second World War.

1943 — In the Moscow Declaration the four Allied Nations undertake to restore Austria's independence after the war and restore the frontiers of 1 January 1938.

1945 —	The Russians occupy Vienna on 11 April. On 27 April a new government forms led by Karl Renner. Austria and Vienna are divided into four occupied zones.

1949-66 — Coalition government formed by the "People's Party" (ÖVP) and the Social Democrats (SPÖ).

15 May 1955 — Following the **Staatsvertrag** treaty, occupying troops withdraw from Austria.

26 October 1955 — Austria declares its neutrality.

1956 — Austria is accepted onto the Council of Europe.

1970-83 — Social democrats form a government under Chancellor Bruno Kreisky, for the first time with an absolute majority in Parliament.

1983-2000 — Government is once again a coalition of the SPÖ and ÖVP.

1989 — Austria applies for membership in the European Union. Death of Zita of Bourbon-Parma, last Empress of Austria and Queen of Hungary, in exile since 1919.

1 January 1995 — Austria joins the European Union.

1998 — Austria is admitted to the European Monetary Union.

2000- — Coalition government formed by the ÖVP and the right-wing Austrian Freedom Party (FPÖ). EU briefly imposes sanctions in protest.

2003 — FPÖ posts huge losses during elections but remains in a coalition government with the ÖVP

2003 — The Danube floods and Austrian ex-body builder Arnold Schwarzenegger is elected governor of California.

2004 — Heinz Fischer is sworn in as Austria's new president. Pope John Paul II beatifies the last Habsburg emperor, Karl I.

MILESTONES

THE EASTERN MARCH

Celtic tribes had established settlements throughout Austria for about 500 years by the time the Romans arrived in the Danube Valley around 15 BC. All along the river there arose a defensive system of forts and castles, of which Carnuntum (Petronell), capital of the province of Pannonia, was the hub.

Starting in the 4C, tribal migrations brought on the decline of the Roman Empire, resulting in a political vaccuum until the territory fell to Frankish ruler Charlemagne (747-814). He established a province called Ostmark or Ostarrîchi, the forerunner to "Österreich." The Magyars gained control of the land in 907 but it was reconquered in 955 by Otto the Great. In 976, Otto, now Holy Roman Emperor, granted the Ostmark to Leopold von Babenberg.

THE HOUSE OF BABENBERG (976-1246)

The Babenbergs ruled first as margraves, then as dukes since 1156, giving them greater independence from imperial power. They chose as residences Pöchlarn, Melk, Tulln, the Leopoldsberg and finally Vienna and founded the abbeys of Kremsmünster, St. Florian, Melk, Göttweig and Klosterneuburg.

The last of the Babenbergs, Frederick II, was killed in 1246 fighting the Magyars.

BOHEMIAN INTERVENTION (1246-78)

Since Frederick died childless, Ottokar of Bohemia laid claim to the possessions of the Babenbergs, even marrying Frederick's sister to solidify his position. When Ottokar refused to swear allegiance to Rudolf of Habsburg, who had beaten him in the election for king of the Holy Roman Empire, war ensued. Ottokar was killed at Marchfeld and Rudolf granted the duchies of Austria and Styria to his two sons, thereby laying the corner stone of the House of Habsburg rule that would last until the 20C.

The Imperial Crown

Austria Est Imperare Orbi Universo – "Austria shall rule the world" was the proud motto of the **Habsburg** dynasty *(see genealogical tree)*. And for a while, it looked as though it would be so.

In the 16C, a clever marriage policy vastly enlarged Austria's territory. Maximilian I acquired the Franche-Comté and the Low Countries by marrying Mary of Burgundy, daughter of Charles the Bold. Maximilian's grandson, **Charles V**, ended up as the most powerful sovereign in Europe, being Holy Roman Emperor, King of Spain, possessor of Naples, Sicily and Sardinia and of territories in the two Americas. Upon his abdication in 1556, the Habsburg territory fell to his brother Ferdinand I.

MARIA THERESIA "THE GREAT" (1740-80)

When Charles VI died without a male heir, the crown went to his daughter Maria Theresia. An intelligent, shrewd and determined woman, she "stood her man" against the Prussians in the War of the Austrian Succession (1740-48) and

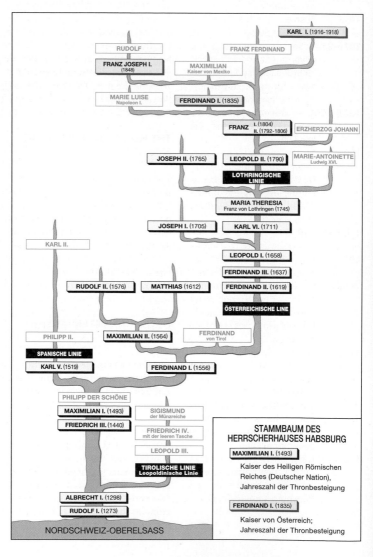

STAMMBAUM DES
HERRSCHERHAUSES HABSBURG

MAXIMILIAN I. (1493)
Kaiser des Heiligen Römischen Reiches (Deutscher Nation), Jahreszahl der Thronbesteigung

FERDINAND I. (1835)
Kaiser von Österreich; Jahreszahl der Thronbesteigung

NORDSCHWEIZ-OBERELSASS

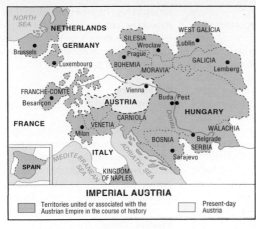

IMPERIAL AUSTRIA

☐ Territories united or associated with the Austrian Empire in the course of history

☐ Present-day Austria

the Seven Years' War (1756-63), winning the respect from other rulers and the affection of her people. An "enlightened despot," she lived unostentatiously introduced a number of popular reforms. She and her husband, Holy Roman Emperor Francis I, had 16 children.

THE STRUGGLE WITH FRANCE (1792-1815)

For the 23 years during which France was at war with the rest of Europe, Austria was, together with England, her most determined opponent.

The accession of Napoleon to the Imperial French throne in 1804 dealt a heavy blow to the Habsburg monarchy. Napoleon I opened his reign with the victories of Ulm and Austerlitz (1805) and forced Franz II to sue for peace and renounce the crown of the Holy Roman Empire.

In 1809 the defeat of the French on the battlefields of Essling and Aspern and the successful Tyrolean rebellion led by **Andreas Hofer** brought new hope to the Austrians. Eventually, though, the humiliating **Treaty of Vienna** forced Austria to relinquish Carniola, Carinthia, Trieste, Rijeka (or Fiume) and Galicia.

In 1810 Napoleon married Marie-Louise, daughter of the vanquished emperor. Metternich, however, refused to accept defeat and threw all of Austria's forces against Napoleon. In 1814 , Austrian troops marched into Paris. The **Congress of Vienna** consolidated not only the triumph of Metternich, the mastermind behind European politics, but renewed the power of the Habsburgs.

THE CENTURY OF FRANZ JOSEPH

Franz Joseph's astonishing 68-year reign (1848-1916) ranks as a particular milestone in Austrian history, largely due to the monarch's personality and policies. Although he had to overcome enormous political and personal difficulties (including the suicide of his only son, Rudolf and the assassination of his wife Elisabeth), his reign is widely regarded as a success. It brought economic prosperity and a relatively easygoing way of life, as reflected in the rise of the middle class and an artistic and cultural revival.

The Republic of Austria

Since adopting a federal constitution in 1920, the Republic of Austria has been a Federal State consisting of nine autonomous provinces.

THE AUSTRIAN PROVINCES (BUNDESLÄNDER)

Every five or six years, each province (Land) elects a **Provincial Diet** with a number of members ranging from 36 and 56 depending on the province's population. Only the Diet of Vienna has 100 members. The diet elects the members of the **Provincial Government** (Landtag), which is the administrative organ of the Land.

Burgenland

3 965km²/1 531sq mi – population 278 700 – capital: Eisenstadt
Predominantly agricultural, this German-speaking province on the border of Hungary has been the republic's easternmost province since 1921. A touristic highlight is the Neusiedler See on the edge of the Central European steppes.

Carinthia (Kärnten)

9 533km²/3 681sq mi – population 560 100 – capital: Klagenfurt

This lake-studded southern province has the only considerable national minority in Austria (4% of its residents are of Slovenian descent). In a 1920 referendum, the southern districts voted in favor of staying with Austria vs becoming part of Yugoslavia.

Lower Austria (Niederösterreich)

19 174km²/7 403sq mi – population 1 575 300 – capital: St. Pölten

Considered the country's historical cradle, this is Austria's largest and most prosperous province. It has extensive agriculture, is rich in oil and other natural resources and boasts a thriving industry, mainly concentrated around Vienna.

Upper Austria (Oberösterreich)

11 980km²/4 625sq mi – population 1 400 000 – capital: Linz

This region between the Salzkammergut and Bohemia is highly developed agriculturally and industrially. Tourism is of great importance in the lake district of the Salzkammergut.

Salzburg

7 154 km²/2 763sq mi – population 526 900 – capital: Salzburg

The former domain of the prince-archbishops of Salzburg did not become part of Austria until 1805. Its economy was based on salt. The Salzburg Festival, ritzy spas and modern ski resorts lure scores of visitors every year.

Styria (Steiermark)

16 388km²/6 327sq mi – population 1 200 000 – capital: Graz

The "green province" of Austria (half its surface is covered by forest) is one of the oldest industrial regions in Europe, with important timber and steel industries, stock-breeding and mining.

Tyrol (Tirol)

12 648km²/4 883sq mi – population 693 700 – capital: Innsbruck

The Tyrol is a world-famous destination that generates more tourist euros than any other Austrian province. Although about 35% of its area is given over to agriculture, industry also plays an important role. Southern Tyrol was ceded to Italy in 1919, separating eastern Tyrol from the rest of the province.

Vorarlberg

2 601km²/1 004sq mi – population 362 250 – capital: Bregenz

The smallest Austrian province has a thriving textile and tourism industry and is a major producer of hydroelectric power. Locals speak a dialect called Alemannisch, which is related to Swiss and Swabian German.

Vienna (Wien)

415 km²/160sq mi – population 1 637 800

The services and ministries of the Federal Government and of the *Land* of Vienna are headquartered in the capital, as are a number of international organizations.

FEDERAL ORGANIZATION

The **Federal Assembly** *(Bundestag)* consists of the members of the National Council and of the Federal Council, who share the legislative power.

The **National Council** *(Nationalrat)* has 183 members elected by a nationwide popular vote for four years. The minimum voting age is 18. It is convoked or dissolved by the Federal President.

The **Federal Council** *(Bundesrat)* is formed by 63 representatives elected by the provincial diets. Its role is to safeguard the rights of the provinces in the administrative and legislative fields *vis-à-vis* the Federation. On the federal level, it has the right to propose laws and its approval is necessary for international agreements and treaties.

The **Federal President** *(Bundespräsident)* is elected for six years and holds executive power together with the Federal Government. The president represents Austria abroad , appoints the chancellor and senior civil servants, and promulgates the laws.

The **Federal Government** *(Bundesregierung)* is made up of a chancellor, a vice-chancellor, ministers and secretaries of state, appointed by the Federal President on advice of the chancellor.

ART AND CULTURE

Architecture

ART AND ARCHITECTURAL TERMS USED IN THIS GUIDE

Apse: semicircular vaulted space terminating the east end of a church

Baldaquin: altar canopy supported on columns

Barrel vault: simple, half-cylindrical vault

Bas-relief: sculpture in which the figures project only slightly from the background

Capital: moulded or carved top of a column supporting the entablature

Cartouche: ornamental panel with inscription or coat of arms (Baroque)

Chapter-house: building attached to religious house used for meetings of monks or clergy

Chiaroscuro: treatment of areas of light and dark in a work of art

Cupola: small dome

Curtain wall: stretch of castle wall between two towers

Entablature: projecting upper part of building supporting the roof

Flamboyant: final phase of French Gothic style (15C) with flame-like forms

Fresco: watercolor wall painting on plaster

Grisaille: monochrome painting in shades of grey

Hall-church: Germanic church in which aisles are of the same height as the nave

Lantern: windowed turret on top of a dome

Lintel: horizontal beam over a door or window

Narthex: rectangular vestibule between the porch and nave of a church

Oriel: bay window corbelled out from an upper floor level

Ossuary: place where the bones of the dead are stored

Pendentive: triangular section of vaulting rising from the angle of two walls to support a dome

Peristyle: colonnade around a building

Pilaster: shallow rectangular column projecting from a wall

Predella: altar platform divided into panels

Putto/i: painted or sculpted cherub

Quadripartite vaulting: vault divided into four quarters or cells

Reredos: screen to the rear of an altar

Reticulated: patterned like a net

Rib: projecting band separating the cells of a vault

Saddleback roof: roof with a ridge between two gables, suggesting a saddle shape

Sgraffito: decoration made by scratching through a layer of plaster or glaze to reveal the color of the surface beneath

Shingle: wooden tile

Stucco or stuccowork: decorative plasterwork

Transept: wing or arm of a church at right angles to the nave

Triptych: set of three panels or pictures, often folding and used as an altarpiece

Trompe-l'œil: use of techniques such as perspective, or the combination of sculptures and painted figures, to deceive the viewer into seeing three dimensions where there are only two

Tympanum: space between the lintel and arch of a doorway

Volute: spiral scroll on an Ionic capital

Art and Architecture

Over the centuries Austria has been a meeting place for varied cultures. Its artistic achievement has often reflected these external influences, which provided some of its best sources of inspiration. At certain periods, however, a style developed which matched the nation's aspirations, particularly in the 18C, under the enlightened rule of the Habsburgs, when Austrian Baroque blossomed so

ABC OF ARCHITECTURE

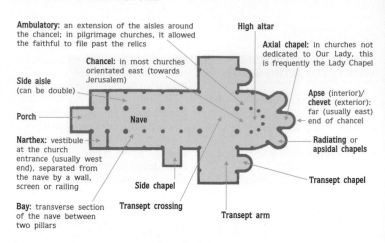

Ambulatory: an extension of the aisles around the chancel; in pilgrimage churches, it allowed the faithful to file past the relics

High altar

Axial chapel: in churches not dedicated to Our Lady, this is frequently the Lady Chapel

Chancel: in most churches orientated east (towards Jerusalem)

Side aisle (can be double)

Porch

Apse (interior)/ **chevet** (exterior): far (usually east) end of chancel

Narthex: vestibule at the church entrance (usually west end), separated from the nave by a wall, screen or railing

Nave

Radiating or **apsidal chapels**

Transept chapel

Side chapel

Transept crossing

Bay: transverse section of the nave between two pillars

Transept arm

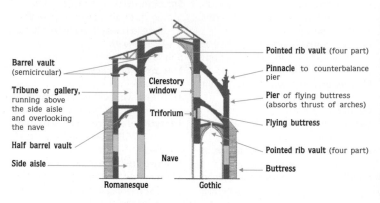

Barrel vault (semicircular)

Tribune or **gallery**, running above the side aisle and overlooking the nave

Half barrel vault

Side aisle

Clerestory window

Triforium

Nave

Romanesque

Gothic

Pointed rib vault (four part)

Pinnacle to counterbalance pier

Pier of flying buttress (absorbs thrust of arches)

Flying buttress

Pointed rib vault (four part)

Buttress

Riesentor (west door) of Stephansdom, Vienna (1230-40)

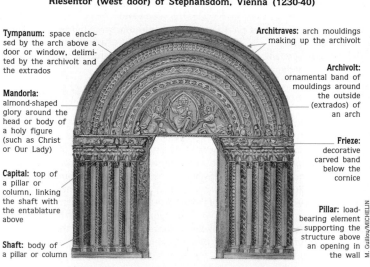

Tympanum: space enclosed by the arch above a door or window, delimited by the archivolt and the extrados

Architraves: arch mouldings making up the archivolt

Archivolt: ornamental band of mouldings around the outside (extrados) of an arch

Mandorla: almond-shaped glory around the head or body of a holy figure (such as Christ or Our Lady)

Capital: top of a pillar or column, linking the shaft with the entablature above

Shaft: body of a pillar or column

Frieze: decorative carved band below the cornice

Pillar: load-bearing element supporting the structure above an opening in the wall

M. Guillou/MICHELIN

Altarpiece: shrine-like structure above the altar, usually framing a painting; can also refer to the painting itself

Squinch: section of wall, often decorated, bridging the gap between a square plan structure and a circular or polygonal superstructure

Cornice: structural moulding running round projecting sections of wall, just below ceiling level

Canopy or baldaquin projecting above the pulpit

Chancel organ: small organ in the chancel or by the wall closing it off from the nave; often as a counterpart to the pulpit opposite

High altar: at the far (east) end of the body of the church

Pulpit: elevated platform for the preacher, usually beneath a canopy or sounding board and reached up a flight of steps

Rocaille cartouches: medallion-shaped ornaments with a coat of arms or other motif, framed in elaborate scroll-like ornamentation featuring shell motifs, characteristic of the Rococo

Tabernacle: ornamental box set in the middle of the altar in which the vessels containing the Blessed Sacrament are kept in Roman Catholic churches

M. Guillou/MICHELIN

Melk Abbey Church (1702-36)

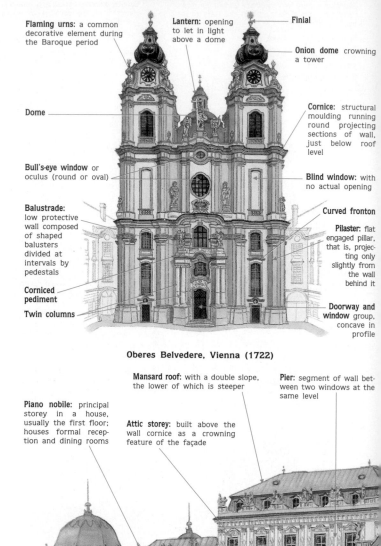

Flaming urns: a common decorative element during the Baroque period

Lantern: opening to let in light above a dome

Finial

Onion dome crowning a tower

Dome

Cornice: structural moulding running round projecting sections of wall, just below roof level

Bull's-eye window or oculus (round or oval)

Blind window: with no actual opening

Balustrade: low protective wall composed of shaped balusters divided at intervals by pedestals

Curved fronton

Pilaster: flat engaged pillar, that is, projecting only slightly from the wall behind it

Corniced pediment

Twin columns

Doorway and window group, concave in profile

Oberes Belvedere, Vienna (1722)

Mansard roof: with a double slope, the lower of which is steeper

Pier: segment of wall between two windows at the same level

Piano nobile: principal storey in a house, usually the first floor; houses formal reception and dining rooms

Attic storey: built above the wall cornice as a crowning feature of the façade

Socle: lowest storey which offers the possibility of compensating for uneven ground

Axis: row of tall windows along the building's façade

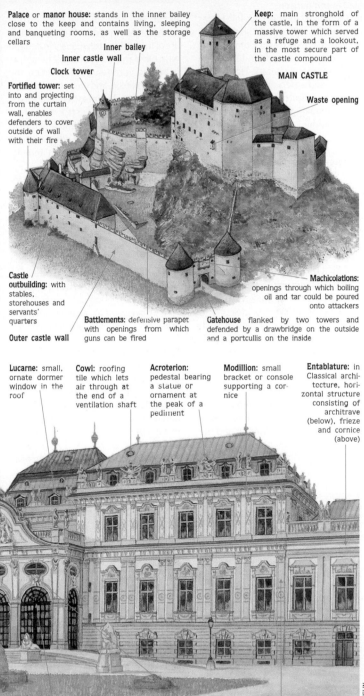

Burg Rappottenstein (12C-16C)

Palace or **manor house:** stands in the inner bailey close to the keep and contains living, sleeping and banqueting rooms, as well as the storage cellars

Keep: main stronghold of the castle, in the form of a massive tower which served as a refuge and a lookout, in the most secure part of the castle compound

Inner bailey

Inner castle wall

Clock tower

MAIN CASTLE

Fortified tower: set into and projecting from the curtain wall, enables defenders to cover outside of wall with their fire

Waste opening

Castle outbuilding: with stables, storehouses and servants' quarters

Machicolations: openings through which boiling oil and tar could be poured onto attackers

Outer castle wall

Battlements: defensive parapet with openings from which guns can be fired

Gatehouse flanked by two towers and defended by a drawbridge on the outside and a portcullis on the inside

Lucarne: small, ornate dormer window in the roof

Cowl: roofing tile which lets air through at the end of a ventilation shaft

Acroterion: pedestal bearing a statue or ornament at the peak of a pediment

Modillion: small bracket or console supporting a cornice

Entablature: in Classical architecture, horizontal structure consisting of architrave (below), frieze and cornice (above)

Portico: colonnaded porch marking the main entrance to a building

Mascaron: ornamental sculpted face, either human or part-human, usually caricatured

Pilaster: engaged pillar with a capital and base

M. Guillou/MICHELIN

vigorously that previous achievements paled in comparison.

The Roman occupation has left traces at Carnuntum (Petronell), in the Danube Valley, downstream from Vienna, which was then called Vindobona, in Enns (Lauriacum) where St Florian was martyred and especially in Carinthia, at Teurnia (near Spittal) and Magdalensberg overlooking St. Veit an der Glan, but also in the Tyrol at Aguntum (near Lienz).

ROMANESQUE

From the 12C onward church building flourished in Austria as in all Christian Europe. The main centers of the Romanesque style were the Episcopal seats of Salzburg, Passau and Brixen. The style was also promoted by the foundation of many Benedictine, Cistercian and Augustinian convents and monasteries, such as those at Melk, Göttweig, Klosterneuburg, Zwettl, Seckau and Heiligenkreuz. The best preserved buildings from this period are the cathedrals of Gurk and Seckau, but the cloisters at Millstatt and the great door of the Stephansdom in Vienna are all outstanding Romanesque examples.

Mural paintings developed most extensively in the Archbishopric of Salzburg The interior of Gurk cathedral and the frescoes at Lambach Abbey are especially noteworth in this context.

GOTHIC

In the 14C and 15C the Gothic style arrived in Austria. Most Gothic churches are of the **hall church** (Hallenkirche) type with nave and aisles of equal height, as in Vienna in the Augustinerkirche, the Minoritenkirche, and the church of Maria am Gestade. The most characteristic Gothic building in Austria, though, is the Stephansdom in Vienna, begun in 1304 by architects who were in touch with their contemporaries in Regensburg and Strasbourg.

Until the 16C there was a preference for sectional vaulting where decorative ribs form a pattern of groined or star vaulting in which richness of design contrasts boldly with the bare walls. This **Late Gothic** (Spätgotik) developed into a style of long straight lines – the exact opposite of the ornamental opulence of the Flamboyant Gothic to be seen in France at this period.

Paired naves were the fashion in the Alps, especially in the Tyrol: two naves at Feldkirch, four at Schwaz.

The great Gothic altarpieces, which were a synthesis of architecture, sculpture and painting have, for the most part, sadly suffered extensive damage over the centuries. Two are of exceptional quality: Kefermarkt, which was restored at the instigation of the writer Adalbert Stifter, and especially St. Wolfgang, painted and carved in 1481 by a Tyrolese, **Michael Pacher**, the greatest Late Gothic artist.

Gurk Cathedral

Kefermarkt Altarpiece

A few 15C secular buildings have been preserved as well, such as the Kornmesserhaus at Bruck an der Mur and the Goldenes Dachl at Innsbruck. The decorative elements adorning their façades, though, herald the Renaissance.

THE RENAISSANCE

Although Austria did not close itself off to new ideas, the Gothic tradition continued to dominate in the 16C. Even the Innsbruck tomb of Emperor Maximilian I (1493-1519), which is regarded as a typical product of the German Renaissance, is still clearly influenced by such famous Gothic tombs as the ones of the dukes of Burgundy in Dijon. Although comparatively rare, there are some fine examples of the Renaissance in Austria, such as the arcaded courtyards at Schloss Schallaburg near Melk, at Schloss Porcia in Spittal an der Drau and at the Landhaus in Graz. Another major exception is Salzburg, which the prince-archbishops essentially dreamed of making into a second Rome.

BAROQUE (17C-18C)

The revolution in the arts originating in Italy at the end of the 16C derives its name from the Portuguese word *"barroco"* meaning something irregularly shaped (originally used of pearls). The Baroque affected all aspects of the arts – architecture, painting, sculpture – as well as literature and music.

In Austria, the style stimulated the richest artistic period since the Gothic. There are various reasons why this new direction in art found such fertile ground in Austria. In essence a religious art, it accorded perfectly with the mood of mystical rejoicing following the Council of Trent. It enjoyed the favor of the Habsburgs, ardent supporters of the Counter Reformation, and benefited from the euphoria after the defeat of the Turks at the gates of Vienna in 1683. At the time, the entire country was seized by a passion for building – at last the danger that had overshadowed the lives of generations of Austrians was no more. Another factor in the triumph of the Baroque style was the Austrian love

for dramatic effects, elegance, color and *joie de vivre*.

The churches, monasteries and palaces of the Baroque can only be understood fully in relation to the new liturgical and festive music that emerged ever more strongly after 1600, in which a dominant melodic line supplanted the older and more complex vocal polyphony. The pomp and circumstance of the new liturgies (in the wake of the Council of Trent, 1545-63) were backed by the rich and powerful sounds of ever more sophisticated church organs.

Austrian Baroque architecture

Austrian Baroque needs to be seen as an essentially home-grown phenomenon, the expression of an authentically Austrian sensibility, and not as an import. With its irregular outlines, abundance of forms and richness of ornament, the Baroque is above all a style of movement. Its dynamism results from color (the use of both bright and delicate colors, the contrast of black, white and gilt), line (curves and undulations), the exuberant treatment of features like pediments, cornices, balustrades, statues and a delight in unexpected effects of angle and perspective.

The great Baroque abbeys

St. Florian, Melk, Altenburg, Kremsmünster, Göttweig... these great abbeys are manifestations of Austrian Baroque at its peak, surpassing in their magnificence any secular buildings of the period. Often prominently sited, these "monuments of militant Catholicism" (Nikolaus Pevsner) draw together bold terraces, elegant entrance pavilions, inner and outer courtyards and main wings of imposing dimensions into harmonious compositions of unparalleled splendor. The scale and lavishness of ornamentation of these vast structures give rise to a certain duality of feeling; places of worship, they are also temples dedicated to art, to which the Baroque assigned a key role in celebrating divine creation.

Churches

All over Austria stand graceful onion-domed churches, their elegant exteriors concealing the delights awaiting within.

It is only once inside the church door that the Baroque, that love of exuberant decoration capable of transforming the most modest of structures, bursts into full and glorious voice.

Many such churches actually evolved from Gothic (Rattenberg, Mariazell) or even Romanesque (Rein, Stams) buildings and were only remodeled in the 17C and 18C. A supreme example of Baroque religious architecture in Austria is the unique Dreifaltigkeitskirche at Stadl-Paura, every aspect of which symbolizes the Trinity.

Secular buildings
Their façades alive with color and movement, palace and town house alike became stage sets for the urban theater. In the 17C, sumptuous residences took shape on the edge of towns like Graz (Schloss Eggenberg) and Salzburg (Schloss Hellbrunn) as well as Vienna (Belvedere).

Great Baroque architects
Numerous famous Italian architects such as Domenico dell'Allio and the Carlones left their mark on Austria's Baroque buildings. But contributing in equal if not greater measure were a number of local masters, many of whom had received their architectural training in Italy or at least undertaken a study tour of the country.

Among them was **Johann Bernhard Fischer von Erlach** (1656-1723), who created a monumental, national style based on his own interpretation of foreign (particularly Italian) influences. The Dreifaltigkeitskirche at Salzburg is one of the prototypes of this style. Many of the most beautiful buildings in Vienna bear the stamp of his genius: the Nationalbibliothek, the Palais Schwarzenberg and the winter palace belonging to Prince Eugene. Most of these buildings were completed after his death by his son, Joseph Emmanuel (1693-1742), who also built the indoor riding school (Winterreitschule) in the Hofburg.

Johann Lukas von Hildebrandt (1668-1745) settled in Vienna after a period of study in Italy and worked with Fischer von Erlach. In Vienna he designed the two palaces at the Belvedere, the Peters-

kirche with its oval cupola, the Piaristenkirche and the Palais Kinsky, and in Salzburg Schloss Mirabell. His considerable body of work had a significant influence on the artists of his generation.

The Tyrolean architect **Jakob Prandtauer** (1660-1726) had a masterly touch in relating massive structures to their landscape setting. Thus, while his church interiors are conventional or even somewhat heavy, his staircase at St. Florian and the two pavilions and great bastion at Melk are achievements of a very high order. The abbey at Melk, a jewel of Austrian Baroque, was completed by Prandtauer's son-in-law, **Josef Munggenast** (1680-1741), who later went on to work at Dürnstein, Altenburg and Geras. Prandtauer did not limit his talents to religious architecture, however. He was also responsible for several gorgeous secular buildings, including Schloss Hohenbrunn.

Baroque painting and sculpture
Baroque architecture is unimaginable without its natural complements of painting and sculpture. Together with delicate stuccowork decorations, they breathe joyful life into the spaces created by the architect. Church walls disappear beneath elaborate altarpieces, myriad saints and angels fill the ceilings and an army of statues puts to flight their Gothic predecessors. Palaces and abbeys are endowed with huge stairways, while cheerfully colored and stuccoed façades lend a theatrical air to both village street and town square.

Great painters and sculptors devoted their talent to the decoration of palaces and churches. Among them were **Johann Michael Rottmayr**, Fischer von Erlach's preferred collaborator and the precursor of a specifically Austrian pictorial style; **Balthasar Permoser** whose famous marble of the Apotheosis of Prince Eugene graces the museum of Baroque art in Vienna; **Daniel Gran** who executed the painting of the Nationalbibliothek in Vienna; **Paul Troger**, master of Austrian ceiling frescoes; **Martin Johann Schmidt** ("Kremser Schmidt") whose altarpieces are to be found all over Lower Austria; **Bartolomäus Altomonte** who decorated the splendid library at Admont, and his uncle **Martin Altomonte** whose airy frescoes and altar paintings grace Wilhering. It is however with **Franz Anton Maulbertsch** that Austrian painting of this period attains its peak. **Georg Raphael Donner**, sometimes referred to flatteringly as the "Austrian Michelangelo," is best-known for the fine fountain in the Neuer Markt in Vienna.

ROCOCO

Inspired by the French rocaille, this style reached its highest form of development in Bavaria. It carries the decorative refinements of the Baroque to their limit, giving them priority over architecture: painting in *trompe-l'œil*, marble, stucco, bronze and wood are used in lavish profusion by artists who allowed their imaginations free rein. The stuccoists combined garlands, medallions, vegetation and shell work. Often two art forms would overlap: a painted figure passes indistinguishably into sculpture, with the head perhaps in *trompe-l'œil* and the body in relief, without the transition between the two being apparent.

The burning passion of the Baroque gives way to a delight in sophisticated effects, monumentality to delicacy and playfulness. Baldaquins, sham draperies, superimposed galleries, niches overladen with gilding and painted in pastel shades add to the prevailing impression of being in a theater rather than a church. The interior of the church at **Wilhering** near Linz is the most accomplished example of a religious Rococo building, while in the east of the country Rococo is found again at **Schloss Schönbrunn.**

19C

Neo-Classicism

After the excesses of Rococo came the triumph of neo-Classicism, inspired by Greece and Rome, a comparatively cold style characterized by the columns and pediments of Classical antiquity. This tendency, which had little in common with the Austrian and even less with the Viennese character, was favored mostly by German rulers, including Ludwig I of Bavaria who transformed Munich. Vienna saw the construction of several buildings of great sobriety like the Technische Hochschule, the Schottenstift and the Münze (Mint). The equestrian statue of Joseph II in the Hofburg by **Franz Anton Zauner** is a typical example of neo-Classical sculpture.

Biedermeier (early 19C)

Biedermeier is the name given to the style which dominated the "Vormärz" (Pre-March), the period between the Congress of Vienna in 1814 and the insurrections of March 1848, the "Year of Revolutions." It is an essentially middle-class style, reflecting the prosperity and settled way of life of this increasingly important section of society.

Comfortable furniture

The cozy interiors inhabited by the rising Vienna bourgeoisie were furnished with simple yet elegant pieces, frequently fashioned in pleasingly light-colored woods, their design reflecting new ideas of function and comfort. Eventually, though, the discretion and modesty of this utterly unpretentious style fell out of fashion. Incidentally, the term "Biedermeier" was only coined around 1900 and is a rather unflattering combination of *"bieder"* (meaning solid or worthy) and "Meyer" (the most common German surname). The Kaiserliches Hofmobiliendepot (national furniture collection) in Vienna has an important collection of Biedermeier furniture and other objects.

Realistic painting

Austrian painting, and Viennese painting in particular, developed in a remarkable way during this period. **Georg Ferdinand Waldmüller** showed himself to be a master of light and color in his rendering of landscape, while **Friedrich Gauermann** captured the atmosphere of the age with great accuracy and left many fine drawings of outstanding quality. The art of watercolor was popular during this period. **Rudolf von Alt** was the greatest master in this medium, becoming honorary president of the Vienna Secession at an advanced age.

M. Hertlein/ MICHELIN

Schloss Schönbrunn seen from the gardens

Historicism (late 19C)

Between 1840 and 1880, on Emperor Franz Joseph's orders, Vienna's encircling fortifications were pulled down and work begun on the great processional way known as the Ringstraße, or "Ring." The buildings along the new boulevard were designed according to the dictates of **Historicism**, an eclectic movement in fashion at the time and drawing on a great variety of past styles for inspiration: Florentine Renaissance (eg, Museum für angewandte Kunst by Heinrich von Ferstel), Greek Classical (Parlament by Theophil Hansen), Flemish Gothic (Rathaus by Friedrich Schmidt), and French Gothic (Votivkirche, also by Heinrich von Ferstel).

Having triumphed in the capital, Historicism went on to leave its mark elsewhere. Towards the end of the 19C, however, opposition to this uncreative and backward-looking style began to grow in Vienna, culminating in open revolt by a number of artists who joined forces to found the famous Vienna Secession movement in 1897.

Late-19C painting and sculpture

Sculpture flourished during this period, not least because of the abundance of public commissions. These included the martial statues of Prince Eugene and Archduke Karl (by **Anton Fernkorn**) in Vienna's Heldenplatz and the moving monument to Andreas Hofer (by Natter) on the Bergisel in Innsbruck.

The late 19C was a turning point for Austrian painting. The great tradition of Realism continued in the work of such landscape painters as **Emil Jakob Schindler**. However, the highly original talent of artists including **Anton Romako** increasingly addressed more serious subjects matter such as decline, decay and death.

JUGENDSTIL (EARLY 20C)

In the final years of the 19C, a new artistic movement known as the Jugendstil swept through all the German-speaking countries, with its epicenter in Munich. It took its name from the widely read magazine *Jugend* (Youth), published between 1896 and 1940, which contained illustrations by artists.

In Vienna, the movement was headed by two exceptionally talented figures, the painter **Gustav Klimt** and the architect **Otto Wagner**. Its influence was felt in the provinces too, albeit in a more subdued form, and there are good examples of Jugendstil buildings in such places as Wels or Graz.

Jugendstil drawing and painting are characterized by a flat surfaces, curvilinear forms and floral decoration. The movement was paralleled by **Art Nouveau** in France, Modern Style in Britain and Stile Liberty in Italy.

The Secession

On 25 May 1897 a small group of friends led by Gustav Klimt founded the **Association of Austrian Artists**, the **Vienna Secession**. The following year, the architect Joseph Maria Olbrich built an exhibition hall – the Secession – in the Karlsplatz. Completed in only six months, this building remains one of the purest expressions of Jugendstil aspirations, even though contemporaries nicknamed it the "Golden Cabbage" because of its dome of gilded laurel leaves. Its façade proclaims the slogan "Der Zeit ihre Kunst – der Kunst ihre Freiheit" (To each age its art, to art its liberty). Olbrich's Secession building was home to numerous exhibitions of contemporary, progressive art, many of them international in scope. It became a focus of opposition to the values represented by Historicism, academic art and the tendency towards pastiche that had characteriszd artistic life in Vienna during construction of the Ringstraße. For the artists of the Secession art was above all a matter of personal expression, requiring sincerity and a quest for truth as well as a rejection of prevailing social and aesthetic conventions.

"To each age its art": the Secession building with a temporary installation as part of an exhibition

M. Hertle n/ MICHELIN

Gustav Klimt (1862-1918)

Painter and interior designer Gustav Klimt was a leading exponents of the Jugendstil and in many ways the typical Secession artist; his elegant and subtle works are world-renowned. Early in his career he put his academic training behind him and abandoned all attempts at naturalism in favor of rich and subtle decorative effects carried out on a two-dimensional surface free of the constraints of perspective. His sinuous line, his original use of color (especially-greens and gold), his stylised foliage, his cult of the sensual and the delicacy of his female portraits provoked a revolution in Viennese artistic circles. Symbolism was an additional influence in the work of this major figure, the forerunner of what was later known as **"Viennese Expressionism,"** represented by painters like Egon Schiele and Oskar Kokoschka.

Otto Wagner (1841-1918)

Wagner was the dominant architectural figure of the Jugendstil period. Born in Biedermeier times and educated in the most classical tradition, he rose to become professor at the Academy of Fine Arts and imperial architectural adviser for the city of Vienna. For more than 20 years his career was one of conventional success; he designed a number of buildings in neo-Renaissance style along the Ring for example. But in 1899 Wagner broke decisively with his past and joined the Secession. He had already outlined his uncompromisingly contemporary views in his *Modern Architecture* (1895), still a standard reference text. Wagner favored the use of glass and steel, a rational approach to spatial design and the omission of superfluous ornament. His finest works include the pavilions for the Karlsplatz underground railway station (1894) in Vienna, the Postsparkasse (1906) near the Ring and the Steinhof Church (1907).

Wiener Werkstätten (Vienna Workshops)

The Wiener Werkstätten were founded in 1903 by the banker Fritz Waerndorfer, the architect Josef Hoffmann and the artist **Kolo Moser**, one of the most gifted members of the Secession movement. They were intended to make good art accessible to all and to put both artist and craftsman on a firm professional

Tea service by Josef Hoffmann (Österreichisches Museum für Angewandte Kunst, Vienna)

footing. A wide range of products was made adopting Jugendstil tenets, from household utensils, furniture and wallpaper to fashion garments and jewelry. Though expensive, these products were much in demand among the wealthier strata of society. Beauty of form and the use of high quality materials ranked as more important than functionality. Financial woes led to the workshops' closure in 1932. Together with Klimt's paintings, the output of the Wiener Werkstätten marks the high point of Austrian Jugendstil and enjoys enduring acclaim.

Josef Hoffmann (1870-1956)

This highly versatile figure was one of Otto Wagner's most talented students. Hoffmann designed not only buildings but also their interior, including furniture and fittings. He was strongly influenced by the work of Scottish architect and designer Charles Rennie Mackintosh, founder of the Glasgow School of Art Nouveau. Hoffmann co-founded the Wiener Werkstätten in 1903 and worked closely with them until 1931. One of the results of this fruitful collaboration is the magnificent **Palais Stoclet** in Brussels. As well as designing material for private clients, Hoffmann also received numerous commissions from the Vienna city council, for whom he produced several housing complexes, including Klosehof. He also designed the interior of the Fledermaus revue theater (1909).

Adolf Loos (1870-1933)

Educated by the Benedictine monks of Melk, this innovative architect called himself a stonemason, though he was considered by Le Corbusier to be the forerunner of architectural Modernism. An admirer of the sober Classicism of Palladio, Loos made a violent attack on the Historicist architecture of Vienna's Ring in 1898, in the pages of the Secessionist journal *Ver Sacrum*. He was soon to break with the architects of the Secession, however, accusing them of "gratuitous ornamentalism." Following a period of residence in the USA (1893-96) and influenced by the Chicago School, he built a number of villas, housing blocks and cafés in Vienna, adopting the principles of a purely functional architectural style. In addition, he designed sculpture and furniture. His work reached maturity in the Golman and Salatsch store (1909) and in his controversial Michaeler Platz building (1908) which attracted bitter criticism because of its total lack of ornament. Loos has gone down in history as one of the high priests of 20C functionalism. His ideas were taken up and developed by architects the world over. He was a particularly strong influence on artists of the International style.

Music

see Wien: *"Vienna, capital of music"*

MIDDLE AGES

9C — Musical culture flourished in the monasteries where Gregorian chant was sung. The earliest examples of written music in Austria are the Lamentations from the abbey at St. Florian and the Codex Millenarius Minor from Kremsmünster.

12C and 13C — The Germanic troubadours known as the **Minnesänger** celebrated the joys and sorrows of courtly love at the court of the Babenbergs in Vienna as well as at St. Veit an der Glan in Carinthia, drawing their inspiration from the Volkslied (folk song), an authentic expression of popular feeling. The most famous were Reinmar von

Hagenau and his pupil Walther von der Vogelweide, Hermann von Salzburg and Neidhart von Reuenthal.

14C and 15C — The burgher-class **Meistersinger** (Mastersingers), organized into guilds, continued the aristocratic *Minnesang* tradition, setting strict rules and testing their skills in competitions.

RENAISSANCE

This was the age of polyphony, pioneered in Austria by the Tyrolean Oskar von Wolkenstein, who worked at the Court at Salzburg. Later it developed throughout the Empire in the work of several musicians belonging to the Franco-Flemish School.

THE 17C

1619 — The accession to the Imperial throne of Archduke Ferdinand of Styria marked the beginning of the supremacy of Italian music in Austria, notably in opera and oratorio. A long line of Italian masters directed the music of the Court Chapel, the last of them being none other than Mozart's great rival, **Antonio Salieri** (1750-1825).

GLUCK AND OPERA REFORM

Vienna was the setting for the reform of opera, thanks to the German composer, Gluck.

1714-1787 — **Christoph Willibald Gluck** considered opera as an indivisible work of art, both musical and dramatic; he sought, above all, natural effects, truth, simplicity and a faithful expression of feeling.

1754 — Gluck is named Kapellmeister of the Opera at the Imperial Court of Maria Theresia.

1774 — Two of his operas inagurate in Paris: *Iphigenia in Aulis* and *Orpheus and Euridice*.

THE VIENNESE CLASSICS

This was the age of Haydn, Mozart, Beethoven and Schubert, all Viennese by birth or adoption. Their primarily instrumental work dominated the musical world for almost a century and made Vienna its uncontested capital.

1732-1809 — **Joseph Haydn**
A conductor and composer attached to the service of Prince Esterházy at Eisenstadt for 30 years, Haydn was the creator of the string quartet and laid down the laws of the classical symphony.

1756-91 — **Wolfgang Amadeus Mozart**
Mozart brought every form of musical expression to perfection, owing to his exceptional fluency in composition and constantly renewed inspiration. His dramatic genius produced great operas of enduring appeal: *The Marriage of Figaro, Don Giovanni, Così fan Tutte* and *The Magic Flute* (see Salzburg for details of Mozart's life and work).

1770-1827 — **Ludwig van Beethoven**
Heir to Haydn and Mozart, Beethoven had a Romantic

Ludwig van Beethoven

ROGER VIOLLET

ROGER VIOLLET

Johannes Brahms

conception of music. He was much affected by the ideas of the French Revolution and felt himself to be the bearer of a message for humankind.

1805 — First performance of Beethoven's only opera *Fidelio* at the theater "An der Wien."

1824 — The Ninth or Choral Symphony concluding with the *Ode to Joy* (fourth movement) with words by Friedrich Schiller. In 1972, this Ode to Joy was adopted as the European anthem.

ROMANTICISM

1797-1828 — Franz Schubert
Blessed with a great sensibility, Schubert was an outstanding improviser, who rediscovered in the Lieder the old popular themes of the Middle Ages. His Lieder, of which he wrote more than 600, even more than his symphonies, masses, impromptus and compositions of chamber music, made him the leading lyrical composer of the 19C.

THE VIENNESE WALTZ AND OPERETTA

1820 — In Vienna, a musical genre, the **waltz**, which had its origins in popular triple-time dance,

was triumphant. Adopted first in the inns and then in the theaters on the outskirts of the city, the waltz scored such success that it appeared at the Imperial Court.

Two men, **Joseph Lanner** (1801-43) and **Johann Strauss** (1804-49), helped to give this musical form such a prominent place that the most popular waltz is now known worldwide as the "Viennese Waltz." The Strauss sons, Joseph and Johann, carried the waltz to a high degree of technical perfection, taking it further and further from its origins to make it a symphonic form.

With the performance at the Carltheater in 1858 of Offenbach's *Die Verlobung bei der Laterne*, Vienna's enthusiasm for **operetta** knew no bounds. Encouraged by Offenbach, **Johann Strauss the Younger** (1825-99) enjoyed equal success with his *Fledermaus* and *Zigeunerbaron* (Gipsy Baron). Other great operetta composers were **Franz von Suppé** (1819-95), **Franz Lehár** (1870-1948, *The Merry Widow, The Land of Smiles*), **Ralph Benatzky** (1884-1957, *White Horse Inn*) and **Robert Stolz** (1880-1975, *Spring in the Prater*).

SYMPHONIC RENEWAL

1824-1896 — Anton Bruckner ranks among the most significant composers of church music, producing nine great symphonies, numerous mass settings and the *Te Deum*. He spent many years as organist of St. Florian and at Linz Cathedral before his appointment as professor at the Vienna Conservatory.

1833-1897 — Of German origin but settled in Vienna, **Johannes Brahms** composed a large body of work of a lyrical nature, inestimable in its impact (1868, *A German Requiem*).

1842 — Founding of the Vienna Philharmonic Orchestra playing under the guidance of illustrious conductors (Richard Strauss, Wilhelm Furtwängler) chosen by the players themselves.

1860-1903 — **Hugo Wolf,** a tormented spirit who eventually became insane, composed fine Lieder in his lucid periods, based for the most part on the poems of Goethe, Mörike and Eichendorff.

1860-1911 — **Gustav Mahler,** a disciple of Bruckner, was the last of the great Romantic composers. An inspired conductor, he composed many Lieder as well as his nine symphonies. He helped to set in motion the revolutionary changes in music at the turn of the century.

20C

From 1903 onwards the "New Viennese School" led by Schönberg is a major influence in the evolution of modern music as seen in the work of composers such as Ernst Krenek and Pierre Boulez.

1864-1949 — The German composer/conductor **Richard Strauss** carried on the Classical/Romantic Austrian tradition, composing symphonic poems and operas. He was one of the founders of the Salzburg Festival.

1874-1951 — **Arnold Schönberg**, whose early works clearly reflect the influence of Wagner and Mahler, revolutionized music by rejecting the tonal system which had prevailed for 300 years. Together with his followers **Anton von Webern** (1883-1945) and **Alban Berg** (1885-1935) he introduced a new method of atonal composition, based on the concept of series. This is known as dodecaphony, or in its more advanced form, as serial composition. His change of style did not meet instant approval with the public, however – the première of his first chamber symphony provoked a riot!

Having pursued his study of atonality in Berlin, Schönberg was exiled from Germany under the Nazis and settled in the United States, where he finally adopted US citizenship.

1894-1981 — The conductor **Karl Böhm** helped to stage two operas composed by his friend Richard Strauss. His fame rests on his seminal interpretations of the works of the great German composers.

1908-1989 — The conductor **Herbert von Karajan** brought classical music to a wide audience by his mastery of audio-visual techniques. For many years he presided over the destinies of the Salzburg Festival as well as directing both the Vienna Philharmonic and the Berlin Philharmonic orchestras.

1947 — Salzburg première of the opera *Danton's Death* by **Gottfried von Einem** (b 1918).

1958 — *"Die Reihe"* ensemble founded by **Friedrich Cerha** (b 1926) and Kurt Schwertsik (b 1935)

1994 — American-born, Vienna-resident **Nancy van de Vate**, one of the most heavily recorded living composers of orchestral music, is granted dual citizenship by Austria.

1996 — Death of **Gottfried von Einem** who had for a long time played an important part in Austrian cultural life.

2006 — Austria celebrates Mozart's 250th birthday with a series of events and concerts throughout the country.

FAMOUS AUSTRIANS OF THE 19C AND 20C

Franz **GRILLPARZER** (1791-1872): poet and dramatist (historical plays).

Adalbert **STIFTER** (1805-68): novelist and short story writer *(Indian Summer)*.

Gregor Johann **MENDEL** (1822-84): biologist specialising in heredity.

Marie von **EBNER-ESCHENBACH** (1830-1916): author, editor of short stories.

Bertha von **SUTTNER** (1843-1914): novelist *(Lay Down Your Arms!)* and prominent pacifist, winner of the Nobel Peace Prize in 1905.

Sigmund **FREUD** (1856-1939): founder of psychoanalysis.

Arthur **SCHNITZLER** (1862-1931): writer. His novella *Leutnant Gustl* introduced interior monologue to German literature as a new mode of expression.

Karl **LANDSTEINER** (1868-1943): pathologist and winner of the Nobel Prize for Medicine in 1930 for his discovery of human blood types.

Hugo von **HOFMANNSTHAL** (1874-1929): poet and dramatist *(Everyman)*, wrote the libretti of a number of Richard Strauss' operas including *Rosenkavalier*.

Rainer Maria **RILKE** (1875-1926): one of the great poets of the 20C.

Karl **KRAUS** (1874-1936): journalist, writer *(The Last Days of Mankind)*.

Lise **MEITNER** (1878-1968): physicist.

Robert **MUSIL** (1880-1942): novelist and short story writer *(The Man without Qualities)*.

Stefan **ZWEIG** (1881-1942): novelist influenced by psychology *(Amok, Schachnovelle)* and biographer *(Marie Antoinette)*.

Erich von **STROHEIM** (1885-1957): filmmaker and actor *(La Grande Illusion; Sunset Boulevard)*.

Georg Wilhelm **PABST** (1885-1967): filmmaker *(The Trial*, 1947).

Karl von **FRISCH** (1886-1982): behaviourist, Nobel Prize for Medicine in 1973.

Fritz **LANG** (1890-1976): film producer *(Metropolis*, 1926; *"M"*, 1931).

Josef von **STERNBERG** (1894-1969): film producer, discovered Marlene Dietrich (*The Blue Angel*, 1930).

Friedrich August **HAYEK** (1899-1992): winner of the 1974 Nobel Prize for Economics; basic principles of economic science.

Ödön von **HORVÁTH** (1901-38): writer *(Tales from the Vienna Woods, Jugend ohne Gott)*.

Konrad **LORENZ** (1903-89): behaviourist, Nobel Prize for Medicine in 1973.

Herbert von **KARAJAN** (1908-89): conductor, founder of the Salzburg Festival (1967).

Kurt **WALDHEIM** (b 1918): Secretary-General of the UNO (1972-81), Austrian President (1986-92).

Ingeborg **BACHMANN** (1926-73): poet (novel *Malina*)

Alfred **HRDLICKA** (b 1928): sculptor and draughtsman.

Friedensreich **HUNDERTWASSER** (1928-2000): painter and architect, whose most famous work is the KunstHaus in Vienna.

Thomas **BERNHARD** (1931-89): controversial novelist and dramatist.

Peter **HANDKE** (b 1942): producer, novelist and film script-writer with Wim Wenders.

Elfriede **JELINEK** (b 1946): playwright and novelist won Nobel prize for literature in 2004.

André **HELLER** (b 1947): multimedia artist, founder of Roncalli Circus among other things.

Arnold **SCHWARZENEGGER** (b 1947): former world champion bodybuilder turned Hollywood actor was elected governor of California in 2003.

Niki **LAUDA** (b 1949): Formula 1 racing driver, three times world champion; founder of LAUDA AIR airline company (1979).

THE COUNTRY TODAY

The Economy

Austria has a population of 8.2 million people, about a fourth of whom live in greater Vienna. Only four other cities have more than 100,000 inhabitants: Graz, Linz, Salzburg and Innsbruck. Austria has a population density of 98 people per km^2 – one of the lowest in Europe (in the UK it is 246 people per km^2). Almost 98% of Austrians speak German as their first language, and there are six recognized ethnic minorities: Slovenians, Croatians, Hungarians, Czechs, Slovaks and Romany-Sinti gypsies. Around 74% of the population is Roman Catholic; only 4.7% are Protestant, only slightly more than Muslims at 4.2%.

Austria has been a member of the European Union (EU) since January 1995. It has been implementing the Schengen Agreement since 1998 and joined the European Monetary Union in 1999. The Euro has been circulating as the official currency since January 2002. In 2005, Austria's gross domestic product was €245 billion.

AGRICULTURE AND FORESTRY

Although vast areas of mountainous land in Austria are not suitable for cultivation, **agriculture** is an important sector of the Austrian economy, providing for almost 100% of national food requirements. About 189,000 people, or around 5% of the country's workforce, are employed in agriculture and forestry. In 2003, there were still 190,400 farm and forestry businesses, although the majority - 115,000 - were smaller than 20ha/49 acres. Only 7,400 were larger than 100ha/247 acres.

Forests represent one of Austria's richest natural resources. Consisting mostly of coniferous trees, they cover about 47% of the country's total surface area – a statistic surpassed within Europe only by Sweden and Finland. In 2005, over 16.5 million m^3/13,400 ft^3 of timber were felled. Agriculture and forestry represent about 2% of Austria's gross domestic product.

NATURAL RESOURCES AND INDUSTRY

The break-up of the Austro-Hungarian Empire in 1919 cut Austria off from its traditional markets and some of its raw material sources. The situation was exacerbated by the fact that in the 19C Austrian industry had been focused purely on meeting the needs of its own huge empire instead of gearing up to compete in international markets.

These days, however, Austria is one of the wealthiest countries in the EU (measured by gross domestic product) and ranks as a highly developed industrial power with a significant services industry sector.

ENERGY SOURCES

As a mountainous country laced by numerous rivers, Austria is a major producer of **hydroelectric power**. Most of its domestic energy requirements are met by the output from some 1 300 power stations. Those along the Danube alone generate a quarter of the state electricity production.

Oil is a natural resource that has been developed since 1937. It still plays a role in the Austrian economy, with production holding more or less steady at just below 1 million tons per year. Most oil fields cluster northeast of Vienna, in the Vienna Basin, which accounts for 95% of the country's oil production. The single largest field is in Matzen. The remaining 5% come from fields in Upper Austria, near Salzburg.

The oil is refined at Schwechat near Vienna, which has a capacity of just below 10 million tons. In addition to domestic oil, it also processes imported crude oil. This travels to Schwechat via the Adria-Wien-Pipeline (AWP), which runs from Trieste/Italy to Vienna and is a branch off the huge Transalpine Ölleitung (TAL; Trieste to Ingolstadt/Germany).

Natural gas from Austria's oilfields is highly prized by the country's industrial concerns. Production hovers around 2 billion m³/70 billion cu ft annually. To meet national demand, though, an additional 6 billion m³/212 billion cu ft has to be imported each year, mainly from Russia.

MINING AND HEAVY INDUSTRY

Austria is a country with a long tradition in mining and heavy industry. In the Tyrol especially, gold, silver and copper were mined intensively up to the 17C. Salt mining and the mining of non-ferrous minerals are still carried out today. In fact, Austria is among the world's most important producers of **magnesite**, a mineral used in fireproofing blast furnaces and smelting ovens and also in construction work.

Of key importance to **heavy industry** in Austria is production in the metallurgical basin in Styria, home of the well-known Erzberg (Iron Mountain). The biggest opencast mine in Europe, it ships about 6000 tonnes of iron ore daily to the blast furnaces of Donawitz, which produce steel sections, and to those of Linz, which produce sheet metal.

SALT MINING

Salt mining is now only of minor importance. Nonetheless, since prehistoric times the precious mineral has played such a part in the civilization of the eastern Alps that it's hard to overlook the various enterprises still operating in the Salzburg area. Moreover, the salt waters of numerous spa resorts such as Bad Aussee, Bad Ischl and Hall in Tirol continue to be prized in the treatment of a variety of illnesses. Place names often include the prefix *Salz* or *Hall* – synonymous terms meaning salt or salt works. Touring a salt mine is a memorable experience. Tour guides are often former miners who stick faithfully to their traditional vocabulary – the greeting *"Glück auf!"* (Hope you come up again!) is still heard. Many also wear their dress uniform and regale you with tales about the underground world.

Melting mountains

Except in the natural springs (*Solequellen*) of Bad Reichenhall/Germany, the mineral deposits in the Salzburg region consist of a mixture, called *Haselgebirge*, of salt, clay and gypsum. The miners begin by making a pit in the bed, which they flood and keep supplied regularly with fresh water. This water dissolves the rock on the spot and so, being saturated with salt (27%), sinks to the bottom of the basin, from which it can be pumped, while impurities are left behind. Modern methods of extraction involve the drilling of boreholes and the dissolving of the deposit by the injection of hot water. The brine (*Sole*) is brought to the surface and pumped into the vats of the salt factories (*Sudhütten*), for the production of domestic or industrial salt.

The first pipelines

By the 17C much of the forest around the salt mines had been burnt up as fuel in the furnaces. This, coupled with the remoteness of many of the mines, led to attempts by the authorities to relocate the centers of salt production closer to the markets. This involved the construction of impressive lengths of pipeline made of timber, lead or cast iron, to bring

SALT-MINING IN THE SALZBURG REGION

● Natural saline springs

✗ Working salt-mine open to visitors

Bad Ischl — Saline spa

▬ ▪ ▬ 'Soleleitung': in service

▬ ▬ ▬ 'Soleleitung': out of service

the brine down from the mountains to the lowlands. The longest of these **Soleleitungen** ran 79km/49mi from Bad Reichenhall to Rosenheim in Bavaria and was in use from 1810 to 1958.

Pumping stations *(Brunnhäuser)* kept up a constant flow of brine, over hill and dale. To prevent too sudden a drop, the aqueducts included long mountain-side sections, as in the water-conduits *(bisses)* of the Swiss Valais. The foot-paths *(Soleleitungswege)* paralleling them made splendid corniche routes. The mine road from Hallstatt to Bad Ischl, for instance, dramatically clings to the mountainside above the lake of Hallstatt.

When the salt had been refined, it was shipped by river – on the Inn below Hall in Tirol and the Lower Traun – or in carts. Many salt roads *(Salzstrassen)* in Austria, one of the best known being the Ellbö-gener Straße (*see Innsbruck: Tour of the Mittelgebirge*), recall memories of this traffic, so fruitful for the country's economy and the public treasury.

OTHER MAJOR ECONOMIC ACTIVITIES

Austria's most important and interna-tionally competitive industry sectors are the machine building and steel industries, chemicals and textiles and engine and automobile parts manufac-ture, most of it for export. Austria also has international standing in the pro-duction of electronic components such as microchips and integrated circuits (it produces components for Airbus and high-speed trains). In general, Austrian industry is strongly export-oriented. About two-thirds of its foreign trade is conducted with fellow European Union countries. The most important customer is Germany, which accounts for fully one-third of exports.

Food production, especially the luxury food sector, contributes about 3.5% of GDP and principally caters to domestic consumption. The largest proportion of gross domestic product, around 68% is generated by the services industry.

TOURISM

Austria is a tourist destination par excellence, offering magnificent scen-ery, major historical monuments, a wide range of leisure opportunities year-round, and an outstanding tour-ist infrastructure. Tourism is extremely important to the Austrian economy both in terms of job creation and as a source of revenue. In 2005, it generated about €15 billion, contributing some 6.4% to the GDP. The number of foreign visitors was 20 million, the majority of whom were German and Dutch. Traditionally, the Tyrol attracts most visitors from home and abroad, followed by Salzburg and Carinthia.

Traditions and Customs

RELIGIOUS BELIEFS

Austria is a country steeped in tradition. Old customs are kept very much alive, particularly in rural communities. A deeply rooted religious faith has left its mark on town and countryside alike.

Roofed crosses *(Wiesenkreuze)*, set up at the roadside or in the middle of a field, are thus very much a feature of Austria's rural landscape and particularly preva-lent in the Tyrol. A common sight in Car-inthia is a post *(Bildstock)* with a little roof protecting a faceted pole decorated with paintings of Biblical scenes. Cru-cifixes are commonly displayed inside Austrian homes, in a part of the house called the *Herrgottswinkel* (God's cor-ner). These are especially prevalent in the Tyrol where you'll find them in virtu-ally every house, including guesthouses and inns.

Religious figures are also a common subject for the paintings to be found on many an Austrian façade *(Lüftlmalerei)*: St Florian features particularly promi-nently in these in his role as protector against fire. Another popular figure is St George, the dragon slayer. You may also come across churches containing an enormous painting of St Christopher (eg in Imst). These arose in response to the popular belief that looking at the image of this saint would protect the viewer from a violent death for another day. The figure of St John of Nepomuk is often to be found adorning bridges and fountains, of which he is the patron saint (having been martyred by being thrown off a bridge in Prague).

A CUSTOM FOR ALL SEASONS

Also see Calendar of Events.
The year begins with processions of masked "Perchten" accompanying St Nicholas through the villages during the "bitter nights" leading up to Epiphany on 6 January. The costumed figures representing good and evil spirits can be beautiful or ugly – the latter are usually clad with shaggy fur and wearing scary horned masks – and are supposed to banish the cold and dark of winter and bring fertility and blessings for the coming year. The feast of the Epiphany itself brings Christmas celebrations to a close by commemorating the journey of the Three Kings guided by the Star of Bethlehem. Festivities involve children's carol singing and processions (*Sternsingen* and *Dreikönigsritte*). In some places, locals parade around sporting giant head-dresses decorated with bells (*Glöcklerläufe*).

Carnival time, or **Fasching** (*Fasnacht* in western Austria), is ushered in as early as January in Vienna with the start of the ball season. Elsewhere, Fasching is celebrated with traditional carnival parades, to which a colorful note is added by the masks handed down from generation to generation. Some of the most famous of these parades include those in the Tyrol, at Imst (*Imster Schemen*) and Telfs (*Schleicherlaufen)*; the Bad Aussee carnival with its original and colorful *Trommelweiber* and *Flinserln*; and the *Fetzenfasching* in Ebensee.

Palm Sunday is marked by the blessing of the "palm branches" – generally willow catkins or box. This is closely followed by May Day celebrations (1 May), complete with maypole (*Maibaum*), climbing competitions *(Maibaumkraxeln)* and dancing. The feast of Corpus Christi sees more processions, which vary according to the particular traditions of the region: carrying 8-10m/25-30ft wooden poles

wound around with garlands of fresh flowers *(Prangstangen)* in Bischofshofen and Zederhaus (24 June); laying down a carpet of flowers *(Blumenteppich)* in Deutschlandsberg; processions on horseback, as in Brixental in Tirol, or on water, as in Traunkirchen and Hallstatt. In August, Murau and Krakaudorf (Styria) are the scene of *Samsonumzüge:* parades involving a giant 5m/16ft figure of Samson carried by one man – this show of strength was believed in the 17C and 18C to protect the religious procession. In August and September many communities celebrate the consecration of their local church (*Kirtag*) with a fair. Fall is the time for the Harvest Festival *(Erntedankfest)* season. This is also livestock is brought down from the mountain pastures to its winter quarters.

The feast of St Hubert is celebrated on 3 November (church services, parades on horseback etc), while St Leonard (patron saint of livestock) gets honored on 6 November. A few days later, the feast of St Martin, with torchlit processions, brightens up a dark winter night. The periods of Advent and Christmas make December full of events, from the feast of St Nicholas (6 December), with the *Nikolospiel* parade in Bad Mitterndorf, through to the Nativity scenes displayed in public sites and inside people's homes (eg Thaur in the Tyrol).

TRADITIONAL COSTUMES

Although traditional local costumes are rarely worn as a daily outfit any more, they occasionally make an appearance at religious and local festivals.

The velvet corsages of the women of Bad Ischl, the embroidered silk blouses of those from the Wachau, the colorful ribbon-laced bodices of the Montafon, the finely pleated costumes of the Bregenzerwald and the lace aprons of the Burgenland are all evidence of a rich tradition of local folklore. Men wear leather or *Loden* wool breeches (tight at the knee) or shorts (which are less restrictive for the brisk movements of Tyrolean dancing), wide braces with a decorated chest panel and short, collarless jackets. The shape of the hat indicates the region its wearer comes from.

House built around a square courtyard
in the Mühlviertel (Upper Austria)

Traditional
Austrian
houses

House in the Bregenzerwald
(Vorarlberg)

Tyrolean country chalet

Rural estate in Lower Austria

The traditional **dirndl** (pleated skirt, pastel colored apron, full white blouse with short puffed sleeves and a buttoned or laced bodice) and the *Steirer Anzug* ("Alpine dinner jacket," consisting of grey or brown *Loden* breeches embroidered in green, white socks and a long flared coat with green embroidery and gilt buttons) are not that common a sight these days. However, they are the original inspiration behind the so-called "traditional Austrian look," which combines modern styles with traditional decorative features and natural materials such as linen, cotton, felt and heavy woollen *Loden*.

RURAL SCENERY

Fences woven from laths were once the most common style delimiting fields in the Salzburg, Tennengau and Pinzgau regions, but they are becoming increasingly rare. Still, it is not unusual to see farmers piling hay at harvest time onto special drying racks made of metal wire or wooden stakes, to keep it off the damp ground while it is drying.

In the Carinthian Alps grains are grown on the sunny slopes up to a height of 1 500m/4 500ft, but the harvest often has to be gathered early to avoid frost. The sheaves are spread out on wooden dryers with horizontal struts, sometimes covered, so the grain is able to ripen.

URBAN SETTLEMENT

In Styria, Carinthia and the Danubian countryside the most interesting examples of urban development usually sprouted around the main road. When a town was first developed, the old road was widened to form a sort of esplanade, known as the **Anger** (green). When all the land on each side of the *Anger* was built over, the resulting form was known as a **Strassenplatz** (street-square). These street-squares, shaped like spindles or regular oblong rectangles, form the heart of the town, approached by the once fortified gateways. The square, which is often called Hauptplatz, is usually dotted with fountains and columns, such as the **Pestsäule** (Plague Column) set up to commemorate the end of a plague.

Food and Drink

Austrian cooking draws from the culinary traditions of the different peoples that once formed the old Empire: German, Italian, Hungarian, Serb and Czech.

Austrian cooking

Soup is served first, followed by the main dish, almost always consisting of meat, fried in breadcrumbs or boiled, accompanied by salad and stewed fruit (such as bilberries: *Preiselbeeren*). Dumplings *(Knödel)* made of liver or flour may be served instead of vegetables. Middle Eastern influences can be detected in the liberal use of spices in many Austrian dishes.

Meat

The most famous dish *(Wiener Schnitzel)* is thin fillet of veal, dusted with egg and breadcrumbs and fried in butter; it's often served with potato salad. Goulash is a highly flavored stew of Hungarian origin, spiced with red pepper or paprika and garnished with tomatoes, onions and potatoes. In Graz and Styria duck or chicken, fried in egg and breadcrumbs, is delicious. Game of all kinds is widely available in season.

Dessert

Austrians are famous for the variety of their sweets. The most famous cake, the *Sachertorte*, invented by Prince Metternich's chef, has a subtle and delicate flavor. It is a large, rich chocolate cake covered with chocolate icing above a thin layer of apricot jam; the original recipe remains a secret (but everyone offers a version of it!). Other favorites include a jam tart *(Linzertorte)*, consisting of pastry made with almonds, filled with apricot or raspberry jam and covered with a pastry lattice; a turnover *(Strudel)* filled with apples, cherries or cream cheese and currants; plum or apricot fritters; and a sweet soufflé *(Salzburger Nockerl)*.

Austrian Wine

Vineyards cover about 48 500ha/120 000 acres in Lower Austria, in the Weinviertel, on the slopes near Vienna, and in the Burgenland and Styria. White wine (81%) is much more popular than red. Annual production is of the order of 2.8 million hectolitres/ 62 million gallons, of which more than a third is exported.

White wines

Well-known Austrian white vintages include Grüner Veltliner, Müller-Thurgau and Welschriesling. Most vintages yield pleasant table wines which are often light and slightly sparkling. New wine, made that year, is drunk in the typical wine taverns called *Heurige* or *Buschenschenken*. The district of Wachau in the Danube Valley produces wines with a delicate bouquet (Spitz, Dürnstein, Weissenkirchen, Krems, Langenlois). Grinzing, the most famous of Vienna's suburban wine villages, makes a pleasant sparkling wine.

Red wines

The red wines, especially the Blauer Portugieser and the Blaufränkischer, are of high quality. In Lower Austria the best-known wines are those from Bad Vöslau, south of Vienna, from Retz (the Retz wine is known as *Spezi*, ie a special), from Haugsdorf and from Matzen, in the Weinviertel. In the Burgenland the wines of Pöttelsdorf, Oggau and particularly Rust, and in Styria those of Leibnitz, have a great reputation.

Wine Regions

Austria is divided into four official wine regions: the Weinland Österreich (Lower Austria and the Burgenland); Steirerland (Styria); Vienna; and Bergland (Upper Austria, Salzburg, Carinthia, Tyrol, Vorarlberg). Weinland Österreich alone accounts for 91.79% of total production while the Bergland, by contrast, only contributes a tiny 0.04%.

The regions are further subdivided into 19 wine-growing areas, of which the Weinviertel, the Neusiedlersee and the Neusiedlersee-Hügelland are the most important, accounting for 32%, 17% and 8% of output, respectively.

For full details, consult:

www.winesfromaustria.com.

The best way to get acquainted with Austrian wine is by exploring the country's wine routes. The most famous of these is the Lower Austria Wine Route, an 830km/518mi-long ribbon meandering through the wonderful countryside of the Carnuntum, Weinviertel, Wachau, Thermenregion, Donauland, Kamptal, Traisental and Kremstal growing areas. A section of this route is described in some detail under Östliches Weinviertel . Styria has eight wine routes, including the delightful Schilcher Trail, Sausal Trail and South Styrian Route, described under Steirische Weinstraße.

Sachertorte

Menu Reader

Backhendl	Fried chicken in breadcrumbs
Baunzerl	White bread roll
Buchteln	Sweet dumplings cooked in milk and sugar
Blunzen	Black pudding
Erdäpfel	Potato
Faschiertes	Mince, meat balls
Fisolen	Green beans
Frittaten	Pancakes cut into strips and put in soups
Gansljunges	Dish made out of goose giblets
Geselchtes	Salted or smoked meats
Golatschen	Small, usually square, filled pastry
G'spritzter	Wine mixed with soda water
G'spritzter Obi	Apple juice mixed with soda water
Häuptlsalat	Lettuce
Hasenjunges	Jointed hare
Heuriger	Young wine (less than a year old) or the inn where you get it from
Hupfauf	Tyrolean dessert
Indian gefüllt	Stuffed baby turkey
Jungfernbraten	Roast loin of pork with caraway seeds
Kaiserfleisch	Cured pork spare ribs
Kaiserschmarren	Dessert made with eggs and raisins
Karfiol	Cauliflower
Kohlsprossen	Brussels sprouts
Kracherl	Fruit-flavoured soft drink
Kren, Apfelkren	Horseradish, horseradish sauce with apples
Kukuruz	Sweetcorn
Marillen	Apricots
Nockerln	Dumplings
Obi	Apple juice
Palatschinken	Thin pancake filled with apricot jam or chocolate sauce
Paradeiser	Tomatoes
Powidl	Plum jam
Quargel	A type of cheese
Ribisel	Blackcurrants
Risibisi	Rice and peas
Schill	Perch
Schlagobers	Whipped cream
Schmankerl	Hot sweet pudding
Schöberl	Little biscuits (similar to croutons), put in soups
Schwämme, Schwammerln	Mushrooms
Seidel Lichtes	Small lager
Steirisches Schöpsernes	Styrian mutton dish
Strudel	Thin pastry roll with various fillings
Tafelspitz	Boiled beef and vegetable stew
Topfen	Type of cream cheese *(Quark)*

Innovation has good prospects whenever it is cleaner, safer and more efficient.

The MICHELIN Energy green tyre offers a shorter braking distance and lasts 25% longer*. It also provides fuel savings of 2 to 3% while reducing CO_2 emissions.

*on average compared to competing tyres in the same category.

MICHELIN

A better way forward

Stephansdom and Haas-Haus, Vienna
Bartl/ Österreich Werbung

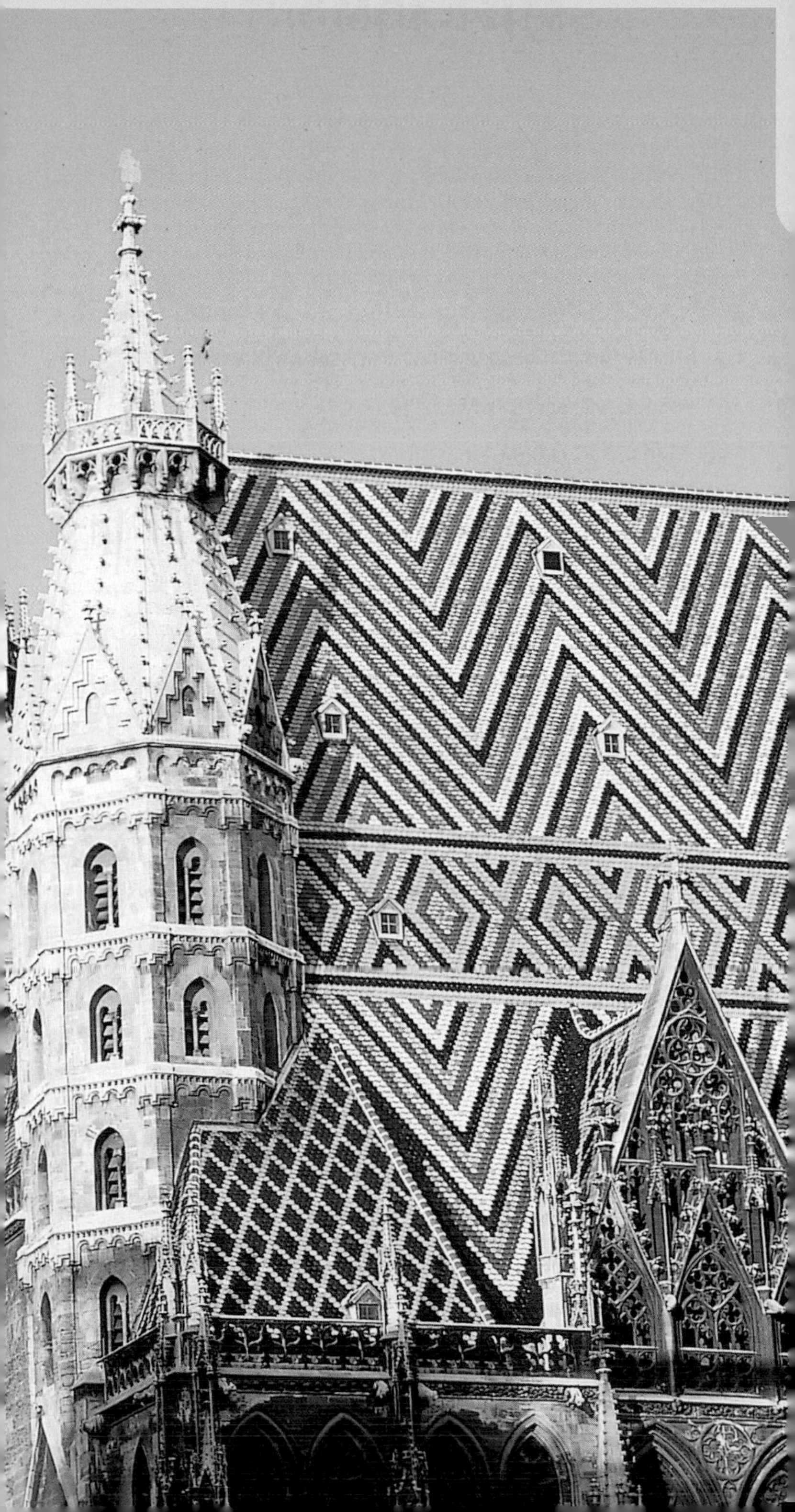

STIFT ADMONT★

STEIERMARK
ALT 641M/2 103FT

The Benedictine Abbey of Admont was founded in the 11C by St Emma of Gurk
(👁 see GURK) and Archbishop Gebhard of Salzburg. The spires of its church are
framed by the summits of the Haller Mauern and the Großer Buchstein, the northern pillar of the Gesäuse. The abbey buildings were completely reconstructed
after a fire in 1865, but fortunately the flames had spared the magnificent library
and its precious collection of manuscripts and books . 🏛 Rathaus, A-8911, ☎ 0 36
13/21 64. www.stiftadmont.at.

▸ **Orient Yourself:** Admont is in northern Styria, at the western entrance of the
  Gesäuse Valley.
👁 **Also See:** Eisenstadt, Eisenerzer Alpen

Stiftsbibliothek (Abbey Library)★★
🕐Open daily Apr-Oct 10am-1pm, 2-5pm. Christmas and school holidays 10am-noon.
👁4,50. ☎ 0 36 13/2 31 26 01.
The exuberant Late Baroque library, completed in 1776, stretches for 70m and is the
world's largest abbey library. Selections from its collection of more than 200,000
volumes are shown on a rotating basis. The seven **ceiling frescoes** by Bartolomeo
Altomonte (1702-83) depict an allegory of theology and the various arts and sciences,
while the bookcases contain valuable medieval illuminated manuscripts, early

Admont Abbey Library

printed books and other prized treasures. Also note the famous statue called **"The Four Last Things"**, a visceral representation of Death, the Last Judgement, Heaven and Hell by Joseph Stammel (1695-1765).

Museums

The **Museum of Fine Arts** displays a small but fine selection of paintings, sculptures, textiles and other objects from the Middle Ages to the Baroque period, including a portable altar dating from 1375 and valuable monstrances. Particularly remarkable are the ceremonial vestments and paraments, all products of the Admont School of Embroidery that flourished in the 17C.

Upstairs are works by contemporary Austrian artists as well as the **Natural History Museum**, which is famous for its insect collection and also presents a good survey of stuffed and preserved animals.

AFLENZER SEEBERGSTRASSE★

STEIERMARK

This 1253m/4111ft mountain pass road links the industrialized Mürz valley with the pilgrimage town of Mariazell and offers sweeping views of the Hochschwab massif along the way.

From Bruck an der Mur to Mariazell *61km/38mi*

Bruck an der Mur★ *See BRUCK AN DER MUR.*

▶ *Start out from Bruck an der Mur northwards on the road to Vienna.*

Leaving Kapfenberg, the road meanders through the narrow Thörlbach Valley to Thörl.

Thörl

This little settlement, lying in a rocky cleft, began as a fortification barring the entrance to the Aflenz basin. Exactly in line with the valley, the ruins of the stronghold of Schachenstein stand on their steep-sided spur. The castle was built in 1464 and was the summer residence of the Abbot of St Lambrecht. Beside the road, to the south, an oratory shelters a Calvary dating from 1530.

Of the gateway *(Törlein)* that gives the village its name there remain, on the mountainside, an 18C building through which the roadway once passed as well as a semicircular tower with an adjacent chapel dedicated to St Barbara. The village is also a a good starting point for hikes in the Hochschwab massif.

Aflenz-Kurort

Aflenz is a popular, medium-altitude climatic health resort in a quiet location. In winter the chair-lift to the Bürgeralm delivers skiers to the sunny Schönleiten plateau, while in summer it serves the mountaineers aiming for the Hochschwab massif. The Late Gothic **church**, which is squat and rustic, boasts a fortified tower and a remarkable south door that has a design of little columns and string-courses superimposed on multilobed archwork. Inside, the most striking features of the pillarless interior are the rib vaulting and the statues of the 12 Apostles. The altars date from the second half of the 18C, while the wooden cross to the left of the choir is Romanesque (1135).

From Aflenz to Au the **road**★ runs along the last foothills of the Hochschwab passing by many houses with wooden galleries that are typical of the area.

The final climb begins at **Seewiesen**, whose 14C Gothic church stands on a small hill. To the west the Seetal is headed by the great blocks of the Hochschwab massif, including the Aflenzer Staritzen and the Mitteralm.

Brandhof

This hunting lodge was created by Archduke Johann. It was here where he secretly got married to Anna Plochl, the daughter of the local postmaster, on 18 February 1829 (see Bad AUSSEE).

The climb to Mariazell offers fine views of the famous pilgrimage church in its wonderful setting.

Mariazell★ See MARIAZELL.

STIFT ALTENBURG★★

NIEDERÖSTERREICH

Founded in 1144, this Benedictine abbey was repeatedly assaulted and all but ruined when a handful of monks set out to reconstruct it in style 1645. The result is a masterpiece of the Baroque, boasting one of the finest abbey libraries in Austria and numerous frescoes by the masterful Paul Troger.

▶ **Orient Yourself:** Stift Altenburg is about 86km (54mi) northwest of Vienna.
 Don't Miss: The library, crypt and the church.
 Also See: Schloss Rosenburg, Eggenburg

Stiftskirche (Abbey church)

The undisputed star features of this beautifully proportioned church are Paul Troger's stunning **ceiling frescoes** depicting the struggle between good and evil. Troger also painted the Assumption above the high altar and several pictures on the side altars. The **stuccowork** is from the workshop of Franz Joseph Holzinger of St. Florian. Also note the **organ** of 1773, elegantly encased in delicately gilded woodwork.

Stiftsgebäude (Abbey buildings)

Guided tour (1hr) Easter Day–1 Nov daily 10am-4pm. €7 0 29 82/34 51.
This is one of the liveliest and most complete groupings of Baroque buildings in the country.

Library

The vestibule, with a dome fresco by Johann Jakob Zeiler, is a mere overture to the magnificence of the church-like library, a collaboration of master archi-

Altenburg Abbey – Frescoes in the "Krypta" (detail)

R. Chéret/MICHELIN

tects, painters and sculptors. Paul Troger painted the ceiling frecoes on the theme of Human and Divine Wisdom. It is at Altenburg more than anywhere else that one can appreciate the Baroque concept of the library as the temple of the spirit and enlightenment.

"Krypta"
This vast, luminous space has no equal among the abbeys of Austria. Its decor, consisting of warmly colored frescoes painted by several pupils of Troger, deals breezily with death, mixing macabre elements with floral motifs.

Sala terrena
Painted with exuberant frescoes, these four rooms are the epitome of Baroque extravagance while also evoking the charm and humor typical of the style. The theme of the first three rooms is water, the source of life and of purity. The fourth, or "Chinese", room is a timeless vision of the Far East.

ARLBERGGEBIET★★

VORARLBERG UND TIROL

Wedged between the Upper Rhine and the Inn corridor, the mountainous region of the Arlberg was for a long time a formidable obstacle to communications. Nowadays, the road to the Arlberg pass, a 10km/6mi long railway tunnel and the 14km/9mi long Arlberg road tunnel link the Vorarlberg and the Tyrol.

A Bit of History

Cradle of Alpine skiing
The Arlberg region is one of the prime skiing destinations in the Austrian Alps with a pedigree going back to 1901 when the country's first skiing club formed here. Twenty years later, local boy **Hannes Schneider** (1890-1955) , whom some consider the 'father of modern skiing' for his inventive techniques, founded Austria's first ski school in St. Anton. Together with British skiing pioneer **Sir Arnold Lunn** (1888-1974). Schneider also organized the first **Arlberg-Kandahar Cup** in 1928, a series of famous downhill and slalom races that continues to this day.

Why Kandahar?

The first downhill race on skis was organised at Montana in Switzerland on 6 January 1911 by Sir Arnold Lunn, who promoted competitive Alpine skiing.

The race was sponsored by Lord Roberts of Kandahar (1832-1914), a British Field Marshal who took his title from the name of a town in Afghanistan which was captured by the Indian army during a military campaign, and his name was therefore adopted for the Kandahar skiing club founded by Lunn in 1924. As this club was joint promoter with the Arlberg skiing club of the skiing championships held at Arlberg from 1928 onwards, which grew into the great international event, this exotic title has been perpetuated.

Skiers who are named five times among the first three in the downhill, slalom or combined event are awarded the Kandahar diamond. Karl Schranz of Austria has gained this honour twice in his career.

The Brotherhood of St. Christoph

Crossing the Arlberg pass used to be a major hurdle for travellers. Many risked, or even lost, their lives due to storms, severe cold or the hazards of the route. For this reason, Heinrich the Foundling from Kempten had an emergency shelter and chapel built just below the pass in 1386. Heinrich founded the brotherhood for the upkeep of the hospice, its charitable works to be funded by donations. Even royalty joined the association and its patrons came from as far afield as Prague, Magdeburg and Strasbourg. The Reformation heralded the decline of the brotherhood and it was finally disbanded under Emperor Joseph II. However, it was reinstated by the Tyrolean bishopric in 1961 and now has more than 11 000 members globally, whose donations go towards helping those in need all over the world.

Arlberg Pass★

① From Bludenz to Landeck *68km/42mi*

Bludenz
This town at the meeting point of five valleys (Walgau, Brandnertal, Montafon, Klostertal and Großwalsertal) centers on a handsome old town and is an ideal base for local excursions.

▸ *An alternative to the Arlberg tunnel road is the old road via Innerbraz, Dalaas, Wald and Klösterle. It is slower and quieter but wll treat you to plenty of delightful mountain views.*

On leaving Bludenz, the craggy outcrop of the Roggelskopf (2 284m/7 494ft) comes into view. After Dalaas, a fresh panorama opens out with the steep wooded slopes of the Batzigg (1 833m/6 014ft) backed by the Rohnspitze peak (2 455m/8 055ft). At **Langen** is the monumental entrance to the **Arlberg tunnel road**, which ends at St. Anton 14km/9mi later.

Stuben
From this tiny, peaceful village, skiers can travel directly to the St. Anton ski slopes. Three chair-lifts give access to the **Albonagrat**★ ridge and there's excellent off-piste skiing as well.

St. Christoph am Arlberg
The Brotherhood of St Christoph has maintained a hospice here since 1386. Travelers can still find shelter in a hospice-hotel and visit the Brotherhood Chapel nearby.

St. Anton am Arlberg ⛷ ⛷
  See ST. ANTON AM ARLBERG.

Stanzertal

After St. Anton, the road traverses the bucolic **Stanzertal**, also known as the Valley of the Rosanna, carving its way between the Lechtal Alps to the north and the Hoher Riffler range to the south. After passing through such attractive resorts as **St. Jakob**, **Pettneu**, **Schnann** and **Flirsch**, the valley narrows and the road runs between forested slopes. Shortly after **Strengen**, the last resort in the Stanzertal, the amazing **Trisannabrücke**★, a steel-construction railway bridge across the River Trisanna, comes into view. A masterpiece of engineering, it was completed in 1884 and is 86m/283ft high and 120m/400ft long.

Landeck

Landeck, where the Arlberg road meets the Inn Valley, lies at the foot of an imposing **castle** (13C-18C), now a local history museum. The nearby **Liebfrauenkirche** is the only Late Gothic church in the northern Tyrol and has an impressive winged altarpiece representing the Adoration of the Magi.

The Flexen Pass★

2 **From the Arlberg road to Warth** 17km/11mi

▶ *The road is open year-round from the turn-off as far as Lech. The stretch further north, between Lech and Warth, is often closed by snow in winter.*

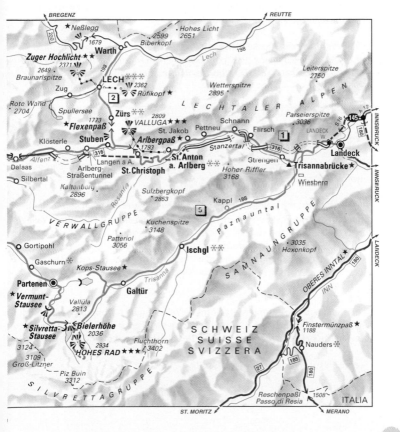

The scenic and winding Flexen pass road branches off the Arlberg pass road east of Stuben and runs over the Flexen pass (1 773m/5 816ft) into the Lech Valley and to the ski resorts of Zürs and Lech.

Zürs 🎿🎿 ⚲ *See ZÜRS.*

After two stretches of tunnel, just before Lech, the valley narrows into a breath-taking rocky ravine only a few meters wide.

Lech 🎿🎿🎿 ⚲ *See LECH.*

On leaving Lech, the road runs halfway up the valley through a less rugged landscape. Softly undulating Alpine meadows alternate with steep rocky cliffs, dotted with majestic spruce trees. At the entrance to Warth, the imposing Biberkopf peak (2 599m/8 527ft) comes into view.

The galleries of the Flexen pass road seen from Stuben

Warth
This small resort is less frenetic than Lech and Zürs and offers great hiking in summer and the full range of snow sports in winter.

▶ *From Warth you can choose between either continuing to Lake Constance through the Bregenzerwald region (⚲ see BREGENZERWALD) or crossing the upper Lech Valley (⚲ see Oberes LECHTAL) towards Reutte.*

Brandner Valley

③ From Bludenz to the Lünersee

▶ *15km/9mi along narrow roads, climbing steeply from Brand onwards, plus a 2hr walk roundtrip.*

On leaving Bludenz the well-built road offers an overview of the town before climb-ing through a forest. Past Bürserberg the view opens out along the Brandner Valley towards the Schesaplana summit (2 965m/9 728ft). Beyond here, the valley gets increasingly narrow. Through a gorge to the left there is a **view**★ of the Zimba peak (2 643m/8 672ft), the "mini-Matterhorn" of the Arlberg region. The route down into the Brand basin reveals the resort's picturesque **setting**★ to full advantage.

Brand
This village founded by immigrants from the Valais region is a popular year-round resort. The road climbs to the foot of the **cirque**★★ , a great natural amphitheater closing off the valley. The road ends after the Schattenlagant refuge.

▶ *Leave the car at the lower cable-car station.*

Lünersee★★

2hr roundtrip, including 10min by cable-car. ©*Operates daily end May-mid Oct 8am-12.30pm,1.10-4.50pm on the hour.* ∞€6,83 *two-way trip.* ☎ 0 55 59/5 14.

The **Lünerseebahn cable-car** delivers you to the lake shore next to the Douglasshütte chalet. In its original state, the Lünersee (1970m/6500ft) was the largest natural mountain lake of the eastern Alps, set in a ring of jagged rocky crests. In 1958 the water level was raised 27m/90ft by a dam, creating a vast reservoir feeding the Lünersee and Rodund power stations more than 1 000m/3 280ft below.

Montafon★

4 **From Bludenz to Partenen** 👍 *See MONTAFON.*

Silvretta Alpine Road★★

5 **From Partenen to Landeck** 👍 *See SILVRETTASTRASSE.*

SCHLOSS-MUSEUM ARTSTETTEN★★

NIEDERÖSTERREICH

Artstetten is most famous for being the final residence of Archduke Franz Ferdinand and his family before their assassination at Sarajevo in 1914. He and his wife are buried below the church. A fortified residence since the 13C, the castle was repeatedly attacked and ravaged by fire. Most of what you see today is from the 17C and 18C, although the complex didn't get its distinctive onion-domed silhouette until 1912. In 1823 it became the property of the Imperial family and it still belongs to its descendants today.

▶ **Orient Yourself:** 18km/12mi west of Melk
👍 **Also See:** Stift Melk, Schloss Schallaburg

A Bit of History

Archduke Franz Ferdinand

In the service of the Empire

Franz Ferdinand was born in 1863 in Graz as the son of Archduke Karl Ludwig and the nephew of Emperor Franz Josef I. Since in his youth there seemed to be no prospect of his ever succeeding to the throne, he decided to embark on a military career. After five years of training, he commanded a regiment of hussars in Hungary and was instrumental in building up Austria's navy, which earned him a promotion to the rank of admiral. The archduke was an accomplished horseman, an excellent shot, a patron of the arts and an avid traveler. With the death of his father in 1896, he became crown prince and heir to the throne. in 1900, against family objections, he married **Sophie Chotek** who, although a countess herself, was not regarded as a suitable match for a future monarch. Together they had three children.

Archduke Franz Ferdinand

Sophie, Duchess of Hohenberg

Schloss Artstetten

Schloss Artstetten

Assassination at Sarajevo

On Sunday 28 June 1914, the archduke and his wife were on an official visit in Bosnia, which had recently been annexed by the Empire. Consequently, the political situation was rather tense, but nobody had an inkling that a group of young Bosnian anarchists was preparing to assassinate the archduke. As the Austrian motorcade drove through the crowds in Sarajevo, one of the conspirators tossed a grenade at the archduke's car. It rolled off the folded-back hood and exploded underneath the following vehicle, injuring a number of attendants and onlookers. The procession fled the scene quickly, reaching the town hall for the official reception without further incident. After the speeches were over, Franz Ferdinand insisted on visiting the wounded attendants in a local hospital, against the advice of local officials who felt they couldn't ensure his safety. Unfamiliar with the changed route, the archduke's driver took a wrong turn. When he tried to back up, another of the seven conspirators, Gavrilo Princip, seemingly coming out of nowhere, fired two shots at almost point-blank range, killing both the archduke and his wife. Princip was quickly apprehended and sentenced to 20 years in prison, where he died of tuberculosis in 1918. The assassination was the direct cause for the outbreak of World War I.

Erzherzog-Franz-Ferdinand Museum★★

○ *Open daily 1 Apr-1 Nov 9am-5.30pm.* € 5,80. ☎ 0 72 13/83 02 30. *www.schloss-artstetten.at.*

An exhibit inside the castle called "For Heart and Crown" chronicles the life and times of Franz Ferdinand and his family. Displays include personal effects, photos, furniture, weapons and other objects once belonging to the Imperial family and associated with events leading to the assassination and outbreak of war in 1914.

BAD AUSSEE⚓

STEIERMARK
POPULATION 5 037

Bad Aussee is the capital of the Styrian Salzkammergut, a region deeply steeped in tradition. It sits at the confluence of two upper branches of the Traun and is surrounded by rugged mountains, including the Dachstein and the Totes Gebirge. The town provides access to two lovely lakes, the Altausseer See and the Grundlsee, and offers an exceptional choice of walks and excursions. Bad Aussee makes both industrial and medical use of the sodium-sulphate waters harvested from the mines of Altaussee. ▯ *Koloman-Wallisch-Platz, A-8990, ☏ 0 36 22/5 23 23. www.ausseerland.at*

▶ **Orient Yourself:** Bad Aussee claims to be at the geographical center of Austria in the southeastern Salzkammergut.
◔ **Also See:** Dachstein Rieseneishöhle (giant ice caves), Hallstatt

A Bit of History

The people's prince
If Bad Ischl owed its fortune to Emperor Franz Joseph, the great man of Bad Aussee was **Archduke Johann**. The prince's controversial romance with Anna Plochl, the daughter of the local postmaster, and their nearly clandestine marriage at Brandhof in 1829 filled the romantic chronicles of the period, confirming the popularity of the "Prince of Styria".
Not surprisingly, in Bad Aussee you will find the prince's statue in the municipal gardens (Kurpark), the medallion of the couple on the bridge over the Grundlseer Traun (Erzherzog-Johann-Brücke) and souvenirs of the Plochl family preserved in the former post office (Alte Pferdepost) at Meranplatz 37.

Sights

Chlumeckyplatz
This central square, anchored by a fountain and a plague column, is a pleasant place for a stroll. Also here is the Kammerhof, once the office of the salt mine regulators

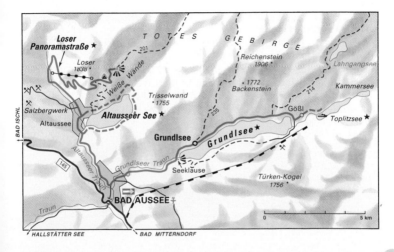

and an impressive Gothic mansion with Renaissance embellishments. Note the marble doorway and window surrounds, the cartouches with cable mouldings and the coat of arms featuring the Imperial eagle above the main entrance. It now houses the local museum, the **Kammerhofmuseum** (*Open daily 15 June-30 Sept 10am-noon, 3-6pm; Palm Sun-14 June & Oct Tues 3.30-6pm, Fri 9.30am-noon, Sun 10am-noon; €3,50 (free admission 26 Oct). 0 36 22/5 25 11 21)* with displays on local history and salt production.

Excursions

Grundlsee★

▶ *5km/3mi to the Grundlsee resort; 10km/6mi to the Gössl fork. Leave Bad Aussee on the Grundlseer Straße.*

At Seeklause (a landing-stage at the head of the lake) there is a **view**★★ over the large Grundlsee, overlooked on the left by the Backenstein promontory. The road skirts the foot of this after passing through the resort of **Grundlsee** from where you have an open view across to the snow-capped summits of the Totes Gebirge.

▶ *Turn back at the end of the lake, at the Gössl fork.*

Another nice side trip *(budget about 3hr from Bad Aussee)* is a visit to the hamlet of Gössl, from where a 20min walk will bring you to the rugged beauty of the **Toplitzsee**. The views from the lake can be seen only by taking the **motorboat excursion** (*Tour of 3 lakes (3hr) daily 13 May-8 Oct 10.20am, 11.35am, 1.20pm & 2.25pm; €6,90. 0 36 22/86 13)*. Beyond the final isthmus lies the little **Kammersee**, hemmed in by the walls of the Totes Gebirge.

Altausseer See★
▶ *5km/3mi to the north.*
The road ends at the climatic resort of **Altaussee,** from where you can walk round the lake *(max 2hr)* or descend into the nearby salt mines **(Salzwelten Altaussee,** *Guided tour (1hr 30min) daily May-end Oct 10am-4pm on the hour; 16-30 Apr & Oct daily 10am, noon & 2pm; Nov-Easter Thur 2.30pm; €10,90 0 61 34/84 00)*. On guided tours through the show-mine you can see the chambers where the Nazis stored looted art during the Second World War and a salt chapel and an underground lake with a sound and light show.

Loser Panoramastraße★
▶ *13km/8mi – about 1hr. Leave Altaussee to the north and follow the "Loser Panoramastraße" signs: toll point after 3.4km/2mi.*
This delightful scenic road climbs to an altitude of 1 600m/5 250ft. From the mountain restaurant (Bergrestaurant) parking lot there is an extensive view over the Altaussee Lake, the sheer "Weiße Wände" ("White Walls") cliffs and, in the distance the Dachstein range and the Hunerkogel. The parking lot is the starting point for a number of marked trails.

BADEN ⚔⚔

NIEDERÖSTERREICH
POPULATION 25,200
ALT 228M/748FT

Baden is a well equipped, modern spa resort with a historic pedigree. It had its heyday in the early 19C when Emperor Franz I spent summers here from 1814 to 1834, attracting such luminaries as Beethoven and Napoleon in his wake. Baden is beautifully located amid vineyards and meadows and noted for its charming villas and elegant Biedermeier architecture. It also hosts a well-known annual summer operetta festival. 🛈 *Brusattiplatz 4, A-2500, ☎ 0 22 52/4 45 31 59. www.baden.at.*

- ▶ **Orient Yourself:** The town lies on the eastern edge of the Vienna Woods along the Schwechat River, about 25km/15mi south of Vienna.
- 🅿 **Parking:** Parking (fee) is available at the Römertherme and at the Parkdeck Zentrum Süd, right by the town's shopping district.
- 👁 **Don't Miss:** Kurpark and Römertherme
- 🕓 **Organizing Your Time:** Take a stroll around town, then spend a relaxing afternoon at a thermal bath.
- 🧒 **Especially for Kids:** The Thermalstrandbad has a playground and special pools for little ones.
- 👣 **Also See:** Wiener Neustadt, Eisenstadt

A Bit of History

Spa resort
It was the Romans who first enjoyed the healing properties of Baden's hot-water springs. Nowadays, the spa's 14 sulfurous springs yield more than 4 million l/ 880 000gal per day, reaching a natural temperature of up to 36°C/97°F. The mineral waters are particulary effective in treating all sorts of rheumatic ailments.

Famous visitors
Musicians displayed a particular fondness for this idyllic town. **Wolfgang Amadeus Mozart** wrote his "Ave Verum" here and **Franz Schubert** came by as well. **Ludwig van Beethoven** visited Baden some 15 times in hopes of curing his deafness. Great waltz and operetta composers, including **Strauss**, Lanner, Millöcker and Zeller, also favored a visit now and then.

Sights

Kurpark★
This fine park sprawls from near the center of town as far as the Vienna woods. At its edge looms the beautifully restored **Casino**, the oldest gambling hall in Austria and also one of its most magnificent. Nearby, the Jugendstil **Sommerarena** (1906), with its movable glass roof, provides a pretty backdrop for the summer operetta festival. Free afternoon concerts take place at the **music pavilion**.

Spa town architecture★
During the first half of the 19C, numerous thermal establishments were built in Baden in the neo-Classical style, many of them under the direction of Josef Kornhäusel. Many still exist, although most now have been given a different purpose. The **Josefsbad**, a

round, domed building in eye-catching yellow ,now serves as a coffee house; the **Frauenbad** (in Frauengasse) with its pillared portico is now an art gallery; the **Franzensbad** is a glass-making workshop; and the **Leopoldsbad** (on Brusatiplatz) houses the tourist information office. The **Sauerhof**, on the other side of the Schwechat, has been converted into a hotel.

The Kaiser-Franz-Ring, the Rainerring and the Breyerstraße feature numerous stately **villas** in the neo-Classical or Biedermeier styles.

Spas

Kids Baden's two main public pools complexes are the summer-only **Thermalstrandbad**, an art deco outdoor playground with a huge sandy beach, and the top-class indoor **Römertherme** (www.roemertherme.at), the largest unsupported span, glass-roofed thermal bath in Europe.

Dreifaltigkeitssäule and Rathaus

Hauptplatz

Baden's central square is dominated by the impressive, columned **Rathaus** (town hall), constructed in 1815 by Joseph Kornhäusel and fronted by the ornate baroque **Dreifaltigkeitssäule** (Trinity Column), a plague column completed in 1718. At No 17 is the **Kaiserhaus**, where Emperor Franz I summered for 30 years and where Austria's last emperor, Karl I, stayed from 1916-18.

Beethovenhaus

Rathausgasse 10. ◐*Open Tues-Fri 4-6pm, Sat, Sun & public hols 9am-11am & 4-6pm. Closed 1 Jan, 24, 25, 31 Dec.* ◉€2,50. ☏ 0 22 52/86 80 02 30
The great composer wrote part of the *Missa Solemnis* and completed his *Ninth Symphony* while staying here between 1821 and 1823. You can see his bedroom and living room as well as a small exhibit on his life and work.

Stadtpfarrkirche St. Stephan

All that remains of the original Romanesque building are the two stumps of towers, between which a Gothic-looking tower with a Baroque dome was added in 1697. Inside there is a dodecahedral baptismal font dating from the 14C and an altarpiece by Paul Troger depicting the *Stoning of St Stephen*.

Doblhoff Park

The main attraction here is the **Rosarium**★, a redolent display of 20 000 roses of 600 different varieties. In June, the Badener Rosentage attract flower-lovers galore.

BRAUNAU

OBERÖSTERREICH
POPULATION 16,260
ALT 352M/1 155FT

Braunau has had a civic charter since 1260, flourished through the salt trade in the 15C, but only became part of Austria in 1779. A bridge over the River Inn connects the town with Simbach in Bavaria, Germany. Although (in)famous as the birthplace of Adolf Hitler, Braunau is really more noteworthy for its pretty town center and the numerous Gothic houses that miraculously survived the great fire of 1874. 🇧 *Stadtplatz 2, A-5280, ☎ 0 77 22/6 26 44. www.tourismus-braunau.at.*

▸ **Orient Yourself:** Braunau is in the Innviertel right on the border with Germany about 60km north of Salzburg and 90km west of Linz.

🅿 **Parking:** Look for fee-based parking lots along Ringstraße, which wraps along the western town center.

Sights

Altstadt
The focal feature of the old town is the **Stadtplatz**, an elongated square framed by houses from various architectural periods. Of particular interest are the **Glockengießerhaus** *(Johann-Fischer-Gasse 18)*, built in 1385, which still has its original bell-foundry workshop, and nearby, the **Herzogsburg**, now a regional museum.

Stadtpfarrkirche St. Stephan
Dominating Braunau's skyline is the landmark steeple of the town's parish church, which ranks as one of the highest in the country. The Late Gothic hall church is filled with treasures, most notably the late 15C **Bäckeraltar** (Bakers' Altar), donated by the bakers' guild.

BREGENZ★★

VORARLBERG
POPULATION 27,900
ALT 398M/1 306FT
HOTELS AND RESTAURANTS: SEE THE MICHELIN GUIDE ÖSTERREICH

Bregenz is the administrative capital of the Vorarlberg and scenically located on the shore of Lake Constance (Bodensee to German speakers), at the point where the mountains spill down to the "Swabian Sea" . The lakeside draws active travelers with its wide variety of water sports and splendid views. Music lovers flood the town during the Bregenz Festival in summer (👢 *see Calendar of Events*). 🇧 *Bahnhofstraße 14, A-6900, ☎ 0 55 74/4 95 90. www. bregenz.ws.*

▸ **Orient Yourself:** Bregenz is on the eastern shore of Lake Constance at the foot of the Pfänder mountain.

🅿 **Parking:** With 2300 spots, Bregenz has public parking aplenty. An automated guide system directs you to the nearest garage or lot with open spaces.

👁 **Don't Miss:** A walk around the Oberstadt, a trip up the Pfänder Mountain.

- ⏱ **Organizing Your Time:** Spend the day in town, then head up the mountain late in the day for sunset views.
- 💧 **Also See:** Bregenzer Wald, Dornbirn

Lower Town *(Innenstadt)*

Lake Shore (ABY)

The main shopping streets (pedestrian zone) cluster at the foot of the former fortified city (Oberstadt or Altstadt) of the counts of Bregenz and Montfort.

In the Middle Ages the lake waters still lapped against the base of the little **Seekapelle** (lakeside chapel – BY). Insulated from road traffic by the railway, the shady quays and flowerbeds of the lake shore stretch from the Seeanlagen to the passenger port. A walk along the landscaped harbour breakwater is particularly pleasant and offers fabulous **views**★ (BY) extending to Upper Swabia with the island of Lindau in

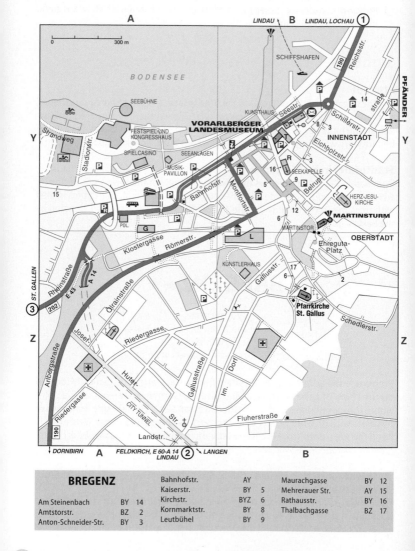

BREGENZ			Bahnhofstr.		AY	Maurachgasse		BY	12
			Kaiserstr.		BY 5	Mehrerauer Str.		AY	15
			Kirchstr.		BYZ	Rathausstr.		BY	16
Am Steinenbach	BY	14	Kornmarktstr.		BY 8	Thalbachgasse		BZ	17
Amtstorstr.	BZ	2	Leutbühel		BY 9				
Anton-Schneider-Str.	BY	3							

the foreground. Further west is the **Festspielhaus** (AY), which hosts cultural events year-round and is a prime venue during the Bregenz Festival. The most spectacular performances, though, are held on the **Seebühne** (AY), a stage jutting above the lake outside the festival hall.

Vorarlberger Landesmuseum★ (BY)

🕐 *Open Tues-Sun 9am-noon, 2-5pm.* 🕐 *Closed 1 Jan, 1 Nov, 25 Dec.* ✆€1,50. ☎ 0 55 74/4 60 50.

The collections are particularly well displayed in the prehistory and Roman departments on the first floor. The second floor presents folkloric costumes and musical instruments, including a fancily carved portable organ from the early 16C. The third floor focuses on religious art scavenged from the richest churches in the province, including an early-16C crucifix from the former abbey church at Mehrerau. On the same floor are works of mythological or religious inspiration and portraits *(Duke of Wellington)* by **Angelika Kauffmann** (1741-1807), considered a native of the Vorarlberg because of her connection with the Bregenzerwald. She lived In Rome, Venice and England, where she was a founding member of the Royal Academy in 1768 and a follower of Reynolds.

On nearby Karl-Tizian-Platz is the 1997 **Kunsthaus Bregenz**★ (BY), an unapologetically modernist structure by Swiss master architect Peter Zumthor. Behind the striking façade of etched glass are changing contemporary art exhibits.

Upper Town *(Oberstadt)* and Church Quarter

With its quiet squares and lanes, this charming quarter makes a peaceful contrast to the bustling lake shore. It can be reached by car via the Kirchstraße, the Thalbachgasse and the Amtstorstraße. If you're walking, stroll up from the central intersection of the Leutbühel by the paved ramp of the Maurachgasse as far as the Martinstor, an old fortified gateway.

Winsquer/BREGENZER FESTSPIELE

Lakeside theatre, Bregenz

Martinsturm (BY)

Open daily May-Oct 9am-6pm. ✆1€. ☎ *0 55 74/4 66 32.*

A Bregenz landmark, this 13C tower only got its huge onion dome (one of the largest in Austria) around 1600. The chapel in the tower base contains a massive Late Gothic altar canopy and fairly well preserved 14C frescoes. Upstairs is a small military museum through whose windows you can enjoy pretty **glimpses**★ of the remains of the wall, the old town, the lake and belfries of Lindau and, in the distance, the Appenzell Alps.

Pfarrkirche St. Gallus (BZ)

This hillside single-nave Baroque church is decorated with the relative restraint typical of the Vorarlberg churches, which contrasts with Tyrolean and Bavarian churches of the same period. The walnut stalls were made about 1740 for the nearby abbey of Mehrerau and are decorated with effigies of saints.

Excursion

Pfänder★★

▶ *Summer mists make it advisable to do this excursion either in the early morning or in the evening before sunset. Leave Bregenz on 1 and the lakeside road to Lindau.*

To drive up the Pfänder, turn right towards the village of **Lochau**. Past the church in Lochau turn right onto the steep and twisting by-road, which reaches a parking lot (fee) after about 6km/4mi. From here, it's about a 15min walk to the Pfänder summit (1 064m/3 491ft).

If you continue driving for another half a mile or so, you reach a plateau with the Pfänder mountain refuge (fee-based parking available). From opposite the mountain hut a small trail leads to the Pfänder summit in a matter of minutes.

An alternative way to get up the mountain is by taking the **Pfänderbahn cable-car** (*Operates daily 9am-7pm every 30min; Closed 2nd & 3rd weeks in Nov;* ✆€9,45 *roundtrip;* ☎ *0 55 74/42 16 00).*

The breathtaking **panorama**★ from the plateau takes in - from left to right - the Allgäu Alps, the snow-covered Schesaplana, the great furrow of the Rhine and the Altmann and the Säntis on the Swiss side.

North of the plateau is the **Alpenwildpark** game reserve where a 30min circuit introduces you to Alpine fauna such as moufflons, ibex, marmots and red deer, housed in generous enclosures. The circuit also takes you past the eagle observation point where there are **bird of prey flight displays** twice a day in summer *(Displays (40min) Open daily1 May-3 Oct 11am, 2.30pm;* ✆€3,70; ☎ *06 63/05 30 40).*

BREGENZERWALD★★

VORARLBERG

Contrary to what the name implies, the Bregenzerwald is not really a dense forest but a wonderfully diverse natural playground with landscapes ranging from softly rolling hills to majestic Alpine peaks. The unspoiled countryside, the traditional wooden houses and villages, and a local population that still cherishes their ancient customs make the Bregenzerwald a popular destination.

▶ **Orient Yourself:** The Bregenzerwald is located between Bregenz on Lake Constance and the Arlberg range.

☺ **Don't Miss:** Rappenlochschlucht
Kids **Especially for Kids:** Inatura in Dornbirn
☼ **Also See:** For a pretty tour of the Vorarlberg, take the Arlbergstraße to Rauz, and then the Flexen pass road to Warth.

The route described below crosses the Bregenzerwald from east to west.

Hochtannenbergstraße★

From Warth to Dornbirn *65km/40mi*

▶ *The road between Warth and Schröcken may be closed for several days at a time between November and March because of risk of avalanches.*

This route crosses the **Hochtannberg pass** (1675m/5495ft) and follows the twisting Bregenzerach River. The crossing of the Bödele pass lends a mountainous character to the final leg of the trip and gives magnificent views of the Rhine Valley. Between Warth and Nesslegg the road runs through the Hochtannberg pastureland.

Nesslegg★

From the viewpoint by the Hotel Widderstein, you'll have a fine overview of the cirque closing the upper valley of the Bregenzerach. From left to right you can see the Mohnenfluh, the Braunarlspitz and its snowfields, the Hochberg, the Schadonapass gap and the Hochkünzelspitze.

From Nesslegg the road plunges down through forest, offering occasional glimpses of the village of **Schröcken**. Downstream from the splendidly engineered Hochtannberg bridge appears the hamlet of **Unterboden**, a typical Valaisian settlement. Between Schoppernau and the resort of **Mellau** the varied structure of the Kanisfluh is revealed; its north face is formed of particularly steep cliffs. The road continues through a succession of idyllic landscapes. Further on, wide valleys with their fruit-growing enterprises are graced by the villages of **Bezau** and Schwarzenberg.

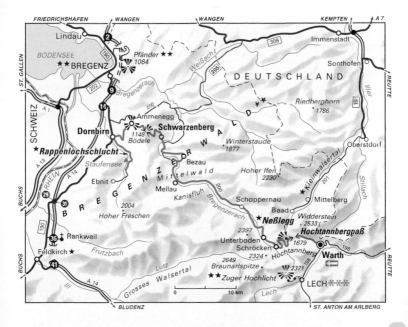

Schwarzenberg

This sleepy village is centered on a pretty **square**★ flanked by flower-festooned houses (eg Gasthof Hirschen). The parish church features several work by the famous artist **Angelika Kauffmann** (1741-1807), including the medallions representing the Apostles and Jesus' disciples and the picture on the high altar. Look for the artist's bust on the north wall of the nave. More of her works can be seen in the Vorarlberger Landesmuseum in Bregenz and the Heimatmuseum in Schwarzenberg.

Traditional costumes from the Bregenzerwald

Crossing the Bödele ridge gives clear **views**★ to the east of the open basin of the Bregenzerwald and the Allgäu Alps marking the German border. On the Rhine slope, after a long run through forest, the **panorama**★ opens out near **Ammenegg** extending, in clear weather, to Lake Constance and the Appenzell Alps.

Dornbirn

Kids The largest town in Vorarlberg, Dornbirn has few tourist-worthy sights. An exception is the kid-friendly **Inatura** (*Jahngasse 9;* ⏲*Open daily 10am-6pm;* ✆€9; ☎ 0 55 72/2 32 35), a modern and edutaining journey into the natural mysteries of the Vorarlberg. Experiences include a visit to an underwater movie theater and a virtual trip back into prehistoric times.

▷ *Leave Dornbirn on the road towards Ebnit/Gütle. After about 3.5km/2mi you reach the parking lot for the Rappenlochschlucht.*

Rolls-Royce-Museum

Gütle 11a. ⏲*Open Apr-Oct Tues-Sun 10am-6pm. Nov-Mar Tues-Sun 10am-5pm.* ✆€8. ☎ 0 55 72/5 26 52.
A 19C textile factory houses the world's largest collection of Rolls Royces with more than 1 000 vehicles, including those once used by the Queen Mum and Spanish dictator General Francisco Franco.

Rappenlochschlucht★

▷ *Allow about 1hr 30min for the walk as far as the road to Ebnit. From July to mid September free guided walks depart every Thursday at 10.30am from the Gasthof Gütle parking lot.* ⏲*Open mid Apr-late Oct.* ☎ 0 55 72/2 21 88. *www.rappenlochschlucht.at.*

About a 20min walk along wooden walkways above the turbulent waters of the Dornbirner Ache brings you to the mighty rocky cliffs of the 72m/236ft Rappenloch gorge. Beyond here, a path along the Staufensee reservoir leads to a the Alploch gorge, which is still impressive if less breathtaking than the Rappenloch. It takes about 20min as far as the Ebnit road. From here, retrace your steps to the parking lot.

BRUCK AN DER MUR★

STEIERMARK
POPULATION 15 090
ALT 481M/1 578FT

Bruck is lorded over by the romantically ruined fortress of Landskron. It's a busy, industrial town whose main sights orbit Koloman-Wallisch-Platz, the main square. ▯ *Koloman-Wallisch-Platz 26, A-860.* ☎ *0 38 62/5 18 11. www.bruckmur.at.*

▶ **Orient Yourself:** Bruck an der Mur lies at the confluence of the Mur and Mürz rivers in northern Styria, about 50km/30mi north of Graz.

Sights

Eiserner Brunnen★★ (A)
The ornate fountain (1626) by local artisan Hans Prasser is considered a superb example of Styrian wrought-ironwork.

Old Houses
Bruck still has several 15C and 16C houses with arcaded courtyards, most notably the **Rathaus** (A R – town hall) and the **Flössmeisterhaus** *(no 5)* (B B). The nicest historic building, though, is the **Kornmesserhaus** ★ (B), named for its builder, the wealthy merchant Pankraz Kornmess.

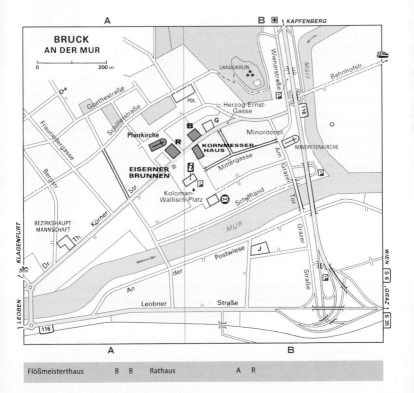

Flößmeisterhaus	B B	Rathaus	A R

Pfarrkirche (A)

This Gothic parish church counts among its highlights a wrought-iron **sacristy door**, believed to come from the Kornmesserhaus, and a fine late-18C **altar of the Holy Cross** in the north side chapel.

CHRISTKINDL

OBERÖSTERREICH

The village of Christkindl (the name means Christ Child) with its charming pilgrims' chapel is associated with a quaint and delightful tradition. Every year around Christmas time, an average of two million Christmas cards and letters are mailed out by the church's special post office. Letters written by children to the Christ Child (baby Jesus), who delivers the gifts in Austria, also get a reply (if return postage is enclosed).

▶ **Orient Yourself:** Christkindl is about 3km/2mi west of Steyr.

Pfarr- und Wallfahrtskirche

The Baroque parish church was begun by Giovanni Battista Carlone and completed by Jakob Prandtauer in 1708. Four semicircular chapels are arranged below a great dome adorned with a fresco of the *Assumption of the Virgin* by Johann Carl Reslfeld (1710).

The main point of veneration, though, is a small, miracle-working wax figure of Jesus, kept above the globe-shaped tabernacle. In 1720 the altar was adorned with 35 gilded statuettes of angels arranged around the trunk of the "Christ tree" in which the effigy was formerly kept. The gilded Rococo pulpit (1751) is also a magnificent piece of work.

Krippenschau

The crib display in the old working quarters of the presbytery is open to visitors from late November to 6 January. Highlights include the early 20C **mechanical crib**, which consists of nearly 300 figures, many of them moveable through a system of cogs and chains. The 1930s **Pöttmesser crib** features a dizzying 778 figures and is considered to be one of the largest in the world.

DACHSTEIN★★

SALZBURG, STEIERMARK UND OBERÖSTERREICH

The Dachstein massif (highest point 2 995m/9 826ft) forms a superb backdrop to several Alpine lakes. The range is also honeycombed by labyrinthine cave systems formed millions of years ago.

▶ **Orient Yourself:** The Dachstein massif forms the southern border of the Salzkammergut region.

⊛ **Don't Miss:** Cable-car ride to the Krippenstein, Dachstein Giant Ice Caves, Hunerkogel.

North Face★

To the north, the Dachstein foothills surround the lakes of Hallstatt and Gosau. From Obertraun, the Krippensteinbahn cable-car serves the Dachstein Giant Ice Cave before terminating near the Krippenstein summit with its superb views. In winter, this is a popular free-riding area for skiers and snowboarders.

Hallstatt★★   *See HALLSTATT.*

Ascent of the Krippenstein★★

Cable-car operates daily May-mid Oct & Christmas-Easter 8.40am-5pm every 15min. Summer ⬤€13 roundtrip, winter €24 ski pass. ☎ 0 61 34/84 00. From Hallstatt 4km/2.5mi in the direction of Obertraun; then bear right 2km/1mi beyond the end of the lake.
The cable car drops off visitors to the caves at the **Schönbergalpe** (alt 1 345m/ 4 413ft) station before continuing to the upper station.
Enjoy sweeping **views★★** of the Dachstein plateau from the chapel at alt 2 109m/ 6 919ft. To get a **bird's-eye view★★** of the lake at Hallstatt, follow the marked path at the beginning of the Krippenstein road to the Pioneers' Cross (*Pionierkreuz, allow an extra 30min*).

Dachstein-Rieseneishöhle★

2hr 30min walk from Obertraun or a ride on the Krippensteinbahn cable-car to Schön- bergalpe followed by 15min walk. Warm clothing is advisable. ⬤*Guided tour (1hr) daily May-mid Oct 8.30am-4.30pm. ⬤90S. ☎ 0 61 34/84 00.*
The spectacular Giant Ice Cave, whose ice draperies, icicles and other formations are illuminated by colored lights, can only be seen on guided tours. It is one of Europe's largest subterranean ice caves.

Mammuthöhle

30min there and back on foot from Schönbergalpe station. 1km/0.5mi walk through the cave. ⬤*Guided tour (1hr) daily mid May-mid Oct 9am-4pm. ⬤90S. ☎ 0 61 34/84 00.*

South face of the Dachstein

P. Mertz/VIENNASLIDE

These limestone caves were carved by a subterranean river and are not as impressive as the Giant Ice Cave, but a tour is still worth it for the excellent sound and light show presented deep inside the mountain.

Gosauseen★★★   🕭   *See GOSAUSEEN.*

South Face★★

The towering bulk of the Dachstein massif drops steeply down to the flower-bedecked pastures of Ramsau.

From Eben im Pongau to Göbming

▶ *62km/39mi*

Filzmoos★
This attractive holiday resort at 1 057m/3 468ft occupies a pretty **site**★ tucked against the western foothills of the Dachstein massif. Towering above the village is the distinctive outline of the **Bischofsmütze** (Bishop's Mitre, 2 454m/8 049ft). There is a small ski slope here and a well laid 14km/8.6mi cross-country track from the mountain station of the Papagenobahn cable-car to the Radstädter mountain refuge. In summer, Filzmoos is a great base for walks in the surrounding mountains. A climb to the **Gerzkopf**★★ summit (1 729m/5 673ft, *4hr roundtrip walk from Schattbach*) is particularly recommended.

Roßbrand★★
After taking the Papagenobahn cable-car, follow the easy ridge trail west to the summit *(about 2hr roundtrip)*. The magnificent **panorama**★★ takes in 150 peaks, mainly of the Dachstein range, the Schladminger Tauern, the Ankogel range, the Hohe Tauern and the Hochkönig.

▶ *Carry on towards Ramsau. After 12km/7.5mi, turn left and then take a small toll road to the right up to the foot of the Hunerkogel.*

Hunerkogel★★★
Alt 1 700m/5 576ft. 🕐*Cable-car operates daily June-end Apr 8.30am-4.50pm.* ⊜⊜€19,98 roundtrip. ☎ 0 36 87/8 12 41, allow at least 1hr roundtrip.
From the end of the toll road, the Hunerkogel (2 700m/8 856ft) can be seen looming like some impregnable fortress. The ascent of the sheer rock face by the **Dachstein-Südwandbahn** cable car (also known as the Gletscherbahn Ramsau) is spectacular. The new Sky-Walk platform at the top offers breathtaking views of the craggy peaks and Ramsua.

Ramsau am Dachstein★
Alt 1 150m/3 772ft. Ramsau clings to a sunny mountain plateau and has plenty of lodging options. It's an oasis of peace and quiet and a hiker's delight, even in winter when 70km/44mi of groomed trails make walking easy.
The **cross-country skiing** ★★★ is excellent here, with over 150km/90mi of tracks of all levels of difficulty between altitudes of 1 000-1 750m/3 281-5 740ft. There are also 40km/25mi of skating tracks. The nearby Dachstein glacier also offers cross-country ski tracks at an altitude of 2 700m/8 858ft.

DONAUTAL★★

The Danube is the longest river in Central Europe (2 826km/1 756mi) and the second longest in Europe, after the Volga (3 895km/2 292mi). It flows through or skirts 10 states, and four capital cities have been built on its banks, bearing witness to its timeless and borderless importance.

▶ **Orient Yourself:** The Danube is Austrian for 360km/224mi from Achleiten, near the German border, to Hainburg, near Bratislava.

☻ **Don't Miss:** Wachau with Melk Abbey, Artstetten Castle & Museum, Krems und Stein, Vienna.

The Austrian section of the Danube is entirely navigable and a vital artery for the country's economy. Its waters may not always be the color evoked in song by *The Blue Danube*, but this epic stream still meanders through plenty of idyllic scenery, particularly between Grein and Krems. Time-worn fortified castles, gracious Renaissance palaces and beautiful churches and abbeys will captivate most visitors.

1 From Passau *(in Germany)* to Linz *86km/55mi*

From Passau to Aschach, our proposed route runs along the south bank of the river. From the north bank rise the granite heights of the Mühlviertel.

Passau★★

The well-preserved old town of Passau occupies a tongue of land between the Danube and the Inn, its cobbled streets clustered around the cathedral of St. Stephan. Overlooking the "town of three rivers" (the Danube, Inn and Ilz converge here) from their hilltop perches are the formidable Oberhaus fortress to the north and the Baroque pilgrimage church of Mariahilf to the south. From either vantage point, you'll have highly photogenic views of the town. ☝ *For a more detailed description see The Green Guide Germany.*

▶ *Leave Passau by crossing the Inn and heading towards Linz.*

The wide and majestic river parallels the road, carving through wooded, rocky slopes. At Obernzell, it spills out into the reservoir of the Jochenstein dam, a magnificent lake. The **Jochenstein power station** generates 850 million kWh annually. From Engelhartszell to Wesenufer the valley narrows. The clifftop road offers some fine views, with various castles occasionally coming into view in the distance. A little after **Wesenufer**, a pretty village with flowered balconies, the road leaves the riverbank and climbs through a wooded gorge to the picturesque Aschach Valley. Beyond here, it crosses the Danube below the **Aschach-Kraftwerk**, one of the largest power stations of its kind in Europe.

▶ *Beyond Ottensheim and its dam, the road follows the river to Linz.*

2 From Linz to Grein 72km/45mi

Linz★ 🕭 See LINZ.

Below Linz, the valley opens out into a wide, fertile basin where wheat, sugarbeet and fruit trees flourish. To the north lie the slopes and forested ridges of the Mühlviertel and further on the Waldviertel.

▷ *Leave Linz to the southeast via St.-Peterstraße towards Grein.*

The road continues through the industrial zone of Linz and crosses the Danube at the Steyregg bridge beyond which it cuts across a plateau to return to the Danube plain at St. Georgen.

▷ *Take the turn towards the camp (Lager) at Mauthausen.*

Mauthausen 🕭 See MAUTHAUSEN.

From Mauthausen to Dornach the road crosses a vast cultivated plain that gradually transitions into a woodsier landscape.

▷ *Near Saxen turn right towards Burg Clam.*

Burg Clam★

Guided tour (45min) daily May–end Oct 10am–5pm. ⌂€6. ☎ 0 72 69/72 17. Dominated by its central tower, the castle rises romantically from its leafy surroundings. The rock on which it stands has been fortified since 1149. The residential part of the castle revolves around the charmingly irregular arcaded Renaissance **courtyard**★. Inside, highlights include an unusually complete **pharmacy** from 1603, fine Vienna and Meissen porcelain and some rare Louis XVI armchairs.

▷ *Return to the Danube road.*

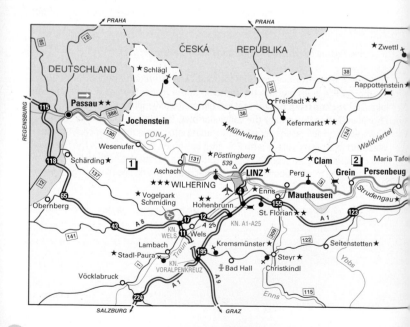

Below Dornach the road hugs the north bank of the river whose watersare hemmed in by rocky, wooded slopes. The approach to Grein is particularly pretty.

Grein

This charming summer resort town is dominated by the hills of the Mühlviertel. Turreted houses frame the pretty town square (Stadtplatz), while the parish church contains an 18C high altar with an altarpiece by Bartolomäus Altomonte. Grein is justifiably proud of its little **Rokoko-Theater** (*Guided tour (20min) daily Apr-end Oct 9am, 11am, 1.30pm and 4pm; €2,50; 0 72 68/70 55)* in the town hall. Entirely made of wood, it dates to the end of the 18C and is still in use every summer.

Greinburg Castle, still under the ownership of the House of Saxe-Coburg-Gotha, is a four-winged structure wrapped around a romantic fountain-studded Renaissance **courtyard**★ with three tiers of arcades. Inside, the **Schiffahrtsmuseum** *(Open June-end Sept Tues-Sun 10am-6pm; May & Oct Tues-Sun 10am-noon & 1-5pm; €2,20; 0 72 68/70 07)* is a local navigation museum with models of bridges, landing-stages and locks as well as works of art evoking the life on the great river in this part of Austria.

③ From Grein to Krems 95km/59mi

Between Grein and Krems stretches the most picturesque section of the Danube Valley in Austria. It is hollowed out of the granite of the Waldviertel, which forms the last foothills of the Bohemian massif.

Grein   *Description under ② above.*

From Grein to Ybbs, the **Strudengau**★, wedged between high wooded cliffs that are often shrouded in mist, provides a heroic and romantic setting. The castle ruins of Burg Struden and Burg Sarmingstein are particularly eye-catching. The river embraces willow-covered islands, then expands into a splendid lake formed by the Ybbs-Persenbeug dam.

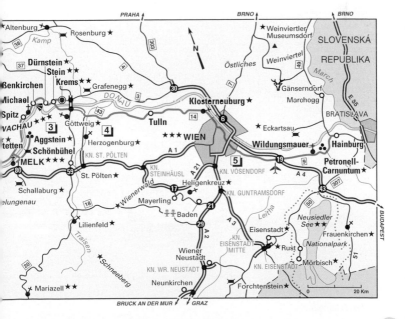

Persenbeug

The last Austrian emperor, Karl I, was born in this rocky castle in 1887. The valley surrounding Persenbeug features in the legendary Nibelungen epic. It was here, in the **Nibelungengau**, that Gunther and Hagen undertook their rides through the forest and where they gathered their knights to go to Attila's court at the invitation of Kriemhild who had married the King of the Huns to avenge the murder of her first husband, Siegfried.

In a splendid **site**★ on a hillock to the left is the 1660 pilgrimage church of **Maria Taferl**, with its splendid facade and dome by Jakob Prandtauer.

Artstetten Castle and Museum★★ ⓖ *See Schloss-Museum ARTSTETTEN.*

▶ *Take the bridge over the Danube to Melk.*

Melk Abbey★★★ ⓖ *See MELK.*

The 35km/22mi stretch of the Danube between Melk and Krems is known as the **Wachau**★★. It's a picturesque and fertile region famous for its apricots (locally known as *Marillen*) and dotted with delightful villages, clifftop fortresses and onion-domed churches.

Schönbühel

From the main road , **Schloss Schönbühel** can be spotted on the south bank, its rocky promontory setting and onion-domed tower creating a charming picture.

▶ *Take the road on the north bank towards Krems.*

Schloss Schönbühel

Burgruine Aggstein★

Its exceptional **site**★ some 300m/1000ft above the Danube and colossal size made this 12C fortress one of Austria's finest strongholds in its heyday. The ruined towers and defensive walls are still an impressive sight today. A steep path *(2hr roundtrip walk)* leads from Aggstein hamlet up to the castle gate. At the top you'll be treated to superb views.

At **Willendorf** a 25,000-year-old limestone statue, known as the "Willendorf Venus", was found in 1906. It is now kept in Vienna at the Naturhistorisches Museum.

Spitz★

Placid Spitz lies half-hidden behind a curtain of fruit trees below a terraced vineyard. Spitz has fine old town houses, especially along Schlossgasse, which leads to the 17C castle. The Gothic **Pfarrkirche** *(◷Open daily Apr-Sept 8am-7pm; daily Oct-Mar daily 8am-5pm; ☎ 0 27 13/22 31)* has an unusual chancel out of line with the nave. The organ loft is adorned with statues of Christ and the 12 Apostles (c 1420). The altarpiece (1799) by Kremser Schmidt over the Baroque altar shows the martyrdom of St. Maurice.

Weissenkirchen

This wine-growing village has an imposing Gothic fortified church with a baroque altar and nice gardens lording above a pretty town with cobbled pathways and fine old houses. *www.weissenkirchen.at.*

Wachaumuseum

◷Open Apr-end Oct Tues-Sun 10am-5pm. ➜€2,18. ☎ 0 27 15/22 68.
The museum is housed in the Teisenhoferhof, a 16C fortified farm with an arcaded courtyard and a covered gallery decorated with garlands of flowers and sheaves of maize. Inside are paintings by Wachau painters working at the turn of the 20C.

Dürnstein★ 👣 *See DÜRNSTEIN.*

The countryside flattens out on the approach to the towns of Krems und Stein.

Krems und Stein★★   *See KREMS und STEIN.*

4 From Krems to Vienna *83km/52mi*

Krems und Stein★★   *See KREMS und STEIN.*

▶ *Cross the Danube on the great steel bridge at Stein, west of Krems.*

A little after Mautern on the right, crowning a wooded hill, stands the impressive Benedictine abbey called **Stift Göttweig**. It has a grand Imperial staircase adorned with a ceiling fresco by Paul Troger and a wonderfully exuberant Baroque church.

Tulln   *See TULLN.*

At Greifenstein, near the Vienna Woods, the valley narrows, and the road squeezes through a passage between the river and high wooded hills.

Klosterneuburg★   *See KLOSTERNEUBURG.*

The road then enters the suburbs of Vienna.

Vienna★★★   *See WIEN.*

5 From Vienna to Hainburg *84km/52mi*

The suggested route follows the south bank of the river through a wide valley.

Vienna★★★   *See WIEN.*

▶ *Leave Vienna on the B 9 for Schwechat, famous for its breweries and giant oil refinery.*

Petronell-Carnuntum   *See PETRONELL-CARNUNTUM.*

The range of hills between Bad Deutsch-Altenburg and Hainburg is the Little Carpathians, the last outrunners of the mountains encircling the Hungarian plain.

Hainburg
Still retaining its ring of walls and fortified gateways below the remains of its castle, Hainburg had an important strategic role in the Middle Ages on the highway linking Vienna and Bratislava.

DÜRNSTEIN ★

NIEDERÖSTERREICH
POPULATION 1 000
ALT 209M/686FT

Dürnstein, considered the 'pearl' of the Wachau region, lies above a scenic bend of the Danube and boasts a bevy of beautiful old houses. Girded by ancient walls, it is crowned by a ruined fortress where Richard I (the Lionheart) was once held prisoner. ℹ *Rathaus, A-3601,* ☏ *0 27 11/2 19. www.duernstein.at.*

▶ **Orient Yourself:** The town is in the heart of the Wachau, about 90km west of Vienna.
ⓘ **Also See:** Krems, Schloss Grafenegg, Stift Göttweig

A Bit of History

Richard the Lionheart

Shortly after being crowned king in 1189, Richard I (1157-99), better known as Richard the Lionheart, set out to lead the ill-fated 3rd Crusade to liberate Jerusalem from the troops of Sultan Saladin. Diplomacy was not his strong suit and so he clashed with the Austrian Duke Leopold V during the conquest of Acre in 1191. Returning from the crusade, he was taken prisoner at an inn near Vienna and held for several months at the fortress in Dürnstein, where according to legend, he was tracked down by his faithful minstrel Blondel. Blondel couldn't do much to rescue his master, however, who was tranferred to Emperor Heinrich VI and held prisoner for almost another year at Trifels Castle (Germany) before finally being granted his liberty at the price of an enormous ransom in 1194.

Sights

Stift Dürnstein

🕐 *Open daily Apr-end Oct 9am (10am Sun)-6pm.* ⊗€2,18. ☏ *0 27 11/3 75. http://stift. duernstein.at.*

The former Augustine canons' monastery was founded in the 15C and got its Baroque look in the 18C courtesy of master architect Josef Munggenast. A splendid gate leads into the courtyard surrounded by old monastic buildings, but the most striking element is the church's landmark blue and white **tower** ★. The church interior is adorned with restrained stuccowork and curved wooden balconies, while the side chapels house paintings by Kremser Schmidt. Enjoy pleasant views of the Danube Valley from the terrace.

Castle Ruins *45min roundtrip walk.*

The trail to the ruins *(Burgruine)* begins at the ramparts east of the town and is worth the climb for the remarkable **view** of Dürnstein and the valley.

Baroque church tower, Dürnstein

Georg Milkes

SCHLOSS EGGENBERG★★

STEIERMARK

This delightful Baroque palace is the largest in Styria. It was begun in 1825 at the behest of Johann Ulrich von Eggenberg, who required a suitably representative building after his promotion to governor of Inner Austria the same year. The palace is surrounded by a lovely park that's perfect for strolling.

▶ **Orient Yourself:** 3.5km/2mi west of Graz
🍴 **Don't Miss:** Planetensaal, Alte Galerie, Strettweg Votive Chariot, Planetengarten
🕐 **Organizing Your Time:** Start with a tour of the state rooms, then check out some of the museums and finish up with a stroll around the gardens.
🚶 **Also See:** Graz, Österreichisches Freilichtmuseum (🚶 see MURTAL).

Architectural theme

Italian architect **Pietro de Pomis** conceived an elaborately detailed allegory of the universe, teeming with images and symbols of the cosmos and the four elements. The four towers stand for the four cardinal points of the compass and there are 365

R. Chéret/MICHELIN

windows for every day of the year. There's also a suite of 24 state rooms symbolizing every hour of the day, which in turn are illuminated by 52 windows, one for every week of the year.

Sights

State Apartments (Prunkräume)★★★
2nd floor. Guided tour (45min) Easter-end Oct Tue-Sun 10am-5pm; tours on the hour except 1pm. € 5,81 (admission free 26 Oct). 03 16/58 32 64. www.museum-joanneum.steiermark.at.
The palace jewel is the **Planet Hall**★★★ (Planetensaal), a sizeable festival hall festooned with elaborate frescoes of the planets, the signs of the Zodiac and the four elements painted by the Styrian artist Hans Adam Weissenkirchner. The hall gives way to a ring of 24 equally lavish staterooms, decorated in a hodgepodge of themes ranging from classical mythology to oriental fables and Biblical scenes. There are also three rooms with Chinese and Japanese decor, a style very much in vogue at the time.

Museums
State room tickets also include admission to the palace's three collections from the Landesmuseum Joanneum, Austria's oldest public museum headquartered in Graz.

Alte Galerie★★
Recently moved here from Graz, the spectacular Old Gallery presents paintings and sculptures from the 13C to the Baroque in 22 rooms, innovatively presented by theme rather than chronology. Stellar pieces worth keeping an eye out for include a stained-glass "Admont Madonna" from 1320, a *Martyrdom of St Thomas à Becket* by Michael Pacher from 1470-80 and a large Mariazell altarpiece from 1518-22. There are also important works by Jan Bruegel the Elder, Pieter Brueghel the Younger, Lucas Cranach the Elder and such German Baroque artists as Johann Michael Rottmayr, Josef Stammel and Paul Troger.

Ur- und Frühgeschichtliche Sammlung
The Pre- and Early History Collection presents archaeological findings from the Stone Age to the early Middle Ages, including the world-famous 2700-year-old bronze **Strettweg Votive Chariot**★★★, a moving work from the Hallstatt period (p000). The chariot is surrounded by soldiers on horseback and on foot, and the artist has captured them performing the swirling movements of a ritual dance.

Münzensammlung
The coin cabinet had its origin in the private collection of Archduke Johann and is the second largest of its kind in Austria.

Planetengarten★★
Just like the main palace, the design of the newly restored Planet Garden is a romantic allegory of the universe. Along the northern edge of the palace grounds, it poetically reflects the seven then-known planets through plants, trees and flowers.

EGGENBURG★

NIEDERÖSTERREICH
POPULATION 3 645
ALT 325M/1 066FT

The town of Eggenburg features some beautiful medieval and Renaissance architecture and can still boast a historic town center, a town wall preserved almost in its entirety and three medieval gate towers, the Holturm, the Wahrsagerturm and the Kanzlerturm. 🏛 *Krahuletzplatz 1, A-3730, ☎ 0 29 84/34 00. www. eggenburg.at.*

▷ **Orient Yourself:** Eggenburg is between the Waldviertel and the Weinviertel regions.

Sights

Hauptplatz

Eggenburg's main square is lined by charming old houses, including the **Gemaltes Haus** with a sgraffito facade sporting images from the Old Testament. Other outstanding features are the **pillory** (Pranger), the Adlerbrunnen (Eagle Fountain), the Mariensäule (Mary column), and the Trinity plague column.

Krahuletz-Museum★

🕙*Open daily Apr-Dec 9am-5pm.* ⚏€5 *(admission free 26 Oct).* ☎ *0 29 84/34 00. www.krahuletzmuseum.at.*
This collection of minerals, fossils and archaelogical finds is of international standing and was assembled by local geology professor Johann Krahuletz in the 19C. Cleverly presented, the informative displays include a **landscape model**★ showing the transformation from the "Eggenburg-on-Sea" of 20 million years ago via the primeval Danube of 11 million years ago to the present. Upstairs exhibits focus on regional cultural history and include an impressive collection of watches and clocks.

Pillory, Eggenburg

R. Chéret/MIECHELIN

"Ausg'steckt Is"

In the "Preßhaus", the grapes are pressed and the must is then stored in barrels for fermentation in the tunnel-like cellar in back. The Preßhaus, however, is not only used for pressing the grapes but also as a wine tavern. Whenever you see a pine or fir branch displayed above the door, this indicates that the vintner is pouring his own wines, alongside such hearty homemade snacks as "Blunzn" (blood sausage), Geselchtes (smoked pork) and Speck (bacon). In fine weather, the nicest seats are in the shade of the walnut trees along Kellergasse.

Österreichisches Motorradmuseum★

  ⏱ *Open Mon-Fri 8am-4pm. Sat, Sun & public hols 10am-5pm.* ⏱ *Closed 21 Dec-5 Jan.*
€4,50. ☎ *0 29 84/21 51.*

Austria's largest motorcycle collection boasts around 320 vehicles in mint condition from every phase of motorcycling history. It's all displayed in a historical factory and a must for motorbike enthusiasts.

Excursion

Stoitzendorf
4km/2.5mi east of Eggenburg on B 303. Follow the signs for "Kellergasse".

Stoitzendorf's **Kellergasse** is an unspoiied example of the roads to be found in Austrian wine-growing areas just outside the villages. It's lined with small, mostly single-storey "Preßhäuser" where the grapes are pressed. Here in the western wine-growing area these buildings are embedded in the soft loam soil.

Pulkau
8km/5mi northwest of Eggenburg

Pulkau is a large wine-producing township near the Czech border. it has a **parish church** with traces of early 14C frescoes and the **Heilig-Blut-Kirche** with a 16C altarpiece carved and painted by artists of the Danube School.

EISENERZ

STEIERMARK
POPULATION 7 800
ALT 694M/2 277FT

Eisenerz is an old mining town at the foot of the mighty stepped pyramid of the Erzberg (Ore Mountain). Its silhouette is oddly impressive, especially in late afternoon light. Since 712, more than 230 million tonnes of ore have been extracted from this mountain, which is the largest opencast ore mine in central Europe. The town istelf is not without charm and is noted for its many historic buildings, especially around Bergmannplatz. 🛈 *Freiheitsplatz 7, A-8790,* ☎ *0 38 48/37 00. www.eisenerz.de.*

▶ **Orient Yourself:** Eisenerz is in northern Styria, about 25km north of Leoben.
Especially for Kids: A tour of the Erzberg will delight young and old.
Also See: Stift Admont, Eisenerzer Alpen

Erzberg★★

Guided 90min tour of exhibition mine daily May-end Oct 10am-3pm. €12,72. Trip on the Hauly truck (1hr): as for tours of the mine €12,72. Joint ticket for mine and truck €21,44. ☎ *0 38 48/32 00*

W. Geiersperger/BILEDAGENTUR BUENOS DIAS

Erzberg, Styria

A tour of the Erzberg is a highlight of any visit to Styria. The mine can be explored in two ways. Descend into the bowels of the earth on the same train that once transported miners until below-ground mining ceased in 1986. An 800m section of this subterranean labyrinth is now a **Schaubergwerk** (exhibition mine), where you learn all about how the ore was extracted and experience an audio-visual simulation of a blasting. Another unforgettable experience is the trip on the **Hauly**, an 860hp truck with a viewing platform that takes you above ground through many of the 42 slopes, from which there is a fine **view**★ of the town, the landscape, and the blue lake which has formed at the foot of the mountain.

St. Oswald★
🕐*Open daily Easter-end Nov 8am-7pm.* ☎ *0 38 48/22 67.*
This Gothic church is the largest fortified house of worship in Styria. it got its for-tress-like ramparts in 1532 in order to keep marauding Turkish troops at bay. The tympanum above the north porch has an *Expulsion from the Garden of Eden* showing Adam as a miner.

Stadtmuseum
Kammerhof, Schulstraße 1. 🕐*Open May-Oct, Tues-Fri 9am-noon, 2-5pm, Sat 10am-noon, 2-5pm; Nov-Apr, Tues-Fri 9am-noon.* 🕸€*3,27.* ☎ *0 38 48/36 15.*
This museum vividly presents the art and culture of those associated with the world of mining, as well as the techniques of mining ore.

EISENERZER ALPEN★

The Eisenerz Alps cradle the astonishing Erzberg on which the industrial power of the former Austrian Empire was built. They join up in the northwest with the limestone Ennstal Alps, whose impressive walls line the Gesäuse Gorge, which became Austria's newest national park in 2003.

▶ **Orient Yourself:** This range is in upper Styria between the Ennstal and Murtal valleys, which are linked by the Präbichl pass.

1 Gesäuse Gorge

From Liezen★ to Hieflau 44km/27mi

The 16km-long **Gesäuse gorge** takes its name from the noise made by the waters of the Enns rushing over their rocky bed. Between Liezen and Admont the road winds along the Enns Valley.

▶ *From the touring route, follow the signposts on the left for Frauenberg.*

Frauenberg
This pilgrimage church in Italianate Baroque style has lavish stucco decoration matching the richly gilded altars and pulpit. The terrace offers a fine **view**★ of Admont and various mountains.

Admont★ *See ADMONT.*

The best **view of the Gesäuse**★★ comes after Admont *(B 146 at kilometre 93.2, by the bus stop and the turn-off for Weng)*, when the magnificent rock faces of the Hochtor unfold before you. There's another fabulous view of this mountain from the Haindlkarbrücke, a bridge over a small tributary of the Enns.

Gstatterboden
This is a popular gateway to the Gesäuse and the starting point for climbing tours.

Hieflau
The village has a wooded setting where the valley widens.

2 Die Steirische Eisenstraße *(The Styrian Iron Road)*

From Hieflau★ to Leoben 50km/31mi

Hieflau *See 1 above.*

From Hieflau to Eisenerz the Erzbach Valley has beautiful, winding gorges and offers fine panoramas of the Tamischbachturm (tower). When reaching the basin of Eisenerz, with a view of the **Erzberg**★★, make a small detour to the Leopoldsteiner See.

Leopoldsteiner See★★
This small lake with its deep green waters lies in one of the finest settings in Styria, below the rock cliffs of the Seemauer in the Hochschwab range.

Eisenerz   *See EISENERZ.*

Past Eisenerz, the road crosses the **Präbichl pass** (alt 1 232m/4 041ft). To the north-west the rocky summit of the Pfaffenstein dominates.

Polster★★

About 1hr 30min roundtrip from the Präbichl, including 30min by **chair-lift** *and 30min on foot. ⏱Chair-lift operates daily 9am-5pm (9am-4pm in winter). Closed Easter-end May, Nov. ☞€7,50 two-way trip. ☎ 0 38 49/6 06 00.*

From the summit (alt 1 910m/6 266ft), there is an excellent **view** of the Erzberg, standing out in all its red-brown mass against the green Alpine pastures.

Vordernberg

Informationszentrum der Steirischen Eisenstraße – ♿ ⏱Open May-Oct, Mon-Sat 10am-4pm; Nov-Apr, Mon-Sat 9am-noon. ☎ 0 38 49/8 32.

This market town has several fascinating **monuments** and **museums of technical interest** associated with iron-working. Ask at the information center about the **Erzbergbahn★★**, a railway running from Vordernberg over the Präbichl to Eisenerz, going both around and through the Erzberg.

Leoben   *See LEOBEN.*

EISENSTADT★

BURGENLAND
POPULATION 12 190
ALT 181M/594FT

The administrative capital of the Burgenland, Eisenstadt has a mild climate allowing grapes, peaches, apricots and almonds to flourish. it is an important market in the region for wine and has a delightful old town. Its main draw card, though, is the legacy of composer Joseph Haydn, who lived here on and off for around 30 years. 🏛 *Schloss Esterházy, A-7000, ☎ 0 26 82/6 33 84 15; Web site: www.eisenstadt-tourism.at.*

▶ **Orient Yourself:** About 60km/37.5mi south of Vienna on the south slopes of the Leithagebirge.
🅿 **Parking:** There are fee-based parking garages at Esterházyplatz, the Rathaus and Hotel Burgenland.
🎭 **Don't Miss:** Schloss Esterházy, Haydnsaal
🎫 **Also See:** Neusiedler See, Burg Forchtenstein, Wiener Neustadt

Haydn's town

The brilliant composer **Joseph Haydn** (1732-1809), was in the employ of Prince Miklós József Esterházy for nearly 30 years, living sometimes at Eisenstadt, sometimes at the Esterháza palace in Hungary. Haydn had been appointed assistant conductor in 1761 and promoted to musical director in 1766. Having an orchestra and a theater at his disposal, Haydn achieved growing fame.

For Haydn's birthplace at Rohrau see PETRONELL-CARNUNTUM: Excursions.

Sights

Schloss Esterházy★ (A)

⏲Open daily Apr-Oct 9am-5pm. ☜€6. ☎ 0 26 82/7 19 30 00; www.haydn-zentrum. at

Eisenstadt was one of the favorite residences of the noble Esterházy clan, the Magyar family that contributed largely to the establishment of the Habsburg's rule in Hungary. The original 17C Baroque palace, a work of Italian architect, Carlo Martino Carlone, was built on the site of a medieval fortress and a century later received some neoclassical touches courtesy of French architect Charles de Moreau. It now houses local administrative offices, but some rooms can be seen on guided tours.

Esterházy Exhibit & Haydnsaal

The highlight of any palace tour is the **Haydnsaal**★, a magnificent hall resplendent with stucco, *grisailles* of Hungarian kings and frescoes with scenes from Greek mythology. In the 18C the marble floor was replaced with parquet for the sake of better acoustics, which you'll get to enjoy during a short concert. It was here that Haydn conducted the court orchestra almost nightly. Other rooms recall the importance of the Esterházy family.

EISENSTADT								
Bürgerspitalgase	B	3	Ing.-Julius-Raab-Str.	B	10	Burgenländisches		
Dompl.	B	4	Johann-Permayer-Str.	B	12	Landesmuseum	A	M²
Esterházypl.	A	6	Josef-Hyrtl-Pl.	B	13	Österreichisches		
Europapl.	B	7	Leopold-Kunschak-Str.	A	15	Jüdisches Museum	A	M¹
Franz-Schubert-Pl.	B	8	Matthias-Marklhl-Gasse	B	16	Rathaus	B	R
			St-Antoni-Str.	B	18			
			Unterbergstr.	A	19			

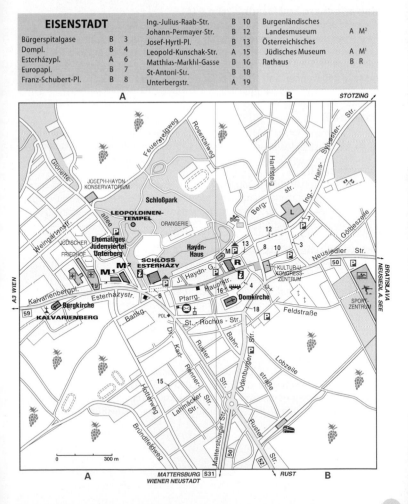

"Court Jews"

Medieval statues forbade Christians to handle interest on loans, which is why, in the 17C and 18C some Jews came to play a crucial role in financial dealings. The Habsburg rulers appointed "court Jews", who enjoyed unrestricted freedom to trade. Among them was Samuel Oppenheimer, a banker from Speyer, Germany, who financed Prince Eugen of Savoy's campaigns against the Turks. Another was his son-in-law Samson Wertheimer, who worked for Leopold I, Joseph I and Karl VI. Such privileges remained reserved for a chosen few, however, while many other members of the Jewish community continued to be oppressed.

Haydn-Haus (A)

⏱*Open Easter-end Oct, daily 9am-noon, 1-5pm.* ✍*€3 (admission free 26 Oct).* ☎ *0 26 82/6 26 52 29; Web site: www.haydnkirche.at.*
At No 21 of a quiet lane called Haydn-Gasse stands the modest Baroque house in which the composer lived from 1776 to 1788. Inside are period rooms, a hammer piano and an organ table from the 18C as well as early prints of his compositions and other mementoes.

Kalvarienberg and Haydnkirche ★ (A)

⏱*Open Easter-31 Oct, daily 9am-noon, 1-5pm.* ✍*€2,50.* ☎ *0 26 82/6 26 38.*
Haydn was buried in the Haydnkirche (also known as Bergkirche), after some vicissitudes – his skull was removed and only reunited with the body in 1954. The church is by an artificial hill known as the Kalvarienberg where 24 **Stations of the Cross**★, made of 260 wooden and 60 stone figures, portray the story of the Passion with dramatic intensity and Baroque flair.

Rathaus (B R)

The 17C Renaissance town hall features a highly original façade with three oriel windows, scrolled gables and a round-arched doorway with diamond-cut stonework.

Domkirche (B)

This Late Gothic hall-church from the 15C and 16C is dedicated to St. Martin, patron saint of the Burgenland. A charming pulpit and the choir, complete with organ, remain of the original Late Baroque interior decoration. Note the beautiful relief of the Mount of Olives, dating from before 1500.

Östereichisches Jüdisches Museum★ (A M¹)

Unterberggasse 6. ⏱*Open 2°May-26°Oct, Tues-Sun 10am-5pm.* ✍*€3,70.* ☎ *0 26 82/6 51 45.*
When Emperor Leopold I expelled the Jews from Vienna in 1671, many sought refuge in Eisenstadt where a thriving Jewish community sprang up in the Unterberg district. In a former private home, this museum has displays on Jewish holidays as well as a private synagogue. The Jewish cemetery is nearby at the end of Wertheimergasse.

Landesmuseum (A M²)

Museumsgasse 5. ♿ ⏱*Open Tues-Sat 9am-5pm. Sun and hols 10am-5pm, Closed 1 Jan, 25, 26 Dec.* ✍*€3 (admission free 26 Oct).* ☎ *0 26 82/6 26 52.*
The regional museum is devoted to the ethnological and cultural history of the region and includes a section on the ethnic minorities that live in the Burgenland.

EISRIESENWELT★

SALZBURG

With over 40km/25mi of subterranean passages, the 'world of the ice giants' is the largest accessible ice cave system in the world. An 800m-long show cave reveals ice formations shaped into fans, curtains, cathedrals and other fantastical features. Bring warm clothing, sturdy shoes and gloves, even in summer.

▶ **Orient Yourself:** The entrance to the caves is at 1641m/5384ft on the western cliffs of the Hochkogel about 6km/4mi northwest of Werfen.

P **Parking:** There is a parking lot at about 1000m elevation on the mountain road.

🕓 **Organizing Your Time:** Allow at least three hours for the trip up and through the caves.

Tour

Caves can only be seen on guided tours (1hr 15min): 👣 *July-Aug, daily 9am-4.30pm; May, June, Sept-26 Oct, daily 9am-3.30pm.* €8. ☎ *06 62/84 26 90 14. Eisriesenwelt-Linie – Bus operates 1 May-26 Oct, daily 8.20am, 10.20am, 12.20pm and 2.20pm, or every 15min if busy. €6 two-way trip.* ☎ *0 64 68/52 93; Web site: www.eisriesenwelt.at.*

Access

Getting to the cave entrance requires a moderate level of fitness, but you'll be spoiled with terrific views all along.

1. From Werfen, the mountain road climbs steeply for 5km/3mi to the parking lot at 1000m. It can be traveled in your own car or on a shuttle bus (journey time: 15min) leaving from the Werden train station and from the bottom of the Eisriesenweltstraße near the village.
2. From the parking lot, it's a 20-minute walk to the Wimmer Hütte (hut).
3. At Wimmer Hütte, catch the **cable car** (🕓*Operates July-Aug, daily 9am-6pm; May, June, Sept-26 Oct, daily 9am-5pm.* €9 *two-way trip.* ☎ *06 62/84 26 90 14)* to the "Dr.-Oedl-Haus" mountain inn (1 575m/5 168ft).
4. From the inn, it's another 20-minute walk to the cave entrance.

Guided tour of the caves

About 1hr 15min.

By the light of acetylene and magnesium lamps visitors enter the ice world of the caves, climbing up to the Posselt-Halle gallery (named after the first explorer to discover the caves in 1879). The "Hrymr Hall" with its Hrymr Mountain and "Niflheimr" with Frigg's Veil are both examples of fantastic ice architecture enhanced by clever lighting. At the back of the "Óðinn Gallery" is a throne-like ice formation called Ásgarðr. Another highlight is the "Cathedral" where the ashes of Alexander von Mörk, the man who led the first full expedition into the caves, rest beneath a plaque. The tour turns around at the ice Palace.

What's in a name…

The origin of many of the names of the galleries in the Eisriesenwelt subterranean complex is Old Norse mythology, as featured in the Old Icelandic saga "Edda": **Óðinn** is the father of the gods, **Frigg** is his wife and at the same time goddess of fertility, **Hrymr** is an ice giant. **Ásgarðr** is the home of the Æsir gods, who are at war with the Vanir, and **Niflheimr** is the world of shadows in the frozen north that existed before this world was created.

ENNS★

OBERÖSTERREICH
POPULATION 10 610
ALT 281M/922FT

Enns is among the oldest towns in Austria founded as a Roman camp in the 2nd century AD. It was here that St. Florian, the patron saint of Upper Austria, suffered martyrdom under Diocletian at the beginning of the 4C. Much of the town's 12C fortifications, including the ramparts, moats and six watchtowers, have survived. 🖹 *Linzerstraße 1, A-4470, ☎ 0 72 23/83 26 10*

▸ **Orient Yourself:** Enns is at the confluence of the Danube and the River Enns.
🅿 **Parking:** Look for parking in lots and garages along or near Stadtgasse.

Sights

Hauptplatz

Enns' pretty medieval old core revolves around the Hauptplatz, the central square, punctuated by the landmark **Stadtturm** (Z). Soaring 60m/197ft high, the tower is adorned with the Imperial eagle and the Habsburg coat of arms. Climb the 156 steps to the gallery to enjoy a marvellous **view**★. Hauptplatz is also orbited by many attractive Gothic burgher houses with Renaissance arcaded courtyards. The former town hall at No 19 contains the **Museum Lauriacum** (Z M; Web site: www. museum-lauriacum.at) with Roman-era archaeological exhibits.

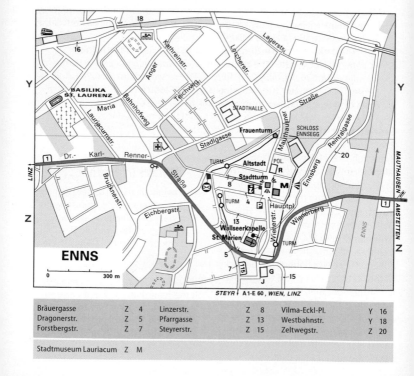

Bräuergasse	Z	4	Linzerstr.	Z	8	Vilma-Eckl-Pl.	Y	16
Dragonerstr.	Z	5	Pfarrgasse	Z	13	Westbahnstr.	Y	18
Forstbergstr.	Z	7	Steyrerstr.	Z	15	Zeltwegstr.	Z	20

Stadtmuseum Lauriacum	Z	M

Pfarrkirche St. Marien★ (Z)

🕐*Open Mon-Sat 7am-7pm (5pm Oct-Apr), Sun 8am-7pm (5pm Oct-Apr).* *Guided tours possible as part of a tour of the town or by appointment.* ☎ *0 72 23/8 28 55.*

This is one of the oldest Mendicant Order churches in Austria, built by the Minorites in 1276-7. It's an austere, two-nave church whose ornamentation is limited to beautifully carved keystones. Three Gothic arches lead into the **Wallseerkapelle**, a chapel named for a former local ruling family. A remarkable painting from 1625 depicts the *Lorcher Bishops*, a view of the town featuring local religious dignitaries. Also note the 13C seated Madonna. The Gothic cloister has a peaceful ambience.

Basilika St. Laurenz (Y)

🕐*Open daily 8am-7pm.* *Guided tour (1hr) mid Apr-mid Oct, daily 4pm. Parts of the church may be visited unaccompanied. Telephone in advance for guided tours.*€3. ☎ *0 72 23/8 74 12.*

The basilica occupies a site on the edge of the ancient Roman camp. Roman stones were used in the construction of the 13C tower, the oldest extant part of the church, which is attached to a 14C choir. Between the nave and chancel archaeological excavations have revealed vestiges of walls from earlier buildings on this site: a Gallo-Roman temple (180), the first Christian church (bishop's see, 370) and early Carolingian church buildings (740). Decorative highlights include a Late Gothic tabernacle and Pietà as well as Austria's two largest oil paintings from the 18C.

FELBERTAUERNSTRASSE★

SALZBURG AND TIROL

The Felbertauern road has made a considerable difference to the lives of residents in the eastern Alps. Its core is a 5.3/3mi long tunnel that has connected eastern Tyrol with Innsbruck in northern Tyrol since opening in 1967. The panoramic road carves through the peaceful Alpine countryside of the Hohe Tauern National Park. Web site: www.felbertauernstrasse.at.

▸ **Orient Yourself:** This scenic road runs from Lienz to Mittersill in the Pinzgau..

◉ **Don't Miss:** Walk to Innergeschlöss

🕐 **Organizing Your Time:** Budget half a day for the Innergeschlöss hike, a full day for the Drei-Seen-Tour.

Combining the Großglockner Hochalpenstraße *(summer only)* and the Felbertauern road into a circular tour gives you magnificent views of the Großvenediger snows.

From Lienz to the Felberntauer Tunnel *41km/25mi*

Lienz *See LIENZ.*

▸ *From Lienz follow the road up the long, wooded valley of the Isel.*

Matrei in Osttirol★ *See MATREI IN OSTTIROL.*

Past Matrei is Schloss Weissenstein, a former outpost of the Salzburg archbishops. The road now continues through the **Tauern Valley★★**, passing through the Prosschegg gorge to reach an open valley overlooked by the hanging glacier of the Kristallkopf.

It is possible at this point to continue north directly via the Felbertauern tunnel (see below) or to make a detour to explore the Großvenediger massif.

Excursions in the Großvenediger Massif★★

▷ *Take a small mountain road to the left of the road leading to the Felbertauern-tunnel (toll), and follow it along the valley floor to the Matreier Tauernhaus (alt 1 512m/4 961ft), a mountain hotel. Allow at least 2hr there and back for a brief visit, or (better) a whole day to include some sightseeing on foot.*

Many beautiful hiking and Alpine routes are located in this massif.

Walk to Innergschlöss★★
4hr roundtrip hike or head up in a horse-drawn carriage or on a little train.
It takes 45min to get to Aussergschlöss (alt 1 695m/5 561ft). The romantic scenery surrounding the chalet almost pales beside the sight of the majestic Großvenediger (alt 3 674m/12 054ft) with its cowl of glaciers. The fairly easy trail continues to Innergschlöss.

Drei-Seen-Tour★★
From Matreier Tauernhaus, walk along the road direction Venedigerhaus, then climb a steep grassy slope from the former valley station of the Venedigerblick chair-lift to the former mountain station at 1982m/6000ft. From here, follow the Pano-

Tauern Valley

ramaweg to the Tauernbach creek and then the creek itself across a meadow to St. Pöltner Hütte mountain lodge at 2481m/7446ft, then along gravelly and rocky trail sections. From the lodge continue along a narrow, rocky path to the St.Pöltner Ostweg past the Grauer See (Grey Lake), Schwarzer See (Black Lake) and Grüner See (Green Lake), then along the Messeling Creek across meadows and back to the mountain station of the chair-lift and down the slope to the valley station.

If you're fit enough, continue on to the Messelingkogel (alt 2 694m/8 838ft – *45min roundtrip*) where you can enjoy a unique **panorama**★★★ over the three lakes, the Großglockner (in the distance), the Tauerntal Valley and the huge glaciers of the Großvenediger.

View of the Großvenediger from the Grüner See

Hike to the Zirbelkreuz★
1hr 45min, 600m/1 970ft difference in altitude down the mountain.
From the former mountain station of the Venedigerbahn chair-lift, the trail leads along the mountainside and finally climbs up to a bridge and then to the cross.

▶ *After exploring the Großvenediger massif, drive back to the main road and go through the tunnel.*

From the Felbertauern Tunnel to Mittersill
16km/10mi

On the north face of the Tauern the road emerges from the tunnel into the upper Amertal, a rugged and more or less deserted high-altitude valley.

▶ *9km/6mi after the exit from the tunnel turn left towards Hintersee. After 500m/550yd park the car on the right to visit the Schößwend gorge.*

Schösswendklamm★
15min roundtrip walk.
Cross the road to the path leading down to the Felberbach and across the river. Following the river bank, the trail offers good **views**★ of the sculptured rock faces carved by the crystal-clear water.

▶ *Drive on for 3km/2mi to the end of the road.*

Hintersee★
This mountain lake surrounded by spruce forest lies in the upper Felber Valley below a magnificent high mountain range, from which a number of waterfalls tumble from great heights. To the south lies the Tauernkogel massif (alt 2 989m/9 806ft). Several information panels explain the geology of the area. It is possible to walk round the lake.

▶ *Turn back to B 108.*

This stretch of road leads through Alpine meadows to the resort of **Mittersill** from where roads lead off to the Thurn *(north)* and Gerloß *(west)* passes.

FELDKIRCH★★

VORARLBERG
POPULATION 26 730
ALT 459M/1 506FT

Feldkirch is the gateway to Austria for travelers coming from the west. Right on the busy road to the Arlberg pass, the little fortified town nestles at the foot of Schattenburg Castle and has preserved the symmetry of its medieval layout and the old-world charm of arcaded squares. *Herrengasse 12, A-6800, ☎ 0 55 22/7 34 67; Web site: www.feldkirch.at.*

▶ **Orient Yourself:** Feldkirch is right on the border with Liechtenstein and Switzerland.

🅿 **Parking:** Several parking lots and garages are near the old town. An automated parking guide system directs you to the nearest one with available spaces.

Sights

Marktplatz
The heart of Feldkirch's old town, this long, arcaded square has retained the charm and tranquillity of a bygone age. Wherever you look, an inn with a colorful façade, an onion-domed corner tower, or a Gothic oriel window catch the eye. To the south the view is bounded by the plain belfry and façade of the Johanniskirche. This is the former church of the monastery of the Hospitallers of St John of Jerusalem, who were entrusted with the protection of the Arlberg pass.

Domkirche St. Nikolaus
🕐*Open daily 8am-7pm. ☎ 0 55 22/7 22 32.*
The twin-nave Late Gothic cathedral sports delicate net vaulting and beautiful, if modern, stained-glass windows (1962). Over the right side altar is a **Descent from the Cross**★ painted in 1521 by Wolf Huber, a leading artist of the Danube School. The pulpit boasts a wrought-iron canopy that was originally a Gothic tabernacle.

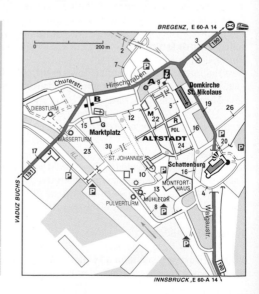

FELDKIRCH	
Ardetzenbergtunnel	2
Bahnhofstr.	3
Burggasse	4
Dompl.	5
Fidelisstr.	7
Ganahlstr.	8
Herrengasse	9
Johannitergasse	10
Kreuzgasse	12
Leonhardsplatz	13
Montfortgasse	15
Neustadt	16
Rosengasse	24
Schillerstr.	17
Schlossgraben	19
Schloßsteig	20
Schmiedgasse	22
Vorstadt	23
Wichnergasse	26
Zeughausgasse	30
Churertor	B
Katzenturm	A

Schattenburg
Heimatmuseum – Open Tues-Sun 9am-noon, 1:30-6pm. €2,50. 0 55 22/7 19 82. Reachable by car via a new access road and Burggasse and on foot via the Schlosssteig stairs.

The Schattenburg has a pedigree going back to 1200 and is one of the best-preserved castles in Austria with great views over the town and surrounds. Originally the seat of the counts of Monfort, it has walls up to 4m/12ft thick and lovely frescoes in the chapel. Some of the Gothic wood-panelled rooms contain the Heimatmuseum, a museum displaying local religious art, Gothic furnishings, arms, armour, coins and other medieval bits and pieces.

Excursion

Basilika Rankweil
19km/12mi roundtrip. Leave Feldkirch on the road to Bregenz.

The hilltop pilgrimage church is dedicated to the Virgin Mary and overlooks the idyllic Austrian Rhine Valley with its profusion of orchards. A church has stood in this spot since the 7C. After a fire in the 15C, it was rebuilt as a fortified Gothic church. In 1986 it was raised to the status of basilica minor.

The **Gnadenkapelle**, or Chapel of Miracles, houses the church's treasured Late Gothic Madonna, attributed to the Swabian School. Above the main altar hangs the so-called "miracle-working" silver cross.

From the **old rampart walk**★ (Wehrgang) you'll have a marvelous view of the upper Rhine valley, the Swiss and Vorarberg Alps and Lichtenstein.

To return to Feldkirch, follow the valley floor to Satteins, bear right at the entrance to Satteins and join the B 1.

FERNPASSSTRASSE★

TIROL

The picturesque road across the Fernpass has been an important Alpine crossing since Roman times when it was part of the Via Claudia Augusta. A vital trade route connecting Augsburg and Venice in the Middle Ages, it now primarily a tourist link between the resorts of the Bavarian Alps and Innsbruck.

From Telfs to Reutte *64km/40mi*

From **Telfs** (*see SEEFELDER SATTELSTRASSEN*) to Holzleiten the road traverses the gentle slopes of the Mieming plateau, from which the well defined crests of the Miemingergebirge rise up. Near Obermieming views of the Inn Valley open out to the left against the snow-capped peaks of the Samnaungruppe.

Driving down towards **Nassereith** from the **Holzleitner Sattel** (alt 1 126m/3 694ft), there is a series of delightful **views**★ of countryside dotted with villages against a mountain backdrop. Several tunnels later, the road reaches Fernstein with "Schloss Fernsteinsee" hotel on the left. To the right of the road, below the parking lot, lies the idyllic **Fernsteinsee**★.

Fernpass
Alt 1 209m/3 967ft. The pass breaches a crest between Fernstein and Biberwier. The road corkscrews up the south slope through rugged, isolated gorges and cirques. About 1km/0.6mi beyond the pass itself, stop at the "Zugspitzblick" restaurant to take

View of the Mieminger range

in the stunning **panorama**★ of the Zugspitze, the distinctive Sonnenspitze peak and other striking summits. Below lies the **Blindsee**★, a long and picturesque lake. *The Blindsee is an ideal spot for a refreshing swim or lakeside walk. Access is on the way down from the Fernpass, from the left of the road (before the information point).*

▷ *Follow the road along the north slope of the Fernpass towards Biberwier.*

At the Biberwier junction, look for **Weissensee** lake on the right. The road from Biberwier to Lermoos, skirting the Lermoos-Ehrwald basin, offers fine **views**★★ of the Wetterstein and the Mieminger range.

Ehrwald★
This resort at the foot of the Zugspitze provides access to numerous lovely hikes, but most people come here to board the **Tiroler Zugspitzbahn** cable-car for the ride to the top of Germany's highest mountain.

Ascent to the Zugspitze★★★
Allow about 2hr, including 10min for the cable-car ride. Operates Whitsun-1 Nov, Christmas-1st week after Easter, daily 8.40am-4.40pm every 20min. Journey time: 10min. €30,50 two-way trip. ☎ 0 56 73/23 09; Web site: www.zugspitzbahn.at.
A 4.5km/3mi-long road runs from Ehrwald to Obermoos and the valley station of the Tiroler Zugspitzbahn cable-car.

Zugspitze summit★★★
The cable-car drops you off on the western peak of the Zugspitze summit (alt 2 964m/9 724ft), where you'll be greeted by a breathtaking panorama taking in four countries and countless peaks, many soaring above 3000m/10 000ft. Information boards help you identify the craggy summits of the Hohe Tauern, the Tyrolean High Alps, the Dachstein and many others.
Also up here is the multimedia exhibit called **Faszination Zugspitze**★ that traces the history of the mountain from its first ascent in 1820 to the present. A highlight is a 3D film that lets you experience the mountains on a virtual flight over the peaks.
In winter, the cable-car gives access to numerous first-class **ski runs**, including the great *Gattlerabfahrt* of nearly 23km/14mi back to Ehrwald *(guide recommended)*.

Lermoos★★

It would be hard to find a better spot than Lermoos from which to admire the Northern Limestone Alps, dominated by the Zugspitze and the fine pyramidal Sonnenspitze summit.

▷ *To cross from the Loisach basin into that of the Lech, follow the valley named Zwischentoren ("between gates").*

Ehrenberger Klause

From the 16C to the 18C, Ehrenberg Fortress was key in defending the Tyrol against Bavarians, Swedes and Frenchmen. The ruins are visible on the wooded hillside to the left of the road.

Before reaching Reutte, it is worth taking a short detour to the Plansee *(about 20km/12mi roundtrip).*

Plansee★

The road runs through a forest, then skirts the lake shore for a 6km/4mi stretch. At the northeast tip you'll find a hotel-restaurant and various kiosks. From here the view stretches southwest through the small strait separating the Plansee from the Heiterwanger See, as far as the Thaneller peak (2 341m/7 680ft).

▷ *From here you can continue to Linderhof and Oberammergau in Germany via the Ammersattel pass.*

Reutte   *See Oberes LECHTAL.*

BURG FORCHTENSTEIN★

BURGENLAND

The fortress of Forchtenstein overlooks charming scenery from its bluff top site in the Rosaliengebirge foothills. it is dominated by its massive 50m/164ft keep, which is the oldest surviving part of the original construction,

▷ **Orient Yourself:** The castle is 23km/14mi southeast of Wiener Neustadt, access is via Mattersburg

☺ **Don't Miss:** Treasury

Especially for Kids: A variety of kid-oriented guided tours are available.

  Also See: Wiener Neustadt, Eisenstadt, Neusiedler See

The fortress was built at the beginning of the 14C by the counts of Mattersdorf. The Esterházy family, owners of Forchtenstein since 1622, added the ring of bastions to

The legend of Rosalia

Legend has it while Giletus, the first lord of Forchtenstein was away on the battlefield, his wife Rosalia ruled the fortress with an iron fist. After learning of his wife's misdoings, Giletus decided to describe the incident to her as if he was talking about some stranger, even asking her opinion on what would be appropriate punishment. Rosalia foolishly recommended imprisonment in the fortress dungeon! And so she ended her days, her restless spirit allegedly haunting the fortress until Giletus had the Rosalienkapelle built to appease it.

stave off marauding Turkish tropps. After the family moved to Schloss Eisenstadt in the early 18C, Forchtenstein became a treasury, arsenal and archive. It is still owned by the Esterházys.

Tour

📞 Guided tour (1hr 15min) on the hour; ⏰Apr 1-Oct 31, daily 10am-6pm. ⊛€5,50. ☎ 0 26 26/8 12 12; Web site: www.burg-forchtenstein.at.

A tour of the castle takes in one of Europe's largest private family collections with about 20,000 items. Highlights include the **treasury** (art and precious objects, clocks and automata, silverware, chinoiseries, porcelain and library); the **picture gallery** (family portraits and battle scenes); and the **arsenal** (arms and armour, trophies from the wars against the French and the Prussians, and the "Turkish booty" from the field campaigns of Prince Paul Esterházy (1652-1713).

Follow the road further uphill from the fortress for 4km/2.5mi to reach the **Rosali-enkapelle** (1670), a chapel dedicated to Rosalia, curer of plagues, from where there is a good **view**★ as far as Eisenstadt and the Neusiedler See.

FREISTADT★

OBERÖSTERREICH
POPULATION 7 300
ALT 560M/1 837FT

Freistadt is a former stronghold on the ancient salt route to Bohemia. Its exten- sive, largely intact, fortifications include a double town wall, towers and gate- ways. With its pretty main square, web of spidery lanes and picturesque houses, Freistadt makes for an idyllic visit. 🛈 *Hauptplatz 12, A-4240, ☎ 0 79 42/7 57 00; Web site: www.freistadt.at.*

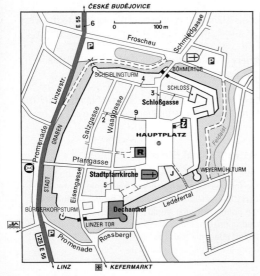

FREISTADT	
Altenhofgasse	2
Böhmergasse	3
Heiligengeistgasse	4
Huterergasse	5
Pragerstr.	6
Samtgasse	9

▶ **Orient Yourself:** Freistadt is in the lower Mühlviertel, about 30km northeast of Linz.

▣ **Parking:** Parking in the historic center is short-term only. Long-term parking is available in lots along Linzerstraße.

⏱ **Also See:** Linz, Kefermarkt

Sights

Hauptplatz★

This rectangular main square is framed by beautiful old pastel-painted houses adorned with delicate stucco; many are fronted by porches or arcades. In the center is a carved fountain dedicated to the Virgin Mary, while on the west side looms the **Rathaus** (R) in a wonderfully pure Italian Renaissance style. Waagstraße, behind the town hall, is lined by exceptionally beautiful buildings, many sporting oriels and sgraffito façades.

Schloss

North of the Hauptplatz is Freistadt's 14C castle with its muscular tower that forms part of the fortifications. Inside, the **Schlossmuseum** examines various aspects and phases of regional history. It is reached via **Schlossgasse**, a quaint and picturesque alley with flower-decked balconies and passages.

Stadtpfarrkirche

The parish church's elegant Baroque tower, just south of the Hauptplatz, is another characteristic feature of Freisach's skyline. The church itself is Gothic and has a tri-ple-aisled nave crowned with a ribbed vaulted ceilings. Also note the **organ case**, beautifully adorned with statues.

FRIESACH★

KÄRNTEN
POPULATION 5 335
ALT 637M/2 090FT

Carinthia's oldest town is greatly appealing with its three ruined castles, six churches and well-preserved fortifications. It belonged to the archbishopric of Salzburg from 960 to 1803 and was a key staging point along the Vienna-Venice trade route. ▯ *Hauptplatz 1, A-9360, ☏ 0 42 68/43 00; Web site: www.friesach.at.*

▶ **Orient Yourself:** Friesach is some 40km/25mi north of Klagenfurt near the border with Styria on the Metnitz River.

☺ **Don't Miss:** Town fortifications, Die Spur des Einhorns

Kids **Especially for Kids:** Die Spur des Einhorns

⏱ **Also See:** Gurk, St Veit an der Glan

Sights

Town fortifications★

The fortifications, including the only water-filled town moat in the German-speak-ing world, encircle the town center with an 820m/0.5mi-long fortified wall. Three of 11 defence towers remain.

Stadtbrunnen★

This Renaissance fountain anchors the Hauptplatz, surrounded by beautiful old houses. Reliefs with scenes from ancient Greek mythology adorn the basin, which is crowned by a small bronze group depicting Poseidon.

Dominikanerkloster & Kirche

Friesach monastery, dating from 1217, was the first foundation of the Dominican Order in a German-speaking country. Its three-nave church is the largest in Carinthia and rather simple in keeping with the rules of the Mendicant order. It does contain a nice winged altar, ornate epitaphs and two precious Early Gothic treasures: a sandstone Madonna and a huge wooden crucifix.

Petersberg

10min walk from the Hauptplatz
For the best view over the town, head to this small hilltop **church** in the northern old town. Nearby, the 28m/92ft-high 12C keep is nearly all that remains of Petersberg castle, the former residence of the Salzburg archbishops. It now houses the **Stadtmuseum** (*Open 1 May- 10 Oct, Tues-Sun 11am-5pm. €3 (admission free 1°May and 26°Oct. 0 42 68/26 00)*), which relates the history of Friesach and the region. Summer open-air theater productions are staged in the former castle courtyard.

Die Spur des Einhorns

(*Open May-Oct, daily 10am-5pm; €5.50; 04268/4300*)
Kids For a memorable break from the church-square-castle sightseeing circuit, visit this multi-dimensional art, sound and light installation that takes you on a virtual journey through medieval mythology. There are interactive encounters with a magic forest, King Arthur's sword Excalibur, a terracotta army of crusaders and a giant wheel of fortune in the moat. It's surreal, fascinating and great fun for young and old.

GAILBERGSATTELSTRASSE

KÄRNTEN

This road runs between Oberdrauburg and Kötschach linking the upper valleys of the Drava (Drau) and the Gail and crossing the pass at 982m/3 222ft.

From Oberdrauburg to the Lesach Valley *67km/42mi*

The most attractive part of the route is the stretch of road climbing the north slope in a series of hairpin bends through larch forest.

Laas

The Late Gothic **Filialkirche St. Andreas** sports doorways and windows framed in local red sandstone and delicate ribbed **vaulting**★★. It is a masterpiece by Bartimä Firtaler, a mason from Innichen in the Pustertal.

Kötschach

The small market community of **Kötschach-Mauthen**, set between the Gailtaler and Karnische Alps, is a popular medium-altitude (710m/2 329ft), mountain-air health resort. The **Pfarrkirche Unsere Liebe Frau** (also known as the "cathedral of the Gailtal") was consecrated in 1485 and completely rebuilt by Bartlmä Firtaler in the early 16C; it embodies the final, exuberantly decorative stage of the Gothic style and has stunning **traceried rib vaulting**★. The fresco on the north chancel wall depicts the Death and Assumption of the Virgin Mary. The "miraculous" statue enclosed in the high altar is a black Madonna.

Lesachtal★

The road follows this charming valley along the Gail, climbing from 900m/2 953ft to 1 200m/3 937ft. Off the beaten track, it has remained largely unspoiled.

St. Lorenzen

This quiet village is dominated by the Late Gothic parish church of St. Laurentius, which boasts some remarkable frescoes. It is set amidst lovely painted farmhouses with shallow gable roofs.

Church vaulting, Kötschach

Maria Luggau

The church, also by Bartlmä Firtaler, was consecrated in 1536. The Baroque tower dates from 1736. The object of veneration is a Late Gothic miraculous image of Our Lady of Sorrows. The statue of the Pietà stands on a valuable tabernacle shrine from the late 18C.

A short steep path leads to the picturesque **Luggau water mills**. These five timber constructions are over 200 years and all that remains of 100 mills once operating in the Lesach Valley.

Kartitscher Sattel

This pass is the highest point along the road (1 530m/5 020ft).

GASTEINER TAL 🎿🎿

SALZBURG

The Gasteiner Tal, a long, wide river valley, is one of the most attractive vacation destinations in Austria. It encompasses three main resorts: Dorfgastein (830m/2 723ft), Bad Hofgastein (860m/2 822ft) and Bad Gastein (1 000m/3 281ft). The latter developed into a leading spa resort as early as the 15C. With its exceptional setting amid medium- and high-altitude mountains, the valley has much to offer both skiers in winter and hikers in summer. www.gastein.com.

▸ **Orient Yourself:** A 40km-long valley in the Hohe Tauern National Park

🖙 **Don't Miss:** Climbing the Stubnerkogel peak in summer and skiing the Kreuzkogel in winter.

🕐 **Organizing Your Time:** Budget at least a couple of days to fully appreciate the magnificent scenery.

Ski slopes 🎿🎿

The Gasteiner Valley is a winter sports mecca. Some 200km/125mi pistes spread over five mountainsides: Fulseck (alt 880-2 030m/2 887-6 660ft) above Dorfgastein; Schlossalm (alt 860-2 300m/2 822-7 546ft) above Bad Hofgastein; Stubnerkogel (alt

1 100-2 250m/3 609-7 382ft) and Graukogel (alt 1 100-2 000m/3 609-6 562ft) above Bad Gastein; and Kreuzkogel (alt 1 588-2 690m/5 210-8 825ft) above Sportgastein. There are 60km of easy runs, 117km of intermediate runs and 24km of difficult runs. The area is part of a super-ski region called Ski Amadé.

Cross-country skiers have 90km/56mi of track at their disposal, covering the whole valley floor from Dorfgastein as far as Sportgastein.

Thermal cures

In the 19C Bad Gastein evolved into one of the ritziest spa towns of the age, visited by emperors and politicians, famous artists and writers alike. It is now a thoroughly modern health resort and home of a balneological research institute.

The thermal water forms from rain water seeping into the Graukogel and Hüttenkogel massifs, which heats up underground and then emerges from 17 thermal springs with a daily output of 5 million litres (about 1.3 million US gallons) and an average temperature of 44.3°C/112°F.

The healing effect of Gastein's thermal water is not so much due to its temperature, however, but to its radon content. This radioactive noble gas can be administered through bathing or inhalation. While in the body, radon gives off helium nuclei that energize the body and regenerate damaged cells. In conjunction with the mild mountain climate, the naturally enriched water helps prevent or soothe rheumatism, respiratory diseases, circulatory problems and other ailments.

Visitors can "take the cure" at numerous hotels, health centers or public pools. Alternatively, spend a session in the *Heilstollen* (www.gasteiner-heilstollen.com), a tunnel in which the temperature is 37.5-41.5°C/99.5-106.7°F.

From Lend to the Tauerntunnel

41km/26mi including excursion to Sportgastein

After leaving Lend, the road makes its way over the Klamm pass. Take the tunnel to avoid the often steep old road along the floor of the gorge. Beyond the tunnel, the Gasteiner Tal soon widens out.

Dorfgastein★

Alt 830m/2 723ft. *Web site: www.dorfgastein.at.*

This pretty village on the valley floor fringed by lush forests perkily shows off its idyllic setting below sun-drenched Alpine meadows. In winter, there are extensive ski slopes nearby, with a connection to the Großarl ski slopes, overlooked by the Fulseck summit (55km/34mi of slopes). The drop in altitude is over 1 100m/3 609ft, and there are good opportunities for off-piste skiing as well.

Bad Hofgastein‡‡

Alt 860m/2 822ft. 🚩 *Bad Hofgastein, Tauernplatz 1, A-5630* ☎ *0 64 32/71 10*

Bad Hofgastein lies in the broadest, sunniest stretch of the valley. This smart and lively health resort has numerous hotels offering the same spa facilities as Bad Gastein. Furthermore, the resort boasts modern, beautifully laid out spa gardens and the new **Alpentherme** thermal pool and sauna complex. Winter brings excellent cross-country skiing in the valley and downhill in the Schlossalm massif. Slopes are linked with those on the Stubnerkogel above Bad Gastein via the Anger Valley.

Pfarrkirche

The parish church is a testimony to Bad Hofgastein's heyday as regional capital when this was the mother church of the valley. The imposing Late Gothic nave has handsome stellar and ribbed vaulting. The church exterior and the niches flanking the main doorway are adorned with elaborate epitaphs of wealthy local gold- and silver-mine owners.

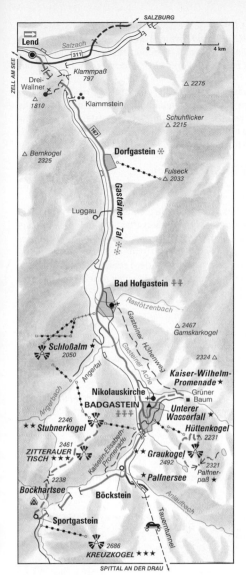

Schlossalm★

Alt 2 050m/6 726ft. *Cablecar, followed by chair-lift.* ⏱*Operates June-mid Oct, Dec-mid Apr, daily 8am-4pm on the hour.* ☜€13,80 two-way trip. ☎ 0 64 32/64 55.

Come here for a good **panorama**★ of the ski slopes and the summits of the Stubnerkogel, Ankogel range, Graukogel and Gamskarkogel. From the second terrace of the restaurant, the view stretches as far as the Dachstein.

Bad Gastein♨♨♨

Alt 1 013m/3 323ft. 🛈 *Bad Gastein, Kaiser-Franz-Josef-Str. 27, A-5640* ☎ 0 64 34/2 53 10. Bad Gastein ranks among the most glitteringly beautiful spas and winter sports resorts in Austria. It is located amid spectacular mountain **scenery**★, flanked by the Stubnerkogel and the Graukogel, and boasts palatial hotels and elegant boutiques. The roaring Gasteiner Ache creates a waterfall right in town. The east bank of the river is paralleled by the **Kaiser-Wilhelm-Promenade**★, which gives lovely views of the town and surroundings.

Bad Gastein has numerous top-notch leisure facilities, including a skating rink, fitness centers, a nine-hole and a new 18-hole golf course, tennis courts and a casino. The **Felsentherme Gastein** is a thermal swimming pool built against the actual rock face.

Local ski slopes include fine runs down the Stubnerkogel and the Graukogel.

Stubnerkogel★★

Alt 2 246m/7 369ft. *Allow 1hr roundtrip. Ascent is in a chair-lift in two stages.* ⏱*Operates June-mid Oct, Dec-end Apr, daily 8.30am-4pm on the hour.* ☜€13,80 two-way trip. ☎ 0 64 32/64 55.

The **panorama**★★ encompasses the Graukogel, the Ankogel glacier massif, the Kreuzkogel and the Anger Valley with the glaciers of the Hohe Tauern in the background, as well as the lower reaches of the Gasteiner Tal.

Tauerntunnel

Regular train service between Mallnitz and Böckstein: Mallnitz 28 May-1 Oct, hourly 6.10am-11.10pm; 2 Oct-9 June, hourly 6.10am-9.10pm; Böckstein 28 May-1 Oct, hourly 5.40am-10.40pm; 2 Oct-9 June, hourly 6.40am-9.40pm. Journey time: 12min. Phone for prices. ☎ 0 47 84/6 00.

The 8.550km/5.3mi double track railway tunnel runs through the Tauern ridge between Böckstein in Salzburg and Mallnitz in Kärnten. Until the opening of the Felbertauern road tunnel this was the only way through the eastern Alps into the Tauern region. Even now, some motorists prefer loading their vehicle onto the train as opposed to driving through the road tunnel.

Excursion to Sportgastein★★

Toll road, free to ski pass holders.

From Bad Gastein, the road reaches Sportgastein, a broad high-altitude plateau set against a majestic backdrop of rocky peaks and glaciers after 6km/4mi. Infrastructure is minimal as of yet, consisting essentially of a large parking lot and a guesthouse. The altitude guarantees excellent snow cover, much to the delight of cross-country (7km/4mi of tracks) and downhill skiers alike. A modern cable-car leads up to the Kreuzkogel summit, from where some exhilarating downhill runs drop more than 1 100m/3 600ft.

Kreuzkogel★★★

Ascent by cable-car in two stages.

Views★★ are impressive from the mountain station, but it's well worth taking the 15min walk up to the summit, marked by a cross, to fully soak up the spectacular **panorama**★★★. Wear mountain boots, as the snow can be quite deep in places.

▶ *Travel back down to Böckstein. It is possible to carry on into Carinthia through the Tauerntunnel.*

Exploring on Foot

With its varied terrain suited to walkers of all abilities, the Gasteiner Tal is one of the best places in Austria for hiking. Walks are especially pretty along the **Kaiserin-Elisa-**

Palfnersee

beth-Promenade, from Bad Gastein to Böckstein, and along the **Gasteiner Hoh-enweg**, which follows the mountain slope from Bad Gastein to Bad Hofgastein.
Be sure to pick up a detailed map and plan your route carefully.

Zitterauer Tisch und Bockhartsee★★★

Allow a full day, including 4hr 30min walking time. Enquire at the tourist office about bus timetables between Sportgastein and Bad Gastein for your afternoon return.
Take the cable-car up to the top of the Stubnerkogel. Turn right at the mountain station and follow the route marked with red and white flashes and red arrows. In just under 1hr the mountain path reaches the Zitterauer Tisch (2 461m/8 074ft). There is a terrific **view★★★** of the entire Gasteiner Tal, especially the upper reaches of the valley. To the northeast, the view stretches as far as the Dachstein.
The path plunges down to pastures, before weaving through a bleak and craggy landscape. After another hour, you'll reach the Miesbichlscharte (alt 2 238m/7 343ft).
On the way down to the Unterer Bockhartsee there are good views of the glaciers and waterfalls of the Schareck massif as well as of the Hocharn and the Ankogel. From the lakeshore climb up to the hut and then down to Sportgastein. Take the bus back to Bad Gastein.

Graukogel★★

2hr 30min roundtrip walk. Difference in altitude of about 500m/1 640ft. This walk is recommended for good walkers wearing sturdy shoes. ⏱Chair-lift operates mid Dec-end Mar, daily 8.30am-4pm on the hour. Closed in poor weather €13,80 two-way trip. ☎ 0 64 34/64 55.
Take the two chair-lifts up to Tonis Almgasthof (alt 1 982m/6 503ft). A path leads from behind the guesthouse up to the Hüttenkogel summit (alt 2 231m/7 320ft) from where you'll have an incredible **panorama★★** of the Hohe Tauern range, and the spectacular Reedsee lake.
Next, follow the path along the ridge (extra care is needed in some of the steeper places) to the **Graukogel** summit for an even broader **view★★** as far as the Dachstein. The Palfnersee can be seen glistening immediately below.

Walk to the Palfnersee★

1hr 45min roundtrip
This is an untaxing walk through some beautiful countryside. Take the two chair-lifts up the Graukogel, walk past the hut and continue straight on. The mountain trail gives you a good **view★** of Schareck, Hoher Sonnblick and Hocharn before climbing up to the Palfnersee (alt 2 100m/6 890ft). From here, you could carry on to the **Palfner pass★** (alt 2 321m/7 615ft) for even better views *(allow an extra hour roundtrip).*

STIFT GERAS★

NIEDERÖSTERREICH

The Premonstratensian abbey of Geras, set in a quiet spot far from the main tourist centers, enjoys considerable renown in Lower Austria. It is surrounded by the Naturpark Geras, a **nature reserve** where fallow deer, roe deer, wild boar and other animals roam within large enclosures. ▯ *Hauptstraße 16, A-2093, ☎ 0 29 12/70 50; www.stift-geras.at.*

▶ **Orient Yourself:** Geras is in the eastern Waldviertel, not far from the Czech border.

Stift *(Abbey)*

👉 *Guided tour (1hr) Easter-1 Nov, Tues-Sat 10am, 11am, 2pm and 3pm, Sun 11am, 2pm and 3pm.* 💶€5. 📞 *0 29 12/9 45.*

This Premonstratensian monastery was founded in 1153 but was redesigned and enlarged in Baroque style by Joseph Munggenast in the 18C. The highlight of the guided tour is the solemn and refined **Marmorsaal**★ (Marble Hall), the former summer refectory, reached via a beautiful staircase with a statue of Pallas Athene, the Greek goddess of wisdom. The hall's magnificent **ceiling fresco**★ by Paul Troger depicts the miracle of the loaves and fishes. Troger is also responsible for the paintings hanging above the two fireplaces, including the *Wedding Feast at Cana*.

Stiftskirche

The colorful abbey church is Romanesque in origin but was completely redone in exuberant Baroque style following a fire in 1730. It has wonderfully delicate stuccowork and sensitive frescoes depicting the life of the Virgin painted by Franz Zoller, a pupil of Paul Troger. Also note the main door, which is decorated with statues of St Norbert and St Augustine, two major figures of the Premonstratensian Order.

Excursion

Perneggg

12km/8mi southwest of Geras.

Set in peaceful, unspoiled countryside, Pernegg was founded in 1153 as a Premonstratensian convent but became affiliated with Geras Abbey following the death of the last nun in 1585. Since 1995 it has been used as a center for religious seminars and fasting retreats. Its church blends Late Gothic, Renaissance and Baroque elements and features a modern high altar decorated with a 16C Crucifixion.

GERLOS-ALPENSTRASSE★

TIROL UND SALZBURG

The Alpine road zigzagging over the Gerlos pass connects the Tyrol with Salzburg and offers panoramic views of the Salzach valley and the Zillertal Alps. It also skirts the spectacular Krimmler Wasserfälle, the highest waterfalls in Europe. Web site: www.gerlosstrasse.at.

▶ **Orient Yourself:** The road links the Zillertal valley with the Oberpinzgau basin.

😊 **Don't Miss:** Krimmler Wasserfälle

🕐 **Organizing Your Time:** Allow plenty of time to negotiate this curvy mountain road. The hike up and down the Krimml falls takes at least 3hr.

Kids Especially for Kids: Wasserwunderwelt at Krimml Falls

From Zell am Ziller to Krimml *38km/24mi*

▶ *The road is steep and narrow in places. Between the Gerlos pass and Krimml, a toll is charged.*

Zell am Ziller   *See ZILLERTAL.*

On leaving Zell am Ziller the road climbs quickly in hairpin bends up the Hainzenberg slope. Soon the pilgrimage chapel of **Maria Rast** (1748), with its distinctive red onion domes ,comes into view. After Hainzenberg the road enters the Gerlos Valley.

Gerlos
At an altitude of 1 250m/4 101ft, this village offers excellent downhill and cross-country skiing in winter and hiking and climbing in summer. Water sports enthusiasts head to the **Durlassbodensee.**
After the toll point the road reaches the rugged moorland landscape of the Gerlos plateau. There are several parking lots here for enjoying superb **views**★★ of the Krimml falls. The walk to the falls starts in the parking lot further downhill, just before the toll booths to the Gerlach pass road.

Krimmler Wasserfälle★★★
The waterfalls can be visited from mid Apr-end Oct or at your own risk in winter. €1,80.
☎ *0 65 64/72 12; www.wasserfaelle-krimml.at.*
The Krimmler Ache, which flows from the glacier of that name at more than 3 000m/10 000ft above sea level, cascades in three stages down the forested cliff sides of the Salzachtalkessel. The falls, the highest in Europe, drop 380m/1 250ft in total and are a magnificent sight, espe-cially in the midday sun when the spray glitters in every color of the rainbow.

Before climbing the 4km path up the falls, be sure to take in the viewpoint at the foot of the lowest fall where the water thunders onto a rocky barrier. The broad path zigzags beneath a canopy of trees to the Schettkanzel at the top of the falls at 1 465m/4 807ft. Just above the middle falls, you can fortify yourself at the Schönangerl mountain inn before the final, steep climb.
At the entrance to the falls is the new **Wasserwunderwelt**★(Water Wonder-land), an interactive theme park with 3D and multimedia exhibits about the falls, playful toys such as a water-powered swing and a look at the falls through a telescope. Just beyond here is a national park information center.

Krimml falls

M. Hertlein/MIC-HELIN

GMÜND

KÄRNTEN
POPULATION 2 700
ALT 741M/2 430FT

Gmünd was founded in the 11C by the archbishops of Salzburg to control the traffic through the Lieser Valley, a stretch along the busy Nuremberg-Venice trade route. The compact center preserves much of its medieval character and is still encircled by fortified town walls entered via two imposing gateways. Gmünd is also home to a thriving artists' community and you'll find its cobbled streets lined by numerous galleries and studios. ⏺ *Rathaus, A-9853, ☎ 0 47 32/22 22; www.stadt-gmuend.at.*

Sights

Alte Burg

An earthquake in 1690 and a fire in 1886 reduced Gmünd's fortress to a mere shadow of its medieval self, but recent efforts have restored it into cultural center hosting art exhibits, seminars, concerts and theater performances. There are also an excellent cafe and restaurant and good views from the keep.

Hauptplatz

Gmünd's handsome main square is bookended by the fortified gateways and lined by elegant town houses splashed in a rainbow of pastels. Near the upper gateway, the 17C **Lodron'sche Schloss**, now a school and public library, opens onto a pretty garden, the entrance to which is flanked by the statues of two massive lions that originally graced the Mirabellgarten in Salzburg.

Off the square's northern end, the old prison *(Kirchgasse 56)* contains the **Eva Faschauerein Heimatmuseum**, a curious exhibit about a local woman accused of poisoning her farmer husband with arsenic soon after their 1770 wedding. After three years of imprisonment and horrific torture, she finally confessed (who wouldn't?) and was executed shortly thereafter.

Porsche-Automuseum, Gmünd

Porsche Museum

Pfarrkirche Maria Himmelfahrt

The Late Gothic church was consecrated in 1339 and enlarged and redecorated in Baroque style in the 18C. Life-size figures of the Apostles flank the fine altar, and there are numerous interesting tombstones as well.

Porsche-Automuseum Helmut Pfeifhofer

Open 15 May-15 Oct, daily 9am-6pm; 16 Oct-14 May, daily 10am-4pm. €6. 0 47 32/24 71; Web site: www.porsche-museum.at.

From 1944 to 1950 Gmünd was the sphere of activity of world-famous engineer **Ferdinand Porsche** (d 1998). It was here where the first car with the "Porsche" marque, the legendary 356, was made. Several of them are on display at this, Europe's only private Porsche museum, alongside prototypes of military and sports vehicles, actual-size wooden models of the first Porsche car bodies and over 400 model cars.

GMÜND

NIEDERÖSTERREICH
POPULATION 6 934
ALT 485M/1 591FT

Gmünd counts an enchanting old quarter, peaceful spots beside the Lainsitz and the Blockheide nature reserve among its assets. *Weitraerstr. 44 A-3950, 0 28 52/5 32 12; www.gmuend.at.*

▸ **Orient Yourself:** Gmünd lies in the northern Waldviertel, near the Czech border, where the Lainsitz and Braunaubach rivers meet.

Sights

Stadtplatz

Gmünd's main square is centered on the Renaissance **Altes Rathaus**, which houses a local history museum and is easily recognized by its gabled tower. On the south side of the square, the **Glas- und Steinmuseum** provides evidence of the glass-making industry that flourished in the region from the 17C to the 20C. At No 31 and 33 are two beautiful Renaissance-era **houses with sgraffito decoration**★ featuring scenes from classical mythology.

Naturpark Blockheide★

Northeast of the town lies this lovely nature reserve, characterized by bizarrely shaped granite blocks with such evocative nicknames as Pilzstein (mushroom rock) and Teufelsbett (devil's bed). A former water reservoir at the park's highest point has been reconfigured as an information center with snack stands nearby. The new viewing tower offers sweeping vistas as far as the Czech Republic.

GMUNDEN⋆

OBERÖSTERREICH
POPULATION 15 075
ALT 420M/1 378FT

Gmunden is a popular lakeside summer resort that experienced its first heyday in the 19C when it became the darling of artists, poets and politicians. These days it is known for its fine ceramics as well as its busy beaches, lake cruises and the Esplanade, an elegant promenade along the northern shore of Lake Traunsee.
🖫 *Am Graben 2, A-4810, ☎ 0 76 12/6 43 05; Web site: www.gmunden.at.*

▶ **Orient Yourself:** Gmunden is on the northern shore of Traunsee lake in the Salzkammergut.
🅿 **Parking:** There is a parking lot (fee) in Seilergasse.
🔅 **Don't Miss:** A stroll along the Esplanade.

Sights

Historic Center

The Renaissance **town hall** on Rathausplatz, the main square, has a ceramic glockenspiel that chimes out several times daily. North of here, the town's medieval warren of lanes is punctuated by the **Stadtpfarrkirche** with a precious high altar by Thomas Schwanthaler depicting the *Adoration of the Magi*.

In the former salt administration building east of the town hall, the **Kammerhofmuseum** (🕙*Open May-Oct, Mon-Sat 10am-noon, 2-5pm, Sun 10am-noon; Dec-mid Jan, daily 10am-noon, 2-5pm. Closed 24 Dec. ⊚€3,05 ☎ 0 76 12/79 42 44)* has exhibits on local history and a selection of local ceramics. Considerably more memorable is the quirky **Klo & So Sanitärmuseum** (🕙 *same hours as Kammerhofmuseum. ⊚€4. ☎0 76 12/9 44 25)* at Traungasse 4, which has a bizarre collection of toilet bowls, chamber pots, sinks and bidets, including one used by Empress Elisabeth.

Seeschloss Ort⋆

On a little island accessed by a wooden bridge, this landmark palace *(www.schlossort. gmunden.at)* wraps around a triangular arcaded courtyard with elaborate sgraffito

Schloss Ort, Gmunden

decoration and a Late Gothic exterior staircase. A popular German TV series called *Schlosshotel Orth* is filmed at the palace.

Excursions

Schloss Scharnstein★

▶ *30km/19mi roundtrip. Leave Gmunden to the east on B 120.*

This Renaissance castle perches above the Alm River and houses two unusual museums and a reptile collection.

The 21 rooms of the **Österreichisches Kriminalmuseum** (Austrian Crime Museum, ◐*Open 1 May-15 Oct, Tues-Sun 9am-5pm.* ✆€5. ☎ *0 76 15/25 50*) traces the fight against crime from the Middle Ages to today. Displays include devices of torture and execution that are not for the faint of heart, let alone kids.

Fans of contemporary Austrian history will likely enjoy the **Zeitgeschichte Museum Scharnstein**, which chronicles all 20C milestones, including the Third Reich years. Down in the cellar is the extraordinary **Reptilienzoo** (Reptile Zoo, ◐*Open May-mid Oct, Tues-Sun 9am-5pm, Nov-Apr, Tues - Sat 1-4pm.* ✆€5. ☎ *0 76 15/77 65*) with over 100 poisonous snakes, scorpions and giant spiders from all over the world.

GOSAUSEEN★★★

OBERÖSTERREICH

The Gosau lakes lie amid the craggy peaks of the Dachstein range and are a fantastic destination for nature-lovers.

▶ **Orient Yourself:** The lakes are some 15km northwest of Hallstadt.

Vorderer Gosausee★★★

Alt 933m/3 061ft. About 5km past the village of Gosau, this lake affords unforgettable **views**★★ of the Hoher Dachstein range. The setting is especially magical early or late in the day for the dramatic interplay of light and shadow between valley and glaciers. It takes about an hour to walk around the lake. For even better views, take the **Gosaukammbahn** to the Zwieselalm (1587m), which is also the starting point for numerous trails.

Hinterer Gosausee★★

The moderately fit might consider continuing for about an hour to the Hinterer Gosausee, a smaller lake encircled by dense forest and a ring of craggy peaks.

Y. Bontoux

Hinterer Gosausee

SCHLOSS GRAFENEGG★

NIEDERÖSTERREICH

Schloss Grafenegg is Austria's most significant example of romanticized late 19C Historicist architecture. Surrounded by an English landscape park, the palace keep with its gallery and turrets rises like a miraculous vision above the Tullner Feld plain. The palace is well known for its exhibitions, readings and concerts. The restaurant serves gourmet-level international cuisine, which is best paired with wine from the palace's own estate.

▶ **Orient Yourself:** The palace is about 12km/7.5mi east of Krems.
⌚ **Also See:** Krems, Stift Göttweig, Schloss Rosenburg

A castle has stood in this spot since the Middle Ages, but what you see today is the product of 19C architect Leopold Ernst. It is a vast neogothic pile surrounded by a dry moat and sporting cream-colored façades festooned with fierce-looking gargoyles. It was severely damaged during 10 years of Soviet occupation after the Second World War but has since been extensively restored.

Tour

Tours by appointment only. ⏱*Open 29 Apr-29 Oct, Tues-Sun 10am-5pm.* ✆*€5.* ☏ *0 27 35/22 05 22; Web site: www.grafenegg.at.*

The ethereal blue **Schlosskapelle** (palace chapel) is a fine example of neo-Gothic architecture and boasts a Late Gothic winged altar depicting the Coronation of the Virgin Mary. The **Great Salon** and the **Dining Room**, with their attractive wooden panelling and carved ornaments and figures, are additional highlights. The **coffered ceiling**★ in the Great Salon is particularly stunning, as is the stairway decorated with the figure of a knight and busts of the builder and his architect. No less remarkable are the **Yellow Salon** and the adjoining bathroom, study and bedroom, the library and the garden room, whose walls and ceilings are covered in exquisite materials.

Coffered ceiling in the Great Salon, Schloss Grafenegg

R. Chéret/MICHELIN

GRAZ★★

STEIERMARK
POPULATION 243 400
ALT 365M/1 194FT

The capital of Styria, Graz is also known as the "Garden City" thanks to its many parks, riverside setting and surrounding rolling hills. In 1999 its extensive historic center was declared a UNESCO world heritage site. Austria's second-largest city is an economic hub that provides employment to around 130,000 people in industries ranging from brewing to shoe making to car manufacturing. Cultural life flourishes tremendously with plenty of performances and festivals taking place year-round. The nightlife is excellent, too, fueled in large part by 50,000 students attending four major universities. ◫ *Kaiserfeldgasse 15, A-8011, ☎ 03 16/8 07 50; www.graztourism.at.*

▶ **Orient Yourself:** Graz is in the valley of the Mur, bounded by the Styrian hills and the last foothills of the Alps in southeastern Austria.

🄿 **Parking:** Garages abound in the center but they are expensive and may only offer short-term parking. You're better off at a Park & Ride lot, for instance the one behind the main train station; take bus No 1 or 7 to the center.

⊘ **Don't Miss:** Zeughaus, Mausoleum, Schlossberg, Kunsthaus

🕒 **Organizing Your Time:** Devote at least a full day to Graz, starting your exploration in the old town around the Hauptplatz, perhaps making time for a museum or two, then heading up the Schlossberg in the afternoon for grand views and a relaxing stroll.

⚲ **Also See:** Schloss Eggenberg, Österreichisches Freilichtmuseum

A Bit of History

In 1379 the Leopoldine branch of the Habsburgs chose Graz as their residence. It became an imperial city when Friedrich III, king of Germany and Austria, was crowned Holy Roman Emperor in 1452. Graz equipped itself with ramparts as early as the 13C as defence against the Turkish invasions in Styria. In 1543 the defences, including the Schlossberg Fortress, were strengthened under Emperor Ferdinand I by the Italian **Domenico dell'Allio**, who was also architect of the Landhaus. The measures

Rooftops of Graz

H. Weissenhofer/ÖSTERREICH WERBUNG

Courtyard of the Landhaus

taken to ward off attack were extensive; a huge arsenal of arms and munitions was built up, the raw material coming from Styria's **"Iron Mountain"** *(◐ see EISENERZ)*. Whenever invasion seemed imminent, the arms were distributed to local volunteers to reinforce the professional troops.

Following the Habsburg partition of the country in 1564, Graz became the capital of a vast area known as **Inner Austria**, comprising Styria, Carinthia, Gorizia, Carniola and Istria. The splendid court of Archduke Karl II brought many cultural and artistic benefits to the city.

The Reformation – By 1568 three-quarters of the population had embraced Protestantism. In this year a school and seminary were founded, where the present Paradeishof stands (CZ 26), and it was here that the German astronomer Johannes Kepler taught between 1594 and 1598.

In 1571 Archduke Karl II called in the Jesuits to implement the Counter Reformation; they founded a college (in the Bürgergasse) and a school (Hofgasse). In 1585 the Archduke founded **Graz University**, which became the intellectual hub of Inner Austria.

The city's fortunes took another turn in 1619 when Karl II's son, Archduke Ferdinand II, was elected Holy Roman Emperor. Ferdinand moved the court to Vienna, and Graz, no longer an Imperial residence, lost much of its importance.

In the 18C, following the reforms of Maria Theresa, the city had to forgo many of its privileges; later, under Joseph II, the university was downgraded to a grammar school. Graz's days of splendor came to a definite end and this is why the city has so few buildings dating from the Late Baroque period.

A Prince beloved by his people, Archduke Johann – The Habsburg Archduke Johann (1782-1859) enjoyed great popularity in Styria and his memory is still honored today. On settling in Graz, he devoted himself to studies of all kinds, roaming through Styria and Carinthia in the company of naturalists, archeologists and painters.

His romantic marriage to Anna Plochl, a postmaster's daughter from Bad Aussee, did nothing to diminish his popularity. He founded model farms, presided over the construction of the Graz-Mürzzuschlag railway (1844) and promoted the development of the Eisenerz area. In Graz itself, the Technische Hochschule is proof of his progressive spirit, as is the Landesmuseum Joanneum, Austria's oldest museum open to the public, founded in 1811.

Old Town★★

Hauptplatz★ (CZ)

The heart of Graz, this is the liveliest of squares. The city trams come and go incessantly, disgorging ever more people to join the motley crowd thronging the market stalls. Behind the brightly painted 17C-19C façades are buildings of much older, medieval date. The flashiest façade belongs to the arcaded **Haus Luegg** (CZ A), which is festooned with luxuriant Baroque stucco work. The city's oldest pharmacy is at no 4; dating from 1535, it still has some of its original fittings. The **Erzherzog-Johann-Brunnen** (fountain) of 1878 lords it over the square. The fact that the statue of the Emperor is relegated to a less important site on the Freiheitsplatz (DY 10) is a tangible reminder of the local people's affection for the enlightened archduke. The four female figures gracing the fountain are allegories of the four main rivers flowing through Styria at the time of the monarchy, though the boundary revisions of 1918 left the province with only two of them (the Mur and the Enns).

The southern end of the square is punctuated by the neo-Renaissance **Rathaus** (Town hall). Standing outside, you'll have a nice view of the Schlossberg with the familiar outline of the Uhrturm (Clock Tower), the emblem of Graz.

The Landhaus is reached via the broad and busy **Herrengasse** (DZ) with its elegant shops and offices. The **Gemaltes Haus** (painted house, at no 3) was residence of the archdukes until the building of the castle in 1450. The murals on historic (notably Roman) themes date from 1742, when they replaced the original decoration by Pietro de Pomis, architect of the mausoleum.

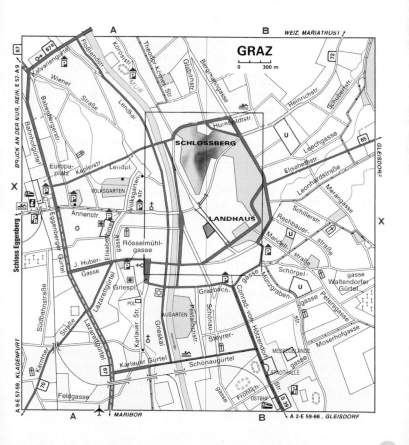

Address Book

PRACTICAL INFORMATION

TOURIST INFORMATION

Graz/Steiermark Information, *im Landhaus, Herrengasse 16, 8010 Graz. Opening times: June-Sept Mon-Fri 9am-7pm, Sat 9am-6pm, Sun and public holidays 10am-3pm; Oct-May Mon-Fri 9am-6pm, Sat 9am-3pm, Sun and public holidays 10am-3pm;* ☎ *03 16/80 75-0.*

Graz Information am Hauptbahnhof, *Europaplatz 6, 8020 Graz. Opening times: Mon-Fri 9am-6pm (summer only);* ☎ *03 16/80 75-0.*

Graz also has its own **Web site** at *www.graztourismus.at*

CITY TOURS

Tour of Old Town (2hr 30min) – *Apr-end Oct daily at 2.30pm, otherwise Sat only at 2.30pm.* Meeting point: Graz/Steiermark Information.

Tours of the Schlossberg – *Easter-Oct daily 9am-5pm on the hour.* Meeting point: at the bell-tower.

Guided tours (in English and German) are available from early April to late October. Departure at 2pm from the Landhausgasse, return at about 7pm. Fridays: Styrian Castle Route
Saturdays: Piber Lippizaner Stud Farm
Sundays: South Styrian Wine Route
Information and bookings from Graz/Steiermark Information, Herrengasse 16.

PUBLIC TRANSPORT

Tickets are available from ticket machines, advance booking offices and tobacconists (Trafiken), and also from tram and bus drivers.

With the **Stundenkarte** you can use any form of public transport in Graz for 1hr, with the **10-Zonenkarte** you can make 10 journeys within the same zone, and there is also a **24-Stundenkarte** and a **Wochenkarte**, giving travel for 24hr and a week respectively.

Further information on public transport can be obtained from the Graz transport authority (GVB) Zeitkartenbüro (Season ticket office), Hauptplatz 14, ☎ 03 16/8 74 08, or from the Informationsstelle on the Jakominiplatz, ☎ 03 16/88 74 11.

BICYCLE HIRE

Bicycles can be hired from the Hauptbahnhof (☎ *03 16/78 48 326*) or Bicycle, *Kaiser-Franz-Josefs-Kai 55 and 66* or *Rechbauerstraße 57*, ☎ 03 16/82 13 57 to explore the city's 75km/47mi of cycle paths.

INNER CITY PARKING

Parking is permitted in the **blue zones** for a fee covering a certain time (*restricted parking is operated between 9am and 7pm on work days*). Parking tickets valid for up to 3hr can be obtained from parking ticket machines. Otherwise you should park in one of the following car parks: Tiefgarage (underground) Mariahilferplatz; Parkhaus (multi-storey) Griesgasse 10; Tiefgarage Andreas-Hofer-Platz; Tiefgarage Rosarium, Hamerlinggasse; Garage Burgring, Einspinnergasse; Schlossberg-Garage, Sackstraße 29; City-Garage Weitzer, Am Entenplatz.

POST OFFICES

Main post office: **Hauptpostamt**, *Neutorgasse 46, Mon-Fri 7am-11pm, Sat 7am-2pm, Sun and public holidays 8am-2pm.*

Station post office: **Bahnhofspostamt**, *Europaplatz 10, daily, 24hr/24hr.*

SHOPPING

The main shopping street is the Herrengasse, but there are also numerous shops in the pedestrian precincts, such as Sporgasse/Murgasse, the streets around the Hauptplatz, and Schmiedgasse/Stubenberggasse/Hans-Sachs-Gasse.

MARKETS

Kaiser-Josef-Platz (farm produce), *daily 6am-noon.*
Lendplatz (farm produce), *Mon-Sat 7am-noon.*
*Karmeliterplatz (*flea market), *3rd Sat in the month.*

SOUVENIRS

Craft goods and traditional costume (Trachten): Steirisches Heimatwerk, Herrengasse 10 and Paulustorgasse 4. Schlossbergkugeln (Schlossberg balls, local speciality chocolates): Konditorei Strehly, Sporgasse 14.

Kernöl (salad oil from pumpkin seeds): farmers' market, Kaiser-Josef-Platz
Styrian wine: Stempfergasse 2.

ENTERTAINMENT

The **"Bühnen Graz"** (☎ 03 16/80 00, Fax 03 16/80 08 565, www.buehnen-graz.com) association includes five theatres:

The **Opernhaus** at Kaiser-Josef-Platz 10, the **Schauspielhaus** (spoken theatre, 12 premieres every season) on Freiheitsplatz, **Next Liberty** (children's and young people's theatre) at *Kaiser-Josef-Platz 10*, the **Orpheum** (venue for rock, pop, jazz and cabaret) at *Orpheumgasse 8*, and in the summer the **Casemates** (open-air theatre) on Schlossberg.

T.i.P. (Theater im Palais), *Leonhardstraße 15*, ☎ 03 16/38 91 016, hosts musical and spoken theatre by students from Graz University of Art.

TheatermëRZ, *Steinfeldgasse 20*, ☎ 03 16/72 01 72. This artists' and authors' theatre can look back on numerous international tours. Its programme focuses on the work of author, director and theatre manager Willi Bernhart: plays, song programmes, children's and young people's theatre.

Theatro, *Neubaugasse 6*, ☎ 03 16/71 60 27. Independent cultural centre which hosts all kinds of theatre as well as concerts of rock pop and world music.

Casino Graz, *Landhausgasse 10*, ☎ 03 16/83 25 78. Austria's second largest casino.

CINEMAS

Large multiple-screen cinema complexes offering a corresponding variety of films are to be found at **UCI Kinowelt Annenhof** (*Annenstraße 29*, ☎ 03 16/72 77) and **Cineplexx** (*Alte Poststraße 470*, ☎ 03 16/29 09). For films other than current mainstream, try the **Filmzentrum im Rechbauerkino** (*Rechbauerstraße 6*, ☎ 03 16/83 05 08), **KIZ Kino im Augarten** (*Friedrichgasse 24*, ☎ 03 16/82 11 86) and **Schubertkino** (*Mehlplatz 2*, ☎ 03 16/82 90 810).

WHERE TO EAT

Altsteirische Schmankerlstube (*Sackstraße 10*, ☎ 03 16/83 32 11); **Franz Schauer's** (*Sackstraße 29, 3rd floor*, ☎ 03 16/83 45 85); **Kehlberghof** (*Kehlbergstraße 83*, ☎ 03 16/28 41 25); **Mohrenwirt** (*Mariahilfstraße 16*, ☎ 03 16/71 20 08); **Landhauskeller** (*Schmiedgasse 9*, ☎ 03 16/83 02 76); **Pichlmaier** (*Petersbergenstraße 9*, ☎ 03 16/47 15 97); **Santa Clara** (*Abraham-a-Santa-Clara-Gasse 1, entrance Bürgergasse 6*, ☎ 03 16/81 18 22); **Stainzerbauer** (*Bürgergasse 4*, ☎ 03 16/8 15 87 50).

CAFÉS AND BARS

Temmel's Kaiserhof (*Kaiserfeldgasse 1*); **Café Promenade am Burgtor** (*Erzherzog-Johann-Allee 1*); **Operncafé** (*Opernring 22*); **Hofbäckerei Edegger-Tax** (*Hofgasse 6*).

The centre of Graz nightlife (known as the "Bermuda triangle") is the area bordered by the Färberplatz, Glockenspielplatz and Herrengasse. Here there are hostelries and wine parlours to suit every taste. In the university quarter (Leonhardtstraße, Zinzendorfgasse and Schillerplatz) is to be found the young scene.

In the **Gasthaus Keplerkeller** (*Stempfergasse 6*), you can drink wine and listen to Styrian music, while special beers are available at the **Bierbaron** (*Heinrichstraße 56*), as well as in the pubs **Eschenlaube** (*Glacisstraße 67*), and **Schillerhof** (*Plüddemanngasse 2*). The **Kulturhauskeller** (*Elisabethstraße 30*) is a pub with music, and the **Café Stockwerk** (*Jakominiplatz 18/I*) offers jazz. You can also have a drink in one of the many bars in Graz, such as the **Ernst-Fuchs-Bar** in the Hotel Erzherzog Johann (*Sackstraße 3-5*), the **Fink** (*Freiheitsplatz 2*), the **Limarutti** (*Prokopigasse 4*) or the **M1** (*Färberplatz 1/III*). There is dancing in the **Monte** (*Sackstraße 27*) and in the **Castello** (*Bürgergasse 4*). The ambiance of an American bar, complete with live jazz, is recreated in the **Hemingway American Bar** (*Klosterwiesgasse 6*).

DATES FOR YOUR DIARY

Diagonale: March-April, Festival of Austrian film.

Storytime in Graz: at Whitsun, Festival of storytelling and fairy tales. Storytellers from all over the world come to Graz to demonstrate how much fun and excitement story-telling can be.

Classics in the city: in summer, open-air performances of classical music in the Renaissance Lanhaushof with international culinary delights.

Generali Hof Jazz concerts: in summer, open-air performances, free of charge, courtesy of the Graz jazz scene.

Styriarte: July, classical music festival.

Jazz-Sommer: July-August, jazz concerts on the Mariahilfer Platz, free of charge.

AIMS: mid July-end August, festival of classical music by the great composers played by students from the **A**merican **I**nstitute of **M**usical **S**tudies.

La Strada: end July-beginning of August, international festival of puppet and street theatre in the old city.

Styrian Autumn: October, international avant-garde festival of contemporary music, theatre, art exhibitions and readings of literary works.

Mountain and adventure film festival: November, international film competition, with the "Grand Prix Graz" awarded in five different categories.

Landhaus★★ (DZ)

The former seat of the Styrian Diet, the Landhaus is a remarkable Renaissance palace built between 1557 and 1565 by Domenico dell'Allio, the military architect who had just completed the total reconstruction of the Schlossberg fortress for Emperor Ferdinand I. Today the Landhaus still serves as the meeting place for the Landtag, the Styrian provincial parliament.

The main façade with its round-arched windows above an elegant doorway prepares us for the splendor of the inner courtyard with its three storeys of arcades, flower-bedecked balconies, staircase wells and loggias. The stairway gracing the chapel in the northwest corner of the courtyard is by another Italian, Bartolomeo di Bosio. The well-head has a fine bronze dais with amoretti and female figures. In summer, the courtyard forms an enchanting backdrop for various performances.

Zeughaus (Arsenal)★★★ (DZ)

🕐*Open 1 Apr-31 Oct, Fri-Wed 10am-6pm, Thurs 10am-8pm; 1 Nov-31 Mar, Mon-Sat 10am-3pm, Sun 10am-4pm. ✆€5 (admission free 26 Oct 26 Nov). ☎ 03 16/82 87 96; Web site: www.zeughaus.at.*

Built in 1642, the Zeughaus was one of many arsenals in the world, but today it is the only one to have been preserved in its original state and with its contents intact. To enter the arsenal is to leave behind the contemporary bustle of the Herrengasse and to be transported back into the world of four centuries ago. You almost expect cavalrymen and foot soldiers to appear, fresh from being mustered in the Landhaus courtyard to be outfitted for battle.

Displayed on four floors are more than 32 000 arms of all imaginable kinds, many of a very high standard of craftsmanship. There are pistols, muskets, arquebuses and other firearms; heavy armour, breastplates and harnesses for use in battle or jousting, plus helmets, pikes, swords - the collection is truly mindboggling. Head to the top floor for a grand view of the Landhaus courtyard, the city's red rooftops and the Schlossberg with clock tower.

Stadtpfarrkirche zum Heiligen Blut (DZ)

The original Gothic church building was remodeled in the Baroque taste, then re-Gothicized in the late 19C. Its Baroque **bell-tower**★, the city's finest, was built entirely out of wood in 1780-81 by the architect Josef Stengg and the master carpenter Franz Windisch. It is topped by a three-barred cross, a reminder of its consecration by the Pope.

Inside, on the altar in the south aisle, is an *Assumption of the Virgin* attributed to Tintoretto. The stained glass of the chancel, the work of the Salzburg artist Albert

Birkle in 1953, has an unusual feature; in the left-hand window, the fourth panel from the bottom on the right shows Hitler and Mussolini observing the flagellation of Christ. Birkle's work had been deemed "degenerate" by the Nazis.

Organ concerts are held in the church on a regular basis.

▶ *Enter Altstadtpassage (DZ 3) at no 7 Herrengasse.*

Walking through Altstadtpassage, the first courtyard has arcaded and vaulted galleries dating from 1648. A little further on, to the right, are a number of courtyards of which one is reminiscent of the Landhaus.

The passageway spills out onto the **Mehlplatz** (DZ 22), flanked by two grand residences with Baroque stucco façades. Go right onto the **Glockenspielplatz** (Carillon Square – *performances at 11am, 3pm and 6pm* – DZ 12) where dancing figures in local costume appear at each carillon performance in the pediment of an imposing house with a bell-turret.

Leave the Glockenspielplatz via the narrow passageway called Abraham-a-Santa-Clara-Gasse (DZ 2), then turn left for a view of no 1 Burgergasse (DZ), the sombre palazzo-like building which once served as a boarding-house for aristocratic pupils of the Jesuits. To the right, a stairway leads to the Mausoleum.

Mausoleum★★ (DZ)

Open Daily 10:30am -12pm,1:30-4pm. Closed public holidays. 4.5€. ☎ *03 16/82 16 83*

Emperor Ferdinand II commissioned Italian architect, **Pietro de Pomis**, to build the Imperial mausoleum. Pomis set to work in 1614, but the structure was finally completed in 1636 by fellow Italian, Pietro Valnegro. Inside, Johann Bernhard Fischer von Erlach designed the exuberant stucco work and some of the frescoes. A particularly fine oval dome surmounts the funerary crypt with the red-marble sarcophagus of Karl II and Maria of Bavaria, the Emperor's parents. Only Maria lies inside, though, while the Emperor was buried at Seckau Abbey. The tomb of Emperor Ferdinand II is to the right of the altar.

Domkirche (Cathedral)★ (DZ)

Next to the mausoleum, the vast and luminous Domkirche only became a cathedral in 1786, having previously served as Imperial court church. It was commissioned by Emperor Friedrich III, whose coat of arms adorns the main entrance, and completed

R. Chéret/MICHELIN

Mausoleum, Graz

in 1464. Frescoes (1485) on the southwest corner of the entrance show the troubles visited on Graz in the 1480s (Turkish attack, plague and locusts).

The **interior** is a harmonious mix of Gothic reticulated vaulting and Baroque decoration. Of the original decor two frescoes of St Christopher (late 15C) have survived. They recall an old belief according to which one would not die on a day on which one had looked at the saint's image.

Near the entrance to the chancel are two magnificent **reliquary chests**★★★. Brought here by the Jesuits, they are works of great sophistication and were once the marriage chests of Paula di Gonzaga, Duchess of Mantua. Made of ebony and decorated with reliefs in bone and ivory, they date from around 1470 and are in the style of Mantegna. Their subject matter goes back to the *Triumphs* of Petrarch, moral and allegorical poems dealing with the various stages of life from the standpoint of a calm acceptance of death. The organ with its 5 354 pipes dates from 1978.

▷ *Leave the cathedral by the north entrance.*

Cross the street by the **Burgtor** (Castle Gate) (DZ) and go through the impressive stone gateway commanding the first courtyard of the 15C **castle** (Burg), the erstwhile residence of Friedrich III. Heavily rebuilt, it now houses the offices of the provincial government (Landesregierung). At the end of the first courtyard, below an archway, is the amazing **Treppenturm**★★ (Staircase Tower, DY B), a highly unusual double spiral stairway. The tower was added in 1499 by his son Maximilian I and is a notable technical achievement in terms of design and the mason's craft.

▷ *Backtrack to Hofgasse and head west to Freiheitsplatz.*

Freiheitsplatz (DY 10)

In the center of the square stands the statue of Franz II, the last Holy Roman Emperor and elder brother of Archduke Johann. The large red building with a neo-Classical pediment closing the square is the city residence of the abbots of St Lambrecht.

Follow Hofgasse to the old **Hofbäckerei** (Imperial Bakery) with its fine shopfront on your left just before Sporgasse. Turning right into the Sporgasse, have a look at the **Palais Saurau** at no 25 with its rusticated Baroque doorway and arcaded doorway; the significance of the Turk brandishing a sword on the gable is a mystery, even to the locals. The Renaissance **Zur Goldenen Pastete** (no 28) is also picturesque.

Follow bright and busy **Sporgasse** (CY) as it winds back to the Hauptplatz. At no 22 is the former Deutschordenshaus (House of the Teutonic Knights); it has an arcaded courtyard in Gothic style. The narrow façade of no 3 is an interesting example of Jugendstil (Art Nouveau).

▷ *Turn right onto Sackstraße.*

Sackstraße (CYZ)

This was once a cul-de-sac (Sack), which was opened by a tower gateway in the 14C whose site is now occupied by the Palais Attems (no 17). The road was lengthened on two occasions in the course of extending the city walls. Because of its proximity to the river, it became the heart of an artisans' district with a great variety of trades: millers, tanners, parchment-makers and many others. After 1650, the oldest part of the street became known as "Lords Blind Alley" because of the aristocratic mansions that are still here today.

The Krebsenkeller at no 12 has a **Renaissance courtyard**★ whose double windows and arcaded loggias create an Italian feel. The **Palais Herberstein** at no 16, once a grand mansion, boasts a monumental staircase as evidence of its past splendor. These days, the Landesmuseum Joanneum has its **Neue Galerie** (New Gallery) here, which displays art from the 19C and 20C in such media as painting, sculpture, photography, video and installations.

The **Palais Khuenberg** at no 18 was the birthplace of ill-fated Archduke Franz Ferdinand (& see ARTSTETTEN), the heir to the throne who was assassinated in 1914. Today it houses the **Stadtmuseum** (M¹) (& ☉Open 6 May-26 Oct, Mon-Sat 9am-7pm, Sun 9am-5pm; Jan-Dec 2001, Tues 10am-9pm, Wed-Sat 10am-6pm, Sun 10am-1pm. ☞€3,65, free on Sunday. ☎ 03 16/872 .7600).

GRAZ					
		Franziskanergasse	CZ 8	Luthergasse	DZ 20
		Franziskanerpl.	CZ 9	Mehlpl.	DZ 22
Abraham-a-Santa-		Freiheitspl.	DY 10	Neue-Welt-Gasse	CZ 23
Clara-Gasse	DZ 2	Girardigasse	DZ 35	Paradeisgasse	CZ 26
Altstadtpassage	DZ 3	Glockenspielpl.	DZ 12	Radetzkybrücke	CZ 27
Färbergasse	DZ 5	Griespl.	CZ 13	Schlossbergpl.	CY 29
Färberpl.	DZ 6	Hauptbrücke	CZ 16	Stempfergasse	DZ 30
		Keplerbrücke	CY 19	Tegetthoffbrücke	CZ 32

Alte Galerie des Steier-		Haus Luegg	CZ A	Steirisches Volkskunde-	
märkischen Landes-		Palais Attems	CY D	museum	DY M²
museums Joanneum	CZ M³	Stadtmuseum	CY M¹	Treppenturm	DY B
Dreifaltigkeitskirche	CY E	Stadtpark-Brunnen	DY F		

Palais Attems (CY D)

Opposite the Stadtmuseum, this is without doubt the finest of all the city's Baroque palaces. Its **façades**★★ repay close inspection, with their profuse decoration of pilasters, mouldings and curvilinear window pediments. The palace was built between 1702 and 1716 for Count Attems on a site previously occupied by six town houses. The nearby city gate was demolished at the same time, having outlived its usefulness.

Dreifaltigkeitskirche (CY E)

Built in 1704, the church seems to be watching over its neighbor, the Palais Attems. It reveals its calm and harmonious façade with its scrolled pediment in an almost shy way, notwithstanding the abundance of iconography referring to the Trinity, to which the church is dedicated.

The view from the church door shows the Schlossbergplatz (CY 29) from which some 260 steep steps climb up to the Schlossberg itself.

Medieval quarter★

Towards the end of the Middle Ages, a cattle market was held between the river and the ramparts, where the Franziskanerplatz (CZ 9) and the Neutorgasse (CZ) are now. The strange name (Kälbernes Viertel meaning Calf Town) still used by locals for the area around the Franciscan church recalls these times. In 1620, the area was brought within the ramparts when the city's defences were being strengthened.

The quarter has kept much of its charm, and a stroll through its narrow **lanes**★ is most enjoyable, particularly the pretty Neue-Welt-Gasse (CZ 23) and the Franziskanergasse (CZ 8), both piled high with the wares of produce vendors.

Franziskanerkirche (CZ)

Traders set up their stalls against the walls of this church, which was rerooofed after the Second World War and given modern glass. It was here in 1240 that the Minorites installed their convent, which passed into the ownership of a closed Franciscan order in the 16C. The oldest part of the church, the Jakobskapelle, dates back to 1330.

Parks★

Schlossberg★ (CY)

Reached by funicular(Schlossbergbahn), from the northern end of the Sackstraße, via the steps leading up from the Schlossbergplatz (CY 29) or by elevator (Schlossberg lift) operating next to the steps. ⏱*Operates every 15min, runs daily May-Sept 9am-11pm; Nov-Apr 10am-10pm. Out of Order 2 Oct-20 Oct.* ⊜€1,70. ☎ 03 16/88 74 50.

Rising 123m/400ft above the city, this impregnable hilltop bristled with redoubts and fortifications right up to the Napoleonic Wars. Even in 1809, when Graz was occupied by French troops, the fortress withstood all assaults. Much to the chagrin of the townsfolk, one of the provisions of the Treaty of Schönbrunn in 1809 involved the demolition of the Schlossberg. Only the payment of a handsome ransom spared the **Uhrturm** (Clock Tower), now the city emblem, and the **Glockenturm** (Bell-tower) whose four-and-a-half ton bell "Lisl" is the biggest in town. The area was later tuned into a park and today is still a popular place for strolling and picnicking.

The Schlossberg is honeycomed by tunnels used as bomb shelters during the Second World War. A section of these is now used as the **Dom im Berg** (www.domimberg. at), an unusual performance and exhibition space right inside the mountain. The entrance is near the steps leading up the Schlossberg.

A wide chestnut-tree-lined avenue leads down to the clock tower rising from a colorful flower bed. The dial is unusual; for a long time it had only a single hand showing the hours. The smaller, minute hand was added later.

Go down the steps leading to the Herberstein gardens. From the terrace there are fine **views**★★ over the city and the Mur Valley.

▶ *Climb back up to the clock tower and then go down the first path on the right which leads backs into town to the Karmeliterplatz.*

Here there is a Trinity Column, erected in 1680 in thanksgiving for relief from the plague.

▶ *Go up the Paulustorgasse.*

Steirisches Volkskundemuseum (DY M²)

☎ 03 16/80 17 9899; Web site: www.volkskundemuseum-graz.at. ◷*Open Tues -Sun 10am-6pm (8pm close Thurs). Admission is* ⊜*€4.50*
This revamped museum devoted to Styrian folk art and traditions forms part of the Landesmuseum Joanneum *(below)* and has been housed since 1913 in a former Capuchin monastery. The exhibit is divided into three major themes: Wohnen (living), Kleiden (clothing) and Glauben (faith). Highlights include the Trachtenraum, a large room with 42 life-size figures showcasing the wealth of folkloric garments through the ages, and the Rauchstube, a smoke room typically found in old farmhouses.

Paulustor (DY)

Together with the Burgtor, this gateway is all that remains of the city walls. Built towards the end of the 16C, it displays the coats of arms, in marble, of Ferdinand II of Austria and of Maria Anna of Bavaria.

Stadtpark★ (DY)

This "English-style" park follows the line of the old walls to the east and southeast of the historic city center. At its center is the **Forum Stadtpark**, a meeting place of avant-garde artists since the 1960s. Outside this building, the **Stadtpark-Brunnen** (F) is a fountain in a luxuriant setting of fine old trees, shrubs and flowerbeds. Also in the park is the **Künstlerhaus**, a contemporary art exhibition space affiliated with the Landesmuseum Joanneum.

▶ *To get back to Hauptplatz, go south through the Stadtpark to the Burgtor, take Hofgasse west, then Sporgasse south and you'll be there.*

Additional Sights

Mariahilf-Kirche★ (CY)

One of the finest of the city's churches, with elegant twin towers and impeccably proportioned Baroque façade, this was the province's most popular place of pilgrimage after Mariazell.
It was begun in 1607-11 by Pietro de Pomis, architect of the Mausoleum and Schloss Eggenberg, who was buried here in 1633. The Late Baroque towers of 1742-44 are by Josef Hueber. Renaissance in structure, the interior of the nave gives an overall impression of harmony and repose. The door on the left of the façade leads to the cloisters, beyond which is a further courtyard with a little building in the style of the Renaissance, albeit designed as late as the end of the 17C. its first floor is given over entirely to the **Minoritensaal** (◷*Open Mon-Fri*

Mariahilf-Kirche, Graz

Georg Mikes

*8am-6pm. Check beforehand. ☎ 03 16/71 31 70), one of the city's concert halls. The building also houses the **Diözesanmuseum** (Diocesan Museum), with several centuries' worth of religious treasures from throughout Styria.*

Landesmuseum Joanneum (CDZ)

⟲*Open Tues-Sun 10am-5pm. Closed 1 Jan, Easter Mon and Whit Mon, 24, 25, 31 Dec.* ⊜€5 (admission free 26 Nov). ☎ 03 16/80 17 97 70; Web site: www.museum-joanneum.at.

The Joanneum is the country's oldest public museum complex and the second-largest museum in Austria after the Kunsthistorisches Museum in Vienna. Exhibits are spread over a number of buildings in and around Graz, including Schloss Eggenberg (Old Masters), the Kunsthaus (contemporary art) and the Volkskundemuseum (crafts and folkore). ⟳ *See individual entries for more on any of these.*

The two original buildings, donated to the city Archduke Johann, are in the heart of the old town. Natural history is the focus of the one in Räubergasse 10, and around the corner, at Neutorgasse 45, is the **Kulturhistorische Sammlung** (Cultural History Collection) where exhibits shed light on the daily lives of Styrians - peasants to nobility - from the Middle Ages to today.

Kunsthaus Graz★

⟲*Open Tue, Wed, Fri-Sun 10am-6pm, Thu 10am-8pm. www.kunsthausgraz.at.*

Opened in 2003, the Kunsthaus is Graz's newest landmark (Fournier & Cook), an architecturally bold exhibition space devoted to presenting art from the 1960s to the present. Sitting on the western bank of the Mur River, the avant-garde building vaguely resembles an alien heart with multiple aortas sprouting from its roof.

Leechkirche (DY)

Built between 1275 and 1293, the university church of Maria am Leech is the oldest religious building in Graz. The Early Gothic, many layered **west front**★ is crowned by a Virgin and Child on the tympanum, a work in Late Romanesque angular style. The **stained glass**★, which dates from 1330 and depicts various saints and the story of Christ's Passion, is of particular interest.

Excursions

Stift Rein★ (AX)

15km/9.5 mi northwest.

Founded in 1129, Rein is the oldest Cistercian abbey in Austria. Its buildings, dominated by the elegant Baroque tower, stand out against a background of wooded hills. Devastated by the Turks, the abbey was fortified in the 15C, then remodeled in the Baroque style in the 18C.

Stiftskirche★★

⟲*Basilica and cloisters open daily 7am-8pm (6pm from Nov to Easter). ☎ 0 31 24/5 16 21. www.stift-rein.at.*

Johann Georg Stengg, a master builder from Graz, presided over the transformation of the old Romanesque abbey church, which now has the rank of minor papal basilica. A new curvilenear façade leads to the light-flooded interior, designed by Josef Adam Mölck, is full of theatrical flourishes. A tour also takes in the abbey's library with its precious collection of calendars, including the oldest German one from 1373 and a calendar table used by Johannes Kepler in 1607.

Wallfahrtskirche Mariatrost

7km/4mi east via road no 72 (BX).

This glorious pilgrimage church (c1714) dedicated to the Virgin Mary is strikingly sited in its leafy suburban setting and easily identifiable by its twin towers.

SCHLOSS GREILLENSTEIN★

This hulking Renaissance castle with its distinctive single tower was built in the late 16C as the residence and representative office of local landowner Hans Georg II of Kufstein. Still owned by the same family today, it preserves many original fittings and is also famous for its Baroque sandstone sculptures of dwarves and other fanciful creatures.

▶ **Orient Yourself:** The Schloss is in the Waldviertel in northern Austria, not far from the Czech border and about 100km/60mi northwest of Vienna.

Kids **Especially for Kids:** The castle runs special programs for kids, including guided tours, ghost tours, birthday parties and staged courtroom trials.

🕓 **Organizing Your Time:** Plan on spending no more than two hours at the castle, including a 40min guided tour.

👁 **Also See:** Stift Altenburg, Eggenburg, Schloss Rosenburg

Tour

🕓*Open Apr-Oct, daily 9.30am-5pm.* ⊜*€4.* ☎ *0 29 89/80 80 21. www.greillenstein.at.*

Exterior

The Baroque balustrade in front of the castle is adorned with sculptures worthy of an entire fable: how a raging lion is transformed into the most gentle of beasts, mirroring the triumph of good over evil. In the inner courtyard with its two-tiered arcaded loggia, you'll find those famous dwarves as well as an expressive dragon fountain.

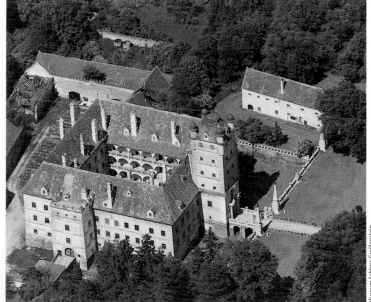

Museum Schloss Greillenstein

Schloss Greillenstein

Interior

From the 16C onwards Greillenstein had jurisdiction over an area covering 14 local villages. The filing cabinets and pigeon holes containing original period documents are still there, as is the baronial **courtroom**★. Also of note is the **Turkish Room**, which contains souvenirs collected by a family member who served as ambassador to Turkey in 1628/9. During his stay he succeeded in signing a peace treaty that resulted in a ceasefire lasting 25 years. The chapel has delicate net-vaulting and an elegant **Renaissance altar**★.

GROSSGLOCKNER-HOCHALPENSTRASSE★★★

SALZBURG UND KÄRNTEN

The Grossglockner Alpine Road is the most famous of all Austrian mountain roads and has exerted its magic on more than 50 million people since opening in 1935. It leads to the celebrated Grossglockner, the highest peak in the Austrian Alps (3797m/12 457ft). The region is an integral part of the Hohe Tauern National Park designated particulary to protect the Alpine flora and fauna. ❰ *Rainerstraße 2, Salzburg, A-5020, ☎ 0662 / 8 73 67 30. www.grossglockner.com.*

▸ **Orient Yourself:** The road runs north-south through western Austria, essentially linking Bavaria (Germany) with Italy.

⊘ **Don't Miss:** Franz-Josefs-Höhe, Edelweissspitze

🕓 **Organizing Your Time:** You'll want to allow plenty of time (up to a full day) to negotiate this steep road and to enjoy its breathtaking vistas.

VIENNASLIDE

The Großglockner

Kids **Especially for Kids:** There's a children's playground at Fuscher Lacke and a snow sliding area at Hochtor.

Promoting tourism loomed large in the concept of this great highway, notably in the construction of two spurs. One leads to the summit of the Edelweiß-Spitze, the other to the Franz-Josefs-Höhe. The road is usually blocked by snow from November to early May. The Edelweiss-Spitze and Franz-Josefs-Höhe may be closed even longer.

From Zell am See to Heiligenblut *75km/47mi*

Zell am See★   *See Zell am See.*

South of Zell am See the road to the Grossglockner begins at Bruck. It plunges into the **Fuschertal**, a dark and sparsely populated valley. Between Fusch and Ferleiten the route gets hillier and passes above the **Bärenschlucht**, a little wooded gorge. Beyond here, you can spot the rocky and jagged **Sonnenwelleck** group and the rounded Fuscherkarkopf.
From **Ferleiten** *(toll point)* to the Fuscher Törl the route begins its twisting climb. Above the Piffkar ravine (alt 1 620m/5 315ft) the **views**★★ are magnificent, especially from the Hochmais parking lot (alt 1 850m/6 070ft). The last larches disappear and the road continues as a corniche as far as the Nassfeld bridges. From here it passes through a rocky wasteland known as Witches' Kitchen (Hexenküche) and climbs across the basins of the Nassfeld. About 2km/1mi before the pass it reaches a nature museum.

Haus Alpine Naturschau★
🕙*Open May-Oct, daily 9am-5pm. Admission free.* ☎ *06 62/8 73 67 30.*
This little museum is devoted to Alpine ecology above the tree-line and gives a clear demonstration of the complex interrelations between flora and fauna. For an introduction, don't miss the multimedia presentation in the movie theater. Outside, a nature trail offers more interesting tidbits about local plantlife and geology.

Edelweißspitze★★
Alt 2 577m/8 455ft. *No access for coaches. Very steep road.*
At the highest point of the road, you'll be rewarded with a spectacular panorama taking in more than 30 mountains above 3000m/9900ft high. The peak of the Grossglockner can be seen just behind the Sonnenwelleck.

Fuscher Törl★
Alt 2 428m/7 964ft. *Park at Fuscher Törl 2.*
The road builders used this "little gate" (Törlein) to form a panoramic bend. **Views**★★ of the Glockglockner and surrounding peaks from the platform are among the best along the road. There's also a memorial to the construction workers who died in building this road.

Fuscher Lacke
Kids Alt 2 262m/7 422ft. An information center here contains displays on the construction of this grand Alpine road. A path leads round the lake for those wishing to stretch their legs. There's also

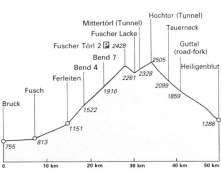

an imaginative **adventure playground** where little ones can fancy themselves as mountain road builders.

Hochtor

Kids The road reaches its highest point (2 505m/8 218ft) at the north end of the tunnel, which marks the boundary between Salzburg and Carinthia. If you feel like a little exercise, follow the 30-minute educational trail starting on either end of the tunnel, where information panels illustrate the story of this 4 000-year-old trade route. Kids love the snow sliding area near the north portal.

The winding descent from the Hochtor passes through Alpine pastures within view of the Schober massif, which forms a crown round the Gössnitz Valley.

From the **Guttal ravine**, turn right onto the "Glacier Road" (Gletscherstraße) leading to Franz-Josefs-Höhe.

During the holiday season and fine weather there can be delays on the trip up to Franz-Josefs-Höhe, as parking lots fill to capacity. In this case, visitors will be directed to overflow lots from where a shuttle service operates to Franz-Josefs-Höhe.

Schöneck

Alt 1 958m/6 424ft. Between the inn at Schöneck and the Glocknerhaus lie the ockhorner Alpine meadows with their wonderful variety of unique plantlife. The **Wunderwelt Glocknerwiesen** nature display and botanical trail at Schöneck give an overview of Alpine flora and insects in this area.

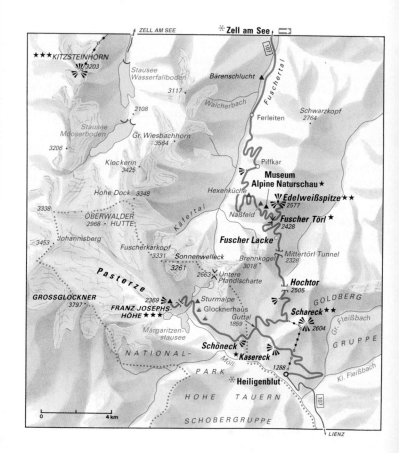

Franz-Josefs-Höhe★★★

The Glacier Road ends at a long panoramic terrace from where you'll have the full-on view of the Grossglockner as well as the longest glacier in the eastern Alps, the 10km/6mi-long **Pasterze**, which is served by a funicular (*"Gletscherbahn" (funicular) operates mid May-end Sept, daily 9am-4pm. €8 roundtrip. ☎ 0 48 24/25 02).*

Views are best from the last platform, the Freiwandeck. From here the Panoramaweg Kaiserstein, laid out as a botanical trail, leads to the **Swarovski observation point**. The glass tower is equipped with free telescopes for close-ups of the surrounding mountain scenery. The visitors' center has four floors of exhibits, including a 'rock and ice path' sensory experience and a new presentation taking you into the frosty world of glaciers. In summer, the area is the starting point for hikes and climbing tours in the Grossglockner massif.

▶ *Retrace the route to the Guttal fork and turn right towards Heiligenblut.*

Kasereck★

Alt 1 913m/6 276ft. More great views of the Grossglockner and the Heiligenblut basin, this spot also has a cheesemaking establishment open to the public.

Driving down to Heiligenblut, note the unusual wooden grain dryers in the form of grilles (known locally as "harps"). The last hairpin bend, curving above the Fleiss Valley, reveals the Sonnblick. A little further on there is the famous view of the church of Heiligenblut, a slender stone spire standing out against the background of the far-off Grossglockner.

Heiligenblut★ *See Heiligenblut.*

GURGLER TAL★★

TIROL

The Gurgl valley, which branches off the **upper valley of the Ötz** (*see Ötztal*), ranks among the most remarkable holiday destinations in the Austrian Tyrol. Its exceptional **setting** makes it a favorite location for hikers and skiers.

▶ **Orient Yourself:** Gurgl Valley is in southwestern Austria, close to the border with Italy.

Also See: Ötztal, Stubaital

Action and accommodation concentrate in **Obergurgl**★ (alt 1 793-1 930m/5 883-6 332ft), which has great **views**★ of the 20 surrounding mountains above 3 000m/10 000ft; and in **Hochgurgl**★ (alt 2 150m/7 054ft), Austria's highest-lying village and a popular winter sports resort.

Ski slopes

These cover 110km/68mi of pistes of varying degrees of difficulty at altitudes ranging from 1 800m/5 906ft to 3 082m/10 112ft. They are equipped with 23 ski lifts. The high altitude guarantees snow cover from November to May. There are 12km/7.5mi of cross-country ski runs.

Hohe Mut★★

Alt 2 653m/8 704ft. *Allow 1hr roundtrip. Take the chair-lift up in two stages. Lifts operate July-end Sept, Dec-end Apr, daily 8.45am-4pm. €12 roundtrip. ☎ 0 52 56/62 74.*

There is a splendid **panorama**★★ of the Rotmoosferner and Gaisbergferner glaciers to the southeast and of the Manigenbach to the west.

The easy walks listed below can be combined to make up a pleasant day's outing.

Hohe Mut to Schönwieshütte★★
400m/1 300ft drop in altitude.

Those in a hurry can reach the Schönwies refuge in about 1hr from the Hohe Mut chair-lift station. It is preferable, however, to follow the trail below the cliff to the foot of the **Rotmoosferner glacier**★★ and then carry on along the valley floor following the Gebirgsbach creek. The path leads through a majestic and captivating Alpine setting.

The refuge can also be reached in about 1hr via a wide trail from Obergurgl.

Around Schönwieshütte★
Allow 1hr 30min roundtrip.

Two easy detours are recommended from the refuge. Go towards the Langtalereck-hütte as far as the so-called **Gurgler Alm** (alt 2 252m/7 388ft), from where there is a **view**★ of the three glaciers higher up with the Schalfkogel (alt 3 540m/11 614ft) at the center.

Backtrack and turn left shortly before the refuge towards the Schönwieskopf (alt 2 324m/7 625ft). From the summit a **panorama**★ stretches across the valley.

Schönwieshütte to Obergurgl via Zirbelwald★
1hr 15min, dropping 330m/1 080ft in altitude.

From the refuge take the trail towards Obergurgl, soon turning left and heading a steep path downhill past the impressive **Rotmoos waterfall**★. Take the left fork into the woods and along the valley floor. You might even spot some chamois.

GURK★★

KÄRNTEN

Gurk is a small village that would be fairly unremarkable were it not for its famous cathedral, which ranks as Austria's most important Romanesque building. A convent was founded here in 1043 by Countess Hemma of Friesach-Zeltschach. However, it was dissolved less than three decades later by Archbishop Gebhard of Salzburg, who instead established a new diocese in an effort to consolidate his power upon the region. The Augustinian canons remained in this secluded valley until 1787, when the diocese was transferred to more prominent Klagenfurt. Since 1932, the convent has been run by Salvatorians.  *Dr.-Schnerich-Straße. 12, A-9342, ☎ 0 42 66/81 25 21; www.dom-zu-gurk.at.*

▶ **Orient Yourself:** Gurk is about 42km/26mi north of Klagenfurt in southern Austria.

⚑ **Also See:** Friesach, St Veit an der Glan

Cathedral *(Dom)*

The High Romanesque cathedral was built between 1140 and 1200 under Prince-Bishop Roman I, councillor to Frederick Barbarossa. Baroque gemel windows and onion domes were added to both towers in 1680.

Porches

The exterior wall of the front porch dates to the Gothic period, but inside there is some stained glass from 1340 along with **frescoes**★ depicting scenes from the Old Testament on the left and from the New Testament on the right. A Romanesque **door**★★ (c 1200) with richly decorated pillars, arches and capitals leads into the main nave.

Interior

◔ *Open Apr-Oct, daily 9am-5pm; Nov-Mar, daily 10am-4pm. 45min tour of cathedral and crypt 10.30am-5pm.* ⊛€4.60. ☏ 0 42 66/82 36 12.

It is immediately evident upon entering that many styles have contributed to this building: the Romanesque triple-nave pillared basilica is surmounted by Gothic net vaulting, the frescoes are from the Gothic and Renaissance periods, while the furnishings are predominantly Baroque.

(1) Jewel-encrusted Hemma reliquary in the form of a tree containing a ring and a pendant thought to have belonged to the saint (1955)

(2) Samson doorway: the **tympanum**★ shows Samson slaying the lion (1200).

(3) and (8): **Carved panels**★ (16C) vividly depicting scenes from the life of St Hemma, commissioned before 1508.

(4) A gigantic **mural of St Christopher** (1250). The doorway to the left with its richly decorated ogee arch was built in 1445.

(5) **High Altar**★★, a gilded masterpiece by Michael Hönel filling the entire apse. Covered in gold, it features full-size, strikingly realistic figures (72 statues, 82 angels' heads) and the four Evangelists at pedestal level with the Church Fathers above them. Created between 1626 and 1632, its central theme is the *Assumption of the Virgin*.

During Lent the altar is shrouded by a **Fastentuch**★ (Lenten veil, 1458), a custom that was abolished almost everywhere in the late Middle Ages. The exquisite veil is 9m/30ft square and is painted with 99 Biblical scenes. (☛ *The Lenten veil can be seen as part of a guided tour, Guided tour (20min) enquire about exact times. €2,91 (free during Lent).* ☏ 0 42 66/82 36 12.)

(6) **Choir stalls**: these richly and decoratively carved stalls are the work of local craftsmen. Each seat, crowned with the head of a cherub, is decorated with charming painted floral motifs (1680).

(7) **Gothic murals**: uncovered at the beginning of the 20C, these illustrate the conversion of St Paul, and Christ enthroned as Judge of the World, surrounded by the Twenty Four Elders of the Apocalypse as narrated by St John the Divine. The donors can be seen at the foot of Christ's throne with their nine children (c 1390).

(8) ♿ *See* (3) *above.*

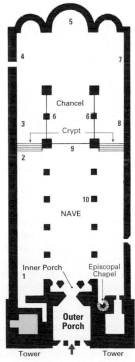

(9) **Altar of the Holy Cross** (1741), with a **Pietà**★ cast in lead by Georg Raphael Donner, his last work.

(10) **Baroque pulpit**★ (1740), an accomplished work by Viennese set designers Giuseppe and Antonio Galli Bibiena. The iconography is fully in keeping with the ideas of the Counter Reformation, taking as its subject the triumph of the Church. The lead reliefs around the body of the pulpit are also by Donner.

Crypt★★

Bathed in somber light, the masterful Romanesque crypt (1174) is supported by a 'forest' of 100 marble pillars. Since 1174 it has sheltered the stone sarcophagus of Hemma, patron saint of Carinthia, who was canonized in 1938. The present tomb is a red-marble extravaganza from the 1720s. It rests on three Romanesque support pillars with marble heads.

Bishop's Chapel

⏲*Open 9am-dusk.* 👣 *Must be seen on guided tour. Guided tour (20min) enquire about exact times and prices.* ☎ *0 42 66/82 36 12.*

The upstairs chapel has some exceptionally well-preserved Romanesque **murals**★★ (c 1260), whose vivid colors have not been touched up. They depict numerous Biblical scenes and characters, including Paradise, Heavenly Jerusalem, the Virgin Mary on King Solomon's throne and the Evangelists.

The stained-glass window on the west wall is contemporary with the frescoes and depicts the Descent from the Cross. This is Austria's earliest stained glass in the angular style.

Excursion

Strassburg

This small town within sight of Gurk is dominated by its **Schloss** (⏲*Open May-26 Oct, daily 10am-6pm;* ⚄*€2,20;* ☎ *0 42 66/23 75),* which for centuries was a bishops' palace until the diocese was relocated to Klagenfurt in 1787. Today it houses a small but fine collection of folkloric items illustrating peasant life and a room dedicated to hunting. The arcaded Renaissance courtyard hosts a summer concert series.

HALL IN TIROL★

TIROL
POPULATION 11 500 – ALT 574M/1 880FT

Hall on the River Inn was the salt town of the Inn Valley. During the Middle Ages, it played a key role in the economic life of the country and ranked among Austria's wealthiest cities, receiving town rights in 1303. In 1477, the local rulers moved the Tyrolean mint from Meran to Hall. The most famous coin produced here was the Haller Silbertaler, which was accepted all over Europe until the early 19C and became the namesake of the US dollar. Modern Hall is still wrapped in the charm of the Middle Ages yet keeps firmly in touch with the present as a highly active cultural and economic center. 🛈 *Wallpachgasse 5, A-6060,* ☎ *0 52 23/56 26 90. www.hall-in-tirol.at.*

▸ **Orient Yourself:** Hall is about 10km east of Innsbruck.

🅿 **Parking:** Look for parking garages on Fassergasse near Stadtgraben and on the corner of Bruckergasse and Stadtgraben.

- **Don't Miss:** Münze Hall, Münzerturm
- **Especially for Kids:** Münze Hall
- **Also See:** Innsbruck, Schwaz

Upper Town★ *(Obere Stadt)*

No traffic is allowed in the Upper Town on Saturday mornings.

▶ *From Unterer Stadtplatz (24), take the Langer Graben up to Oberer Stadtplatz.*

Oberer Stadtplatz

Hall's main square is the heart of the old town and hemmed in by attractive medieval buildings. This is where you'll find the **Stadtpfarrkirche**★ (A), the late-13C parish church that was repeatedly enlarged, resulting in a generously proportioned but asymmetrical three-nave hall church. The decoration is now largely Baroque. Note the ceiling frescoes by Joseph Adam von Mölck and a high altar adorned with a painting by Quellini, a pupil of Rubens. The **Waldaufkapelle** (late 15C) to the left of the high altar houses a Late Gothic figure of the Virgin Mary from the circle of Michael Pacher alongside sumptuously decorated reliquaries.

On the west side of the square is the **Rathaus** (R), which was originally the residence of Heinrich, King of Bohemia, and donated to the town by Duke Leopold IV in 1406. The council chamber is particularly handsome with its beamed ceiling from 1451.

▶ *Follow Agramgasse (2), Quarinongasse (12) and Schulgasse (16) to the Stiftsplatz.*

Stiftsplatz *(20)*

This square is bounded in the east by the austere façade of the Jesuitenkirche (Jesuit church, now a concert hall), and in the south by the Baroque ones of the **Damenstift**, a former convent for noble ladies founded by Archduchess Magdalena, the sister of Archduke Ferdinand II in 1579. The **west front**★ with its four full-length fluted pilasters is a fine example of the transition from the Renaissance to the Baroque style.

HALL IN TIROL	
Agramsgasse	2
Eugenstr.	3
Guarinonigasse	4
Krippgasse	5
Langer Graben	7
Milserstr.	8
Rosengasse	13
Salvatorgasse	14
Scheidensteinstr.	15
Schulgasse	16
Schweighofferstiege	17
Speckbacherstr.	18
Stiftspl.	20
Unterer Stadtpl.	24
Wallpachgasse	25
Rathaus	R
Stadtpfarrkirche	A

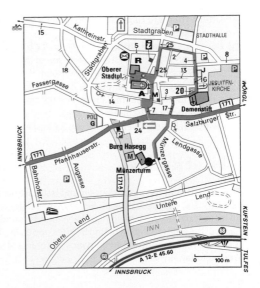

▶ *Return to Unterer Stadtplatz via Eugenstraße (3) and the Schweigerhofstiege steps (17) to the left. Follow Münzergasse to Burg Hasegg.*

Burg Hasegg

🕒*Open Apr-Oct, Tue-Sun, 10am-5pm; Nov-Mar, Tue-Sat, 10am-5pm.*✆€6. ☎ 0 52 23/5 85 51 65. www.muenze-hall.at.

📷 Dominated by its landmark tower, Hall's castle originated in the 13C to protect the city, the salt mines and the river traffic. Its historical importance soared in 1567, when the Tyrolean rulers transferred their mint here. Closed in 1809, it reopened in 1975 and still produces commemorative coins on a regular basis.

The city's minting history is creatively chronicled at the **Münze Hall**★ inside the castle. You'll see a cylindrical stamping press, interactive coin displays and even get to mint your own coin. Admission includes audio-guides (also in English).

Climb the architecturally distinguished **Münzerturm** *((admission €4, or €8 in combination with museum)* with its new spiral staircase for splendid views of the town and the impressive mountain range to the north.

The castle also harbors the **Stadtmuseum** (local history museum), which was being revamped at the time of writing and expected to reopen in 2009.

HALLSTATT★★

OBERÖSTERREICH
POPULATION 950 – ALT 511M/1 677FT

Hallstatt crouches beneath the Salzberg in a breathtaking setting on the Hallstätter See★★, a deep and dark green lake backed by the craggy peaks of the Dachstein range. Often deluged by day trippers, it provides the quintessential picture of romantic Austria with streets so steep and narrow that the famous Corpus Christi procession has to take place mostly in boats on the lake. In 1998 the Hallstatt region, including the Dachstein range and central Salzkammergut, was declared a UNESCO world heritage site. 🚇 *Seestr. 169, A-4830,* ☎ *0 61 34/82 08. www.hallstatt.net.*

▶ **Orient Yourself:** Hallstatt on the southwestern shore of the Hallstätter See in the Salzkammergut

📍 **Parking:** Central Hallstatt is closed to traffic from 10am-5pm May-Oct. An automated parking guide system directs you to the nearest parking lot.

🚫 **Don't Miss:** Salzwelten Hallstatt, Museum Hallstatt

🕒 **Organizing Your Time:** Budget half a day for the Salzbergwerk and another half day for the Museum Hallstatt and the church.

📷 **Especially for Kids:** Salzwelten Hallstatt, Museum Hallstatt

👁 **Also See:** Eisriesenwelt, Dachstein, Gosauseen, Bad Aussee

A Bit of History

The salt mines in the mountains around Hallstatt have been exploited since the Neolithic Era, but the first major heyday came in the Bronze Age around 1200 BC. So many traces of salt mining have been found around Hallstatt that it coined the name of the Hallstatt Period dating from 850 to 500 BC. The most startling evidence is a vast Iron Age cemetery with over 4000 graves. The salt mines are still being worked today.

Sights

Pfarrkirche Mariae Himmelfahrt

Overlooking the lake from its perch above the central Marktplatz, Hallstatt's parish church has 12C Romanesque origins but only a squat tower to prove it, while the rest of the building is mostly 15C Late Gothic. The three winged **altars**★ also date to this period. The most accomplished of these is the one on the right, which shows the Virgin flanked by Sts Barbara and Catherine.

Perhaps more interesting than the church itself is the two-story Michaelskapelle across the tiny graveyard, which houses the macabre but fascinating **Beinhaus**★. This small charnel house contains some 600 skulls, all stacked up neatly and painted with flower motifs, the name and other personal details of the person. New skulls are still being added once in a while.

Museum Hallstatt

Open May-Sept, daily 10am-6pm; Apr, Oct, daily 10am-4pm; Nov-Mar 11am-3pm Wed-Sun. €7.50; 0 61 34/82 80 15. www.museum-hallstatt.at.

This completely revamped and updated museum takes visitors on an educational, high-tech romp through 7000 years of regional history. Special emphasis is given to the Hallstatt Period with an impressive selection of archaeological finds, including weapons, tools and human bones. Other themed sections zero in on periods of Celtic and Roman occupations, religious strife, the big fire of 1750, coin minting, tourism and many other topics.

Salzwelten Hallstatt

Allow 3hr for this excursion. ☞ *Tours (70min) every half-hour; 29 Apr-17 Sept, daily 9am-4.30pm; 18 Sept-1 Oct, daily 9am-3.30pm; 2 Oct-26 Oct, daily 9am-3pm. Temperature is 8oC/46oF inside the mine. €15.50. 0 61 34/84 00. www.saltwelten.at.*

Hallstatt's salt mines in the Salzberg above town are considered the oldest in the world. It was here where a salt-preserved corpse, the so-called Man in Salt, was found in 1734. Sections of this warren of mines have been developed into an exhibition mine, which can be explored on a guided tour (in German and English). It takes in a salt crystal room, an underground salt lake, technical exhibits, displays about mining during the Bronze Age and the Hallstatt Period and other themes. Kids love schussing down the wooden slides once used by miners to travel quickly from one level to the next.

The mine can be reached on a 45-minute walk from the town center or a three-minute ride aboard the Salzbergbahn funicular (€8.50, or €21 with tour of the mines). From the mountain station, it's a 10min walk across the famous Iron Age graveyard to the mine entrance. Views are great from the **Rudolfsturm**, a tower built to defend the mine; it now houses a restaurant.

HEILIGENBLUT

KÄRNTEN
POPULATION 1 260 – ALT 1 288M/4 226FT

Postcard-pretty Heiligenblut is a gateway to the Hohe Tauern National Park and the Grossglockner Hochalpenstraße and often deluged with visitors. Its slender-spired church stands photogenically in silhouette against the Grossglockner. A-9844, 0 48 24/20 01 21. www.heiligenblut.at.

▶ **Orient Yourself:** Heligenblut is at the foot of the Grossglockner in southern Austria, about 38km/24mi north of Lienz.

◔ **Also See:** Grossglockner Hochalpenstraße

Ski slopes ☜

Heligenblut's slopes stretch between the Schareck, Gjaidtroghöhe and Viehbühel peaks at altitudes from 1 300m/4 265ft to 2 912m/9 554ft. There are 14 ski lifts and 55km/34mi of pistes with a variety of descents, well laid out through the rugged, treeless mountain landscape. In spite of the high altitude, snow conditions can begin to deteriorate as early as March.

Pfarrkirche★

Open daily 7am-7pm. Heiligenblut's parish church was built in the 15C by the monks of Admont to shelter a tiny vial of blood said to be Christ's, thereby giving the village its name. The twin-aisled crypt contains the tomb of Briccius, an officer of the Imperial Court of Byzantium, who allegedly brought the vial north in the 10C. Works of outstanding artistic merit include the **altarpiece**★ on the high altar (1520), attributed to the school of Michael Pacher, and the Gothic canopy (1496), ornately carved in pale sandstone.

Opposite the church is the **Hohe Tauern National Park Information Center** with a small but interesting exhibition on the Grossglockner.

Schareck★★

Alt 2 604m/8 543ft. *Cable-car ascent in two stages, then 10min walk to the summit.* ⏱*Operates mid June-end Sept, mid Dec-mid Apr, daily 9am-noon, 1pm-4pm.* ✆*€15.50 roundtrip.* ☎ *0 48 24/22 88.*

From the top of this mountain, the impressive **panorama**★★ encompasses 40 peaks towering to 3 000m/10 000ft, including the pyramidal Schildberg and the Grossglockner range to the west and the Gjaidtrog to the east.

STIFT HEILIGENKREUZ★

NIEDERÖSTERREICH

The Cistercian abbey of Heiligenkreuz was founded by the Babenberg Margrave Leopold III as a burial place for his dynasty. A fine example of Romanesque-Gothic architecture with Baroque embellishments, the abbey owes its name to a relic of the Holy Cross donated in the 12C by Duke Leopold V. It is the oldest continuously operating Cistercian abbey in the world and still has around 70 monks.

▶ **Orient Yourself:** The abbey is in the Wienerwald, about 15km west of Vienna.

◑ **Organizing Your Time:** Tours last 45min.

Tour

☜ *Tours Mon-Sat 10am, 11am, 2pm, 3pm and 4pm, Sun 11am, 2pm, 3pm and 4pm. Closed Good Friday, 24 Dec.* ✆*€6,20.* ☎ *0 22 58/87 03. www.stift-heiligenkreuz.at.*

Stiftskirche★

Behind the austere Romanesque façade lies the nave from the same period and a Gothic chancel from the 13C with fittings dating from the 19C. The other furnishings are Baroque in style, including fine **choir stalls** by Giovanni Giuliani. The Holy

The Cistercian Order

This reforming Benedictine order took its name from the monastery of Cîteaux in France, founded by Robert of Molesmes in 1098. The order grew rapidly in the 12C under Bernard of Clairvaux, who forbade the levying of tithes and the acquisition of land. He also encouraged precise observance of the Benedictine rules.

Cistercian architecture also adheres to strict principles. Churches are simple yet harmonious in their proportions and distinguished by purity of line. There is no bell-tower, only a ridge turret, and no stained glass, only *grisaille* painting. The initial austerity of Cistercian architecture mellowed over the centuries, with the result that pictures and statues are now to be seen in Cistercian churches.

The order still remains true to the *charta caritatis* promulgated in 1115, and has 300 monasteries and convents all over the world.

Cross reliquary is kept in a modern side church, the 1982 **Kreuzkirche**, off to the left of the chancel.

Cloister

The 13C cloister beautifully bridges the Romanesque and the Gothic, with rounded arches on its north side and pointed Gothic ones on the opposite side. There are two sculpture groups by Giuliani and a nine-sided fountain room (late 13C) with fine tracery and a Renaissance basin for the ablutions. The grey-black medieval **stained-glass windows** show members of the Babenberg dynasty.

Several chapels are just west of the cloister, including the square **Kapitelsaal** (chapterhouse), where the Babenbergs are buried and also depicted in murals.

Next door is the **Totenkapelle** (Chapel of the Dead) where the monks are laid out before burial. Giuliani was responsible for the decoration, including the somewhat macabre "dancing skeletons".

Sacristy

Tours conclude in the sacristy, reached across a small courtyard. The attractively decorated room has an old lavabo recess, and is 18C in style, even with some Rococo touches. The four splendid **sacristy cupboards** with exceptionally fine marquetry were made by lay brothers in the early 19C.

Detail of a sacristy cupboard, Heiligenkreuz

SCHLOSS HERBERSTEIN★

STEIERMARK

The fortress of Herberstein perches on a rocky spur, surrounded on three sides by the course of the Feistritz, in the middle of a rugged gorge. It has been modified numerous times during its 700-year existence and boasts Gothic, Renaissance and Baroque elements. The counts of Herberstein have occupied the castle without interruption since 1290.

▶ **Orient Yourself:** Herberstein is in southeast Austria, about 57km/29mi northeast of Graz.

Tour

Tickets cost €13 and include a palace tour (Apr-Oct only), the animal park, the gardens and the museums. ☎ *0 31 76/8 82 50. www.herberstein.at.*

Schloss
Guided tour (50min) Apr-Oct, daily noon, 1pm, 2pm, 3pm, 4pm.
Tours take in some of the oldest parts of the building, including a kitchen in use since the 16C , and provide glimpses into daily life at the palace during the 19C.

Tier- und Naturpark
Open Mar-Oct, daily 9am-5pm, Nov-Feb, daily 10am-4pm.
The zoo at Herberstein is a modern animal park with a history dating back to the 17C. It is home to animals from five continents, including bison, timberwolves, kangaroos, lions and leopards. The latter are in a special new enclosure that allows them to "hunt" for their dinner. For young visitors, there's also the Tikiba petting zoo.

Historical gardens
Open Mar-Oct, daily 9am-5pm; Nov-Feb, daily 10am-4pm.
These were restored in 1997 following old designs and a picture dating from 1681. In the center of the park stands the rose pavilion with a fountain of youth. The geometrically arranged beds symbolize different times of the day and types of human temperament. The "multimedia space" in the Siegmund garden forms a bridge between old and new.

Museums
Since 2004, Herberstein is home to the **Gironcoli-Museum** (*Open daily 10am-5pm*), devoted to the avant-garde sculptures of Bruno Gironcoli, one of Austria's most important contemporary artists. It's housed in a converted 16C barn with a modernist annex. Another building, the Kunsthaus, houses Gironcoli's impressive collectionof African masks and changing exhibits by contemporary artists.

BURG HOCHOSTERWITZ★

KÄRNTEN

Looking like everyone's idea of a romantic fairy-tale castle, Hochosterwitz occupies a dramatic **site**★★ on a rounded limestone rock rising 150m/490ft above the surrounding countryside. Its impressive towered and turreted outline and defence works can easily be spotted from several miles away.

▶ **Orient Yourself:** The fortress is in St Georg am Längsee, about 22km/14mi northeast of Klagenfurt in southern Austria.
P **Parking:** Below the castle.
⚲ **Also See:** St Veit an der Glan, Maria Saal, Klagenfurt

First documented in 860, the castle remained in the hands of the lords of Osterwitz until 1475, then reverted to the emperor and in 1571 was finally bought by Georg von Khevenhüller, an imperial counsellor and chief stablemaster. He greatly expanded

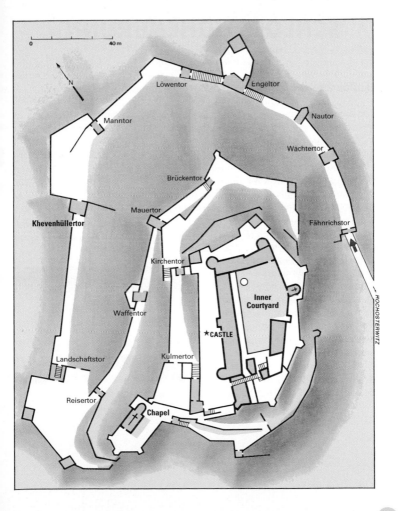

and fortified the castle to defend it against Turkish invasion, adding the 14 gateways and an arsenal. His descendents still own it today.

Tour

&⃝*Open May-Sept, daily 8am-6pm; Apr, Oct, daily 9am-5pm.* ☞*€7,50.* ☏ *0 42 13/20 20; www.burg-hochosterwitz.at.*

From the parking lot, a ramp passing through all 14 gates leads up to the castle in about 30min with some lovely views along the way. The grandest of the gates is the seventh, known as the **Khevenhüllertor** (1582), surmounted by a lion's head, the family coat of arms and a bust of Georg Khevenhüller dressed as a military leader. The ramp passes the **Burgkapelle** (castle chapel) and reaches the **Innere Burghof** (inner courtyard) with a restaurant. Some rooms in the castle have historical exhibits about the Khevenhüller family, family portraits and a fine collection of arms and armour. A faster but considerably less scenic way to get up to the castle is via an elevator (€5 roundtrip) ingeniously carved straight through the rock.

SCHLOSS HOHENBRUNN★

OBERÖSTERREICH

▶ **Orient Yourself:** The palace is about 1.5km/1mi west of St. Florian.

Too large for a hunting lodge and too open to the surrounding countryside ever to have made any pretense at defense, Schloss Hohenbrunn is set like a Palladian villa in attractive natural surrounds.
Schloss Hohenbrunn was built in the 18C as a hunting lodge for the abbey of St. Florian (&⃝ *see entry*) by one of Austria's most celebrated Baroque architects, the Tyrolean **Jakob Prandtauer**. Hohenbrunn is in fact the only castle that can definitely be attributed to him. The palace owes its name (Hoher Brunnen meaning high fountain) to the pumping appliance originally installed in a tower flanking the south façade.

Jagdmuseum★

Quite appropriately, the Schloss now houses the **Jagdmuseum**★ *(⃝Open Apr-Oct, daily 10am-noon and 1pm-5pm. €2.20)*, a thorough and informative exploration of hunting in Upper Austria. Expect plenty of weapons, models, plaster casts of footprints and stuffed animals but also hunting clothes once worn by Emperor Franz Joseph I and an extraordinary rifle (3.12m/10ft 3in long) belonging to Archduke Karl Salvator.

Schloss Hohenbrunn

Fremdenverkehrsamt Oberösterreich, Linz

INNSBRUCK★★

TIROL
POPULATION 140 000 – ALT 574M/1 883FT

Innsbruck (literally, Bridge over the Inn) is the capital of the Tyrol and a major cultural and tourism center that has twice hosted the Winter Olympic Games, in 1964 and 1976. Local life is closely linked with the mountain, and it's not uncommon for people to spend their midday break on the slopes. In summer, Innsbruck is often deluged with visitors milling about the pedestrianized historic center. The relative lack of industry has enabled the city to keep its charming provincial character, at least once the main thoroughfares are left behind.
🚊 *Burggraben 3, A-6021, ☎ 05 12/5 98 50 or* 🚊 *Hauptbahnhof, ☎ 05 12/58 37 66. www. innsbruck tourism.at.*

▸ **Orient Yourself:** Innsbruck is in the Inn Valley in western Austria, about 30km north of the Brennerpass to Italy.
🅿 **Parking:** Inner city parking garages and lots include: Congress-Garage, Herrengasse/Rennweg (daily until midnight); Europahaus, Meinhardstraße (daily 7am-10pm); Parkgarage Landhausplatz, Wilhelm-Greil-Straße (daily 7am-1am); Sparkassengarage, Erlerstraße (Mon-Fri 7am-9pm, Sat 8am-5pm); Maria-Theresien-Garage, Erlerstraße (daily 24hr), Parkgarage Altstadt, Tschamlerstraße (daily 7am-1am); City Parkgarage, Kaiserjägerstraße (daily 24hr).
🅰 **Don't Miss:** Dom zu St Jakob, Hofburg, Hofkirche
🕓 **Organizing Your Time:** Devote the better part of a full day to seeing the sites of Old Innsbruck, then spend half a day on a trip up the Hafelekar. Add another day if you're planning on touring the Mittelgebirge.
👟 **Also See:** Hall in Tirol

A Bit of History

The Tyrol came into existence as a state in the 12C under the jurisdiction of the counts of Tyrol but passed into Habsburg control in 1363. Duke Friedrich IV made Innsbruck his residence in 1420, ushering in a long heyday that reached its pinnacle under **Maximilian I** (1459-1519) who positioned the city as a European center of culture and politics. Through clever marriages, first to Maria of Burgundy, then to Bianca Maria Sforza of Milan, he managed to extend his sphere of influence to territories encompassing today's Belgium, Netherlands, northern France and northern Italy. In 1508, he became Holy Roman Emperor. Maximilian always nursed a special fondness for the Tyrol whose silver and copper mines brought him wealth, while its rich hunting grounds provided entertainment.
In 1806, during the Napoleonic Wars, the Tyrol fell under Bavarian rule and Innsbruck became the hub of a resistance movement led by Andreas Hofer, who is now celebrated as a national folk hero. The region reverted to Austria at the Vienna Congress in 1815.

General View

In town, the **Stadtturm** (tower – 👟 *see below)* offers the best view. For sweeping views over the city and the surrounding peaks, go up to the **Hungerburg**★ (AY), reached by car via the Alte Innbrücke (Old Bridge over the Inn), the Höttinger Gasse, the Hötting Church and the Höhenstraße. A new **funicular**, still under construction at the time of writing, should be completed in 2007.

Address Book

PRACTICAL INFORMATION

TOURIST INFORMATION

Innsbruck-Tourismus *Burggraben 3/11* Opening times: Mon-Fri 8am-6pm, Sat 8am-noon. Closed on Sun.

Innsbruck-Information (sales and bookings office for tickets, Innsbruck Cards, room reservations, city tours etc), *Burggraben 3, 6021 Innsbruck,* ☎ *05 12/53 56,* Fax *05 12/53 56 14.* Opening times: Mon-Sat 8am-7pm, Sun and public holidays 9am-6pm. Ticket office open Mon-Fri 8am-6pm, Sat 8am-5pm. Closed on Sun.

Tirol-Werbung, *Maria-Theresien-Straße 55, 6020 Innsbruck,* ☎ *05 12/53 20 0.* Opening times: Mon-Fri 8am-6pm. A monthly events calendar is available from Innsbruck-Tourismus and Innsbruck-Information.

INNSBRUCK CARD

These special visitors' tickets are available from Innsbruck-Information for 24hr (€23), 48hr (€28) or 72hr (€33) and cover free travel on public transport, including roundtrip cable-car rides on the Hungerburg-, Nordketten- and Patscherkofelbahn, and free or discounted entry to numerous museums and sights (including the Swarovski Kristallwelten at Wattens). For further details, call ☎ *05 12/53 56.*

CITY TOURS

Walks (1hr) – May-Oct, Dec 2pm, additional walk at 10am in June-Sept; €8.

Imperial Hofburg (1hr) – May-Oct, Dec 12.15pm, additional tour at 3.15pm June-Sept; €8.

PUBLIC TRANSPORT

Buy tickets before boarding the bus, since drivers only sell single tickets and charge a little extra. The 24hr pass entitles to unlimited trips within the city limits. Alternatively there are four-journey tickets, and weekly and monthly tickets to choose from. Tickets are available from Innsbruck-Information, the Innsbruck transport authorities (Stainerstraße 2, ☎ *05 12/5 30 70)* and tobacconist's shops with the appropriate sign. Further information can be found on the Internet *(www. ivb.at).*

POST OFFICES

Main post office: **Hauptpostamt**, *Maximilianstraße 2,* Mon-Sat 7am-11pm.

Station post office: **Bahnpostamt**, *Bruneckerstraße 1,* Mon-Sat 6.30am-9pm. ☎ *05 12/50 00.*

SHOPPING

The main shopping streets are Maria-Theresien-Straße, the pedestrian zone in the old town center around Herzog-Friedrich-Straße, and Museumstraße.

MARKETS

Franziskanerplatz: farm produce every Thurs 9am-1.30pm, bric-à-brac every Sat 7am-1pm.

Sparkassenplatz: farm produce every Fri 9am-2pm.

Rathaushof: flea market every 1st and 3rd Sat in the month 7am-1pm.

Christmas markets (Christkindlmärkte) are held in the old town and on Landhausplatz from late Nov to just before Christmas.

SOUVENIRS

Crafts and traditional costume (Trachten): Tiroler Heimatwerk, Meraner Straße 2-4.

ENTERTAINMENT

Tiroler Landestheater, *Rennweg 2,* ☎ *05 12/5 20 74.*

Kellertheater, *Adolf-Pichler-Platz 8,* ☎ *05 12/58 07 43.*

Theater an der Sill, *Kravoglstraße 19,* ☎ *05 12/36 29 29.*

Tiroler Volksbühne Blaas, *Maria-Theresien-Straße 12,* ☎ *05 12/58 60 01.*

Kulturgasthaus Bierstindl, *Klostergasse 6,* ☎ *05 12/57 57 57.* Old Innsbruck folk theatre, chivalry plays.

Treibhaus, *Angerzellgasse 8,* ☎ *05 12/57 20 00.* Range of performances including cabaret, jazz and world music.

Utopia Kulturzentrum, *Tschamlerstraße 3,* ☎ *05 12/58 85 87.* Concerts, events, performances, exhibitions.

Casino Innsbruck, *at the Hilton Hotel, Landhausplatz/Salurner Straße 15,* ☎ *05 12/5 87 04 00.*

CINEMAS

Cineplexx, *Wilhelm-Greil-Straße 23,* ☎ *05 12/58 14 57.*

Metropol Multiplex, *Innstraße 5*, ☎ *05 12/28 33 10*.

Central, *Maria-Theresien-Straße 17*, ☎ *05 12/58 80 78*.

Metropol, *Innstraße 5*, ☎ *05 12/28 33 10*.

Cineplexx, *Tschamlerstraße 7*, ☎ *05 12/58 14 00*.

Original-version films are shown at **Cinematograph** (*Museumstraße 31*, ☎ *05 12/57 85 00*) and **Cine-Royal** (*Innrain 16*, ☎ *05 12/58 63 85*).

WHERE TO EAT

Ottoburg – *Herzog-Friedrich-Straße 1*, ☎ *05 12/58 43 38*. Top-quality restaurant in one of Innsbruck's oldest buildings. Several tastefully fitted wood-paneled rooms. Reservation recommended.

Goldener Adler – *Herzog-Friedrich-Straße 6*, ☎ *05 12/57 11 11*. Elegant Tyrolean style restaurant. The illustrious guest list for the hotel of the same name includes Mozart, Heine, Camus and Sartre.

Weißes Kreuz – *Herzog-Friedrich-Straße 31*, ☎ *05 12/5 94 79*. Traditional Tyrolean inn with rooms decorated in rustic style.

Hirschen Stuben – *Kiesbachgasse 5*, ☎ *05 12/58 29 79*. Charming contrast between modern decor and old vaulting, with rotating exhibitions of works by contemporary artists.

Fischerhäusl – *Herrengasse 8 (by cathedral passage)*, ☎ *05 12/58 35 35*. Hidden restaurant with a peaceful, inviting garden.

CAFÉS AND BARS

Café Central – *Gilmstraße 11*. Viennese coffee house-style decor: stucco ceiling, chandeliers, palms – very classy!

Konditorei-Café Munding – *Kiesbachgasse 16*. This coffee house with a pleasant summer terrace is supposed to be the oldest cake shop in the Tyrol.

Krahvogel – *Anichstraße 12*. Cozy bar with a limited selection of food and a garden in the back courtyard.

Bellini's – *Meranerstraße 5*. This modern café-bar offers a taste of Italy in the middle of Innsbruck.

Theresienbräu – *Maria-Theresien-Straße 53*. Slightly off-the-wall bar

Herzog-Friedrich-Straße

aimed at a younger clientele with tasty beer brewed on the premises.

Sweet Basil – *Herzog-Friedrich-Straße 31*. Restaurant and two bars occupying several floors. Elegant, welcoming and very enjoyable.

Elferhaus – *Herzog-Friedrich-Straße 11*. Wide selection of beers from all over the world and a small food menu.

Piano – *Herzog-Friedrich-Straße 5*. Long café-bar with small picture gallery and several comfortable sofas conducive to taking the weight off your feet after a day of sightseeing.

Papa Joe's – *Seilergasse 12*. Grill, fast-food and bar. Hint of Latin America in the eclectic decor with fans and even a small "waterfall."

Hofgarten-Café – Very popular summer meeting place with a large terrace in the Hofgarten.

Café-Club Filou – *Stiftgasse 12*. Bar, restaurant and disco. Variety of seating ranging from bar stools to chairs and sofas. Drinks include beer, cocktails and even champagne.

Tip: in the **Ing.-Etzel-Straße** (level with the junction with Dreiheiligen-Straße) in the arches beneath the railway line there is something to suit every taste, from pizza outlets to music bars and trendy wine bars.

DATES FOR YOUR DIARY

Tanzsommer: June-July. High quality dance performances by international artistes.

Innsbruck Festival of Old Music/ Ambraser Schlosskonzerte: July-Aug.

Travelers coming from the Brenner via the B182 have another remarkable **view**★★ of the city panorama from the Sonnenburgerhof at one of the last road bends.

Old Innsbruck★

Maria-Theresien-Straße★ *(CZ)*

This lively "street-square" has an imposing **vista**★★ of the Nordkette (2 334m/7 657ft). Along here are several attractive old houses with beautiful façades, most notably Palais Lodron at no 7, Palais Troyer at no 39, Palais Trapp at no 38 and Palais Sarnthein at no 57.

Triumphpforte (CZ F)

This landmark triumphal arch was built to commemorate the marriage of Archduke Leopold to the infanta of Spain, Maria Ludovica in 1765. Since the wedding was overshadowed by the death of the duke's father, Emperor Franz I, the arch became a memorial to both the joys and the sorrows that year brought for the Imperial court. Medallions of Franz I and Maria Theresa are among the features gracing the north side, while imagery on the other side honors the newlyweds.

Altes Landhaus (DZ)

This palace at No 43 is an excellent example of secular Baroque architecture. It was designed by Georg-Anton Gumpp, completed in 1728 and is now the seat of the provincial government.

Annasäule (CZ A)

This monumental column (1706) commemorates the defeat of Bavaria on St Anne's day 1703. The Virgin Mary perches atop the slender column, with St Anne appearing only on the base beside St George and the dragon.

Stadtturm (tower) (CZ B)

◷*Open Jul-Aug, daily 10am-8pm; Sept-May, daily 10am-5pm.* ⊜€4,50. ☎ *05 12/56 15 00.*

Shortly past the column, Maria-Theresien-Straße segues into **Herzog-Friedrich-Straße**, eventually reaching this 51m-high Gothic tower that was originally part

Triumphpforte

A. Niederstrasser/ÖSTERREICH WERBUNG

of the old town hall of 1358. It's well worth climbing the 148 steps to a platform from where you'll enjoy a splendid **panorama**★.

Goldenes Dachl★ (Little Golden Roof) (CZ)

The Golden Roof is Innsbruck's most famous symbol. Consisting of 2738 gilded copper shingles, it tops a Late Gothic balconied oriel added to an existing building in 1500. It was commissioned by Maximlian I to mark his wedding to Bianca Maria Sforza and intended to show off his wealth and disperse rumors about financial woes. From the balcony, the imperial entourage observed festivals, tournaments and other events taking place on the square below.

The oriel itself is lavishly decorated. The balustrade on the first floor is adorned with eight delicately carved coats of arms. Above is a band of reliefs that includes pictures of the emperor (in the middle) and his two wives. All decorations are replicas, but the originals are on view at the Tiroler Landesmuseum Ferdinandeum (& see below).

Helblinghaus

M. Hertlein/MICHELIN

Maximilianeum

🕔*Open May-Sept, daily 10am-6pm; Oct-Apr, Tue-Sun 10am-5pm.* ✆€3,80. ☎ 05 12/58 11 11.

You can stand in the spot from where the imperial couple used to observe the square's goings-on by visiting this small Maximilian memorial exhibit in the building behind the Goldenes Dach. The 20min video about the emperor's life and times is well worth watching and an audio-guided tour (in English) provides additional insights.

Helblinghaus★ (CZ)

Opposite the Goldenes Dachl, the Helblinghaus has Gothic origins but got a frilly Rococo façade in the 18C.

▶ *Continue north on Pfarrgasse, which leads to the Domplatz.*

Dom zu St. Jakob★ (CZ)

&🕔*Open 12 May-25 Oct Mon-Sat 7.30am-7pm, Sun 8am-8pm; 26 Oct-11 May, Mon-Sat 7.30am-6pm, Sun 8am-6.30pm.* ☎ 05 12/58 39 02.

There has been a church on this spot since 1180, but successive buildings were destroyed by fire or earthquake, and the cathedral did not receive its characteristically curving, two-towered façade and great dome until the early 18C.

The Baroque **interior**★ was decorated in 1722 by the famous Asam brothers from Munich, Cosmas Damian (painter) and Egid Quirin (stucco artist). Their compositions, with their clever effects of perspective, glorify the Trinity and the intercessions of St James. The painting of *Our Lady of Succour* (Mariahilf), by Lucas Cranach the Elder, graces the **high altar**★. In the north transept is the canopied tomb of Archduke Maximilian III, a grand master of the Teutonic Order, who died in 1618. Daily at 12.15pm the **Friedensglockenspiel** (peace carillon) sounds from the north tower.

▶ *Backtrack south on Pfarrgasse,then turn left onto Hofgasse, then, after a covered alley, left again onto Rennweg.*

Hofburg★ (CZ)

&⊙*Open daily 9am-5pm (last admission 4.30pm). Closed 15 Aug. €5,45 (free admission 18 May and 26 Oct).* ☎ *05 12/58 71 86. www.hofburg-innsbruck.at.*

It's hard to imagine now, but this glorious palace has origins as a humble medieval castle. These are well concealed due partly to Maximilian I but, more importantly, to Maria Theresia who had the complex completely redesigned in the style of the Viennese rococo in the late 18C.

The state rooms are devoted to the glories of the Tyrol and of the Habsburg monarchy, especially the **Riesensaal**★★ (Giants' Hall), which is about 31.5m/100ft long and lined with stucco panels with a porcelain finish. The main theme of the ceiling fresco, by Franz-Anton Maulpertsch, is the triumph of the House of Habsburg-Lorraine. On the walls are full-length portraits of Maria Theresa's children following the Imperial couple in procession.

▶ *Return to the Rennweg and enter the Hofkirche (enter through the Tiroler Volkskunstmuseum to the left of the church).*

Hofkirche (CZ)

&⊙*Open Mon-Sat 9am-5pm (5.30pm July-Aug), Sun and public holidays 12.30pm-5pm. Closed 1 Jan, afternoon of Shrove Tues, Easter Day, Whit Sun, Corpus Christi, 1 Nov, 25 Dec. €3, incl Silberne Kapelle.* ☎ *05 12/58 43 02. www.hofkirche.at.*

This three-nave hall church is still largely Gothic, although the Renaissance style is already in evidence at the tower and the entrance porch, and there are Baroque embellishments as well. It was commissioned by Ferdinand I in the 1560s to house the mausoleum of his grandfather, Maximilian I, even though the emperor was actually buried in the castle chapel at Wiener Neustadt, his birth place.

Maximilian's Mausoleum★★ *(Grabmal Kaiser Maximilians I)*

This tomb is a premier example of German Renaissance sculpture and was personally designed by the Emperor Maximilian I. The lavish design centers on a cenotaph of the kneeling emperor atop a sarcophagus adorned with 24 alabaster reliefs showing scenes from his life carved by Flemish sculptor Alexandre Colin. Colin also created the four cardinal virtues positioned at the corners of the sarcophagus, which is surrounded by a splendid wrought-iron grille. Standing guard between the red marble pillars are 28 larger-than-life-size bronze statues (40 were planned) representing ancestors. Some were designed by such famous artists as Albrecht Dürer and Peter Vischer.

The Hofkirche also contains the tomb and memorial of **Andreas Hofer** (1767-1810), hero of the Tyrolean uprising against Napoleon. Look for it in the northern aisle.

The famous **Renaissance organ** in the choir is a work of Jörg Ebert of Ravensburg and has been largely preserved in its original state.

R. Chéret/MICHELIN

Mausoleum of Maximilian I – detail

Silberne Kapelle★★

This separate chapel, built by Archduke Ferdinand II so that he might rest beside Philippine Welser, his commoner wife, was finished in 1587. It owes its name to a large embossed silver Madonna. The first bay on your left contains the tomb of the duke's wife and is one of the most accomplished works of Alexandre Colin. Colin also sculpted the funeral statue of Ferdinand showing him in full armour. His actual armour is displayed separately on a console, in a kneeling position, facing the altar. A small 16C cedarwood organ, of Italian origin, completes the collection of works of art housed in the chapel.

Hofgarten (DZ)

This public park with free-roaming parrots was laid out in the 16C under Archduke Ferdinand II and was one of the most ambitious gardens north of the Alps at the time. Given a Baroque character under Maria Theresa, it was landscaped as a less formal park in the early 19C.

Tiroler Volkskunstmuseum★★ (CDZ)

Open Mon-Sat 9am-5pm (5.30pm July-Aug), Sun 9am-noon. Closed 1 Jan, afternoon of Shrove Tues, Easter Day, Whit Sun, Corpus Christi, 1 Nov, 25 Dec. €5. 05 12/58 43 02. www.tiroler-volkskunstmuseum.at.

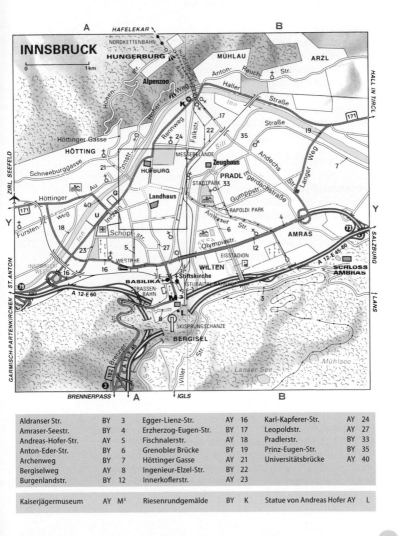

Aldranser Str.	BY	3	Egger-Lienz-Str.	AY	16	Karl-Kapferer-Str.	AY	24
Amraser-Seestr.	BY	4	Erzherzog-Eugen-Str.	BY	17	Leopoldstr.	AY	27
Andreas-Hofer-Str.	AY	5	Fischnalerstr.	AY	18	Pradlerstr.	BY	33
Anton-Eder-Str.	BY	6	Grenobler Brücke	BY	19	Prinz-Eugen-Str.	BY	35
Archenweg	BY	7	Höttinger Gasse	AY	21	Universitätsbrücke	AY	40
Bergiselweg	AY	8	Ingenieur-Elzel-Str.	BY	22			
Burgenlandstr.	BY	12	Innerkoflerstr.	AY	23			

Kaiserjägermuseum	AY	M³	Riesenrundgemälde	BY	K	Statue von Andreas Hofer AY	L

Next to the Hofkirche, this museum exhaustively covers the gamut of folk art from the entire Tyrol, including South Tyrol in today's Italy. The ground floor has special exhibits and a beautiful collection of Nativity scenes. Upstairs, displays include models of farmhouses, Gothic rooms and intriguing carnival masks and costumes. The top floor features Renaissance and Baroque period rooms, folkloric festival garments and a valuable collection of religious folk art.

▶ *Take the Angerzellgasse onto Museumsstraße to get to the "Ferdinandeum."*

Tirolermuseum Ferdinandeum★ (DZ M²)

Ⓖ🕓*Open Mon-Wed, Fri-Sun 10am-6pm, Thur 10am-9pm. Closed 1 Jan, 25 Dec. (free admission 26 Oct).* €8. ☎ 05 12/59 48 91 10. www.tiroler-landesmuseum. at.
Although it possesses not inconsiderable prehistory and early history collections, displayed in the basement, this museum is devoted essentially to the development of the fine arts in the Tyrol from the Romanesque to the present. Highlights include masterworks from the Gothic age (Multscher, Pacher) and the Baroque (Troger). There is also a good collection of Dutch masters as well as historical musical instruments on the 2nd floor and modern art on the 3rd.

Zeughaus★

🕓*Open June-Sept, daily 10am-5pm; Oct-May, Tue-Sun 10am-5pm. Closed Dec 25 and Jan 1.* €5.50. b 05 12/5 94 89 311. www.tiroler-landesmuseum.at.
The former armoury, commissioned by Maximilian I in 1503 and completed in 1506, now houses the Tyrolean cultural history collection of the Tiroler Landesmuseum. The eight themed rooms take you on a journey through the ages, covering such subjects as the importance of silver and salt mining to the region's development, the story of resistance leader and local hero Andreas Hofer and post-WWII Tyrol.

Additional Sights

Riesenrundgemälde (Bergisel Panorama) (ABY K)

🕓*Open 1 Apr-30 Oct, daily 9am-5pm.* €3. ☎ 05 12/58 44 34.
This huge circular oil painting depicting the Battle of Bergisel on 13 August 1809 was painted in 1896 in honor of Andreas Hofer, hero of the Tyrolean uprising against Napoleon. It is an amazing technical achievement (10m/33ft high by 100m/330ft long) that took only six months to complete.

Hungerburgbahn (CZ)

Still under construction at press time, the new Hungerburgbahn is a funicular running below ground from the Congresshaus to the Löwenhaus where it crosses an elegant bridge designed by star architect Zaha Hadid before entering a tunnel. It re-emerges at the Alpenzoo (🐾 *see next*) and ends at the Hungerburg mountain station, which was also completely resdesigned by Hadid. From here you can continue up the mountain aboard an equally brand-new two-stage cable-car to the Nordpark-Seegrube ski area and the Hafelekar peak at 2 334m/7 657ft. From here, you'll have a fabulous **view** ★★ over the Inn Valley, the Stubai Alps and the rugged Karwendel cliffs.

Alpenzoo (AY)

🕓*Open daily 9am-6pm (5pm in winter).* €7. ☎ 05 12/29 23 23.
Halfway up the Hungerburgbahn, Innsbruck's zoo is the highest In Europe and is home to 2000 animals from 150 species, most of them found in the Alpine region. Rare indigenous species of fish tumble around the cold-water aquarium.

Innsbruck-Wilten, Bergisel and Amras

Wilten

Dominating the southeastern suburb of Wilten is the twin-towered **Basilica**★ (**AY**; ⏰*Open 15 May-1 Oct, Mon-Fri 8.30am-5pm, Sat 8.30am-noon, Sun 8am-7pm; 2 Oct-14 May 8am-7pm daily except Sat* ☎ *05 12/58 33 85*). Completely restored in the 1750s, this former parish church was raised to basilica in 1957 and has a sumptuous rococo **interior** decorated by a team led by stucco artist Franz-Xaver Feichtmayr of the Wessobrunn School, and Matthäus Günther from Augsburg. The latter's ceiling paintings depict the Virgin Mary as an intercessor (chancel) and Esther and Judith (nave). The statue of the Virgin Mary, which is the main object of veneration with pilgrims, is enthroned in glory at the high altar, under a baldaquin supported on marble columns.

M. Hertlein/MICHELIN

Wilten Abbey Church

Nearby is the **Stiftskirche (ABY; ⚷** *closed for restoration until at least 2008.* ☎ *05 12/58 30 48)*, a Baroque church with a distinctive yellow-red façade. According to legend, the abbey was founded by the giant Haymon in atonement for slaying fellow giant Thyrsus. That's them in stone, guarding the main portal.

Bergisel *(ABY)*

Reached by car via the Brennerstraße, the Bergiselweg and the park avenue .
The Bergisel hill was the setting of the bloody battle between Franco-Bavarian troops and the victorious Tyrolean insurgents led by Andreas Hofer. The event is commemorated by a statue of Hofer and the **Kaiserjägermuseum** *(Memorial to the Imperial Light Infantry,* ⏰*Open Apr-end Oct, daily 9am-5pm.* ⬥€*3.50.* ☎ *05 12/58 23 12)* (AY M³). The hill itself is now a popular spot for strolling. Also here is the Bergisel ski jump, also by Zaha Hadid. This is where the third of the famous four-part Vierschanzentournee ski jumping competition is held annually on January 4.

Schloss Ambras★ (BY)

Take Olympiastraße east; turn right at the skating rink; after passing under the autobahn turn left onto Aldranser Straße; after 500m/550yd turn left to Schloss Ambras. ⏰*Open daily 10am-5pm.* ⬥€*8. Apr-Oct ,* €*4 Nov-Mar (admission free 26 Oct, 24 Dec).* ☎ *05 12/52 52 47 45. www.khm.at/ambras.*
This fanciful Renaissance palace served as the residence of Archduke Ferdinand II (1529-95) and his beloved commoner wife, Philippine Welser. An avid collector, the prince had the **Unterschloss** (lower palace) built to house his own private museum. Present-day displays include his famous **Kunst- und Wunderkammer**, a cabinet of curiosities, and the arms and armor of the **Rüstkammern★**.
The former residental quarters in the **Hochschloss** (upper palace) now shelter the **portrait gallery★** with works by Cranach, Titian, Velásquez and other famous artists. Late medieval art is shown on the ground floor, where the **Georgsaltar★** (Altar of St George) is a star exhibit. The inner courtyard sports remarkable frescoes.
South of the Hochschloss is the magnificent **Spanischer Saal★** (Spanish Hall) built by the archduke for entertaining on a grand scale and now a concert venue.

Tour of the Mittelgebirge★★

105km/65mi including final ascent to the Brenner pass. The route follows a narrow corniche road with hairpin bends and a steep gradient not suitable for motorhomes. Leave Innsbruck by the Hall in Tirol road (BY on town plan).

Hall in Tirol★   *See Hall in Tirol.*

▶ *The road to Tulfes crosses the Inn and, as it climbs, gives attractive views of the town of Hall.*

Church of St Charles Borromeo at Volders★
🕐*Open daily 7am-7.15pm.*
The unusual 17C main building has a clover-leaf ground plan, six cupolas and an onion dome with three corner turrets at its base. Inside, the most masterful features are the ceiling frescoes illustrating the life of Milan cardinal Charles Borromeo and the painting above the high altar, both by Troger's pupil **Martin Knoller**.

▶ *Continue towards Wattens and follow the signposts to "Kristallwelten."*

Swarovski Kristallwelten in Wattens★
Kids 🕐*Open daily 9am-6pm. Closed 6-17 Nov, 1 Jan, 25 Dec.* €8. ☎ 0 52 24/51 08 00. www.swarovski.com/crystalworlds.
Although essentially a publicity vehicle for the Swarovski crystal company, this underground exhibition is nonetheless a satisfying experience. An overgrown fountain shaped like a giant head guards the entrance to this magical sparkling world of crystal designed by Vienna artist André Heller. The blue entrance foyer displays the world's largest crystal as well as crystal art by Keith Haring, Andy Warhol, Salvador Dalí and other internationally famous artists. This is followed by 13 "magic chambers" containing fantastic, mystical and meditative installations combining sound, light, objects and natural crystals in every shape and hue. Recently added highlights include an ice installation by fashion designer Alexander McQueen and a lab where kids can get creative with crystals.

▶ *Retrace the route to St Francis Borgia Church, and turn left to Rinn and Tulfes.*

Igls★
🕐*Cable-car operates end May-end Oct, daily 9am-noon, 12.45-4.30pm; end Nov-early Apr, daily 9am-4pm.* €14,90 two-way trip (Summer) €26,50 day pass (Winter). ☎ 05 12/37 72 34. www. patscherkofelbahnen.at.
Igls hosted the Winter Olympic Games in 1964 and 1976 and consequently boasts a substantial tourist infrastructure. The **Patscherkofel** (2 247m/7 372ft), served by **cable-car**, offers excellent walking tours in summer and skiing until well into the spring. Other attractions include a vast stone pine forest and the highest botanical gardens in Austria (open all hours from June to September, by the upper cable-car station at 1 964m/6 444ft).

▶ *Carry on towards Patsch/Matrei.*

Ellbögener Straße★★
This mountain road, which was once used for carting salt, leads through several tiny villages and hamlets, giving fine views of the Sill Valley. The approach to Patsch offers a splendid **view**★ along the length of the Stubaital and the Europa bridge (*see below*). After Gedeir, the road drops down into the valley, ending at Mühlbach. It then crosses the Sill and joins the Brenner road (B182) in Matrei am Brenner.

At this point, you can either take a detour left as far as the Brenner pass and Italian border *(32km/20mi roundtrip)*, or turn immediately right towards Innsbruck.

Brennerstraße★

The Brenner pass (alt 1 375m/4 510ft) is the lowest Alpine crossing and the only one negotiated by a main railway line in the open air (since 1867). The first Brenner road was built in 1772. The Brenner toll autobahn (A 13) was opened in 1969 to speed up through-traffic. A slower but more scenic alternative route is the B182.

From Matrei am Brenner to the Brenner pass

After leaving pretty Matrei, the road reveals a view of the **Navistal** (valley), with the tiny white churches of St. Kathrein (left) and Tiezens (right), before running along the idyllic Sill valley. On leaving Gries, the **chapel of St. Christopher and St Sigmund** at Lueg is worth a stop. The road then continues its climb to the pass and Italian border.

▶ *Retrace your route back to Matrei.*

From Matrei am Brenner to Innsbruck

On leaving Matrei the road runs above the River Sill, then drops down towards Innsbruck in a seemingly never-ending series of hairpin bends. After crossing the **Europa bridge**★ (785m/0.5mi long, 190m/623ft high), it arrives at a parking area with a panoramic viewpoint. The road then leads to the city center via Wilten.

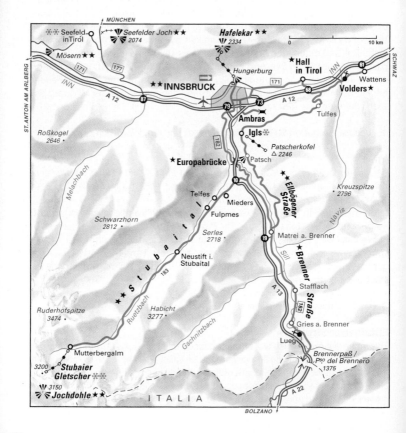

OBERES INNTAL★

TIROL

The Inn Valley has become the backbone of the Tyrol. For 185km/115mi, from the Finstermünz ravine to the Kufstein gap, the scenery is typical of the longitudinal furrows of the Alps shaped by the last phases of the Ice age.

From Nauders to Imst *104km/65mi*

Nauders ⚡
Nauders is a popular winter sports resort dominated by Schloss Naudersberg. The cross-country Skiparadies Reschenpass offers 111/69mi of tracks. In summer, mountain biking is the main sport here, with 600km/370mi of tracks covering the sprawling terrain. Past Nauders the road plunges into the Finstermünz gorge.

Finstermünzpass★
This grim gorge forms the natural frontier between the Tyrolean Inn Valley and the Lower Engadine and Alto Adige. Downstream from the Hochfinstermünz hotel the road clings precariously to the cliffs of the right bank, reaching a viewing terrace after three rock-vaulted tunnel passages. Further on, it drops down to the valley floor at the Kajetanbrücke (St Gaëtano) bridge.

▶ *After the bridge, head for the Lower Engadine Valley (signposted St. Moritz).*

After crossing the Inn, the road runs past **Pfunds**. Between **Ried** and **Prutz** look for the ruins of Laudeck to the left, flanked by the little, white church tower of **Ladis**.

▶ *In Prutz the road forks off to the right into the* **Kaunertal**★★★ *(👣 see entry).*

Landeck 👣 *See* Arlberggebiet①.
In Landeck, the ruins of **Schrofenstein** can be seen half way up a mountain slope, all the way to Zams. Past Zams look for **Kronburg** fortress perched atop a forested mountain peak. After **Schönwies**, the road climbs again and has several pull-outs where you can stop to enjoy the views. At last it reaches the wide Imst basin in sight of the jagged crests of the Stubaier Alps (east).

Imst
The delightful upper town (Oberstadt), with its numerous pretty fountains, is punctuated by the imposing 15C **parish church** with a neo-Gothic interior and original 16C murals on the west and south façades. At 84.5m/277ft the tower is the tallest in the Tyrol.

Behind the church starts the trail through the 1.5km/1mi-long **Rosengartenschlucht**★ *(Budget 90min for the roundtrip and wear sturdy shoes)*, which passes by roaring waterfalls and steep, rugged cliffs and offers fine views of the mountains. The well-known Imst carnival, with its procession of ghosts *(Schemenlaufen)*, takes place only every fourth year *(👣 see Calendar of events)*, but the **Fasnachtsmuseum** has a permanent display of masks and costumes used on the occasion. The world's first SOS-Children's Village was founded in Imst in 1949.

Carnival time at Imst

ISCHGL

TIROL
POPULATION 1 350 - ALT 1 377M/4 518FT

Ischgl on the **Silvretta-Hochalpenstraße**★★ undoubtedly ranks among the most beautiful of Austria's winter sports resorts. It's a modern village that's well developed for the tourist trade, offering the gamut of lodging options, an intense après-ski scene and off-piste fun in the Silvretta and Freizeit Centers with their indoor pools, saunas, tennis courts, billiards room and bowling alley. In summer, Ischgl morphs into a peaceful vacation resort. 🛈 *Ischgl 320, A-6561, ☎ 0 54 44/5 26 60. www.ischgl.com.*

▶ **Orient Yourself:** Ischgl is in the Paznauntal, a valley in the far southwestern corner of Austria, right on the border with Switzerland.

🕭 **Also See:** Silvretta-Hochalpenstraße

Ski slopes

The ski slopes at Ischgl and the neighboring Swiss resort of **Samnaun** (alt 1 840m/6 037ft) belong to the Silvretta Arena (alt 1 400-2 900m/4 600-9 500ft; www.samnaun.ch), which has 40 lifts and 230km/143mi of pistes suitable for all skill levels. Almost the entire terrain lies over 2 000m/6 550ft and snow cover remains excellent from late November until early May.

For **cross-country skiers** there is a ski track towards Galtür (🕭 *see Silvretta-Hochalpenstraße),* from where there are more possibilities available.

Pardatschgrat★

Alt 2 624m/8 609ft. *From Dec-May* take *the Pardatschgratbahn (Operates daily 8.30am-4pm); in summer and winter the Silvretta Seilbahn gives access as far as the Idalp at 2 320m/7 612ft (Operates 8.30am-noon, 1pm-4pm).* ⊜ *€40.50 day pass.* ☎ *0 54 44/6 06. www.silvretta.at.*

Ischgl

Mallaun/ÖSTERREICH WERBUNG

From the mountain station there is a good view of the ski slopes surrounded by the Vesulspitze, Bürkelkopf, Flimspitze and Piz Rots summits. Directly to the south lies the Fimbatal, a valley dwarfed by the Fluchthorn massif.

Trida Sattel★★

Alt 2 488m/8 163ft. *Cable-car up from Samnaun or follow the ski tracks from Ischgl.* From the terrace of the mountain restaurant, the **view**★★ extends southwards over the sheer Stammerspitze, Muttler and Piz Mundin peaks, and to the southeast over the Ötztaler Alps.

An even more far-ranging **panorama**★★ can be enjoyed from the Visnitzbahn and Mullerbahn chair-lifts.

BAD ISCHL⚓

OBERÖSTERREICH
POPULATION 14 000 – ALT 469M/1 539FT

Bad Ischl is one of Austria's most famous spa towns and for 60 years was the favorite summer retreat of Emperor Franz Joseph I. It gained fame in the 1820s when his mother, the Archduchess Sophie, came to town for a saline cure to treat her infertility. It wasn't long before she became pregnant with the future emperor; four more children, nicknamed the 'salt princes', followed. Franz Josef's presence lured a who's who of European royalty, artists and politicians to Bad Ischl, including composer Franz Lehár whose house is now a museum. Today, the town still bathes in the genteel glow of its 19C heyday, although it is also an attractive, modern health resort and gateway to the five lakes of the Salzkammergut. 🚉 *Bahnhofstraße 6, A-4820, ☎ 0 61 32/2 77 57; Web site: www.badischl.at.*

▶ **Orient Yourself:** Bad Ischl is in the Salzkammergut, about 54km/34mi east of Salzburg.
🏛 **Don't Miss:** Kaiservilla
👁 **Also See:** St Wolfgang, St Gilgen, Hallstatt

The Town

The central square, **Auböckplatz** (B), is bordered by the Trinkhalle (pump room, 1831) and the parish church. East of here, **Pfarrgasse** (B 16), the main shopping street, leads to the Elisabethbrücke across the River Train. It retains such survivals from 19C spa life as the elegant Zauner Café and pastry shop. Just before the bridge, it merges with the **Esplanade** (A), a shady riverside walk, where rich *Salzfertiger* (salt refiners) once stored salt for the Treasury before it was sent downstream. In one of their dwellings, the **Seeauer House** (no 10), with a Rococo façade and triple gables, Franz Josef got officially engaged to his 15-year-old cousin, Elisabeth of Bavaria ('Sisi') in 1853. A hotel until 1982, the building now houses the **Stadtmuseum** with exhibits on the salt trade, local folklore and the town's rise to spa resort and imperial summer residence.

Kaiservilla★ (A)

🚶 *Guided tour (45min) May-mid Oct, daily 9-11.45am, 1-4.40pm. ⊛€9,50. ☎ 0 61 32/2 32 41. www.kaiservilla.com.*

The Imperial villa north of the town, on the left bank of the Ischl, was a wedding present from Archduchess Sophie to Franz Josef and Sisi. It was later enlarged to form the shape of an 'E' in honor of Elisabeth. A tour of the private apartments includes the emperor's study where he signed the fateful declaration of war with Serbia

BAD ISCHL			Kaltenbachstr.	A	9	Pfarrgasse	B	16
			Kurhausstr.	A	12	Steinfeldstr.	B	18
Johannes-Brücke	B	5	Leitenbergerstr.	A	13	Traunkai	A	20
Kaiser-Franz-Josef-Str.	B	7	Maxquellgasse	B	15	Voglhuberstraße	B	2
Marmorschlößel	A	M¹						

on 28 July 1914. Scores of antlers and various stuffed animals attest to the ruler's passion for hunting. The complex still belongs to his descendents, some of whom are occasionally in residence. The villa is surrounded by a magnificent landscape garden, the **Kaiserpark**.

Marmorschlössl (M¹)

🕐 *Open Apr-end Oct, daily 9.30am-5pm.* 👁 *€1,50.* ☎ *0 61 32/2 44 22.*
In the park is the little "marble palace," which served as Elisabeth's tea house and favorite retreat. It now houses the **Photomuseum**.

KAISERGEBIRGE★★

TIROL

The limestone massif of the Kaisergebirge is popular with hikers and mountaineers. It actually consists of two ranges, separated by the Kaisertal valley: the Wilder Kaiser, a higher and more rugged chain to the south and the lower and Zahmer Kaiser characterized by gentler, pasture-covered slopes.

▸ **Orient Yourself:** The Kaisergebirge range is in western Austria, on the border with Germany, not far from Kitzbühel.

Wilder Kaiser

☐1 **From Lofer to Kufstein** *68km/42mi*

Lofer★
The village of Lofer, backed by the delicately chiseled, snow-flecked cliffs of the Loferer Steinberge, makes a delightful scene. Imposing houses adorned with deep overhanging balconies and ornate façades decorated with flowers and paintings line its narrow lanes, in which traffic is restricted. The town is a hiker's paradise with favorite destinations including the Auerwiesen, the Loferer Alm and the **Maria Kirchental pilgrimage church** (👣 *see Saalachtal*).

▶ *Leave Lofer on B 312 towards St. Johann.*

Beyond Lofer, the valley narrows into a ravine known as the Pass Strub where there is a memorial to the 1809 resistance fighters led by Andreas Hofer. Those with time should make a brief detour to **Strub**, by turning left about 3km/2mi after the memorial. The stretch of road between Strub and Waidring skirts many splendid traditional Tyrolean farmhouses whose living quarters, stables and granary are all under the same roof.

▶ *Return to B 312 and carry on towards St. Johann.*

Erpfendorf
Turn left off the road towards the town center.
The church, finished in 1957, is the work of Clemens Holzmeister, who also designed the new building for the Salzburg Festival. Inside is a monumental Crucifixion group, integrated into the roof beam construction above the nave.

St. Johann in Tirol★ 👣 *See St. Johann in Tirol.*

Spitalskirche zum Hl. Nikolaus in der Weitau★

▶ *Shortly after leaving St. Johann, turn right towards Rettenbach/Weitau. After about 1km/0.5mi the road re-enters St. Johann (signpost). The church is just beyond here on the right, surrounded by the Weitau agricultural college.*

The church was founded in 1262 as a home for the poor and converted into the Gothic style in c 1460 and the Baroque style in the 18C. In 1744 Simon Benedikt Faistenberger from Kitzbühel painted the ceiling frescoes (showing St Nicholas as patron of the poor, the Fourteen Auxiliary Saints and St John of Nepomuk). In 1745 Josef Adam Mölk from Vienna created the murals. Behind the altar is the oldest preserved stained-glass window in the Tyrol (c 1480). The church also houses the province's oldest bell (1262).

Ellmau
Ellmau's trademark feature is the hilltop **Maria-Heimsuchungs-Kapelle** (1719), from where you'll have a fine view of the town against the backdrop of the Kaisergebirge mountains.

Hintersteinersee
About 4km/2.5mi after Ellmau, turn right towards Scheffau/Hintersteinersee. The road reaches the lake after a steep, winding stretch of about 5km/3mi.
The crystal clear waters of this mountain lake reflect the rocky crags of the Wilder Kaiser. It's a nice spot for swimming or a lakeside walk.

▶ *Return to B 312 and carry on towards Wörgl.*

Söll

This charming little town is grouped around the richly decorated Baroque church of Sts Peter and Paul. To the south lies the Hohe Salve with its rounded summit.

Hohe Salve★★

Alt 1 829m/6 000ft. Cable-car and chair-lift to the summit. Lower station is about 1km/0.5mi southwest of Söll. ◷*Operates mid-May–mid-Oct, daily 9am–5.30pm, Dec–Easter, daily 8.30am–5pm, depending on snow.* ◉€13. ☏ 0 53 33/52 60.

From the summit with its tiny church and a restaurant there is a marvellous **panorama**★★, extending to the Kitzbüheler Alps, the Hohe Tauern and the Zillertaler Alps. To the north, the jagged peaks of the Wilder Kaiser dominate.

A path to the left of the lower station leads after 500m/550yd to the **Stampfanger pilgrimage chapel**, idyllically situated above a little creek and reached via a covered bridge.

Skiwelt Wilder Kaiser-Brixental ⛷

Austria's largest contiguous ski region encompasses nine winter sports resorts in the Wilder Kaiser (Going, Ellmau, Scheffau, Söll, Itter) and the Brixen Valley (Brixen, Westendorf, Kelchsau, Hopfgarten) with 250km/155mi of ski runs and 90 ski lifts. It is ideal for skiers preferring a more gentle and relaxed style of skiing. Access to the ski area is easiest from Scheffau, Söll and Brixen.

Cross-country skiers have 170km/68mi of ski runs to play with.

▷ *Take B 312 back northeast and after 2km/1mi turn right towards Kufstein.*

Kufstein ⓖ *See Kufstein.*

Zahmer Kaiser

② From Kufstein to St. Johann in Tirol *61km/38mi*

The road continues first along the slopes of the Zahmer Kaiser and then through a harsher landscape towards the imposing Wilder Kaiser rockface.

Kufstein ⓖ *See Kufstein.*

Take B 172 east towards Kössen. Between Durchholzen and the Walchsee it opens out into an attractive valley overlooked by a few peaks of the Zahmer Kaiser.

Walchsee

The road parallels the north shore of Walchsee lake, which is used for water sports and has attracted a healthy level of tourism to the village.

Maria Klobenstein

▶ *A side road leads for about 8km/5mi up the Klobenstein pass. In Kössen, turn onto B 176 towards Schleching. After about 3km/2mi, follow the signpost to "Wallfahrts-kirche Maria Klobenstein."*

The Ache, which surges down from the Kitzbüheler Alp, forces itself through a narrow gap just behind **Kössen**, forming a natural border between the Tyrol and Bavaria. The pilgrimage chapel of Maria Klobenstein unusually features two church interiors, one inside the other (1707 and 1733). Beneath the chapel a rock split into two and several meters high can be seen – this is the namesake "Klobenstein" (cleft rock).

▶ *Take B 176 back, heading south, until it reaches Griesenau and the Kaiserbach Valley. A toll is charged beyond the junction. After 5km/3mi, park by the Griesener Alm.*

Ascent of the Stripsenkopf
4hr roundtrip hike. Nearly 800m/2 623ft elevation gain.
From Griesener Alm (1 024m/3 360ft) the trail brings you to the Stripsenjoch mountain refuge at 1 605m/5 266ft in about 90min. Beyond here, following the red-white "Stripsenkopf" waymarkings should deliver you to the summit (1 807m/5 928ft) in about another half hour. However, as the path is rather steep and strewn with rocky patches, it may be too challenging for those with little experience or not wearing the right footwear. At the top, you'll be rewarded with excellent close-up **views**★ of the imposing north face of the Wilder Kaiser.

▶ *Return to B 176 and continue south. The road ends after Gasteig, with a panoramic descent through the meadows above the Leukental and St. Johann in Tirol.*

St. Johann in Tirol★ ♿ *See ST. JOHANN IN TIROL.*

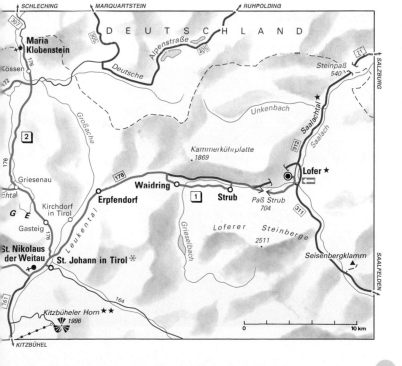

KAPRUN

SALZBURG
POPULATION 2 800 – ALT 786M/2 579FT

This peaceful town at the foot of the Grossglockner Alpine Road offers year round skiing thanks to the linking of the Schmieding glacier with the Kitzsteinhorn. Together with **Zell am See**★ (see entry), a mere 7km/4mi away, Kaprun has evolved into a huge recreational zone under the name of Europa-Sportregion. In summer you could ski in the morning and swim in the lake in the afternoon.

- ▶ **Orient Yourself:** Kaprun is in the Hohe Tauern National Park in western Austria.
- **Don't Miss:** Kitzsteinhorn
- **Organizing Your Time:** Allow a full day to explore the Kapruner Valley
- **Also See:** Zell am See

During the summer the Kapruner Valley, famed for its magnificent mountain setting, is laced with numerous interesting trails. The **Alexander-Einziger-Weg** from the Alpincenter (upper section of the Kitzsteinhorn) to the summit of the Maiskogel is well worth a detour.

Kaprunertal★★

Allow at least 2hr 30min for the Kitzsteinhorn and at least 4hr for the reservoirs, which are only accessible between late May and mid-October.
The Kapruner Valley lies between the ice-capped summits of the Hohe Tauern and the green, shimmering waters of the **reservoirs**★★ serving the Glockner-Kaprun power station. Park at the Kitzsteinhorn cable car station.

Kitzsteinhorn★★★

Cable-cars operate daily 8am-4.30pm (closed 2 weeks in June and September); €22.
☎ 0 65 47/8 70 00. www.kitzsteinhorn.at.

Markowitsch/ÖATERREICH WERBUNG

Kapruner Valley

The **trip**★★ between two particularly sheer rock faces is most impressive. At the Langwied station (alt 2 000m/6 562ft), switch to the Langwiedbahn which drops you at the **Alpincenter** station (alt 2 452m/8 045ft, restaurant). There is a beautiful view of the Kitzsteinhorn massif and the summer ski slopes.

From Alpincenter, another cable-car climbs to 3 029m/9 938ft, reaching a snow-covered mountain ridge just below the summit (alt 3 203m/10 503ft, accessible only to mountaineers). From the upper station climb to the second level of the viewing terrace. Straight ahead, the Grossvenediger dominates the **panorama**★★★. On a clear day the view stretches as far as the Zugspitze, Germany's highest mountain, on the other side of the Karwendel range. For another dose of impressive Grossglockner **views**★★, head down to the terrace of the Glocknerkranzl.

Kitzsteinhorn ski slopes 🎿 🎿

Open year-round, the area is relatively modest in size (15 ski lifts and 35km/22mi of ski runs), but it offers fantastic snow conditions in a spectacular setting between 2 000m/6 500ft and 3 000m/10 000ft above sea level. The facilities are among the most modern and comfortable anywhere in Austria. The ski runs are suitable for all levels of ability, with a slight preponderance of easier runs.

Hydroelectric dams★

Beyond the cable-car station, a road runs to the Wasserfallboden and Mooserboden reservoirs but it is only open to private vehicles as far as the Kesselfall Alpenhaus, about 2km/1mi past the station. Here, you must leave your car in a huge parking lot and board a bus taking you to the Lärchwand funicular. During the ascent there is a good view of the valley and Kaprun.

Limbergsperre

At the upper station of the Lärchwald funicular, the Limberg dam (alt 1 672m/5 486ft) comes into view. The power station at the foot of the dam wall receives water from the Mooserbodenspeicher reservoir opposite and expels it into the Wasserfallboden reservoir behind the dam.

From the funicular station, another bus travels through a number of tunnels to the Mooser dam offering scenic glimpses of the **Wasserfallboden reservoir**★.

Mooser- und Drosensperre★

Alt 2 036m/6 680ft. Both valley exits of the Mooserboden are blocked by arch gravity dams to the east and west of the so-called Höhenburg. The **Mooserboden reservoir**★★, amid spectacular Alpine scenery at the foot of the ice-draped Hohe Tauern, is especially scenic.

Crossing the first dam, there is a wonderful **view**★★ down onto the green waters of the Wasserfallboden.

KARWENDELGEBIRGE★

TIROL UND BAYERN (GERMANY)

The impressive limestone massif of the Karwendel, with the Birkkarpitze as its highest point (2 749m/9 019ft), can also be seen from Mittenwald (in Germany) and from the road to the Achensee. Only an excursion into the Rissbach Valley, with a possible detour through Bavaria, gets you near the greyish, pitted cliffs (the Kar) that give these mountains their character. If time is scarce, it is still worth driving as far as the Achensee, the largest lake in the Tyrol.

▶ **Orient Yourself:** This range is north of Innsbruck in western Austria.
🕙 **Don't Miss:** Achensee
🕓 **Organizing Your Time:** This region can be explored on a leisurely day trip.
Kids **Especially for Kids:** Achensee
🕐 **Also See:** Hall in Tirol, Innsbruck, Schwaz

1 From the Inn Valley to the Sylvenstein Dam
(Germany) 39km/24mi

Beginning at the Inn Valley *(take the autobahn exit "Wiesing-Achensee"),* the panoramic road climbs up to Eben.

Kanzelkehre★★
From this terraced **viewpoint**★★ you'll look down on the Inn Valley and the lower Ziller Valley, dotted with steeples. The scale of these valleys makes a fascinating contrast to the surrounding mountains. The Rofangebirge mountains tower to the north.

Eben
The church of this village contains the chalice of St Notburga, who is much revered in Bavaria and the Tyrol as the patroness of workers.

Erfurter Hütte
Alt 1 834m/6 033ft. *Rofanbahn cable-car operates May-end Oct, mid Dec-Easter, daily 8am-5pm every 15min. €14.50 roundtrip.* ☎ *0 52 43/52 92.*
This hut, the departure point for climbing expeditions into the Rofangebirge massif, is set in a magnificent panorama above the Achensee and the Karwendel.

Achensee★★
Kids This fjord-like, 10km/6mi-long lake wedged between the Karwendel and the Rofan range is the largest in the Tyrol and a popular and family-friendly destination for water sports and other outdoor recreation. The villages dotted along the shore, including Maurach and Achenkirch, have excellent tourist infrastructure. The lake is also served by the **Achenseebahn** *(⊜ €26 roundtrip; www.achenseebahn.at),* a historic steam-powered cog railway that chugs from Jenbach as far as Seespitz.

▶ *To drive along the edge of the lake, turn round at the village of Achensee and use the old road (one way: north-south). Austro-German border just after Achenwald. Turning right and crossing the Achen pass takes you to the Tegernsee in Bavaria (about 18km/11mi from the border). Turn left onto B 307 to the Sylvenstein dam.*

Sylvenstein-Staudamm
This dam regulates the dreaded floodwaters of the Isar. Water is conducted from the vast reservoir into an underground power station to generate electricity.

2 From the Sylvenstein Dam *(Germany)* to Eng
37km/23mi

▶ *The road, for part of which a toll is charged, is narrow and winding and closed from November to May.*

Sylvenstein-Staudamm 🕐 *See above.*

On leaving the reservoir and reaching Vorderriss, turn left into the deep Riss Valley and cross the Austro-German border.

Hinterriss

The hunting lodge built in the 19C for the Duke of Coburg-Gotha is a favorite vacation resort of the Belgian royal family. Use binoculars to scan the slopes and steep cliffs overlooking the road, to see some of the 5 000 chamois which still live on the massif.

Eng

The road ends here, in the **Großer Ahornboden**★, a grassland where the maples are ablaze with color in the fall, brightening an otherwise severe landscape.

The walls of the Spritzkarspitze (alt 2 605m/8 547ft) and the Grubenkarspitze (alt 2 661m/8 727ft) form a natural amphitheater marking the end of the valley.

KAUNERTAL★★★

TIROL

This long valley, traversed by one of Europe's highest roads, the Kaunertaler Gletscher-Panoramastraße (Kaunertal Glacier Panoramic Road; highest point: 2 750m/9 022ft), makes for an ideal day trip thanks to magnificent mountain scenery and a large reservoir. Skiing is possible from September to June on the Kaunertal glacier.

▶ **Orient Yourself:** The Kaunertal is in western Austria, not far from the Swiss border.

From Prutz to the Kaunertal Glacier 40km/25mi

In Prutz, turn left off the B 315 towards Switzerland and Italy. The road parallels the Faggenbach River throughly a deeply incised, green valley below the Köpfle and Peischlkopf peaks.

A toll (⊜ €20) is charged beyond Feichten, reached after 12km/7.5mi. This is where the valley widens, letting you catch glimpses of the glacier in the distance. After 10km/6mi of steep climbing through a beautiful forest, the road arrives at the Gepatsch reservoir, the largest in western Austria, from where you'll have a pretty **view**★ of the lake and the Weissseespitze (alt 3 535m/11 665ft). The road skirts the left bank for 6km/4mi, sprayed by numerous **waterfalls**★. The best view of the pine-fringed lake is just past the Faggenbach bridge.

As the vegetation thins, the landscape becomes ever more rocky. There is a **view**★ to the right of the picturesque Krummgampen Valley with its reddish cliffs. Shortly after this, the Weisssee comes into sight. The road ends after a final, steep stretch on the edge of the Kaunertal glacier (alt 2 750m/9 022ft), where **skiing** ⤸ is possible from September to June. Another attraction here is a 40m/120ft-long icy walk-through glacier crevasse - ⊜ not for the claustrophic!

▶ *Drive back down to the Faggenbach bridge.*

KITZBÜHEL

TIROL
POPULATION 7 872 – ALT 762M/2 500FT

Kitzbühel is one of the oldest and most exclusive resort towns in the Austrian Alps with a stellar reputation as a winter sports destination. The village developed thanks to silver and copper mining and its position along a trade route from Venice to Munich. Kitzbühel retains some of the atmosphere of the fortified medieval village it once was. The nucleus of the town is formed by two pedestrian streets, the "Vorderstadt" and the "Hinterstadt", which are lined by elegant gabled Tyrolean houses housing smart boutiques and cafes. ▯ *Hinterstadt 18, A-6370,* ☎ *0 53 56/7 77. www. kitzbuehel.com.*

▶ **Orient Yourself:** Kitzbühel is in the eastern Tyrol, wedged in between the Kitzbühel Alps and the Wilder Kaiser range.

🅿 **Parking:** Hahnenkamm, Hornbahn and Pfarrau are all parking lots within a five-minute walk of the town center.

🎯 **Don't Miss:** Skiing or hiking from the Kitzbüheler Horn

🐾 **Also See:** Kaisergebirge, St Johann in Tirol

A Bit of History

Kitzbühel's winter sports history was kickstarted in the 1890s by one man: skiing pioneer Franz Reisch. Inspired by Fridtjof Nansen's "The First Crossing of Greenland," Reisch ordered a pair of skis from Norway and started exploring the mountains. Others villagers soon followed in his tracks and and it wasn't long before the first small races were staged. However, several decades would pass before Kitzbühel's inaugural **Hahnenkamm downhill race** in 1931, which has since become a World Cup classic taking place every January. The downhill and the Super-G races are held on the **Streif**, the Hahnenkamm's most famous slope. Besides skiing, winter activities in Kitzbühel include ice-skating, curling and swimming (indoor pool with a health center). There's also a casino.

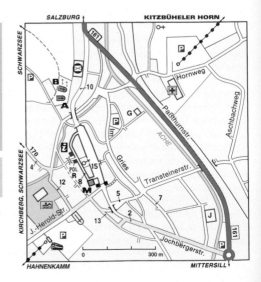

KITZBÜHEL	
Bichlstr.	2
Franz-Reich-Str.	4
Graggaugasse	5
Hammerschmiedstr.	7
Hinterstadt	8
J.-Pirchl-Str.	10
Klostergasse	12
Malinggasse	13
Vorderstadt	15

Liebfrauenkirche	B
Museum Kitzbühel	M
Pfarrkirche	A

Kitzbühel is also a popular summer destination. It has made quite a name for itself as the hub of Austria's tennis circuit (the clay court Generali Open is held here in July) and also ranks among the country's leading golf venues with two nine-hole and two 18-hole courses. There's even a hang- and paragliding school and several riding centers. However, the main summer activity is hiking with 200km/124mi of waymarked trails, mostly running along the ski slopes. They're great for those in search of an untaxing hike, picturesque scenery and spectacular views *(lifts give access to some of the best viewpoints)*.

Kitzbühel Alps

Between the Wörgl-Saalfelden gap and the upper valley of the Salzach, the smoothly rounded Kitzbühel Alps reach an altitude of 2 362m/7 749ft at the Großer Rettenstein. Known locally as Grasberge (grass mountains), they form a charming and tranquil pastoral landscape.

The contrasting shapes and colors of the surrounding massifs – the jagged walls of the Wilder Kaiser in the north and the towering ridge of the Hohe Tauern in the south – make the Kitzbühel Alps much sought-after for the quality of their views.

Ski slopes 🎿 🎿

Slopes spread over four separate areas, all served by ski buses: **Hahnenkamm-Steinbergkogel-Pengelstein** (alt 750-1 970m/2 450-6 450ft), **Kitzbüheler Horn** (alt 750-2 000m/2 450-6 550ft), **Stuckkogel** (alt 900-1 580m/2 950-5 180ft) and **Pass Thorn** (alt 930-1 980m/3 050-6 500ft). There are 56 ski lifts leading to 55 ski runs covering a total distance of 168km/105mi. Although international competitions are held here, the slopes are principally suited to more gentle skiing, with long, pleasant runs through pine forests. Only about 12km/7.5mi cover steeper terrain, mainly in the area of the Steinbergkogel peak. Because of the resort's relatively low altitude, snow starts disappearing as early as March.

To avoid the long lines at the Hahnenkamm massif, day trippers would be better off traveling to the neighboring **Kirchberg** peak, where the Fleckalm cable-car takes you to the heart of the mountain range in 15min. Good snow conditions on the flank of the Kitzbüheler Horn opposite make it possible to ski right down into the valley.

Sights

Pfarrkirche (A)

Like the neighboring Liebfrauenkirche (🕐 *see next*), the church is set off by its raised site. The nave shows off the talents of a local artist family, the **Faistenbergers**, who were all well-known artists in the 17C and 18C. Benedikt Faistenberg created the painting in the high altar, while the ceiling painting of the Chapel of St Rosa of Lima was done by his grandson, Simon-Benedikt.

Liebfrauenkirche (B)

This two-storeyed church is distinguished by a massive square tower that seems to dwarf the nave. The Baroque interior of the upper church includes a ceiling fresco of the Coronation of the Virgin by Simon-Benedikt Faistenberger (1739) and a Rococo grille (1778). In the high altar is a 17C painting of Our Lady of Succour (Maria-Hilf) after Cranach the Elder.

Museum Kitzbühel (M)

🕐 *Open 10 July-20 Sept daily 10am-6pm, 21 Sept-5 Dec, Tue-Sat 10am-1pm, 6 Dec-10 Mar Tue-Sat 10am-1pm, 5pm-8pm, 11 Mar-9 July, Tue-Sat 10am-1pm;* ⊘€4. ☎ 0 53 56/6 72 74.

This local museum is housed in the oldest building in the town, a former grain store, and has exhibits on the town's mining era, ski history and folklore.

Excursions

Kitzbüheler Horn★★
Alt 1 996m/6 549ft. *Allow 1hr 30min. Cable-car, in two stages.* ⏱*Operates mid May-end Oct and mid Dec-early Apr 8.30am-5pm.* €*15 roundtrip.* ☎ *0 53 56/6 28 57.*
There is a fabulous **panorama**★★ of the jagged peaks of the Kaisergebirge, the Kitzbühel ski slopes and the Hohe Tauern range. In the summer, the Kitzbüheler Horn is a departure point for an interesting **hike to the Bichlalm** (alt 1 670m/5 479ft – *allow 3hr and wear sturdy shoes*). From here, take the chair-lift back down into the valley, and then the bus back to town *(check the timetable with the tourist office).*

Ehrenbachhütte (Hahnenkamm-Massiv)★
Alt 1 802m/5 912ft. *Cable-car from Klausen (near Kirchberg), 45min roundtrip.*
There is a good **view**★ of the Wilder Kaiser, the Hohe Salve, the Kitzbüheler Horn and the Großer Rettenstein peaks. In winter, it is possible to ski to the **Steinbergkogel** summit (alt 1 975m/6 480ft) with more great **views**★★ of the Hohe Tauern and the Leoganger Steinberge. In summer, the hike from the upper cable-car station to the Jufenkamm ridge is popular. From here, you could follow the ridge trail south to the Pengelstein mountain refuge and on to the **Schwarzkogel**★ summit.

Schwarzsee
5km/3mi on the Kirchberg road and the lake road to the right (level crossing). A lovely walk also leads to the lake via the Liebfrauenkirche and the Lebenberg road.
This lake offers the opportunity of bathing within view of the Kaisergebirge.

KLAGENFURT

KÄRNTEN
POPULATION 90 000 – ALT 446M/1 463FT

Klagenfurt is a hugely popular vacation destination thanks to its mild southern climate and setting near the Wörther See, Europe's warmest Alpine lake, to which it is linked by a lovely canal. The city was founded in the 12C and quickly evolved into an important center for trade, although it didn't become capital of the province until elevated in 1518 by Emperor Maximilian. ⬚ *Neuer Platz/Rathaus, A-9010,* ☎ *04 63/53 72 23. www.info.klagenfurt.at.*

▶ **Orient Yourself:** Klagenfurt is near the southern edge of Austria, close to the borders with Slovenia and Italy.
🅿 **Parking: No charge lots -** St. Ruprechter Straße; Messegelände exhibition center; Krassnigstraße. **Long-stay fee-paying** - Waaggasse lot; Geyerschütt garagee; Domplatz garage; Apcoa garages on Neuer Platz, Heiligengeistplatz (Woolworth's store) and Dobernigstraße.
😊 **Don't Miss:** Lindwurmbrunnen, Landhaus, Landesmuseum Rudolfinum
🕐 **Organizing Your Time:** Plan on spending at least one full day in Klagenfurt, another half day if visiting Minimundus.
Kids **Especially for Kids:** Minimundus
👶 **Also See:** Wörther See, St Veit an der Glan, Maria Saal

Old Town★★

The idyllic old town, which is at its most animated in summer, reflects almost 800 years of local history. In the 16C and 17C architects from Italy masterminded its distinctive grid pattern of streets as well as over 50 picturesque arcaded courtyards, many of them open to the public. Numerous fine squares also present lovely architectural accents.

Neuer Platz (Y)

This large square is at the heart of the old town. Its focal point is the **Lindwurmbrunnen**★ or Dragon Fountain, which has become the city emblem. The great monster was created around 1590 by Ulrich Vogelsang, although the basin and Hercules figure weren't added until a few decades later. Completing the ensemble is the country's first-ever monument to Maria Theresa, placed here in 1764.

The square is lined with historic houses, including the 16C **town hall** (Rathaus) and the Adler-Apotheke with charming Rococo stucco decoration.

KLAGENFURT			Heiligengeistpl.	Y	6	Pernhartgasse	Y	10
			Herbertstraße	Y	19	Purtscherstr.	Y	12
August Jaksch Str.	Z	2	Herrengasse	Y	7	St. Veiter Str.	Y	13
Benediktinerpl.	Z	3	Heuplatz	Y	16	Sterneckstraße	Y	20
Domgasse	YZ	11	Karfreitstraße	YZ	14	Theaterpl.	Y	15
Feldkirchner Str.	Y	4	Kramergasse	Y	9	Wienergasse	Y	17
Feldm.-Conrad-Pl.	Y	5	Landhaushof	Y	8	Wiesbadener Str.	Y	18
Diözesanmuseum	Z	M²			Landesmuseum	Z	M¹	

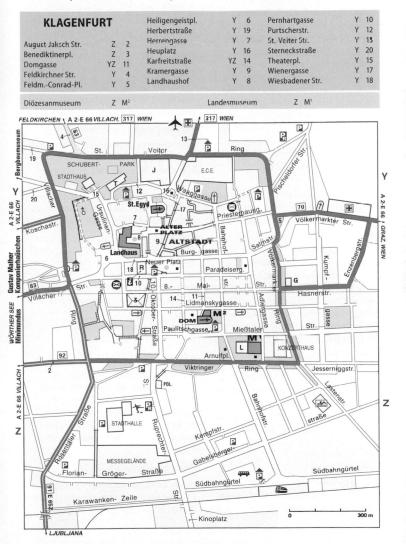

Address Book

PRACTICAL INFORMATION

TOURIST INFORMATION

Klagenfurt-Tourismus, Rathaus, Neuer Platz; ⏰May-mid Oct Mon-Fri 8am-8pm, Sat, Sun and public holidays 10am-5pm; mid Oct-Apr Mon-Fri 8am-6pm, Sat, Sun and public holidays 10am-1pm.

The tourist office issues a monthly calendar of events from May-Sept. Otherwise refer to the annual calendar of events.

"KÄRNTEN CARD"

This "Carinthia Card" is useful further afield than just in Klagenfurt. It is available May-Oct and is valid for up to three weeks. Almost 90 sites/activities of interest (museums, cable-cars, boat trips, leisure parks and swimming pools) in Carinthia can be visited free of charge and in some cases as often as you like with this card (however, the card is not transferable). It also entitles you to free travel by local rail and bus. It is on sale at local Carinthian tourist offices for €34. For further details, call the hotline ☎ 04 63/30 00.

CITY TOURS

A variety of guided city tours is usually available, especially in the peak summer months. Check with the tourist office for details.

PUBLIC TRANSPORT

Buy your ticket before boarding the bus to avoid paying a supplement. The **Stadtkarte** (town ticket) is good for unlimited trips within 1hr within Klagenfurt. The applies for the **24-Stunden-Karte** (24hr ticket) and the **7-Tage-Karte** (weekly ticket), which are transferable.

Tickets and public transport information is available from the ticket sales office on the Heiligengeistplatz (Quelle-Passage, ⏰ Mon-Fri 6.30am-2.30pm, ☎ 04 63/52 15 42) or from tobacconists' shops (Trafiken). Or call the hotline ☎ 04 63/52 15 34 (⏰5am-midnight) for timetable information.

POST OFFICES

Hauptpostamt (main post office): Benediktinerplatz; ⏰Mon-Fri 7.30am-8pm, Sat 7.30am-1pm.

Post am Bahnhof (station post office): open round the clock.

SHOPPING

Most of the department stores, general shops and exclusive boutiques are on Alter Platz and Neuer Platz, and in the Bahnhofstraße, Kramergasse, Wienergasse, Burggasse and Paradeisergasse. The pedestrianized area encompasses Kramergasse, Wienergasse, Tabakgasse, Renngasse, Alter Platz and Dr.-Arthur-Lemisch-Platz.

MARKETS

Benediktinerplatz: weekday market ⏰daily except Wed 8am-5pm, Grand Market ⏰Thur and Sat 7am-noon. Pfarrplatz: organic farm produce every Fri 6am-noon.

SOUVENIRS

Crafts and traditional costume (Trachten): Kärntner Heimatwerk, Herrengasse 2.

ENTERTAINMENT

Stadttheater, *Theaterplatz 4, ☎ 04 63/5 40 64.* Theater, music and dance.
klagenfurter ensemble, *Glashüttenstraße 10, ☎ 04 63/31 03 00.* This professional troupe with its own theater was founded in 1979 and now puts on plays, music and children's productions.

CINEMA

Kammerlichtspiele, *Adlergasse 1, ☎ 04 63/5 40 51.*
Wulfenia Kinozentrum, *Luegerstraße 5, ☎ 04 63/2 22 88.*
Volkskino, *Kinoplatz 3, ☎ 04 63/31 98 80.*
Carinthia Lichtspiele, *Ehrentaler Straße 28, ☎ 04 63/4 22 56.*

EATING OUT

Gasthaus Pumpe, *Lidmanskygasse 2;* **Gasthof Pirker**, *Adlergasse 16;* **Hirter Botschaft**, *Bahnhofstraße 44;* **Restaurant Wienerroither**, *Neuer Platz 10;* **Restaurant 5er**, *Kaufmanngasse 5;* **Restaurant Landhauskeller**, *Landhaushof 1.*

CAFÉS AND BARS

Cafés: **Café Domgassner**, *Domgasse 12;* **Café Janach**, *Bahnhofstraße 5;* **Café Musil**, *10.-Oktober-Straße 14;* **Café**

Segafredo, *Alter Platz 30*; **Café am Neuen Platz,** *Neuer Platz*; **Café 7. Himmel,** *Osterwitzgasse 12*.

Popular bars: **Bierhof zum Augustin,** *Pfarrhofgasse 2*; **Biergarten Marhof,** *Stift-Viktring-Straße 18*; **Künstlerhauscafé,** *Goethepark 1*; **Napoleonstadel "Haus der Architektur",** *St. Veiter Ring 10*. Live music is played in the blues and jazz cellar **Kamot,** *Bahnhofstraße 9*. There is dancing at **Scotch Dancing,** *Pfarrplatz 20*; **Fun Factory & Filoy Dancing,** *Gerberweg/Südring*. Genuine cocktails are prepared in these bars: **Meyer Lansky,** *Herrengasse 6*; **Camino,** *Rennplatz 2*; **Lemon Bar,** *Pfarrplatz 20*; **Gates Internet Café,** *Waagplatz*; **Rock-** **efeller Bar**, *Osterwitzgasse 5*; **Joe's Bar**, *Arcotel Hotel Moser-Verdino, Domgasse 2*.

DATES FOR YOUR DIARY

Singing, dancing and music under the maypole: in May, traditional shows in the Landhaus courtyard.

Musikforum Viktring: in July and Aug. Master classes and series of concerts on modern music and jazz. Details from ☎ 04 63/28 22 41.

Altstadtzauber ("Old town magic"): last weekend in Aug. Brings together internationally known artists and music groups performing on several stages, with a big flea market.

Christkindlmarkt (Christmas market): in Dec on the Neuer Platz.

Alter Platz★ (Y)

Kramergasse links Neuer Platz with Alter Platz, a lively street-square that derives a certain grandeur from its plethora of beautiful 16C mansions. Many sport elegant Baroque façades or charming Renaissance arcaded courtyards, such as the **old town hall** (Altes Rathaus), now called the Palais Orsini-Rosenberg. To the west, the Haus zur Goldenen Gans (Golden Goose), a gift from Emperor Friedrich III and one of the town's oldest houses, closes off the square. On the southwest corner stands the **Palais Goess** with a Late Baroque pilastered façade.

The Trinity Column (Dreifaltigkeitssäule) from 1680 was placed here in gratitude for the town's deliverance from the plague; the crescent moon and cross were added after the 1683 victory over the Turks.

Turn out of Alter Platz into Wiener Gasse, at the end of which is the **Ossiacher Hof**, another architectural gem from 1627 with two fine inner courtyards and a neo-Classical façade added in the late 18C.

Stadthauptpfarrkirche St. Egyd

North of Alter Platz, this 17C church is richly decorated with galleries, sumptuous fittings and fine ceiling paintings by Joseph Mölck (nave) and Joseph Fromiller (chancel). There are tombstones spanning four centuries, including one from 1998 erected to French-American author Julien Green, whose final wish was to be buried in Klagenfurt. Climb the church tower for a fine **view**★ of the town.

Landhaus (Y)

This imposing building west of Alter Platz has another harmoniously proportioned **Renaissance courtyard**★ with a two-story arcaded gallery. Completed in 1590 as the town's armoury, it is now used by the Carinthian provincial government.

Grosser Wappensaal★

🕐 *Apr-Oct daily 9am-5pm.* ☞€2. ☎ *04 63/57 75 72 15.*

The remarkable Heraldic Hall was decorated by one of Carinthia's most important Baroque painters, **Joseph Fromiller** (1693-1760). His masterpiece is the magnificent ceiling fresco, framed by *trompe-l'œil* galleries and depicting a scene showing members of the States of Carinthia paying homage to Emperor Karl VI. Fromiller also painted most of the 665 coats of arms of local noblemen adorning the walls and window embrasures.

Großer Wappensaal, Landhaus, Klagenfurt

Trumler/ÖSTERREICH WERBUNG

Dom★ (Z)

The cathedral was built in 1578 as a Protestant house of worship but fell under the control of the Jesuits in 1604 during the Counter Reformation. They made numerous alterations, resulting in the Baroque look you still see today. The **high altar**, framed by columns, is the work of Daniel Gran, while the magnificent **pulpit** (1726) is attributed to Carinthian artist Christoph Rudolph. Opposite, the *Apotheosis of St John of Nepomuk* by Joseph Fromiller counterbalances the pulpit beautifully. The **side altars**★ are a symphony of colored marble. Of special note is the one in the **Ignatius-von-Loyola Chapel** in the south aisle, which boasts an altar painting by the great Paul Troger.

Museums

Landesmuseum Rudolfinum★ (Z M¹)

🕐*Year-round Tues, Wed, Fri 10am-6pm, Thu 10am-8pm, Sat & Sun 10am-5pm.* 🕐*Easter Mon and Whit Mon.* &♿⊛€5. ☎ 04 63/53 63 05 52. www.landesmuseum-ktn.at.

This vast museum offers a comprehensive window on Carinthia's intriguing history and culture. A new highlight is the **Glocknerama**★, a multimedia installation taking you on a virtual climb of the great Grossglockner mountain. Other exhibits are more traditional and drawn from such themes as geology, early- and pre-history, Roman archaeology and folk art. There are plenty of fascinating items, including the famous "**dragon skull**", a fossilized rhinoceros cranium found in 1335 in a gravel pit near Klagenfurt. It is said to have inspired the designer of the Lindwurmbrunnen. Also impressive is a large Dionysius **mosaic floor**★ from the ancient Roman provincial capital of Virunum in today's Zollfeld plain near Maria Saal (♿ *see entry*).

The 15C and 16C are represented by numerous works of religious art, including the imposing St. Veit altarpiece. Note also Paola Gonzaga's **bridal chests**★ decorated with colorful reliefs based on designs by Andrea Mantegna.

Diözesanmuseum★ (Z M²)

🕐*1 June-14 June Mon-Sat 10am-noon, 15 June-14 Sep 10am-noon and 3pm-5pm, 15 Sep-15 Oct 10am-noon.* ⊛€2.30. ☎ 04 63/5 77 70 10 64.

The seven-room museum aims to give a good general picture of religious art in Carinthia from the 12C to the 18C. It displays the gamut of artistic endeavor, from gold- and silverwork to tapestry and embroidery, sculpture and painting. Endearing folk art is presented alongside works of outstanding artistic merit, such as a rare 12C **processional cross** and the fine **Magdalenenscheibe**★ , which is the oldest piece of stained glass in Austria, dating from 1170.

Bergbaumuseum★ (Y)

Access via the botanical gardens. Dress warmly, as the temperature is 9°C/48°F. ◔Apr-Oct *daily 9am-6pm.* ♿✆€5. ☎ *04 63/51 12 52. www.bergbaumuseum.at.*

The warren of air-raid galleries from the Second World War carved into the local Kreuzbergl hill is now home to galleries illustrating Carinthian mining history. An impressive sampling of minerals is displayed as if in a treasure chest, including an enormous chunk of cairngorm weighing about 200kg/440lb. Elsewhere you can study the skeletons of fossilized animals, admire an original historic coin mint and try to imagine working under ground by examining various mining equipment.

Excursions

Europapark & Minimundus

3km/2mi west of Klagenfurt. Leave via the Villachr Straße (YZ). ◔July-Aug daily 9am-9pm; May, June, Sep daily 9am-6pm; mid-Apr-end Apr and Oct daily 9am-5pm. ♿✆€12. ☎ 04 63/21 19 40. www.minimundus.at.

🧒 The Europapark is a large leafy recreational area encompassing a mini-golf course, a reptile zoo and an old-fashioned Strandbad (lakeside pool), although the biggest attraction here is Minimundus. This family-friendly theme park centers on 150 scale models (1:25) of world monuments made of authentic materials, from Big Ben to the Statue of Liberty, and the Eiffel Tower to St Mark's in Venice, all displayed in a park-like setting. It's an "edutaining" experience, enhanced by audio-guides that provide background information and virtual 3-D walks through some of the buildings. Tickets also include admission to the nearby planetarium.

Minimundus – tour the world on foot

R. Chéret/MIECHLEIN

Gustav-Mahler-Komponierhäuschen

Follow the southern shore of the Wörthersee from Minimundus and park opposite Maiernigg beach from where it's a 15min walk. ⊙*May-Oct daily 10am-4pm.* ⊸€1. ☎ *04 63/5 37 56 32; www. gustav-mahler.at.*

This log cabin hidden in the forest is pretty unprepossessing, but lovers of **Gustav Mahler**'s music are sure to be moved by it nonetheless. The composer created some of his masterpieces here between 1900 and 1907, including Symphonies Four to Eight and the Rückert Lieder. Employed as director of the Hofoper in Vienna at the time, Mahler only got the chance to compose during his summer vacation.

Pörtschach★

10km/33mi west of Klagenfurt along road 83.

This is a popular and rather exclusive resort on the Wörthersee, located on a peninsula and dotted with elegant villas and hotels half-hidden under abundant foliage. A flower-lined promenade runs all round the tiny tongue of land. Other good strolling destinations are Schloss Leonstein on a rock southwest of town and the classic walk from Pörtschach to the "Gloriette" belvedere giving a view of the lake and the Karawanken mountains *(30min; ☜ a lot of steps).*

KLEINWALSERTAL★

VORARLBERG
POPULATION 5 300
ALT OF RESORTS: 1 086M/3 563FT TO 1 244M/4 081FT

The Kleinwalsertal is a petite region isolated from the rest of Austria by the Allgäu Alps and is thus exclusively oriented towards Germany – whether it be economically or through tourism. It shares a ski area with Oberstdorf across the border and is a departure point for scenic mountain hikes during the warmer seasons. ▯ *Walserstraße 64, A-6992, ☎ 0 55 17/5 11 40 , www.kleinwalsertal.de; or* ▯ *Oberstdorf, Marktplatz 7, D-87561, ☎ 0 83 22/70 00, www.oberstdorf.de.*

From Oberstdorf *(Germany)* to Baad *14km/8.6mi from the border*

Oberstdorf★★

This is a charming mountain spa resort and winter sports center at the foot of the majestic Nebelhorn. ⇝ *Traffic is barred from the town center.*

▸ *From Oberstdorf head south on B 19, reaching the Austrian border after 5km/3mi.*

The road through the Kleinwalsertal (B 201) serves **Riezlern**, **Hirschegg**, **Mittelberg** and its offshoot **Baad**. The highest mountain at the end of the valley is the imposing Grosser Widderstein (2 533m/8 311ft).

Walsermuseum

At Riezlern tourist office. ⊙*Year-round Mon-Sat 2-5pm.* ⊙*one week after Easter until Whitsun and 1 Nov-20 Dec.* ⊸€4. ☎ *0 55 17/53 15 34 (from Austria),* ☎ *0 83 29/53 15 34 (from Germany).*

This is an exhibition on the history and way of life (including traditional costume) of the valley and its inhabitants. The second floor has reconstructions of a typical Valaisian chalet and an Alpine dairy hut.

Skimuseum
In the Walserhaus in Hirschegg. ◷*Daily 8am-6pm.* ✆*no charge.* ☎ *0 55 17/54 17 (from Austria),* ☎ *0 83 29/5 11 40 (from Germany).*
The evolution of various winter sports from the late 19C to around the Second World War is retraced here with the help of numerous exhibits on the first and second floors of the Walserhaus.

Bergschau 1122
In the Walserhaus in Hirschegg. ◷ *Mon-Sat 8am-7pm, Sun 8am-4pm.* ✆*free.* ☎ *0 55 17/5 11 40. www.bergschau.de.*
Also in the Walserhaus, this is a small but engaging exhibit about life in the Allgäu Alps from prehistoric times onward. Discoveries include the magic world of crystals seen through a video microscope and an interactive relief model of the valley.

KLOSTERNEUBURG★

NIEDERÖSTERREICH
POPULATION 24 500 – ALT 192M/630FT

In 1113 Babenberg Margrave Leopold III moved the court from Melk to Klosterneuburg, founding an abbey there the following year. According to legend, it stands in the spot where the Margrave miraculously found his wife's veil that had blown off many years earlier while the couple was standing on their castle balcony. The abbey, which is still run by Augustinian canons, remains the town's sightseeing trump card to this day. ▯ *Neidermarkt 4, A-3400, 0 22 43 /3 43 96, www. klosterneuburg.at.*

▶ **Orient Yourself:** Klosterneuburg is about 12km/8mi north of Vienna.
◷ **Organizing Your Time:** Klosterneuburg is an easy half-day to day-trip from Vienna.
🄺🄸🄳🅂 **Especially for Kids:** Kids can learn about life at the abbey during hands-on workshops held in the Kinideratelier (children's studio) on Sunday afternoons.

Abbey *(Stift)*

◷*9am-6pm daily.* ◷*25, 26 Dec.* ✏*Guided tours (1hr) 10am-5pm.* ✆*€7. The abbey museum may be visited without a guide.* ☎ *0 22 43/41 10. www.stift-klosterneuburg.at.*

Stiftskirche (Abbey church)
This three-nave Romanesque basilica has origins in the 12C but has been modified repeatedly, most notably in 1634 when it was given the full Baroque treatment courtesy of the great Giovanni Battista Carlone and Andrea de Retti. The **ceiling**

Nicolas of Verdun

Little is known of Nicolas of Verdun (late 12C/early 13C) other than that he was a goldsmith and enameler from Lorraine. The side panels of the Dreikönigsschrein (Shrine of the Three Kings) in Cologne Cathedral are attributed to him, but his name is only known to us from inscriptions on two works, the Mary Shrine in Tournai Cathedral and the enameled panels in Klosterneuburg, both considered masterpieces of medieval art.

frescoes in the nave were executed by Georg Greiner c 1689, although the ones by Johann Michael Rottmayr depicting the *Assumption* in the chancel are considered more accomplished. Other decorative standouts include the high altar by **Matthias Steinl** and the richly gilded **choir stalls** decorated with 24 Habsburg coats of arms. The Baroque organ of 1636 is famous for its exquisite sound and was greatly admired by Anton Bruckner.

Abbey church

Kreuzgang (Cloisters)

These date from the 13C and 14C and are a fine example of Early Gothic architecture with Burgundian influence. The old pump house contains a remarkable seven-armed **bronze candelabrum**, a 12C Veronese work symbolizing the Tree of Jesse. In the southwest corner is the Freisingkapelle, which contains the tomb of the Bishop of Freising (died 1410).

Leopoldkapelle

East of the cloisters, the Leopoldkapelle has ethereal 14C **stained glass**★, although the true show-stopper is the **Verdun altarpiece**★★. This amazing winged altar was fashioned in the 12C by Nicolas of Verdun and consists of 50 gilded enamel panels arranged in three rows and depicting famous scenes from the Old (upper and lower rows) and New (middle row) Testaments.

The chapel also contains the tomb of Leopold III, who was canonized in 1485. His bones are kept in the reliquary above the altarpiece.

Stiftsbau (Abbey building)★

Emperor Charles VI envisioned an abbey modeled on nothing less than the grand Escorial near Madrid. Construction began in 1730 but only a quarter of the plans were fully realized because of Charles' sudden death in 1740 and a total lack of interest in the project by his daughter, Maria Theresa. Visitors are greeted by eight giant Atlases by Lorenzo Mattielli in the unfinished **Sala terrena**, the former garden room. There are exhibits about the abbey's history leading to the grand **Chorher-renstiege** (staircase), which is lined by video installations informing you about the canons' daily life. The stairs drop you off at the imperial apartments where you'll want to linger in the Gobelin Hall, adorned with priceless tapestries from Brussels, and the **Marble Hall**★ with its giant oval dome decorated with frescoes by Daniel Gran glorifying the Habsburgs. After the tour, the Weinweg (wine path) leading back to the Sala terrena has displays about the abbey's four large wine estates.

Stiftsmuseum★

⏱9am-6pm daily. ⬤€5.50; ☎ 0 22 43/41 11 54.

The abbey museum is filled with interesting items, most famously a huge painting depicting the geneaology of the Babenbergs, a statuette of Mercure by Raphael Donner, richly carved ivory decorative objects, and four early works by Egon Schiele.

Additional Sights

Sammlung Essl★
⏱Tues, Thu-Sun 10am-7pm; Wed 10am-9pm. ⏱1 Jan, 24, 25 Dec. ♿,♨€7 (free Wed after 7pm). ☎0 22 43/3 70 50. www.sammlung-essl.at.

An der Donau-Au 1. An unexpected contrast to the Baroque abbey is delivered by this stellar collection of post-1945 Austrian paintings. It was gathered by Karlheinz and Agnes Essl, owners of a huge home improvement store chain. Changing selections are on view in a strikingly angular, modernist building by Heinz Tesar located south of the Stift near the Danube. Encompassing more than 5 500 works, the collection represents a far-reaching survey of all major stylistic periods, including Abstract Expressionism, Vienna Actionism and New Paintings. Friedensreich Hundertwasser, Max Weller and Maria Lassnig are among the artists you'll find here.

Excursion

Kierling
Heading west from the Stadtplatz along Kierlinger Straße takes you to this village where, in 1924, **Franz Kafka** died of tuberculosis at age 40 in the former sanatorium. There is a small museum with memorabilia of the great writer.

KREMS UND STEIN★★

NIEDERÖSTERREICH
POPULATION 23 120 – ALT 221M/725FT

Krems is a delightful wine village snuggled against terraced vineyards on the left bank of the Danube. More than 1 000 years old, it actually consists of three towns in one: Krems, Stein and Und, giving rise to the saying: "Krems Und (and) Stein are three towns." It is part of the Wachau region, which was declared a UNESCO world heritage site in 2000. Krems was the long-time home of the painter Martin Johann Schmidt (1718-1801), better known as **Kremser Schmidt**, whose work graces many churches and abbeys around the country. 🗎 Undstraße 6, A-3504, ☎ 0 27 32/8 26 76, www.krems.at.

▸ **Orient Yourself:** Krems is at the eastern edge of the Wachau, about 77km/42mi west of Vienna.
🅿 **Parking:** There are pay-parking garages at Steiner Tor, on Kasernenstraße and on Ringstraße and a free Park & Ride lot at the Bahnhof (train station).
☺ **Don't Miss:** Piaristenkirche, Weinstadtmuseum, Kunsthalle Krems
☟ **Also See:** Dürnstein, Stift Göttweig, Schloss Grafenegg

Krems

Piaristenkirche★ (BZ)
First run by Jesuits, this church was handed over to the Piarists, an educational order who's still in charge today, by Maria Theresa in 1776. Dominating the old town, it is a beautiful three-nave Late Gothic hall church with exquisite net vaulting and a bonanza of works by Kremser Schmidt. The most famous among these are the **high altar** painting of the *Assumption* and the right side altar showing the founder of the

Piarist order. Notable too are the **choir stalls**, still with stylistic features of the Early Renaissance although dating from well into the 17C.

Pfarrkirche (BZ)

This Early Baroque church, completed in 1630 under the Italian architect Cyprian Biasino, has a sumptuously decorated interior. The nave and chancel vault are adorned with Kremser Schmidt frescoes.

Weinstadtmuseum★ (BZ M)

🕐 *Mar-Nov Tue-Sat 10am-6pm.* ◉€4. ☎ 0 27 32/80 15 67. www.weinstadtmuseum.at.

This former Dominican monastery provides a delightful setting for the imaginatively presented displays on Krems' cultural history. Wine takes center stage, naturally, but there are also some fine works by Kremser Schmidt as well as the famous **Fanny of Galgenberg★**. Standing a mere 7.2cm/2.8in tall and made of greenish slate, this little statuette is believed to be about 32 000 years old, making it the world's oldest female figurine unearthed so far. The 700-year-

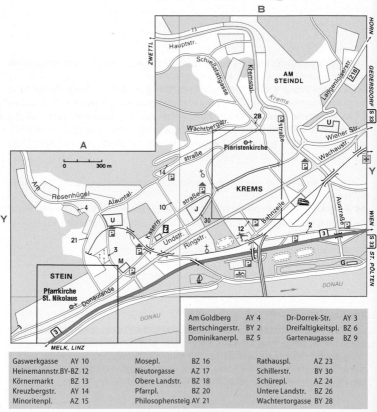

Am Goldberg	AY 4	Dr-Dorrek-Str.	AY 3
Bertschingerstr.	BY 2	Dreifaltigkeitspl.	BZ 6
Dominikanerpl.	BZ 5	Gartenaugasse	BZ 9

Gaswerkgasse	AY 10	Mosepl.	BZ 16	Rathauspl.	AZ 23
Heinemannstr.	BY-BZ 12	Neutorgasse	AZ 17	Schillerstr.	BY 30
Körnermarkt	BZ 13	Obere Landstr.	BZ 18	Schürepl.	AZ 24
Kreuzbergstr.	AY 14	Pfarrpl.	BZ 20	Untere Landstr.	BZ 26
Minoritenpl.	AZ 15	Philosophensteig	AY 21	Wachtertorgasse	BY 28

old monastery church impresses with its crisp Gothic architecture that was never adulterated by Baroque embellisment.

Obere und Untere Landstraße (BZ 18, 26)

Historic Krems' main artery, the pedestrian-only Landstraße is lined with Renaissance and Baroque façades and punctuated by the Steiner Tor, a monumental 15C gateway. Deserving closer inspection is the **Bürgerspitalkirche** (BZ), an elegant Gothic chapel whose single rib-vaulted nave exudes a peaceful atmosphere. The high altar is flanked by two superb gilded wooden statues, the work of Matthias Schwanthaler.

Stein

About 1km/0.6mi west of the Steiner Tor, Stein is charmingly hemmed in by the Danube and terraced vineyards. The main drag, **Steiner Landstraße**, which opens out here and there into small squares, is lined with well-preserved, elegant town houses and arcaded courtyards, both a reflection of local wealth.

Approaching Stein from the west, you can't miss the **Kunsthalle Krems** (①10am–6pm daily. ⊗€8. ☎ 0 27 32/90 80 10. www.kunsthalle. at), a well-respected art exhibition hall skillfully converted from an old

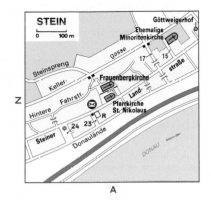

tobacco factory. The progressively minded shows also spill over into the nearby former **Minoritenkirche**, a three-nave pillared basilica whose 14C frescoes provide an interesting backdrop on view here.

Further west looms the mighty west tower of the **Pfarrkirche St Nikolaus** with its delicate Baroque dome. Inside, Kremser Schmidt worked his magic with the ceiling fresco and the altar paintings. The **Frauenbergkirche**, right behind the Pfarrkirche, is now a war memorial.

Excursions

Stift Göttweig★

6km/4mi south of Krems on the road to St. Pölten (BY). ①*June-Sep daily 9am-6pm; 21 Mar-end May and Oct-mid Nov daily 10am-6pm.* ①*Good Fri.* ⊗*€2.50, full access €7.* ☎ *0 27 32/85 58 12 31. www.stiftgoettweig.or.at.*

The prominent hilltop setting and striking architecture of this Benedictine abbey has garnered it the nickname "Austria's Monte Cassino," after the Italian abbey where the order originated. Founded in 1083, it was nearly destroyed by fire in 1718 and restored in Baroque style. The church **interior**★ dazzles with elaborate stuccowork and a number of interesting features, most notably the mighty high altar (1639) and the pulpit, both by Dutch master Hermann Schmidt. Medieval remnants include the Erentrudiskapelle (chapel) and the crypt. Full admission also provides access to the monumental **Imperial staircase**★ with a ceiling fresco by **Paul Troger** (1739); the imperial state rooms and the museum with its changing roster of items from the abbey's treasury. Since 2001, the abbey has been include on UNESCO's prestigious list of World Heritage Sites.

KREMSMÜNSTER★

OBERÖSTERREICH
ALT 384M/1 260FT

The impressive Benedictine abbey of Kremsmünster is a rambling compound in a dramatic bluff-top setting overlooking the Krems Valley. According to legend, it was founded in 777 by Bavarian Duke Tassilo III in the spot where his son was killed by a wild boar in a hunting accident. Nothing remains of the original abbey, which now grandstands in Baroque splendor thanks to a large cast of talented architects and artists. From its silhouette rise not only the church's two domed towers but also the bulky "Mathematical Tower," a former astronomical observatory. ▯ *Rathausplatz 1, A-4550, ☎ 0 75 83/72 12, www.kremsmuenster. at.*

▶ **Orient Yourself:** Kremsmünster is 43km/27mi south of Linz and 25km/16mi west of Steyr.
▯ **Parking:** Park in the outer court of the abbey.
🕓 **Organizing Your Time:** Budget about half a day for a complete visit.
👁 **Also See:** Steyr, Wels

Abbey *(Stift)*

Guided tours of abbey and art collection (1hr) May-Oct daily 10am, 2pm, 3pm, 4pm, also Mon-Fri 11am, Sat-Sun 11.30am and 1pm; Nov-Apr daily 11am, 2pm, 3.30pm. €6.50. Guided tours of natural science collection (1hr 30min) May-Oct daily 10am and 2pm, July-Aug also 4pm. €7.50. Tickets on sale in the abbey shop in the first courtyard, near the fish pond. ☎ 0 75 83/5 27 51 51. www.stift-kremsmuenster.at.

Fischbehälter★
No admission, can be seen without guided tour.
An unexpected feature in the first abbey courtyard is the five **fish basins** framed by arcades and adorned with water-spouting statues of Samson, David, Neptune, Triton and other mythological creatures. They were designed by Carlo Antonio Carlone around 1690 and enlarged by Josef Prandtauer a couple of decades later.

Stiftskirche (Abbey Church)
The basilica, which is structurally Romanesque-Gothic in style, was given its Baroque look by Carlone after 1680. The ceiling frescoes by the three Grabenberger brothers are set amid richly sculpted stuccowork. Your eyes will also be drawn to the huge altar painting by Johann Andreas Wolf depicting the *Transfiguration of Christ on Mt Tabor.* It is framed by an impressive flock of cherubs, although the ones in the side altars, hewn in marble by Michael Zürn, are even more artistic. The tomb of Tassilo III's son, Gunter, is under the south tower.

Trumler/ÖSTERREICH WERBUNG

Tassilo chalice

Stiftsgebäude (Abbey Buildings)

The **Kaisersaal** (Emperors' Hall) owes its name to 17C portraits by Martino Altomonte of the Holy Roman Emperors from Rudolf of Habsburg to Charles VI. Ceiling frescoes and stucco mouldings of great delicacy adorn this state hall.

The star exhibit in the abbey treasury is the 8C **Tassilo chalice**★★★, an exquisite work made from gilded copper with silver inlay. It was used in 765 in the duke's wedding and later presented to the abbey's monks.

The abbey **library**★ is divided into four rooms that again bear the decorative stamp of Carlone and contains some 160 000 volumes. There's also a smattering of paintings exhibited in several galleries on the second floor.

Mathematischer Turm★

The "mathematical tower," or observatory, is about 50m/164ft high and has a decidedly modern appearance despite its 18C pedigree. Inside are extensive collections relating to paleontology, physics, mineralogy, zoology, anthropology and astronomy. Views from the top stretch as far as the Alps.

KUFSTEIN

TIROL

POPULATION 14 500 – ALT 499M/1 637FT

Kufstein, the last Austrian town in the Inn Valley, lies at the foot of a rocky outcrop crowned by a mighty fortress. The town has become a lively and popular tourist resorts thanks, in part, to the proximity of the Kaisergebirge range (see entry), easily reached by the Wilder Kaiser chair-lift (Y). *Unterer Stadtplatz 22, A-6330, ☎ 0 53 72/60 20, www.kufstein.at.*

▶ **Orient Yourself:** Kufstein is on the Inn River, just 5km from the border with Germany.

🕐 **Organizing Your Time:** Spend a couple of hours visiting the castle, ideally built around a 15min organ concert at noon or 6pm.

👁 **Also See:** Kaisergebirge

General view (Z)

The best **view**★ of the fortress is from the Heldenhügel, a wooded rise topped by a memorial statue to Tyrolean freedom fighter Andreas Hofer.

Fortress *(Festung) (Z)*

🕐 *8 Apr-Oct daily 9am-5pm.* ⊜*€8.* 🕐*Nov-7 Apr daily 10am-4pm (museum closed)* ⅙ ⊜*€7.* ☎ *0 53 72/60 23 50. www.festung-kufstein.at.*

Kufstein owes much of its character to the citadel that dominates the town. Starting from the Unterer Stadtplatz, an archway above the church leads to the Festungshof *(left)* with the auditorium for the Heldenorgel *(see below)*. Here you can catch the funicular (included in admission tickets) or continue via a covered stairway.

A gateway takes you to the Tiefer Brunnen, a 60m/197ft-deep well. From here, a tunnel carved through the rock leads to the "Peacock tail" (Pfauenschweif) gateway, and then left to the Wallachen and Caroli bastions, from where you'll enjoy good **views**★ over the Inn River.

In summer, tickets also include admission to the **Heimatmuseum**, which presents an array of objects collected by the Kufstein local history society. Of particular interest are the rooms illustrating the fortress through the ages.

Kaiserturm★

This colossal 16C tower, with walls up to 4.5m/15ft thick, rears up on the highest point of the rocky bluff. The cells on the third floor are reminders of the tower's use as a state prison in the 19C.

Heldenorgel

⏱ *Organ recitals daily noon; July-Aug also 6pm.* ♿ ⬤ €0.80. ☎ 0 53 72/60 23 50.
This giant instrument, known as the "Heroes' organ," was first played in 1931 to commemorate the fallen of the First World War. It is on the top floor of the Bürgerturm, one of the fortress towers, and boasts 4 307 pipes and 46 registers. The organist's keyboard and the gallery for the audience are at the foot of the rock. The recitals can be heard throughout the town or you can buy a ticket to sit in the auditorium. Since the organ is exposed to the air, it has to be constantly retuned.

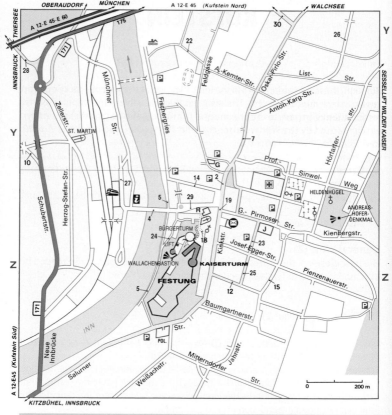

Excursions

Schloss Mariastein
12km/7.5mi southwest of Kufstein. Park in the valley and climb up to the castle.
In the 14C, a fortified tower was built on a huge rocky outcrop in a small peaceful valley paralleling the Inn. It was called "Stein" (rock) and became a site of Marian pilgrimage after a Lady Chapel was built here.

▶ *Cross the courtyard and climb the tower staircase.*

The Knights' Hall (Rittersaal) upstairs houses the **Schlossmuseum** (⊙*daily 9am-5pm.* ☎ *0 53 32/5 64 85)* whose collection includes a Tyrolean royal crown and scepter, and numerous ex-votos. Two chapels have been built one above the other on the upper storeys: the lower Late Gothic **Kreuzkapelle** (Chapel of the Cross) and the upper **Gnadenkapelle** (Chapel of Miracles), decorated in the Baroque style. The venerated statue of the Virgin Mary and Child dates from 1450.

Ursprungpassstraße★
25km/15.5mi from Kufstein to Bayrischzell (Germany). Leave Kufstein on the Thierseestraße, northwest of town.
The road climbs rapidly into the forest from Kufstein, and on leaving the Inn Valley loses sight of the fortress.

Thierseetal
The green valley with scattered settlements stretches almost as far as the German border. Thiersee, venue of a Passion play every six years (⊙see Calendar of events), lies on a small round lake of the same name.
A succession of combes and gorges leads to the Ursprung pass (alt 849m/2 785ft), which marks the Austro-German border. After the pass, the road runs through the thickly forested **Ursprungstal** in Germany, a valley that bears hardly any traces of human settlement. In Bayrischzell, at the foot of the Wendelstein, the road joins the **German Alpine Road** (Deutsche Alpenstraße) which runs between Lindau and Berchtesgaden (⊙for description, see The Green Guide Germany).

LAMBACH

OBERÖSTERREICH
POPULATION 3 170 – ALT 349M/1 145FT

In the Middle Ages, this small town on the River Traun built its wealth on the salt trade. To this economic function was added the prestige of a Benedictine abbey, founded by Bishop Adalbero in the 11C and still an active monastery today. ▯ *Marktplatz 8, A-4650, ☎ 0 72 45/28 35 50, www.stift-lambach.at.*

▶ **Orient Yourself:** Lambach is about 15km/9mi southwest of Wels or 48km/30mi southwest of Linz.
⊙ **Also See:** Wels

Abbey★ (Stift)

Stiftskirche (Abbey Church)

🕭 *Guided tour by reservation only (1hr 30min) Easter-end Oct, daily 2pm.* ✺€5.
☏ 0 72 45/2 17 10.

The abbey church, which contains the tomb of Adalbero, was largely rebuilt in the 17C according to Baroque precepts, although some exquisite Byzantine-influenced **frescoes**★★ survive from the Romanesque period. Uncovered and restored in 1967, they are considered among the oldest in Europe. The scene in the central dome shows the Virgin Mary with the Infant Jesus, flanked to the left by the Three Wise Men bearing gifts and to the right by Jerusalem and Herod interrogating the Wise Men.

Klostergebäude (Abbey Buildings)

Highlights in the main abbey buildings include the Baroque **library** with frescoes by Melchior Seidl and 50 000 precious volumes; the well-proportioned **summer refectory** with outstanding stucco decoration by Carlo Antonio Carlone (now a concert hall); the former abbey tavern, now a **pharmacy**, which also contains some beautiful stuccowork; and the **ambulatory** by Diego Carlone.

Lambach even has its own theater, the beautiful 18C Rococo **Kleines Theater**★, the only one of its kind to have surived in Austria.

Pfarr- und Wallfahrtskirche Stadl-Paura★

2km/1m. Leave Lambach to the south. Cross the River Traun and turn right after 500m/550yd.

This church is a symmetrical ode to the Trinity. It has a triangular floorplan, three towers, three chancels, three marble portals, three altars, three small organs and three sacristies. Even the frescoes in the dome and the altar paintings are by a trio of famous artists: Carlo Antonio Carlone, Martino Altomonte and Domenico Parodi.

Dreifaltigkeitskirche, Stadl-Paura

LECH

VORARLBERG
POPULATION 1 270 – ALT 1 447M/4 747FT

Lech is indisputably the prettiest holiday destination in the Austrian Alps and one of the few resorts in the northern Alps to have made a name for itself as an international winter sports venue. Upscale and imbued with an air of exclusivity, it is a favorite haunt of royalty, celebrities and the merely moneyed. 🗓 A-6764, ☏ 0 55 83/2 16 10, www. lech-zuers.at.

▸ **Orient Yourself:** Lech is in the far western reaches of Austria, close to the borders with Germany, Lichtenstein and Switzerland.
ᕦ **Also See:** St Anton am Arlberg, Arlberggebiet

Lech has won its reputation thanks in part to its merging with the neighboring resorts of **Zürs** 🎿 🎿 and **St. Anton** 🎿 🎿 (👤 *see separate entry*) to create a ski area capable of meeting the most demanding standards, but most of all because of its insistence on quality above quantity. Here, biggest is not allowed to be best, and tourist facilities have been built very much with the welfare of the natural environment in mind.

For this reason, guest capacity is only about 7 000, or three to six times smaller than the demand in the other major European winter sports resorts listed above. Accommodation consists mainly of hotels and family guesthouses in the luxury category with an après-ski scene to match. Expect plenty of exclusive boutiques, elegant cafés, gourmet restaurants and upscale cultural activities.

Lech also has plenty to offer in the summer months, when life takes on a much calmer pace. Although there are no particularly breathtaking panoramas, the soft green meadows of the surrounding countryside are most restorative. The area is great for hiking (👤 *see Excursions below*) and mountain bike tours, most popularly in the Formarin, Ferwall and Moos valleys. One of Lech's major attractions is the vast open-air swimming pool in a pretty woodland setting. Anglers can choose between lakes such as the Formarinsee, Spullsee, Zürssee or Zugweiher (🎣 *enquire about fishing permits at the Lech tourist office*).

Town Setting★

The town of Lech lies on a mountain plateau (alt 1 444-1 717m/4 738-5 633ft). Limestone peaks (the Mohnenfluh and Braunarlspitze to the north, Rote Wand to the west, Schafberg and Omeshorn to the south and Rüfispitze to the east) tower above the lush Alpine pastures and forests that grow at up to 1 800m/5 900ft above sea-level. Although difficult access roads and the sheer cliff faces of Omeshorn and Rüfikopf lend the area an undeniably mountainous aspect, the mountains around Lech are not in fact that high. None of the surrounding peaks are taller than 2 700m/8 850ft, and there is not a single glacier in sight.

The town of Lech is spread along the banks of its namesake river. It retains little physical evidence of its past, although the Gothic **church**, a few farmhouses from the days of the Valais (eg Haus Anger no 19) and the court in the Weisses Haus (16C) opposite the Hotel Krone are noteworthy exceptions.

Gritscher/ÖSTERREICH WERBUNG

Lech center

Further uphill, the resort of **Oberlech** (alt 1 700m/5 577ft) hugs a slope of the Kriegerhorn and is blessed with plenty of sunshine, excellent snow conditions and a sweeping view. In winter, Oberlech is car free and only accessible by cable-car.

If you're seeking respite from the hubbub of the ski slopes and fellow skiers, the hamlets of Zug to the west and Stubenbach to the east offer calmer alternatives.

Ski Slopes

The **Arlberg ski slopes** 🎿 🎿 🎿, which encompass from north to south the resorts of Lech, Zürs, Stuben and St. Anton, are the largest and most varied in Austria. They include over 260km/162mi of maintained and 180km/112mi of open slopes, to which 84 ski lifts give access. It is possible to ski from Lech to Zürs and back, and likewise from Stuben and St. Anton. To get from Zürs to Stuben or St. Anton, however, it is necessary to take the bus.

The **ski area** 🎿 attached to Lech extends over two mountains. Most of the ski runs are on the Kriegerhorn and the Zuger Hochlicht (alt 1 450-2 377m/4 757-7 799ft). The guaranteed snow cover and the gentle slopes make skiing here an enjoyable and relaxing experience. The Mohnenmähderpiste (very easy) and the Steinmähderpiste (intermediate) are definitely worth a try. Experienced skiers will prefer the Rüfikopf (alt 1 450-2 362m/4 757-7 749ft). This is the departure point for two off-piste runs (the Langerzug and the Tannegg), which can be tackled with a ski instructor.

Views

Zuger Hochlicht★★

Alt 2 377m/7 799ft. *In winter accessible to skiers only, allowing 1hr 30min roundtrip. Take the Schlegelkopf and then the Kriegerhorn chair-lifts, followed by the Mohnenfluh cable-car. In summer, it is possible to take the **Petersboden chair-lift** from Oberlech, and then do the tour of the Zuger Hochlicht round via the Mohnenfluhsattel gap and on to Butzensee Lake (2hr 15min roundtrip walk).* ○*Operates daily 8.30am-5pm.* ⊚€5.80 *roundtrip.* ☏ 0 55 83/2 16 10.

From the Kriegerhorn (alt 2 173m/7 129ft) there is a broad view of the Zuger Valley against a backdrop of the Rote Wand cliffs, to the west, and of the Zuger Hochlicht ski slopes, to the north. To the south lies Zürs, at the foot of the majestic Rüfispitze and the precipitous Roggspitze.

The Zuger Hochlicht reveals a beautiful **panorama**★★ of the Arlberg region, the Lechtal Alps and the Rätikon. There is an all-round panorama from the peak itself, reached in a few minutes from the far left end of the cable-car station. The Hochtannberg pass road can be seen further below.

Rüfikopf★

Alt 2 362m/7 749ft. ○*Cable-car Nov-Apr and mid-June-late Sep daily 8.30am-5.30pm.* ⊚€12 *roundtrip.* ☏ 0 55 83/2 16 10.

There is a beautiful overall view from this summit of the resort town and the Lech ski slopes against the rocky Mohnenfluh and Braunarlspitze peaks. The Rüfikopf is a good departure point for a ski trip to Zürs.

Excursions

The Lechtal Alps offer numerous possibilities for walking and hiking tours, with 200km/124mi of marked trails.

Spullersee★

▶ *The toll road to the lake is closed to cars from 9am to 3pm, but buses make the trip in 30min from the Lech post office (the tourist office has timetables). You can park in the Anger underground garage (free during summer) opposite the post office.*

This beautiful **drive**★ leads through bucolic countryside. Level with the toll booth, there is a municipal swimming pool set in the woods. Then the road passes through the pretty village of Zug, with Alpine pastures, through which the Spullerbach creek winds a course in between clumps of fir and larch.

Finally, after a very steep climb, the road reaches the **Spullersee**★, which lies in a spectacular natural amphitheater 1 827m/5 994ft above sea-level. The major summits are the Plattnitzer Spitze and Rohnspitze to the south, the Wildgrubenspitze to the east and the Spuller Schafberg (alt 2 679m/8 789ft) and Pfaffeneck to the north.

Formarinsee★

▶ *Take the bus to the lake. The first half of the trip is identical to that described above. Allow 30min for the bus ride and then 10min walk downhill on a well-maintained trail.*

The Formarinsee (alt 1 789m/5 869ft) lies at the foot of the Rote Wand (alt 2 704m/8 871ft).

Walk from the Formarinsee to the Spullersee★★

Allow 4hr for this quite taxing walk, parts of which should be tackled with care. Difference in altitude is about 600m/2 000ft. Climbing boots are essential. ⊙ This excursion is dangerous in mist or fog, or if the ground is damp.

Take the bus to the Formarinsee, but instead of walking down to the lake, take the trail climbing gently up to the left *(waymarked in yellow)*. The path, dotted with Alpine roses, leads right along the edge of the cliff, offering lovely views of the Formarinsee below before reaching the **Freiburger Hütte** (mountain refuge).

From here take path no 601 towards the Ravensburger Hütte *(waymarked in red)*. After 30min of easy climb towards the Formaletsch range the path crosses a picturesque limestone plateau, a real sea of rocks, known aptly enough as **Steinernes Meer** (⊙ *Take care! Do not leave the waymarked path.*)

Beyond here, the trail again becomes defined more clearly, climbing steeply up to the **Gehrengrat**, where chamois and ibex may be spotted. There is a good view of the Verwall range, the Kloster Valley and the Rätikon. A very steep path leads from the summit down to the Spullersee *(allow 1hr 30min; follow signs to Ravensburger Hütte, or "RH")*. On reaching the lake, turn left. After about 5min, the trail comes to the bus stop for the return trip to Lech.

OBERES LECHTAL

VORARLBERG UND TIROL

Upstream from Reutte, the Upper Lech Valley hollows out a deep 60km/37mi-long furrow between the Allgäu and Lechtal Alps. It's a sparsely inhabited area due, in large part, to poor agricultural soil, forcing many locals to leave the valley to seek employment elsewhere. However, having made their fortune, many return to their home villages for retirement, which accounts for the many grand houses, often sporting beautifully painted façades.

▶ **Orient Yourself:** The Upper Lech Valley is in the far western reaches of Austria.

◔ **Also See:** Fernpassstraße, Lech

From Warth to Reutte *61km/38mi*

Avalanches may temporarily close the road between Warth and Steeg. Generally, it is rarely possible to drive between Lech and Warth in winter.

Between Warth and **Steeg** the road travels through a series of gorges, before entering a harsh landscape of forest and rocks where it runs along mountain slopes with the Lech gushing along beneath them. In the hamlets of Hägerau and Holzgau, beyond Steeg, there are several houses with especially fine painted façades, the work of the Zeiller family of painters from Reutte (◔ see below).

Elbigenalp

The Tyrolean tradition of woodcarving is still very much alive in this village. In 1768 the painter **Joseph Anton Koch**, well known for his "heroic" landscapes and one of the most talented figures among the German Romantics, was born in the suburb of Untergiblen. Elbigenalp is also the birthplace of artist **Anna Stainer-Knittel** (1841-1915) who became a famous local figure better known as "**Geierwally**" and immortalized in novel, and on stage and screen.

Pfarrkirche St. Nikolaus

The sharp pointed spire of this church has made it one of the most distinctive images of the upper Lech Valley. The exuberant Baroque interior with a riot of almost luminous fresco decoration is the work of Johann Jakob Zeiller (◔ *see Reutte below*). Alongside the main church is the small 15C Martinskapelle whose crypt once served as a charnel house. The chapel interior is decorated with 15C frescoes and a painted panel representing *The Dance of Death*, a traditional 19C work.

Reutte

Reutte is the economic capital of the Ausserfern district and a good starting point for walks in summer and skiing in winter. Reutte is the home town of the Zeiller family of painters, whose Baroque frescoes adorn many a church interior in the Tyrol and south Germany. The most notable family member is **Johann Jakob Zeiller** (1708-83), whose masterworks include the frescoes in the Bavarian Benedictine foundations

Ceiling fresco in St. Nikolaus church, Elbigenalp

M. Hertlein/MICHELIN

at Ettal and Ottobeuren. In Reutte itself, the painted façades of the "Grünes Haus" (Green House) at Untermarkt 25, and "Schönes House" (Beautiful House) or "Zeiller-Haus" at Untergsteig 1 are attributed to him.

Heimatmuseum

In the Grünes Haus. ⓒ *early May-end Oct Tue-Sun 10am-noon and 2-5pm.* ⊛€5. ☎ *0 56 33/52 13.*
The local museum collections focus mainly on works by the Zeiller family and their pupils, as well as the history and customs of the local district.

LEOBEN

STEIERMARK
POPULATION 32 010 – ALT 541M/1 775FT

Leoben has been the center of the Styrian metalworking industry since the Middle Ages thanks to its proximity to the Erzberg with its vast iron ore deposits (ⓒ see Eisenerz). The city's industrial suburbs form a striking contrast to its medieval center and the Alpine surroundings. *Hauptplatz 12, A-8700,* ☎ *0 38 42/4 06 20, www.leoben.at.*

▸ **Orient Yourself:** Leoben is about 20km/12mi west of Bruck an der Mur, on the Mur River in central Austria.
ⓒ **Also See:** Eisenerz, Bruck an der Mur

Sights

Old town

The **Hauptplatz** is lined with gracious façades, such as the red 17C **Hacklhaus** with its sculpted decoration. West of here is the **Stadtpfarrkirche St. Xaver** (ⓒ *daily 8am-7pm.* ☎*0 38 42/4 32 36),* an early Baroque church once part of a Jesuit College. The interior preserves the original **furnishings★** of 1670, including the richly gilded main altar with its twisted columns framing a painting of St Francis Xavier by Heinrich Schönfeld.

MuseumsCenter & Kunsthalle★

Kirchgasse 6 & 8. MuseumsCenter ⓒ *year-round Tue-Sun 9am-6pm.* ⊛€5.50. *Kunsthalle* ⓒ*daily 9am-6pm.* ⊛*fee varies.* ☎ *0 38 42/4 06 24 08.*
In 2004, the sweeping collections of Leoben's local history museum were dusted off, rearranged and presented in a modern, appealing fashion using clever lighting techniques and multimedia technology. Seven themed sections spotlight Leoben's industrial heritage as well as major historical milestones such as the signing of the peace treaty between Napoleon and Emperor Franz II in 1797. It's all housed in a former Jesuit monastery. A modern annex, the **Kunsthalle Leoben**, often presents large-scale, high-caliber temporary exhibits, usually with an ethnological bent.

Stiftskirche Göss

ⓒ *by appointment only.* ☎ *0 38 42/2 21 48.*
In the southern suburb of Göss, this **church** counts an early Romanesque **crypt**, unusual twisted pillars resting on star-shaped bases and a richly carved **south porch★** among its outstanding features. It is surrounded by a former Benedictine convent whose buildings now house the **Gösser brewery**, which is open for tours and also contains a small museum.

LIENZ

TIROL

POPULATION 12 040 – ALT 678M/2 224FT

Lienz lies in the shadow of the deeply wrinkled, rocky slopes of the Dolomites and is the southern terminus of the transalpine Grossglockner and Felbertauern roads. Early settlers included the Romans and a hint of Italy, only 40km away, still pervades the town today. 🖹 *Europaplatz 1, A-9900, ☎ 0 48 52/6 52 65, www. lienz-tourismus.at.*

▶ **Orient Yourself:** Lienz is at the confluence of the Drava and Isel Rivers in eastern Tyrol.

⚅ **Also See:** Felbertauernstraße, Grossglockner-Hochalpenstraße

Sights

Schloss Bruck and the Regionalmuseum Osttirol

🕐 *mid May-end Oct daily 10am-6pm.* ⚅€7. ☎ 0 48 52/6 25 80.
The former seat of the counts of Görz, this 13C hilltop castle dominates Lienz' silhouette and offers wonderful views of the town. It now houses a regional museum, which displays local antiquities, folklore, crafts and Roman stone fragments.
The large **Albin-Egger-Lienz Gallery** gives a comprehensive survey of the work of this painter (1868-1926), who was often inspired by the Tyrol and the suffering of its people. In 2006, Egger-Lienz's famous *Totentanz 1806* (Dance of Death 1806), which had been seized by the Nazis, was restored to its rightful owner in the USA. It fetched €912 000 at a Vienna auction, a record for a work by this painter.
The museum also exhibits paintings and sculpture by contemporary artists.

LIENZ		Grafendorferstr.	6	Muchargasse	15
		Haugerpl.	7	Patriasdorferstr.	16
		Hauptpl.	8	Rosengasse	17
Albin-Egger-Str.	2	Johannespl.	10	Schweizergasse	20
Andrä-Kranzgasse	3	Kärntner Str.	12	St-Michaelsgasse	18
Emanuel-von-Hibler-Str.	4	Messinggasse	13	Südtirolerpl.	21

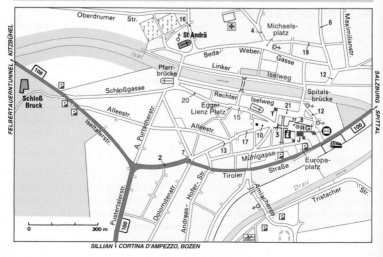

The two-storey late 13C **chapel** has fanciful cross-ribbed vaulting and 15C frescoes by Nikolaus Kentner and Simon von Talsten, a pupil of Friedrich Pacher.

Stadtpfarrkirche St. Andrä

Northwest of the town center, across the river, this Gothic church is famous for its **murals**, uncovered during a 1968 restoration. The **organ**, a 1618 work by Passau master Andreas Putz, is one of the oldest in Austria. Under the gallery are the magnificent **tombstones**★, in red Salzburg marble, of Count Leonhard (1506-07), the last of the Görz-Tirol line, and of his successor, Michael von Wolkenstein.

Within the once fortified graveyard stands the **war memorial chapel** containing the tomb of Albin Egger-Lienz as well as his cycle of paintings depicting the unflinching brutality of war. *Key to the chapel can be obtained from Pfarrgasse no 13.*

STIFT LILIENFELD★

NIEDERÖSTERREICH

Founded in 1202 by Babenberg Duke Leopold IV as a Cistercian abbey, Stift Lilienfeld is the largest medieval monastery complex in Austria. Upon returning from a Crusade, the duke presented the monastery with a relic of the Holy Cross, which is still a major object of veneration today. Affiliated with Heiligenkreuz near Vienna, the abbey is a superb example of the transitional style bridging Romanesque and Gothic architecture.

▶ **Orient Yourself:** The abbey is about 25km/15mi south of St Pölten.

👣 **Also See:** St Pölten, Mariazell

Tour

🚶 *Guided tour (1hr) Mon-Sat 10am and 2pm, Sun and holidays 2pm.* ☞€7 *with tour, €3 without.* ☎ *0 27 62/5 24 20. www.stift-lilienfeld.at.*

Stiftskirche

This is the largest church in Lower Austria, 82m/269ft long by 21m/69ft wide. The pillared basilica is essentially Romanesque in concept with its cruciform ground plan and round-arched windows, although the Gothic period

Nepomuk group, Lilienfeld

R. Chévret/MICHELIN

The bridge saint

Bohemia-born **St John of Nepomuk** went to Prague in 1370, serving first as a priest and later as vicar-general to the archbishop. In a dispute between the archbishop and King Wenceslas I, he defended the rights of the church and especially the sanctity of the confessional. For this reason, in 1393, the king had him tortured and thrown from the bridge into the Vltava. Hence, statues of this martyr have come to grace many bridges in southern Germany, Bohemia and Austria.

brought the addition of flying buttresses. Have a look at the **west doorway**★, then take in the uplifting ambience of the interior with its Gothic vaulting and **Baroque furnishings**★ that blend beautifully with the medieval architecture. The predominant tone is the black of the Türnitz marble from which the altars, the pulpit, the choir organ case and the Leopold memorial are made, lavishly lit up by gleaming gold leaf. The painting of the *Assumption of the Virgin Mary* on the high altar is by **Daniel Gran** (1746).

Cloister★

The ribbed vaulting is supported on finely proportioned consoles by clustered pillars of attractively colored stone. On the north side are remarkable stained-glass windows from the first half of the 14C. The **chapter-house** is one of the oldest parts of the whole complex, with stone benches lining the square room. Over the cellarium, a well-preserved storage cellar, is the impressive two-aisled, lay brothers' **dormitory**, the only one of its kind in Austria to have survived from the Middle Ages.

Library★

As is always the case in a monastery, the library is one of the finest rooms. Dating from 1700, it has magnificent stucco decoration and ceiling frescoes as well as richly inlaid bookcases and doors. Also sneak a peek inside the adjoining picture gallery.

LINZ★

OBERÖSTERREICH
POPULATION 197 960 – ALT 266M/873FT

Linz, the capital of Upper Austria and the country's third-largest city, straddles the Danube at a widening of the river valley. Three bridges link the city with its suburb of Urfahr, on the left bank. In fact, Linz owes a good deal of its prosperity to the Danube. Today it is an important industrial city, whose strong support for culture and the art garnered it the title of European Capital of Culture 2009. Austria's oldest and largest churches are both in Linz. ⓘ *Hauptplatz 1, A-4010, ☏ 07 32/70 70 17 77, www.linz.at.*

▶ **Orient Yourself:** Linz is in northwestern Austria, not far from Germany.
🅿 **Parking:** An automated parking guide system directs you to the nearest garage (fee-based), of which there are several in the center. Parking is free in lots by the train station and across the river on Urfahrmarkt.
👁 **Don't Miss:** Lentos Kunstmuseum, Ars Electronica Center, Neuer Dom
🕐 **Organizing Your Time:** It takes a full day to do Linz justice.
🧒 **Especially for Kids:** Ars Electronica Center, Grottenbahn
🕑 **Also See:** Stift St Florian

A Bit of History

Although settled since around 4 000 BC, Linz wasn't really put on the map until the Romans founded a camp called Lentia here in 1AD. In the Middle Ages, the town became a major trading center and even enjoyed a brief stint as imperial capital under Friedrich III from 1489 to 1493. Protestantism fell on fertile ground here, drawing the astronomer Johannes Kepler in its wake who wrote his best-known work, *Harmonice mundi*, while in town. Eventually, though the Counter Reformation struck back with a vengeance and Linz remained a provincial backwater until the

Industrial Age arrived in the 19C, bringing factories and the railroad. Adolf Hitler took a particular liking to the city and locals largely returned the affection. The Nazis built the large steel and ironworks along the Danube that still provide employment to many today. Since the end of the Second World War industrial development has accelerated with emphasis on chemicals and other heavy industries.

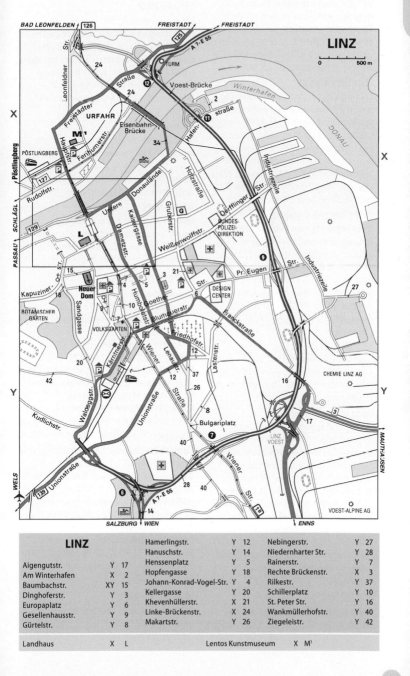

Address Book

PRACTICAL INFORMATION

TOURIST INFORMATION

Tourist-Information, *Hauptplatz 1*, 🕐 Mon-Fri 8am-7pm, Sat 9am-7pm, Sun and public holidays 10am-7pm (Nov-Apr until 6pm in each case).
Tourist-Information, *Urfahrmarkt 1, 4040 Linz,* 🕐 daily July-Sept 10am-6pm, Oct-June Mon and Thur 8am-4pm, Tue and Fri 8am-1pm. ☎ *07 32/70 70 29 39.*

LINZ CITY TICKET

This entitles you to a city sightseeing-tour, a 20% reduction on a river trip on the Danube, free entry to 12 museums, the botanical gardens and the zoo, a roundtrip on the Pöstlingberg mountain railway and the no 3 tram, a Grottenbahn ride and a €10 food and drink voucher. The Linz City Ticket is sold at tourist offices and costs €20.

TRIPS ON THE DANUBE

Boat trip between Passau-Linz-Passau: Donauschiffahrt Wurm & Köck, *Untere Donaulände 1, 4020 Linz,* ☎ *07 32/78 36 07,* or *Höllgasse 26, 94032 Passau, Germany,* ☎ *+49 8 51 92 92 92.*
Boat trip between Krems-Linz-Krems: Donauschiffahrt Ardagger, *3321 Ardagger 155,* ☎ *0 74 79/6 46 40.*

CITY TOUR

Linz-City-Express: tour in a miniature train with commentary (25min) – in season 🕐 10am-6pm, hourly (if demand is heavy, every 30min). Leaves from the Hauptplatz and costs 🎫 €5.

PUBLIC TRANSPORT

Individual tickets Single tickets and day passes (Tageskarten) can be obtained from the ticket vending machines, while **multiple tickets** (Mehrfahrtenkarten) for six journeys and transferable **runabout tickets** (Netzkarten), valid for several days and giving unlimited travel on buses and trams, are available from ticket offices in Trafiken (tobacconists' shops). Information on public transport services is provided by ESG-Kundenzentrum, Landstraße 85/1 ☎ *07 32/78 01 70 02.*

POST OFFICES

Main post office: Hauptpostamt, *Bahnhofplatz 11,* 🕐 daily 6am-midnight

Branch post offices *Domgasse 1, Bismarckstraße 2, Volksfeststraße 2, Schmiedegasse 14 (usually* 🕐 *8am-noon and 2-6pm).*

SHOPPING

Shops and department stores concentrate along Landstraße, which is pedestrianized for about 2km/1.25mi from Hauptplatz to Bürgerstraße, and its side streets. There are exclusive boutiques in the arcade on the Landstraße. The Herrenstraße has another pedestrian shopping precinct.

MARKETS

Südbahnhof: daily market in the mornings, with a large market on Tues and Fri.
Hauptplatz: farmers' market Fri 10am-2pm, flea market Sat 6am-2pm.

SOUVENIRS

Crafts: Heimatwerk, Landstraße 31; Linzer Torte (local speciality, a jam-filled cake): Café Jindrak (several branches, including Herrenstraße 22).

ENTERTAINMENT

Landestheater (Provincial Theater), *Promenade 39,* ☎ *07 32/7 61 11 00.*
Theater Phönix, *Wiener Straße 25,* ☎ *07 32/66 65 00.*
Konzerthaus Brucknerhaus, *Untere Donaulände 7,* ☎ *07 32/7 61 20.*
Posthof, *Posthofstraße 43,* ☎ *07 32/7 70 54 80.* Cabaret, stand-up, theater, dance, broad range of musical events.
Casino Linz, *Rainerstraße 2-4,* ☎ *07 32/65 44 87.*

CINEMAS

Central Kinocenter, *Landstraße 36,* ☎ *07 32/77 16 60.*
Kolosseum, *Schillerplatz 1,* ☎ *07 32/66 30 86.*
Hollywood Megaplex, *Pluskaufstraße 12, in Pasching,* ☎ *0 72 29/6 93 00 15.*
Art-house cinemas:
Café Kino Cinematograph, *Obere Donaulände 51,* ☎ *07 32/78 56 03.*
Moviemento, *Dametzstraße 30,* ☎ *07 32/78 40 90 50.*

WHERE TO EAT

Kremsmünsterer Stuben, *Altstadt 10,* ☎ *07 32/78 21 11.*

Josef – Das Stadtbräu, *Landstraße 49,* ☎ *07 32/77 31 65.*
Stieglbräu zum Klosterhof, *Landstraße 30,* ☎ *07 32/77 33 73.*
Sturm's Wirtshaus, *Am Pöstlingberg 12* (with a panoramic view of the town), ☎ *07 32/73 14 83.*
Ursulinenhof, *Landstraße 31,* ☎ *07 32/77 46 86.*

CAFÉS AND BARS

Cafés

Café Glockenspiel, *Hauptplatz 18;*
Café Jindrak, *Herrenstraße 22.*
Many of the most popular bars are in the old town, such as **Grand Café-Daniel Sassi** (in the arcade, *Spittelwiese 8*). Other good places to go include the **Irish Pub** (*Hessenplatz 19*), **S'Kistl** (*Altstadt 17*), and **S'Linzerl** (*Hofberg 5*). To listen to music, head for **17er Keller** (*Hauptplatz*) or the **Kasper-Keller** (*Landstraße 24,* food available, jazz jam session every Tues, admission free),

Stieglitz im Klosterhof (*Landstraße 30*) or **Joe's bar** in the Arcotel (*Untere Donaulände 9*).

DATES FOR YOUR DIARY

Linz Fest: May. Wide range of musical entertainment including pop, hip-hop, jazz, soul, folk and popular Viennese music.
Klangplatz Hauptplatz: June-Aug, every Fri. Jazz, pop or rock music concert on the Hauptplatz.
Linzer Pflasterspektakel: one weekend in July. Cabaret artists, musicians and travelling entertainers from all over the world transform the centre of Linz into a big stage.
Festival Ars Electronica: Sept. Performances using and discussions on the use of electronic media (symposia, happenings etc).
Internationales Brucknerfest: Sept-Oct. Concerts of classical music.

General View

Pöstlingberg★ (X)

Kids 4.5km/3mi northwest. The Pöstlingberg narrow-gauge railway links Linz-Urfahr (north bank) with the Pöstlingberg. To get to the valley station, take tram no 3 or cross Nibelungenbrücke to the left bank of the Danube. Turn left into Rudolfstraße, then right into Hagenstraße, right again by the oratory and park in the lot below the church. ⏱Departure from Pöstlingberg station "Bergbahnhof" Mon-Sat 5.20am-8.20pm every 20min; Sun and public holidays 7.15am-11.15 every 30min, 11.15-8.20 every 20min. €3.50 roundtrip train only, €5.60 roundtrip tram and train. ☎ 07 32/78 01 75 45.
Europe's steepest narrow-gauge mountain railway covers the 2.9km/1.8mi journey to the top of the Pöstlingberg with its Baroque church in 16min. From a flower-decked terrace below the church there is an extensive **view**★ from nearly 300m/1 000ft down into the Danube Valley. Also up here, and a winner with kids, is the **Grottenbahn**, a dragon-pulled miniature-train chugging through a fairy-tale landscape.

Old Linz★ (Z)

Hauptplatz

This strikingly large square was laid out in the 13C and has at its center a Trinity Column (*Dreifaltigkeitssäule*), erected to commemorate the town's escape from plague, fire and Turkish invasion.

▶ *Leave the square along the Domgasse (5).*

Linz headdress

Alter Dom St. Ignatius

🕐 *Mon-Sat 7am-7pm; Sun 7am-8pm.* ☎ *07 32/77 08 66.*
This 17C Jesuit church by Pietro Francesco Carolone is the city's most important Baroque house of worship. The simple façade forms a striking contrast to the interior, where stucco, pink marble columns, an elaborately carved pulpit and choir stalls, and a high altar adorned with marble statues make up a highly elaborate decor. Bruckner served as church organist from 1855 to 1868.

▷ *Turn right into the Graben (Moat); continue into the Promenade (30); turn right to the Landhaus.*

Landhaus (L)

This 16C building, now the seat of the provincial government, wraps around an inner courtyard lined on two sides by arcades and anchored by an octagonal fountain. The seven figures on its base represent the planets and recall the years 1612 to 1626 when Kepler taught at the regional secondary school, then based at the Landhaus.

Trinity Column on the Hauptlatz, Linz

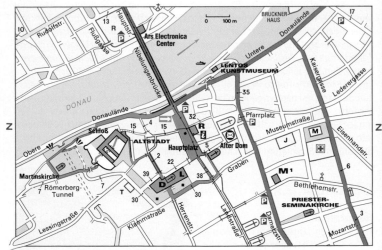

LINZ			Fiedlerstr.	Z	13	Promenade	Z	30
			Hagenstr.	Z	10	Rathausgasse	Z	32
Altstadt	Z	2	Hofberg	Z	4	Rechte Donaustr.	Z	35
Dinghoferstr.	Z	3	Hofgasse	Z	15	Römerstr.	Z	7
Domgasse	Z	5	Honauerstr.	Z	17	Schmidttorstr.	Z	38
Elisabethstr.	Z	6	Klosterstr.	Z	22	Theatergasse	Z	39

Landhaus	Z	L	Neue Rathaus	Z	R¹
Minoritenkirche	Z	D	Nordico - Museum der Stadt Linz	Z	M²

Composers Welcomed

Linz was a staging-post for **Mozart** in the course of his many tours; in 1782 he wrote his 36th symphony, the "Linz Symphony", here in just four days for a concert he was due to give at the city theater. **Beethoven** too composed a symphony in Linz, his Eighth, but more than any other composer, the city cherishes the memory of **Anton Bruckner** who was cathedral organist here for 12 years. Every year Linz keeps his memory alive through its international festival of classical music, the Brucknerfest.

Minoritenkirche (D)
May-Oct daily 8.30am-4pm; Nov-Apr daily 8.30am-11am. ☎ *0732-7 72 01 13 64.*
The Gothic church, founded in the 13C by the Franciscans, was remodelled in the Rococo style in the 18C. The altarpiece on the high altar by Bartolomäus Altomonte represents the Annunciation; the altarpieces on the six side altars are the work of Kremser Schmidt.

▶ *Take the Altstadt north.*

Schloss
The oldest part of the palace, which was the residence of Emperor Friedrich III, dates from the end of the 15C. It houses the art and historical collections of the provincial museum.

Schlossmuseum★
Tues-Fri 9am-6pm; Sat-Sun 10am-5pm. *1 Jan, 24, 25, 31 Dec.* ♿ ⬤€4. ☎ *07 32/77 44 19. www.schlossmuseum.at.*
This museum offers insight into the art and cultural history of Upper Austria. If you have limited time, focus on the collection of paintings from the Gothic period and the 19th and early 20th century with some fine examples by Gustav Klimt, Oskar Kokoschka and Egon Schiele. You'll also find plenty of gems among the fine traditional costumes and hats, the impressive arms and armour and the Gothic and Renaissance period rooms.

▶ *Walk west on Römerstraße.*

Martinskirche
First documented in 799, this is considered Austria's oldest church. It was built using pieces of debris left over from the 1C Roman camp and combines various Romanesque and Gothic features. A glass door separates you from the interior which can only be seen during Mass and on guided city tours.

▶ *Return to the Hauptplatz via the embankment (Obere Donaulände).*

Additional Sights

Priesterseminarkirche★ (Z)
The 18C seminary church, designed by Johann-Lukas von Hildebrandt, is a small building with great majesty. The graceful stuccowork is by Paolo d'Allio, while the moving Crucifixion over the high altar stems from the brush of Altomonte.

Neuer Dom (Y)
This neo-Gothic edifice is the largest church in Austria, able to accommodate 20 000 parishioners. Consecrated in 1924, its spire soars to a lofty 134m/440ft, only 3m/10ft shorter than the one of the Stephansdom in Vienna. The stained-glass windows

are particularly interesting, especially the "Linz Window" depicting scenes from town history.

Nordico Museum der Stadt Linz (Z M²)

🕑*Mon–Fri 8am-5pm; Sat-Sun 2-5pm.* ♿🎫*€4.* ☎ *07 32/70 70 19 12. www. nordico.at.*
This museum presents changing exhibits on city history and also draws crowds with its big exhibitions on nature and Linz' cultural history. Its name goes back to the 17C and 18C when the Jesuits used the building to train young Catholics from Northern Europe.

Lentos Kunstmuseum★★

🕑*Year-round Wed, Fri-Mon 10am-6pm, Thu 10am-10pm.* 🎫*€6.50.* ☎*07 32/70 70 36 14. www.lentos.at.*
The Lentos is a spectacular showcase of modern art featuring an international cast of artists, including Gustav Klimt, Lovis Corinth and Max Pechstein as well as post-1945 masters such as Andy Warhol and Keith Haring. Changing exhibitions of equally high caliber supplement the permanent galleries. Since 2003, the collection has been housed in a bold new building by the Swiss architects Weber & Hofer, which is especially stunning after dark when its façade color toggles between blue and red.

Ars Electronica Center

🕑*Wed-Sun 10am-6pm.* 🕑*24, 25 Dec.* ♿🎫*€7.* ☎ *07 32/72 72 12. www.aec.at/en/index. asp.*
Kids An unapologetically modern building houses this "museum of the future", a high-tech palace entirely devoted to the latest in digital technology and media. This is where you can explore virtual worlds in 3-D in the CAVE installation; experience Linz from a bird's eye perspective by boarding the flight simulator "Humphrey"; or interact with Nuvo, the humanoid robot - to mention just a few of the often mind-bending experiences. Fun and educational at once, the exhibit is indeed a window on the future.

Excursions

Mühlviertel
Roundtrip of 90km/56mi

The Mühlviertel district derives its name from the small Mühl river, which flows into the Danube above Linz. It is a hilly upland region with wide, forested valleys extending as far as the Czech frontier.

▶ *Leave Linz on the road (no 126) north to Bad Leonfelden.*

Leaving Linz the road enters a little verdant gorge and climbs gently, sometimes among rocks, sometimes among orchards. The wild nature of the hills, where

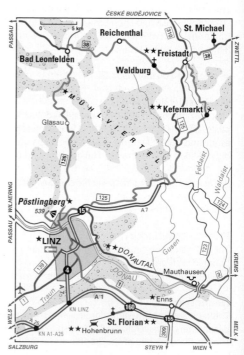

meadows alternate with fir forests, grows more marked near Bad Leonfelden. About 500m north of this town bear right towards Freistadt.

Freistadt★ ⚫ *See Freistadt*

▶ *Right past Freistadt, leave the Linz road and cross to the east bank of the small Feldaist River.*

Kefermarkt

Kefermarkt on the Feldaist is surrounded by a restful, hilly landscape marking the transition between the Mühlviertel and the granite plateaux of the Waldviertel.

St. Wolfgangskirche

🕒 *Daily 8am-5pm.* ☎ *0 79 47/62 03.*

This Gothic church contains a remarkable **altarpiece**★★ carved of wood by an unknown sculptor. More than 13m/40ft high, it is outstanding as much for its size as for the beauty of its proportions and the delicacy of the limewood carvings. The three figures in the central panel are St Wolfgang, flanked by St Peter and St Christopher. On the shutters are depicted the Annunciation and the Birth of Christ *(above)* and the Adoration of the Magi and the Assumption of Mary *(below)*.

▶ *At the main crossroads in Kefermarkt turn right towards the railway station; cross the track and the Feldaist. After 7km/4mi turn left onto the main road, no 125, connecting Freistadt and Linz.*

MALTATAL★★

KÄRNTEN

A 30km/18.5mi stretch of road leads through this magnificent valley, one of the most beautiful destinations in Carinthia. It became famous after the construction of the Kölnbrein dam and reservoir, but its main appeal really lies in its highly diverse landscape. Until reaching the village of Malta the valley is wide and characterized by alternating meadows and forested patches. Beyond here it narrows, then opens up again to reveal the magnificent glacier panorama of the Ankogel massif and the Hochalmspitze peak. The area is also a terrific launch pad for medium- and high-altitude Alpine hikes.

▶ **Orient Yourself:** The valley extends from Gmünd (⚫ see Gmünd, Kärnten) to the foothills of the Hohe Tauern National Park in southern Austria.
🔶 **Don't Miss:** A drive on the Malta-Hochalmstraße.
⚫ **Also See:** Gmünd

Sights

Village of Malta

The village at 840m/2 755ft above sea-level is an entrancing holiday spot. The church of Maria Hilf, which dates from the 15C, houses some fine frescoes from the same period, including a rare image of Mary in labour on the south wall. The Baroque decor is beautifully uniform. The high altar and pulpit were made in 1730.

Malta-Hochalmstraße★★

A toll is charged past Malta.

This excellently laid out road meanders over nine bridges and through seven tunnels, including a memorable one designed as a hairpin bend. Attractions include the luxuriant vegetation (spruce, larch, alder and birch) and the waterfalls, 30 in all, roaring down into the valley. The Fallbach, the Melnikfall and the Hinterer Maralmfall are particularly impressive.

Kölnbreinsperre★

During high season, ⚊⚊ there are guided tours of the dam on the hour.

The road ends at this dam located 1 900m/6 233ft above sea-level. It is the largest dam in Austria measuring 200m/656ft high, 41m/134ft thick at the base and 626m/2 054ft wide. Apart from its phenomenal technical prowess, the design of this concrete colossus with its flowing, parabolic shape, is just as impressive. Inside the panoramic look-out tower is an **information center** (🕐*mid-May–early Oct daily from 7am;* ⚊*free;* ☎ *04 63/2 37 16)* with films about the Hohe Tauern National Park and a multimedia display on the dam's construction. Also here is the **Tauernschatzkammer**★, a treasure trove of local rock crystals and other minerals.

The dam is the point of departure for some wonderful walks. Even the easy hike around the lake provides wonderful views over the **surrounding Alpine landscape**★★. If you can muster the stamina, you should tackle the Arlscharte (see next).

Hike to the Arlscharte and the Arlhöhe★★

3hr 45min roundtrip from the dam. Head towards the "Osnabrücker Hütte" mountain lodge.

The trail skirts the northern lakeshore and soon proffers a magnificent view over the Ankogel glaciers. After walking for 45min, you will reach a memorial to a tragic accident that occurred during the building of the dam. Turn right and continue along a relatively steep Alpine flower trail. After 10min, when the trail forks, head left for the steep 45min climb to the peak (look for the red and white markings). At

Y. Bontoux

Kölnbrein dam

the top, your efforts will be rewarded with magnificent views over lakes, valleys, a small glacier and the towering Hochalmspitze peak.

For another dose of impressive views, continue to the Arlhöhe (alt 2 326m/7 631ft). Walk a few steps towards Pfringersee, then turn left and pick up a kind of ridge trail *(marked with a red cross on a white background)* taking you to your destination in about 20min. An orientation map helps identify mountains and other natural landmarks. Backtrack along the same trail.

Excursion to the Gösskarspeicher★

Total trip involves a 1hr drive and 45min walk.

Halfway between Malta and the toll point, turn to the left towards the Giessener Hütte mountain lodge. The narrow 12km/7.5mi mountain road is quite steep and follows the course of the Gössbach, even fording the river bed at one point (danger, especially during bad weather; watch out for flood warnings). The countryside is rugged and refreshingly unspolled.

Leave your car in the lot and continue on foot to the Gösskar reservoir *(15min climb)*. This is a beautiful **wooded area**★, lorded over by the Grosser Gössspitze and the Dösnerspitze peaks.

Walk along the left shore of the lake for fantastic **views**★ over the Hochalmspitze peak and its glacier, from which waterfalls thunder down.

Return to the reservoir, continue to its end and then to the right along the meadow (through a fence) until you reach a wide, moderately steep trail for a **view**★ over the rocky peaks of the Riekenkopf and the Pfaffenberger Nocken. Return to the parking lot or, if you're feeling ambitious, climb up to the Giessener Hütte mountain lodge, the starting point for the climb to the legendary Hochalm peak.

MARIA SAAL★

KÄRNTEN
POPULATION 3 850 – ALT 504M/1 654FT

Maria Saal is a small, sleepy town famous for its pilgrimage church, which jauntily perches atop a fortified hill, its twin towers visible from far away. The current Late Gothic incarnation dates from the 15C and stands atop the original one founded by Bishop Modestus of Salzburg in the 8C as a launch pad for the re-Christianization of Carinthia following the Barbarian invasions. 🛈 *Am Platzl 7, A-9063, ☎ 0 42 23/22 14. www.maria.saal.at.*

▶ **Orient Yourself:** Maria Saal is about 7km/4mi north of Klagenfurt in southern Austria.

🅿 **Parking:** Look for public lots along Hauptstraße and Arnsdorfer Straße near the open-air museum.

⟳ **Also See:** St Veit an der Glan, Gurk, Klagenfurt

Dom ★★

Exterior

With its twin towers of volcanic stone and its vast stone roof, this church makes a striking impression. Completed in 1460, it is protected by a fortified enclosure and fronted by an octagonal **charnel house** that is encircled by a two-story arcaded gallery. The south facade incorporates numerous stone reliefs and **tombstones**, including several scavenged from the nearby ruined Roman settlement of Virunum. Stand-outs include a relief showing Achilles dragging the corpse of Hector, and the **Roman postal wagon**★, a symbol for the journey of a dead soul into the afterlife. The magnificent **Keutschacher Epitaph**★ (c 1510), a red marble tombstone, depicts the Coronation of the Virgin. In the porch is another interesting Roman gravestone featuring a she-wolf feeding Romulus and Remus.

Interior

The triple-nave church is a typical Late Gothic building. The bays of the ribbed vaulting above the nave are decorated with frescoes depicting the genealogy of Christ.

The Baroque **high altar** is the place of honor for the stone figure of the Madonna (1425) that's still much venerated by pilgrims. Two other altars deserving closer inspection are the splendid **Arndorf Altar**★ in the north chancel, which shows the Coronation of the Virgin Mary, and the Altar of St George in the south chancel, which depicts the saint as the Dragon-Slayer, symbolizing the triumph of Christianity. Also of interest are the **tomb of St Modestus**★ in the left side aisle in the Saxon chapel and the **fresco** of the Three Magi on the north wall of the chancel.

R. Chéret/MICHELIN

Keutschacher Epitaph, Maria Saal

Kärntner Freilichtmuseum★

300m/330yd north of the village center. Allow 45min. ⓍMay-mid-Oct Tue-Sun 10am-6pm (last admission 5pm). ♿☎€5. ☎ 0 42 23/31 66. www.freilichtmuseum-mariasaal.at.

Some 33 historic farmhouses, stables, barns and other outbuildings offer unique insights into rural life in 16C and 17C Carinthia. All were taken down and reassembled at this open-air museum, nicely located in a hilly wooded setting. Most are log cabins and either thatched with straw or roofed with shingles. The living quarters have a smoking room with an oven and an open hearth.

A reconstructed covered wooden bridge leads to the mill area. Here, a mill wheel, a turbine-like mill and a saw-mill illustrate both the difficult working conditions endured by the millers and the ingenuity of early mechanization.

Log cabin construction

This type of construction has been typical in Carinthia for centuries. It is used for living quarters and such outbuildings as barns and drying sheds. Beams of straight-grained pine or larch are laid horizontally on top of each other, alternating crown and root end. To build corners, the beams are dovetailed into each other to strengthen the joint. Since this corner joint has taken on various forms since the 16C – swallow's tails, bells, faces – it often points to the age of a building. The gaps between the beams were padded with a special kind of moss or straw matting, while the façades were sometimes filled in with a clay wash.

MARIAZELL★

STEIERMARK
POPULATION 1 930 – ALT 868M/2 848FT

Mariazell is the most important place of pilgrimage in Austria. It is also a popular year-round resort, occupying a charming site★ on the gentle, forested slopes of the extreme eastern end of the Alps. For a bird's-eye view of the region, ride the cable-car to the top of the **Bürgeralpe** , the local mountain. *Hauptplatz 13, A-8630, ☎ 0 38 82/23 66, www.mariazell.at and www.basilika-mariazell.at.*

▶ **Orient Yourself:** Mariazell is 150km/94mi north of Graz and 130km/80mi southwest of Vienna in central Austria.

☉ **Also See:** Bruck an der Mur

A Bit of History

It wasn't long after the Benedictines from St. Lambrecht Abbey founded a priory here in 1157 that pilgrims started flocking to Mariazell to worship a small wooden, miracle-working Madonna. Its popularity really took off when King Ludwig of Hungary attributed his victory over the Turks in 1370 to this statuette and had a chapel (the Gnadenkapelle) built in thanksgiving. From that time on, the worship of the Virgin of Mariazell increasingly came to symbolize the spiritual forces that guaranteed the cohesion of the Austrian Empire. To this day pilgrims from all over central Europe descend upon Mariazell, especially in summer for the Saturday evening torchlight processions and for special ceremonies on Assumption Day (15 August) and the Birth of Mary (September 8).

Basilica★

In the 17C the growing number of pilgrims made it necessary to enlarge the earlier Gothic building from the 14C. Architect **Domenico Sciassia** lengthened and widened the nave and topped the eastern end with a dome. He also added two much squatter onion-capped towers on either side of the central 90m-high Gothic spire, resulting in a slightly awkward design that has nonetheless become an emblem of this pilgrimage site. The main doorway still sports the original carved tympanum.

Gnadenkapelle (Chapel of Miracles)

The object of veneration is enshrined in this small, trapezoidal chapel at the center of the church. Dressed like a precious doll, the seated Madonna is placed beneath a valuable silver baldaquin resting on 12 columns; it was designed by Johann Emmanuel Fischer von Erlach the Younger (1727). The enclosing grille, also of silver, was ordered by Maria Theresa from Viennese silversmiths in 1756.

West Nave

By enlarging the nave, Sciassia made room along the aisles for a series of side chapels, and on the first storey for a gallery whose large windows flood the church with natural light. To appreciate fully the details of the Baroque decoration – stucco and paintings – one should walk along these galleries.

The chapel in the north aisle, dedicated to St Ladislas, King of Hungary, until fairly recently housed the mortal remains of Cardinal Mindszenty, Primate of Hungary, now transferred to Esztergom in that country.

East Nave

This truly monumental piece of Baroque architecture is superbly proportioned. It forms a second, inner nave, beyond a false transept. The first bay is lit by an oval lantern-dome which harmonizes with the extended shape of the whole church. The second square bay, which closes the perspective, contains the majestic high altar by Johann Bernhard Fischer von Erlach, which shows the Crucifixion and was completed in 1704. Lorenzo Mattielli's statues of the Crucifixion group, like those of the great angels guarding the Gnadenkapelle, are silver-plated wooden copies of the solid silver statues melted down to meet the needs of the Austrian treasury during the Napoleonic Wars.

Schatzkammer (Treasury)

May-end Oct Tues-Sat 10am-3pm, Sun 11am-4pm. €3. 0 38 82/2 59 50.
A staircase in the southwest tower leads up to the treasury, which is filled with six centuries of often endearing votive offerings left here by pilgrims. A particular highlight is the church's second-most important object of veneration, a 14C painting of the Virgin also donated by Ludwig of Hungary. It is believed to be the work of Siennese artist Andrea Vanni.

MATREI IN OSTTIROL

TIROL

POPULATION 4 900 – ALT 1 000M/3 300FT

The popular holiday resort of Matrei in East Tyrol lies in beautiful and diverse surroundings and boasts an exceptionally pleasant climate. The market town lies in a restful low-mountain area at the foot of the Grossvenediger and Grossglockner, the highest and most impressive peaks in Austria. Thanks to its extraordinary setting, it has become a well-known gateway for **hikes**★★★ into the Eastern Alps.

▶ **Orient Yourself:** Matrei lies at the junction of the Tauerntal, Virgental and Iseltal, about 30km/19mi north of Lienz.
Organizing Your Time: Budget a full day for the trip to the Karl-Matrei pass and Grossdorf.
Especially for Kids: Hiking the Europa-Panoramaweg.
Also See: Felbertauernstraße

In winter, the **ski area**★ offers satisfactory conditions for skiers. Three chair-lifts and three T-bar lifts lead to 30km/18.5mi of pistes of between 1 000m/3 300ft and 2 400m/7 900ft in length, some with artificial snow. It is a particularly attractive resort for lovers of long distance skiing and ski tours, with 24km/15mi of long pistes and vast off-piste areas.

Sights

St. Nikolauskirche

Approach by car. From the main square in Matrei, cross the bridge to Lienzer Straße, then turn left onto the Bichler Straße. The road leaves the village, leading over another bridge and then right past a wooden well. Turn right at the next two intersections. The road is now unpaved but is quite drivable. Turning right onto the next small road leads you straight to the church.

In a meadow above Matrei, St. Nikolaus is a 12C church with Romanesque and Gothic elements. An outstanding architectural feature is the unusual two-story Romanesque choir decorated with **frescoes**★. The lower level represents scenes from Genesis, while the upper storey - reached via a double staircase - shows the four elements carrying the 12 Apostles and the Evangelists.

Excursions

Europa-Panoramaweg★★
Budget about 4hr for the entire trip, including about 2hr walking time.

[Kids] This is a wonderful, family-friendly hiking excursion, where you'll be treated to panoramic **views**★ taking in 60 peaks over 3 000m/10 000ft, including the Grossglockner. From Matrei, catch the Goldriedbahn cable car to the mountain station at 2 150m/ 7054ft, then embark

A fresco in St. Nikolauskirche

Y. Bontoux

on the easy walk to the **Kals-Matrei-Törlhaus**★★ along a wildflower-lined path. Stop here for refreshments or continue to the mountain station of the Blauspitzbahn where there is another restaurant as well as a high-altitude children's playground. Take the Blauspitzbahn down into Kals where buses run back to Matrei (weekdays only, enquire about departure times at the tourist office).

Virgental★
18km/11mi drive from Matrei to Ströden.
This beautiful valley to the south of the Grossvenediger glacier makes for a delightful summer excursion. The dense forests in the lower part and the Alpine mountain scenery in the upper part are impressive. Prägraten is the most beautiful holiday resort in the valley. The Umbal falls at the end of the road are well worth a visit.

BURG MAUTERNDORF★

SALZBURG

On a trade route in use since Roman times, this 13C castle served as a residence for the archbishops of Salzburg who wished to keep a close eye on their possessions in the Lungau region. Today, the ancient walls house family-oriented exhibits taking you on a fun-filled trip back to the late 15C and the castle at the time of Archbishop Leonhard von Keutschach.

▶ **Orient Yourself:** The castle is in the southern Salzburger Land, about 120km/75mi southeast of Salzburg.
🕓 **Organizing Your Time:** Budget about 2hr and 30min for a visit, including a tour and spin around the museum.
[Kids] **Especially for Kids:** Ask about the kids' version of the audio guide. There's also a terrific, castle-like playground with a superlong "dragon slide".
👣 **Also See:** Radstätter Tauernstraße, Tamsweg

Tour

👣 *Guided tour May-Oct daiiy10am-6pm. ✑€8, incl castle tour and museum; 26 Dec-23 Apr Tue-Fri 10.30am-6pm. ✑€6.50, incl castle tour. ☎ 06472/74 26. www. salzburg-burgen.at.*

A ramble around this castle includes a 90-minute self-guided audio-tour during which you'll be "eavesdropping" on the castle residents as they prepare for a lavish feast back in the 15C. Scores of authentically costumed figures - from the archduke to his servants - have been arranged in scenes and impart interesting tidbits about what daily life was like in those days. The tour ends in the original Gothic watchman's tower from where you'll enjoy fabulous views over the town and countryside.

In the south tower is the **Lungauer Landschaftsmuseum**, which takes an often intriguing look at local customs and history.

"The Archbishop's Turnip"

The story goes that **Leonhard von Keutschach** led a lively student life, rarely heeding his family's advice. One day, on a visit to Pinzgau, he was walking in a turnip field with his uncle Wolf zu Alm, who soundly berated him for neglecting his studies. Piqued by the young man's impertinent reply, the uncle threw a turnip at him saying, "If you don't mend your ways, I will never receive you again!" The turnip changed Leonhard's life; he applied himself to his studies and later became Prince-Archbishop of Salzburg. In gratitude, he had a turnip included in his coat of arms.

MAUTHAUSEN

OBERÖSTERREICH

POPULATION 4 350 – ALT 250M/820FT

About 25km/16mi east of Linz, Mauthausen would be just like any other sleepy, historic riverside town had it not been chosen, in 1938, as the site of a notorious Nazi concentration camp thanks to the proximity of several quarries. 🛈 *Heindlkai 13, A-4310, ☎ 0 72 38/22 43.*

KZ Mauthausen (Concentration Camp)

🕐 *Apr-Sep daily 8am-6pm, Feb-Mar and Oct-mid Dec daily 8am-4pm. ✑€2. ☎ 0 72 38/22 69. www.gusen.org.*

About 200 000 people were imprisoned at Mauthausen and its 49 subsidiary camps. Over half perished working in the granite quarries or, if they had become too sick or weak, being executed in horrific fashion. Some of the huts and rooms where the prisoners were kept still exist. Another building is now a museum with photographs and other documentary material on the horrors perpetrated in this sinister place. Outside the camp limits are memorials set up by countries whose people perished here. Below the plateau is the infamous "Todesstiege" (Stairway of Death), leading down to the quarry. Famous survivors include Simon Wiesenthal, who dedicated his life to tracking down Nazis and bringing them to justice.

MAYERLING

NIEDERÖSTERREICH

At the end of the 19C Mayerling was the setting of one of the greatest mysteries in Austrian history: the death of the 30-year-old Crown Prince Rudolf in 1889. Many novels, plays and movies deal with this tragedy that made headlines around the world.

▶ **Orient Yourself:** Mayerling is 36km/22mi southwest of Vienna and 6km/4mi southwest of Heiligenkreuz.

A Bit of History

In 1888, **Crown Prince Rudolf**, only son of Emperor Franz Joseph and estranged husband of Stephanie of Belgium, fell madly in love with the teenaged Baroness Maria Vetsera. Not surprisingly, the Emperor did not approve of such a scandalous affair. A vociferous argument between the ruler and Rudolf resulted in the latter storming off with his mistress in tow and taking her to the family's hunting lodge at Mayerling. What transpired next has been the source of endless speculation for more than a century. Fact is that on the morning of 30 January 1889, the lifeless bodies of both Maria and Rudolf were found at the lodge, seemingly killed by gunshot in an apparent suicide pact. But why did the fun-loving crown prince kill himself

ROGER VIOLLET

Archduke Rudolf

and his lover? Theories have him suffering from clinical depression or an incurable venereal disease. Or was it heart failure, a hunting accident or perhaps politically motivated murder? Nobody will ever know, but the mystery still makes Mayerling a place of pilgrimage for the curious to this day.

Chapel and Memorial

○*Daily 9am-6pm.* ⊙€2. ☎ 0 22 58/22 75.
Grief-stricken by the death of his only son, Emperor Franz joseph had the hunting lodge demolished and replaced with a Carmelite convent. A neo-Gothic chapel now occupies the site where the bodies were found, and there is a small memorial exhibit with original furniture, photographs and drawings as well.

STIFT MELK★★★

NIEDERÖSTERREICH
ALT 213M/699FT

The majestic abbey of Melk, which crowns a rocky bluff overlooking the Danube, is the apogee of Baroque architecture in Austria and a must-see along the Danube. It has origins in the 10C as the castle of the ruling Babenberg family but became a monastery in 1089 when Margrave Leopold II donated the building to the Benedictines. Famous for its scholarship, the abbey has been a spiritual , cultural and intellectual center for nearly a millennium. 🔢 *Rathausplatz 11, A-3390, ☎ 0 27 52/5 23 07, www.stiftmelk.at.*

▶ **Orient Yourself:** Melk is 27km/17mi west of St Pölten in northeastern Austria.
🕐 **Organizing Your Time:** Budget at least half a day for your visit.
👣 **Also See:** Burg Aggstein, Dürnstein, Krems und Stein, St Pölten

Tour

🕐*mid Apr-31 Oct daily 9am-5pm (6pm May-Sep). Last admission 1hr before closing.*
🚶*From Nov-May the abbey can only be viewed as part of a guided tour at 11am and 2pm; ☞€7 without tour, €8.80 with tour. ☎ 0 27 52/55 52 32.*

Exterior
The original abbey was gutted by fire during the Turkish invasion in 1683 and entirely rebuilt from 1802 onward by **Jakob Prandtauer** and completed after his death by his pupil **Josef Munggenast**. The outer gateway, giving access to the first courtyard, is framed by statues of the abbey patrons St Leopold and St Coloman and flanked by two bastions. On the inner gate is the abbey coat of arms. Beyond a vestibule with a ceiling painting of St Benedict is the **Prälatenhof** (Prelates' Courtyard), a fine group of buildings adorned with statues of the Prophets.

Kaisergang
Access via the Imperial staircase.
The Emperors' gallery, which is 196m/644ft long, provided access to the chambers reserved for important visitors. Some of these rooms now house a **museum**★,

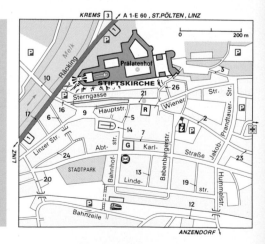

MELK	
Abbe-Stadler-Gasse	2
Abt-B.-Dietmayr-Str.	3
Bahngasse	5
Fischergasse	6
Fisolengasse	7
Hauptpl.	9
Hubbrücke	10
Josef-Büchl-Str.	12
Kaiblingerstr.	13
Kirchenpl.	14
Kremser Str.	16
Nibelungenlände	17
Pischingerstr.	19
Prinzlstr.	20
Rathauspl.	21
Roseggerstr.	23
Stadtgraben	24
Stiftsweg	26

Abbey of Melk

which presents the abbey's history and its treasures in an engaging and visually appealing fashion using light, sound and such modern media as video installations and computer animations.

Marmorsaal

The Marble Hall impresses less with its lavishness than with the strength of its design. It is dominated by a series of reddish pilasters, which incidentally, are not made of marble at all but of colored stucco. The undisputed highlight here is the ceiling fresco by **Paul Troger**, which centers on the goddess Athena riding a lion-drawn carriage in an allegory of wisdom and enlightenment.

Bibliothek (Library)

A terrace offering sweeping views of the surrounding countryside links the Marble Hall with the abbey library, which contains 100 000 books and 1 800 manuscripts. It too has a fine ceiling painting by Paul Troger symbolizing Faith. The gilded wood statues by the doors represent the four faculties.

Stiftskirche★★★

The church interior gives a great impression of lightness, which is due to the sweep of fluted pilasters, a judicious use of color and the many windows. The decoration is nothing if not lavish, with the dominating brownish red color offering the perfect contrast to the liberal use of gold leaf.

A veritable who's who of Baroque master artists contributed to this spectacular church. The ceiling frescoes and most of the side altars show off the exquisite style of **Johann Michael Rottmayr**; some of the altar paintings are the work of Paul Troger. Giuseppe Galli-Bibiena was responsible for the extraordinary high altar dedicated to Sts Peter and Paul. There are sculptures wherever you look, most of them the work of Lorenzo Mattielli and Peter Widerin. The left side altar in the transept contains the bones of St Koloman.

Excursion

Schloss Schallaburg★
6km/4mi south of Melk towards Anzendorf. ⊙May-Oct Mon-Fri 9am-5pm; Sat-Sun to 6pm. &⊕€10. ☎ 0 27 54/63 17. www. schallaburg.at.

The castle has substantial Romanesque remains and a Gothic chapel, but it is the great 16C **Renaissance arcaded courtyard**★ with its extraordinary profusion of terracotta ornamentation that makes the most striking impression. Statues, atlases, caryatids, floral motifs, cartouches and ornamental keystones boldly and harmoniously form a masterly composition.

Today, Schallaburg is an exhibition and cultural center for the province of Lower Austria, used every summer for prestigious exhibitions.

MILLSTATT★

KÄRNTEN
POPULATION 3 200 – ALT 604M/1 982FT

Millstatt lies on the north shore of the **Millstätter See**, a lake boasting summer water temperatures of up to 26oC/82oF. Owing to its lakeside beach and its favorable climate, Millstatt has become a very popular summer resort. Between May and October, it hosts a series of concerts, the Internationale Musikwochen.
🛈 *Marktplatz 8, A-9872, ☎ 0 47 66/20 22, www.millstatt-see.co.at.*

▶ **Orient Yourself:** Millstatt is in southern Austria, about 10km/6mi east of Spittal an der Drau and 83km/52mi northwest of Klagenfurt.
◔ **Also See:** Spittal an der Drau, Gmünd

Abbey *(Stift)*★

The abbey began life in the 11C as a Benedictine monastery, then became the seat of the Knights of St George in 1469 before falling into the hands of the Jesuits in 1598. They ran it until the order's dissolution In 1773. A small **museum** *(⊙June-end Sep daily 9am-noon, 2-6pm; &⊕€2.20; ☎ 06 76/4 60 64 13)* provides good insight into the abbey's history and the works of art, both religious and secular, that it contains.

Stiftshof (Abbey courtyard)★
The elegant courtyard framed by two-tiered arcades reveals the riches of the Order of St George founded by Emperor Friedrich III to assist in the defence of Christianity against the Turks. Also here is a 1 000-year-old **Gerichtslinde**, a lime tree below which court was held back in the Middle Ages.

Ph. Roy/EXPLORER

Abbey cloisters at Millstatt

Kreuzgang (Cloister)★

Enter from the east side of the courtyard. In summer, the cloisters may only be seen as part of a visit to the abbey museum. ⊙*daily 9am-noon, 2-6pm.* ⚒. ☎ *06 76/4 60 64 13.* The peaceful 12C cloister is a superb example of Romanesque architecture despite the addition of Gothic vaulting in the 15C. Its arches are held aloft by slender pillars whose capitals are decorated with animals, plants, gargoyles and faces.

▶ *Return to the abbey courtyard to go up to the church.*

Stiftskirche

Surviving elements from the Romanesque period include the magnificent **door** in the west porch and its tympanum showing Abbot Heinrich II (1166-77) paying homage to Christ. The **high altar**★ (1648) features gilded columns and larger-than-life-size statues of St Domitian (left) and Margrave Leopold III (right). Though faded, the most noteworthy **fresco**★ adorning the church is Urban Görtschacher's *Last Judgment* (1515) on the south wall (at the far end of the aisle). Two side chapels contain the red-marble tombs of various grand masters.

MÖLLTALER GLETSCHER★★

KÄRNTEN

This particularly picturesque mountain region is home to long Alpine lakes, which are used to generate hydroelectricity, along with a year-round ski area.

▶ **Orient Yourself:** The glacier is near Flattach in southern Austria.
⚒ **Also See:** Lienz, Spittal an der Drau, MIllstadt

Mölltaler Gletscherbahnen★★

Alt 1 250-3 120m/4 101-10 237ft. 9km/5.5mi from Flattach to Innerfragrant and the lower cable-car station for the new Stollenbahn (alt 1 250m/4 101ft). From here take the underground funicular and a cable-car on up to the Eissee mountain restaurant at 2 798m/9 180ft (allow about 40min there and back). www.gletscher.co.at.
The ski area on the glacier, where snow is guaranteed virtually all year round, offers a total of 53km/33mi of downhill pistes. Hikers have plenty of options in summer, including treks up to the Schareck peak (3 122m/10 243ft) and the Baumbach peak (3 108m/10 197ft). The Schareck peak can also be reached by chair-lift leaving from the upper cable-car station. You can pick out some 30 summits over 3000m/10 000ft in the Hohe Tauern range, including the Grossglockner.

MONDSEE

OBERÖSTERREICH
POPULATION 3 015 – ALT 481M/1 578FT

Mondsee lies below the cliffs of the Drachenwand and the Schafberg and sprouted around a Benedictine abbey founded in the 9C and dissolved in 1791. It is named for the nearby lake, which is shaped like a crescent moon and whose temperate, clean waters attract scores of water sports enthusiasts in the warmer months. *Dr.-Franz-Müller-Str. 3, A-5310, ☎ 0 6 2 32/22 70, www.mondsee.at.*

▶ **Orient Yourself:** Mondsee is in western Austria, 32km/20mi east of Salzburg.
⚲ **Also See:** Salzkammergut, St Gilgen, St Wolfgang

Sights

Basilika Mondsee⋆
The wedding church from the *Sound of Music* has been a basilica minor since 2005. Swiss-born sculptor **Meinrad Guggenbichler** (1649-1723) spent 44 years in Mondsee, creating seven of the 13 black-and-gold altars, including the masterful altar of the Holy Sacrament, on the lower left-hand side, with its twisted columns supported by cherubs.

Museum Mondseeland & Pfahlbaumuseum
late June-early Sep Tue-Sun 10am-6pm, May-late June Tue-Sun 10am-5pm. ⊜€3. ☎ 0 62 32/22 70.
The Pfahlbaumuseum sheds light on a phase of the Neolithic Era known as the "Mondsee Culture" (about 5000 years ago) when residents lived above the water in buildings sitting on stilts.

Freilichtmuseum Mondseer Rauchhaus
Tue-Sun May-Aug 10am-6pm, Tue-Sat Sep 10am-5pm, Sat-Sun Oct 10am-5pm. ⊜€2. ☎ 0 62 32/22 70.
Of the traditional farmhouses relocated to this open-air museum the Rauchhaus (smoke house) is the most interesting. It combines living spaces for humans and animals under a single roof.

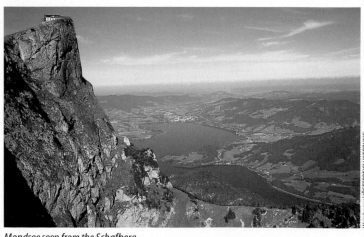

Mondsee seen from the Schafberg

MONTAFON★

Montafon is a charming, densely populated valley surrounded by three major massifs: the Rätikon in the northwest, the Silvretta in the south and the Verrwall in the northeast. It is a relaxing region dotted with pretty villages and offering good hiking, skiing and mountain-biking as well as access to the famous Silvretta-Hochalpenstraße★★ (👆 see entry), one of Austria's most scenic Alpine roads. 🔲 ☎0 55 56/72 25 30, www.montafon.at.

▶ **Orient Yourself:** The valley is 39km/24 long and near the far western edge of Austria, close to Switzerland.

🕐 **Organizing Your Time:** Allow at least one day to cover the route described below.

From Bludenz to Partenen 40km/25mi

Bludenz 👆 See Arlberggebiet 1.

▶ *Turn left in St. Anton in Montafon towards Bartholomäberg.*

Bartholomäberg
This settlement is beautifully scattered along a sunny terrace. From the parish church there is an impressive **panorama**★ of the villages of Vandans, Schruns and Tschagguns backed by impressive mountains such as the spiky Zimba peak and the Drei Türme massif. The church's **Baroque interior**★ boasts numerous fine art treasures. Stand-outs are the high altar and pulpit, both by Georg Senn, and the triptych dedicated to St. Anne on the right-hand side of the nave. The organ(1792) is one of the finest instruments in Austria.

▶ *Continue towards Innerberg, turn right towards Silbertal, then left on the main road at the bottom of the valley to the Kristbergbahn railway.*

Kristbergbahn★
🕐 *28 May-26 Oct and Dec-Apr daily 7.50am-6.15pm.* ☞ €10.30 roundtrip. ☎ 0 55 56/7 41 19. www.kristbergbahn. at.
The Kristberg inn (alt 1 430m/4 691ft), with a chapel nearby, can be reached in 5min from the cable car mountain station. It affords an especially beautiful **all-round view**★ over the Montafon. Hikers can climb up to the Kristbergsattel and then follow the ridge path to the **Ganzaleita** viewpoint (alt 1 610m/5 282ft) for views of the Lechtaler Alps and the Rote Wand.

▶ *Continue towards Schruns.*

Y. Bontoux

Drei Türme mountains

Schruns 🚞

Alt 690m/2 264ft. This resort and capital of the Montafon is located in a broad section of the valley and has plenty of lodging and leisure facilities. In summer, it is an ideal departure point for hikes in the medium-altitude mountains. In winter, the **ski area** 🚞 (40km/25mi of pistes) is especially suitable for beginners and for relaxed skiing. More experienced ski hounds can explore the off-piste section at Sennihang. Thanks to the area's considerable differences in height (700-2 400m/2 300-7 100ft), you will be skiing through a rather varied landscape. Snow machines make it possible to ski all the way down into the village.

Ski passes are valid for the entire Montafon Valley with its 62 ski lifts and 222km/138mi of pistes. Free buses link the various areas in the villages of Tschagguns-Vandans, Schruns, Kristberg, Gargellen, St. Gallenkirch and Gaschurn.

Cross-country skiers are restricted to 13km/8mi of easy tracks around Schruns. For more demanding exploits head to Kristberg (11km/7mi), Tschagguns (6km/4mi), Vandans (8km/5mi) or the extensive cross-country ski area in the Hochmontafon.

Sennigrat★

Allow 1hr. 🕐*Hochjochbahn cable-car late June-mid Oct daily 8am-4.30pm; Zamangbahn mid-Oct-Apr daily 8am-4.30pm; Sennigrat chair-lift late June-mid-Oct daily 8am-4.30pm.* 🎫*€15.90 roundtrip.* ☎ *0 55 56/7 21 26.*

From Schruns, take the Hochjochbahn or Zamangbahn cable-car to the **Kapell** (alt 1 850m/6 069ft). Enjoy the view down into the valley and the many scattered chalets of Schruns. In summer only, another chair-lift goes up to the Sennigrat (alt 2 210m/7 250ft), where the **panorama**★ takes in the Kreuzjoch area, the Madrisa massif and the Rätikon.

Hike to the Kreuzjoch and the Zamangspitze★★

4hr roundtrip. To shorten the route to 2hr, go as far as the mountain lodge and follow the lake path. Climbing boots are recommended.

From Sennigrat, the Wormser Hütte mountain lodge (alt 2 305m/7 562ft) can be reached in 20min. From the lodge, follow a ridge path to the Kreuzjoch and then on to the Zamangspitze peak (alt 2 386m/7 828ft), from where a **panorama**★★ opens up over the Silvretta massif and the Hochmontafon. Backtrack to the lodge and take the lake trail past **Herzsee** and **Schwarzsee** lakes back to the Kapell, returning to Schruns in the cable-car.

▶ *Follow the road into the Hochmontafon.*

Silvretta Nova ski area 🚞

The villages of St. Gallenkirch and Gaschurn have joined together to create an extensive, varied ski area with 114km/71mi of pistes between 900m/2 950ft and 2 300m/7 550ft. Good skiers use the black Buckelpiste and the 14km/8mi ski run into the valley from the Schwarzköpfle, and, on powdered snow, the Ziglamstrecke run for remarkable **views**★★ over the Silvretta group. Beyond here, **Gargellen,** the highest village in the Montafon (alt 1 423m/4 668ft), also offers good pistes.

For **cross-country skiers** there are connected ski runs along the valley floor between St. Gallenkirch and Partenen. In addition, a 15km/9mi cross-country track around the Silvretta reservoir can be reached by funicular and bus.

MURAU

STEIERMARK
POPULATION 2 630 – ALT 829M/2 720FT

Murau is a delightful town on the sprightly Mur River snuggled into the upper Mur Valley amid forested hillsides and Alpine meadows. Its historic center imparts undeniable southern charm with its warren of narrow streets lined by handsome merchant houses painted in a rainbow of pastel colors. *Bundesstraße 13A, A-8850, ☎ 0 35 32/2 72 00. www.stadtmurau.at.*

▶ **Orient Yourself:** Murau is in southwestern Styria, about 80km/50mi north of Klagenfurt.
🅿 **Parking:** Look for lots along Friesacherstraße, Bahnhofstraße and the B 97.
Also See: Hohentauernpassstraße, Radstätter Tauernstraße

Sights

Stadtpfarrkirche St. Matthäus★

The Gothic character of the parish church, with its majestic nave and splendid decorations, was not destroyed by 17C Baroque alterations. There are several beautiful **frescoes** from the 14C to the 16C, including one showing St Anthony and his pig, an *Entombment of Christ*, and an *Annunciation*. The north transept was decorated in the late 16C with numerous small paintings representing epitaphs of members of the local Liechtenstein ruling family. The magnificent **Baroque high altar★** was wrought by local artists and centers on a Gothic Crucifixion (1500); the sky-blue tabernacle is complemented by wood and gilt work.

Schloss Murau

Access via the wooden stairway north of the church. 👣 *Guided tours (1hr) mid-June-mid-Sep Wed, Fri 2pm.* ☜ *€3.* ☎ *0 35 32/23 02 58.*
All that remains of the original castle, commissioned in 1232 by Ulrich von Liechtenstein in a commanding spot above the Mur River, are the cellars and a well 48m/157ft deep. The present 17C Renaissance-era palace was built by Count Georg-Ludwig von Schwarzenberg. Tours start in the inner courtyard and take in the chapel. the Knight's Hall and other rooms.

Murtalbahn

74km/46mi roundtrip – about 5hr. ⏱*July-Sep Tue-Wed.* ☜ *€16.80 each way.* ☎ *0 35 32/22 33.*
This privately-run steam train chugs through attractive scenery between Murau and Tamsweg. The stations in both villages rent bicycles, which may be taken on the train for free.

Oberwölz

27km/17mi northeast of Murau. Leave town on B 96 going east; in Niederwölz take the road to Oberwölz.
This small medieval town below the 12C Rothenfels castle grew wealthy on the

Murau

salt trade and silver-working. Large sections of the fortified town wall have survived, including several towers and three gateways. The remains of the wall encircle the pretty old town, which is ablaze with flowers in season.

MURTAL

STEIERMARK

The Mur River has carved out a 483km/300mi-long route from the Radstädter Tauern in the Salzburg district to Hungary, where it joins the Drava, a tributary of the Danube. The stretch described below covers about one-seventh of the full length and runs through the deeply wooded Mur Valley.

▶ **Orient Yourself:** The valley is north of Graz in southern Austria.
⊚ **Don't Miss:** Österreichisches Freilichtmuseum

From Graz to Leoben 70km/43mi

Graz★★ ⚭ *See Graz.*

▶ *Leave Graz on the road to Bruck an der Mur (AX).*

Österreichisches Freilichtmuseum (Austrian Open-air Museum)★★
In **Stübing**. ⓞ Apr-Oct Tue-Sun 9am-5pm. ⚭≋€7.50. ☎ 0 31 24/5 37 00. www.freilichtmuseum.at.
Framed by forest, meadows and fields in a little side valley of the Mur, this open-air museum features 100 original farmhouses from throughout Austria, grouped by province - from Burgenland in the east to Vorarlberg in the far west. All the buildings are authentically furnished and provide a nostalgic glimpse of the way of life and working methods of yesteryear. The museum also puts on temporary exhibitions on rural life and traditional culture, while craftspeople give daily demonstrations of their work. Wear comfortable shoes as the complex sprawls for about 2km/1mi.

▶ *Continue north past industrial Peggau to the Lurgrotte.*

Lurgrotte★ (Peggau entrance)
⊚ *Dress warmly as the cave temperature hovers around 10°C/50°F year round.*
≋ *Guided tours (1hr/2hr) Apr-Oct, daily 9am-4pm; Nov-Mar by appointment only; 1hr/2hr tour ≋€5.50/9; ☎ 0 31 27/25 80; www.lurgrotte.com.*
The walk beside the underground river formed from melt-water leads deep into the cave, past several bizarre formations, including the impressive "Prince" stalactite, which weighs 3t and is almost 4m/13ft long.

Bruck an der Mur★ ⚭ See Bruck an der Mur.

West of Bruck, the road follows the south bank of the Mur with the Brucker Hochalpe off to the left. The valley now widens and becomes more and more industrial until it reaches Leoben.

Leoben ⚭ See Leoben.

NEUSIEDLER SEE★★

The vast Neusiedler See (Fertö in Hungarian) is the most westerly example of a steppe-type lake. It one of the great attractions of the Burgenland and a popular weekend getaway for Vienna folks. Most of the lake belongs to Austria; only the southern tip is in the Hungarian Puszta. It is a paradise for water sports enthusiasts and ringed by swimming beaches that have been slashed out from the reed-fringed shore. To preserve this unique habitat with its profusion of plants, rare animals and migratory birds, the region was designated a national park in 1992 and garnered a spot on UNESCO's list of World Heritage Sites in 2001. The lake is also at the center of an important wine region. ⓘ *Rathaus, A-7071 Rust;* ☎ *0 26 85/5 02, www.neusiedlersee.com and www.nationalpark-neusiedlersee.org.*

▶ **Orient Yourself:** The lake is on the eastern edge of the country, about 50km/31mi southeast of Vienna.

🕐 **Organizing Your Time:** This is an easy day trip from Vienna, although the lake also warrants an overnight stay or two.

🧒 **Especially for Kids:** There's great swimming and boating on the lake.

👁 **Also See:** Eisenstadt, Petronell-Carnuntum

From Neusiedl to Eisenstadt *69km/43mi*

Neusiedl am See
The place that gives the lake its name has a ruined medieval castle and a 15C church, but otherwise there's little reason to spend much time here.

▶ *Head northwest towards Eisenstadt; after Donnerskirchen turn left for Rust.*

Rust★
Rust is famous for its storks' nests, to which the birds return faithfully every year, and for being a prosperous wine-growing center. Since 1989 a wine academy has offered seminars and other wine-related events.

It's an attractive town with charming Renaissance and Baroque façades, arcaded inner courtyards and a partially preserved fortified town wall. A highlight on the west side of Rathausplatz is the **Fischerkirche**, which has impressive **frescoes**★ from the 14C and 15C. Also note the Late Gothic statues on the altar to the Three Magi in the side aisle and the fine organ from 1705.

From the village a causeway through the rushes leads to the **Seebad Rust** (🕐*May-mid Sep daily 9am-7pm;* ♿ ◉€4; ☎ *0 26 85/59 14)*, a lakeside resort with buildings on piles connected by pontoons.

A capricious lake

The Neusiedler See is fringed by enormous reed beds, has no permanent outflow and only one tributary, the tiny Wulka. Being replenished mostly by rain, snow melt and ground water keeps the water level rather shallow (up to 2m/7ft deep), saline and warm. The lake has even been known to dry up altogether, although not since the late 19C. Consistent winds blowing from the same direction can drive the water towards one shore, leaving the other shore temporarily dry.

Nightingale

European Bee-eater

Whinchat

Little Ringed Plover

Partridge

Lakeside Birdlife

Coot

Bar-tailed Godwit

Great Egret

M. Guillou/ MICHELIN

Mörbisch am See★

With its web of picturesque alleyways, Mörbisch is one of the prettiest places on the Neusiedler See. The whitewashed houses nearly all have stone steps leading up to pillared porches, brightly painted doors and window shutters, corn cobs hanging up to dry and flowers everywhere.

Leaving the village to the east through the reed-beds takes you a swimming place and the floating **Seebühne** stage where an operetta festival is held in summer.

▶ *Return to Rust, then bear left for St. Margarethen.*

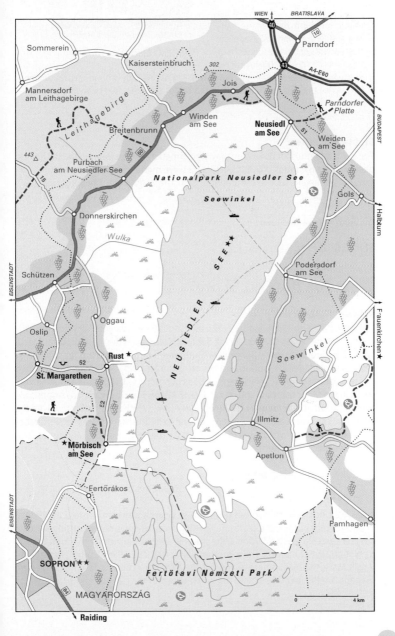

Between Austria and Hungary

As a result of the Treaty of Saint-Germain-en-Laye (1919), parts of the three western *comitats* (provinces) of Hungary passed to Austria. These form the present province of Burgenland, which clearly shows a certain Magyar influence, for example in its cultural and musical traditions.

The Burgenland has retained its ethnic mix with Hungarian, Romany and Sinti minorities, as well as descendants of Croat refugees from the time of the Turkish invasions.

House in Apetion

M. Guillou/MICHELIN

These minorities settled in this province - and particularly around the Neusiedler See - since the area had formed part of a buffer zone that had been intentionally depopulated by the Hungarian rulers.

St. Margarethen

The town is famous for its Passion play, performed every five years in the old Roman quarry. Several famous buildings in Vienna were made from St. Margarethen's calcareous sandstone, such as the Stephansdom, the Votivkirche, the Burgtheater and the Parlament.

▶ *Continue towards Eisenstadt.*

Eisenstadt★   *See Eisenstadt.*

Sights on the East Shore

Schloss Halbturn

Apr-Oct Tue-Sun 10am-5pm. €7. ☎ 0 21 72/85 94. www.schloss-halbturn.at.
Built in 1701 by Lukas von Hildebrandt, **Schloss Halbturn** is the most important secular Baroque building in the Burgenland and served as a hunting lodge for Emperor Charles VI. Ravaged by looting and fire after the Second World War, the building has now been completely restored to its former glory, with its façade looking very smart in shades of pale blue and cream. **Franz Anton Maulbertsch** was responsible for the remarkable **frescoes**★ in the garden room, which fortunately survived the 1949 fire. The palace hosts important cultural exhibitions from May to September and also operates a well-respected wine estate (tastings possible) and restaurant. Extensive gardens invite strolling and picnicking.

Basilika Frauenkirchen★

May-Sep daily 8am-8pm; Oct-Apr Mon-Fri 8am-6pm, Sat-Sun 8am-8pm. ☎ 0 21 72/22 24)
A basilica since 1990, the famous **pilgrimage church** was commissioned by Prince Paul Esterházy in 1702. It radiates Italian elegance, which is not surprising since its architect was Francesco Martinelli, the stuccowork was done by Pietro Conti and the frescoes by Luca Columba. The sumptuous altar frames an Early Gothic statue of the Virgin Mary, the main object of veneration. Note the painting of a breast-feeding Madonna in the first side altar in the north aisle and the painted choir stalls.

OBERTAUERN

SALZBURG

POPULATION 400 – ALT 1 739M/5 705FT

Obertauern lies on a broad terrace on the Radstädter Tauernpass in one of the most beautiful ski areas in the northern Alps. Unlike most Austrian mountain resorts, it did not grow from an existing village, but was developed purely as a winter sports destination. In summer, hiking is the main lure. ⓘ *A-5562 Obertauern, ☎06456/72 52. www.obertauern.at, www.obertauern.com, www.ski-obertauern.at.*

▶ **Orient Yourself:** Obertauern is about 90km/56mi southeast of Salzburg

Ski area

Obertauern boasts good, reliable snow levels, 28 ski lifts and 95km/60mi of pistes, nearly all of them for beginning and moderate skiers. The resort's fairly modest size is more than made up for by the quality of the facilities, which are among the most modern and comfortable in the country.

ÖTSCHERMASSIV★

NIEDERÖSTERREICH UND STEIERMARK

The mountainous area south of St. Pölten, between the Wienerwald and the Eisenerz Alps, is part of the limestone Pre-Alps. The wooded foothills give way to a succession of minor ranges, reaching an altitude of 1 893m/6 211ft at the massive peak of the Ötscher (from an old Slavonic word Otan meaning godfather).

▶ **Orient Yourself:** The Ötschermassif is south of St. Pölten, between the Wienerwald and the Eisenerz Alps in central Austria.

☺ **Don't Miss:** Mariazell, Stift Lilienfeld

Round Trip from Mariazell *112km/70mi*

Mariazell★ ☃ *See Mariazell.*

Leave Mariazell by road no 21 (east), which closely follows the Salza River through the Salza Valley. In Terz, the picturesque road turns north and plunges into a gorge.

▶ *In Freiland turn right onto road no 20 to Lilienfeld.*

Stift Lilienfeld★ ☃ *See Stift Lilienfeld.*

▶ *From Lilienfeld return south; in Freiland continue southwest on road no 20.*

The road, which is pleasant and picturesque, becomes more and more enclosed, first between wooded slopes, then in a rocky gorge. Beyond Türnitz, it climbs steadily, offering wide views of ridges. A series of hairpin bends culminates at Annaberg.

Annaberg

Annaberg's beautifully situated church is a popular stop for pilgrims headed to Mariazell. The first building, a timber chapel, was erected here in 1217, though the present church is 14C-15C. It is dedicated to St Anne, as the Madonna and Child with St Anne (15C) on the high altar attest. There are Baroque frescoes and stuccowork in the south chapel and a mass of gilding and carving on the pulpit and the organ-loft.

During the hairpin bend descent, the Ötscher sticks out clearly to the west. Josefsberg is the start of a pleasant downhill run among firs, with fine vistas towards the Gemeindealpe on the right. The road also skirts the Erlaufstausee reservoir. On leaving Mitterbach turn right and drive beside a second lake, the natural Erlaufsee.

▶ *Return to Mariazell.*

ÖTZTAL★★

TIROL

The Ötztal, which is famous for its series of shining glaciers, is one of three deep river valleys running north from the Ötztaler Alps into the Inn. This section of the Alps encompasses the highest point in the northern Tyrol, the Wildspitze (alt 3 774m/12 382ft) and the highest parish in Austria (Obergurgl at 1 927m/6 321ft). Until the First World War the valley communities were more closely connected with the Alto Adige to the south, from which their people originally came, than with the Inn Valley. Only in 1969, when the Timmelsjoch road was completed, did the isolation of the Ötztal come to an end, at least in summer.

▶ **Orient Yourself:** The Ötztal runs north-south through western Austria, about 55km/34mi west of Innsbruck.

⊚ **Don't Miss:** Stuibenfälle, Sölden

From the Inn Valley to San Leonardo in Passiria
(St. Leonhard in Passeier) 88km/55mi

On the Austrian side, the road is generally open all year round, at least to Hochgurgl. On the Italian side, however, it is generally only snow free from mid-June to mid-October. The route demands care and has an irregular surface, especially in tunnels. Trailers, caravans, buses and trucks are not allowed.

The B 186, turning off the busy Inntal road, runs through pleasant pine woods among piles of debris brought down from the Ötztaler Ache creek. This flows beneath the picturesque covered bridge at Ebene to enter the Ötz basin dominated by the rocky tooth of the Acherkogel. Chestnuts, fields of maize and peach and apricot orchards show that the Ötztal corridor, running due south, attracts the warm air of the Föhn.

Oetz

This village on a sunny slope sports several traditional buildings with flower-bedecked oriels and painted façades. A popular walk leads to the romantic Piburgersee lake.

Österreuten

This hamlet is among the most architecturally harmonious in the valley. Note the buildings' overhanging upper storeys sheltering verandas.

▶ *Continue to Umhausen, gateway to the Stuiben Falls.*

Stuibenfälle★★
About 1hr 30min roundtrip walk beginning at the Umhausen tourist office.
The path to this large and powerful waterfall leads first to a restaurant-chalet, crosses the torrent and continues up the left bank to the 150m/492ft-high **waterfall**. A second wooded ravine lies downhill, near the swiftly flowing Ötztaler Ache.

Längenfeld
Together with nearby **Huben**, Längenfeld offers 150km/93mi of hiking trails, several climbing training courses and two actual climbs, as well as a 50km/31mi network of mountain bike tracks.

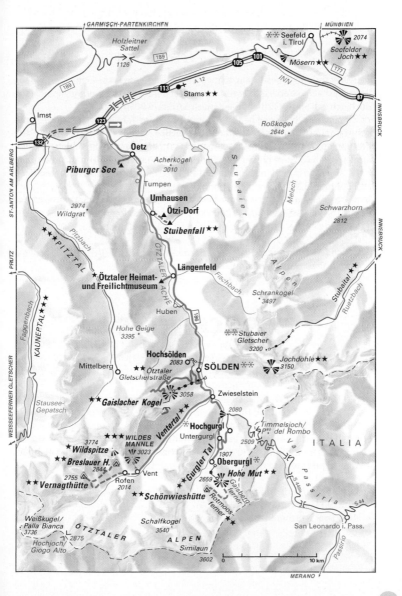

"Ötzi"

In 1991 a pair of climbers discovered a mummified body in the Similaun range in the Ötztaler Alps. Their discovery soon became an archaeological sensation, as the body turned out to about 6 000 years old! The mummy, fondly nicknamed "Ötzi," had been particularly well preserved due to the environmental conditions in the glacier. Even the organs were still intact, so that it was possible to draw conclusions about his diet and the circumstances of his death. Apparently, Ötzi froze to death in a snow storm despite his good thick clothing of furs and a grass cloak. As the mummy was found on Italian territory, it is now on display in the South Tyrol Archaeological Museum in Bolzano (Bozen).

Beyond Huben, a long ravine begins, narrowing after the bridge at Aschbach to a larch-covered **gorge**★. Below the road, the Wildbach churns over massive rocks.

Sölden🛏️🛏️ 👍 *See Sölden.*

The valley forks in Zwieselstein: to the right lies the **Ventertal**★★ (👍see Sölden), the valley that gave access to two of the earliest border passes over the Alpine ridge (Hochjoch 2 875m/9 432ft and Niederjoch 3 019m/9 905ft).
For this itinerary, however, head left into the **Gurgler Tal**★★ (👍 *see entry*), home of the famous winter sports resort of **Obergurgl**★.
After a steep climb, the Timmelsjoch road drops briefly to reach the **Windegg viewpoint**★★ with vistas of the Gurgl Valley, the Great Gurgl glacier and the cleft of the Ötztal. The road now climbs through an austere landscape up to the Timmelsjoch (alt 2 509m/8 232ft) on the Italian border.
On the steeper southern slope of the pass, you'll pass through a tunnel before plunging into the Val Passiria enjoying impressive crest views along the way, particularly of the Monte dei Granati (Granatenkogel). The road continues as far as Moso.

▶ *At San Leonardo one can join the road from Merano to the Brenner by way of the Monte Giovo (Jaufenpass).*

OSSIACHER SEE★

KÄRNTEN
LOCAL MAP SEE WÖRTHER SEE

Ossiach Lake, which is not yet deluged by tourists, lies a little set back from the Villach basin, tucked amid the wooded slopes of the Gerlitzen, the Hexenberg and the Ossiacher Tauern. It is Carinthia's third largest lake, measuring 11km/7mi long by 1.5km/1mi wide and reaching a depth of 46m/150ft. Its inviting shores are perfect for swimming and generally chilling out. From spring to fall, boats provide regular service to all the lakeside resorts.

▶ **Orient Yourself:** The Ossiach Lake is in southern Austria, about 40km/25mi west of Klagenfurt.
👍 **Also See:** Wörther See, Klagenfurt

Tour of the Lake★

Starting from Villach 66km/41mi

Villach★ 🕭 See Villach.

From Villach, the B 94 skirts the ruins of Landskron fortress and follows the north shore overlooked by the steep slopes of the Gerlitzen.

Gerlitzen★★

The Gerlitzen summit (alt 1 909m/6 263ft) dominates central Carinthia, its foothills cascading down to the Ossiach Lake. In winter, its numerous hotels, the cable-car from Annenheim up to the Kanzel, the ski lifts and sunny slopes attract an international crowd of skiers.

Ascent of the Gerlitzen

From Bodensdorf on the north shore head to Tschöran for the little mountain road to Gerlitzen (12km/7.5mi, toll levied).
After winding through woods and pastures, the road ends at 1 764m/5 787ft at a complex including restaurants and lodging. Finish the climb on foot or, if necessary, by **chair-lift** (🕭 mid June-late Sep daily 9am-5pm; Dec-Apr daily 8.30am-5.15pm, depending on snow levels. ☞ €15.50 roundtrip. ☎ 0 42 48/27 22).
The **panorama**★★ embraces the Ossiach, Wörth and Faak lakes and, beyond the Drava Valley, the long barrier of the Karawanken. The permanently snow-covered slopes of the Hochalm and Ankogel glaciers glitter in the northwest.

▶ *Return to the lake.*

The road carries on east to Steindorf. Turn right off the main road and follow the road paralleling the south shore.

Ossiach

The Benedictine **abbey** of Ossiach (now a hotel) was founded in the 11C. In the 16C and 17C it went through periods of splendor, even receiving Emperor Charles V in

Ossiacher See

1552. In 1783 the abbey was dissolved on the orders of Emperor Joseph II. It subsequently took on various roles, becoming a stud farm, a military base and a convalescence home, all of which took their toll on the building. These days, Ossiach is well known far beyond national borders as a venue of the Carinthian Summer festival.

Church★

◷*May, June, Sep, Oct daily 10am-6pm; July-Aug daily 9am-12pm and 1.30pm-6pm.* ⌖☞*€1.50.* ☎ *0 42 43/22 80.*

Ossiach's triple-nave pillared basilica was originally of Romanesque design but completely transformed into the Baroque style between 1741 and 1745. Delicately colored, lace-like **stuccowork** by masters from the Wessobrunn School in Bavaria adorns the interior. The ceiling painting is the work of famous local artist **Joseph Ferdinand Fromiller**, who also worked in the Landhaus at Klagenfurt. The Gothic baptistry on the left contains a valuable **carved altarpiece**★ whose central panel depicts the Virgin Mary flanked by St Margaret and St Catherine; on the side panels are the Apostles.

▶ *Take the road back to Villach.*

PACK- UND STUBALPENSTRASSE★

STEIERMARK UND KÄRNTEN

These routes cut across the gentle, wooded heights of the Pannonian Pre-Alps between the valleys of the River Mur and River Lavant and the Graz basin. Known as the Koralpe, the Packalpe, the Stubalpe and the Gleinalpe, these mountains form a barrier less by their height, which hardly exceeds 2 000m/6 500ft, than by their remoteness. The inter-regional road from Graz to Klagenfurt passes over the Packsattel, whereas the old road from Graz to Judenburg via Köflach crosses the Stubalpe, cutting off the wide bend of the River Mur.

▶ **Orient Yourself:** These routes are in southern Austria, just west of Graz.
Kids **Especially for Kids:** Gestüt Piber

Stubalpe★

From Judenburg to Köflach *44km/27mi*

Judenburg

Judenburg, at the convergence of five trade routes, is the oldest commercial center in Styria. Records show that a Jewish community was established here as early as 1103 but driven out in 1496 by order of Emperor Maximilian I. Numerous old buildings and courtyards from the historic town center cluster around the **Neue Burg**.

From Weisskirchen, the winding road climbs gradually through the fir trees to the crest. The main Stubalpe ridge is crossed at the **Gaberl** pass (alt 1 547m/5 075ft). Beyond the pass, the road drops suddenly into the wild and narrow wooded **Salla Valley** to a tiny village of the same name. Here and there you'll pass old sawmills and scythe factories that once brought industry to the valley, though many are now in ruins. (Styrian scythes were famous worldwide.)

Köflach

This town is near an opencast lignite mine considered among the most productive in Austria. In early September the "Lipizzaner Almabtrieb" takes place here. This is when the famous white stallions are driven down from the Alpine pastures to their winter quarters at the Piber stud farm.

Gestüt Piber★

3km/2mi northeast of Köflach. ⏰ 🚗 *Guided tours (1hr 10min) Apr-Oct Tue-Sat 9am-5pm, Nov-Mar by prior arrangement.* 🚻 ♿ *€11.* ☎ *0 31 44/33 23.*

Kids Piber's claim to fame rests on the graceful **Lipizzaner stallions**, which are bred here and then sent to the Spanische Reitschule in Vienna (♿ *see Wien)*. For close-ups of the horses, visit the stables or take a walk in the nearby fields. The animals are born bay or black and only acquire their white coats between the ages of four and 10. In rare cases a Lipizzaner may retain its dark coat, making it a highly prized "Hofburg bay."

Packsattel★

From Köflach to Wolfsberg *52km/32mi*

Köflach ♿ *See above.*

After leaving Köflach, the route skirts the opencast lignite pits and then climbs up a hill offering views back down into the industrial valley, although you can also espy the bright white outline of the pilgrimage church at Maria Lankowitz.

▶ *Continue as far as Pack.*

Pack

Close to the **Packer Stausee** (an artificial lake with boating and swimming facilities), this little community enjoys a peaceful **panorama**★ of the wooded foothills of the Pannonian Pre-Alps and the Graz plain.

In gentle pastoral surroundings the road reaches the **Packsattel**, which is also known as the Packhöhe or the Vier Tore (Four Gates – alt 1 166m/3 825ft), before dropping into an even quieter and more thickly wooded zone.

Lipizzaner stallions at Piber stud farm

Wiesenhofer/ÖSTERREICH WERBUNG

A series of hairpin bends below the Preitenegg ridge lends a little variety to the descent. The route leads past the sombre Schloss Waldenstein, then continues along the ravine of the Waldensteiner Bach to join the Lavant Valley at Twimberg.

Lavant Valley Motorway Bridge (Autobahnbrücke)★

At 1 079m/3 500ft long and 165m/541ft high, this bridge is taller than the Stephansdom in Vienna. It is among the 10 longest bridges in Austria and Europe's second highest bridge built on pylons.

Wolfsberg

The town is characterized by a Tudor-style 19C castle and wraps around the Hoher Platz, a square adorned with a column to the Virgin Mary and flanked by fine Biedermeier houses.

PETRONELL-CARNUNTUM★

NIEDERÖSTERREICH
POPULATION 1 200 – ALT 330M/1 082FT

Excavations on the site of Petronell and in the neighboring community of Bad Deutsch-Altenburg have unearthed remnants of an ancient Roman town from around the 1C AD. ▯ *Kirchengasse 57, A-2404, ☏ 0 21 63/22 28, www.petronell.at.*

- ▶ **Orient Yourself:** Petronell-Carnuntum is on the eastern edge of the country, about 40km/26mi east of Vienna.
- ▯ **Parking:** There's parking at the Freilichtmuseum and at the Museum Carnuntinum.
- ◷ **Organizing Your Time:** Distances between sights are quite large, so allow at least half a day to see it all.
- ▦ **Especially for Kids:** Freilichtmuseum Petronell
- ◔ **Also See:** Neusiedler See

A Bit of History

The Capital of Upper Pannonia – Carnuntum was founded as a Roman military winter camp by Emperor Tiberius in 6 AD and became the capital of the Roman province of Upper Pannonia in the 2C. In 171 Emperor Marcus Aurelius drove back the Marcomanni and Quadi tribes from here, while also writing part of his *Meditations*. In 308 Emperor Diocletian convened an Imperial Conference in Carnuntum in order to try to hold the Roman Empire together. But for the town the end was near as first the Goths and then the Huns overran and devastated it around 400 AD.

Sights

Archäologischer Park Carnuntum

Information Center, Hauptstraße 296; ◷1 Mar-12 Nov daily 9am-5pm. ♿ ⊜€8, audioguide €3.50. ☏ 0 21 63/3 37 70. www.carnuntum.co.at.
The archaelogical park consists of two main areas: the Zivilstadt (civilian town) in the town of Petronell-Carnuntum and the Militärstadt (military town) in Bad Deutsch-Altenburg. For orientation and to pick up maps and an audio-guide (in English, recommended), start your visit at the information center. One ticket is good for all Roman sites and the museum.

Zivilstadt★

The main excavation area is now the **Kids Freilichtmuseum Petronell**, an open-air museum where you can stroll along actual Roman streets lined with ancient foundations and reconstructed buildings such as the Temple of Diana. A new highlight, open since 2006, is the **House of Lucius★**, an authentically decorated and furnished home of a textile merchant that provides rare insight into the lifestyle enjoyed by rich Romans.

About 700m west of here are the remnants of one of the city's two **amphitheaters**, which had two gateways and a capacity of 13,000 spectactors. Another stroll takes you to the **Grosse Therme**, one of the largest and fanciest Roman bathing complexes north of the Alps and once decorated with colored marble and mosaic floors. These days, only bits and pieces of floor heating, water canals and the pools survive.

Harrach'sche Gemäldegalerie – The Concert (c 1500)

Graf Harrach'sche Familier sammlung/SCHLOSS ROHRAU

South of the open-air museum is the **Heidentor** (Heathen's Gate), a 4C stone arch that once formed part of a much larger monument to Emperor Constantin II. Its curious name dates to the Middle Ages, when people erroneously thought that it was built by non-Christians, even though Christianity had already taken root among the Romans.

Militärstadt

The only surviving remnant from the military camp is the **Amphitheater Bad Deutsch-Altenburg**, where gladiators fought, soldiers paraded and meetings gathered There's more to see here than at the theater in Petronell, includeing cages, tunnels and gateways. A permanent exhibit offers insights into the forms of entertainment enjoyed by Roman society.

Museum Carnuntinum★

Badgasse 40-46. ◷21 Mar-12 Nov Mon noon-5pm, Tue-Sun 10am-5pm. ☏ 0 21 63/3 37 70.

The archaeological museum in Bad Deutsch-Altenburg occupies a beautiful replica Roman villa and was opened by Emperor Franz Joseph in 1904. It houses a remarkable collection of ancient artefacts, including exceptional sculpture such as a striking marble statuette of the **Dancing Maenads of Carnuntum★**. The exhibits on the ground floor mainly relate to the **Mithras cult** and come from the Mithraeum, an underground place of worship unearthed by the excavations. Mithras was a Persian god who was venerated by Roman soldiers in the 2C before the advent of Christianity.

Rundkapelle

Opposite the Information Center in Petronell.

This unusual Romanesque round chapel from 1200 has a pointed roof and semicircular choir. The individual character of the building is further emphasized by the simplicity of the façade with its three-quarter columns and arcades carried on consoles. The **tympanum relief★** over the entrance shows the baptism of Christ, an indication that the chapel must originally have been used as a baptistry.

Excursion

Rohrau

4km/2.5mi south of Petronell-Carnuntum.

The 16C Schloss Rohrau contains the **Harrach'sche Gemäldegalerie**★★ (*Easter-Oct Tue-Sun 10am-5pm; €7; 0 21 64/22 53*), which ranks among the largest and most prestigious private art collections in Austria, with works by 17C and 18C masters from Spain, Naples and Rome, and 16C and 17C masters from Holland and Flanders. Of outstanding merit is *The Concert* (16C), a particularly graceful painting of female figures playing musical instruments, presumably by a Dutch artist.

The composer **Joseph Haydn** was born in 1732 in the thatched **Geburtshaus Joseph Haydns** (*year-round Tue-Sun 10am-4pm; €1.50; 0 21 64/22 68*) on the main village road. It now contains a memorial exhibit about the man, his works and his life.

PITZTAL★★★

TIROL

The long Pitztal Valley, which runs north-south, is flanked in the west by the Kaunertal Valley and in the east by the Ötztal Valley. It is famous for the extraordinary Alpine scenery in its upper reaches. It is enclosed by a massive glacier basin over which towers the 3 774m/12 382ft high **Wildspitze** peak, the highest point in the Tyrol.

▸ **Orient Yourself:** The Pitztal is in western Austria, about 58km/36mi west of Innsbruck.

Don't Miss: Hinterer Brunnenkogel

Organizing Your Time: Allow 45min for the drive to Mittelberg and 2hr for the trip up the Hinterer Brunnenkogel.

Also See: Ötztal, Kaunertal

Sights

Road from Arzl to Mittelberg★

The 39km/24mi long road offers views of the glaciers and passes through villages and forest, past little waterfalls and along the Pitzbach creek to Mittelberg where lifts take you up to the glaciers.

Hinterer Brunnenkogel★★★

Alt 3 440m/11 286ft. *Pitzexpress funicular daily 8.30am-4.30pm. Pitz-Panorama-bahn cable-car daily 9am-3.15pm. late May-July. combined ticket €22 roundtrip. 0 54 13/8 62 88.*

The Pitzexpress funicular travels underground for 3.7km/2.3mi to the foot of the Pitztal glacier at 2 860m/9 383ft. Continue on the Pitz-Panoramabahn, the highest cable-car in Austria. The peak, which offers a fantastic **Alpine panorama**★★★, is only a short hike from the upper mountain station. The Wildspitze towers majestically over this grandiose landscape. Take sunglasses, sturdy shoes suitable for snow and warm clothing (even in summer).

Pitztal Glacier & Rifflsee ski areas

🕐 *mid-Sep–early June daily 8.30am-4.30pm.* ✆€34.50 ski day pass, also includes Rif-
flsee area. ☎0 54 13/8 62 88. www.pitztaler-gletscher.at.

Seven lifts lead up to 25km/15.5mi of pistes that are usually well covered in snow
from fall through May. The ski area is suitable for skiers of all levels, although easy
runs predominate. There's also skiing on the slopes of the Rifflsee.

Excursion to the Rifflsee★

Park in Mandarfen, 1km/0.5mi below Mittelberg. Cable-car 🕐*late June-Apr daily
8.30am-4.30pm.* ✆€13.50 roundtrip in summer. ☎ 0 54 13/8 62 88.

From the mountain station at 2300m/7546ft, take a walk around the lake or, if you
have more stamina, head for the Fuldaer Höhenweg ridge trail to the **Taschachhütte**
mountain lodge at 2 432m/7 979ft. During the trip you will enjoy interesting **views**
over the valley, and of the Kerlesferner glacier to the south.

PÖLLAU★

STEIERMARK
POPULATION 1 860 – ALT 427M/1 401FT

Pöllau, a charming town with red-tiled houses, lies away from the major tourist
routes in the heart of the Pöllauer Tal (Pöllau Valley). Much of the surrounding
countryside has been turned into a large game park laced by 100km/62mi of
trails. In an area of limited agricultural activity, vines occupy a significant niche
in the local economy. In season, great places to sample the local product are
the traditional taverns called Buschenschenken. 🄸 *Schloss 1, A-8225,* ☎ *0 08 00
/84 72 68 37.*

▸ **Orient Yourself:** Pöllau is in southeastern Austria, about 62km/39mi northeast
of Graz.

◔ **Also See:** Schloss Herberstein

Sights

Marktplatz

This traditional market place, with its column to the Virgin Mary, has southern flair
thanks to its many old façades. To the north of the square, an old door leads to the
Schloss, a former Augustinian abbey with origins as a moated 12C castle.

Stift

Founded in 1504, the fledgling abbey had a troubled time during the 16C, when
Styria was racked by religious disputes and Turkish raids. Despite such adversity, it
grew prosperous by the late 17C and was rebuilt in the Baroque style. During secularization under Emperor Joseph II it was closed in 1785 and turned into a private
residence. It now belongs to the town.

Abbey church★

The imposing Baroque church was designed by **Joachim Carlone**, a member of the
celebrated family of Graz architects, and has impressive dimensions: the nave and
chancel are 62m/203ft long, the transept is 37m/121ft wide and the cupola 42m/138ft
high, creating an unusually generous space for such a small community. Because of
its size, the church is sometimes called the "Styrian Petersdom."

Georg Mikes

Pilgrimage church at Pöllauberg

The remarkable **decor** is a delightful blend of paintings, gold, stuccowork and opulent sculptures. The frescoes in the nave and cupola are by Styrian artist **Matthias von Görz** and clearly show off his hallmark bright colors, a passion for light, and considerable skill at *trompe-l'œil*. The enormous painting on the **high altar** depicts the martyrdom of St Vitus and is a work of Joseph Adam von Mölk.

The 24-stop **organ**, built in 1739, stands on an arcaded gallery, beneath a ceiling fresco of David playing the harp.

Excursions

Pöllauberg★

6km/4mi northeast of Pöllau. ☎0 33 35/23 81. *www.poellauberg.at.*

Pöllauberg is a tiny village that grew up around its celebrated 14C **pilgrimage church** crowning the top of a steep hill and visible for miles around. Its unusual design features twin naves of equal size separarated by three pillars and with intersecting ribbed vaults. The large and sumptuously decorated 18C high altar centers on a statue of the Virgin Mary that is the main object of worship. The lavishly gilded pulpit dates from 1730.

RADSTÄDTER TAUERNSTRASSE★

SALZBURG

Already a well-used thoroughfare in Roman times, this road was one of the major lines of expansion towards the south pursued by the archbishops of Salzburg in the Middle Ages. The **Lungau**, in the upper Mur Valley, is the only remaining relic of these ambitions. Until the opening of the Tauern autobahn, this was one of the most remote and tradition-bound areas of the Alps.

▶ **Orient Yourself:** The road in southcentral Austria links the upper valleys of the Enns and Mur rivers across the summit of the Niedere Tauern (1 700m/5577ft)

⊙ **Don't Miss:** Burg Mauterndorf, Schloss Moosham

Ⓒ **Also See:** Dachsteinstraße

From Radstadt to St. Michael im Lungau *67km/42mi*

Radstadt

Radstadt is a pretty town at the crossroads of the Dachsteinstraße and the Radstädter Tauernstraße. It is still enclosed by its tower-studded medieval town wall and a partial moat. In the charming surrounding countryside, you will come across traditional manor houses, such as those of Tandalier and Mauer, with their characteristic wide, overhanging roofs, corner turrets and watchtowers.

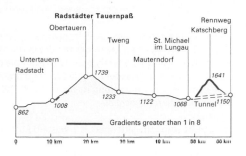

The run from Radstadt to Untertauern travels through sprawling meadows, dotted here and there with big farms. Above Untertauern, hills and ravines, cooled by the shade of maples and the Taurach cascades, lead to the upper part of the valley.

Gnadenfall

This lusty cascade of the Taurach leaps a wooded shelf in two light falls. Hotels crouch between the larches and spruces below the pass at 1 739m/5 705ft. About 800m/0.5mi short of the pass a modern (1951) statue of a Roman legionary stands guard over the bridge.

Obertauern★★   *See Obertauern.*

Beyond the pass, the road enters a forbidding section, but between Tweng and Mauterndorf pleasant clearings appear on the banks of the calmer Taurach. Soon the roofs of Mauterndor castle peer out from among the trees.

Burg Mauterndorf★   *See Burg Mauterndorf.*

Tamsweg★   *See Tamsweg.*

Schloss Moosham★

Guided tours (1hr) Apr-Sep Tue-Sun hourly 9am-4pm; mid-Dec-Mar 11am, 1pm and 2.30pm. €8. 0 64 76/3 05. www.schloss-moosham.info.

This former fortified palace of the archbishops of Salzburg was restored and refurnished in the last century. In the pine-paneled rooms on the second floor and in the vaulted chancelery there are considerable collections of furniture and art objects. Ask for the explanation of the comical picture of people classified by their characteristic features in the bedroom on the second floor.

St. Michael im Lungau

This attractive resort is flooded with sunshine year-round and especially busy in winter when numerous lifts ferry skiers up the fine slopes. Next to the Gothic parish church, the Wolfgangkapelle is an elegant octagonal chapel.

RATTENBERG★

TIROL
POPULATION 440 – ALT 514M/1 686FT

This tiny frontier town once built its prosperity on silver-mining but essentially stopped evolving when the mines ran dry in the 17C. As a result, Rattenburg's old town is an almost perfectly preserved example of Renaissance urban design. The town is also famous for its engraved and finely modeled glassware, available in numerous stores along its main street. *Klostergasse 94, A-6240, ☎ 0 53 37/6 33 21. www.rattenberg.at.*

▶ **Orient Yourself:** Rattenberg is in western Austria, about 48km/30mi northeast of Innsbruck.
🅿 **Parking:** There are two large lots north and south of the train station.
🕙 **Also See:** Kaisergebirge, Karwendelgebirge

Sights

Augustinermuseum★
Pfarrgasse 8. ⏱*May-2nd Sun in Oct daily 10am-5pm.* ☞€3. ☎ *0 53 37/6 48 31.*
The Augustinian monastery was founded in 1384 and is now a museum displaying Tyrolean art treasures, including exquisite Gothic sculpture in the cloisters and fine examples of local goldsmithing. Processional items are exhibited up in the church gallery; stand-outs include a seated Madonna and the Mocking Group.

Pfarrkirche St. Virgil★★
The twin naves of this Gothic church, separated by four graceful columns, are a harmonious pink and white confection. In former times, the larger nave was reserved for the burghers, while the smaller one was set aside for the miners. Abundant statuary, delicate stuccowork, and elegant frescoes make up the scintillating Baroque decorative scheme. The masterly **Last Supper** is the work of the Bavarian artist Matthäus Günther, while the *Transfiguration* in the chancel is by Simon Benedikt

Bohnacker/ÖSTERREICH WERBUNG

Rattenberg

Faistenberger. The statues around the **altar** in the miners' chancel were sculpted by Meinrad Guggenbichler, the famous sculptor from Mondsee.

Schlossberg
30min roundtrip walk.
From this vantage point there is a good **general view** of the town, hemmed in between the Inn and the mountain, with the belfry of the Servitenkirche (13C-18C) rising above the roof ridges. Downstream, the Kaisergebirge comes into view.

Excursion

Freilichtmuseum Tiroler Bauernhöfe★
*7km/4mi away in **Kramsach**. The parking lot is shortly after the hamlet of Mosen.* ○*mid -Apr-Oct daily 9am-6pm (last admission 5pm).* ⊜€5.50. 0 53 37/6 26 36.
More than a dozen farmhouses and their outbuildings, including a sawmill and a school, gathered from throughout the Tyrol have been reassembled here in a quiet Alpine setting. Budget about 2hr to see it all at a leisurely pace.

Alpbach★
12km/7.5mi southeast of Rattenberg.
idyliic and postcard-pretty Alpbach has been settled since 1000 AD and wraps around its church, the **Pfarrkirche St Oswald** whose pointed spire stands out against the mountainous backdrop. The plain exterior does not hint at its rich interior with fine frescoes and superb altars. The High Altar bears the figures of St Oswald, St Martin and St Catherine, while the two side altars are framed in Rococo carvings. The left-hand one with its miraculous picture of *Our Lady of the Victory* has attracted pilgrims for centuries.
Since 1945, the town has hosted the Alpbach European Forum, an annual gathering of academics, politicians, economists and artists of all nationalities who discuss contemporary issues facing the world.

REISSECK-MASSIV★★

KÄRNTEN

The Reisseck massif, which towers over the Möll Valley, is one of the most unspoilt places in Carinthia. Only the arrival of a funicular and a railway line to serve the power station at Kolbnitz opened it up to a greater degree. Its beautiful location and good snow conditions attract ski hounds in winter, while summer draws in-the-know hikers who cherish the many lakes and glorious viewpoints .

▶ **Orient Yourself:** The Reisseck massif is in southcentral Austria, about 56km/35mi northwest of Villach.
○ **Organizing Your Time:** Budget at least half a day to get up and around the mountain.

Reisseckbahn★
From Kolbnitz. 25min each way by funicular plus 10min on the train. ○*May-mid-Oct daily 8.30am-5pm.* ☎0 47 83/24 10.
This is an awe-inspiring trip to the top of the Reisseck mountain. The funicular follows a very steep gradient for 3.5km/2.2mi to the Schoberboden station (alt 2 237m/7 339ft), from where there is a beautiful **view**★ of the valley and the rocky

foothills of the Reisseck massif. From here the Höhenbahn train travels underground for 3.2km/2mi, arriving at a pleasant hotel.

Hike to the Grosser Mühldorfer Seen★

From the Höhenbahn mountain station, an easy 30min walk leads to the Grosser Mühldorfer See, a reservoir from where there is a **view**★ to the east over the Hohe Leier. Beyond here, the trail is quite stony, so sturdy shoes are essential *(follow the red and white markings)*. After 10min the path emerges above the Kleiner Mühldorfer See dam. There is a beautiful **open view**★ over both lakes, which lie in an unspoiled rocky landscape. Keen hikers can continue for another hour to the **Riekentörl pass** (alt 2 525m/8 284ft), for a magnificent **panorama**★★ over the entire Reisseck massif. The hike climbs along a rocky trail, but presents no technical difficulties.

RETZ

NIEDERÖSTERREICH
POPULATION 4 370 – ALT 252M/827FT

Retz, near the Thaya Valley, is an important wine-growing and farming center in a hilly region forming part of the Bohemian Forest. The old town still has its medieval grid plan, ramparts and defensive towers. Its emblem is a windmill, built in 1772 and still operational. ▪ *Hauptplatz 30, A-2070,* ☎ *0 29 42/27 00*

▶ **Orient Yourself:** Retz is in northcentral Austria, right on the border with the Czech Republic, about 78km/48mi northwest of Vienna.

Hauptplatz★

This fine, central square is anchored by a column to the Holy Trinity and surrounded by several architecturally remarkable buildings. Stand-outs are the crenelated **Verderberhaus** on the north side and the **Sgraffitohaus**, opposite, a handsome building with a carved doorway and a façade covered with inscribed maxims. Also here is the **Rathaus** (town hall), which was converted from a Gothic church in the 16C.

To sample the local wines, meet outside the Rathaus for a tour of the **Retzer Erlebniskeller** *(Guided tours 1hr 30min May-Oct daily 10.30am, 2pm, 4pm; €7; ☎ 0 29 42/27 00)*. At 21km/13mi long, this is Austria's largest historic wine cellar.

SCHLOSS RIEGERSBURG★

NIEDERÖSTERREICH

The unspoilt, peaceful landscape of the northeastern Waldviertel provides a backdrop for the most important Baroque mansion in Lower Austria. The former moated castle was bought by Sigmund Friedrich Count Khevenhüller, governor of Lower Austria and converted into a four-winged Baroque palace by the masterful **Franz Anton Pilgram**. The decoration is rich, but not ostentatious. Still owned by the same family, the building is a fine example of an 18C country seat.

▶ **Orient Yourself:** The Schloss is in the far north of Austria, close to the Czech border.

Tour

Guided tour (45min) Apr-June and Sep-mid-Nov daily 9am-5pm; July-Aug daily 9am-7pm. €9, combination ticket with Burg Hardegg €14. ☎ 0 29 16/4 00. www. schloss-riegersburg.at.

State rooms

The palace interior is filled with high-quality furnishings. The surprisingly plain but beautifully proportioned **banqueting hall** (Festsaal) features stuccowork above the door showing Count Johann Joseph Khevenhüller-Metsch, Maria Theresia's Chief Lord Chamberlain, whose diaries are said to have inspired the libretto for Richard Strauss' opera *Der Rosenkavalier*. The portraits of Maria Theresia and her mother Elisabeth Christine are by court painter Martin van Meytens. The **Baroque room** houses a view of Naples composed of 35 copper engravings dating from 1730 to 1775. The furniture in the Salon includes Queen Anne and Chippendale pieces, as well as furnishings in the Austrian Baroque style and a handsome tabernacle cupboard.

The **tower room**, hung with plate-printed cotton, contains furniture from the 18C. Note the pretty portable desk from England. The **dining room** contains French furniture and houses a famous portrait of Prince Eugene of Savoy by Austrian painter Auerbach.

The **stucco ceiling**★ of the **Yellow Salon** depicts an allegory of princely virtue. The room is furnished with Marie-Antoinette chairs and two beautiful Florentine commodes with delicate inlaid work. The **Chinese Salon** also features a magnificent stucco ceiling.

In the north wing is the elegant **Schlosskapelle** (chapel), consecrated in 1755. The altar is integrated into the architectural structure and is surmounted by rich stuccowork. The altarpiece depicts St Sigismund.

The **Schlossküche** (kitchen) on the ground floor, in use until 1955 and still featuring its original appointments, working equipment and large brick oven, is the only remaining manorial kitchen in Austria.

From the café in the right wing, you can access the park with its pond.

Atlas carrying the world

Schloss Riegersburg

Excursion

Burg Hardegg

8km/5mi to the east. ⏱Apr-mid Nov daily 9am-5pm;July-Aug daily 9am-6pm. €6.90, combination ticket with Riegersburg €14. ☎ 0 29 16/4 00. www.burghardegg.at.
Hardegg on the Thaya River is dominated by its blufftop castle whose formidable keep and thick walls create an impression of impregnability. The origins of this strategically important fortress date back to 1000 AD, but extensions were added right up to the 14C. After a chequered history, the fortress passed into the hands of the Khevenhüller family in 1730 and at the end of the 19C it was converted into a mausoleum for the Lower Austrian line of this dynasty. Some of the rooms are dedicated to the memory of the ill-fated Emperor Maximilian of Mexico, a comrade-in-arms and close confidant of Count Johann Franz Carl Khevenhüller.

SCHLOSS ROSENBURG★

NIEDERÖSTERREICH

More than 1 000 years ago, the Babenbergs freed central Austria from the Magyars so that this region could at last be settled. In order to counter effectively the constant threat from Bohemia, the nobles built a series of castles in the strategically important Kamptal. Of these, the Rosenburg, built in the first half of the 12C, is one of the most attractive and important. It has been owned by the counts of Hoyos since the 17C.

▶ **Orient Yourself:** This Schloss is in northcentral Austria, about 84km/52mi northwest of Vienna, near the Abbey of Altenburg.
⏱ **Organizing Your Time:** Two hours should be plenty for this palace.
Kids Especially for Kids: Falconry demonstrations.
Also See: Stift Altenburg, Schloss Greillenstein

Tour

Guided tour (45min) May-Sep daily 9.30am-5pm; Apr and Oct Thur-Sun 9.30am-4.30pm . €10. ☎ 0 29 82/29 11. www.rosenburg.at.
Kids Passing through the gateway, one comes to the 1614 courtyard surrounded on three sides by double galleries and once used for equestrian games. The square **keep** is part of the original castle, but was altered in the Renaissance period by the addition of a balcony.

After standing nearly empty in the 18C, the living rooms and grand public rooms were furnished mainly in the style of the German Renaissance. The **library** with its remarkable wooden **coffered ceiling**★ is of particular interest, as are the Marble Hall and the palace chapel.

Schloss Rosenburg is a center for falconry. Kids especially love the **free flight demonstrations**★ in which hunting falcons, eagles and vultures perform their routines.

Flight demonstration, Schloss Rosenburg

SAALACHTAL

SALZBURG UND BAYERN (GERMANY)

The valley of the River Saalach, which breaches the Northern Limestone Alps, forms the quickest link between Salzburg, Zell am See and the Grossglockner.

▶ **Orient Yourself:** This valley runs north south between Salzburg and Zell am See.
🕐 **Organizing Your Time:** With stops, this tour can easily turn into a day trip.
Kids **Especially for Kids:** Vorderkaserklamm, Lamprechtshöhle

From Salzburg to Zell am See *95km/59mi*

Salzburg★★★ & *See Salzburg.*

▶ *Leave Salzburg on road no 1.*

Shortly past the airport, consider making a 6km/3.7mi detour to **Grossgmain** and the Salzburg open-air museum.

Salzburger Freilichtmuseum
🕐*Apr-Oct Tue-Sun 9am-6pm; 26 Dec-6 Jan Tue-Sun 10am-4pm.* €7. ☎ *06 62/85 00 11. www.freilichtmuseum.com.*
Kids More than 60 original buildings from throughout Salzburg province representing six centuries' of traditional architecture have been reassembled in this woodsy open-air museum village. In addition, there are specialized exhibitions, such as a collection of old tractors, a multimedia presentation and a House of Sounds as well as live craft demonstrations.

▶ *Carry on to Bad Reichenhall (Germany).*

Bad Reichenhall★
This Bavarian town sits atop some of the richest salt springs in Europe and is a major producer of table salt. The saltwater spa helps cure respiratory diseases.

Branching off at Schneizlreuth from the Deutsche Alpenstraße, the Lofer road runs within view of the Drei Brüder mountains, then turns away from the Saalach and climbs up to Melleck. The Steinpass marks the Austrian border. The road returns to the Saalach.

Lofer★ & *See Kaisergebirge* 1.

In contrast to earlier scenery, the enclosed section from Lofer to Saalfelden, in a former glacial gorge, is strikingly uniform.

Wallfahrtskirche Maria Kirchental
4km/2.5mi south of Lofer. At St. Martin bei Lofer turn right off B 311 onto a narrow toll road. 🕐*daily 7am-7pm.* & ☎ *0 65 88/85 28.*
Nicknamed the "Pinzgau Cathedral," this rustic yet graceful late-17C pilgrimage church was designed by the renowned Johann Bernhard Fischer von Erlach. It was steadily redecorated and furnished over the 18C and 19C as the offerings of the pilgrims mounted up.

About 6km/4mi beyond Lofer the road reaches the Vorderkaser gorge, the first of the trio of natural attractions (*www.naturgewalten.at*) described next. A combination ticket costs €6.90.

Vorderkaserklamm

May-Oct daily 9am-6pm. €2.80. 0 65 88/85 10.

Kids This wildly romantic gorge shaped by a thundering torrent is reached via an easy 2.5km/1.5mi trail through an idyllic natural recreation area, complete with pools for swimming and barbecue areas. From here an initially quite steep path leads up through the forest to the entrance to the gorge, which is 400m/1 300ft long, 80m /260ft deep and only 80cm/2.6ft wide in some places. Footbridges run past waterfalls and beneath wedged rocks. Budget about 45min roundtrip for the gorge only.

Lamprechtshöhle

8km/5mi beyond Lofer. Dress warmly as the cave is only about 5-7°C/41-45°F. *Guided tours (45min) year-round Fri-Wed 9am-6pm, Thur 9am-5pm.* €3.40. 0 65 82/83 43.

Kids The Lamprechtshöhle is one of Europe's most extensive underground cave networks extending for some 51km/32mi. Tours cover 700m/765yd and end at a viewing platform, from which visitors can peer down into the depths of a giant cave.

▶ *1km/0.6mi after the Lamprechtshöhle, turn left for the Seisenberg gorge.*

Seisenbergklamm

Allow about 1hr. *May-Oct daily 9.30am-6.30pm.* €2.80. 0 65 82/8 35 24.

Steps, footbridges and trails give access to the Weissbach as it roars through this narrow gorge, about 600m/650yd long and up to 50m/164ft deep. Highlights are the tortured rock formations, gouged out by the water, of the dark **Dunkelklamm**. Beyond here, a trail climbs through the forest along the Weissbach for 30min to the Gasthof Lohfeyer, idyllically situated in an Alpine pasture.

▶ *From the town of Weissbach the road runs through a steep, long canyon and eventually reaches the Saalfelden basin.*

Saalfelden

This market town with 12 centuries of history under its belt has plenty to offer visitors: a beautiful site, a historical town center and rich and varied leisure facilities. In winter Saalfelden is particularly favored by cross-country skiers who have 80km/50mi of ski tracks to play with. The number goes up to 160km/99mi when factoring neighboring Saalach Valley communities. Towering above the resort are the imposing rock faces of the Steinernes Meer.

▶ *Continue to Zell am See.*

Zell am See★   *See Zell am See.*

SAALBACH-HINTERGLEMM

SALZBURG
POPULATION 2 700 – ALT 1 003M/3 291FT

Together with neighboring Hinterglemm, Saalbach is one of the largest winter sports resorts in Austria. Its main attraction lies in its wooded rural setting and the harmonious contours of its broad, gently falling slopes. In winter, its tougher runs attract world championship-level downhill races. Summers are relaxing here and great for hikers who have more than 400km of trail to choose from, including the Pinzgau path and the hike to the Tristkogel and Torsee Lake. ⓘ A-5753, ☎ 0 65 41/68 00. www.saalbach.at.

▶ **Orient Yourself:** The resort is in western Austria, about 18km/11mi northwest of Zell am See.
♨ **Also See:** Zell am See, Grossglockner-Hochalpenstraße

Visit

Ski slopes
Saalbach's ski slopes extend between 900m/2 950ft and 2 100m/6 890ft and offer good snow conditions from Christmas to April. Some 55 ski lifts open up 200km/124mi of pistes for skiers of all levels. Experienced ski hounds will enjoy the slopes of the Zwölferkogel and the northern downhill section of the Schattberg-Ost. A relaxing 8km/5mi run links the latter with Vorderglemm. The second run on the Bernkogel is recommended for beginners. Some pistes are reserved for snowboarders. Cross-country skiers will find only 18km/11mi of track between Vorderglemm and Saalbach and above Hinterglemm.

Ski slope down into the town center

Sochor/ÖSTERREICH WERBUBUNG

Viewpoints

Schattberg-Ost★★

Alt 2 020m/6 627ft. *Cable-car from Saalbach.* ⏱*July-late Sep daily 9am-11.45am, 1pm-4.15pm; early Dec-mid Apr daily 8.30am-4pm.* ≈€*15.40 roundtrip (summer),* €*37.50 one-day area ski pass.* ☎ *0 65 41/6 27 10.*
From the top you'll have an **overall view** of the Glemmtal Valley and its ski area with the Loferer and Leoganger Steinberge and the Hohe Tauern in the distance.

Zwölferkogel★

Alt 1 984m/6 509ft. *Cable-car from Hinterglemm.* ⏱*late May-late Oct daily 9am-11.45am, 1-4.15pm; Dec-mid Apr daily 8.30am-4.15pm.* ≈€*15.40 roundtrip (summer),* ≈€*37.50 one-day area ski pass.* ☎ *0 65 41/6 32 10.*
Views from here stretch over the entire area around Hinterglemm and are dominated by the Hohe Penhab and by the Schattberg-West.

SALZACHTAL★

SALZBURG

The Alpine valley of Salzach is an artery of the province of Salzburg, whose hooked shape conforms with the bent course of the gushing Salzach River. Strung out between the Krimml waterfalls and Salzburg is a series of basins called the Pinzgau, the Pongau, the Tennengau and the Flachgau. Until the coming of the railway, each of these isolated sections of the valley tended to lead its own life, quite separate from that of its neighbors.

▸ **Orient Yourself:** The valley extends south of Salzburg in western Austria.
⊛ **Don't Miss:** Eisriesenwelt, Golliinger Wasserfall, Salzburger Salzwelten
🕐 **Organizing Your Time:** This route can be done as a day trip from Salzburg, although if you stop at every site, you'll probably need two days.

Hochkönig mountains

[Kids] **Especially for Kids:** Eisriesenwelt, Erlebnisburg Hohenwerfen, Salzwelten Salzburg

1 From Lend to Radstadt★ *70km/44mi*

Via the Hochkönig road and the Wagrainer Höhe

The mountain section between Dienten and Mühlbach has many bends and is usually blocked by snow in winter.

Leave industrial-flavored **Lend** on the minor road to Dienten and cross the Salzach. The church at **Dienten** soon emerges against the Hochkönig crests whose vertical white cliffs are particularly impressive in the evening sun. The road reaches its highest point at the Dientener Sattel (1 370m/4 493ft) at the foot of the **Hochkönig.** Beyond here, it still has several steep sections, including the sharp descent into **Mühlbach**, a center for mountain walking.

▶ *Take road no 311 south to St. Johann im Pongau.*

St. Johann im Pongau is recognisable by its trademark twin-towered church, a neo-Gothic confection from the late 19C. Between here and the Enns Valley, the road traverses lovely countryside, particularly around **Wagrain**★.

Radstadt 👓 *See Radstätter Tauernstraße.*

2 From Lend to Salzburg *89km/55mi*

The Salzach Valley, closely hemmed in as far as Lend (👓 1 *above*), opens out north of Schwarzach to form the Pongau basin.

▶ *Turn right off road 311 to St. Johann im Pongau, and follow the signposts to "Liech-tensteinklamm."*

Liechtensteinklamm★
Allow 1hr roundtrip walk. ⏱ *mid May-Sep daily 9am-6pm, Oct daily 9am-4pm.* 👓*€3.50.* ☎ *0 64 12/60 36.*

Sheer – at times overhanging – rock walls and the varied and unusual formations wrought by water billowing over the shiny, white-streaked rock contribute to the charm of the gorge. At the end of the walkways with handrails you'll be rewarded by the sight of a majestic **waterfall**★.

▶ *Return to road no 311 and go north towards Salzburg.*

Bischofshofen
The largest town in the Pongau occupies a fine **setting**★, with the Tennengebirge to the north and the Hochkönig to the west. Bischofshofen is well-known to ski jumping fans as the fourth and final

Y. Bontoux

Liechtenstein gorge

venue of the world-famous Vierschanzentournee. Competitions are held annually on January 6.

Pfarrkirche
This church is the lowest of three built on a slope and linked by a narrow road, thus forming a typical example of a "family group" of churches. The present building dates to 1450 and was commissioned by the bishop of Chiemsee, who is buried in a marble tomb in the north transept. A copy of the **Rupertuskreuz**, a processional cross that is Austria's oldest religious work of art (c 700), is on display as well. The original is in the cathedral museum at Salzburg.

▷ *Carry on towards Salzburg. After Imlau, the fortress of Hohenwerfen comes into view. Before reaching the fortress, turn right in Werfen for the Eisriesenwelt caves.*

Eisriesenwelt★★ ♿ *See Eisriesenwelt.*

Erlebnisburg Hohenwerfen★
Allow 3hr. ⟳ *Interior by guided tour only (1hr). The castle entrance is a 15min uphill walk from the parking lot.* ◷ *July-Aug daily 9am-6pm; May, June, Sep daily 9am-5pm; Apr Tue-Sun 9am-4.30pm; Oct daily 9am-4.30pm.* ⬤ *€10 or €13 with lift.* ☎ *0 64 68/76 03. www.salzburg-burgen.at.*

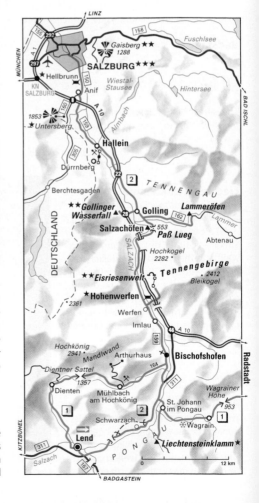

🄺🄸🄳🅂 The fortress dates back to the 11C but was extended to its present form in the 16C and 17C by the archbishops of Salzburg, who used it as a military base, residence, hunting lodge and prison. Tours take in the chapel, the torture chamber and the armory. There is also a museum of falconry and a birds-of-prey trail in the front castle. The birds kept here – long-legged buzzards, white-tailed eagles and red kites – perform in **flight displays**★ daily at 11am and 3pm.

▷ *The road continues through the impressive Werfen-Golling section of the valley. Before reaching the tunnel at Lueg pass, turn right to the Salzach gorge.*

Salzachklamm (Salzachöfen)
This gorge is one of three impressive natural features close to the pass, along with the Lammeröfen gorge and

Gollinger waterfall. From the Gasthof Pass-Lueg Höhe, a steep path *(45min round-trip)*, slippery in rainy weather, leads to a jumble of rocks forming a natural bridge over the Salzach.

▷ *About 2km/1.3mi beyond the tunnel at Lueg pass, turn right towards Abtenau/Lammertal for the Lammeröfen gorge. Detour of 14km/8.7mi.*

Lammeröfen
After the entrance to Oberscheffau, 7km/4mi beyond the junction, park next to Lammerklause guesthouse. The walk (1hr roundtrip) begins after the bus stop. ⏰*May-Oct daily 9am-6pm.* ✆*€2.50.* ☎ *0 62 44/84 42. www.lammerklamm.at.*
After about 20min walk through the relatively wide gorge, the trail reaches the ticket booth. From here there is a shorter but more rewarding walk up concrete steps to a viewpoint beneath a natural rock vault, where a narrow cleft in the rock lets light down into the gorge below.

▷ *Take road B 162 to Golling. Turn left in front of the Zur Goldenen Traube inn and follow the signposts to "Wasserfall."*

Gollinger Wasserfall★★
30min roundtrip walk to the foot of the waterfall, 1hr 30min to the top; ✆*€2.*
The Golling Falls tumble down 75m/246ft from the Hoher Göll (2 522m/ 8277ft) and can be more or less spectacular depending on the time of year and the amount of water. Park at the Torrener Hof inn, then follow the road for a short stretch in the direction of Kuchl and pick up the trail to the fall *(follow the red/white markings)* leading through forest. From the bridge and ticket booth, the path climbs gently up from the bottom of the cascade to where the water emerges.

▷ *Return to Golling and carry on to* **Hallein** *and from there to the Salzwelten Salzburg in Bad Dürrnberg.*

En route to the salt mine, you'll pass a pilgrimage church and the **Keltendorf am Dürrnberg**, a reconstruction of a Celtic village.

Salzwelten Salzburg★
Allow about 2.5hr. Not suitable for children under 4 years. 🎧*Guided tour (70min) Apr-Oct daily 9am-5pm; Nov-Mar daily 11am-3pm.* ✆*€16.50, ticket includes admission to Keltendorf.* ☎ *0 61 32/2 00 24 00. www.salzwelten.at.*
Kids Salt harvested in the Dürrnberg mountain brought wealth to the archbishops of Salzburg and production continued until 1989. Now a small section of the underground warren of tunnels has been developed as a show-mine where guides dressed as Archbishop Wolf Dietrich von Raitenau lead entertaining tours. The visit ends with a romantic raft trip across the floodlit underground salt lake.

▷ *Continue to Salzburg.*

Salzburg★★★ 🕭 *See Salzburg.*

SALZATAL★★

STEIERMARK

The Salza River, a tributary of the upper Enns, has carved out a 70km/45mi-long remote and romantic valley. It is almost completely uninhabited, except for the villages of Wildalpen and Greith, and offers nature lovers plenty of opportunities for delightful expeditions through the forest. The river's sprightly rapids and churning pool draw scores of white-water enthusiasts.

▶ **Orient Yourself:** The valley is in central Austria, about 100km/60mi northwest of Graz.

From Hieflau to Mariazell *80km/50mi*

Between Hieflau and Grossreifling the route follows the Enns, which is dammed in several places. Between Grossreifling and Palfau the road follows a winding, uphill course to Wildalpen.

Wildalpen
Tiny Wildalpen has an attractive setting and is primarily known as a starting point for white-water sports on the Salza (using rafts, kayaks and canoes). The interesting **Heimat-, Pfarr- und Wasserleitungsmuseum**★ (�*May-26 Oct Mon-Fri 10am-noon, 1-3pm, Sun 10am-noon;* �*€2;* ☏ *0 36 36/45 10)* gives a visual account of the building of the pipeline that supplies Vienna with drinking water. The **Pfarrkirche St. Barbara** with its scalloped tower roof has fine frescoes and remarkable furnishings.

▶ *Turn right Immediately after the Postbus stop (at kilometer stone 31.6).*

Brunn
From the Brunn wayside shrine, only a few yards from the road, there is a **view**★ down into the bottom of the Brunntal, in the heart of the Hochschwab.
There is also a splendid **view**★★ along the north slope of the massif with its fantastically eroded cliffs.

From here the road winds its way through **Prescenyklause** with its old-fashioned logging dam, then on to **Weichselboden**, dominated by its Baroque parish church. The road now climbs steadily as far as Greith. Beyond, the landscape becomes gradually less mountainous and the road begins its descent to Gusswerk and then on to **Mariazell** (� *See Mariazell).*

SALZBURG★★★

POPULATION 147 000 – ALT 424M/1 391FT
LOCAL MAPS UNDER SALZACHTAL AND SALZKAMMERGUT

Salzburg, Mozart's birthplace, is a delight the moment you spot the silhouette of the Hohensalzburg fortress floating above roofs and the meandering Salzach River. Its picturesque streets with their wrought-iron signs, its spacious squares with sculptured fountains, and the noble architecture of its buildings leave memories that linger for years. Every summer, scores of music lovers descend for the famous Salzburg Festival, one of the most prestigious concert series in the world. In 1997, Salzburg's Old Town was ranked a World Heritage Site by UNESCO. *Auerspergstraße 7, A-5020, ☎ 06 62/88 98 70, www.salzburginfo.at*

▸ **Orient Yourself:** Salzburg is on Austria's western edge, right on the German border.

▣ **Parking:** Park & Ride Süd (Alpenstraße), Altstadt-Garage (Mönchsberg), Bahnhof-Garage (Südtiroler Platz), Mirabell-Garage (Mirabellplatz); Airportcenter (Innsbrucker Bundesstraße), Parkgarage Auersperg (Auerspergstraße), Parkgarage Linzer Gasse (Glockengasse), Raiffeisen-Garage (Schwarzstraße). Public lots on Akademiestraße, Gebirgsjägerplatz, Hellbrunn, Mülln, Petersbrunnstraße, Salzburg Airport

☺ **Don't Miss:** Hohensalzburg, Residenz, Stiftskirche St. Peter, Mozart's Geburtshaus

◷ **Organizing Your Time:** Allow at least two days for a visit, three if taking in Hellbrunn or other outlying attractions.

▦ **Especially for Kids:** Haus der Natur, Stiegl's Brauwelt, Schloss Hellbrunn, Zoo Salzburg

A Bit of History

The heritage of the prince-archbishops – The See of Salzburg was founded shortly before 700 by St Rupert and was raised in the following century to an archbishopric. In the 13C the bishops were given the title of Princes of the Holy Roman Empire. Their power extended as far as Italy, while their coffers were filled to bulging with revenue from the Salzkammergut salt mines. Three of these rulers showed a taste for building and in just over half a century converted the little medieval town into a grand residence in the Italian style.

Wolf Dietrich von Raitenau was elected archbishop in 1587. He was a typical representative of the Renaissance: brought up in Rome and closely connected with the Medicis, he longed to make Salzburg the Rome of the North. After a fire destroyed the central cathedral quarter, he hired the Italian architect Scamozzi to build a new house of worship even larger than St Peter's in Rome. Raitenau had 15 children with Salome Art, a great beauty for whom he built Schloss Mirabell. After losing a conflict with the dukes of Bavaria over the salt trade, he was imprisoned in 1612 in Hohensalzburg Castle where he died after five years of captivity. His only completed building project was his own mausoleum in St. Sebastian cemetery.

Raitenau's successor, **Markus Sittikus**, downscaled the cathedral and entrusted the work to another Italian architect, Santino Solari. The mansion of Heilbrunn to the south of Salzburg is another of his architectural legacies.

It fell to **Paris Lodron** to complete the work begun by his predecessors, including the cathedral which was solemnly consecrated in 1628. Lodron also finished the Residence and opened new streets in the town, creating the face of Salzburg for generations to come.

Address Book

PRACTICAL INFORMATION

VISITOR INFORMATION
Salzburg Information (see introductory paragraph). Other tourist information outlets are:

Mozartplatz, *Mozartplatz 5*, ☎ *06 62/88 98 73 30;*

Hauptbahnhof (Main station), *Platform 2a*, ☎ *06 62/88 98 73 40;*

Salzburg Centre, *Münchner Bundesstraße 1*, ☎ *06 62/88 98 73 50;*

Salzburg South, Park & Ride Car Park, Alpensiedlung-Süd, *Alpenstraße*, ☎ *06 62/88 98 73 60;*

Airport Arrivals Hall, ☎ *06 62/85 12 11 or 85 20 91 or 8 58 09 99.*

Open June-Sept:

Salzburg North, *Kasern autobahn service station*, ☎ *06 62/88 98 73 70.*

SALZBURG CARD
This ticket, valid for 24, 48 or 72hr, gives free travel on nearly all public transport in the city, as well as free entrance to most sights in and around Salzburg. From Jun-Sep, the cost is €23/29/34 for 24/48/72 hours, respectively. From Jan-May and Oct-Dec, prices drop to €20/27/32. It is available at tourist offices, travel agencies and hotels.

SALZBURGERLAND CARD
If you're spending most of your time in Salzburg province and only want to visit the city for one day, this discount may be a better alternative. It is good for free or discounted admission to 190 regional attractions and integrates a 24hr Salzburg Card. It is available from May-Oct and is valid for either six days (€37) or 12 days (€46). Buy it at tourist offices, hotels and even some gas stations. For further details, see www.salzburgerlandcard.com.

CITY TOURS AND GUIDED TOURS
Auf den Spuren Mozarts (In Mozart's Footsteps; 1hr 30min coach tour and 1hr in Mozart's house) – Departures daily at 9.30am, 11am, noon, 2pm and 4pm, or by request.

Panorama City Tour (1hr) – Departures daily at 10am, 11am, noon, 1pm, 3pm, 4pm and 5pm, or by request.

Information and reservations from Salzburg Panorama Tours, Schrannengasse 2, ☎ 06 62/88 32 11 0 (Web site: *www.panoramatours.at*).

Mozart City Tour (2hr) – Departures daily at 9.30am, 11am and 2pm.

Salzburg-Informativ (1hr) – Departures daily at 10am, noon, 3pm, 4pm and 5pm.

Salzburg-Exklusiv with bus trip, walk and wine-tasting (4hr) – 15 May-15 Sept daily at 2pm.

Information and reservations from Salzburg Sightseeing Tours, Mirabellplatz 2, ☎ 06 62/88 16 16.

PUBLIC TRANSPORT
Information and tickets for the city bus network can be obtained from the ticket offices of the Salzburg public transport authorities (*Griesgasse 21*, ☎ *06 62/44 80 62 62; Lokalbahnhof (at the Hauptbahnhof)*, ☎ *06 62/44 80 61 66; Alpenstraße 91*, ☎ *06 62/44 80 62 63*). Tickets can also be bought from bus drivers, in tobacconists (Tabaktrafiken) and from ticket machines at the bus stop (tickets for a single trip should be bought in advance in blocks of five, before starting on a journey, as a supplement is charged when they are bought separately from the bus driver or a ticket machine). Tickets must be date-stamped as soon as you get on the bus.

The Salzburg transport authorities also offer transferable daily, weekly, monthly (valid from time of first use) and family-day-trip travel cards for the city area, and a 24hr ticket (valid for the whole transport network, only available in blocks of five), with which you can make as many journeys as you like. These are available from tobacconists and ticket offices (daily, weekly and monthly tickets also from ticket machines).

POST OFFICES
Hauptpostamt (Main post office): *Residenzplatz 9*, open Mon-Fri 7am-7pm, Sat 8am-10am.

Postschalter im Hauptbahnhof (counter at the main station): *Südtirolerplatz 1*, open daily 6am-11pm.

SHOPPING

The main shopping areas include the Altstadt (Old Town), left and right of the Salzach, the areas around the Getreide-gasse, the area around the Festspiel-häuser, the Mozartplatz, the Kaigasse, the Alter Markt, the Linzer Gasse, the Makartplatz and the Mirabellplatz.

MARKETS

Around the Andräkirche: Schrannen-markt (fresh food, vegetables, flowers) Thur (or Wed if Thur is a public holiday) 6am-1pm.
Universitätsplatz and Wiener-Phil-harmoniker-Gasse: Vegetable market Mon-Fri 6am-7pm, Sat 6am-1pm.

SOUVENIRS

Craft goods and traditional costume (Trachten): Salzburger Heimatwerk, Residenzplatz 9; Wood carvings, busts of Mozart: Kopfberger, Judengasse 14; hand-crafted wax goods, Lebkuchen specialities: Nagy Johann & Söhne, Linzergasse 32; Mozart souvenirs: Mozartland, Getreidegasse 10; sou-venir shop in Mozarts Geburtshaus, Getreidegasse 9; **Mozartkugeln** (round chocolates with marzipan and truffle filling): Café-Konditorei Fürst (inventors of the original recipe), Brodgasse 13, Sigmund-Haffner-Gasse and Mirabell-platz 5; Schatz Konditorei, Getreide-gasse 3.

ENTERTAINMENT

Grosses and **Kleines Festspielhaus**, *Hofstallgasse 1*, ☎ *06 62/8 04 50*. Thea-tre and musicals, concerts.
Landestheater, *Schwarzstraße 22*, ☎ *06 62/8 71 51 20*. Theatre, musicals and dance.
Kleines Theater, *Schallmoser Haupt-straße 50*, ☎ *06 62/87 21 54*. Theatre and cabaret.
Salzburger Marionettentheater, *Schwarzstraße 24*, ☎ *06 62/87 24 06*. Mozart operas feature predictably quite highly on the programme of this world-famous marionette theatre, which also includes master works by Rossini, Offenbach, Strauss and Tchaik-ovsky, on recordings by prestigious orchestras. The audience in the old Hotel Mirabell with its Rococo decor is transported into another world of magic and fantasy.

Kammerspiele, *Schwarzstraße 24*, ☎ *06 62/87 15 12*. Youth theatre, cabaret.
SZENE-Salzburg, *Anton-Neumayr-Platz 2*, ☎ *06 62/84 34 48*. Theatre, music and dance.
Rockhouse Salzburg, *Schallmoser Hauptstraße 46*, ☎ *06 62/88 49 14*. Jazz, folk, blues, reggae, heavy metal and rock music concerts.
Kulturzentrum Nonntal, *Mühlbach-erhofweg 5*, ☎ *06 62/84 87 84 0*. Live concerts and other events.
Casino Salzburg, *Schloss Klessheim in Wals Siezenheim*, ☎ *06 62/85 44 55*.

CINEMAS

Central Kino, *Linzer Gasse 17-19*, ☎ *06 62/87 22 82*.
Elmo-Kino-Center, *St.-Julien-Straße 3-5*, ☎ *06 62/87 23 73*.
Mozartkino, *Kaigasse 33*, ☎ *06 62/84 22 22*.
Salzburger Filmkulturzentrum, Das Kino, *Giselakai 11*, ☎ *06 62/87 31 00*.

WHERE TO EAT

Brandstätter – *Salzburg-Liefering*, *Münchner Bundesstraße 69*, ☎ *06 62/43 45 35*. Restaurant in the hotel of this name; rooms range from the rustic Schankstube to the elegant Zirbelstube. Some of the best cooking in town.
K+K Restaurant am Waagplatz – *Waagplatz 2*, ☎ *06 62/84 21 56*. This

Salzburger Marionettentheater

restaurant's unique selling point is as "Salzburg's first eatery": guests are fed and entertained in medieval style in a 900 year old vaulted cellar (starts at 8pm; costs 570S for a seven-course meal, welcome drink and programme of entertainment with musicians; enquire about dates; booking recommended). There is also a more "traditional" restaurant in a number of rooms spread over four floors.

Alt Salzburg – *Bürgerspitalgasse 2,* ☎ *06 62/84 14 76.* Cosy, tastefully decorated rooms, in which local products cooked in a truly authentic Austrian fashion are served.

Bei Bruno – *Makartplatz 4,* ☎ *06 62/87 84 17.* Separately run, elegant restaurant belonging to a luxury hotel with excellent food.

Stadtkrug – *Linzer Gasse 20,* ☎ *06 62/87 35 45.* Small, intimate and stylish local restaurant with an extensive wine list. The ideal venue for a candle-lit dinner!

Eulenspiegel – *Hagenauerplatz 2,* ☎ *06 62/84 31 80.* Self-declared as "Austria's most original restaurant" with the Eule bar on the ground floor and its small dining rooms full of nooks and crannies divided over several floors. For a very special experience, you might try the **Mozart Dinner Concert**, on offer all year round in the Baroque room of the Stiftskeller St. Peter (St. Peter Bezirk I/4): 3 course menu (drinks not included) by candlelight, to the accompaniment of works by WA Mozart (performed by musicians in historical costumes). 560S. Details of dates: ☎ *06 62/82 86 95 0 or 84 84 81.* Booking recommended.

The **Stiftskeller St. Peter**, ☎ *06 62/84 12 68 0,* with its tradition dating back to 803, in any case offers a pleasant setting (several banqueting rooms and dining rooms) for eating out in style.

Blaue Gans – *Getreidegasse 41-43,* ☎ *06 62/84 24 91 0.* Old vaulted premises and correspondingly traditional Austrian cooking using authentic old recipes.

Sternbräu – *Griesgasse 23/Getreidegasse 34,* ☎ *06 62/84 21 40.* A staggering 14 different dining rooms to cater to every taste, fine arcaded courtyard.

Programme of evening entertainment from May to October.

Pitter Keller – *Auerspergstraße 23,* ☎ *06 62/88 05 52.* Earthy beer cellar with local food.

Alter Fuchs – *Linzer Gasse 47-49,* ☎ *06 62/88 22 00.* Informal atmosphere. Daily menus are good value for money.

Krimpelstätter – *Müllner Hauptstraße 1,* ☎ *06 62/43 22 74.* Traditional inn with a large beer garden.

CAFÉS AND BARS

Tomaselli – *Alter Markt 9.* Classic coffee house, where visitors never outstay their welcome.

Fürst – *Brodgasse 13.* Parent branch of the Konditorei-Confiserie, where the original Salzburger Mozartkugeln are made.

Bazar – *Schwarzstraße 3.* Stylish café with terrace overlooking the Salzach.

Café-Restaurant Winkler – *Mönchsberg 32.* Marvellous view of the city.

Augustiner-Bräu – *Augustinergasse 4.* Abbey brewery since 1621. Beer served in stone tankards. Enormous halls with something of a beer-tent atmosphere and a large, shady beer garden.

Die Weisse – *Rupertgasse 10.* Rustic inn with its own brewery, serving Weissbier made on the premises (since 1901).

Zum fidelen Affen – *Priesterhausgasse 8.* Beer and wine cellar with warm wooden panelling.

Zebra – *Imbergstraße 11.* Ultra-modern cocktail bar. Italian antipasti for anyone feeling a bit peckish.

Daimler's – *Giselakai 17.* Small restaurant and friendly bar on two floors.

Fridrich – *Steingasse 15.* Smart bar specialising in wine.

Saitensprung – *Steingasse 11.* Cocktails and wines in a homely brick-vaulted room, which stays open into the early hours.

Zwettler's – *Kaigasse 3.* Rustic, relaxed atmosphere for a light meal or simply to enjoy a little drink.

Shamrock Irish Pub – *Rudolfskai 12.* Typical exported pub, rough-stone walls, live music: rustic, but agreeable.

Vis-à-vis – *Rudolfskai 24.* Café, bar with brick-vaulted ceiling, bathed in blue neon light.

Salzburg Festival – "Everyman"

Salzburger Altstadtkeller
– *Rudolfkai 26*. Live music every day at the "musical landlord's".

DATES FOR YOUR DIARY

Mozartwoche: 3rd and 4th weeks in Jan. Solo recitals, chamber, choral and orchestral concerts.

Osterfestspiele: Sat before Palm Sun until Easter Mon. Easter music festival with opera and concerts.

Salzburger Pfingstfestspiele (specialising in Baroque music): Sat before Whit weekend until Whit Mon. Whitsun music festival with opera and concerts.

Salzburger Festspiele: end of July to end of Aug. Salzburg Festival with opera, concerts, theatre, literature and poetry readings, Lieder evenings (Ⓒ *see also below*).

SommerSzene: July. Festival of alternative art: theatre, dance, performances, exhibitions (various venues around the city and immediately surrounding area).

Kulturtage: mid to end Oct. Cultural festival with opera and concerts.

Internationaler Salzburger Jazz-Herbst: early Nov. Autumn jazz festival with jazz, spirituals and Gospel music.

Krampusläufe: Exhibition of traditional customs on 2, 3 and 4 Dec in Getreidegasse; 1st Sat in Dec in Linzer Gasse.

Weihnachtsmärkte (Christmas markets): Mirabellplatz and Domplatz (late Nov to 24 Dec) and in the castle courtyard of Hohensalzburg (every weekend in Advent).

Wolfgang Amadeus Mozart (1756-91)

Mozart was born in Salzburg on 27 January 1756.

A child prodigy

Leopold Mozart, a talented composer and violinist in the service of the archbishop of Salzburg, recognized early on the exceptional gifts of his son Wolfgang and his older daughter Nannerl. Young Wolfgang had a remarkable musical memory and sophisticated ear, started composing by age five and was a keyboard virtuoso by age six. He had also started learning the harpsichord at age four. Leopold gave his son a serious musical education and together they undertook a memorable four-year tour of Europe, getting enthusiastic receptions in Munich, Vienna, Augsburg, Frankfurt, Paris, London and The Hague. At Schönbrunn, Empress Maria Theresa herself embraced the talents of young Wolfgang. Mozart remained in Salzburg for three years after the family's return in 1766. In 1772, Mozart was made concertmaster of the court orchestra of the Salzburg prince-archbishop.

Wiesenhofer/ÖSTERREICH WERBUNG

First disappointment

Until 1777, Mozart spent long periods in Salzburg. His employer, Archbishop Hieronymus Colloredo, did not approve of his many journeys abroad and relations were consequently rather strained. After a major quarrel with the prince-archbishop in 1777 Mozart resigned his post and left for Paris where he came under the influence of opera reformer Christoph Willibald Gluck. During the following years he produced much religious music, of which the *Coronation Mass* is a supreme example, and symphonic and lyrical pieces such as *Idomeneo*, an opera reflecting the influence of the French School. In 1781, after a further heated altercation with the prince-archbishop, the breach was complete. Mozart left Salzburg for Vienna.

Independence in Vienna

Arriving in Vienna, the 26-year-old Mozart had only limited means of support. He married Constanze Weber the same year and got initiated into the ideals of Freemasonry. Discovery of Handel's oratorios and of further works by Bach, together with the influence of his friend and mentor Haydn, contributed to the development of his mature style. The public adulation occasioned by works such as *The Abduction from the Seraglio* of 1781 and the Mass in C Minor of 1783 was not repeated, at least in Vienna, where the public even failed to appreciate *The Marriage of Figaro* (1786) and *Don Giovanni* (1787). A somber period began.

The final years (1788-91)

Mozart's career was to end in poverty and destitution. Though nominated "Composer to the Imperial Chamber" by Joseph II, he never received a commission. His final operas, *Così fan Tutte* (1790) and *La Clemenza di Tito* (1791) met with a cool reception, barely mitigated by the success of *The Magic Flute* (late 1791).

The great composer was to die before his time, alone and haunted by the specter of his own death.

On 6 December 1791 the paupers' hearse carried Mozart's corpse to a communal grave in St Mark's Cemetery in Vienna. His remains have never been identified.

Mozart's musical legacy

Mozart's astonishing output was equalled only by the ease with which he mastered every form of musical expression. His style has a charm that makes him a favorite with a wide public and is appreciated even by the unpracticed ear. Pleasant and sparkling motifs ripple beneath a rhythmic counterpoint of sprightly liveliness.

But spontaneity and brio need not mean lack of depth. His works are characterized by an exquisitely pure melodic line, sometimes tinged with melancholy. Towards the end of his life this vague sadness turned into despair, forcefully expressed in the 40th Symphony in G minor, *Don Giovanni*, the late string quartets, the "tragic" quintet in G major (K 516) and the *Requiem* (K 626), composed shortly before Mozart's own death (and not completed). Chopin was

Wolfgang Amadeus Mozart

Roger Viollet

Ball/BILDAGENTUR BUENOS DÍAS

so affected by this great choral work that he requested it to be played at his own funeral. These late works reflect the emotional frustration of Mozart's life and his struggle against poverty and illness.

Salzburg Festival

Guided tour (45 min) Jan-Aug 9.30am, Sep 2pm, 3pm. €5. Meet at the entrance to the Kleines Festspielhaus. ☎ 06 62/84 90 97.

Many years passed before his native city acknowledged Mozart's outstanding place in musical history. His biography was written in 1828 by Constanze's second husband, Georges Nicolas de Nissen. In 1842 Salzburg put up a statue to Mozart and later founded a musical academy named the **Mozarteum**. Finally, in 1917 the poet Hugo von Hoffmansthal, the composer Richard Strauss and the producer Max Reinhardt conceived the idea of a Mozart Festival.

The festival was inaugurated in 1920 and is held from late July to the end of August each summer, attracting the cream of the world's musical talent and scores of music

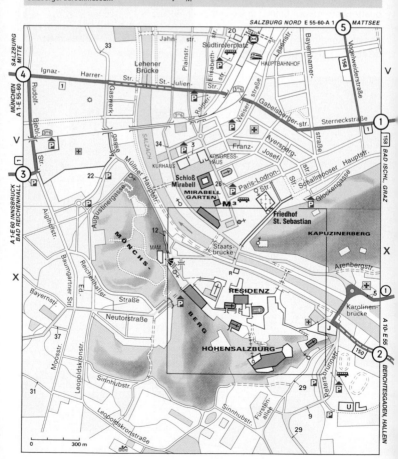

lovers. Performances take place at the great **Festival Hall** (Grosses Festspielhaus – Z), built in 1960 by the architect **Clemens Holzmeister**, the small festival hall (Kleines Festspielhaus) , the old Summer Riding School (Felsenreitschule), the **Mozarteum**, the **Landestheater** (Y), the Residenzhof and the disused salt mines on Perner Island in Hallein. Non-Mozart works are performed as well, including Hoffmannsthal's *Jedermann (Everyman)* on the cathedral forecourt.

Viewpoints★★

Mönchsberg★★ (Z)

Lift ◷daily 9am-11pm (7pm Mon). ⬭€2.90 roundtrip. ☎ 06 62/44 80 62 85.
From the Gstättengasse (X 12) a lift goes up to a terrace just below the Café Winkler, from which there is a fine general view of the city with modern Salzburg along the right bank of the Salzach and the old town between the river and the Hohensalzburg Fortress. To the south are the Tennen- and Hagengebirge, the Untersberg and the Salzburg Alps; eastwards the Kapuzinerberg and the Gaisberg.

SALZBURG		Herbert-von-Karajan-		Max-Reinhardt-Pl.	Z 33
		Platz	Y 16	Residenzpl.	Z 32
Alter Markt	Y 2	Judengasse	YZ	Sigmund-Haffner-	
Bürgerspitalgasse	Y 4	Kaigasse	Z	Gasse	YZ 35
Dreifaltigkeitsgasse	Y 6	Kajetaner-Pl.	Z 21	Theatergasse	Y 39
Getreidegasse	Y	Linzer Gasse	Y	Universitätspl.	Y 40
Hanusch-Pl.	Y 15	Makartpl.	Y	Waagpl.	Z 43

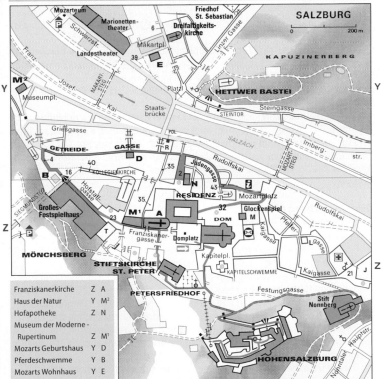

Franziskanerkirche	Z A
Haus der Natur	Y M²
Hofapotheke	Z N
Museum der Moderne -	
Rupertinum	Z M¹
Mozarts Geburtshaus	Y D
Pferdeschwemme	Y B
Mozarts Wohnhaus	Y E

Hettwer Bastei★★ (Y)

Climb up to the Kapuzinerkirche via the steep walkway reached from the Linzergasse through the covered passageway. From the church, go downhill again for about 50m/55yd, turn left and follow the sign "Stadtaussicht-Hettwer Bastei" to the viewpoint.

The Hettwer Bastei (bastion) on the south side of the Kapuzinerberg gives fine **views** over Salzburg, particularly when the morning light enhances the green of the many copper-clad roofs.

▶ *Return via the series of steps leading to the Steingasse.*

Old Town★★

Domplatz (Z)

Three arches link the buildings surrounding this square, the cathedral and the Residenz, the former ecclesiastical palaces. In the center is a Virgin Mary Column.

Dom★ (Z)

○*Mon-Sat 6.30am-5pm, Sun 8am-5pm (summer to 7pm). ☎ 06 62/80 47 79 50.*

The monumental Early Baroque cathedral is largely the work of Italian architect Santino Solari and was consecrated in 1628. Its west front, flanked by two towers, is of light-colored local marble and graced by numerous statues, including those of Sts Rubert, Virgil and Peter and Paul in front of the main door. The **interior** is impressive in both size and the richness of its decoration. Mozart was baptized in the Romanesque font in 1756. The tombs of the prince-archbishops and a Romanesque Crucifix may be seen in the **crypt**.

Dommuseum

○*Apr-early Jan Mon-Sat 10am-5pm, Sun 1-6pm. ○early-mid Nov, early Jan-Mar.* ♿.☞€5. ☎ 06 62/84 41 89.

Featured here is the cathedral treasure and a fabulous *Kunst- und Wunderkammer*, a gallery of objet d'art, minerals, crafts and precious knickknacks amassed by Archbishop Guidobald von Thun. It's all presented in a similarly haphazard way as it was in the 17C. Upstairs is the usual array of religious art from the Middle Ages to the present.

Behind the cathedral, in Kapitelplatz, the **Kapitelschwemme** is a drinking trough for horses in the form of a monumental fountain. From here, a street leads up to the station of the **Festungsbahn** (○*May-Aug daily 9am-10pm; Sep-Dec daily 9am-9pm. Jan-Apr 9am-5pm; ☞€9.80, includes entrance to fortress, museums and audio-guide; ☎ 06 62/84 26 82)*, the funicular providing access to the great Hohensalzburg fortress.

Hohensalzburg★★ (Z)

Allow about 2hr. Ascent on foot (20min) or by Festungsbahn funicular. ○*July-Aug daily 9am-7pm; Jan-Apr, Oct-Dec daily 9.30am-5pm; May, June, Sep daily 9am-6pm. ☞€6.90, includes entrance to fortress, museums and audio-guide; ☎ 06 62/84 24 30 11. www.salzburg-burgen.at. www.hohensalzburg.com.*

The former stronghold of the prince-archbishops stands on a block of Dolomite rock, about 120m/400ft above the Salzach. The castle was begun in 1077 by Archbishop Gebhard, frequently enlarged and eventually remodeled into a comfortable residence with state rooms by Archbishop Leonhard von Keutschach in the 15C. The archbishops often stayed here until the end of the 15C, reinforcing it considerably by the addition of towers, bastions for cannons and barbicans and the construction of magazines and arms depots.

At the exit from the upper station of the funicular, turn left to the panoramic terrace from which stairs and a postern lead into the fortress. Go past the guided tours office and a little way downhill, bearing right along the lists and round the fortified nucleus of the inner castle until you come to a courtyard opposite the south wall of the **St. Georgskirche**. This is decorated with two beautiful marble reliefs: a group of statuary in red Salzburg marble of Archbishop Leonhard von Keutschach flanked by two priests, and above it a Crucifixion.

The door to the right of the church leads to the terrace of the **Kuenburgbastei** from where there is a good **view**★★ of the old town's domes and belfries.

State Rooms and Museums

The state rooms and museums are best explored on a 90-minute self-guided audio tour. From the Reck watchtower there is a **panorama**★★, which is particularly interesting towards the Tennengebirge and the Salzburg Alps (south).

The state rooms, formerly the archbishops' apartments, were fitted out by Leonhard von Keutschach and are largely in their original state. There are walls adorned with Gothic woodcarvings, doors fitted with complicated ironwork, and coffered ceilings with gilded studs. In the Gilded Room is a monumental porcelain stove, dating from 1501, decorated with flowers and fruit, Biblical scenes and the coats of arms and portraits of sovereigns of the period.

The Hall of Justice has a coffered ceiling whose beams feature coats of arms of the provinces, dioceses or abbeys under the archbishop's jurisdiction as well as those of the dignitaries of his court.

Tickets are also good for admission to a marionette museum, a multivision show and the **Rainer-Regiment-Museum** displaying weapons, uniforms and mementos of Archduke Rainer's Infantry Regiment stationed here from 1871 to 1918.

▷ *Go back down the ramps and follow the path on the right to Nonnberg convent.*

Stift Nonnberg (Z)

This Benedictine convent was founded around 700 by St Rupert, whose niece, St Erentrud, was its first abbess. It is the oldest convent in the German-speaking world.

The **Stiftskirche**, enclosed by its churchyard, is in Late Gothic style and dates from the end of the 15C. The main doorway was built between 1497 and 1499; it incorporates the older Romanesque tympanum showing the Virgin Mary flanked by John the Baptist and St Erentrud on one side and by an angel and a kneeling nun on the other. The high altar is adorned by a fine carved and gilded altarpiece. In the central section is a Virgin and Child attended by St Rupert and St Virgil, while the wings depict scenes from the Passion. The vast crypt contains the tomb of St Erentrud.

In the **Johanneskapelle** there is a Gothic altarpiece of 1498, attributed to Veit Stoss, with a lively central section showing the Nativity.

▷ *Go down to the lower station of the funicular via the Festungsgasse, then into the Petersfriedhof immediately on the left.*

Petersfriedhof★★ (Z)

Cemetery: *Apr-Sep 6.30am-7pm, Oct-Mar 6.30am-6pm. free.* Catacombs *May-Sep Tue-Sun 10.30am-5pm, Oct-Apr Wed-Thu 10.30am-3.30, Fri-Sun 10.30am-4pm. €1. 06 62/8 44 57 60.*

This touching cemetery abuts the vertical rock wall of the Mönchsberg, which is hollowed with early Christian catacombs that can be seen on a short guided tour. The cemetery itself features wrought-iron grilles under Baroque arcades enclosing the chapels where several generations of the patrician families of Salzburg lie. Famous names include Nannerl Mozart, the architect Santino Solari and Michael Haydn. The 15C Margaretenkapelle is a delicate construction dating from the late Gothic period.

Stiftskirche St. Peter★★ (Z)

The triple-aisled Romanesque basilica was drastically remodeled in the 17C and 18C, but the serenity and harmony of the original structure can still be sensed amid the Baroque decor. The best view of the interior is from the gilded **wrought-iron grille**★ separating the porch from the nave. It is an elaborate work of art made in 1768 by Philip Hinterseer. The building's architectural simplicity, heightened in effect by the white walls, emphasizes the elegance of Benedikt Zöpf's Rococo decoration, with its fine paintings and fresh pastel shades that enhance the delicate stuccowork.

The ceiling of the nave is frescoed with scenes from the life of St Peter painted by the Augsburg artist, Johann Weiss. On each of the walls above the great arches, note, among other compositions, an Ascent to Calvary and a Raising of the Cross by Solari. Beneath the upper windows is a set of paintings by Franz X König representing *(right)* the life of St Benedict and *(left)* the life of St Rupert. The altarpiece on the high altar and those in the nave, with their red-marble columns, make an ensemble of great richness. Most of the altarpiece paintings are the work of Martin Johann Schmidt ("Kremser Schmidt"). Only the south aisle has chapels and also contains the tomb of St Rupert. In the chapel furthest from the chancel there is a fine marble tomb built by Archbishop Wolf Dietrich for his father, Werner von Raitenau.

▶ *Cross the abbey courtyard, turn right into the covered passageway and go along the side of the Franziskanerkirche which is entered through the west doorway.*

Franziskanerkirche★ (Z A)

🕒 *daily 6.30am-7.30pm*

The church was consecrated in 1223 but has been remodeled several times since. It offers a comparison between the Romanesque and Gothic styles.

The plain Romanesque nave, divided from the side aisles by massive pillars with capitals adorned with foliage and stylized animals, makes a striking contrast with the well-lit chancel from the final Late Gothic 15C. The star vaulting is supported by palm-shaped cylindrical columns.

The impressive high altar is the work of Johann Bernhard Fischer von Erlach (1708). The finely modeled statue of the Virgin Mary adorning the Baroque high altar was formerly part of a Gothic altarpiece made by Michael Pacher in the late 15C.

▶ *Exit through the side door and follow Franziskanergasse westwards.*

Museum der Moderne (Z M¹)

Wiener-Philharmoniker-Gasse 9 and Mönchsberg 32. 🕒 *year-round Tue, Thu-Sun 10am-6pm, Wed 10am-9pm.* 🕒 *24, 25 Dec.* ♿ ☞ *€6 Rupertinum, €8 Mönchsberg, combination ticket €12, audio-guide €2.* ☏ *06 62/8 42 22 03 51. www.museumder-moderne.at.*

Salzburg's modern art museum now occupies two spectacular locations. The original one is the **Rupertinum**, a Baroque townhouse built as a seminary by the archbishops in the 17C. It contains a fine collection of 20C art covering all major media, including painting, sculpture, graphic works and photography. The collection features works by numerous heavy hitters of the art world, including Gustav Klimt and Oskar Kokoschka as well as Austrian Expressionists Herbert Boeckl, Eduard Bäumer and Hans Fronius as well as such sculptors as Alfred Hrdlicka and Fritz Wotruba.

The museum recently expanded into a new, unapologetically modern building atop the **Mönchsberg**, easily reached by the Mönchsberglift. The minimalist space frequently hosts temporary (often traveling) exhibits of cutting-edge contemporary art. **Views**★ over the city are especially stunning from the restaurant, M32.

North of Max-Reinhardt-Platz stands the massive Baroque **Kollegienkirche** (University Church), another work of Johann Bernhard Fischer von Erlach. Continue west past the Grosses Festspielhaus (Festival Hall).

From Herbert-von-Karajan-Platz (36) there is a tunnel (the Siegmundstor), about 135m/150yd long, which was made in 1767 to go under the Mönchsberg hill. Look back for a fine view of the Hohensalzburg Fortress and the Stiftskirche St. Peter.

Pferdeschwemme (Y B)

This vast horse trough was built about 1700 and was exclusively used by the horses in the archbishops' stables. It is adorned with a sculpture group, the *Horsebreaker* by Mandl, and murals depicting fiery steeds.

Haus der Natur★★ (Y M²)

Budget at least 2hr. ⏱*daily 9am-5pm.* €5. ☎ *06 62/8 42 65 30.*

🧒This is a vast and well-presented natural history museum with many lively and engaging displays. Particularly interesting sections are those on dinosaurs, the world of outer space with its diorama depicting the first moon landing, human and animal characters in myth and fable, giant rock crystals and the aquarium and reptile house.

Getreidegasse★ (Y)

This is one of the main streets of old Salzburg. Like the rest of the Old Town, which, being crowded between the Mönchsberg and the Salzach, could expand only vertically, it is narrow and lined with five- and six-storey houses. A lively shopping street, Getreidegasse is adorned with many wrought-iron signs which provide a picturesque touch, while the houses with their carved window frames lend the street a certain elegance.

Getreidegasse

Mozarts Geburtshaus (Y D)

Getreidegasse 9. ⏱*July-Aug daily 9am-7pm; Jan-June, Sep-Dec daily 9am-6pm.* €6, *combo ticket with Mozart Wohnhaus* €9.50. ☎ *06 62/84 43 13. www.mozarteum.at*
The Mozart family lived on the third floor of this building from 1747 to 1773. It was here where Wolfgang was born on 27 January 1756 and where he composed many of his early works. In late 2005, the hallowed rooms were turned into a light, sound and design installation by the American set designer and director Robert Wilson. It incorporates instruments played by Mozart, including his harpsichord, his piano and the violin he played as a child, as well as musical manuscripts, a selection of portraits and letters and furniture and everyday objects from the times of Mozart.
Particularly passionate Mozart fans may also like to visit the Mozart Wohnhaus (👉 *see below*).
Continue along Getreidegasse past the town hall (Rathaus, R) on the left and on the right the Alter Markt (Old Market Square), with a fountain to St Florian and a curious **Hofapotheke** (YZ N), a chemist's shop with a lavish Rococo interior.

Judengasse (YZ)

This street cuts through the former Jewish Ghetto. It is narrow and picturesque and, like the Getreidegasse, adorned with wrought-iron signs. At no 4, note a sculptured group in stone representing the Virgin of Maria Plain (👉 *see Excursions below*).
Pass through the Waagplatz to Mozartplatz, with the predictable bronze statue of the composer, then continue to Residenzplatz.

Residenzplatz (Z 32)

Until the 16C there was a cemetery on this site. Prince-archbishop Wolf Dietrich created the present square, which got its fine fountain in the 17C. The square is bounded on the south by the cathedral and to the west by the Residenz. On the east is the **Glockenspiel** (Z), a carillon of 35 bells cast in Antwerp at the end of the 17C and set up in Salzburg in 1705.

Residenz★★ (Z)

The main residence of Salzburg's prince-archbishops was begun during the reign of Wolf Dietrich and completed under his successor Markus Sittikus. It was here where Emperor Franz Joseph received Napoleon III in 1867 and the German emperor, Kaiser Wilhelm I, in 1871.

State rooms

⏱*daily 10am-5pm.* ✆*€8, includes self-guided audio tour and gallery.* ☎ *06 62/80 42 26 90.*

The Residenz is entered from Residenzplatz via a marble gate festooned with the coats of arms of various prince-archbishops. A sweeping staircase leads to the Carabinieri Hall beyond which are the state rooms. These were redecorated in the early 18C by Johann Lukas von Hildebrandt and feature ceiling frescoes by Johann Michael Rottmayr and Martino Altomonte.

The young Mozart gave his first court concert at age six in the Conference Hall and later also performed in the Rittersaal (Knight's Hall), which has grand acoustics and is still used for concerts today. A testament to the wealth and power of the religious rulers is the opulent **Audienzsaal** (reception hall), where precious Gobelin tapestries form part of the decoration.

Residenzgalerie

⏱*Tue-Sun 10am-5pm, daily during Salzburg Festival.* ✆*€6.* ☎ *06 62/8404510. www. residenzgalerie.at*

The gallery houses a collection of important European paintings from the 16C to the 19C. The particularly exceptional array of 17C Dutch painting includes works by great masters such as Rembrandt, Rubens and Brueghel. The valuable exhibition, which occupies 15 state rooms, is rounded off with a display of 19C masterpieces.

Mirabell Schloss & Garten★ (V)

Little is left of the mansion built at the beginning of the 17C by Prince-archbishop Wolf Dietrich as a residence for his mistress Salome Alt. It got a complete overhaul courtesy of the architect Johann Lukas von Hildebrandt in the following century but suffered severe damage during the great fire sweeping through the city in 1818. The final reconstruction resulted in the rather sober building you see today, which rather fittingly houses part of the city administration.

The Trapp Family

Rodgers and Hammerstein's 1959 Broadway musical *The Sound of Music* (film version starring Julie Andrews from 1965) was based on the true story of the Von Trapp family. The young novice Maria Kutschera (1905-87) became governess to widower Baron Georg von Trapp's seven children and finally married the baron himself. Together they formed a family choir in the mid-1930s but then fled Nazi-occupied Austria in 138 and continued their career in the USA.

Salzburg locations used in the film include Nonnberg Abbey, Hohensalzburg Fortress, Mirabell Schloss and gardens, the Felsenreitschule, where the family sing their farewell song, and Schloss Leopoldskron, where the front facing the lake is used as Baron Trapp's house, and in whose music pavilion the love duet takes place.

Of the original building, the monumental **marble staircase**★★ with its sculptures by Georg Raphael Donner has survived, together with the Marmorsaal (Hall of Marble), a gilt and colored stucco extravaganza that is now used for wedding ceremonies and chamber concerts.

Considerably more noteworthy are the exquisite **Mirabell gardens** laid out in 1690 by Fischer von Erlach. With their abundance of flowers, statues and sculptures, they are a favorite place for relaxing. From a terrace there is a fine view over the gardens towards the old fortifications and the Hohensalzburg.

The old orangery has been restored and encloses a pretty courtyard with bright flowerbeds. Its south wing houses a small museum of Baroque art.

Salzburger Barockmuseum★ (M³)

🕐*Tue-Sat 9am-noon, 2-5pm (9am-5pm July-Aug), Sun 10am-1pm.* ✦€3. ☎ 06 62/87 74 32. www.barockmuseum.at.

Designs for frescoes, paintings and sculptures and a collection of master sketches form the contents of this little museum which sets out to give a general view of 17C and 18C European art.

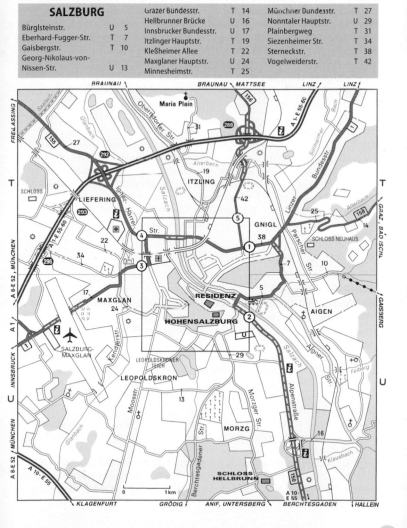

Mozart-Wohnhaus (Tanzmeisterhaus) (Y E)

Makartplatz 8. ⏰daily 9am-6pm (7pm July-Aug). ⚌€9, combination ticket with Mozart Geburtshaus €9.50. ☎ 06 62/87 42 27 40. www.mozarteum.at.

The so-called Tanzmeisterhaus, which was the Mozart family home from 1773 to 1787, was largely destroyed by bombs in 1944 and completely rebuilt in 1994-95. Mozart lived in the house until 1780 and composed a number of his works here.

The self-guided tour using nifty headsets with infrared-activated commentary and music takes you through rooms filled with period furniture, old instruments, literature and documentary items on the Mozart family and their contemporary environment. Special emphasis has been placed on Mozart's extensive travels. The tour concludes with a multivision show called "Mozart and Salzburg."

Die-hard Mozart fans might also like to pop into the **Mozart-Ton- und Filmmuseum**, where you can pick your favorite clips from an extensive audio and video archive and watch or listen to them for free.

Friedhof St. Sebastian (VX)

The cemetery behind the church of St. Sebastian, the original of which fell victim to the big fire of 1818, was conceived by Prince-archbishop Wolf Dietrich, whose grand mausoleum naturally dominates the grounds. Its interior is tiled with multi-hued porcelain. Other famous people buried here include Mozart's wife and father (in the central lane) and Paracelsus, a doctor and philosopher of the Renaissance who died in Salzburg in 1541 (in the southwestern corner behind a wrought-iron grille)

Dreifaltigkeitskirche (Y)

Completed in 1699, this Baroque church is the work of the great architect Fischer von Erlach and features frescoes by Michael Rottmayr.

Stiegl's Brauwelt

Bräuhausstraße 9. From the center, take Neutor-, Moos- and Nussdorfer Straße (X 31). Bräuhausstraße is the fourth turning on the left. ⏰daily 10am-5pm (July-Aug 10am-7pm) ⚌€9, includes beer, pretzl & souvenir. ☎ 06 62/83 87 14 92. www.brauwelt.at.

Kids The exhibition in the old malthouse of one of Salzburg's largest breweries covers the whole world of beer, obviously with the emphasis on Austria and Salzburg. Themes include ingredients, beer production around the world and advertising. Tours ends with a tasting session in the brewing room.

Excursions

Gaisbergstraße★★

13km/8mi. Leave Salzburg on R, B 158 towards St. Gilgen. After about 4km/2.5mi turn right for the scenic drive to Gaisberg

Park at the end of the road below the Gaisberg summit. There is a **view**★ of Salzburg, the Salzach gap and the Salzburg Alps. A path runs between the guesthouses and past the transmitting station, quickly taking you to the summit at an altitude of 1 288m/4 226ft. From here, the mountain **panorama**★ takes in the Salzkammergut and the Dachstein massif.

Schloss Hellbrunn★ (U)

🔊Guided tour (fountains: 35min, palace: 20min) July-Aug daily 9am-6pm; May, June, Sep daily 9am-5pm; Apr, Oct daily 9am-4.30pm. ⚌€8.50. ☎ 06 62/8 20 37 20. www.hellbrunn.at.

Kids This palace in the style of an Italian palazzo began life as the summer residence of Prince-archbishop Markus Sittikus in 1615. A self-guided audio tour of the interior takes in the banquet hall, with its *trompe-l'œil* painting, and the domed Octagon or Music Room.

Considerably more memorable, especially for kids, is a guided spin around the attractive **gardens**★★, filled with whimsical trick fountains originally built to entertain the fun-loving prince-archbishop. There is a mechanical theater with 13 figures that are set in motion by the action of water, amazing shell-encrusted grottoes, and fountains that suddenly start spurting, taking unwary visitors by surprise.

Tickets also include admission to the **Volkskundemuseum**★ (Apr-Oct 10am-5pm; €2 without Schloss; 06 62/6 20 80 85 00), a regional folklore museum with displays covering traditional customs, costumes, popular religion and daily life in Salzburg province.

Zoo Salzburg

Access via the Schlosspark or main entrance in Hellbrunner Allee. July-Aug daily 8.30am-6.30pm; Apr-June, Sep-Oct daily 8.30am-5pm; Nov-Dec daily 8.30am-4pm. Jan-Mar. €8. 06 62/8 20 17 60. www.salzburg-zoo.at.

Kids Salzburg's modern zoo houses around 500 animals representing 140 species in three beautifully landscaped habitats representing Eurasia, Asia and Africa. All the usual crowd-pleasers are there, including lions, pumas and monkeys.

Untersberg★

12km/7.5mi 1hr roundtrip drive, plus 15min by cable-car. Leave Salzburg on 2 towards Berchtesgaden. Just after the major St. Leonhard intersection, bear right and continue to the cable-car station. July-Sep daily 8.30am-5.30pm; Mar-June, Oct daily 9am-5pm; 20 Dec-Feb daily 9am-4pm. two weeks in Apr, Nov-mid Dec. €18 roundtrip. 0 62 46/72 47 70.

From a height of 1 853m/6 079ft, there is a splendid **panorama** of the Salzburg basin, the Salzburg Alps (Watzmann, Steinernes Meer, Staufen), the Wilder Kaiser and the Dachstein.

Schloss Leopoldskron (U)

Mirrored in its tranquil lake, complete with ducks and swans, Leopoldskron was built in 1744 as a summer residence for Prince-archbishop Leopold Anton Firmian. It was acquired in 1918 for cultural and artistic purposes by Max Reinhardt, one of the founders of the Salzburg Festival. Its charming setting, its car-free lakeside walk, its modern swimming pool and other recreational facilities make Leopoldskron a pleasant place to relax in, especially in summer.

Wallfahrtskirche Maria Plain (T)

After crossing Plain bridge, turn right onto Plainbergweg, the road which ends at the church of Maria Plain. Park the car by "Plainwirt" inn.

This bluff-top Baroque church (1674) was built to shelter an image of the Virgin Mary with the infant Jesus, which miraculously remained unharmed during a fire. It has been an object of pilgrimage ever since and is prominently displayed in front of the altar. The interior is distinguished by fanciful choir stalls, elaborate stucco decorations and an altar painting of the Assumption by Frans de Neve.

SALZBURGER SPORTWELT

SALZBURG

One of five areas forming the massive Ski Amadé winter sports region, the Salzburger Sportwelt is a paradise for skiers, snowboarders and cross-country enthusiasts. Its mountains are crisscrossed by 350km/218mi of pistes served by 100 lifts. Slopes extend between 800m/2 624ft and 2 000m/6 650ft and are especially suitable for beginning and intermediate skiers. The main villages are Flachau, Wagrain, St. Johann-Alpendorf, Radstadt, Altenmarkt-Zauchensee, Kleinarl, Eben and Filzmoos, all embedded in a lovely setting and with legendary apres ski scenes. *Hauptstraße 159, ☎ 0 64 57/29 29, www.salzburgersportwelt.at.*

▶ **Orient Yourself:** The ski area is located between the Tenner range and the Radstädter Tauern, about 70km/43mi southeast of Salzburg.

⌚ **Also See:** Radstädter Tauernstraße, Dachstein

Zauchensee★

Alt 1 361m/4 465ft. Zauchensee is by far the highest-lying resort in the Salzburger Sportwelt and consequently offers the best snow cover. Keen downhill skiers are able to indulge their passion in a beautiful **low-altitude mountain setting**★ with ski runs of varying degrees of difficulty.

If you are after a more authentic village atmosphere and a more extensive range of leisure facilities, visit the charming village of **Altenmarkt im Pongau.**

Schwarzwand-Seilbahn★★

Alt 2 100m/6 890ft. *For skiers only.* The cable-car leads to the foot of the Schwarzkopf, from where there is a magnificent **panorama**★★ of the Tennengebirge, the Dachstein and the Radstädter Tauern.

Rosskopf★★

Alt 1 929m/6 329ft. *Travel up on the* **Flachau cable-car**. ⌚*1 Dec-25 Apr daily 8.30am-4pm; 10 June-30 Sep daily 9am-noon, 1-5pm.* ☞€12 roundtrip. ☎ 0 64 57/22 14.
At the top of the cable-car ride there is a remarkable **view**★ over Modermandl and Faulkogel. Continue by chair-lift up to the Rosskopf. Climbing up to the peak takes only a few minutes and rewards you with a stunning **panorama**★★ over Zauchensee and Flachau, the Dachstein, the Radstädter Tauern and the Hohe Tauern.

Mooskopf★★

Take the Kleinarl chair-lift and the Bubble-Shuttleberg chair-lift, then walk a few minutes to the summit. ⌚*15 Dec-20 Apr daily 9am-4pm.* ☞€35 day pass. ☎ 0 64 57/22 14.
From the peak a splendid **panorama**★★ opens up taking in the Tennengebirge range, the Dachstein, the Ennskraxn massif and other impressive peaks.

Wagrain★

Alt 838m/2 749ft. Besides having the area's best lodging and most extensive network of ski lifts, the town also enjoys a certain fame as the home of Atomic, the largest Austrian ski manufacturer. The snow cover, though, is fairly unreliable.

Koglalm★

Alt 1 878m/6 161ft. **Panorama**★ over Wagrain, Flachau and Kleinarl with the Tennengebirge range, the Dachstein and the Niedere Tauern in the background. Good skiers and hikers are able to reach the **Saukarkopf**, where even broader **views**★★ open up.

SALZKAMMERGUT★★★

OBERÖSTERREICH, SALZBURG AND STEIERMARK

Salt has given the Salzkammergut its name and, until recently, exceptional economic importance. For about 4 000 years the "white gold" was the region's main source of prosperity, as is reflected in its towns' proud architecture. Tourism has boomed since the early 20C thanks to dozens of lakes, legendary mountains such as the Dachstein and the Totes Gebirge and long-estabiished spa resorts like Bad Ischl. In 1997, UNESCO honored the region's exceptional beauty and cultural significance by placing it on its list of World Heritage Sites, together with Hallstatt and the Dachstein. *Götzstraße 12, A-4820 Bad Ischl, ☎ 0 61 32/24 00 00, www.salzkammergut.co.at.*

▶ **Orient Yourself:** The Salzkammergut is east of Salzburg in central Austria.
🕐 **Organizing Your Time:** Starting from Salzburg it is possible to tour the Salzkammergut in four days, by following, in succession, itineraries 1, 2, 3 on day one, and itinerary 4 on days two, three and four.

Tour of the Lakes★★

1 **From Salzburg to Bad Ischl** *84km/52mi*

Salzburg★★★ & *See Salzburg.*

▶ *Leave Salzburg and take the A 1 autobahn to the Mondsee exit.*

Between Salzburg and Mondsee, the autobahn affords open views of the Drachenwand cliffs and the Schafberg spur.

Mondsee★ & *See Mondsee.*

The north shore of the Mondsee, which is calm and welcoming at first, becomes a little more severe beyond the Pichl promontory, where the road climbs over a wooded rise.

Burggrabenklamm
5km/3mi south of Au along the B 152 to the southern tip of the Attersee at Burgbachau. Park near the Gasthof Jägerwirt; 30min roundtrip walk.
This little but dramatic gorge with an 18m/60ft waterfall is one of the most beautiful in the Salzkammergut. The trail, which is short and often slippery, leads past a statue of St Mary .

▶ *Backtrack on the B 152 to the south shore of the Mondsee.*

Floating Corpus Christi Festival

Since 1632 a famous procession has been held on the lake here every year in celebration of the feast of Corpus Christi. In days gone by, boats called "Trauner" which were used for shipping salt were pressed into service for the procession. Nowadays, these have given way to the rather less romantic motor boat.

The pass road connecting Scharfling and St. Gilgen has remarkable **panoramic views**★★ from a parking lot above St. Gilgen. Beyond the slender onion-domed village bell-tower, the **Wolfgangsee**★★ lake stretches towards the Rinnkogel massif.

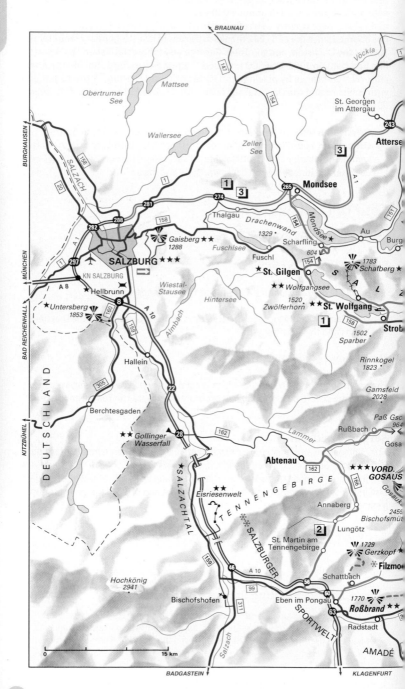

St. Gilgen★

Delightful St. Gilgen, at the northwestern tip of the **Wolfgangsee**, is a former out-post of the prince-archbishops of Salzburg and the birthplace of Mozart's mother, Anna-Maria Pertl. His sister Nannerl settled here after marrying the local magistrate. The family legacy is kept alive with a Mozart fountain on the central Mozartplatz square and a small **memorial exhibit** (🕐*Jun-Sep Tue-Sun 10am-noon, 2pm-6pm;*

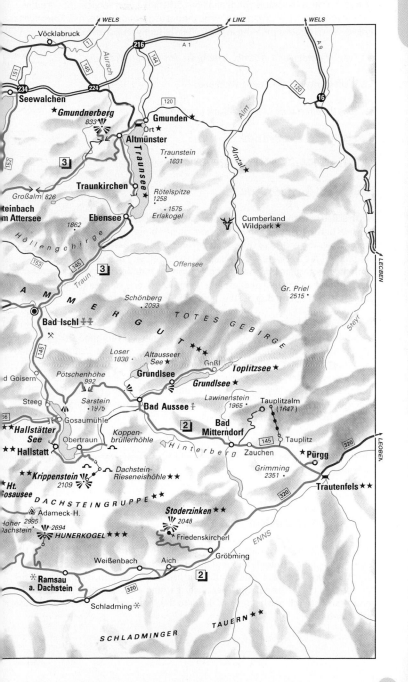

∞€1; ☎ 0 62 27/23 48) in the former law court at Ischlerstraße 15, the very building where Anna was born and where Nannerl later lived with her family.
Another pleasant diversion in town is the **Musikinstrumente Museum**, which displays medieval and exotic instruments from around the world.

The lake, meanwhile, attracts numerous watersports enthusiasts, especially sailors who appreciate its favorable wind conditions. Scheduled boat service stops at numerous sites around the Wolfgangsee, while the nostalgic paddle-steamer *Kaiser Franz Joseph*, which began operating in 1873, offers leisurely lake cruises.

▸ *Leave the main road at Strobl to make the detour to St. Wolfgang.*

St. Wolfgang★★ 👣 *See St. Wolfgang.*

▸ *Take the direct road to Bad Ischl, avoiding Strobl.*

Bad Ischl⚓ 👣 *See Bad Ischl.*

② From Bad Ischl to Gmunden 34km/21mi

Bad Ischl⚓ 👣 *See Bad Ischl.*

North of Bad Ischl, the Traun corridor, which was one of the great European salt routes, unwinds between the Höllengebirge and Totes Gebirge foothills. Beside the road, a track follows the course of the saltwater conduit *(Soleleitung)*, which since the 17C has brought the salt waters from Hallstatt to the refinery at Ebensee.
From the spectacular **cliff road**★ from Ebensee to Traunkirchen, which runs above the **Traunsee**★, Austria's deepest lake (191m/527ft), one can see the golden peak of the Rötelspitze, and then further north, the Traunstein itself.

Traunkirchen
Perched on a **promontory**★, Traunkirchen is a popular stop among Salzkammergut explorers who come to appreciate the splendid vistas over the Traunsee lake and the rugged mountains. While here, also pop into the **Pfarrkirche** (parish church) surrounded by a terraced graveyard overlooking the lake. It has splendid Baroque furnishings, particularly the **Fisherman's Pulpit**★, made in the form of the Disciples' fishing boat, complete with dripping nets. Since 1632, the town has staged an annual **Corpus Christi festival** on the lake.

Altmünster
Altmünster has a Late Gothic hall-church with sumptuous decoration and a stone high altar dating from 1518.

Gmunden★ 👣 *See Gmunden.*

③ From Gmunden to Salzburg 117km/73mi

This route links the Traunsee, the Attersee and the Mondsee. The road leaves the Traunsee to enter a tranquil, hilly region dotted with whitewashed farmhouses and clumps of huge lime trees. After skirting the hamlet of Grossalm, it burrows into the forest below the Höllengebirge, eventually reaching a pass (alt 826m/2 710ft). The most scenic stretch on the descent down to the Attersee, is between Kienklause and Steinbach.

Steinbach am Attersee
The composer **Gustav Mahler** spent his holidays in Steinbach, working in his "Komponierhäuschen" (composing shed).

The road skirts the **Attersee**✶ (aka Kammersee), the largest lake in the Austrian Alps and popular for fishing and boating. it is bordered to the south by the last cliff-like slopes of the Schafberg. Between Seewalchen and Attersee on the western shore, the road runs through charming sun-drenched hills where orchards flourish. Only the cliffs of the Höllengebirge lend a note of harshness to the scene. For good lake views, stop by the Buchberg chapel.

Attersee
This well-known resort has a pilgrimage church, Mariae Himmelfahrt, with fine Baroque furnishings, including works by Meinrad Guggenbichler.

▸ *Leave the lake at Attersee and take the A1 autobahn towards Salzburg.*

Mondsee   *See Mondsee.*

▸ *Continue on the A1 autobahn to Salzburg.*

Salzburg★★★   *See Salzburg.*

Tour around the Dachstein★★

④ **Leaving from Bad Ischl** *267km/166mi*

Day one: Bad Ischl, Hallstatt, Krippenstein, Gosauseen
Day two: Filzmoos, Rossbrand, Hunerkogel, Ramsau
Day three: Stoderzinken, Bad Aussee, Bad Ischl

Bad Ischl✝   *See Bad Ischl.*

Head south from Bad Ischl via Bad Goisern to Steeg, which marks the beginning of the road along the western shore of the **Hallstätter See**★★. The **view**✶ opens out onto the town of Hallstatt.

▸ *Enter the tunnel to by-pass Hallstatt. Park at the viewing terrace and walk into town.*

Hallstatt★★   *See Hallstatt.*

Ascent to the Krippenstein★★   *See Dachstein.*

▸ *Continue south through the tunnel and on emerging turn round to head back north via the south-north tunnel. At Gosaumühle turn left.*

After passing under the saltwater aqueduct *(Soleleitung)* the road enters a valley carved by the Gosaubach creek. Where it widens, the magnificent Gosaukamm crest unfolds on the left.

▸ *Turn towards the Gosauseen lakes and park at the end of the road.*

Gosauseen★★★   See Gosauseen.

▷ *Backtrack north to Gosau; turn left onto the Gschütt pass road.*

Abtenau
This little resort at the foot of the enormous Kogel is a popular departure point for hikes and excursions. The drive to St. Wolfgang along the **Postalmstraße** *(toll payable)* is especially scenic. The Postalm is the largest area of Alpine meadows in Austria, and the second largest high-lying plateau in Europe.

▷ *Return east; turn right to Annaberg along the "Salzburg Dolomites" road.*

From Eben im Pongau to Gröbming★★   See Dachstein.
The road follows the Enns Valley. To the right there appears the massive bulk of Trautenfels Palace.

Schloss Trautenfels
🕐8 Apr-Oct daily 9am-5pm. ⊘€6. ☎ 0 36 82/2 22 33.
With origins in the 13C, this is a lovely Baroque country palace with richly decorated rooms, including stuccowork and valuable frescoes by Carpoforo Tencalla. The stunning collection of antlers also impresses. In addition, the palace houses a recently revamped museum on the natural and cultural history of the Enns Valley and the Ausseerland; it is affiliated with the Graz-based Landesmuseum Joanneum.

▷ *At the Trautenfels crossroads, turn left on road no 145.*

Pürgg
Park at the village entrance.
Art-lovers should go up to the bluff-top **Johanneskapelle**, a small chapel endowed with some terrific **Romanesque frescoes** depicting the Annunciation, the Birth of Christ, a fabulous fight between cats and mice, the Wise and Foolish Virgins and other scenes. The crucifix on the altar was carved around 1220.

The road travels through a narrow stretch of the Grimming-Bach Valley into a dip known as the Hinterberg Plateau. In the foreground the chiseled walls of the Grimming face the slab-like shapes of the Lawinenstein. This crest masks the Alpine pastures of the **Tauplitzalm**, a popular winter sports area.

Bad Mitterndorf
This place is known both as a spa and a winter sports resort. The local museum displays a colorful collection of masks worn during the Nikolospiel, a traditional play staged on St Nicholas' Day.

Bad Aussee⚕   See Bad Aussee.

Grundlsee★ and Toplitzsee★   See Bad Aussee: Excursions.

▷ *Return to Bad Ischl via the Pötschenhöhe pass (alt 992m/3 255ft) and road no 145.*

ST. ANTON AM ARLBERG

TIROL
POPULATION 2 400 – ALT 1 304M/4 278FT
LOCAL MAP SEE ARLBERGGEBIET

St. Anton, draped into a deeply incised valley, is something of a shrine for winter sports aficionados. It was here in 1921 where ski pioneer Hannes Schneider, who is considered the "father of modern skiing," founded Austria's first ski school. From then on, the sport took St. Anton by storm and today it is one of the largest resorts in the Northern Alps with a youthful, sporty atmosphere and a lively apres-ski scene. Summer brings a degree of calm, although the scenic Arlbergstraße does draw its share of tourist traffic. Atractions include an enormous leisure park and 90km/56ml of hiking trails. 🛈 *Arlberghaus, A-6580,* ☏ *0 54 46/2 26 90, www.stantonamarlberg.com.*

▶ **Orient Yourself:** St. Anton is in western Austria, about 100km/60mi southwest of Innsbruck.
🅿 **Parking:** Look for lots along the main Arlbergstraße.
Don't Miss: Skiing, trip up to the Valluga viewpoint
Also See: Arlberggebiet, Lech, Zürs

Arlberg ski area

St. Anton is part of the Arlberg ski region that also includes **Lech** , (*see Lech)*, **Zürs** (*see Zürs, served by bus)* and **Stuben** (*see Arlberggebiet).* A single ski pass is good for the entire area, which lies at an altitude of 1 300-2 650m/4 250-8 700ft and has 260km/162mi of marked and 180km/112mi of unmarked pistes, accessed by a total of 80 ski lifts. St. Anton is especially suitable for experienced skiers, offering steep, undulating pistes from the Schindler Spitze, Kapall and Pfannenkopf peaks. Less proficient skiers will find suitable runs on the Galzig, Gampen and Gampberg slopes.

Arlberg-Kandahar-Haus

This is a museum on the history of skiing and the development of tourism in the Arlberg area.

Arlberg ski slopes seen from the Valluga ridge

Y. Bontoux

Viewpoints

Valluga★★★

Alt 2 811m/9 222ft. About 2hr 30min roundtrip. ◐*mid Dec-end Apr, early July-end Sep daily 8.30am-4pm.* ⊜*€20 roundttrip.* ☎ *0 54 46/2 35 20.*

This excursion starts with a ride aboard the new **Galzigbahn**, a gondola with Ferris-wheel-style boarding housed within a spectacular glass shelter designed by Tyrolean architect Georg Driendl. From the mountain station (alt 2 185m/7 169ft), there is a wonderful **view**★★ over the ski slopes..

Next, take the Valluga I gondola to the Valluga ridge (alt 2 650m/8 695ft) for more impressive **views**★★, although for the truly breathtaking **360° panorama**★★★ catch the short Valluga II gondola to the peak itself.

Kapall★★

Alt 2 330m/7 644ft. About 1hr roundtrip aboard the Nassereinbahn cable-car or the Gampenbahn chair-lift, followed by the Kapall chair-lift. ◐*Dec-end Apr, June-end Aug daily 8.45am-3.45pm.* ⊜*€18 roundtrip.* ☎ *0 54 46//2 35 20.*

This trip drops you at the at the foot of the rocky Weissschrofenspitze peak (2752m/9 028ft and treats you to a very beautiful **panorama**★★ over the entire St. Anton Valley and across to the Swiss Alps, the Rätikon and the Verwall range.

STIFT ST. FLORIAN★★

OBERÖSTERREICH

The abbey of St. Florian, the largest in Upper Austria and an eminent cultural center, has been run by Augustinian canons since the 11C. The present buildings are in the purest Baroque style, since the monastery was entirely rebuilt between 1686 and 1751 under the direction of Carlo Antonio Carlone and Jakob Prandtauer. The latter was also the architect of Hohenbrunn, the palatial edifice built nearby for one of the abbey's provosts.

▶ **Orient Yourself:** The abbey is 18km/11m southeast of Linz.
◐ **Also See:** Linz, Schloss-Museum Hohenbrunn, Stiftskirche Wilhering

Tour

🔊*Guided tour (1hr 30min) Easter-1 Nov daily 10am, 11am, 2pm, 3pm and 4pm; otherwise by appointment only.* ⊜*€6.* ☎ *0 72 24/8 90 20. www.stift-st-florian.at.*

The Legend of St Florian

Florian was head of the Roman administration in Noricum province, who was martyred after converting to Christianity in 304. After suffering considerable torture, he was thrown into the Enns River with a stone around his neck. The abbey that bears his name was allegedly built near the spot where a local woman first discovered his mangled body. St. Florian is the patron saint of Upper Austria as well as of Poland and of firefighters. In fact, there is hardly a church in Austria without a statue of this saintly protector.

Exterior

An elegant doorway with two balconies, carved columns and statues leads into the abbey's inner courtyard, which is adorned by a remarkable sculptured fountain, the Eagle Fountain (Adlerbrunnen), and a wrought-iron well-head, dating from 1603.

Bibliothek (Library)

Guided tours start in the library, one of the oldest and most prestigious abbey repositories in the country. The exquisite allegorical ceiling paintings by Bartolomeo Altomonte represent the union of religion and science. Marquetry in walnut, encrusted with gold, sets off the 150 000 valuable manuscripts and books.

ST. FLORIAN

0 — 50 m

Stiftskirche

Kaiserzimmer

Adlerbrunnen

Doorway

Bibliothek

★★★Altdorfer Galerie

Inner Courtyard

Marmorsaal

WELS

ENNS

STEYR

Marmorsaal

Prandtauer designed the magnificent Marble Hall, whose ceiling fresco by Martino and Bartolomeo Altomonte glorifies Prince Eugene of Savoy's victory over the Turks. It was originally conceived as an imperial dining room but also served as a concert hall.

Kaiserzimmer (Imperial Apartments)

The Imperial apartments are reached via a magnificent grand staircase whose balustrades are adorned with statues, while the walls and ceilings are embellished with

St. Florian Abbey

H. W. Partaj/BILDAGENTUR BUENOS DIAS

Anton Bruckner at St. Florian

Anton Bruckner, Austria's greatest 19C composer of church music, was born near St. Florian in 1824. After his father's early death, the boy attended choir school at the abbey, where he was first introduced to religious music.

Bruckner trained as a teacher and eventually managed to win an appointment at St. Florian in 1845. To his great joy, he was also appointed abbey organist. It was here that Bruckner decided to devote himself to music. In 1856 he became cathedral organist in Linz, where he composed several masterpieces, including three masses and two of his nine symphonies. Next he went to Vienna to teach at the conservatory. Despite his increasing fame, Bruckner always had a soft spot for St. Florian, and it was there where he wished to be buried beneath the very organ that had been so instrumental on his way to success as a composer and organist.

stuccowork and frescoes. Until 1782 the apartments received such illustrious visitors as Pope Pius VI, emperors and princes.

Amid the succession of halls and state rooms note the Faistenberger room, the bedrooms of the emperor and empress, the reception room and the Gobelin room.

Altdorfer Galerie★★★

The most valuable pictures in the abbey' art collection are by **Albrecht Altdorfer** (1480-1538), a master of the Danube School whose work is noted for its balanced composition and rich, warm colors. The 14 pictures were painted for the abbey church's Gothic altar to St Sebastian and form the world's most important collection of Altdorfer's work.Four panels depict the martyrdom of St Sebastian, while the other eight show scenes from the Passion.

Stiftsbasilika

Organ recitals (20min) mid-May-mid-Oct Sun, Mon, Wed-Fri 2.30pm. €3.
The Baroque basilica was built under the direction of Carlo Antonio Carlone to replace the old Gothic church. Carlo's brother Bartolomeo was responsible for the stuccowork. The entire ceiling is swathed in frescoes executed by Johann Anton Gumpp and Melchior Steidl from Munich. The great organ was built by Franz Xaver Chrisman (1770-74) and has more than 103 stops and 7 836 pipes. It is now named the **Bruckner Organ** after Anton Bruckner, who worked at the abbey as organist and composer. He's buried in a crypt beneath the organ.

ST. JOHANN IN TIROL

TIROL
POPULATION 8 500 – ALT 670M/2 198FT
LOCAL MAP SEE KAISERGEBIRGE

The market town boasts a number of Baroque houses with façades charmingly decorated with painted, sometimes *trompe-l'œil*, scenes typical of the Tyrolean region. Its location at the intersection of several valleys makes St. Johann a lively tourist resort,especially in winter. The wide, sun-drenched bowl of the valley is enclosed by the Wilder Kaiser and Kitzbüheler Horn peaks. *Poststraße 2, A-6380, 0 53 52/6 33 35, www.ferienregion.at.*

▶ **Orient Yourself:** St. Johann is in western Austria, about 11km/7mi north of Kitzbuehel.

👁 **Also See:** Kitzbühel, Kaisergebirge

Ski slopes

Downhill ski slopes are concentrated on the north face of the Kitzbüheler Horn. All in all there are 60km/37mi of pistes, 28km/17mi of which can be supplemented with snow machines in case nature fails to deliver.

Cross-country skiers have 74km/46mi of tracks, including two of 16km/10mi in length classified as difficult. If you factor in tracks in neighboring Oberndorf, Going-Ellmau, Kirchdorf-Erpfendorf and Waidring, the number goes up to almost 200km/124mi.

Pfarrkirche

This Baroque building, designed by Abraham Millauer, has remarkable ceiling paintings by **Simon Benedikt Faistenberger**, a student of Rottmayr. The altar paintings are by Jacob Zanusi, court painter at Salzburg.

Spitalskirche zum Hl. Nikolaus in der Weitau★ 👁 *See Kaisergebirge* 1.

STIFT ST. LAMBRECHT

STEIERMARK

The Benedictine abbey of St. Lambrecht has a pedigree going back to the 11C. Little remains of the original Romanesque abbey church, which was replaced by the current High Gothic triple-nave hall church in the 14C. The main buildings were built in 1640 based on plans by Domenico Sciassia. Dissolved by Joseph II in 1786, the abbey was re-established by Franz II in 1802.

▶ **Orient Yourself:** The abbey is in the Murtal, a valley in southern Austria, about 70km/44mi north of Klagenfurt.

👁 **Also See:** Friesach, Gurk

Benedictine abbey of St. Lambrecht

303

Tour

🔊 Guided tour (1hr 30min) mid May-mid Oct Mon-Sat 10.45am, 2.30pm; Sun after the morning service and 2.30pm. 🎧€6. ☎ 0 35 85/23 45, www.stift-stlambrecht.at

Exterior

As you enter the abbey courtyard, the impressive west façade extends for 135m/443ft on your right, while on your left is a bastion adorned with statues by Johann Matthias Leitner in 1746. An open staircase leads up to the Gothic **Peterskirche**, which features a winged altar with a Crucifixion scene and works by the Master of Lambrecht. Behind the church are the remains of an early 15C castle.

Stiftskirche

An elaborate marble doorway opens into the narthex, which houses a 14C Lettner crucifix in a Baroque framework. Medieval frescoes embellish the vaulted ceiling above the chancel and the walls of the nave. Star of the show, though, is the enormous 1632 **high altar**★ by Valentin Khautt, which centers on a painting of the *Assumption*. The decoration of the altar to St Emmeram in front on the right, the statues of the church Elders on the organ gallery, and the Madonna in the narthex are all works of the famous sculptor Michael Hönell.

ST. PAUL IM LAVANTTAL★

KÄRNTEN

ALT 400M/1 312FT

The Benedictine abbey of St. Paul, half-hidden in the trees and slightly above the Lavant Valley, was founded in 1091. It boasts one of Austria's finest Romanesque churches and a well-respeced collection of art treasures. 🏠 A-9470, ☎ 0 43 57/20 19 22 , www.stift-stpaul.at

▶ **Orient Yourself:** The abbey is in the far south of Austria, near the border with Slovenia, about 85km/53mi east of Klagenfurt.
🕐 **Organizing Your Time:** Plan on spending about two hours.

Stiftskirche (Abbey church)

🕐 *daily 8am-5pm.* ♿
The church, which was begun in 1180, follows a cruciform layout culminating in three half-rounded apses. After a fire in the 14C Gothic vaulting was added and decorated with frescoes by the masterful Friedrich and Michael Pacher. The south doorway features an image of the Adoration of the Magi, and the west door one of Christ in Majesty.

Stiftsgebäude (Abbey buildings)

🕐 *May-Oct daily 9am-5pm.* 🎧€7, 🔊 *guided tour €9.*
The abbey is home to a veritable treasure trove that includes a precious numismatic collection, paintings (eg by Rubens, Rembrandt and Van Dyck), drawings (eg by Dürer, Holbein and Troger), objets d'art, silverwork, porcelain, woodcarvings and valuable pieces such as Rudolf of Swabia's imperial cross.

ST. PÖLTEN★

NIEDERÖSTERREICH
POPULATION 54 600 – ALT 271M/889FT

Founded by the Romans in AD 1, St. Pölten only became provincial capital of Lower Austria in 1987, when the government moved its offices from Vienna to the brandnew Landhausviertel quarter on the Traisen River. Today, the quarter's modern architecture and entertainment venues inject a dose of life into what is otherwise a rather sleepy town. Its heyday dates back two centuries to the Baroque period when a Who's of Who of artists, including Jakob Prandtauer, Josef and Franz Munggenast, Daniel Gran, Paul Troger and Bartolomeo Altomonte, lived and worked here. Evidence of their creativity is found at every turn, making a stroll around the old town a lesson in Baroque. *Rathausplatz 1, A-3100, ☎ 0 27 42/35 33 54, www.st-poelten.gv.at.*

- **Orient Yourself:** St. Pölten is about 65km/41mi west of Vienna.
- **Parking:** Look for parking garages on Eybnerstraße, Dr.-Karl-Renner-Promenade, Bräuhausgasse, Rossmarkt, Rathausplatz and in the Landhausviertel. Parking is free in the Landesviertel garages from Friday 7pm to Monday 5am.
- **Don't Miss:** Dom, Landesmuseum, Klangturm
- **Organizing Your Time:** Devote at least one full day to St. Pölten.
- **Especially for Kids:** Klangturm, Landesmuseum
- **Also See:** Stift Melk, Stift Lilienfeld, Mariazell

Sights

Rathausplatz

The main town square is bordered by beautiful patrician houses and punctuated by the massive marble **Trinity Column**, completed in 1782 by Andreas Gruber. It shows St Hippolytus, St Florian (recognizable by his attribute of a burning house), St Sebastian (arrow) and St Leopold (model of a church).

Lording over the square is the pinkish **Rathaus** (town hall), created in the 16C by connecting two existing Gothic houses. In 1727 Josef Munggenast added the Baroque façade. The tower has become the emblem of St. Pölten.

To the left of the Rathaus is the 16C **Schuberthaus**, in which the composer stayed in 1821, holding "Schubertiade" musical evenings.

On the square's north side, the **Franziskanerkirche** (1757-79) with its lively Rococo façade is noted for its exuberant high altar by Andreas Gruber and the four side altar paintings by Kremser Schmidt.

To the right of the Rathaus is the 1707 **Prandtauerkirche**, named for its builder. The Crucifixion scene on the

Herzberger/ÖSTERREICH WERBUNG

Rathaus tower and Trinity Column, St. Pölten

Address Book

PRACTICAL INFORMATION

VISITOR INFORMATION

Tourismusninformation *(Rathaus-platz 1, ⏰Apr-Oct Mon-Fri 8am-5pm, Sat 9am-5pm, Sun 10am-5pm; Nov-Mar Mon-Fri 8am-5pm)* The local **Calendar of events** on the city and its surroundings comes out monthly between May and October and can be obtained from the tourist office and hotels.

CITY TOURS

The tourist office organizes various themed walking tours of varying length. Check for a current schedule. For self-guided tours (in English), the office rents out **audio-guides** (€1.45). The tours take in old town and the Landhausviertel and last about 2hr 15min.

For an easy introduction to St. Pölten, catch a ride aboard the free **Haupts-tadtexpress** (⏰Apr-Oct, Dec Thu-Sat 10am-5pm hourly, free), a little tourist train stopping at major attractions throughout the city centre.

PUBLIC TRANSPORT

City buses tickets can be bought from the bus drivers, and so can bus timetables at a cost of 15S. A single-trip ticket costs 18S (valid for 1hr; allows change of vehicle and of direction of travel). Multiple-trip tickets cost 80S and are valid for six single trips. A weekly ticket costs 90S. Timetable and price details can be obtained by calling ☎ 0 27 42/25 23 60. After 8.40pm, a taxi service (Sammel-Taxis) operates, ☎ 0 27 42/25 35 45.

POST OFFICES

City centre post office *(Wiener Straße 12, ⏰Mon-Fri 8am-noon, 2-6pm)*
Main post office *(Bahnhofsplatz 1a, ⏰Mon-Fri 7am-8pm, Sat 7am-1pm)*

SHOPPING

The main axes of the pedestrian shopping zone are Kremser Gasse and Wiener Straße. There is a wide variety of shops here, catering to every taste.

ENTERTAINMENT

Theater der Landeshauptstadt
– *Rathausplatz 11*, ☎ 0 27 42/35 20 26 19. Theatre, musicals, operettas, children's theatre. Closed for a summer break in July and August.

Bühne im Hof – *Linzer Straße 18*, ☎ 0 27 42/35 22 91. Cabaret, dance, concerts.

Festspielhaus – *Franz-Schubert-Platz*, ☎ 0 27 42/20 10. Wide range of entertainment on offer: concerts of classical music, folk music, jazz, pop, rock, opera, operettas, musicals, ballet, folk dancing.

Kultur Gasthof Figl – *Ratzersdorf, Hauptplatz*, ☎ 0 27 42/25 74 02. Inn with cabaret.

CINEMAS

The **Hollywood Megaplex** (☎ 0 27 42/28 80; Engelbert-Laimer-Straße 1 on the right of the Traisen) offers eight cinema screens and various options for eating out or other entertainment under a single roof.

WHERE TO EAT

Galerie – *Fuhrmannsgasse 1*, ☎ 0 27 42/35 13 05. Top quality restaurant, considered the best in town.

Parzer & Reibenwein – *Riemerplatz 1*, ☎ 0 27 42/35 30 17 30. Restaurant with stylish decor in a 12C building (Baroque façade, arcaded courtyard).

Gasthof Winkler – *Mühlweg 64*, ☎ 0 27 42/36 49 44. Menu varies with the seasons, idyllic garden for clientele.

Zum Gwercher – *In Stattersdorf (right of the Traisen, southeast of city centre), Schiffmannstraße 98*, ☎ 0 27 42/23 05 90. Welcoming restaurant with a large garden inside the courtyard. International selection of wines and cigars.

CAFÉS AND BARS

Kaffee-Konditorei Amler
– *Brunngasse 4-6*. Traditional coffee house.

Café Punschkrapferl – *Domgasse 8*. More than 80 pastries to choose from and, as if that were not enough, ice cream and a salad bar.

Zum Rothen Krebs – *Kremser Gasse 18*. Modern daytime bar with a library corner, where visitors feel as if they have been transported to some grand mansion.

Winzig ("Little", *Kremser Gasse 25*) and **Riesig** ("Large", *Wiener Straße 24*) are two bars, which despite their names are both relatively small, where a pleasant evening can be spent over a light meal or a drink or two (beer or wine).

Mitt'n Drin – *Wiener Straße 10*. Visitors barely need to set foot over the threshold to be in the thick of things. Good for a quick drink to recharge the batteries.

Drunter & Drüber – *Kugelgasse 6*. Bar with comfortable sofa corner and garden. During the colder months, there is also live music ranging from rock to blues.

Narrenkastl – *Wiener Straße 33*. Small bar with a platform overlooked by the figure of a dwarf. During summer, the pretty courtyard is where most of the action takes place.

Salzamt – *Linzer Straße 18*. Bar atmosphere beneath a fine vaulted ceiling.

Cabrio – *Linzer Straße 30*. Local bar serving beer to a youthful set, with plenty of greenery adorning the premises (not all of it real, however).

Flieger-Bräu – *Ferstlergasse 9*. House-brewed naturally dark beer. Rustic local bar, where flying is the main theme of the decor (as the name suggests).

DATES FOR YOUR DIARY

Meisterkonzerte: Dec to Apr. Concerts of classical music in the Stadtsaal and Festspielhaus.

St. Pöltner Festwochen: early May to early June. Concerts, plays, cabaret.

Film am Dom: early June. The "Cinema Paradiso" association presents a discriminating programme of open-air cinema on the Domplatz.

Hauptstadtfest: second Fri in July. Music, cabaret, children's entertainment at various venues in the city centre. Fireworks display.

Sonnenblumenfest: July. "Sunflower Festival": musical and culinary delicacies on offer on the Rathausplatz.

Film-Festival: one-month film festival between late July and early Sept. Films and food from all over the world on the Rathausplatz.

St. Pöltner Seefest: Aug. Ballet, concerts, children's entertainment by the Ratzersdorfer Lake.

Musica Sacra: late Sept to early Oct. Performances of international church music in the cathedral and the abbey churches of Herzogenburg and Lilienfeld.

More precise details about dates and other information is available from the tourist office on ☎ *0 27 42/35 33 54*.

---

high altar by Johann Lukas von Hildebrandt is attributed to the Spanish painter José de Ribera (1588-1652).

Stadtmuseum

🕐*Tue-Sat 10am-5pm.* 🕐*24 Dec-6 Jan.* ✎*€1.60.* ☎ *0 27 42/3 33 26 43. www.stadtmuseum-stpoelten.at.*
The city history museum is part of a cultural center inside a converted Carmelite nunnery attached to the Prandtauerkirche. Exhibits, which include archaeological finds and Jugendstil works, were in the process of getting a makeover at press time.

Institut der Englischen Fräulein★

From Prandtauerstraße turn left onto Linzer Straße (no 11).
The most outstanding Baroque façade in St. Pölten belongs to this girls' school that was originally affiliated with an order founded by the English nun Mary Ward in 1709. Prandtauer designed the sumptuous pink and white exterior whose black wrought-iron grills make a striking contrast. Four portals, richly decorated with scrolls and busts of angels, divide up the long building, as do several sculpture-filled niches. The small **Institutskirche** (church) is lavishly decorated with frescoes by Paul Troger and Bartolomeo Altomonte.

Cathedral District

Dom Mariä Himmelfahrt★

Enlivened only by an ornate spire and the two figures of St Hippolytus and St Augustine, the cathedral's austere façade belies the Baroque splendor that awaits behind its portals. The soft tones of the stucco marble and paintings, the sheen of the liberally applied gilding and the inlaid work combine to create a rich and warm effect.

The conversion into the Baroque style began in 1722 under Jakob Prandtauer and was completed in 1735 under Josef Munggenast. The 1658 high altar painting by Tobias Pock depicts the *Assumption of Mary*. The splendid **choir stalls**★ with their elaborately carved wooden decoration and the organ case are by Peter Widerin. The ceiling frescoes and the 10 large **wall-paintings**★, which show scenes from the life of Christ, are the work of Thomas Friedrich Gedon and clearly demonstrate the influence of Daniel Gran. Gran himself, along with Bartolomeo Altomonte, painted the frescoes in the side aisles as well as the altarpieces in the side altars.

The **Rosenkranzkapelle** is the only remaining section from the original medieval church. It has cross-ribbed vaulting and pillars with intricately decorated capitals. The entrance to this chapel is via the choir stalls.

Diözesan-Museum★

On the upper floor of the cloister courtyard. ⏱*May-Oct Tue-Fri 10am-noon, 2-5pm; Sat, Sun, holidays 10am-1pm.* €4. ☎ 0 27 42/32 43 31.

This museum houses religious art from the Romanesque period to the present, in particular Gothic altarpieces and sculptures, and works by leading Austrian Baroque artists. The crowning glory is the sumptuous library, the **Stiftsbibliothek**★, with sculptures attributed to Peter Widerin and frescoes by Daniel Gran and Paul Troger. These depict the four faculties: theology, philosophy, medicine and law.

Stöhr Haus

This is an important example of a Jugendstil building, at Kremser Gasse no 41, built in 1899 by Joseph Maria Olbrich, creator of the Vienna Secession building.

Landhausviertel

Since becoming the seat of the Lower Austrian government, St. Pölten has built a new government and cultural district about 500m southeast of the old town by the Traisen. The quarter's main commercial artery is the Landhaus Boulevard, which culminates in the elegant new state parliament building. Beyond here are the main cultural institutions, including the Festspielhaus concert hall designed by Klaus Kada, and the Landesmuseum (see next).

For a birds-eye view of the quarter, head to the 46m/150ft viewing platform of the **Klangturm** ("Sound tower", ⏱*year-round Mon-Sat 8am-7pm, Sun 9am-5pm; exhibits late Apr-Oct Tue-Sun 9am-5pm;* ♿free. ☎ 0 27 42/90 80 51; *www.klangturm.at*), designed by Ernst Hoffmann, which is illuminated at night. The tower also doubles as an information center and houses changing exhibitions (mostly interactive) of artistic installations experimenting with sound.

Landesmuseum

Kids ⏱*Tue-Sun 9am-5pm.* €8. ☎ 027 42/90 80 901 00. *www.landesmuseum.net*.

Housed in a radically modern building by Hans Hollein, the Lower Austrian provincial museum presents exhibits on nature, art and history in engaging fashion that often makes clever use of interactive technology. The prized art collection presents the entire spectrum of works from the Middle Ages to today. Elsewhere you can take a virtual journey into the past with the help of multimedia installations and a 3D film.

The overarching theme is "water," which pops up in unusual places throughout the museum. Special exhibits and child-oriented events add additional dimensions.

Excursions

Stift Herzogenburg★
12km/7.5mi north of St. Pölten. ⏱ ⚊ *Guided tour (1hr) Apr-Oct daily 9.30am, 11am, 1.30pm, 3pm, 4.30pm; Nov-Mar by appointment.* ♿ ⊛ *€7.* ☎ *0 27 82/8 31 12 11. www. stift-herzogenburg.at.*

The Augustinian canons' monastery was founded in 1112 by Bishop Ulrich of Passau and given a complete Baroque makeover in the 18C in a collaboration of three of the era's greatest architects: Jakob Prandtauer, Johann Fischer von Erlach and Joseph Munggenast. Franz Munggenast rebuilt the **church**, which was adorned with frescoes by Bartolomeo Altomonte who also painted the altarpieces on the side altars. The picture on the high altar is by Daniel Gran.

A highlight of the monastic buildings is the **Festsaal**★ (festival hall), a work of Fischer von Erlach crowned by Altomonte's huge allegorical fresco to the glory of the prince-bishops of Passau. Tours also take in the **library**, which is liberally decorated with pictures, frescoes and *grisailles* (paintings in tones of grey), and a room filled with Late Gothic works by artists belonging to the Danubian School.

Kirchstetten
15km/9mi east. This village was for many years the summer retreat of the poet **WH Auden** (1907-73), who was buried here.

ST. VEIT AN DER GLAN

KÄRNTEN

POPULATION 13 775 – ALT 476M/1 562FT

St. Veit was the seat of the dukes of Carinthia until 1518 when the role of regional capital passed to Klagenfurt. The well-preserved town wall, the picturesque narrow streets, the two town squares with their handsome houses and arcaded courtyards all contribute to the charming flair of this town. 🚩 *Hauptplatz 1, A-9300,* ☎ *0 42 12/55 55*

▸ **Orient Yourself:** St. Veit is in southern Austria, about 19km/12mi north of Klagenfurt.
☺ **Don't Miss:** Fuchs Palast
⏱ **Organizing Your Time:** The town warrants about a half day visit.
⚲ **Also See:** Burg Hochosterwitz, Gurk, Maria Saal, Magdalensberg

Sights

Hauptplatz★
Most places of interest in St. Veit are on or near this central square, which is at the heart of a mostly pedestrianized web of lanes. The **Schüsselbrunnen** is a fountain surmounted by a grotesque bronze figure in a 16C miner's costume that has become the town mascot. The square's other fountain honors Walther von der Vogelweide, the most famous of the German troubadours who once worked at the court of St. Veit. Also have peek inside the **Stadtpfarrkirche,** notable for its Late Baroque high altar and chancel, both by local master woodcarver Johann Pacher.

Fuchs Palast, St. Veit

Rathaus★

This elegant building was built during the Late Gothic period but did not get its grand pilastered **stucco façade**★ until 1754, the work of Joseph Pittner. On the pediment is the double-headed eagle of the Holy Roman Empire, embossed with the statue of the city's namesake Saint Veit. A vaulted Gothic passageway leads to the sgraffito-decorated **Renaissance courtyard**★, one of the finest in Carinthia. The great hall, or **Rathaussaal**★ (⏰*Mon-Fri 7am-6pm;* ♿; ☎ *0 42 12/5 55 56 68)* on the first floor is decorated with lacey stuccowork.

Museum der Stadt Veit

Hauptplatz 29. ⏰*Jul-Aug daily 9am-6pm; Apr-Jun, Sep-Oct daily 9am-noon, 2pm-6pm.* ☞€3. ☎ *0 42 12/55 55 64, www.museum-stveit.at.*

Transport and communication are the main themes of this small museum where you can admire a huge model railway with 200m/220ydm of tracks or fancy yourself a locomotive engineer in a clever simulator. The century-old post office provides an endearing window on the past.

Fuchs Palast

Professor-Ernst-Fuchs-Platz 1. ☎ *0 42 12/4 66 00.* *www.fuchspalast.com*

Probably what you'll remember more than anything about St Veit is this must-see-to-be-believed art hotel, a whimsical composition by painter Ernst Fuchs. With its patterned red, white and blue façade and equally fantastical interior, it blithely defies all conventions. For the full immersion, book one of the 60 rooms.

Excursions

Magdalensberg★

15km/9mi – about 2hr. Leave St. Veit on the road to Klagenfurt. ○*May-mid Oct daily 9am-7pm.* ○€5. ☎ *0 42 24/22 55. www.landesmuseum-ktn.at.*

After 7km/4mi turn left onto an uphill road on the flank of the Magdalensberg. The road ends at the **Archaeological Park Magdalensberg**, an open-air museum leading through the excavated traces of an early Roman town, built on the remains of an even older Celtic settlement.

Walk *(45min roundtrip)* to the top of the mountain (alt 1 058m/3 470ft) to enjoy the majestic **panorama**★ and to pop into the Gothic pilgrims' chapel dedicated to Sts Helen and Mary Magdalene. It houses a beautiful, paneled 15C altarpiece from the woodcarving workshops at St. Veit.

ST. WOLFGANG★★

OBERÖSTERREICH
POPULATION 2 790 – ALT 549M/1 801FT
LOCAL MAP SEE SALZKAMMERGUT

A deluge of visitors is no novelty for St. Wolfgang on the lake of the same name. Its church, which is a feast of magnificent works of art, has been a place of pilgrimage since the 12C. Today the faithful are joined by music lovers who come to see the original of the "White Horse Inn" and the beautiful landscape and magnificent **lake**★★ praised in the comic opera of that name *(Im Weissen Rössl)*. The charm of St. Wolfgang is most strongly felt in the less busy periods either side of the main summer season and during the winter. ▯ *Pilgerstraße 28, A-5360,* ☎ *0 61 38/80 03, www.stwolfgang.at.*

▶ **Orient Yourself:** St. Wolfgang is in the Salzkammergut, about 48km/30mi east of Salzburg.
▣ **Parking:** Parking is tight in summer. Try the garages at the village entrance and at the Schafberg station, 1km/0.5mi beyond the church.
○ **Organizing Your Time:** Budget half a day, more if going up the Schafberg.
◔ **Also See:** St. Gilgen, Bad Ischl, Mondsee,

Access

In high season a pleasant alternative to driving is to arrive by **boat** (○*May-Oct;* ☎ *0 61 38/2 23 20).* Regular services operate from Strobl and St. Gilgen, calling in at Schafberg and the center of St. Wolfgang.

Sights

Pfarrkirche

○*daily 8am-6pm.* ☎ *0 61 38/23 21.*

St. Wolfgang's parish church is the successor to the chapel of a hermitage built, according to legend, by St Wolfgang, the bishop of Regensburg who came to seek solitude on the shores of the lake that would later bear his name. The present late 15C structure on a rocky spur abuts onto the elegant 16C priory. The outer cloisters, lined with arcades that yield bird's-eye views of the lake, complete the charming ensemble.

R. Dietrich/BILDAGENTUR BUENOS DIAS

Altar by Michel Pacher, St. Wolfgang

Michael-Pacher-Altar★★

This 12m/39ft high masterpiece (1481) shows rare unity in composition and is considered to be an outstanding example of Gothic art. The central panel shows a heavily gilded Coronation of the Virgin, while the complementary paintings depict scenes from the life of Mary. Pacher reveals himself to be a master of perspective and detail in this work.

Schwanthaler-Doppelaltar★

This Baroque masterpiece was created by Thomas Schwanthaler in 1675-76 and features more than 100 carved figures full of life and energy. The left panel, executed in black and gold, shows the Holy Family on their pilgrimage to Jerusalem, while the right panel depicts St Wolfgang.

It is said that Thomas Schwanthaler dissuaded the abbot of Mondsee from replacing Pacher's altarpiece with his own when the church was redecorated in Baroque style, but there is no evidence to corroborate this story.

A third great artist has left his legacy in this church: the Mondsee master **Meinrad Guggenbichler**, to whom the three altars on the north side of the church, including the majestic Rosenkranzaltar, and the pulpit are attributed. His *Man of Sorrows* is particularly heart-rending. Near the church is the famous **Weisses Rössl** (White Horse Inn).

A family of artists

The **Schwanthaler family,** from Ried im Innkreis, produced no less than 21 artists in a period of 250 years, the majority of whom were sculptors. A 19C descendant, Ludwig Ritter von Schwanthaler, Court Sculptor to King Ludwig I of Bavaria, was responsible for the sculpted figure of Bavaria on the Theresienwiese in Munich.

Excursion

Schafberg★★

Alt 1 783m/ 5 830ft. About 4hr roundtrip, including 1hr 30min by Schafbergbahn rack railway and 30min walk. ◷*May-Oct 8.25am-3.55pm.* €*24 roundtrip.* ☎ *0 61 38/2 23 20., www.schafbergbahn.at.*

From the mountain station, make for the hotel on the summit, which is a short distance from the impressive precipice on the north face. From here you can spot numerous lakes, including the Mondsee, Attersee and Wolfgangsee and any number of major Alpine peaks and ranges, including the Höllengebirge, the Totes Gebirge and the Dachstein.

SCHÄRDING★

OBERÖSTERREICH

POPULATION 5 640 – ALT 318M/1 043FT

This picturesque little town on the Inn River belonged to the royal Bavarian Wittelsbach family almost without interruption from 1248 to 1779 when it was ceded to Austria. There are no major sights here, but the lovely Baroque old town with cobbled lanes and remains of the medieval fortifications make Schärding a pleasant stop nonetheless. 🛈 *Innbruckstraße 29, A-4780 Schärding,* ☎ *0 77 12/4 30 00, www.oberoesterreich.at/schaerding*

▸ **Orient Yourself:** Schärding is on Austria's western edge, right on the border with Germany, about 107km/67mi west of Linz.

Silberzeile, Schärding

R. Chéret/MICHELIN

🅿 **Parking:** Look for parking lots on Bahnhofstraße and Alfred-Kubin-Straße. There's also a garage on Tummelplatzstraße.

🕓 **Organizing Your Time:** Plan on spending about a couple of hours in town.

🕯 **Also See:** Donautal

Old Town

Schärding's old town centers on **Stadtplatz**, the main square divided by a row of buildings called a *Grätzel*. Its most distinctive feature, though, is the **Silberzeile**★, a phalanx of statuesque Baroque houses painted in a rainbow of colours. The name, which translates as "Silver Row," is a reference to the deep-pocketed merchants who had them built back in the 17C.

Just off the square, the Late Baroque **Stadtpfarrkirche** (parish church), dedicated to St George, has fine proportions that give the well-lit nave a lofty dignity, emphasized by soaring pillars. The left side altar has a panel by Michael Rottmayr (Christ appearing to St Theresa) from about 1690.

The upper square is closed off by the Linzer Tor (Linz Gate), while the Rathaus (town hall) marks the beginning of the lower square anchored by the St.-Georgs-Brunnen (St George's Fountain) of 1607. To get to the Inn River, walk through the **Wassertor** (Water Gate), where high water marks provide evidence of disastrous flooding.

Taking a stroll along the **Innlände** riverside promenade opens up attractive perspectives on the town. River steamers stop here as well.

SCHLADMINGER

TAUERN 🎿 🎿

STEIERMARK

This mountain chain stretches for 40km/25mi and towers over the broad **Ennstal**. On the other side of this valley is the muscular **Dachstein massif**★★, which has the appearance of a fortress with its limestone rocks, steep jagged cliffs and harsh features. The Schladminger Tauern, by contrast, are characterised by long, densely wooded and easily accessible valleys with lakes and rivers. It is precisely these varied landscapes that lend the Ennstal its special appeal. Since the 1960s, the area has been a popular winter sports resort. In summer, hikers have access to wide-open, unspoiled areas with spectacular views.

▸ **Orient Yourself:** The area is in central Austria, about 84km/53mi southeast of Salzburg.

◉ **Don't Miss:** Hunerkogel

🕯 **Also See:** Dachstein

Dachstein-Tauern Ski Area

Ski hounds will find 78 lifts, 140km/87mi of downhill ski runs and 350km/217mi of off-piste slopes to play with, but need only a single ski pass for the combined Schladminger Tauern and Dachstein area.

The **downhill ski runs** concentrate mainly on the Schladminger Tauern and consist of five areas: the **Reiteralm** (alt 800-1 860m/2 625-6 102ft) above Pichl; the **Hoch-**

wurzen (745-1 850m/2 444-6 069ft) above Rohrmoos; the **Planai** (745-1 894m/2 444-6 213ft) above Schladming; the **Hauser Kaibling** (752-2 015m/2 467-6 611ft) above Haus; and the **Gaisterbergalm** (680-1 976m/2 231-6 483ft) above Pruggern. Most are connected to each other and are also served by buses. Fageralm, Stoderzinken and the Dachstein glacier are smaller areas.

Moderately good skiers will be especially happy here, but less those who like open spaces and large differences in altitude. The snow cover is generally good, but the moderate altitude can sometimes pose problems. Snow-making equipment is often used on the lower pistes.

For cross-country skiers, the Schladminger Tauern provide 60km/37mi of tracks around Rohrmoos in beautiful, sunny surroundings, and a further 28km/17mi around Schladming. Dedicated skiers should steer towards **Ramsau am Dachstein** (👤 *see Dachstein*) whose internationally renowned **cross-country ski area** 🎿🎿🎿 is distinguished by a particularly enchanting setting.

Schladming 🎿

Alt 745m/2 444ft. The World Cup downhill races held on the Planai slopes since 1973 have given Schladming plenty of publicity. Après-ski entertainment is also provided for, with generous sports facilities (themed swimming pool, indoor tennis courts etc). Golfers will find a demanding 18-hole course at Oberhaus. Schladming's pedestrian zone is a joy to stroll around.

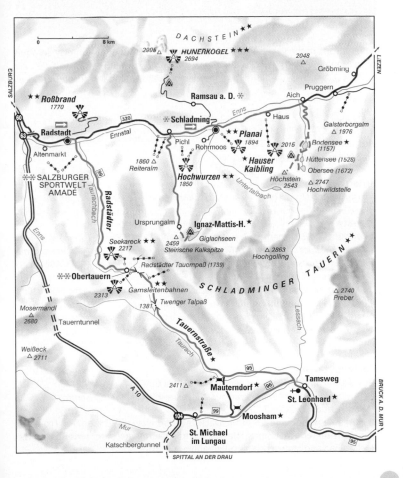

Bodensee, Schladminger Tauern

Other resorts in the valley include **Rohrmoos**, Pichl, **Haus** (with a pretty Baroque church) and Pruggern. Another alternative is the sunny plateau of **Ramsau** *(see Dachstein)*, which is famous for its unspoiled countryside and delightful setting.

Viewpoints

Hunerkogel★★★
Alt 2 694m/8 836ft. *See Dachstein.*

Rossbrand★★
Alt 1 770m/5 807ft. *28km/17mi west of Schladming. See Dachstein.*

Planai★★
Alt 1 906m/6 253ft. *1hr roundtrip from Schladming. Take the cable-car in two stages (sit facing the back).* ◷*11 June-22 Oct, Dec 1-May daily 9am-4.30pm (summer to 5pm).* ∞*€13 roundtrip (summer), €31.50 day pass (winter).* ☎ *0 36 87/2 20 42 13. Also accessible via a small mountain (toll) road.*
The view from the mountain station is rather limited, but if you make the 24km/15mi climb to the summit you'll enjoy a wonderful **panorama**★★. Skiers can make the journey via the Burgstallalm piste and also the chair-lift of the same name. Hikers can climb up to the **Krahbergzinken** (alt 2 134m/7 001ft) in 2hr 30min roundtrip. The less ambitious can take an easy nature trail round the summit of the Planai in 45min.

Hochwurzen★★
Alt 1 849m/6 066ft. *30min roundtrip via cable-car from Rohrmoos* ◷*11 June-22 Oct, Dec-1 May daily 9am-4.30pm (summer to 5pm).* ∞*€9.70 roundtrip (summer), €16.50 (winter).* ☎ *0 36 87/2 20 42 13.*
Remarkable **panorama**★★ of the Dachstein and view of Schladming. From the mountain inn terrace it is possible to see the Schladminger Tauern massif with the Hochgolling and Steirische Kalkspitze summits.

Hike

Schladming and other Ennstal villages are ideal starting points for **walks and hikes**★★ in the relatively low-lying surrounding mountain ranges. A magnificent panorama can be enjoyed from such summits as Höchstein and Hochgolling, but because of the long climb involved, plan on overnighting at the mountain lodge.

Dreiseen circuit★

17km/11mi east of Schladming. Allow 4hr hiking time for the entire circuit. Drive on E 651 towards Liezen then turn right onto a small toll road towards the Bodensee.
An easy trail leads to the **Bodensee**★ with its beautiful waterfall in about 15min. From the far end of the lake, an arduous trail climbs up to the Hans-Wödl-Hütte mountain lodge (alt 1 528m/5 013ft) on the idyllic **Hüttensee** in about 1hr. A beautiful spruce forest and two waterfalls form the backdrop. After another 45min through luxuriant vegetation, the trail reaches the crystal-clear **Obersee** (alt 1 672m/5 485ft). Return the same way.

SCHNEEBERG★

NIEDERÖSTERREICH

Since the completion of the Semmering railway in the mid 19C, the Schneeberg region has been a popular getaway for outdoor enthusiasts from Vienna. Hiking and touring are popular in summer, while skiers hit the slopes at first snowfall.
🅘 *Reichenau an der Rax, Schlossplatz 9, A-2651, ☎ 0 26 66/5 28 65 and* 🅘 *Semmering, Passhöhe 248, A-2680, ☎ 0 26 64/2 00 25, www.semmering.at.*

▶ **Orient Yourself:** The area is in eastern Austria, some 70km/44mi south of Vienna

Tour of the Schneeberg *102km/63mi*

From Neunkirchen to Semmering★

The route described below includes steep and narrow stretches of road, especially between Hirschwang and Semmering.

Neunkirchen
North of the Hauptplatz with its Trinity Column, the parish church of Mariä Himmelfahrt (mid 12C-16C, Baroque interior) towers above the rooftops. Because of the town's frontier setting, the church was fortified and once even surrounded by a moat.

▶ *In Neunkirchen, turn off B 17 onto B 26 towards Puchberg.*

Puchberg am Schneeberg
This pleasant mountain resort is distinguished by idyllic spa gardens laid out around a lake and a 12C ruined castle. From Puchberg station, the rack railway **Schneebergbahn** (🕐*May-Oct daily 9am-5.30pm; ⌖€28 roundtrip; ☎ 0 26 36/36 61; www.schneebergbahn.at*) makes several trips up the Schneeberg daily. From the mountain station next to a refuge (with restaurant), an easy trail leads to the summit in about 90min, treating you to fabulous **views**★ along the way.

▶ *Leave Puchberg on B 26 towards Wiener Neustadt, turn left towards Waldegg. In Reichental turn left again towards Gutenstein.*

Gutenstein

In the 19C Gutenstein was a popular summer resort, attracting artists such as Lenau, Brahms and Waldmüller. The town's annual Raimundspiele open-air theater festival (*www.raimundspiele.at*) commemorates the Austrian actor and playwright **Ferdinand Raimund**, who committed suicide here in 1836, fearing that he had caught rabies from a dog. He is buried in the town graveyard.

Wallfahrtskirche Mariahilfberg

3km/2mi from Gutenstein. Turn left before the church towards Mariahilfberg.
Various Habsburg emperors are among those who have made the pilgrimage to this Baroque church. An altarpiece in the left aisle features a striking depiction of an angel coming to the rescue of a soul burning in Purgatory.

▶ *2km/1.2mi beyond Gutenstein turn left into the Klostertal.*

Klostertal★

About 16km/10mi.
This valley is sparsely populated and largely unspoiled. Towards the end, it narrows considerably, already heralding the Höllental.

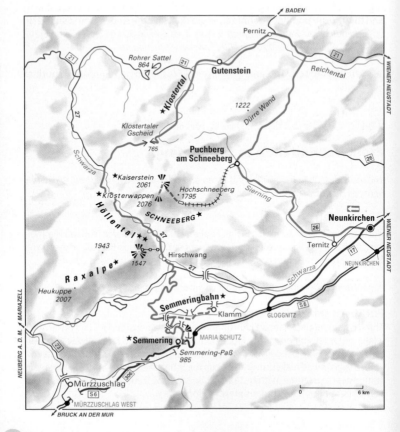

Höllental★★

About 14km/8.5mi.

The Höllental, or Hell Valley, was carved by the River Schwarza between the two limestone massifs of the Schneeberg and the Raxalpe. There is quite a contrast between the delightful Klostertal and the harsher Wildbach Valley, where the green water gushes over the boulders and gravel of the deeply embedded riverbed.

▶ *At Hirschwang, the valley station of the Rax cable-car is to the right of the road.*

Raxalpe★

Ascent by Raxseilbahn cable-car in 8min. 🕐*daily 8am-4.30pm every 30min;* 🕐*two weeks in Nov;* ✆*€16.70;* ☏ *0 26 66/5 24 97; www.raxseilbahn.com*

This steep-sided limestone massif has become a climbing center with several routes departing from the upper station at 1 547m/5 075ft. You can also undertake multi-day tours that have you overnighting in mountain huts. For details, check with the Reichenau tourist office. Along the way you will enjoy charming **viewpoints**★ over the Schneeberg, the Höllental and Semmering.

▶ *Exiting Hirschwang turn right towards Prein, then left towards Gloggnitz and right towards Semmering.*

The winding road leaves the Schwarza Valley and cuts across the picturesque, rugged Semmering region. Dropping down to Breitenstein it affords first glimpses of the superbly engineered viaducts of the **Semmering railway**★ (👆 *see box below*).

▶ *Shortly after the "Semmering" signpost turn left towards "Haltestelle Wolfsbergkogel". After a couple of hundred yards turn left again and follow the wooden "Aussichtswarte Doppelreiterkogel" signs. Park and follow the marked trail for about 10min to the look-out point.*

The **Doppelreiterkogel look-out point**★★ offers a magnificent view of the Semmering railway, which cuts a particularly fine route at this point, with numerous viaducts and tunnels.

Semmering railway

Rail links already existed between Vienna and Gloggnitz and between Mürzzuschlag and Bruck an der Mur, but crossing the Semmering range still required the use of horse-drawn carts. In order to complete the final gap in the southern railway network, Venetian engineer Carlo di Ghega (1802-60) was invited to take over the Semmering railway project. Between 1848 and 1854, up to 20 000 workers were busy building the track of Europe's first standard-gauge mountain railway (some 1 000 of them died in accidents or from epidemics during construction). On the 41km/25mi stretch between Gloggnitz and Mürzzuschlag (21km/13mi above ground) the train passes through 15 tunnels, crosses 16 viaducts and more than 100 smaller bridges, overcoming an altitude difference of 480m/1 584 ft. In spite of the tremendous feats of construction – 1.4 million m3/49 million cu ft of rock alone had to be blasted – the railway blends harmoniously into the beautiful landscape around Semmering. After the railway's inauguration in 1854 by Emperor Franz Joseph and Empress Elisabeth, the region's popularity soared, especially as a summer retreat for the Viennese. Originally, steam engines trundled over the Semmering range at 6kph/4mph, but speeds increased to 60kph/37mph after the line was electrified in 1956. In 1999, UNESCO declared the railway and surrounding countryside a World Heritage Site.

Archiv Zwicki/ ÖSTERREICH WERBUNG

The Semmering railway

▶ *Backtrack and follow the signposts to "Hochstraße/Südbahnstraße" to get to Semmering.*

Semmering★

After the construction of the Semmering railway, this climatic mountain spa and winter sports center, built on terraces between 985m/3 231ft and 1 291m/4 235ft, experienced a steep economic boom.The village is dotted with smart villas and hotels, mostly built between 1850 and 1910. Adding to the area's appeal is the exceptionally sunny climate. Information on the Semmering railway is available from the local tourist office.

SCHWAZ★

TIROL
POPULATION 12 500 – ALT 538M/1 765FT

From the 15C to the 16C when its silver and copper mines were in full production, Schwaz was the largest town in the Tyrol, after Innsbruck. Its one-time prosperity is attested to today by the unusual size and the decoration of its most representative buildings, all erected between 1450 and 1520. *Franz-Josef-Straße 2, A-6130, ☎ 0 52 42/6 32 40, www.silberregion-karwendel.at/schwaz*

- ▶ **Orient Yourself:** Schwaz is in western Austria, about 30km/19mi northeast of Innsbruck.
- **Parking:** Parking is free for the first two hours in the Stadtgarage.
- **Don't Miss:** Haus der Völker
- **Organizing Your Time:** Budget half a day to a day.
- **Especially for Kids:** Silberbergwerk, Schloss Tratzberg
- **Also See:** Hall in Tirol, Karwendelgebirge

Sights★

Pfarrkirche

Schwaz's parish church on Franz-Josef-Straße is the largest Gothic four-aisle hall church in the Tyrol with an impressive roof covered with 15 000 copper shingles Consecrated in 1502, half the church was originally reserved for the burghers, the other for the miners. The finest piece of religious sculpture is the **altar of St Anne** in the south side aisle. Its Baroque altarpiece (1733), honoring the patron saints of Austria, St George and St Florian, frames a fine early 16C group of the Holy Family

Haus der Völker★

Christoph-Anton-Mayr-Weg 7. About 15min walk north of town center via Husslstraße. ⏱daily 10am-6pm. ☞€6. 0 52 42/6 60 90, www.hausdervoelker.com.

Kids This private museum of ethnology presents the fantastic collection of non-European art and artefacts assembled by local photojournalist Gert Chesi. The main focus is on Africa with great Yoruba masks, sculpture and voodoo cult objects. There's also exquisitely carved sculpture from Burma (Myanmar), Thailand and China .

Silberbergwerk★ (Silver mine)

Alte Landstraße 3a. Bring a sweater as the temperature is about 13°C/55°F. ⏱👣Guided tour (1hr 30min) May-Sep daily 9am-5pm; Oct, Feb-Apr daily 10am-4pm. ☞€15 ☎ 0 52 42/72 37 20, www.silberbergwerk.at

Kids A little train whisks visitors 800m/0.5mi into the Sigmund gallery, created about 500 years ago when Schwaz was a vast silver mining center employing 11 000 miners. Steps give access to a labyrinth of galleries where the techniques of mining and excavation of shafts are graphically explained.

Schloss Freundsberg

⏱Apr-Oct Fri-Wed 10am-5pm. ☞€3. ☎ 0 52 42/6 39 67.

The square keep gives this castle a defiant appearance as it sits picturesquely on its knoll, commanding **views**★ of the Inn Valley and the town. The castle is the 12C ancestral seat of the knights of Freundsberg who sold it to a local duke in 1467.

Bohnacker/ÖSTERREICH WERBUNG

Schloss Tratzberg

The Late Renaissance palace kitchen is a jewel, while the keep houses the town museum.

Excursion

Schloss Tratzberg★

5km/3mi. Leave Schwaz on the road to Stans. 20min walk from the parking lot. Guided tour (1hr) 25 Mar-May, Sep-Oct daily 10am-4pm; Jun-Aug daily 10am-5pm. €9. 0 52 42/6 35 66 20, www.schloss-tratzberg.at.

Kids This castle served as a hunting lodge for Emperor Maximilian and the Fuggers, the powerful merchant dynasty from Augsburg, who had interests in Schwaz's silver mine. Guided tours, including special fairytale-themed ones for children, take you to rooms containing original furniture, pictures and weapons. The coffered ceiling of the royal chamber (Königinzimmer) of 1569 is magnificent and held together without a single nail. The Habsburg Room features a a 46m/151ft long wall painting depicting 148 of Emperor Maximilian's ancestors in the form of a family tree.

ABTEI SECKAU

STEIERMARK

The extensive abbey complex, whose corner towers lend it a somewhat military air, was founded in 1140, run by Augustinian canons and served as the seat of the diocese from 1218 until its dissolution by Joseph II in 1782. Benedictine monks have been in charge since its refounding in 1883.

▶ **Orient Yourself:** The abbey is at the foot of the Seckau Alps (Niedere Tauern) about 74km/46mi northwest of Graz and 11km/7mi north of Knittelfeld.

Basilica★

May-Oct daily 10am-5pm. €1.50. 0 35 14/5 23 41 00. www.abtei-seckau.at
The abbey's Romanesque basilica has lavish net vaulting that was added in the 15C but is otherwise a rather minimalistic place. The main visual focus therefore is the simple but moving **Crucifixion** (1260) above the main altar. The figures of Mary and Joseph probably date from earlier, c 1200.

In the **Bischofskapelle** (Bishop's Chapel) attention is drawn to the **altarpiece**★★ (1489) depicting the *Coronation of the Virgin*. Besides Mary it shows three other figures representing the Holy Trinity, all enclosed in a circular, carved framework.

In the adjacent **Gnadenkapelle** (Chapel of Grace), the key piece is a 12C alabaster image of the Virgin and Child, considered the oldest Marian image venerated in Austria.

The chapel to the left of the high altar contains the **Mausoleum of Archduke Karl II**, which was designed by the Italian artist Alessandro de Verde in 1612. The chapel itself blends Late Renaissance and Baroque style elements.

SEEFELD IN TIROL

TIROL
POPULATION 2 800 – ALT 1 180M/3 871FT
LOCAL MAP SEE SEEFELDER SATTELSTRASSEN

Seefeld lies on a sunny, broad mountain plateau surrounded by thick forest and offering good views of the rocky ridges of the Hohe Munde, Wettersteingebirge and Karwendel range. It is a popular cross-country ski resort, which hosted the Nordic skiing events during the 1964 and 1976 Olympic Games as well as the World Skiing Championship in 1985. Off the pistes, you find a sophisticated resort with numerous leisure faciliities, including a modern swimming pool complex with water slides and saunas; ice rinks; riding centers; tennis courts and golf courses. Paragliding, rafting and mountain biking are other diversions. Seefeld is also terrific hiking territory, even in winter when 143km/90mi of trails are kept snow-free. ◪ *Klosterstraße 43, A-6100, ☎ 05/0 88 00, www.seefeld.at.*

▶ **Orient Yourself:** Seefeld is in western Austria, close to the German border and about 22km/14mi west of Innsbruck.

◔ **Also See:** Seefelder Sattelstraßen, Stift Stams

Ski slopes

Seefeld boasts one of the largest **cross-country ski areas** in the Alps, with 260km/160mi of tracks and good snow cover from Christmas to March.

For downhill skiers, the resort has 25 ski lifts leading to slopes that are ideal for beginners or those who prefer gentle skiing. The most interesting runs are on the **Seefelder Joch** and the **Härmelekopf.**

The Seekirchl, Seefeld

The Miraculous Host

The **Golden Chronicle of Hohenschwangau** records the following miraculous event: One day after Mass, the knight Oswald Milser and his cohorts confronted the priest. insisting that his rank gave him the right to eat the same special wafer as the priest. When the man of God offered it to Milser, the ground opened up beneath the sacrilegious knight. His whole body shaking with fear, he barely grabbed the altar, where his fingers left their mark as if in wax. The priest retrieved the wafer and the ground closed again, though shortly afterwards the wafer turned blood-red.

Sights

Pfarrkirche St. Oswald

This lovely 15C Gothic church was built to perpetuate the worship of a miraculous host, which had been an object of pilgrimage since 1384 and was kept here until 1949. Note the tympanum above the south door which represents, on the right, the martyrdom of St Oswald of England, the patron saint of the church, and, on the left, the miracle of the host. The same themes are picked up by the frescoes decorating the chancel and in a picture (1502) to the right of the chancel.

Seekirchl

South of the village, this church is noteworthy mostly for its postcard-pretty setting against a mountainous backdrop.

Excursions

Seefelder Joch★★

Alt 2 074m/6 804ft. *Funicular to Rosshütte mountain lodge, then Seefelderjochbahn.* ⏱*June-mid Oct, Dec-Mar Mon-Fri 9am-noon, 1pm-5pm; from 8.30am Sat-Sun.* ⌖*€15 roundtrip.* ☎ *0 52 12/2 41 60.*

it is just a short walk from the mountain station to the summit where a beautiful **panorama**★★ takes in the Karwendel mountains, the Wetterstein range with the Zugspitze plateau and other peaks. If you wear sturdy shoes, it is possible to walk back down into the valley, even in winter.

SEEFELDER SATTEL-STRASSEN★★

TIROL AND BAYERN (GERMANY)

The Seefelder Sattel (Seefeld Saddle), high above the Inn Valley and the Scharnitz ravine, cuts a broad breach in the Northern Limestone Alps along the Munich-Innsbruck route.

▸ **Orient Yourself:** This area rubs against the German border in western Austria.

⊛ **Don't Miss:** Mösern

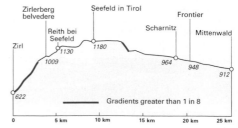

Zirlerberg★

⒈ **From Innsbruck to Mittenwald** *(Germany) 38km/24mi*

Innsbruck★★ 🚶 *See Innsbruck.*

▶ *Leave town on the B 171.*

Between Innsbruck and Zirl the road runs along the floor of the Inn Valley beneath the steep slopes of the **Martinswand**, which provided the setting for an episode dear to the hearts of the Tyrolean Emperor Maximilian is said to have fallen down the cliff in the excitement of the hunt and been saved from a perilous plight by an angel, appearing in the guise of a peasant.

▶ *Rather than driving into Zirl, turn right towards Seefeld.*

The road passes the Baroque Kalvarienbergkirche (1803-05) and the ruined fortress of Fragenstein outlined above Zirl. The notoriously steep **Zirlerberg★** road connects Zirl and Reith bei Seefeld. From the **viewpoint★** at the hairpin bend you can enjoy a great view of the saw-tooth ridges of the Kalkkögel to the south of Zirl.

Reith bei Seefeld★
The local church stands in a charming **setting★** facing the small Roskogel range and the jagged crests of the Kalkkögel.

Seefeld in Tirol ⛷⛷ 🚶 *See Seefeld in Tirol.*

Mittenwald★
Described by Goethe as a "living picture-book," this violin-making town on the old Augsburg-Verona trade route is a popular tourist destination and starting point for numerous hikes into the mountains. Its high street is lined with fine painted **houses★★** and leads to the church fronted by a memorial to Matthias Klotz, the man who brought the fine art of violin making to Mittenwald in 1684. Learn more about him at the local **Geigenbau-und Heimatmuseum**.

Leutasch Valley★★

⒉ **From Mittenwald** *(Germany)* **to Telfs** *32km/20mi*

This route combines a run through the Leutasch Valley and a visit to Mösern, one of the most attractive viewpoints in the upper Inn Valley.

Mittenwald★ 🚶 *See above.*

South of Mittenwald the road leaves the Isar Valley and immediately climbs above the **Leutasch Gorge** (Leutaschklamm) within view of the Karwendel range. After crossing the Leutascher Ache, it runs into the grassy combe of Unterleutasch, majestically bounded by the Ahrnspitze and the Wettersteinwand. A few roofed crosses and farm houses dot this lonely valley, preserving its primitive air.

Leutasch
This community consists of 24 village segments, strung out along the valley. The road passes through some, then forks left in Gasse towards Seefeld. At the junction, there is a splendid view of the majestic Hohe Munde to the right.

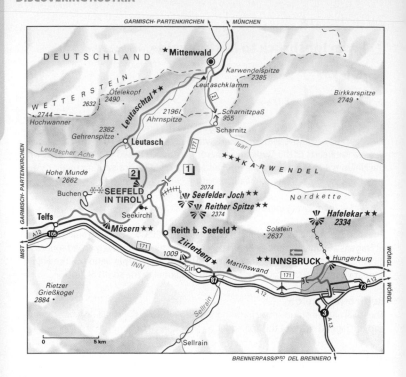

Seefeld in Tirol 🎿🎿 🏌 *See Seefeld in Tirol.*

The **Seekirchl** church marks the beginning of a short valley which climbs up (5km/3mi) to Mösern, located 600m/2 000ft above the Inn Valley.

Mösern

This superbly sited village is a perfect place for a picnic with particularly fine **views**★★. The Inn winds along the floor of the Telfs furrow before slipping into a tangle of crests. Further to the right, the green terrace of the Mieming Plateau snuggles against the Mieming range culminating in the great dome of the Hohe Munde. South of the valley rise the Sellrain mountains and, in the middle distance, the jagged crests of the Kalkkögel.
After Mösern, the road drops down into the Inn Valley in a series of hairpin bends.

Telfs

This bustling market town is home to the interesting Fasnacht- und Heimatmuseum, a local museum displaying costumes and masks used during the **Telfser Schleicher-laufen**, a carnival celebration held every five years.

SILVRETTA-HOCHALPENSTRASSE★★

The Silvretta-Hochalpenstraße links the Ill Valley (**Montafon**★ (ᵢ *see entry*) with the Trisanna Valley (Paznaun Valley) via the Bielerhöhe pass (2 036m/6 680ft). The rugged character of this high-lying pass is mitigated by the shimmering green-blue waters of the reservoirs. The road is usually blocked by snow from November through May and closed to trailers and caravans at any time. There are 30 narrow bends to negotiate on the western slope.

▶ **Orient Yourself:** This scenic route is in the far western corner of Austria, right on the Swiss border, about 130km/84mi southeast of Innsbruck.
⊛ **Don't Miss:** Walk around the Silvretta-Stausseeand ascent to the Hohes Rad.
⊙ **Organizing Your Time:** Allow at least one day, including the hike up to the Hoher Rad.
(ᵢ **Also See:** Montafon

From Partenen to Landeck *73km/45mi.*

⊛ *Gaschurn/Partenen, Galtür or Ischgl are ideal places to look for lodging.*

The road climbs from **Partenen** (1 051m/3 448ft) over the Bielerhöhe at 2 031m/6 664ft into Paznaun and the Tyrol. Along the way it corkscrews past some of the Vorarlberg's highest peaks (eg Piz Buin 3 312m/10 867ft) and the deep blue waters of Alpine reservoirs.

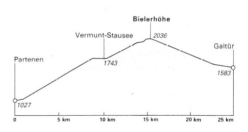

Vermunt-Stausee

This lake forms an intermediate reservoir between Partenen and the Silvrettatal valley, at an altitude of 1 743m/5 718ft. The **view**★ stretches as far as the ridges of the Grosser Litzner and the Grosser Seehorn. As the road winds upwards to the mountain pass, which has been polished smooth by glaciers, the Silvretta dam and mountain summit come gradually into view above the upper lake.

Bielerhöhe

The **Silvretta-Stausee**★ reservoir blends superbly into the Alpine landscape and makes for a pleasant stopping point. Motor boat trips are available on the lake, which is the highest in Europe offering such a service. A walk along the dam (432m/1 417ft long and 80m/262ft high) gives a remarkable **view**★ of the surrounding mountains. An even better way to appreciate the lovely countryside is on the 1hr 45min walk round the **lake**★★. This easy trail passes by several waterfalls and numerous Alpine rose bushes and offers splendid views of the surrounding peaks.

Ch. Heeb/VIENNASLIDE

Vermunt reservoir

Ascent to the Hohes Rad★★★

Allow 5hr 30min roundtrip. Park in the lot at the east end of the lake. This is a great hike for experienced walkers. Waterproof climbing boots and warm, knee-high socks are essential. Those with less stamina should steer towards the Wiesbadener Hütte mountain lodge (about 4hr 15min roundtrip).

It takes about 45min to walk the length of the entire reservoir from where a trail leads uphill along the gushing waters of the Jil, which is fed by numerous waterfalls and brooks. Gradually, several peaks come into view, with the most eye-catching sight being the glacial cirque that closes off the valley.

From the **Wiesbadener Hütte** mountain lodge (alt 2 443m/8 015ft), there is a wonderful **view**★★ of the highest peak in the Silvretta group, the **Piz Buin** (alt 3 312m/10 866ft), which is flanked by the Vermunt glacier on the left and the Oschsental glacier on the right.

Next comes a 1hr 30min climb to the Radsattel. Turn left past the mountain lodge and follow the **Edmund-Lorenz-Weg** trail, which first climbs steeply but then levels out somewhat. It leads down to a small lake (alt 2 532m/8 307ft), shimmering in a kaleidoscope of color from orange to green and lying in a splendid setting below the Rauherkopf glacier. It is all uphill from here as far as the **Radsattel** (alt 2 652m/8 701ft), which marks the boundary between Vorarlberg and the Tyrol. There is a superb **panorama**★★ of the Grosser Litzner and all the glaciers already mentioned. To the east lies the Bieltal valley, which likewise has a glacier towering above it.

The trails climbs slightly towards the rocky foothills of the Hohes Rad, then crosses numerous glacial snowfields before arriving, after 45min, at the **Radschulter**★★ (alt 2 697m/8 843ft). Shortly before the pass, the Radsee, its frigid waters tinged a dark green, pops into sight beneath the Madlener Spitze peak. From the pass, there is an impressive **view**★★ of the Bieltal and Rauerkopf glaciers.

Experienced hikers not prone to vertigo may like to continue along a rocky trail for at least another 45min up to the **Hohes Rad**★★★ summit (alt 2 934m/9 626ft). It is a demanding detour, but one that will reward you with a **360° panorama** of the Silvretta range and reservoir.

The walk down from the Radschulter takes 1hr 30min. The very steep **route**★★ is usually covered by snow well into August and leads through a long rocky stretch before finally turning green again. For the last part of the walk, the trail is flanked by splendid alpine roses and yellow gentians, and provides a number of magnificent **views**★★ of the Silvretta reservoir with the Hochmaderer in the background.

Piz Buin peak and glacial cirque

After 5km/3mi, the road reaches the **Kops-Stausee**★ (alt 1 809m/5 935ft), flanked by the Ballunspitze to the south, the Versalspitze to the west and the Fluhspitzen peaks to the north. Return to the main road and drive on to Galtür.

Galtür

Alt 1 584m/5 197ft. This pretty village on the slopes of the Ballunspitze provides access to a small but interesting ski area above the Kops reservoir. A total of 11 ski lifts lead to 40km/25mi of pistes covering all degrees of difficulty. With 45km/28mi of cross-country tracks and good snow cover, Galtür also has plenty to offer cross-country skiers.

Ischgl ✺ ✺ ⛷ *See Ischgl.*

The Trisanna Valley now narrows further and becomes increasingly picturesque and rugged, with villages clinging to mountain plateaux. The road parallels a rushing creek through fairly dense forest. After a long drive, the appearance of the Burg Wiesberg heralds the famous **Trisanna bridge**★.

Landeck ⛷ *See Arlberggebiet* 1.

SÖLDEN

TIROL
POPULATION 3 056 – ALT 1 377M/4 518FT
LOCAL MAP SEE ÖTZTAL

Geographically speaking, Sölden is the largest municipality in Austria, stretching across 468km²/181sq mi. Yet only a tiny portion (1km²/0.4 sq mi) of the area is inhabited. Surrounded by some 90 peaks soaring above 3 000m/10 000ft, this classic Tyrolean village has developed into an important year-round vacation resort and hub of the **Ötz Valley**★★ (*see Ötztal*). It is well known for its après-ski entertainment and sports facilities as well as its many lively bars, cafés and clubs. The little village of Hochsölden (alt 2 090m/6 857ft) occupies a beautiful plateau and offers excellent snow cover and extensive views. *A-6450; ☎ 0 52 54/51 00; www.soelden.com.*

▶ **Orient Yourself:** Sölden is in the Ötztal valley in western Austria, about 84km/53mi southwest of Innsbruck.

Don't Miss: Ascent of the Wildes Mannle (experienced hikers only).

Also See: Ötztal, Stubaital, Pitztal

Ski slopes (1 377-3 260m/4 518-10 696ft)

Sölden is the main town of the Ötztal Arena, which has 35 ski lifts, 30 artificial snow machines and 150km/94mi of pistes (53km/31mi blue, 63km/39mi red and 28km/17mi black). Ski conditions are good from mid December to early May.

The long descents from the Gaislachkogl to the Stabele chair-lift valley station and the one linking the Hainbachjoch with Sölden are recommended. Less experienced skiers should use the pistes above Hochsölden and the broad trail through the woods from the Gaislachalm.

The **Ötztaler Gletscherstrasse**★★ climbs to 2 822m/9 258ft, making it one of the highest roads in the eastern Alps. It gives access to another ski area (29km/18mi of piste and 10 ski lifts) in a beautiful Alpine landscape on the Rettenbachfern and Tiefenbachfern glaciers.

Cross-country skiers have 8km/5mi of tracks available to them in Sölden, 8km/5mi in Zwieselstein and 3km/1.9mi in Vent.

Viewpoints

Gaislachkogl★★

Alt 3 058m/10 033ft. *1hr round trip. Gaislachoglbahn cable-car ⏰daily 9am-4pm, ⏰ 8 May-23 June. ⟂€19.50 roundtrip, one-day ski pass €40.50. ☎ 0 52 54/5 08.* The ascent is in two stages. From the top mountain station, the summit can be reached on foot in a few minutes (wear sturdy shoes) to take in a splendid **panorama**★★ of the peaks and glaciers of the Ötztal Alps.

Giggijochbahn

⏰*mid Dec-May daily 9am-4pm, ⏰8 May-23 June. ⟂€12.50 roundtrip, one-day ski pass €40.50 ☎ 0 52 54/5 08.* From the terrace of the mountain station there are beautiful **views** of the Sölden ski slopes extending from the Gaislachkogl to the Hainbachjoch. To the east lie the Söldenkogel, the Rotkogel and the Gurgler Tal valley.

Excursions

Ventertal★★

This beautiful glacier-framed valley is a hiker's paradise.

Road from Zwieselstein to Rofen★

16km/10mi. The road first travels through a delightful wooded area, passing the hamlet of Heiligenkreuz with its pretty, onion-domed chapel. It soon reaches **Vent** (alt 1 900m/6 234ft), an unpretentious winter sports resort distinguished by remarkably good snow cover and steep slopes. It has 15km/9mi of pistes at altitudes of between 1 900m/6 234ft and 2 680m/8 793ft, and four ski lifts. Most visitors, though, arrive in summer to take advantage of a seemingly inexhaustible range of trips into the high mountains.

After Vent, the valley splits into two parts on either side of the imposing Talleit-spitze peak (alt 3 406m/11 174ft). The **Rofental** valley, on the right, runs alongside the **Wildspitze** and the **Hochvernagtspitze** peaks before being blocked by the **Weisskugel**. The **Niedertal** valley on the left of the Talleitspitze peak runs along the Ramolkogel and the Schalfkogel, ending in the glacial basin of the **Similaun**. All these peaks have been the goal of legendary mountain expeditions.

Wildspitze-Sesselbahn★

Park at the chair-lift in Vent. ○ *mid June-end Sep daily 8am-5.30pm; mid Dec-mid Apr daily 9.30am-4pm.* ○€7.50 roundtrip. ☎ *0 52 54/81 54.*

At 3 774m/12 450ft the Wildspitze is the highest peak in the Tyrol. From the mountain station (alt 2 356m/7 730ft) there is a beautiful **view**★ of the ski area and various peaks and glaciers. This is also the starting point of numerous hikes, a couple of which are detailed below.

Wildes Mannle★★★

This hike covers 670m/2 198ft difference in altitude and requires a fair level of fitness and experience as well as sturdy footwear. Allow at least 3hr roundtrip, or 4hr if continuing on to the Breslauer Hütte mountain lodge.

From the chair-lift mountain station start hiking towards the Breslauer Hütte. After a 30min walk, veer to the right *(waymarker)* onto a narrower trail. As the view becomes ever more breathtaking, look out for the markers and "WM" indications. The path gets steep and rocky, but does not present any real difficulties.

From the peak (alt 3 023m/9 918ft), which is marked with a cross, there is a terrific **panorama**★★★ of about 15 glaciers belonging to the Ötztal Alps, the most impressive and closest of which is the Rofenkar glacier. Chamois can often be spotted in this region. To the west, notice the Breslauer Hütte lodge at the foot of a rocky , reddish natural amphitheater. A detour to this mountain lodge is a pleasant extension of this hike. Those with a poor head for heights should first follow the same trail as on the way there and then turn off towards the right *(waymarked on the rocks)*. Experienced hikers can take a walk of about 15min across the ridge of the Wildes Mannle as far as a metal sign *(towards Breslauer Hütte via Rofenkarsteig)*. Be sure to pay attention to the markers *(stone cairns)*. At the sign, turn off onto a steep, narrow trail which leads down to the foot of the Rofenkar glacier *(ropes available)*.

The path then leads over a narrow ridge to give beautiful **views**★★ of the glacial cirque. Very soon afterwards, turn off to the right *(waymarked "BH" on a rock)* and reach the Rofenbach brook which is crossed in two stages, the last on wooden planks. Then follow the brook for about 10m/11yd without attempting to climb the slippery rock walls, before regaining the path, which leads up to the Breslauer Hütte mountain lodge. From here, there is a splendid **panorama**★★ (○ *see below*). The descent *(1hr)* to the chair-lift back to Vent is easy.

Breslauer Hütte★★

Alt 2 844m/9 331ft. *Easy hike with a difference in altitude of 500m/1 640ft. Allow 2hr 30min roundtrip starting from the mountain station.*

From the hut, there is a very beautiful **panorama**★★ across the Wildspitze and the ridges of the Wildes Mannle to the north, the glaciers above the Niedertal Valley to the east and the Kreuzspitze peak and its glaciers to the south.

SPITTAL AN DER DRAU

KÄRNTEN
POPULATION 16 000 – ALT 554M/1 818FT

Charming Spittal lies at the confluence of the Lieser and the Drava (Drau) at the foot of the Goldeck peak and close to the Millstättersee (lake). Thanks to its strategic position on a major trade route between Germany and Venice it flourished over the centuries as an economic and cultural center. Nowadays, it is still an important hub in Upper Carinthia. *Burgplatz 1, A-9800, ☎ 0 47 62/34 20, www.spittal-drau.at*

▶ **Orient Yourself:** Spittal is in southern Austria, 37km/23mi west of Villach.
🅿 **Parking:** Central options include the City Center garage and the Hauptplatz.
👁 **Don't Miss:** Museum für Volkskultur
🧒 **Especially for Kids:** Erlebniswelt Eisenbahn, Museum für Volkskultur
👁 **Also See:** Millstatt

Schloss Porcia★

This Italian Renaissance palazzo was built for Gabriel Salamanca, a Spanish aristocrat who served as general treasurer to Archduke Ferdinand until 1526. From 1662 to 1918 the palace was the residence of the princes of Porcia, a noble family from northeastern Italy. The park and the three-story **arcaded courtyard**★ are open to the public at any time. The latter features antique medallions, balustraded pillars, door frames and other

Schloss Porcia

Trumler/ÖSTERREICH WERBUNG

ornamentation typical of the Renaissance style. Also note the splendid 16C wrought-iron **gates**★. Theater performances are held in the courtyard in summer.

Museum für Volkskultur★★

🕐 *mid May-Oct daily 9am-6pm; Nov-mid May Mon-Thu 1-4pm.* 🚻 ♿ €4.50. ☎ 0 47 62/28 90. www.museum-spittal.com.

📷 On the upper floors of Schloss Porcia, this museum chronicles local history, culture and folklore in 47 attractively presented themed displays (education, farming, mining etc). A new highlight is the **3D flight simulator**★ that lets you soar like a bird above the Hohe Tauern National Park.

Affiliated with the museum is the **Erlebniswelt Eisenbahn**★, which is home to Austria's largest model railway featuring some 600m/2 000ft of track, 85 locomotives and 350 cars. Find it on the first floor of the Gerngross City Center mall on Neuer Platz square.

Goldeckbahn

🕐10 June-24 Sep, 17 Dec-26 Mar daily 9am-5pm. ♿€15.50 roundtrip, one-day ski pass €28. ☎ 0 47 62/28 64. www.goldeck-spittal.at.

This 4km/2.5mi cable-car ride leads in two sections to 2 050m/6 726ft, an altitude increase of 1 500m/4 922ft. From the upper station there is a fine **view**★ of Spittal, the surrounding mountains and the Millstättersee lake.

Excursion

Teurnia Ausgrabungen (excavations)★

4km/2.5mi west of Spittal at St. Peter in Holz. Turn off left from the road to Lienz.

The area around St. Peter im Holz has been settled since the 12C BC, first by Celts, then as the Roman city of Teurnia around 50 AD. Excavations have uncovered the remains of this latter settlement, including residential terraces, the forum, a bathing house and a temple. In the 5C and 6C, Teurnia was a fortified provincial town and episcopal seat. The remains of the diocesian church are now protected by a modern shelter. Nearby, the newly revamped **Römermuseum Teurnia**★ (🕐*May-mid Oct Tue-Sun 9am-5pm;* ♿€5; ☎ 0 47 62/3 38 07) presents artefacts unearthed by the excavations, including reliefs, everyday objects and coins.

Outside the city wall is the early Christian Friedhofskirche with a famous **mosaic floor**★ (5C) featuring animal motifs.

STAINZ

STEIERMARK
POPULATION 2 000 – ALT 377M/1 237FT
LOCAL MAP SEE STEIRISCHE WEINSTRASSE

Lying in the valley and watched over by its ancient Schloss (palace), the town of Stainz reveals many hints of its 16C and 17C period of prosperity based on the wine trade. It still boasts a number of old houses with smart façades, particularly in the main square. The Schloss began life in 1229 as an Augustinian abbey, was secularized in 1740 and became the residence of Archduke Johann in 1840. 🔖 *Erzherzog-Johann-Str. 3, A-8510,* ☎ 0 34 63/45 18

▶ **Orient Yourself:** Stainz is 25km/16mi southwest of Graz.
📷 **Especially for Kids:** Jagdmuseum
🍇 **Also See:** Steirische Weinstraße

Church

🕐*daily 8am-6pm.* ☎ *0 34 63/22 37.*
Of the original Gothic abbey church only the two west towers survive while the rest was rebuilt in 1686 in a subdued Baroque style. Only the vault has been decorated – with painted medallions within a stucco composition. At the center of the elevated high altar (1695) is a work by Hans Adam Weissenkircher.

Jagdmuseum (Hunting Museum)★★

🕐*Tue-Sun 9am-5pm.* ⊜*€4.50.* ☎ *0 34 63/2 77 20.*
Kids This state-of-the-art museum, a section of the Landesmuseum Joanneum in Graz, opened at the Schloss in 2006 and is perhaps the first such museum examining the hunt in a historical, natural and ethical context. Baroque trophies, historical weapons, paintings and objets d'art trace its evolution from the Stone Age to the royal courts of the 17C and 18C. Another part of the exhibit looks at the effects of tourism, sports, transportation and industrial production on the Earth's ecological balance.

STIFT STAMS★★

TIROL

The Cistercian abbey of Stams was founded in 1273 by Count Meinhard II of Görz-Tirol as the burial place for his dynasty. The majestic architectural ensemble is purely Baroque in style, the result of a thorough make-over between 1650 and 1750 that also added the distinctive twin onion-domed towers. ▯ *A-6422;* ☎ *0 52 63/62 42; www.stiftstams.at*

▶ **Orient Yourself:** Stams is about 35km/23mi west of Innsbruck.
🅿 **Parking:** Park at the foot of the 14C village church.
♿ **Also See:** Seefeld in Tirol, Ötztal

Stams Abbey

Y. Bontoux

Tour

Guided tour (30 min) year-round daily 9am, 10am, 11am, 2pm, 3pm, 4pm; also May 5pm, June-Sep 1pm and 5pm, additional tours Jul-Aug. €4.

Stiftskirche★★

As you enter the church, elevated to basilica minor by Pope John Paul II in 1984, note on your right the famous **Rose Grille**★. This screen, a masterpiece in ironwork dating from 1716, closes the passage leading to the Heiligblutkapelle (Chapel of the Holy Blood). A balustrade in the nave surrounds the open crypt with 12 gilded wood statues representing the princes of the Tyrol who are buried here. The church's showpiece is the **high altar**★ (1613), whose altarpiece represents the Tree of Life in the form of interlacing boughs supporting 84 carved figures of saints surrounding the Virgin Mary.

Bernardisaal★

The Bernardi Hall is reached from the porter's lodge by a **grand staircase** with a fine wrought-iron balustrade. The hall's ceiling is decorated with paintings (1722) recalling outstanding episodes in the life of St Bernard.

Also have a look at the **museum**, which displays changing art exhibits.

STEIRISCHES THERMENLAND

STYRIA

The **Styrian spa region is** comprised of the five spa towns of Bad Waltersdorf, Blumau, Loipersdorf, Bad Gleichenberg and Bad Radkersburg in the southeast corner of Styria. It is one of Austria's most fertile belts of land, as illustrated by the numerous vineyards, orchards and fields of pumpkins and cereal crops.

▶ **Orient Yourself:** The spa region is east of Graz in the far southeastern corner of Austria, close to the border with Hungary.

Don't Miss: Riegersburg, Styrassic Park

Organizing Your Time: Simply driving through the region takes less than a day but for a more thorough look, and perhaps a spa treatment, allow two days.

Especially for Kids: Kids-themed tours of Riegersburg, Styrassic Park

Blumau

About 7km/4mi north of Fürstenfeld.

Blumau would be just your run-of-the-mill health resort were it not for the **Rogner Bad Blumau**, the avant-garde spa and hotel complex designed by the late Viennese architect **Friedensreich Hundertwasser**. It is a brightly pigmented fairy-tale composition where people, architecture and nature are intended to harmonize with each other. Whimsical touches include roofs covered with lawns and buildings shaped like eyes. Access is open to hotel or spa day guests or to those participating in a **guided tour** *(about 45min)* (*daily 9am-5pm;* *free;* *0 33 83/51 00 90 02*).

Riegersburg★

On the B 66, 10km/6mi north of Feldbach. ◷*May-Sep daily 9am-5pm; Apr, Oct daily 10am-5pm.* ◷☞☞*Guided tours for kids Jul-Aug Sun 12.30pm, 3pm (included in admission).* ☞€9.50, lift €2, combination ticket with Styrassic park (see below) €14. ☎ 0 31 53/8 21 31. www.veste-riegersburg.at

🄺🄸🄳🅂 The 12C Riegersburg castle is one of the most imposing strongholds to have guarded Austria's eastern frontiers. Protected by 3km/2mi of ramparts and 11 bastions, it successfully withstood the onslaught of both the Hungarians and the Turks. Its site alone, on the remains of a 482m/1 581ft high volcano above the village that shares its name, is impressive. Since 1822, the castle has belonged to the royal family of Liechtenstein and now houses a museum on witches in the cellars and an exhibition on prominent 17C women associated with the castle. Architectural highlights include the **Knight's Hall** with its intricately inlaid wooden doors and coffered ceiling and the Early Baroque **White Hall** with its delicate stuccowork. Perhaps even more memorable, though are the wonderful **views**★ of the Styrian countryside enjoyed from up here.

Bad Gleichenberg⚕

On the B 66, 11km/7mi south of Feldbach.
After Graz and Mariazell, the spa town of Bad Gleichenberg is the most popular vacation destination in Styria. Near the Hungarian and Slovenian borders, it is famous for its medicinal springs and mild climate and became a favorite with Austrian aristocracy in the 19C. The town still boasts some beautiful **Biedermeier-style villas and hotels** and is set amid countryside reminiscent of a landscaped garden.

Styrassic Park
Take B 66 and follow the signposts. ◷*Apr-Sep daily 9am-5pm; Oct 9am-4pm.* ☞€9.50, combination ticket with Riegersburg €14. ☎ 0 31 59/28 75 11, www.styrassicpark.at.

🄺🄸🄳🅂 Dinos on the loose in Austria? Well, almost. This sprawling forest park is inhabited by more than 75 life-size model dinosaurs made of steel and concrete. On your tour you will encounter the entire cast of characters, from the long-necked Brachiosaurus to the vicious Velociraptors to the terrifying Tyrannosaurus rex. Display panels give brief explanations on the chronology, fossil discoveries and dimensions of each species. A dino-movie theater, a huge children's playground with the largest slide in the country and a petting zoo further add to the fun.

"Wait 'til the ranger sees that…!" – A Diplodocus in Styrassic Park

Bad Radkersburg★

On the B 69, 26km/16mi south of Bad Gleichenberg right before the Slovenian border.
Radkersburg is an increasingly popular spa town whose calcium and bicarbonate-rich springs are helpful in easing illnesses affecting the nerves and the urinary tract. Since its foundation in 1182, it has been one of the leading trading centers in Styria and was also an important bastion during the wars against the Turks. The partly preserved **fortifications**, with moats, six bastions and towers still attest to this period.
A walk around town will inevitably lead to the **Hauptplatz**, the main square whose many merchant mansions with beautiful stone doorways and courtyards give an indication of the town's former wealth. In the center is a Virgin Mary Column erected in 1680 by the townspeople as a thank you for their deliverance from the plague. The onion-domed octagonal **town hall tower** has become Radkersburg's emblem.

STEIRISCHE WEINSTRASSE★

STYRIA

The **Styrian vineyard trail** is a delightful journey into traditional Austria; a tranquil, timeless world in the midst of outstandingly beautiful countryside. The region is dotted with taverns (**Buschenschenken**) where people meet over a glass of wine and listen to accordion music. It is particularly lovely in the fall when the vines are cloaked in a kaleidoscope of brilliant colors. The vast majority (80%) of wine produced in Styria is white with dry Welschriesling, fruity Weissburgunder and sprightly Müller-Thurgau being the dominant varietals. Zweigelt is the most important red wine, but **Schilcher**, a rosé, is actually better known.

▶ **Orient Yourself:** The wine routes detailed below are all southwest of Graz in southeastern Austria.
⚫ **Also See:** Graz, Steirisches Thermenland

Tour Starting from Graz *180km/112mi*

▶ Leave Graz on the B 70 (AX). *Take either the autobahn as far as Steinberg or the B 70 to Krottendorf, and then follow signs to Stainz.*

① Schilcher Trail

The south-facing vines grown in the Schilcher hills, which back onto the Koralpe range, are often so steep that harvesting by machine is impossible.

On leaving the autobahn, the road immediately begins to climb, providing charming **views**★★ of the Graz plain, the undulating hills northwest of the town and the Schöckl (alt 1 445m/4 741ft) with its flat summit.

Gundersdorf
As you enter this typical wine-growing village, keep an eye out for the strange wooden stake topped with a four-bladed propeller. This is a familiar sight in the Styrian vineyards because its noise scares away the birds as the grapes start ripening. The local speciality is Schilcher wine, which can sometimes be bought directly from the vintner.

Schilcher

Schilcher is made from the Blauer Wildbacher grape and has only been officially known as Schilcher since 1976. Records show that this late-ripening, acidic grape (a distinction is made between the late blue and sloe varieties of Wildbacher), with its characteristic flavour and pretty "onion-skin" colour, has been cultivated in west Styria since as early as 1580. Schilcher vineyards cover about 80ha/198 acres.

Grape-pickers' cottages

Grape-pickers ("Weinzierle") traditionally had no property of their own, but lived in small cottages owned by their vineyard-owning employers. The typical west Styrian grape-picker's cottage, called a "Winzerei," consisted of two rooms, a kitchen and a front veranda with an attached garden. A separate wooden hut would be used to store coal and fodder.

▶ *Turn right after Gundersdorf, then left towards Langegg and Greisdorf.*

Langegg

This village is filled with numerous traditional wine taverns, often housed in simple wooden-roofed summer cottages or on terraces attached to wine-growers' houses. The wine goes rather well with slices of **Verackertbrot**, black bread with chopped, spiced bacon, or perhaps with a **Brettljause**, cold meats served on a wooden platter.

From Langegg there is a delightful **view**★★ of the Mur Valley, the Schöckl and the vine-clad hills of Sausal.

▶ *Turn left at Marhof and follow the signs to Stainz.*

Stainz ⚭ *See Stainz.*

Bad Gams ob Frauental

This village is well known in Styria for its traditional pottery; there is a potter's workshop on the outskirts of the nearby town of Furth.

En route to Deutschlandsberg the road descends into a plain encircled by forests.

Deutschlandsberg

The hub of the Schilcher Wine Trail, this town at the foot of the Koralpe near the Slovene border takes its name from the fortified castle of Landsberg. The prefix *"deutsch"* was not added until the 19C, and then because of its location on German-speaking territory. Deutschlandsberg is famous throughout Styria for its lively and colorful Corpus Christi celebrations featuring flower-bedecked processional altars. The town's grapes benefit from a favorable climate with 280 days of sunshine.

To the north of the town stands the castle of Wildbach, where Schubert is supposed to have composed his famous Lied *The Trout*. Only the 12C keep is original, the rest of the castle having been reconstructed. A number of trails through the vineyards start in the parking lot, which also offers a fine **view**★ of the surrounding plain.

▶ *Rejoin the road from Stainz; continue south in the direction of St. Andrä-Leibnitz via St. Martin; to reach St. Andrä, turn left onto the valley road which joins up with the Sausal Vineyard Trail.*

2 Sausal Trail

St. Andrä is the point of entry to the Sausal hills which rise to 670m/2 198ft and produce mostly **Rheinriesling**, a noble, crisp white with an excellent bouquet.

Styrian vineyard landscape with the local version of a scarecrow ("Klapotetz")

Kitzeck★

Set on a ridge at 564m/1 850ft, this is the highest wine-growing village in Europe and provides **panoramic views**★★ over a sea of hills. The **Wine Museum** (◷*Apr-Aug Sat-Sun 10am-noon, 2pm-5pm; Sep-Oct Tue-Sun 10am-noon, 2pm-5pm; ◌€2.20; ☏ 0 34 56/35 00*), which occupies a wine-grower's estate from 1726, contains articles and tools, including a reconstructed device for smoke curing, an old press and a wagon for transporting barrels.

▷ *Drive towards Fresing, then continue to Klein Klein.*

Celtic tombs dating from the 6C-4C BC have been discovered in the forest near **Grossklein**. The finds are kept in Schloss Eggenberg (⟲ *see entry*).

▷ *In Grossklein turn left towards Heimschuch, then right to Eichberghof.*

The road meanders through wild and hilly country where small south-facing vine-yards alternate with fields of maize and woodsy patches.

▷ *Continue to Leutschach.*

③ South Styrian Route

On either side of the road near **Leutschach** you will pass fields planted not with wine but with hops growing on tall poles.

▷ *In Leutschach turn left before the church and follow the green road sign to the "Südsteirische Weinstraße" (South Styrian Wine Route).*

This is the most southerly wine-growing area in Austria, where the route hugs the border with Slovenia. This region is also known as the **Styrian Tuscany** because of its sunny climate and similarity to the Tuscan countryside in Italy.

A forest of conifers gives way to rows of vines which cover the gently contoured hills of what is the very heart of Welschriesling and Samling country.

Ehrenhausen

Near the Slovenian frontier, a wooded bluff overlooking the Mur and the village of Ehrenhausen was chosen by the Eggenberg princes as the site of a castle and a mausoleum. The **Pfarrkirche** on the main square has a fine bell-tower with a particularly elaborate roof. The church was remodeled in the Baroque style in 1752.

Mausoleum★

Obtain the key from the parish office (8am-6pm). ☎ *0 34 53/25 07.*

This curious funerary monument shelters the tomb of Ruprecht of Eggenberg, who distinguished himself in the struggle against the Turks at the end of the 16C. Completed in 1640, the building was decorated by pupils of Johann Fischer von Erlach. He is buried in the crypt alongside his successor, Wolfgang von Eggenberg. The mausoleum interior is especially striking for the elaborate stuccowork decorating the central dome.

▶ *Take the autobahn back to Graz.*

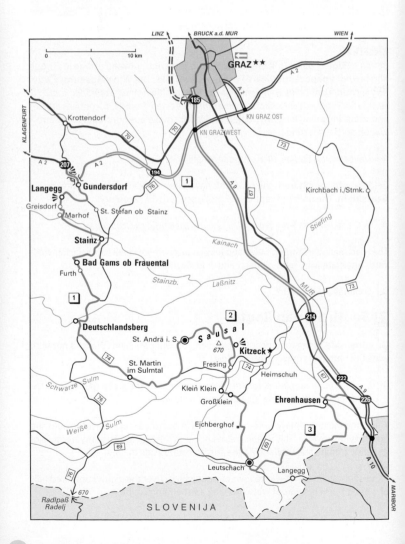

STEYR★

OBERÖSTERREICH
POPULATION 43 000 – ALT 310M/1 017FT

Steyr had a glorious past and for a while even rivaled Vienna in terms of economic and political importance. It is now Upper Austria's third largest town (after Linz and Wels) and still an important economic and industrial center. The picturesque old town, which has preserved its medieval character and charm, clusters at the confluence of the Enns and the Steyr. *Stadtplatz 27, A-4400, ☎ 0 72 52/53 22 90, www.tourism-steyr.at*

▶ **Orient Yourself:** Steyr is about 50km/30mi southeast of Linz.
Don't Miss: Museum Arbeitswelt
Also See: Christkindl

Old Town

Stadtplatz★ (Y)

Steyr's elongated main square is lined with fine Late Gothic and Renaissance houses and centered on the 17C **Leopoldibrunnen** (A). Standout buildings include the **Rathaus** (R) with its Rococo façade surmounted by a tower, and the Gothic **Bummer-**

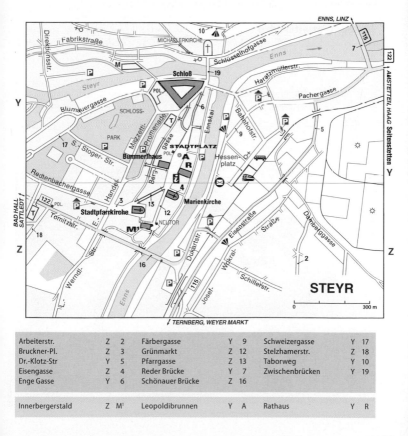

Arbeiterstr.	Z	2	Färbergasse	Y	9	Schweizergasse	Y	17
Bruckner-Pl.	Z	3	Grünmarkt	Z	12	Stelzhamerstr.	Z	18
Dr.-Klotz-Str	Y	5	Pfarrgasse	Z	13	Taborweg	Y	10
Eisengasse	Z	4	Reder Brücke	Y	7	Zwischenbrücken	Y	19
Enge Gasse	Y	6	Schönauer Brücke	Z	16			

Innerbergerstald	Z	M¹	Leopoldibrunnen	Y	A	Rathaus	Y	R

Ihaus (no 32), which sports a triangular gable and characteristic first-floor overhang. Also duck into the lovely courtyards of the houses at no 9, no 11 and no 36/38.

Marienkirche (Z)

The former Dominican church is decorated in the Baroque style and features a high altar overloaded with gilding, a Virgin and Child of 1704 and a Rococo pulpit.

Museum der Stadt Steyr (Z M¹)

Dec-7 Jan daily 10am-5pm; Nov, 7 Jan-Mar Wed-Sun 10am-4pm; Dec-7 Jan daily 10am-5pm. no charge. ☎ *0 72 52/57 53 48.*

A 17C granary known as the **Innerberger Stadl** houses Steyr's charming local history museum, which has a fabulous collection of Baroque religious figurines as well as a huge Nativity scene carved from olive wood in Bethlehem.

Stadtpfarrkirche (Z)

Behind the Innerberger Stadl, the 15C Gothic parish church is the work of Hans Puxbaum, the architect of the Stephansdom in Vienna. Puxbaum also designed the **tabernacle**★, with its delicate tracery, and the tripartite chancel baldaquin.

Schloss Lamberg (Y)

At the confluence of the Steyr and the Enns.

A fortress has stood here for a thousand years but the present Baroque incarnation only dates to the 18C. It is now used mostly by the municipal administration, although it's still worth coming here to pop into the Schlossgalerie with its changing contemporary art exhibits or to take a stroll around the park.

Museum Arbeitswelt★

Wehrgrabengasse 7. ☎*Tue-Sun 9am-5pm. €5.* ☎ *07252/77351. www.working-world. net.*

Ceiling fresco by Paul Troger in the Marble Hall, Stift Seitenstetten

R. Chéret/MICHELIN

The completely revamped permanent exhibit at the "Working World Museum" details the fundamental changes at the workplace in the Age of the Internet and globalization. The high-tech presentation uses videos, text animations, room installations and other modern media to explore the challenges of today and the future.

Excursions

Stift Seitenstetten★
19.5km/12mi east of Steyr on the B 122. 👣👣*Guided tour (1hr 15min) Easter Mon-Oct daily 10am and 3pm.* ✆€6.50. ☎ *0 74 77/4 23 00.*
This Benedictine abbey was founded in 1112 and is still active today, operating a famous grammar school.

Stiftskirche (Abbey church)
The three-aisled Early Gothic basilica turned Baroque in the 17C has rich stucco decoration and frescoes. The high altar is dominated by an *Assumption of the Virgin*, a major work by Johann Karl Reslfeld of Garsten. Behind the church is the **Ritterkapelle** (Knight's Chapel), the oldest part of the abbey, whose apse and side walls date back to the 14C.

Stiftsgebäude (Abbey buildings)
The main abbey buildings are mostly the work of Josef Munggenast, but numerous famous artists contributed to its decoration. Above the festive **Abteistiege** (abbey staircase) is a ceiling fresco by Bartolomeo Altomonte, while those in the **Marmorsaal** (Marble Hall) and the library are by **Paul Troger.** Tours also take in 12 fine paintings by **Kremser Schmidt** in the Maturasaal and the mineral collection displayed in its Rococo cabinets. The abbey's **art collection**★ also includes some fine works by Kremser Schmidt and Paul Troger.

STUBACHTAL★★★

SALZBURG

About 20km/12mi long, the Stubachtal is among the most beautiful Alpine valleys in Austria. A well-built scenic road leads from Uttendorf (alt 804m/2 638ft) to Enzingerboden (alt 1 480m/4 856ft). From here, the Weissee Gletscherbahn cable-car transports skiers in the winter and hikers in the summer to mountain lakes and the magnificent glacial massif of the Hohe Tauern National Park.

▶ **Orient Yourself:** The valley is in western Austria, about 34km/21mi southeast of Kitzbühel.

🅿 **Parking:** Park at the valley station of the Weissee Gletscherbahn in Enzigerboden.

🕓 **Organizing Your Time:** Allow a good day for the drive and the trip to the Kaiser Tauern.

Road from Uttendorf to Enzingerboden ★★
17.5km/11mi. Start in Uttendorf, 6km/4mi east of Mittersill on B 168.
The road provides views of the Steinkarlhöhe range and then runs through a beautiful spruce forest.

Kaiser Tauern★★★

2hr 30min roundtrip, including 1hr walk. Sturdy footwear required. ⏲*mid June-late Sep daily 9.30am-5pm.* ⚬*€23 roundtrip.* ☎ *0 65 63/2 01 50.*

The trip starts with a 25min ride aboard the Weisseebahn gondola to the Rudolfshütte hotel and restaurant (alt 2 315m/7 595ft) through luxuriant vegetation with lovely views of the Grüner See. From here, a 10min walk brings you down to the Medelz chair-lift, which travels through a majestic Alpine massif and treats you to a magnificent **panorama**★★★ during its 15min ascent. From the top, a 25min hike (look for the red and white markers) leads through the rock to the Kaiser Tauern pass, from where you will enjoy more beautiful **views**★ of the lake and the Dorfertal valley.

STUBAITAL★★

TIROL
LOCAL MAP SEE INNSBRUCK: TOUR OF THE MITTELGEBIRGE

The Stubai Valley is a popular day trip for people based in the Innsbruck area. In summer, it is an ideal launchpad for hiking expeditions and also provides access to one of the largest all-year ski areas in Europe.

▸ **Orient Yourself:** This valley is southwest of Innsbruck in western Austria.

From Innsbruck to Mutterbergalm★ *44km/27mi*

▸ *Leave Innsbruck via the Brenner-Bundesstraße. After crossing the Europa bridge, turn off into the Stubai Valley at Schönberg. Alternatively, take the Brenner autobahn (toll).*

On entering the valley, you will soon face the enormous glacial massif of the **Zuckerhütl** (alt 3 511m/11 520ft). The well-built road runs past the valley's five resorts. First up are **Schönberg**, **Mieders** and **Telfes** on a sunny terrace opposite. Then comes **Fulpmes**, which specializes in the manufacture of mountaineering equipment and tools. Lastly, **Neustift** is dominated by the striking silhouette of its 18C parish church by Franz de Paula Penz.

Over the last 7km/4mi of the journey, the gradient becomes ever steeper and the landscape more rugged. The road finally leaves the forest and arrives at the Mutterbergalm (alt 1 728m/5 669ft) at the foot of a rocky cirque.

Stubai Glacier 🎿 🎿 *(Stubaier Gletscher)*

This popular ski area offers downhill enthusiasts slopes of varying degrees of difficulty covering a total of 53km/33mi between altitudes of 2 300m/7 546ft and 3 200m/10 499ft. The area's appeal lies in its outstanding snow cover and excellent transportation infrastructure. The ski season generally runs from October to the beginning of July. Good skiers will appreciate the 10km/6mi long **Wilde Gruben** descent to Mutterberg through splendid, unspoiled **countryside**★★.

There is also a 4.5km/3mi long cross-country course at an altitude of 2 600m/8 530ft (starting from the Gamsgarten cable-car).

The most important viewpoints, which can be reached by lift or on foot, are indicated next *(take warm clothing, sunglasses and thick-soled, waterproof footwear).*

Eisgrat★★
Alt 2 900m/9 514ft. A cable-car in two stages leads to the glacial cirque and the foot of the Stubaier Wildspitze peak (alt 3 340m/10 958ft) and Schaufelspitze peak (alt 3 333m/10 935ft). Walk round the restaurant to see the lower part of the valley.

Daunferner★★
Skiers can reach the glacier (alt 3 160m/10 367ft) by means of the Daunfern ski tow, the Wildspitz double chair-lift and the Rotadl chair-lift. Enjoy impressive **views**★★ over the rocky cliffs framing the glacier from the Stubaier Wildspitze peak to the Ruderhofspitze peak.

TAMSWEG★

SALZBURG

POPULATION 6 000 – ALT 1 024M/3 360FT

Tamsweg is the capital of the remote Lungau region and fosters many old traditions. Most famous among these is the so-called Samsonumzug (Samson Procession) headed by a huge dummy representing Samson and accompanied by two dwarfs. It takes place several days each summer (👁 see Calendar of events).
🅸 Kirchengasse 107, A-5580, ☎ 0 64 74/21 45, www.tamsweg.at

▷ **Orient Yourself:** Tamsweg is about 50km/31mi south of Radstadt in southcentral Austria.

👁 **Also See:** Radstädter Tauernstraße, Mauterndorf

Sights

Marktplatz
Tamsweg's main square is framed by pretty houses, including the 16C **Rathaus** (town hall) with fanciful corner turrets, and the old **Schloss Kuenburg**, now home to offices and a cultural center. Further off, an old hospice now houses the **Heimatmuseum**, which offers glimpses into the local way of life of yesteryear. The varied collection includes a good assortment of Roman artefacts found in the area.

St. Leonhardkirche

▷ *Drive south from Tamsweg on the Murau road over the River Mur. Cross the railway and park at the bottom of the road (right) that climbs straight up to the church. A footpath further right is less steep.*

The 15C pilgrimage church of St Leonard has kept its Early Gothic plan and design – tall light windows, network vaulting etc. Its original **stained glass** is among the finest in Austria and includes the famous "**gold window**" (Goldfenster), on the right of the chancel, which consists entirely of yellow and blue glass. Near the high altar, the small altar to St Leonard features a statuette of the saint held in the branches of a juniper tree. The discovery of the statuette is the basis of the pilgrimage.

TULLN

NIEDERÖSTERREICH
POPULATION 14 650 – ALT 180M/591FT
LOCAL MAP SEE DONAUTAL

Tulln grew up on the site of the Roman camp of Comagena founded in the 1C AD. Between 1042 and 1113, the town was the residence of the Babenberg dynasty, predecessors of the Habsburgs. Tulln's most famous son is the painter Egon Schiele (1890-1918). *Minoritenplatz 2, A-3430, ☎ 0 22 72/6 75 66, www.tulln.at*

▶ **Orient Yourself:** Tulln is on the Danube, about 40km/25mi west of Vienna.

▣ **Parking:** Look for parking on the Hauptplatz or in garages in Albrechtsgasse, Frauentorgasse or at the main train station.

☺ **Don't Miss:** Egon-Schiele-Museum, Karner

Kids **Especially for Kids:** The fire engine collection in the Minoritenkloster.

⌚ **Also See:** Klosterneuburg, Donautal

Sights

Egon-Schiele-Museum

Donaulände 28. ⏲Apr-Oct Tue-Sun 10am-noon, 1pm-5pm. ☞€5. ☎ 0 22 72/6 45 70. http://egonschiele.museum.com

The old local prison now houses an exhibition on the life and work of Tulln-born painter Egon Schiele (1890-1918). On the ground floor are a biographical documentation as well as the reproduction of a jail cell in Neulengbach where he was held for a few days in 1912 for possession of child pornography. Upstairs are a smattering of originals, including drawings, lithographs, watercolors and a few oil paintings, most of them early works (1905-08). Admission also includes entry to the room in the main train station where Schiele was born (his father was stationmaster). Let museum staff know if you would like to see it and they will make arrangements.

Römerturm

This fortified tower has survived almost unchanged in shape and height since being built under Roman Emperor Diocletian (AD 284-305). In the Middle Ages it was used as an arsenal and from the early 19C as a salt storehouse, which explains why locals also call it the Salzturm (salt tower).

Pfarrkirche St. Stefan

Wiener Straße. This 12C Romanesque basilica was transformed in the 15C to the Gothic style and then remodeled in the Baroque style in the 18C. Outstanding elements include the Romanesque western portal, which is adorned with busts of the 12 Apostles. The altarpiece dates to 1786 and represents the stoning of St Stephen. The church's most memorable feature is the 13C polygonal **Karner**, one of the finest **funerary chapels** (ossuaries) in Austria. The **doorway**★★ is decorated with palm-leaf capitals and geometrical motifs, while the domed interior is adorned with fantastical Romanesque frescoes that were drastically restored in 1874 in the 19C style.

Minoritenkirche

Minoritenplatz. This Baroque building constructed in 1739 was dedicated to St John of Nepomuk. Inside, to the left of the high altar, there is a glimpse of the sacristy with a magnificent inlaid cabinet dating from the 18C.

Minoritenkloster and Minoritenkirche, Tulln

M. Hertlein/MICHELIN

Minoritenkloster Museums★

Minoritenplatz 1. ◷*Mar-Oct Tue-Sun 10am-6pm.* €3. ☏ *0 22 72/6 19 15.*
Tulln's old monastery has been successfully recycled into a museum complex. The collections of the **Stadtmuseum** take up most of the space and include items from Roman to recent times discovered during excavations beneath the monastery; an exhibit tracing the region's geological evolution; an assortment of historic fire engines; rooms chronicling daily life in the city during the 18C and 19C; and other aspects of local history. In the attic is the first **Austrian Sugar Museum** (Tulln is a major producer of the sweet stuff), which traces the evolution of sugar production, from primitive sugar cane mills to modern factories. A changing roster of contemporary art exhibits is also housed under the same roof.

Fans of the Austrian painter Friedensreich Hundertwasser should ask museum staff for access to the **Hundertwasser-Schiff "Regentag"** moored in the harbor behind the monastery. It contains a small exhibit about the journeys made by the artist.

VILLACH★

KÄRNTEN
POPULATION 54 640 – ALT 501M/1 644FT
LOCAL MAP SEE WÖRTHER SEE

Frequently referred to as the "secret capital" of Carinthia, Villach is the province's second largest town and a regional economic and cultural hub. Settled since Celtic times, it has an attractive location on the Drava (Drau) River and is considered a gateway to both Italy and Slovenia. In 1007, Emperor Heinrich II donated Villach to his newly founded bishopric at Bamberg, some 540km/337mi north in Bavaria. This arrangement shaped Villach's fortunes until Maria Theresa bought the town back in 1759. Today, part of its appeal lies in its thermal mineral springs and proximity to the Faaker and Ossiach lakes . ▯ *Rathausplatz 1, A-9500,* ☏ *0 42 42/2 05 29 00, www.villach.at*

▶ **Orient Yourself:** Villach is on the far southern edge of the country, close to the Slovenian border, about 40km/25mi west of Klagenfurt.
▣ **Parking:** There are plenty of pay lots and garages in central Villach as well as a large free parking lot by the train station, about a 15min walk away.
◉ **Don't Miss:** Villacher Alpenstraße
Kids Especially for Kids: Burg Landskron, Affenberg

⏱ **Also See:** Ossiacher See, Velden, Maria Wörth, Wörther See

Sights

Old town★
The old town is hemmed in to the north and east by the Drava. The **Hauptplatz**, an elongated square, is flanked by several interesting houses, including the Paracelsushof (no 18), named after the great physician who spent his youth in Villach; and the Khevenhüllers' house (now the Hotel Post) where Emperor Karl V stayed for seven weeks in 1552.

Hauptstadtpfarrkirche St. Jakob
Behind the parish church's simple exterior awaits a lovely hall-church with stellar and ribbed vaulting, a high altar with magnificent sculptures, and a canopied stone pulpit (1555). There are also several 15C-18C **tombs**★on the south wall. In summer it is possible to climb up the free-standing church tower for sweeping views.

Museum der Stadt Villach★
Widmanngasse 38. ⏱*May-Oct daily 10am-6pm.* ⬤*€3.* ☎ *0 42 42/2 05 35 00.*
This Renaissance-style building with its arcaded courtyard forms a fine backdrop for the local historical collections. Exceptional items include the two Gothic panel paintings by **Master Thomas of Villach**, the 1557 death plaque of local governor Christoph Khevenhüller, and large iron chests from the 16C-19C that were used as fire-proof storage places for valuables.

Wallfahrtskirche Heiligenkreuz
▶ *Follow Peraustraße as far as the junction with Ossiacher Zeile.*
This Late Gothic pilgrimage church with its striking twin-towered façade stands on the south bank of the Drava. The richly decorated high altar with the Crucifixion scene, the Lamentation altarpiece in the north transept and the extremely rare depiction of the Thief on Christ's Right in the south transept all contribute to the overall harmony of the church interior.

Villach – a year-round destination

Markowitsch/ÖSTERREICH WERBUNG

Villacher Fahrzeugmuseum

Draupromenade 12. ⏰*mid June–mid Sep daily 9am–5pm; mid Sep–mid June daily 10am–noon, 2–4pm.* ⬤*€5.50.* ☎ *0 42 42/2 55 30. www.oldtimermuseum.at*

This small museum is devoted to means of transport manufactured between 1927 and 1977 and has some endearing old Fiats and Puch motorcycles. The collection will eventually move to new facilities still under construction at press time in the Villach suburb of Zauchen. Check with the tourist office for details.

Warmbad-Villach

About 3km south of town.

Every day, 24 million l/5 million gal of therapeutic spring water bubbles up from the six warm springs (29°C/84°F) in the southern suburb of Warmbad-Villach. When Villach was part of the French Illyrian Provinces between 1809 and 1813, Napoleon nursed plans to develop it into a spa resort of world renown. These came to nothing back then, but today's modern spa has all the facilities one has come to expect.

Excursion

Villacher Alpenstraße★

16.5km/10mi (toll road). ⏰*mid June–mid Sep 5am–10pm; May–mid June, mid Sep–Oct 6am–8.30pm.* ⬤*€13.* ☎ *0662/8736730. www.villacher-alpenstrasse.at*

This modern mountain road runs from Villach-Möltschach (550 m) up the Dobratsch as far as 1 732 m/5 700 ft. Many viewpoints have been constructed for views of Villach, the Julian Alps and Dobratsch tiself.

Alpengarten Villacher Alpe★

Access from parking lot P6. ⏰*June–Aug daily 9am–6pm.* ⬤*€2.* ☎ *042 42/5 91 38.*

This Alpine garden devoted to the flora of the southern Alps should not be missed. It covers an area of 10 000m²/11 960sq yd and is home to 900 types of Alpine plant, with explanatory panels.

Dobratsch★★

From the end of the road, a trail leads to the peak of the **Dobratsch** (alt 2 167m/7 107ft) in about 2hr. As a reward for your effort, you get to enjoy a famous **panorama** taking in the Karawanken, the Carinthian lakes, the Julian Alps and the Tauern.

Burg Landskron

5km/3mi north of Villach.

Kids A Habsburg stronghold in the Middle Ages, this castle passed to the Khevenhüller family in the 16C who refitted it in sumptuous style but later lost the place as punishment for supporting the Reformation. It is now a hotel-restaurant with a fabulous **view**★ of the Villach basin, the Karawanken and Ossiacher See from the terrace.

Not only kids will be impressed by the **flight demonstrations**★ (⏰*Jul–Aug daily 11am, 2.30pm, 5.30pm; May, June, Sep daily 11am, 2.30pm;* ⬤*€8;* ☎ *0 42 42/4 15 63)* staged at the castle and starring a cast of kites, falcons and eagles.

En route to Landskron, you pass the **Affenberg** (⏰*Apr–Oct daily 9.30am–5.30pm;* ⬤*€8;* ☎ *0 42 42/43 03 75; www.affenberg.com)* where a colony of Japanese macaco monkeys lives in the open countryside.

Ossiacher Lake★ ♿ *See Ossiacher See.*

VÖCKLABRUCK

OBERÖSTERREICH
POPULATION 12 000 – ALT 430M/1410FT

Vöcklabruck bestrides the old main road halfway between Salzburg and Linz and has a pedigree going back to the 12C. Today, the place is still a busy market town and educational center for the surrounding countryside. It also benefits from its proximity to the famous Salzkammergut tourist area and the nearby Attersee and Traunsee lakes. ▯ *Hinterstadt 14, A-4840, ☎ 0 76 72/2 66 44*

Sights

Stadtplatz
As is frequently the case in Austria, the town square is simply a widening of the main road. Most buildings are decorated with Baroque façades but are in fact much older, including no 14, which has an arcaded courtyard very much in the style of the Italian Renaissance. The square is bookended by two towers. One of them, the **Unterer Stadtturm** (Lower Tower), features the coats of arms of the various possessions of Burgundy as well as those of the Habsburgs. This is a visual reminder of the marriage of **Emperor Maximilian I**, who owned a house in town, to Mary of Burgundy.

Dörflkirche St. Ägidius
Leave the town via the Unterer Stadtturm and cross the river; the church is just over the bridge on the right. If the door is closed, ring at the presbytery. ☎ 0 76 72/7 26 08.
This elegant building is the successor to a much earlier church, first consecrated in 1143. It was built in 1688 by the architect **Carlo Antonio Carlone** and decorated by Giovanni Battista Carlone. Its Baroque splendor was restored in 1980.

WAIDHOFEN AN DER THAYA

NIEDERÖSTERREICH
POPULATION 5 650 – ALT 510M/1 673FT

Waidhofen is situated on the left bank of the River Thaya in bucolic surroundings of farmland and forest. The town grew up from a fortified settlement first recorded in 1171. The parish church stands on the highest point, while the town fortress was built on the lowest ground, to the east. ▯ *Bahnhofstr. 2, A-3830, ☎ 0 28 42/5 15 00, www.waidhofen-thaya.at*

▸ **Orient Yourself:** Waidhofen is in the Waldvietel, near the Czech border and about equidistant (120km/75mi) from Vienna and Linz.

⟳ **Also See:** Gmund (Lower Austria), Riegersburg

Sights

Altstadt
In the old town, the north promenade with the powder tower and the south promenade with a partially preserved defence tower are all that remain of the original fortifications. There are some interesting old houses along Wienerstraße (no 14, the Heimathaus), Böhmgasse and Pfarrgasse.

Hauptplatz

In the center of the town square stands the **Rathaus**, a beautiful example of an essentially Gothic town hall, even if it owes its stepped gables to the Renaissance. The ridge turret was added in 1721. The **Dreifaltigkeitssäule** column was put up in 1709 to protect the town from plague, fire and war.

Pfarrkirche

The church's modest, if finely proportioned, exterior offers no hint of its lavish Baroque interior. The vault of the nave is decorated with frescoes and stuccowork by Josef Michael Daysinger and depicts scenes from the life of Mary. The magnificent **high altar** (1721) fills the chancel with its lofty columns. Also note the beautifully carved **stalls** with a double-headed eagle on the upper part to symbolize the church's function in an Imperial parish, as well as the pulpit and the organ gallery.

Church, Waidhofen an der Thaya

R. Chéret/MICHELIN

ÖSTLICHES WEINVIERTEL

NIEDERÖSTERREICH

Austria's **Eastern Wine Country is still** a region somewhat off the beaten tourist track. Its remote position in Austria's far northeastern corner means that the countryside has remained relatively unspoiled. It is a delightful area filled with natural and cultural treasures. Be sure to sample the excellent local wine, preferably along a charming *Kellergasse*, a strip of tiny wine cellars.

▶ **Orient Yourself:** The Weinviertel is northeast of Vienna, rubbing up against the borders with the Czech Republic and Slovakia.

☺ **Don't Miss:** Weinviertler Museumsdorf, Kellergassen in Poysdorf

◷ **Organizing Your Time:** The Weinviertel makes for a nice day trip from Vienna.

Kids Especially for Kids: Weinviertler Museumsdorf, Museum für Urgeschichte

From Gänserndorf to Poysdorf 62km/39mi

☺ *Watch out for unmarked railway crossings along this drive!*

Start in the district capital of **Gänserndorf** *(26km/16mi northeast of Vienna; reached via the B 8)* and continue to Prottes.

Erdöl-Erdgas-Lehrpfad

Along the road from Gänserndorf to Prottes are numerous pumps, extracting oil or gas in perpetual motion. To learn more about the subject, follow the 4.5km/3mi educational trail through charming countryside starting at the affiliated **museum**

"Eing'richt"

This painstaking craft in which tiny scenes, mainly on religious themes, are patiently crafted – often from very simple materials – and then inserted *("eingerichtet")* into bottles used to keep many a farming family occupied on long winter evenings. A small collection of this naive art form is on display in the Niederösterreichisches Museum für Volkskultur in Gross-Schweinbarth.

(🕐*Easter Sun-Oct Sat-Sun & holidays 9.30am-11.30am, 2pm-4pm;* ⊜*€1.50;* ☎ *0 22 82/21 82*) in Prottes (*follow red and white markings*). Along the way you will encounter display panels with background information and numerous original pieces of machinery connected with the extraction of this raw material, including oil detection probes, mobile drilling gear, production derricks etc. There is no admission for the trail, which is open year-round.

▷   *Drive on via Matzen towards Gross-Schweinbarth.*

Niederösterreichisches Museum für Volkskultur

In Gross-Schweinbarth. *Right by the B 220; from Prottes keep left heading towards Gänserndorf.* 🕐*mid Apr-mid Nov Tue-Sun 9am-5pm.* ⊜*€4.* ☎ *0 22 89/23 02. www. museum.gross-schweinbarth.at.*
This museum of traditional regional culture (complete with wine section) has found the perfect home in an old dairy that once supplied the neighboring castle. Displays include traditional costumes, furniture and crockery as well as a broad range of items dealing with local customs, religious practices and craftwork. The history and role of the dairy farm is also explained. An entire wing is dedicated to amber, explaining the formation, extraction and use of this fossilized resin. There are even specimens enclosing 50 million-year-old animals, conjuring visions of "Jurassic Park."

▷   *Take the B 220 towards Pirawarth. At the exit to Gross-Schweinbarth turn right towards Hohenruppersdorf. From there head towards Zistersdorf and then to Niedersulz.*

Weinviertler Museumsdorf★

In Niedersulz. 🕐*Apr-Oct Mon-Fri 9.30am-4pm, Sat-Sun 10am-6pm.* ⊜*€6.50.* ☎ *0 25 34/3 33, www.museumsdorf.at.*
Kids This large open-air museum re-creates an entire Weinviertel village as it might have looked in pre-industrial times. More than 60 buildings, including farmhouses, barns, sheds, chapels and mills whose existence in their original sites had been threatened, have been reassembled here. The museum site has been planted with flora typical of the region. The realistic layout of houses around a central square, complete with church, inn, presbytery and even a graveyard, creates the impression of walking around a village whose inhabitants are all out working in the fields. The houses contain authentic furnishings or exhibitions on rural life. There's also a "living farm" where domestic and farm animals make their home.

The "living farm" at the Weinviertler Museumsdorf

M. Hertlein/MICHELIN

▶ *Drive on through Obersulz and Schrick towards* **Mistelbach**. *In Lanzendorf turn left and follow the signposts to "Schloss Asparn/Zaya – Museum für Urgeschichte".*

Asparn an der Zaya

This town at the foothills of the Leiser Berge boasts a fine ensemble of historic buildings. These include the **Baroque Minorite convent** from the18C, which now houses a museum on wine-growing and the local region; the elegant parish church of St Pancras and St Francis; and the Renaissance castle with its prehistory museum.

Museum für Urgeschichte

In the castle. ⏱Apr-late Nov Tue-Fri 9am-5pm, Sat-Sun 10am-6pm. ⊛€3.50, audio-guide €1.50. ☏ 0 25 77/80 39. www.urgeschichte.com

Exhibits at this prehistory museum illustrate the evolution of humankind and human culture through to the year 1C. There are reproductions of cave paintings from Altamira, Lascaux and other famous sites alongside jewelry, ceramics, tools and many other objects once in use thousands of years ago.

The **open-air museum**★ behind the castle is a particular highlight, with reconstructions of walk-in dwellings from the Paleolithic Age to the New Iron Age (25 000 BC to 2C AD)

▶ *From Asparn drive on towards Hörersdorf and then turn left onto the B 46 to Laa an der Thaya.*

Burgruine Staatz

At the Laa-Poysdorf crossroads, carry straight on, following the signposts to "Ruine." Park by the Musikerheim and walk along the fortified wall. Guided tours (1hr) May-Oct Sun and holidays 3pm.

The castle ruins can be seen from miles away perching on the relatively low Staatzer Berg (331m/1 086ft). From the top, there is a sweeping **view**★★ across the Weinviertel and the Carpathian mountains to the northeast.

▶ *Carry on to Poysdorf.*

Shortly before reaching Poysdorf, the road passes the **pilgrimage church of Maria Bründl** in an idyllic, tree-shaded setting. It was completed in 1751 according to plans by Italian architect Donato Felice d'Allio, who was also the mastermind behind the abbey church at Klosterneuburg (see entry).

Poysdorf

The self-titled "wine town of Austria," which ironically produces mostly sparkling wine *(Sekt)*, is a great place for exploring the romantic *Kellergassen*. Particularly fine examples of these wine-cellar-lined lanes can be found in Bürsting *(via Singergasse from the tourist office)* and on Berggasse *(below the parish church)*. A 1hr loop trail on the theme of *Kellergassen* leaving from the Stadtmuseum also takes in some of the delightful vineyards on the edge of town *(follow the beige-white markers)*. From May to October, wine-growers take turns in opening their premises for public tours and wine tasting sessions.

WELS

OBERÖSTERREICH
POPULATION 56 500 – ALT 317M/1 040FT

Wels on the Traun River evolved from a small Celtic settlement into the Roman town of Ovilava, which became an important supply center and was eventually raised to the status of colony. Today, it is the second-largest town in Lower Austria after Linz and known for its trade fairs and lovely historic town. 🛈 *Stadtplatz 55, A-4600,* ☎ *0 72 42/4 34 95*

▶ **Orient Yourself:** Wels is about 35km/22mi southwest of Linz.
🅿 **Parking:** There are pay parking garages on Kaiser-Josef-Platz, below the Traun-park Hotel and on the Marktplatz. Parking is free at the Messe on non-trade show days.
🕓 **Organizing Your Time:** Taking in all the museums, it's easy to make a day of it in Wels.
🔢 **Especially for Kids:** Zoo Schmiding
👶 **Also See:** Lambach, Stadt-Paura, Schloss-Museum Hohenbrunn

Sights

Stadtplatz
Wels' historic town centers on the elongated **Stadtplatz**★, the main square with a flower-bedecked fountain and rows of attractive buildings, mostly sporting Baroque façades. The golden **Rathaus** (town hall) is certainly striking, although the star of the parade is the **Haus der Salome Alt** at no 24, named after a mistress of Wolf Dietrich of Raitenau, the prince-archbishop of Salzburg. Distinctive features include the Late Gothic oriel and the Renaissance fresco paintings.

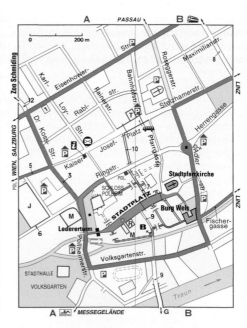

WELS		
Adlerstr.	B	
Altstadtgasse	B	2
Bäckergasse	A	10
Bahnhofstr.	A	
Dragonerstr.	A	5
Dr-Koss.-Str.	A	
Dr-Salzmann-Str.	A	3
Dr-Schauer-Str.	B	8
Eisenhower-Str.	A	
Herrengasse	B	
Kaiser-Josef-Pl.	A	
Karl-Loy-Str.	A	
Maria-Theresia-Str.	A	6
Maximilianstr.	B	
Pfarrgasse	B	
Pollheimerstr.	A	
Rainerstr.	A	
Ringstr.	A	
Roseggerstr.	B	
Schmidtgasse	B	7
Stadtpl.	B	
Stelzhamerstr.	B	
Traungasse	B	9
Vogelweiderstr.	A	12
Volksgartenstr.	AB	
Wegkapelle	B	B

North of this house is the **Stadtpfarrkirche** (B), the local parish church, with some fine 14C stained-glass windows in the chancel. To the south looms the Kaiserliche Burg, the imperial castle. The western end of the Stadtplatz is punctuated by the 13C **Ledererturm** (Leather Tower) (A), the last surviving town gate.

Burg Wels (B)

Tue-Fri 10am-5pm, Sat 2-5pm, Sun 10am-4pm. €3.70. 0 72 42/2 35 73 50.
The restored imperial castle, where Emperor Maximilian I died in 1519, now houses four **museum collections**: the Local History Museum, with a remarkable display of Biedermeier items; the Museum of Agriculture, arranged on the theme of the "farmer's year"; the Austrian Museum of Baking, the only one of its kind; and the Museum of Displaced Persons.

Stadtmuseum Minoritenkloster (A R)

Minoritengasse 5. *Tue-Fri 10am-5pm, Sat 2pm-5pm.* €3.70. 0 72 42/23 56 94.
Each excavation within the town uncovers yet more evidence of its past, particularly the Roman period. This has resulted in a particularly rich archaeological collection housed In a former monastery. One section re-creates a mock Roman village where you can peek inside tradesmen's workshops, private living quarters and tombs.

Excursion

Zoo Schmiding★

In Krengelbach. *7km/4mi north of Wels.* *daily 9am-7pm (last admission 5pm).* €11. 0 72 49/1 62 72. www.zooschmiding.at

What once used to be merely a bird park has evolved into a full-fledged, modern zoo where animals live in re-created habitats. These include a tropical rainforest (squirrel monkeys, crocodiles, sloths, etc) and the African Savannah (zebras, giraffes, etc). Another highlight is the giant aviary inhabited by birds of prey.

A resident of Zoo Schmiding

Vogelpark Schmiding

WIEN★★★

VIENNA
POPULATION 1 539 848, ALT 156M/512FT
LOCAL MAPS SEE DONAUTAL AND WIENERWALD
HOTELS AND RESTAURANTS: SEE THE RED GUIDE EUROPE
FOR LONGER VISITS TO THE CITY, CONSULT THE GREEN GUIDE VIENNA

Vienna was the residence of the Imperial court for six centuries and is indelibly stamped with the seal of the Habsburg dynasty. Even now as capital of the Republic of Austria, Vienna has retained its incomparable grandeur and considerable prestige as one of Europe's most important cultural and artistic centers. For many, the name Vienna evokes the rhythm of the waltz or the shape of the Prater's Giant Wheel. The city's global renown, however, is due above all to its historic buildings, to the magnificent art collections, to its excellent museums, to the musical tradition preserved by the opera and Vienna's famous choirs and orchestras, and to the elegance of the shops lining its grand avenues. Even politically Vienna plays a pivotal role on the world stage as the permanent headquarters of OPEC (Organization of Petroleum Exporting Countries) since 1965. Several UN organizations, including the International Atomic Energy Agency (IAEA), are also based in the city. ▯ *Am Albertinaplatz 1, A-1025, ☏ 01/21 11 40*

Michaelertor, entrance to the Hofburg

3BIS/MICHELIN

Address Book

PRACTICAL INFORMATION

TOURIST INFORMATION

If arriving by car -

From the north: Floridsdorfer Brücke, "Donauinsel" exit (May-Sep daily 9am-7pm). **From the south** (via A2): "Zentrum" exit (Jul-Sep 8am-10pm, week before Easter-Jun, Oct 9am-7pm). **From the west** via A1: Wien/Auhof gas station (Apr-Oct 8am-10pm, Nov-Mar 10am-6pm).

If arriving by rail –

Westbahnhof (Apr-Oct 7am-10pm). **Südbahnhof** (May-Oct 6.30am-10pm; Nov-Apr 6.30am-9pm).

If arriving by air –

Wien-Schwechat airport (daily 8.30am-9pm; 01/70 07 3 28 75).

City center: Am Albertinaplatz 1, 1. Bezirk (district). daily 9am-7pm, 01/21 11 40. The tourist office publishes a free monthly cultural calendar of events.

Vienna on the Internet:
www.info.wien.at (tourist information); www.wien.gv.at (city government); www.aboutvienna.org (cultural and tourist information).

WIENKARTE

The **Vienna Card** (€18.50; www.wienkarte.at) entitles to unlimited travel on the city's underground/subway (U-Bahn), bus, tram and most night buses for 72hr, starting from the moment it is first validated. In addition, you qualify for four consecutive days of discounts at museums, sights and attractions, and for certain purchases and meals. Full details are included in the coupon booklet that comes with the ticket. It is available from many hotels, tourist information offices, some ticket agencies and information offices belonging to the Viennese transport authorities (Wiener Linien; for example, Stephansplatz, Karlsplatz, Westbahnhof) or online using a credit card.

CITY TOURS

City bus tours

Vienna Sightseeing Tours, *Stelzhamergasse 4/11, 3. Bezirk,* 01/71 24 68 30. City tour with the "Vienna Line Hop on Hop off". This operates hourly between 13 stops (for example, Staatsoper, Heldenplatz, Prater) from 9.30am to 6.10pm. Commentaries in English and German. Cost of a ticket valid for two days is 250S, available from any hotel in Vienna, or any travel agency in Austria as well as abroad.

Cityrama, *Börsegasse 1, 1. Bezirk,* 01/53 41 30. City tours daily at 9.30am and 2.30pm with a guided tour of Schloss Schönbrunn. Takes about 3hr 30min. Tour costs 400S per person (including pick-up from hotel).

Robin Reisen-Stattwerkstatt, *Kolingasse 6, 9. Bezirk,* 01/3 17 33 84. City tour entitled "Dream and Reality" focussing on Jugendstil and "Red Vienna" (1920s social-democrat housing projects). Departures: Tues and Thur at 1pm, Sat at 10am, sometimes also at 2pm. Takes about 3hr. Tour costs 330S. Booking necessary.

Round tour in an old-fashioned tram – Early May-early Oct, Sat and Sun and public holidays at 11.30am and 1pm. On Sun and public holidays the "Oldtimer" tram also runs at 9.30am. Departure from Karlsplatz. Takes about 1hr. Tickets available from "Wiener Linien" information office at Karlsplatz U-Bahn station. 01/7 90 94 40 26.

City tour by horse-drawn carriage – The horse-drawn carriage stands are located on Albertinaplatz behind the Staatsoper as well as on Heldenplatz and Stephansplatz.

Vienna on foot – The city of Vienna organises themed walks around town, such as Musical Capital of the World, Jugendstil, Unadulterated Habsburgs, The Viennese Coffee-house, Old Houses and Quiet Courtyards, Underground Vienna. Takes about 90min. Monthly programme available from the tourist office at Albertinaplatz 1.

City tour with a difference "On the Trail of the Third Man" – This tour naturally takes place underground in the Viennese sewer system: greetings from Orson Welles's classic film "The Third Man". The tour (which takes about 25min) leaves from opposite the Café

Diejun/ÖSTERREICH WERBUNG

Horse-drawn carriage

Museum (JS) in the Esperantopark (cross Friedrichstraße, ticket office in metal container). During heavy rain, tours understandably do not take place; only children older than 12 years old are admitted; sturdy closed-in footwear is recommended; tour participants should have a good command of German. If all these criteria are met, this tour is a lively and interesting experience, full of all kinds of surprises. Advance booking and information from MA 30 – *WienKanal, A-1030 Wien, Friedrichstraße/Esperantopark*, ☎ *01/5 85 64 55.*

Cycle tours – Cyclists in Vienna have some 700km/435mi of cycle paths at their disposal. Those arriving in Vienna by train can hire bicycles from the following stations: West- and Südbahnhof, Wien Nord and Florisdorf, and Franz-Josefs-Bahnhof. These can be returned at any station with luggage check-in facilities. Further cycle hire outlets can be found on the Donauinsel or at the Hundertwasserhaus (cost from about 40S per hour with some form of identification such as a passport left as a security).

"Pedal Power" cycle tours through Vienna are offered in various languages May-Sept daily at 10am; takes about 3hr; 280S (180S with your own bicycle); further details from ☎ *01/7 29 72 34.* The brochure entitled **Tips für Radfahrer**, available free from tourist offices, gives full details of the above.

Boat tours – DDSG Blue Danube Schiffahrt GmbH offers boat tours on the Danube Apr-late Oct; for example a Hundertwasser tour on the *Vindobona* (departure from Schwedenplatz, takes 1hr 30min). Details from DDSG Blue Danube Schiffahrt GmbH, Friedrichstraße 7, A-1010 Wien, b 01/58 88 00, Fax 01/58 88 04 40.

Air tours – *Vienna Aircraft Handling, Hangar 3, A-1300 Flughafen Wien-Schwechat,* ☎ *01/70 07 2 22 04, Fax 01/70 07 2 24 64* offers airborne circuits (30min) in a CESSNA 210 (single-engine plane). Recommended price: 1 100S per person.

PUBLIC TRANSPORT

Viennese transport authorities, Wiener Linien, operate services in the central zones of the Vienna city area (all districts) and are linked with the east Austrian transport authority (Verkehrsverbund Ost-Region, VOR). Written enquiries and requests for information by telephone can be addressed to either organisation:

Wiener Linien, *Erdbergstraße 202, A-1031 Wien,* ☎ *01/79 09 105.*

Verkehrsverbund Ost-Region, *Neubaugasse 1, A-1070 Wien, information hotline* ☎ *08 10/22 23 24.*

Further details on public transport in Vienna are to be found on the Internet at the relevant Web site *www.wienerlinien.co.at or www.vor.at.*

Tourists in Vienna are advised to pay a visit in person to one of the **information and ticket offices** in the following U-Bahn stations: Stephansplatz, Schwedenplatz, Karlsplatz, Landstraße/Wien-Mitte, Westbahnhof, Spittelau, Schottentor, Reumannplatz, Philadelphiabrücke, Hietzing, Florisdorf or Kagran. *To find your way around: a map of the U-Bahn network is included on the city map published by the Vienna tourist office and available from most hotels, among other places.* These outlets can also supply timetables for Vienna's transport system or the more comprehensive timetable book, as well as selling tickets (runabout or magnetic strip tickets).

Tickets – Tickets are valid for travel on the underground/subway (U-Bahn), tram, high-speed rail (Schnellbahn) and bus. Single tickets can be validated using ticket machines on the transport in question or in U-Bahn stations. It is cheaper, however, to buy tickets in advance from ticket offices or an authorised tobacconist's (Tabaktrafik). Tickets that are well-suited to the needs of tourists include the **24-** (60S) and **72-** (150S) **hour runabout ticket** or the **8-day ticket** (300S; this allows the bearer unlimited travel within Vienna city center limits per strip validated, on the date it was validated). The "**Wiener Einkaufskarte**" (Viennese shopper's ticket) offers another interesting deal: for 50S you can make unlimited trips in the city center for one day (between Mon and Sat) 8am-8pm.

Of course, there is always the option of the "Wien-Karte" (*see above*), which allows three days of unlimited travel on Viennese public transport.

Night line – When normal city transport finishes running for the day (after about 12.30am until about 4.30am), 22 night bus lines operate in the city center every 30min, for which special rates apply (runabout tickets are not valid on these night buses; single ticket 15S; tickets available from ticket machines on the bus or as strip tickets bought in advance – 45S for four trips). Further details and a map of the night line services are available from indicated Vienna transport authority ticket offices.

INNER CITY CAR PARKS
Vienna old town and the surrounding districts (Bezirke 1-9 and 20) are

fee-paying short-stay parking zones. However, these are only signposted as such at the entrance to each district concerned (no further indication is given in the streets themselves – a paid-up parking ticket is obligatory from the minute you park). In commercial streets, parking regulations may vary, for example concerning how long you may park, in which case these will be specifically indicated. Pre-paid parking tickets can be bought from most authorised tobacconists (Tabaktrafiken) and banks, stations and from Vienna transport authority (Wiener Linien) ticket offices. Visitors who have booked a hotel should phone ahead of their arrival and confirm where to leave their car.

The most practical solution to the difficulty of parking in the city center is offered by numerous multi-storey or underground **car parks**, which are open daily 24hr/24hr. In the 1. Bezirk these are the following underground car parks: *Am Morzinplatz (Franz-Josefs-Kai), Rathauspark (Ring/Stadiongasse), Operngarage (Kärntner Straße 51), Am Hof, Beethovenplatz 3, Cobdengasse 2.* An overview of car parks in Vienna can be requested from the tourist office (☎ 01/21 11 42 22) or found on the Internet *(www.wkw.at/garagen).*

POST OFFICES
The second and third digit in Viennese **post codes** denote the district (Bezirk) in question, thus 1070 denotes the 7. Bezirk, Vienna.
The main post offices are open daily 24hr/24hr:
Hauptpostamt, *Fleischmarkt 19, 1. Bezirk*, ☎ 01/51 50 90
Post am Westbahnhof, *Mariahilfer Straße 132, 15. Bezirk*, ☎ 01/89 11 50
Post am Franz-Josef-Bahnhof, *Althahnstraße 10, 9. Bezirk*, ☎ 01/3 19 14 70

SHOPPING
Most department stores and specialist boutiques are located in the pedestrian zones in Kärntner Straße, Graben, Kohlmarkt, Naglergasse, Tuchlauben, Stephansplatz, part of Krugerstraße and Franz-Josefs-Kai, Wolfengasse, Seitenstettengasse, Rabensteig, Griechen-

gasse, Ballgasse and Vienna's main shopping street – **Mariahilfer Straße**.

SOUVENIRS

Augarten GmbH, *Stock-im-Eisen-Platz 3-4, 1. Bezirk*. In Schloss Augarten, 2. Bezirk. Sales outlet for the famous porcelain manufacturer, whose origins date back to 1717.

Backhausen, *Kärntner Straße 33, 1. Bezirk*. This textile factory sells furnishing materials, curtains and silk scarves with Jugendstil designs.

Frimmel, *Freisingergasse 1, 1. Bezirk*. This is *the* shop for buttons, which used to supply the Imperial court.

J. & L. Lobmeyr, *Kärntner Straße 26, 1. Bezirk*. A glassware specialist which used to supply the Imperial court, and which is famous for its extremely fragile and delicate "Musselinglas".

Maria Stransky, *Hofburg. Burgpassage 2, 1. Bezirk*. This is the home of typical Viennese petit point embroidery.

Piatnik, *Kandlgasse 33, 7. Bezirk*. This establishment founded at the end of the 19C sells such beautiful playing cards that they can almost rank as works of art.

Schau Schau Brillen, *Rotenturmstraße 11, 1. Bezirk*. Spectacles in the strangest shapes are the speciality here, signed by Peter Kozich. One of his clients is no less a figure than Elton John.

FOOD MARKETS

Naschmarkt, *Linke Wienzeile/Kettenbrückengasse. 4. and 6. Bezirk*. This is divided into the **Naschmarkt** proper (fruit and vegetables): Mon-Fri 6am-6.30pm, Sat 6am-5pm, and the **Bauernmarkt** (farm produce): Mon-Thur 6am-noon, Fri 6am-1pm, Sat 6am-5pm.

Markt auf der Freyung, 1. Bezirk, May-Nov Tues and Thur 10am-6.30pm.

FLEA MARKETS

Naschmarkt: *Linke Wienzeile. 4. and 6. Bezirk*. The flea market is located at the south end of the Naschmarkt: Sat 6am-6pm.

Art and antiques markets
Kunst- und Antikmarkt am Donaukanal (art and antiques market on the promenade along the banks of the Danube on the old town side by the

Augarten porcelain workshop

Marienbrücke, 1. Bezirk): May-Sept Sat 2-8pm, Sun 10am-8pm.

Am Hof (1. Bezirk): Mar-Christmas Fri and Sat 10am-8pm.

Kunst- und Handwerksmarkt im Heiligenkreuzerhof (art and crafts market, *Schönlaterngasse, 1. Bezirk*): every first weekend in the month, in Dec every weekend.

CHRISTMAS MARKETS

Christkindlmarkt Rathausplatz mid Nov-Christmas

Weihnachtsmarkt am Spittelberg late Nov-Christmas

Altwiener Christkindlmarkt Freyung late Nov-Christmas

Kultur- und Weihnachtsmarkt in front of Schloss Schönbrunn late Nov-Christmas

Kunsthandwerksmarkt in front of Karlskirche late Nov-Christmas

ENTERTAINMENT

THEATER

Burgtheater, *Dr.-Karl-Lueger-Ring 2, 1. Bezirk*. ☏ *01/5 14 44 44 40*. A European theater offering the entire range of theatrical repertoire. Tickets sold in advance from the 20th of the month preceding the month in question, for the whole calendar month. Written applications for tickets should be addressed at least 10 days in advance of the date in question to the Servicecenter Burgtheater, *Hanuschgasse 3, A-1010 Wien (Fax 01/5 14 44 41 47)*. Tickets can be ordered by telephone (payment by credit card) daily 10am-9pm from ☏ *01/51 31 513*. For performances that are not sold out, tickets can be obtained at 50% of their original price from 1hr

H. Wiesenhofer/ÖSTERREICH WERBUNG

before the performance starts from the "Abendkasse" (☎ 01/51 44 44 44 0). Other theaters linked with the Burgtheater are the **Akademietheater** (Lisztstraße 1, 3. Bezirk, ☎ 01/51 44 44 740) and the **Kasino** (Schwarzenbergplatz 1, 3. Bezirk, ☎ 01/51 44 44 830).

Theater in der Josefstadt, Josefstädter Straße 24, 8. Bezirk. ☎ 01/42 70 03 00. Venue for theatrical productions since 1788, where such famous Austrian names as Nestroy and Raimund made their debut: both classic and modern theater.

Volkstheater, Neustiftgasse 1, 7. Bezirk, ☎ 01/524 72 63. Broad spectrum of plays from the classics to the avant-garde.

gruppe 80, Gumpendorfer Straße 67, 6. Bezirk, ☎ 01/586 52 22. Predominantly Austrian plays from the classics to contemporary drama.

Schauspielhaus, Porzellangasse 19, 9. Bezirk, ☎ 01/3 17 01 01. Young, unconventional theater.

Komödie am Kai, Franz-Josefs-Kai 29, 1. Bezirk, ☎ 01/533 24 34. Popular comedies from all over the world for a pleasant evening.

English Theater, Josefsgasse 12, 8. Bezirk, ☎ 01/40 21 26 00. English-language theater productions from both Britain and America have been staged here since 1963 (classics, comedies, guest performances by solo artists).

MUSICAL VENUES

Staatsoper (Herbert-von-Karajan-Platz, 1. Bezirk) and **Volksoper** (Wahringer Straße 78, 9. Bezirk) – the opera venues of the Austrian capital. Tickets go on sale one month before the performance date. Written applications for tickets must be submitted at least three weeks before the performance to the Österreichischer Bundestheaterverband, Bestellbüro, Hanuschgasse 3, A-1010 Wien. Tickets can be ordered by telephone (payment by credit card) from ☎ 01/5 13 15 13. Remainder tickets can be purchased from the Bundestheater ticket offices, Hanuschgasse 3, ☎ 01/51 44 29 60 or from the Volksoper itself (Mon-Fri 8am-6pm, Sat, Sun and public holidays 9am-noon). For programme details call b 01/15 18 (recorded message).

Neue Oper Wien: The independent opera group, which stages only a few productions per year, has dedicated itself to premieres and 20C works that have some relevance to current affairs and that concern humanitarian and social-political matters. Information on the programme and performances from ☎ 01/5 97 30 37 or on the Internet at Web site (www.neueoperwien.music.at).

Musikverein: Vienna's association for friends of music (Bösendorferstr. 12, A-1010 Wien, ☎ 01/5 05 81 90, Fax 01/5 05 81 94) puts on about 500 concerts of classical music per year. Tickets go on sale about three weeks before the concert date, Mon-Fri 9am-7.30pm, Sat 9am-5pm. For programme details call ☎ 01/5 05 13 63 (recorded message).

Concerts by the Vienna Boys' Choir (Wiener Sängerknaben): The Vienna Boys' Choir perform from Apr-June and Sept-Oct Fri at 4pm in the Brahms Room at the Musikvereins. Tickets (390-550S) are on sale in hotels and from Reisebüro Mondial (travel agent's), Faulmanngasse 4, A-1040 Wien, ☎ 01/58 80 41 41, Fax 01/5 87 12 68, e-mail: ticket@mondial.at

Sung Masses in the Burgkapelle at the Hofburg on Sundays and 25 Dec (with the Vienna Boys' Choir and members of the chorus and orchestra of the Vienna State Opera): These begin at 9.15am. Seats cost 60 to 340S; there is no charge for standing room. Orders must be placed in writing (please do not enclose either cash or cheques) at least 10 weeks in advance to: Hofmusikkapelle, Hofburg, A-1010 Wien, Fax 01/5 33 99 27 75. Collection and payment of pre-ordered tickets is on Fri 11am-1pm and 3-5pm or on Sun from 8.15-8.45am in the Burgkapelle. Availability permitting, tickets for seats for a particular Sun are sold at the Burgkapelle Tageskasse from 3-5pm on the immediately preceding Fri.

Wiener Konzerthaus, Lothringerstraße 20, 3. Bezirk, ☎ 01/7 12 12 11. Orchestra and soloists from all over the world as well as performances by the concert house's resident company. Top-quality **musical productions** are presented by Vereinigte Bühnen Wien GmbH (Linke Wienzeile 6, A-1060 Wien,

☎ 01/58 83 02 00, Web site: www. musicalvienna.at), which incorporates three venues:

Theater an der Wien, Linke Wienzeile 6, 6. Bezirk.

Raimund-Theater, Wallgasse 18-20, 6. Bezirk.

Ronacher, Seilerstätte 9, 1. Bezirk.

WUK, Währinger Straße 59, 9. Bezirk, ☎ 01/4 01 21 10. Self-administered "**W**erkstätten- **u**nd **K**ulturhaus" (workshops and cultural center): music, dance, concerts, readings and exhibitions.

Szene Wien, Hauffgasse 26, 11. Bezirk, ☎ 01/74 93 341. Live concerts by advertised bands, world music.

Planet Music, Adalbert-Stifter-Straße 73, 20. Bezirk, ☎ 01/3 32 46 41. Venue for all sorts of musical varieties – hip-hop, pop through Blues, reggae, jazz to rock and heavy metal. There are also events specially for children and families.

Ticket reservations – The following organisation also deals with ticket reservations from abroad, principally for musicals and classical music: **Vienna Ticket Service**, Börsegasse 1, A-1010 Wien, ☎ 01/5 34 17 75 (Mon-Fri 9am-5pm, Fax 01/5 34 17 26). For rock and pop concerts, contact **Österreich Ticket**, Kärtner Straße 19, (1. Bezirk, Kaufhaus Steffel, 3. Stock), A-1010 Wien, ☎ 01/96 0 96 (Mon to Sat 9am-9pm, Sun 10am-9pm).

OTHER VENUES

Orpheum, Steigenteschgasse 94b, 22. Bezirk, ☎ 01/481 17 17. Entertainment venue (with adjoining inn – ☎ 01/2 03 12 54), in which cabaret, music and readings are on offer.

Kulisse, Rosensteingasse 39, 17. Bezirk, ☎ 01/485 38 70. Musicals, cabaret, children's theater and its own inn (☎ 01/4 85 44 02).

Wiener Metropol, Hernalser Hauptstraße 55, 17. Bezirk, ☎ 01/40 777 40. Venue for concerts (ballads and songs, world music), cabaret and home-produced musical productions.

Vindobona, Wallensteinplatz, 20. Bezirk, ☎ 01/3 32 42 31. The place to go for cabaret; Sat and Sun children's theater. There is also a restaurant close at hand

so that visitors will be well taken care of all evening.

MISCELLANEOUS

Spanische Reitschule: Ticket reservations for performances (gala performances, 80min, seats 250-900S, standing room 200S; classic displays of riding skills to music, 60min, 250S) should be addressed as far in advance as possible to the Spanische Reitschule, Hofburg, A-1010 Wien, Fax 01/53 50 186, e-mail: office@srs.at, or alternatively to authorised Vienna theater ticket offices or travel agencies (there will be a supplementary charge of at least 22% in this case). Reservations are not necessary for morning training sessions ("Training der Lipizzaner"). Tickets (100S) for this can be bought on the same day at the entrance to the Spanische Reitschule (Hofburg, Josefsplatz).

A folder in several languages is available from the Vienna tourist office giving details of precise dates and terms and conditions.

Casino Wien, Palais Esterházy, Kärntner Straße 41, 1. Bezirk, ☎ 01/5 12 48 36.

CINEMAS

The following are only a small selection, away from the mainstream, of the numerous cinemas that there are in Vienna. For the current cinema programme and additional addresses, consult wienside, the weekly calendar of events available from cinemas, local "in" bars etc or the daily press.

Österreichisches Filmarchiv, Obere Augartenstraße 1, 2. Bezirk, ☎ 01/2 16 13 00. Classics from the history of film.

Schikaneder Kino, Margarethenstraße 24, 4. Bezirk, ☎ 01/5 85 28 67. Small-screen, committed mainly to recent arts films.

Votiv Kino, Währinger Straße 12, 9. Bezirk, ☎ 01/3 17 35 71. Preview cinema.

Imax-Filmtheater (next to the Technisches Museum, AZ), Mariahilfer Straße 212, 14. Bezirk, ☎ 01/8 94 01 01; info hotline: 01/15 47.

(Especially English-language) films in their original versions are shown at:

Burg, Opernring 19, 1. Bezirk, ☎ 01/5 87 84 06. In summer, but also on most weekends throughout the year, Carol Reed's **The Third Man** is screened here.

English Cinema Haydn, *Mariahilfer Straße 57, 6. Bezirk,* ☎ *01/5 87 22 62.*

American Flotten Center, *Mariahilfer Straße 85-87, 6. Bezirk,* ☎ *01/5 86 51 52.*

WHERE TO STAY

The following lists of hotels and restaurants make a distinction between three categories: "Budget" includes addresses that are within the means of even modest budgets. "Our selection" regroups hotels or restaurants which offer a slightly higher level of comfort at correspondingly higher prices. "Treat yourself!" denotes really outstanding establishments – a taste of luxury that it would probably not be possible to afford every day.

BUDGET

Pension Franz – *Währinger Str. 12, 9. Bezirk,* ☎ *01/34 36 37, Fax 01/34 36 37 23.* Family guesthouse with decor in the style of the turn of the 19C-20C. 24 rooms. Single room from 590S.

Pension Pertschy – *Habsburger-gasse 5, 1. Bezirk,* ☎ *01/53 44 90, Fax 01/5 34 49 49.* Family guesthouse in a 250 year old Baroque palace with Louis XV style furniture. 47 rooms. Single room from 700S.

Zur Wiener Staatsoper – *Kruger-str. 11, 1. Bezirk,* ☎ *01/5 13 12 74, Fax 01/51 31 27 41 5.* Grand Viennese town house, small friendly hotel, with rooms furnished with period furniture. 22 rooms. Single room from 900S.

Kaiserpark Schönbrunn – *Grünberg-str. 11, 12. Bezirk,* ☎ *01/81 38 61 00, Fax 01/8 13 81 83.* City hotel right next to Schloss Schönbrunn. 45 rooms. Single room from 900S.

Park-Villa – *Hasenauerstr. 12, 19. Bezirk,* ☎ *01/3 19 10 05, Fax 01/3 19 10 05 41.* Jugendstil building dating from 1888, tasteful rooms, pleasant area to stay. 21 rooms. Single room from 950S.

Landhaus Fuhrgassl-Huber – *Rathstr. 24, 19. Bezirk,* ☎ *01/4 40 30 33, Fax 01/4 40 27 14.* Country house in the middle of the Heurige district, furnished with period and rustic furniture; quiet rooms facing the garden. 22 rooms. Single room from 960S.

OUR SELECTION

Theater-Hotel in der Josefs-tadt – *Josefstädter Str. 22, 8. Bezirk,* ☎ *01/4 05 36 48, Fax 01/4 05 14 06.* Modernised inner city hotel near the Ringstraße. 54 rooms. Single room from 1 250S.

Am Stephansplatz – *Stephans-platz 9, 1. Bezirk,* ☎ *01/53 40 50, Fax 01/53 40 57 10.* Located directly opposite the Stephansdom; rooms at the front have a view of the cathedral. 60 rooms. Single room from 1 330S.

Dorint Rogner Hotel Biedermeier im Sünnhof – *Landstraßer Haupt-str. 28, 3. Bezirk,* ☎ *01/71 67 10, Fax 01/71 67 15 03.* Biedermeier style room decor. 203 rooms. Single room from 1 550S.

König von Ungarn – *Schulerstr. 10, 1. Bezirk,* ☎ *01/51 58 40, Fax 01/51 58 48.* Comfortable little hotel redolent of Vienna in the old days. 33 rooms. Single room from 1 610S.

TREAT YOURSELF!

Sacher – *Philharmonikerstr. 4, 1. Bezirk,* ☎ *01/5 14 56, Fax 01/51 45 68 10.* Vienna's classic Grand Hotel – and home of the world-renowned Sachertorte. 108 rooms. Single room from 2 500S.

Im Palais Schwarzenberg – *Schwarzenbergplatz 9, 3. Bezirk,* ☎ *01/7 98 45 15, Fax 01/7 98 4/ 14.* Former royal palace from the 18C, novel decor with some antiques, 7.5ha/18.5 acre private park. 44 rooms. Single room from 3 000S.

EATING OUT

BUDGET

Figlmüller – *Wollzeile 5, 1. Bezirk,* ☎ *01/5 12 61 77,* main dishes starting at 80S. One of several local eateries serving the famous Wiener Schnitzel.

Pfudl – *Bäckerstr. 22, 1. Bezirk,* ☎ *01/5 12 67 05,* main dishes starting at 85S. Ranks among the inns that have become a Viennese institution.

Haas & Haas – *Stephansplatz 4, 1. Bezirk,* ☎ *01/5 13 19 16,* main dishes starting at 95S. One of the most popular local restaurants in the immediate vicinity of the cathedral; in the evening the cathedral garden is a pleasant place to sit.

OUR SELECTION

Fadinger – *Wipplingerstr. 29, 1. Bezirk,* ☎ *01/5 33 43 41,* main dishes starting at 120S. A simple bar at the front, with a more sophisticated restaurant at the back, serving interesting modern Viennese dishes.

Eckel – *Sieveringer Str. 46, 19. Bezirk,* ☎ *01/3 20 32 18,* main dishes starting at 130S. Cosy rustic restaurant with an elegant side room.

Hedrich – *Stubenring 2, 1. Bezirk,* ☎ *01/5 12 95 88,* main dishes starting at 165S. Simple restaurant, calling itself a fast-food restaurant, but which in reality offers an interesting regional menu at a very reasonable price.

Vikerl's Lokal – *Würffelgasse 4, 15. Bezirk,* ☎ *01/8 94 34 30,* main dishes starting at 165S. Really comfortable little local restaurant with wooden panelling where Viennese nouvelle cuisine is on the menu.

Hietzinger Bräu – *Auhofstr. 1, 13. Bezirk,* ☎ *01/87 77 08 70,* main dishes starting at 170S. The classic restaurant for Viennese Tafelspitz (boiled beef and vegetable stew) and other beef dishes.

K & K Restaurant Piaristenkeller – *Piaristengasse 45, 8. Bezirk (below the Piaristenkirche),* ☎ *01/406 01 93,* main dishes starting at 175S. In a 300 year old vaulted cellar where traditional Viennese dishes are served, there is the additional option of visiting two museums – the Kaiser-Franz-Joseph Hat Museum (souvenir photos are available, of visitors taking part in the "Old-style Viennese Hat Parade") and the K & K Weinschatzkammer (treasure trove of four centuries of wines from the Imperial wine cellars). For further details, consult the Internet (*www.piaristenkeller.com*).

Plachutta – *Wollzeile 38, 1. Bezirk,* ☎ *01/5 12 15 77,* main dishes starting at 185S. Restaurant dedicated to the Viennese beef tradition.

Salut – *Wildpretmarkt 3, 1. Bezirk,* ☎ *01/5 33 13 22,* main dishes starting at 185S. Small friendly restaurant in several welcoming rooms in the city center.

Hauswirth – *Otto-Bauer-Gasse 20, 6. Bezirk,* ☎ *01/5 87 12 61,* main dishes starting at 190S. Typical Viennese restaurant with a pretty garden in the courtyard.

Cantinetta Antinori – *Jasomirgottstr. 3, 1. Bezirk,* ☎ *01/5 33 77 22,* main dishes starting at 200S. The Italian restaurant in the 1.Bezirk.

Windows of Vienna – *Wienerbergstr. 7, 10. Bezirk,* ☎ *01/6 07 94 80,* main dishes starting at 200S. Restaurant on the 22nd floor of a business center, with an excellent view of Vienna and its surroundings.

Mraz & Sohn – *Wallensteinstr. 59, 20. Bezirk,* ☎ *01/3 30 45 94,* main dishes starting at 240S. Modern restaurant, in which a father and son team produce some outstanding results.

TREAT YOURSELF!

Steirereck – *Rasumofskygasse 2, 3. Bezirk,* ☎ *01/7 13 31 68,* lunchtime menu from 395S, evening main dishes starting at 320S. Located near the Hundertwasserhaus. Arguably the best food in Vienna, with a substantial wine cellar which you can visit.

HEURIGE (Wine taverns)

Mayer am Pfarrplatz – *Pfarrplatz 2, 19. Bezirk,* ☎ *01/32 24 16.* Wine tavernbuffet. Comfortable local tavern with a beautiful garden.

Altes Presshaus – *Cobenzlgasse 15, 19. Bezirk,* ☎ *01/3 20 02 03.* Wine tavernbuffet. The oldest Heuriger in Grinzing (house dates from 1527), parts of the vaulted cellar are very old, as are the winepresses it contains.

Buschenschank Wolff – *Rathstr. 46, 19. Bezirk,* ☎ *01/4 40 23 35.* Wine tavernbuffet. Typical wine tavern in cosy rooms with an extensive, magnificently maintained garden.

Fuhrgassl-Huber – *Neustift am Wald 68, 19. Bezirk,* ☎ *01/4 40 14 05.* Wine tavern-buffet. Earthy rustic atmosphere spread over several rooms with Viennese "Schramml-Musik" (popular music played on violin, accordion and guitar).

CAFÉS, BARS AND NIGHTCLUBS

COFFEE-HOUSES

The coffee house is a Viennese institution, and visitors should therefore make sure that they try out one of the numerous speciality coffees, with perhaps an accompanying slice of cake, in at least one such establishment.

Kalmar/ÖSTERREICH WEBUNG

Café Central

Central, *Herrengasse 14, 1. Bezirk,* ☎ *01/5 33 37 63 26.* Specialities are the "Mazagran" (iced coffee with rum) and "Pharisäer" (hot coffee with rum and whipped cream). Piano music between 4pm and 7pm (Mon-Sat 8am-10pm; July and Aug only to 8pm).

Hawelka, *Dorotheergasse 6, 1. Bezirk,* ☎ *01/5 12 82 30.* Specialities include "Buchteln" (pastry filled with plum jam), served only after 10pm (Wed-Mon 8am-2am, Sun and public holidays 4pm-2am; closed on Tues).

Imperial, *Kärntner Ring 16, 1. Bezirk,* ☎ *01/50 11 03 89.* Both Sigmund Freud and Anton Bruckner were regular clients at this coffee house which opened in 1873 (daily 7am-11pm).

Landtmann, *Dr.-Karl-Lueger-Ring 4, 1. Bezirk,* ☎ *01/5 32 06 21.* Near the Parlament, Rathaus and Burgtheater, this café is a popular meeting place, which also boasts a beautiful summer terrace (daily 8am-midnight).

Café Museum, *Friedrichstraße 6, 1. Bezirk,* ☎ *01/5 86 52 902.* Coffee house designed by Adolf Loos in the late 19C near the Secession building (daily 8am-midnight).

Sacher, *Philharmonikerstraße 4, 1. Bezirk,* ☎ *01/5 14 56 0.* The legendary *Sachertorte* is on sale here, an absolute must on the Viennese cake list (daily 8am-midnight).

Im KunstHaus, *Weissgerberlände 14, 3. Bezirk,* ☎ *01/7 12 04 97.* Superb garden and inside room almost overgrown with plants – a coffee house with a difference (daily 10am-midnight).

CONFECTIONERY AND PATISSERIE

Altmann und Kühne, *Graben 30, 1. Bezirk,* ☎ *01/5 33 09 27.* Fantastically packed confectionery.

Central, *Herrengasse 17, 1. Bezirk,* ☎ *01/535 99 05.* This patisserie shop sells the **Imperialtorte**, rival to the Sachertorte, in five different packages (guaranteed to last four weeks).

Demel, *Kohlmarkt 14, 1. Bezirk,* ☎ *01/53 51 71 70.* The prices are high, but you get something special for your money.

Lehmann, *Graben 12, 1. Bezirk,* ☎ *01/5 12 18 15.* Apfelstrudel to die for.

BARS

The "**Bermuda triangle**" of the Viennese bar scene is located in the 1. Bezirk around the Ruprechtskirche and Rudolfsplatz (KPR). There is something to cater to every taste here. Just dive right in.

Flanagans Irish Pub, *Schwarzenbergstraße 1-3, 1. Bezirk,* ☎ *01/5 13 73 78.* The stone floor comes from an Irish chapel, and the bar has spent a century of its life in Ireland. Open Thur-Sat 11am-4am, Sun-Wed 11am-2am.

Kolar-Beisl, *Kleeblattgasse 5, 1. Bezirk,* ☎ *01/5 33 52 25.* Open daily 5pm-2am.

Krah Krah, *Rabensteig 8, 1. Bezirk,* ☎ *01/5 33 81 93.* Open daily 11am-2am. Popular local bar offering more than 50 varieties of beer.

Loos-Bar, *Kärntner Straße 10, 1. Bezirk,* ☎ *01/5 12 32 83.* Open daily 6pm-4am. Small, but to be recommended, and not only because it was designed by Adolf Loos.

Panigl, *Schönlaterngasse 11, 1. Bezirk,* ☎ *01/5 13 17 16.* Open 4pm-4am. Small Italian wine bar.

Philosoph, *Judengasse 11, 1. Bezirk,* ☎ *01/5 35 45 32.* Open Sun-Wed 6pm-2am, Thur-Sat until 4am. Good music.

Planter's Club, *Zelinkagasse 4, 1. Bezirk,* ☎ *01/5 33 33 93.* Open 5pm-4am. Those wishing to spend the evening in this chic, Colonial style bar room must be prepared to queue for quite some time to get in.

Reiss, *Marco-d'Aviano-Gasse 1, 1. Bezirk,* ☎ *01/5 12 71 98.* Open Sun-Wed 11am-2am, Thur, Fri 11am-3am, Sat 10am-3am. Champagne-set hang-out with interior design by architects' office Coop Himmelblau.

Zum Basilisken, *Schönlaterngasse 3-5, 1. Bezirk,* ☎ *01/5 13 31 23.* Open daily noon-2am, Fri and Sat until 4am.

Zum Bettelstudent, *Johannesgasse 12, 1. Bezirk,* ☎ *01/5 13 20 44.* Open 10am-2am, Fri, Sat until 3am.

JAZZ

Jazzland, *Franz-Josefs-Kai 29, 1. Bezirk,* ☎ *01/5 33 25 75.* International groups appear in this vaulted jazz cellar beneath the Ruprechtskirche. Great atmosphere. Music from 9pm.

Miles Smiles, *Lange Gasse 51, 8. Bezirk,* ☎ *01/4 05 95 17.* Not only for fans of Miles Davis.

Jazzclub Porgy & Bess, *Riemergasse 11, 1. Bezirk,* ☎ *01/50 37 009.* Concerts by Austrian and international jazz musicians, live music every day.

Otto, *Altmannsdorfer Straße 101, 12. Bezirk,* ☎ *01/8 04 76 50.* Oct-Apr Sun at 11.30am pre-lunch drinks with jazz.

NIGHTCLUBS

P1, *Diskothek. Rotgasse 9*, 1. Bezirk. House, techno, soul.

Havanna Club, *Krugerstraße 8, 1. Bezirk,* ☎ *01/5 13 32 25.* Latin-American music: DJ and dance courses.

U4, *Diskothek. Schönbrunner Straße 222, 12. Bezirk.* Techno, Dance Floor.

B72, *Hernalser Gürtel-Bogen 72, between 8. and 17 Bezirk,* ☎ *01/4 09 21 28.* Live music and DJs.

ON THE BANKS OF THE BLUE DANUBE

Donauinsel (Neue Donau) – *Linie 1, U-Bahn-Station: Donauinsel.* A total of 42km/26mi of beach, with cycle, surfboard and boat hire outlets, and a rich selection of local bars and restaurants on the "**Copa Cagrana**" (after the Viennese suburb of Kagran, with apologies to Rio) on the river banks attract not only the Viennese – this is a great place to escape the heat of the city and really chill out.

Alte Donau – *Linie 1, U-Bahn-Station: Alte Donau.* The Viennese also come here to enjoy themselves in summer. The old branch of the Danube offers meadows, beaches and numerous bar-restaurants in which you can while away a pleasant evening on the banks of the Danube.

DATES FOR YOUR DIARY

Wiener Eistraum – Jan-Mar. Ice-skating in front of the Rathaus.

Wiener Festwochen – May-June. Avant-garde festival of theater, music and art.

Donauinselfest – Late June. Free open-air concerts which lure thousands to the Donauinsel.

Im-Puls-Tanzfestival – July-Aug. International dance performances which you can watch, or in which you can take part, in the museum district.

KlangBogen – July-Aug. Wide range of musical events at various venues around town. ☎ *01/40 00 84 10*

Filmfestival am Rathausplatz – July-Aug. Free open-air video shows on a giant screen with recordings of classical music, in front of the Vienna Rathaus.

Viennale – Oct. International film festival. Details: *www.viennale.or.at.*

Wiener Ballsaison – Nov-Ash Wednesday. Viennese Ball Season, the highlight of which is of course the world renowned Vienna Opera Ball.

▸ **Orient Yourself:** Vienna is in the northwest corner of Austria, not far from the borders with the Czech Republic, Slovakia and Hungary.

🅿 **Parking:** Finding parking is easy thanks to an electronic guide system that directs you to the nearest garage and also shows the number of available spaces. 24hr parking garages in the center (1. Bezirk) include: Am Morzinplatz (Franz-Josefs-Kai), Rathauspark (Ring/Stadiongasse), Operngarage (Kärtner Straße 51), Am Hof, Beethovenplatz 3, Cobdengasse 2. For a complete list, check www.wkw.at/garagen.

⌾ **Don't Miss:** Hofburg, Kulturhistorisches Museum, Stephansdom, Schloss Schönbrunn

🕔 **Organizing Your Time:** Budget at least three days for your Vienna stay.

Kids **Especially for Kids:** Zoom Kindermuseum, Prater, Tiergarten, Technisches Museum, Naturhistorisches Museum

A Bit of History

From Antiquity to the Habsburgs – Vienna began its existence as a modest Roman camp called Vindobona, founded around 15 BC. It gradually grew into a larger settlement and trading site but didn't gain capital status until 1155 when Heinrich II Jasomirgott moved his residence to Vienna. The town flourished economically and culturally in the early 13C under Leopold the Glorious, whose rule saw the construction of a massive fortified wall and the Church of St Stephen, which became a bishop's seat in 1469. By the time the last of the Babenbergs died in 1246, Vienna had become, after Cologne, the most important city on German-speaking soil. Its growth, from then on, was inseparably linked with the fortunes of the Habsburgs, who reigned over Austria from 1273 to 1918.

The Turks – A major impediment to Vienna's development was the persistent threat posed by the Ottoman army, which numbered as high as 300 000 men. The city was besieged twice, first in 1529 and then again in 1683. During the latter siege, the Emperor and the court fled Vienna, leaving its defense in the hands of 24 000 troops who managed to stave off all attacks for nearly two months. In the end, a relief force of 80 000 Austrians, Poles, Bavarians, Swabians and Franconians led by the Emperor's close ally, the Polish King Jan III Sobieski, succeeded in driving back the Turkish army for good. This battle marked a turning point in the power strug-

Donauinsel

M. HERTLEIN/MICHELIN

Metternich

The career of Klemens Lothar Wenzel, Prince of Metternich-Winneburg, began in 1806, when he was appointed ambassador to Paris. In 1809 Metternich was given the heavy burden of directing Austria's foreign policy. He proposed a *rapproche-ment* with France and succeeded in forging an alliance between the two countries by negotiating Napoleon's marriage to Archduchess Marie-Louise. With remarkable diplomatic insight he made Austria a buffer state between the Russian and French empires, ultimately enabling him to use his skills and cunning as mediator at the Congress of Vienna.

gle between the central European powers and the Ottoman army, which had been waged for three centuries.

Following this famous victory, the western sovereigns recognized the pre-eminence of the Emperor. The Austrian Empire now entered a long period of prosperity, finally allowing Vienna to blossom into a glamorous Imperial capital, marked by the influence of Baroque architecture. Palaces, mansions and churches sprang up, eventually overflowing the narrow limits of the 17C city walls and leading to the development of new quarters and extensive suburbs.

The Congress of Vienna – Napoleon occupied Vienna twice, in 1805 and again in 1809, but when his empire collapsed in 1814, it fell to the Austrian capital to host the famous international gathering that was to redraw the map of Europe. For a year the Congress of Vienna furnished a pretext for splendid festivities. Receptions and balls were held at the embassies, in the state rooms at the Hofburg, and in the Great Gallery at Schönbrunn Palace. *"Le Congrès ne marche pas, il danse"* (The Congress is not working, it is dancing), Prince de Ligne summed it up so poignantly. More than any other city, Vienna could offer choice entertainment to its guests: exquisite art collections, theater, opera and classical concerts. Ludwig van Beethoven himself conducted a gala concert and his opera *Fidelio* was received with enthusiasm. Even after the delegates left, the idyllic Vienna of the Biedermeier continued its carefree lifestyle, with people idling their time away in cafes, relaxing over wine in the Vienna Woods or listening to Schubert's dreamy Lieder (songs).

Growth of Vienna – Vienna had to await the reign of **Franz Joseph** (1848-1916) for the large-scale planning and building that made it what it is today. In 1857 the Emperor ordered the removal of the bastions and the formation of a circular boulevard - the **"Ring"** - around the old town. Famous architects and artists contributed to this great project, which is lined by Vienna's most important public buildings as well as by the numerous tenement blocks characteristic of the city. In 1890, the outer boroughs were incorporated as well and the second ring of fortifications razed, making space for an outer circular road, known as the **"Gürtel"** (belt).

Vienna, Capital of Music

Venerable traditions

St Peter's in Salzburg may have been the cradle of sacred music in the German-speaking world but, by the 12C, Vienna under the Babenbergs had become an important center of secular music performed by Minnesänger (minstrels or troubadours). Vienna's status as musical capital was further cemented when Maximilian I moved his dazzling court choir here from Innsbruck, which still thrills modern audiences as the **"Hofkapelle."**

The great days of Viennese music

The 18C was dominated by **Joseph Haydn**, the initiator of Classicism in Vienna. The princely palaces became veritable musical workshops, places for great performers and composers to meet, including Mozart, Beethoven and Gluck. Around 1825 the musical soirées known as **"Schubertiades"** began, at which Schubert interpreted Lieder for a circle of friends and which ended in dancing.

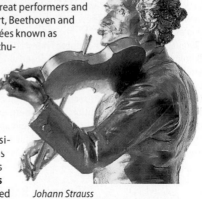

Johann Strauss

After the revolution of 1848, music societies proliferated, promoting high standards of concert performance and of musical education. The most illustrious of these societies was the "Friends of Music," which counted **Brahms** among its conductors. Brahms enjoyed unparalleled prestige, but **Bruckner**, who had left his native Linz to become court organist, found his sacred masterpieces to be beyond the comprehension of the Viennese public. **Mahler** used his 10 years in Vienna as Kapellmeister (orchestra leader) to undertake the reforms that helped usher in a new musical era.

The force of destiny (1770-1827)

Few other artists were more captivated and inspired by the romantic countryside surrounding Vienna than **Ludwig van Beethoven**. Beethoven arrived in the city at age 20 and soon charmed its people with his virtuosity as a pianist. It was in Vienna where he created the works that revolutionized the language of music: the Eroica Symphony, the opera *Fidelio*, the Fifth Symphony, and the monumental Ninth Symphony, the great "Ode to Joy". He died in his beloved city on March 26, 1827.

The triumph of the Viennese Waltz

One byproduct of the Congress of Vienna was the popularization of the Viennese **waltz**. This vigorous and light-hearted dance kept the city on its toes throughout the 19C. Polished, refined, and made a genre in its own right by **Joseph Lanner** and Johann Strauss the Elder, the waltz came to dominate the dance floor under **Johann Strauss the Younger**, whose tributes to the city (*Vienna Blood*, *Tales from the Vienna Woods*) got an enthusiastic reception. Today, the statue of Strauss the Younger in Vienna's Stadtpark has become a city emblem.

Rock me Amadeus

Two hundred years after Mozart, another Austrian musician won world-wide fame. We're of course talking about Vienna's own Hans Hölzl, better known as the eccentric stage persona of **Falco**. In 1985, he not only won over European audiences with his mega-hit song "Rock me Amadeus," but even skyrocketed to the top of the American charts, an outstanding feat for a German-language pop song. With his characteristic combination of speech-song and catchy tunes, Falco is the only Austrian pop star to have made it big on the world stage. He was killed in a car accident in the Dominican Republic in 1998 and - unlike his illustrious predecessor - was awarded an "honorary grave" by the City of Vienna in the Zentralfriedhof.

The "New School" of Vienna

New School refers to the movement founded by the Viennese **Arnold Schoenberg**, promoter of a veritable musical revolution whose effects would reverberate through the century. His theories of 12-tone composition are set out in his *Treatise on Harmony* in which he established new relationships between sounds freed from traditional harmonic conventions.

Originally self-taught, Schoenberg later studied with the opera composer Alexander Zemlinsky (1871-1942) and first composed works like the *Gurrelieder* that still show affinities with the post-Romantic style. But he soon left behind the boundaries of tonality with such works as the Second String Quartet (1908) and the 1912 *Pierrot Lunaire*, a melodrama in 21 sections for narrator and five instruments, which brought him international recognition. Schoenberg exercised a profound influence on a number of his pupils, most notably Webern and Berg, both Viennese. Of the three composers, it was Webern who strayed furthest from classical tonality, while Berg enjoyed the greatest public success with his operas *Wozzeck* and *Lulu*.

Viennese Ball Season

During the winter in Vienna, one ball follows close on another. The famous Emperor's Ball is held on New Year's Eve, reawakening the elegance and splendor of the former Imperial court at the Hofburg. During Carnival time (Fasching), the various associations and professional guilds put on about 300 balls, many in magnificent surroundings (Rathaus, Hofburg, Musikverein). These include the Floral Ball, organized by gardeners and florists, the Rudolfina-Redoute Masked Ball, and balls of the Viennese Coffee-Houses, the Vienna Philharmonic Orchestra and the Technicians' Circle. Doctors and lawyers each have a ball, and so do hunters and firemen.

The ball to end all balls in terms of sheer elegance is the **Opera Ball**, held in February at the Staatsoper. This event draws the rich and famous from Austria and abroad, and is *the* High Society event of the year. The ball is opened by ballet dancers from the Vienna State Opera and a committee of young ladies and gentlemen dancing a Polonaise with fans.

Opera Ball, Vienna

Pratt-Pries/DIAF

Sampling new wine in one of Vienna's Heurigen

Life in Vienna

The coffee house, a Viennese institution

When the Turks fled in 1683, they left behind a large quantity of coffee beans, thereby inadvertently launching a great Viennese tradition. Since the 19C the coffee house has been an indispensable social part of middle class and intellectual life, a place for people to meet, converse and read the newspapers.

The city's classic coffee houses fill up as the working day ends. Discreetly attired waiters serve the traditional glass of water alongside the coffee, which is available in a bewildering variety (⟨ *see boxed text*) and often paired with a piece of cake or pastry. Once the coffee is finished, the waiter collects the cup and brings another glass of water while also keeping the customer supplied with newspapers and magazines. In fact, it is not unusual to linger for hours without repeating the order.

Wine bars, inns and taverns

A convivial atmosphere can be enjoyed in the **Keller**, not unlike a German beer hall, where snacks and cold meals are downed with a glass of beer or wine. Some establishments (*Gasthäuser, Weinhäuser*) offering good home cooking are known as **Beisel**. Other popular places for locals to wind down at the end of the work day are taverns *(Weinstuben)* and the cheerful wine pubs called **Heurige**. The latter are located in the wine-growing villages surrounding the city, such as Grinzing, Nussdorf, Sievering and Gumpoldskirchen. Usually run by the wine-growers themselves, they are recognized by the pine branch fastened above the entrance. In cozy rooms or leafy courtyards, you can sample the new wine *(Heuriger)* along with snacks or a simple meal. **Schrammelmusik,** played by a pair of violins, an accordion or clarinet plus a guitar, often enlivens this utterly Viennese experience.

Exploring Vienna

Tour of the Ring★

By car or tram (circular routes nos 1 and 2). Start at the Stubenring (LR) to the east and continue in a clockwise direction.

Driving along the Ring is a good overture to exploring the historic city center and is especially lovely at night when many buildings are floodlit.

Guide to Coffee, Viennese style

Listed below are some descriptions of the more commonly served types of Viennese coffee, among the 30 or so preparations which are available:

Großer/kleiner Schwarzer large/small cup of black coffee
Großer/kleiner Brauner large/small cup of black coffee with a dash of milk
Verlängerter Schwarzer/Brauner "Schwarzer"/"Brauner" diluted with water
Einspänner black coffee served in a glass with whipped cream (Schlagobers)
Fiaker black coffee in a glass with a tot of rum
Franziskaner coffee mixed with chocolate chips
Kaffee verkehrt coffee with more milk than coffee
Kaisermelange coffee with egg yolk and alcohol
Kapuziner black coffee with a small blob of whipped cream
Konsul mocca diluted with cold water
Mazagran iced coffee with rum
Melange milky coffee (can be served with whipped cream)
Türkischer Kaffee strong coffee prepared in a small copper coffee pot, served hot in tiny cups
Verlängerter mocca diluted with hot water

A further tip: never ask for a cup of coffee (eine Tasse Kaffee) in Vienna – it is *"eine Schale Kaffee"* (literally, a bowl of coffee). Depending on how high a milk content you would like, coffee can be ordered "Braun", or even "Gold".

Postsparkasse★ (LR)
This important Jugendstil (Art Nouveau) building was designed at the start of the 20C by Otto Wagner.

Österreichisches Museum für Angewandte Kunst (MAK)★★ (LR)
The applied arts museum is housed in a monumental building designed in Florentine Renaissance style, its stone and brick façade articulated by round-headed bays and twin windows.

Stadtpark (KLRS)
South of the MAK, this attractively landscaped park was laid out in 1862 and is famous for its statues of musicians, including Franz Schubert, Anton Bruckner, Franz Lehar and Robert Stolz. Pride of place goes to the memorial honoring Johann Strauss.

Oper★★ (JS)
Austria's national opera house, with its elegant arcades in French Renaissance style, was the first of the great public edifices to be erected along the Ring. The main façade was all that was left standing when the building burnt down in 1945.

Burggarten (JRS)
Between the Ring and the Hofburg, the palace gardens, first laid out in the 19C, have been open to the public since 1919. At the entrance stands a statue to Goethe, and there are other memorials to Franz Joseph, Franz I (on horseback) and Mozart.

Neue Burg (JR)

The Neue Burg was the last wing to be added to the Hofburg, completed just before the First World War and now housing several museums.

Maria-Theresien-Platz (HRS)

This square's central element is the 1888 monument to Maria Theresa, which is buttressed by equestrian statues of several of her generals. Other figures represent statesmen and the composers Gluck, Haydn and Mozart.

The two domed buildings facing each other across the square were constructed between 1872 and 1891 and house the Imperial collections in the **Kunsthistorisches Museum**★★★ and the **Naturhistorisches Museum**★.

MuseumsQuartier (HS)

Vienna's newest museum cluster awaits on the other side of the Ring, across Museumsplatz, where the former Imperial stables designed by Fischer von Erlach have been reborn as the MuseumsQuartier. This vast cultural center harbors theaters, a dance studio as well as the city's top art showcases, the Leopold Museum, the Museum Moderner Kunst, and the Kunsthalle.

Volksgarten★ (HR)

This pleasant, quiet park with its pools, statues and famous rose garden is great for strolling and picnicking. A replica Greek temple adds an exotic element.

Parlament (HR)

Opposite the Volksgarten and adjacent to the law courts, this is Austria's seat of government (1873-83) with its elegant classical Greek façade.

Neues Rathaus (HR)

🕐 ⏏️*Guided tour (45min) Mon, Wed, Fri 1pm (except when council is in session).* 🕐 *public holidays.* ✑*free.* ☎ *01/5 25 50.*

The neo-Gothic city hall is linked to the Ring by attractive gardens. The tower is topped by the famous "Rathausmann" carrying the city flag. Summer concerts are held in the arcaded courtyard. The reception rooms, council chambers and the huge banqueting hall are all open to the public.

Burgtheater (HR)

⏏️*Guided tour (1 hr) daily 3pm and Sun 11am, also daily 2pm Jul-Aug, by prior reservation only.* ✑*€5.* ☎ *01/5 14 44 41 40.*

Opened in 1888, this theater replaced the Hofburgtheater (Court Theater) on the Michaelerplatz founded in 1741 under Maria Theresa. Gottfried Semper was responsible for the Renaissance façade, while Carl Hasenauer designed the neo-Baroque interior. The Burgtheater has long been considered among the most important German-language theaters, and an engagement here was, and still is, the summit of an acting career. Tours take in the **ceiling frescoes**★ painted by Gustav Klimt, his brother Ernst, and Franz Matsch.

Universität (HP)

On the north side of the Rathausplatz, the Italian Renaissance-style university by Heinrich von Ferstel houses the second-oldest German-language university (after Prague). Beyond it, on the left, as the Ring makes its final bend, is the Votivkirche.

Votivkirche (HP)

Two tall spires flank the west door of this neo-Gothic church, completed in 1879. Note the Antwerp Altar in the right-hand chapel beyond the transept and the tomb of Count Salm from 1530, with its **reclining figure**★ in the baptistry.

After passing the **Börse** (Stock Exchange – JP) on the right, the tour ends by the Donaukanal at the Franz-Josefs-Kai.

City viewpoints

The **Kahlenberg**★ and the **Leopoldsberg**★★ (BX) are two splendid viewpoints in the hills overlooking the city from the northwest.

The **Donauturm** (CX) (Danube Tower, ⟡*daily 10am–midnight. Elevator:* ⊚*€5.30.* ☎ *01/2 63 35 72*) was built on the north bank of the river in 1964. From its two revolving restaurants or its viewing terraces 150m/500ft above the Donaupark there is a far-ranging **view**★★ over the city and its surroundings. There is a similar **panoramic view**★ from the **Riesenrad**★★ (Giant Wheel) in the Prater (GU).

Hofburg★★★

The Imperial palace, the winter residence of the Habsburgs, was progressively enlarged during the centuries, resulting in a hodgepodge of styles. The oldest section, built in the 13C, is the Schweizerhof (Swiss Court), while the Burgkapelle (castle chapel) was erected in the mid 15C. Next came the Amalienburg and the Stallburg in the 16C, followed by the Leopoldinischer Trakt (now the official office of the Federal President) in the 17C. The 18C saw the addition of the Reichskanzleitrakt (Imperial Chancellery), the Spanische Reitschule (Spanish Riding School) and the Nationalbibliothek (National Library). The Neue Burg (New Imperial Palace), completed just before 1914, marked the end of the structural history of the Hofburg.

Exterior

Michaelerplatz★

Designed by JE Fischer von Erlach, this complex was not completed until 1893. The semicircular façade overlooking the square is decorated with two monumental statue-studded fountains. The main arches are closed by bronze gilded grilles. A magnificent gateway, the **Michaelertor**★, flanked by figures from the Hercules legends,

Neue Burg from Heldenplatz

gives access to the octagonal rotunda beneath the famous **Michaelerkuppel**★, one of Vienna's most elegant domes. The square known as "In der Burg," anchored by a monument to Emperor Franz II, is reached via this rotunda. From the courtyard, the **Schweizertor**★, a fine Renaissance gateway bearing coats of arms and inscriptions, leads to the **Schweizerhof** and the stairs up to the Hofburgkapelle.

Josefsplatz★

Arched passageways lead into this square, regarded as Vienna's finest because of its ideal proportions. It owes its name to the fine equestrian statue of Joseph II, the base of which is adorned with low-relief sculptures in bronze. On the south side is the early-18C **Österreichische Nationalbibliothek** by Fischer von Erlach.

Heldenplatz★

Heldenplatz overlooks the concave façade of the Neue Burg, built in Italian Renaissance style between 1881 and 1913. The square is bounded to the north by the shady Volksgarten and boasts two grand equestrian statues of Prince Eugene of Savoy and Archduke Karl by the sculptor Anton Dominik Fernkorn.

The monumental gateway (1824) on the southwest side is the Äusseres Burgtor, which leads to the Ring and has served as a war memorial since 1934.

Interior

Schatzkammer★★★

🕐*Wed-Mon 10am-6pm.* ♿❄€8. ☎ *01/5 33 79 31.www.khm.at*

A highlight of any Vienna visit, the treasury displays the insignia of Habsburg power, as well as mementoes and holy relics collected by the family. Listed below are the must-see exhibits:

Room 1 – The regalia of the archdukes of Austria used in ceremonies of homage: the **orb and scepter** (Prague, 14C) and the ducal mantle (Vienna, 1764).

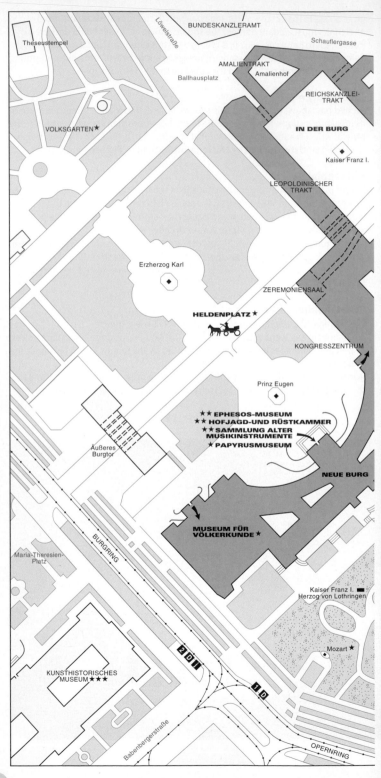

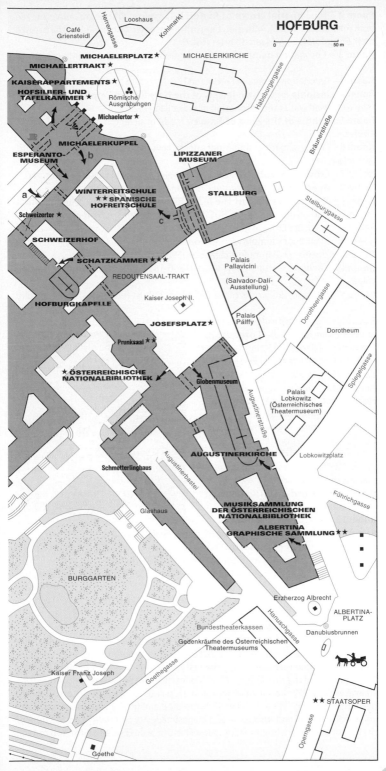

HOFBURG

0   50 m

MICHAELERPLATZ ★

MICHAELERTRAKT ★

KAISERAPPARTEMENTS ★

HOFSILBER- UND
TAFELKAMMER ★

Römische
Ausgrabungen

Michaelertor ★

MICHAELERKUPPEL

ESPERANTO-
MUSEUM

b

MICHAELERKIRCHE

Herrengasse

Café
Griensteidl

Looshaus

Kohlmarkt

Habsburgergasse

Bräunerstraße

LIPIZZANER
MUSEUM

STALLBURG

Stallburggasse

WINTERREITSCHULE
★★ SPANISCHE
HOFREITSCHULE

a

Schweizertor ★

c

SCHWEIZERHOF

SCHATZKAMMER ★★★

REDOUTENSAAL-TRAKT

HOFBURGKAPELLE

Kaiser Joseph II.

JOSEFSPLATZ ★

Prunksaal ★★

★ ÖSTERREICHISCHE
NATIONALBIBLIOTHEK

Globenmuseum

Palais
Pallavicini

(Salvador-Dalí-
Ausstellung)

Palais
Pálffy

Dorotheergasse

Dorotheum

Spiegelgasse

Palais
Lobkowitz
(Österreichisches
Theatermuseum)

Lobkowitzplatz

Augustinerstraße

AUGUSTINERKIRCHE

Schmetterlinghaus

Augustinerbastei

Glashaus

MUSIKSAMMLUNG
DER ÖSTERREICHISCHEN
NATIONALBIBLIOTHEK

Führichgasse

ALBERTINA
GRAPHISCHE SAMMLUNG ★★

BURGGARTEN

Erzherzog Albrecht

ALBERTINA-
PLATZ

Hanuschgasse

Danubiusbrunnen

Bundestheaterkassen

Gedenkräume des Österreichischen
Theatermuseums

Kaiser Franz Joseph

Goethegasse

Goethe

★★ STAATSOPER

Operngasse

377

Room 2 – The **Imperial crown of Rudolf II**★, made in Prague by Jan Vermeyen from Antwerp (early 17C), with matching orb and scepter. Also notable is the **bronze bust of Rudolf II** by Adriaen de Vries (1607).

Room 3 – Coronation mantle (1830) and ceremonial robes. Insignia of various Orders.

Room 4 – Coronation regalia of Ferdinand I.

Room 9 – **Insignia and crown jewels of the Holy Roman Empire**. The last time they were used was at the coronation of Franz II in 1792.

Room 5 – **Cradle of the King of Rome**★ made of silver gilt. **Portrait of Marie Louise**★.

Room 6 – Christening robes and other effects; keys to the coffins in the Kaisergruft (*see below*).

Room 7 – **Crown of Stephan Bocskay**★. Jewelery, emerald vessel (2 680 carat).

Room 8 – **Agate bowl**★ (4C). Narwhal horn measuring 2.43m/8ft.

Room I – **Miniature replica of the Mariensäule**★ (Virgin Mary column), which formerly stood on the square Am Hof. It is decorated with 3 700 precious stones.

Room II – Reliquary cross of King Ludwig I of Hungary (c 1370).

Room III – Small ebony temple with an ivory figure of Christ by Christoph Angermair; Florentine crucifix by Giambologna (about 1590).

Room IV – Reliquary altars from Milan (1660-1680); altar furniture in Dresden china.

Room V – 18C and 19C works of art including 22 bust reliquaries, some in solid silver.

Room 10 – Ceremonial robes of the Norman kings, including the **Coronation mantle**★★ of Roger II of Sicily (Palermo, 1133); ceremonial sword of Friedrich II.

Room 11 – The most outstanding item among the crown jewels of the Holy Roman Empire is the **Imperial crown**★★★, probably made for Otto I (962) in the monastery on the island of Reichenau in Lake Constance, or possibly in Milan. Imperial cross of 1024 with a base added in 1352. An astonishing reliquary is the **Holy Lance**★★ (8C), while the **Imperial sword**★ (11C) is attributed to St Maurice.

Room 12 – Reliquaries, jewel boxes.

Room 13 – Robes and heraldic coats of arms from the Duchy of Burgundy.

Imperial crown
Kunsthistorisches Museum

Room 14 – Items from the treasure of the dukes of Burgundy.

Room 15 – Items associated with the Order of the Golden Fleece, including the **potence**★★ (mid 15C).

Room 16 – **Mass vestments**★★ of the Order of the Golden Fleece.

Kaiserappartements★

🕐*Jul-Aug daily 9am-5.30pm, Sep-Jun daily 9am-5pm.* ♿☕€8.90, *includes admission to Sisi Museum and Silberkammer.* ☎ *01/5 33 75 70. www.hofburg-wien.at.*

The **Imperial apartments** occupy the first floor of the Chancellery wing (Reichskanzleitrakt) and the Amalientrakt and are reached via the Kaiserstiege (Emperor's staircase). Only 20 of about 2 600 rooms in the palace are open to visitors. They are decorated in rococo style with fanciful stucco ornamentation, luxurious furniture, crystal chandeliers and Aubusson and Flemish tapestry and date from the time of the last royal occupant Emperor Franz-Josef I and his wife Elisabeth (Sisi). You can see the bedroom, study, audience chamber, bathroom and Sisi's dressing and exercise room, complete with wall bars and rings.

Admission includes a spin around the new **Sisi Museum**, which traces the empress' childhood, life at court and tragic death while also addressing the myth that developed around her.

Also worth a look is the **Silberkammer**★ (Imperial Silver Collection), a magnificent spread of items used by the family until the monarchy's demise in 1918. Displays include an enormous **vermeil service**★ for 140 guests and the famous **Milanese centerpiece**★★ of 1838, designed for a table more than 30m/100ft long. There are also several Sèvres services, including the green service of 1776, numerous Empire-style ones from the Vienna Porcelain Factory, and fine sets of crystal glassware.

Hofburgkapelle

Mon-Thu 11am-3pm, Fri 11am-1pm. Jul and Aug and public holidays. €1.50, 01/5 33 99 27. www.wsk.at.

The Gothic palace chapel was built in the middle of the 15C and is the oldest part of the present palace. The famous Vienna Boys' Choir performs during Sunday mass (*9.15am; reservations required*).

Spanische Hofreitschule★★

Guided tours (1hr) most Tue-Sat 2pm, 3pm and 4pm, Sun 10am, 11am, 1pm, 2pm and 3pm. €15. Morning training sessions most Tues-Sat 10am-noon. €12. Tickets are available on the same day at the entrance, Josefsplatz Tor 2 and from the Besucherzentrum (visitors' center) at Michaelerplatz 1 Tue-Sat 9am-4pm. Performances (45min) selected days, usually Sun. €26-165. Make ticket reservations as early as possible by phone or online. 01/5 33 90 31. www.srs.at.

Feats of dressage dating back to the late 16C are performed In the all-white, indoor **Winter Riding School**, the work of Joseph Fischer von Erlach. The riders wear brown tailcoats, white buckskin breeches, riding boots and cocked hats. The white Lipizzaner stallions (*see Piber under Pack- und Stubalpenstraße),* their tails and manes plaited with gold ribbons, go through their paces with stunning precision, culminating in the school quadrille with a group of horses.

The **morning training session** (*Morgenarbeit*), although less spectacular, shows the horses performing difficult jumps, steps and other movements.

The Spanish Riding School

WIEN					
Adalbert-Stifter-Str.	CX 3	Donaustadtstr.	CXY 24	Grenzackerstr.	CZ 45
Altmannsdorfer Str.	AZ 6	Erdberger Lände	CYZ 28	Grinzinger Allee	BX 48
Breitenfurter Str.	AZ 16	Erdbergstr.	CY 30	Grinzinger Str.	BX 49
Döblinger Hauptstr.	BXY 21	Erzherzog-Karl-Str.	CY 31	Hietzinger Kai	AZ 60
		Floridsdorfer Brücke	CX 36	Hirschstettner Str.	CX 63
		Freudenauer Hafenstr.	CDZ 37	Hoche Warte	BX 64

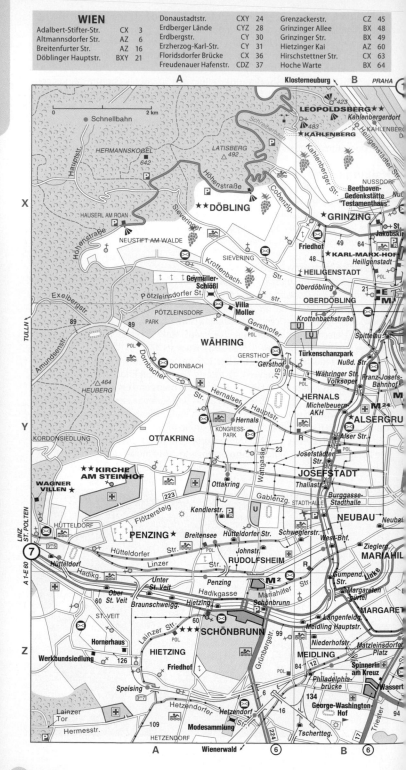

Kulmgasse	AY 23	Raxstr.	BZ 94	Eroicahaus	BX	E
Lassallestr.	CY 74	Schlachthausgasse	CY 98	Technisches Museum	AZ	M²
Margaretenstr.	BCYZ 82	Schönbrunner Str.	ABZ 99	Weinbaumuseum	BX	M¹
Meidlinger Hauptstr.	BZ 84	Speisinger Str.	AZ 109	Wiener Strassenbahn-		
Neuwaldegger Str.	AY 89	Veitingergasse	AZ 126	museum	CY	M³
Prinz-Eugen-Str.	CY 93	Wienerbergstraße	BZ 134			

381

Lipizzaner-Museum

Reitschulgasse 2. ⏱daily 9am-6pm. ⊚€5. ☎ 01/52 52 45 83. www.lippizaner.at.
The stallions reside in the nearby **Stallburg**, which also houses this museum whose genealogical tables, uniforms, harness and audio-visual displays provide a comprehensive chronicle of this world-famous breed of horses. You even get to sneak a peek inside some of the stables, albeit only through a thick glass screen.

Österreichische Nationalbibliothek★

Josefsplatz 2. Enter on 1st floor. ⏱Tue, Wed, Fri-Sun 10am-6pm, Thu 10am-9pm. ⊚€5. ☎ 01/53 41 04 64. www.onb.ac.at.
The core collection inside this early 18C building by Joseph Emanuel Fischer von Erlach is formed by the Imperial library, established in the 14C. The **Prunksaal**★★ (Great Hall) is a masterpiece of Baroque architecture and decoration with **ceiling frescoes** by **Daniel Gran** in the oval dome and statues by the Strudel brothers. It holds Prince Eugene of Savoy's magnificent library and also hosts special exhibitions

Kaisergruft★★

Enter to the left of the Kapuzinerkirche. ⏱daily 10am-6pm. ⊚€3. ☎ 01/5 12 68 53.
For more than three centuries the vaults of the Kapuzinerkirche, completed in 1632, have served as the burial place of the Imperial family. The remains of 12 emperors, 16 empresses and more than 100 archdukes are buried here, while their hearts are in the Augustinian church and their entrails in the catacombs of the Stephansdom.
In the Karlsgruft (Charles's vault) are the sarcophagi of Leopold I and Joseph I by Johann Lukas von Hildebrandt, as well as the **sarcophagus of Charles VI**. Decorated with coats of arms and an allegorical figure of Austria mourning, it is a masterwork by Balthasar Moll. Maria Theresa and her husband, Francis of Lorraine, lie in a beautiful **double sarcophagus**★★, also by Moll, fronted by the coffin of their son, Joseph II.
The sarcophagus of Emperor **Franz Joseph**, his wife **Elisabeth** and their son, Archduke Rudolf, are in a separate room. The so-called Neue Gruft, or new vault, built in 1961, contains the sarcophagi of **Marie-Louise**, empress of France, and **Maximilian of Mexico**. The last Habsburg emperor, Karl I, was buried on Madeira, but in 1989 his wife Zita became the last person to be entombed in the Imperial vault.

Augustinerkirche

Built in the 14C within the Hofburg, this Gothic court church hosted the marriages of Maria Theresa and Francis of Lorraine (1736), of Napoleon and Marie Louise (1810) and of Franz Joseph and Elisabeth of Bavaria (1854).
In the south aisle is the **tomb**★ of Archduchess Maria Christina, Maria Theresa's favorite daughter. This white marble mausoleum is considered a masterpiece of the Italian sculptor Canova, who worked in Vienna from 1805 to 1809. The **Loretokapelle** *(access via the right side aisle, ⏱⚐Guided tour (15min) by appointment and Sun after mass. ☎ 01/5 33 70 99)* holds in its **crypt** 54 urns containing the hearts of the Habsburgs. The Georgskapelle nearby was a meeting place for the knights of the Order of St George, and later for those of the Order of the Golden Fleece. It contains the cenotaph of Emperor Leopold II.

Albertina★★

⏱Thu-Tue 10am-6pm, Wed 10am-9pm. ⚐⊚€10. ☎ 01/5 81 30 60 11. www.albertina.at.
With about 45 000 drawings and watercolors, 35 000 publications and 1.5 million prints, the Albertina is considered the world's greatest collection of graphic art. Of particular importance is the **Dürer collection**, which contains such famous works as the *Praying Hands* and the *Hare*. Other masters represented are Hans Baldung Grien, Bruegel, Cranach the Elder, Chagall, Goya, Holbein, Klimt, Picasso, Rembrandt, Schiele and Leonardo da Vinci.

Tomb of Archduchess Maria Christina, Augustinerkirche

Schmetterlinghaus

Apr-Oct Mon-Fri 10am-4.45pm, Sat-Sun 10am-6.15pm; Nov-Mar daily 10am-3.45pm.
€5. 01/5 33 85 70.

Feel transported to a magical world upon entering the Jugendstil glasshouse in the palace garden, in which myriad colorful butterflies flutter through a re-created tropical rainforest. Some have even been known to land on the tip of a visitor's nose.

Neue Burg

Heldenplatz. Wed-Mon 10am-6pm. €8. 01/52 52 40. www.khm.at.
The Neue Burg harbors the following collections, all accessible on the same ticket:

Hofjagd- und Rüstkammer★★

This exceptionally rich collection of arms and armor was created in the 15C from the collections of the archdukes Ernst of Styria (1377-1424) and Ferdinand of the Tyrol (1527-95), and then merged in 1806 with the Imperial Court weaponry collection. The filigree work and elaborate decoration on the ceremonial harnesses, helmets and saddles that were made for kings and emperors reflect European history.

Sammlung alter Musikinstrumente★★

This is a great collection of Renaissance instruments. Of particular historical and artistic interest are a **rebec**★, or early bowed instrument, made from a single piece of wood (an animal's feeding trough) in 15C Venice; a **harpsichord**★ (Venice 1559); a **cittern**★★ made in Brescia in 1574; a **reed-organ**★ from Innsbruck (before 1569). Other highlights include six magnificent, partly gilded, **trumpets**★ (Vienna 1741 and 1746), and a **piano**★ (Vienna 1867) made by **Ludwig Bösendorfer** for the Paris World Exhibition, with ornate inlaid work.

Ephesos Museum★★

Archaeological findings from Ephesus in Turkey form the core of this exhibit, augmented by items uneared at Samothrace on the Aegean. Star items include fragments of the altarpiece of Artemis in the stairway and the 40m/131ft-long marble **Frieze of the Parthian Monument**★★ (c AD 170) in the mezzanine. It depicts the adoption of Marcus Aurelius, battle scenes from the wars with the Parthians, and the

Alte Backstube	EU	B	Kaiserliches Hofmobilien-			Museum der Gold-		
Bezirksmuseum			depot	EU	M11	und Silberschmiede	EU	M12
Alsergrund	ET	M20	KunstHausWien	GU	G	Österreichisches Museum für		
Dreifaltigkeitskirche	ET	K1	Lichtentalkirche	FT	K7	Volkskunde	EU	M7
Schubert-Geburtshaus	FT	M5	Liechtenstein-			Piaristenkirche Basilika		
Haus des Meeres	EU	M9	museum	FT	M27	Maria Treu	EU	A
Haydnhaus	EV	M10	Mariahilferkirche	EU	K2	Theater in der Josefstadt	EU	T1
Hundertwasserhaus	GU		Müllverbrennung-			Volksoper	ET	T2
			Fernwärme-Heizwerk	FT	S	Wagnerhaus	EU	M13

Map of Wien (Vienna)

WIEN

Alserbachstr.	EFT	4	Heiligenstädter Lände	FT	5	Schönbrunner Str.	EV 99
Billrothstr.	ET	12	Heiligenstädter Str.	FT	58	Spitalgasse	EU 111
Erdberger Lände	GU	28	Kundmanngasse	GU	71	Spittelauer Lände	FT 112
Favoritenstr.	FV	34	Landstr. Hauptstr.	GUV	72	Webgasse	EV 68
Gaudenzdorfer Gürtel	EV	39	Lange Gasse	EU	73	Weissgerberlände	GU 129
Gregor-Mendel-Str.	ET	43	Lassallestr.	GT	74	Wiedner Gürtel	FV 131
Hasenauerstr.	ET	54	Margaretenstr.	EFV	82	Wiedner Hauptstr.	FV 132
			Neubaugasse	EU	86	Zieglergasse	EU 135
			Prinz-Eugen-Str.	FUV	93		

consecration and apotheosis of Lucius Verus. On the upper floor are the impressive **Athlete of Ephesus**★★ and the **Boy with the Goose**★.

Museum für Völkerkunde★

🔑 *Closed for renovation until early 2007. Call 01/52 52 40 for details.*

The ethnological museum features a Japanese section with a complete Samurai horseman's suit of armor from the 17C. There's also a well documented exhibition on Polynesia, with some items attributed to Captain James Cook. The Early American section includes an **Aztec feather headdress**★★ from Mexico.

Old Vienna★★ *Start from Stephansplatz (KR 115)*

Wedged between the cathedral and the Danube canal, the heart of Old Vienna still evoke a special atmosphere in spite of reconstruction.

Stephansdom★★★ (KR)

🕐*Mon-Sat 6am-10pm, Sun 7am-10pm.* ♿☜€1 (Jul-Sep only, free Oct-Jun). Audioguide €4.90. ☜Guided tours Mon-Sat 10.30am, 3pm, Sun 3pm, Jun-Sep also Sat 7pm. ☜€4.90. ☎ *01/5 15 52 35 26.*

Vienna's cathedral is its most dramatic landmark. With its vast roof (exactly twice the height of its walls) of glittering tiles and its mighty south tower (the famous **Steffl**), its magnificence and significance are unparalleled in Austria.

A bit of History

On the site of the present building originally stood a Romanesque basilica consecrated in 1147. This church was badly damaged by the great fire of 1258 and today only the west front with the **Riesentor**★★ (Giants' Gate – 👁 *Introduction: ABC of architecture)* and the **Heidentürme** (Towers of the Heathens) remain. The first Gothic building was begun in 1304, and the Stephansdom as we now know it was built over the next two centuries. It became a cathedral in 1469.

Damaged during the Turkish siege of 1683, the cathedral again suffered serious damage in 1945 when flying sparks from nearby burning houses set fire to the north tower. After the war, it was swiftly restored to its former beauty.

Exterior

The small size of the Stephansplatz, center of the medieval city, accentuates the vastness of the cathedral, whose one complete steeple, the **Stephansturm**★★★ or "Steffl," soars to a height of 136.7m/449ft. The north steeple was never completed but contains the great 21.3t bell known as the **Pummerin** (the largest bell in Austria), which peals only on special occasions and to ring in the New Year. The bronze bell was cast in 1711 from 180 Turkish cannons captured in 1683, and hung originally in the south steeple. It was shattered in 1945, and a new Pummerin bell was cast from the remains in 1951.

The intricately carved Romanesque west door, called the **Riesentor**★★ (Giants' Gate), is crowded with statues, including one of Christ in Majesty on the tympanum and others of the Apostles in the recessed arches. If you encircle the

Pulpit, Stephansdom

H. A. Jahn/VIENNASLIDE

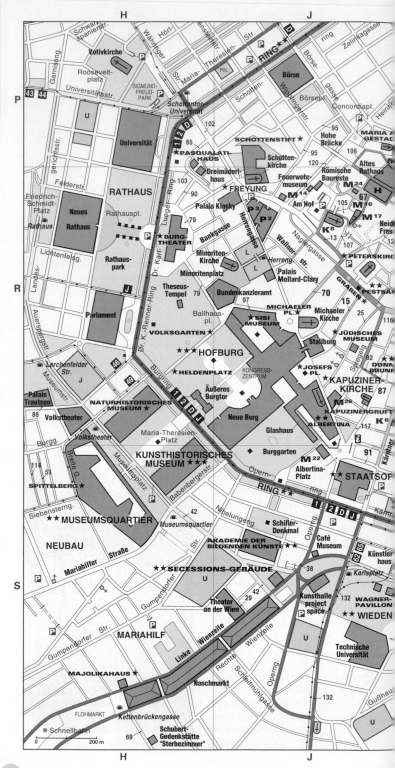

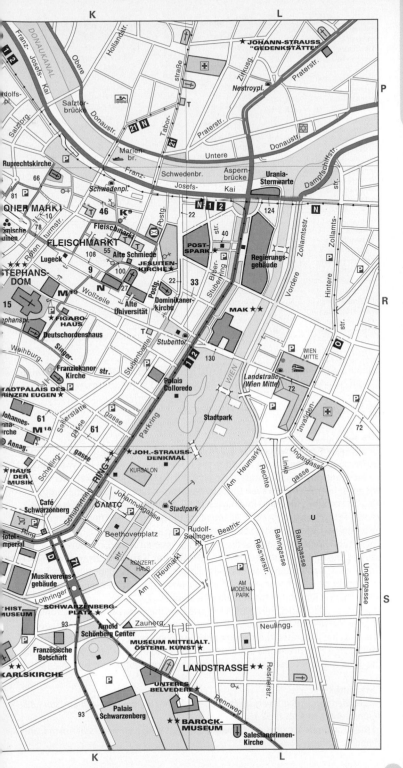

WIEN

Babenbergerstr.	HJS		Judenpl.	JR	67	Salvatorgasse	JPR	96
Bäckerstr.	KR	9	Kärntner Str.	JRS		Schauflergasse	JR	97
Bauernmarkt	KR	10	Kettenbrückengasse	HS	69	Schönlaterngasse	KR	100
Bognergasse	JR	13	Kohlmarkt	JR	70	Schottengasse	HJP	102
Bräunerstr.	JR	15	Landstr. Hauptstr.	LR	72	Schreyvogelgasse	HR	103
Dominikanerbastei	KR	22	Lichtensteg	KR	78	Schulhof	JR	105
Dorotheergasse	JR	25	Löwelstr.	HR	79	Schwertgasse	JP	106
Dr-Ignaz-Seipel-Pl.	KR	27	Marc-Aurel-Str.	KPR	81	Seitzergasse	JR	107
Falkestr.	KLR	33	Mariahilfer Str.	HS		Sonnenfelsgasse	KR	108
Friedrichstr.	JS	38	Millöckergasse	JS	29	Spittelberggasse	HS	114
Georg-Coch-Pl.	LR	40	Mölkerbastei	HP	85	Stephanspl.	KR	115
Getreidemarkt	HJS	42	Neuer Markt	JR	87	Stock-im-Eisen-Pl.	JR	116
Graben	JR		Neustiftgasse	HR	88	Tegetthoffstr.	JR	117
Griechengasse	KR	46	Oppolzergasse	HR	90	Tiefer Graben	JPR	120
Gutenberggasse	HS	51	Philharmonikerstr.	JS	91	Tuchlauben	JR	123
Heiligenkreuzer Hof	KR	55	Plankengasse	JR	92	Uraniastr.	LR	124
Himmelpfortgasse	KR	61	Prinz-Eugen-Str.	KS	93	Weiskirchnerstr.	LR	130
Judengasse	KR	66	Renngasse	JPR	95	Wiedner Hauptstr.	JS	132
			Rotenturmstr.	KR		Wollzeile	KR	

Akademie der Wissenschaften	KR	N	Griechisch-orientalische Kirche zur Hl. Dreifaltigkeit	KR	K[9]	Palais Harrach	JR	P[3]
Ausstellung der Österreichischen Freiheitskämpfe	JPR	M[21]	Kirche zu den neun Chören der Engel	JR	K[8]	Puppen- & Spielzeug- Museum	JR	M[16]
Böhmische Hofkanzlei	JR	H	Kunstforum Bank Austria	JR	M[1]	Salvatorkapelle	JR	K[4]
Dom- und Diözesanmuseum	KR	M[19]	Malteserkirche	JR	K[6]	Uhrenmuseum der Stadt Wien	JR	M[17]
Gedenkräume des Österreichischen Theatermuseums	JS	M[22]	Museum Judenplatz	KR	M[24]	Ursulinenkirche und kloster	KR	M[18]
			Österreichisches Theatermuseum	JR	M[26]			
			Palais Ferstel	JR	P[2]			

cathedral anticlockwise, you'll come to the copy of a Gothic lantern of the dead from the old cemetery of St. Stephan (now Stephansplatz) at the southwest corner.

▶ *Enter the cathedral through the Giants' Gate.*

Interior

Clearly inspired by the traditional Germanic hall church, the long, majestic nave (107m/352ft) is ingeniously linked to the three-aisled chancel. The magnificent carved stone **pulpit**★★★ dates from c 1480 and is a Gothic masterpiece. Its creator has never been identified even though he portrayed himself, under the ramp, holding his sculptor's tools and looking out of a half-open window (which is why he is known as the "Fenstergucker"). All round are the exceptionally finely carved busts of St Augustine, St Ambrose, St Gregory the Great and St Jerome.

The left apsidal chapel, known as the Frauenchor (women's choir), contains a beautiful painted and gilded altarpiece known as the **Wiener Neustadt altarpiece**★(15C). On the central panel are the Virgin and Child flanked by St Barbara and St Catherine and, up above, is the Coronation of the Virgin Mary. The altarpiece on the high altar in the chancel represents the stoning of St Stephen.

The right apsidal chapel, the Apostelchor, preserves the remarkable late-15C **tomb**★★ of Emperor Friedrich III, made of red Salzburg marble by Nikolaus Gerhart of Leyden. The artist has illustrated the struggle between Good and Evil, symbolizing the evil spirits in the form of animals trying to enter the tomb to disturb the Emperor, while the good spirits, represented by local personages, prevent them from doing so.

Catacombs

◈ *Guided tour (30min) every half hr Mon-Sat 10am-11.30am, 1.30-4.30pm, Sun 1.30-4.30pm. ◈€3. ☎ 01/5 15 52 35 26.*

In the catacombs are urns containing the organs of the emperors of Austria, and chapels established since 1945.

Cathedral towers
Hochturm: daily 9am-5.30pm. ∞€2.50. Nordturm (high-speed lift to "Pummerin" great bell): Apr-Oct daily 9am-5.30pm (6pm Jul-Aug); Nov-Mar daily 8.30am-5pm. ∞€3.50. ☎ 01/5 15 52 35 26.

The south tower (Hochturm) can be climbed to a height of 73m/240ft, while the platform of the north tower (which houses the Pummerin bell) 60m/197ft above ground is reached by lift. In fine weather there are good **views**★★ over the city, the Kahlenberg heights and the Danube plain to the east.

Dom- und Diözesanmuseum★ (KR M¹⁹)
Stephansplatz 6. ◷Tue-Sat 10am-5pm. ∞€5. ☎ 01/5 15 52 36 89. www.dommuseum. at.

This museum in the 14C former Zwettler Hof displays a fine collection of painting and sculpture alongside the cathedral's most precious treasures.

▷ *Cross Stephansplatz to Singerstraße.*

Deutschordenskirche (KR E)
This church was built by the Teutonic Order, a German hospitaller order founded in 1190. The church, a 14C Gothic building remodeled in the Baroque style, contains a beautiful 16C Flemish gilded and carved **altarpiece**★ with painted panels.

Treasure of the Teutonic Order★
◷Tue, Thu , Sat 10am-noon, Wed, Fri 3-5pm. ∞€3.60. ☎ 01/5 12 10 65.

The wealth accumulated by the order over the centuries is impressive: robes and mementoes of Heads of the Order, such as a **chain of the Order**★ (c 1500), sacred vessels, silverware, arms decorated with gold and precious stones, and also clocks, including a **longcase clock**★ carried by Hercules (about 1620).

Franziskanerkirche (KR)
This church was transformed into the Baroque taste in the 18C. On one of the right hand altars is a painting of St Francis by Johann Georg Schmidt, known as **"Wiener Schmidt,"** and an Immaculate Conception of 1722 by Johann Michael Rottmayr. The nearby **Franziskanerplatz** has a Moses fountain (1798) and, like the Ballgasse leading off it to the south, is bordered by picturesque old houses.

▷ *From Singerstraße turn right onto Blutgasse (13).*

Mozarthaus Vienna★ (KR)
Domgasse 5. ◷daily 10am-8pm. ∞€9. ☎ 01/5 13 62 94. www.mozarthausvienna. at.

The house where Mozart lived from 1784 to 1787 is now a museum with newly organized exhibits about his life and times. Visits start on the third floor, which focuses on his daily life, his sponsors, his passion for gambling and the relationship with the freemasons. The second floor zeroes in on his opera compositions, while on the first you can take a spin around the actual apartment where he lived.

▷ *Domgasse and Strobelgasse lead to busy Wollzeile. Take Essiggasse (40) almost opposite, then turn right onto elegant Bäckerstraße (9).*

Jesuitenkirche★ or Universitätskirche (KR)
Dr-Ignaz-Seipel-Platz. ◷Mon-Sat 7am-7pm, Sun 8am-8pm. ♿ ☎ 01/5 12 52 32.

Like the Salzburg Cathedral, this church was inspired by the church of Gesù in Rome and is in Baroque style. Interesting features include the **pulpit**★, inlaid with mother-of-pearl, and the dome with *trompe-l'œil* painting by Andrea Pozzo, the Jesuit lay brother who was also responsible for the high altar.

▶ *Take Sonnenfelsgasse (108) and then Schönlaterngasse (100).*

Heiligenkreuzerhof (KR 55)

The courtyard of this 18C mansion, a former dependence of Heiligenkreuz Abbey (& Stift Heiligenkreuz), is a popular retreat with artists and writers. The chapel of St. Bernhard has an altarpiece by Martin Altomonte.

▶ *Take Postgasse (97) to the Fleischmarkt.*

Hoher Markt (KR)

Interesting remains were found here of the Roman camp of Vindobona. In medieval times, this was the heart of the city, the "High Market", and also where the gallows stood. Today the square is dominated by the 1732 **Virgin Mary's Wedding fountain** (Vermählungsbrunnen) by Joseph Emmanuel Fischer von Erlach. At no 10 is a Jugendstil **clock** (1913) by Franz Matsch where figures in period dress come to life every day at noon.

▶ *Take Judengasse (KR 66) to the Ruprechtskirche.*

Ruprechtskirche (KPR)

◷*Mon-Fri 10am-1pm.* &.☎ *01/5 35 60 03.*

This church is said to have been founded in 740 by St Virgil, Bishop of Salzburg, and is the oldest building in Vienna. The nave and the foundations of the tower date from between 1130 and 1170 and the chancel and the doorway from the mid 13C. The church was finally completed in the second half of the 15C. The Romanesque belfry, Austria's oldest surviving stained-glass windows in the apse, and contemporary stained-glass windows by Lydia Roppolt (1953, 1992-93) are striking features.

▶ *Return to Sterngasse, a narrow street with some steps. Turn left onto Fischerstiege, then right onto Salvatorgasse.*

Maria am Gestade★ (JP)

Salvatorgasse; enter through the south door.

Built on a terrace above the Danube, this church was originally built in the 12C and later replaced by a Gothic edifice, of which the general outline survives. The western façade is ornamented with sculptures, and the doorway is covered by a canopy (about 1410). The seven-sided Gothic tower is surmounted by a delicately pierced **stone cap**★, which is one of the loveliest products of Viennese Gothic.

Inside, the chancel has interesting stained-glass windows, and elegant statues on the pillars of the nave.

▶ *Walk down Schwertgasse (106) – Interesting Baroque doorway at no 3.*

Wipplingerstraße

In Wipplingerstraße are two handsome Baroque buildings. On the left, the **Altes Rathaus** (JR) served as Vienna's town hall from the 14C to 19C and features the **fountain of Andromeda**★ (1741) by Raphael Donner in its courtyard. On the opposite side is the old **Böhmische Hofkanzlei** (Chancellery of Bohemia – JR H) with its outstanding façade by Johann Bernhard Fischer von Erlach (1708-14).

▶ *Skirt the chancellery to arrive at Judenplatz (JR 67), the heart of Vienna's medieval Jewish ghetto, then follow narrow Parisergasse to Am Hof.*

Uhrenmuseum der Stadt Wien★ (JR M[17])

Schulhof 2. ◷*Tue-Sat 9.30am-4.30pm.* ☜€3.60. ☎ *01/5 33 22 65.*

Three floors of displays illustrate the way clocks have changed mechanically and in appearance since the 15C. All types of clocks are represented, from the sundial to the electronic clock, not forgetting the cuckoo clock. Note the amazing **astronomical clock**★ (1769) by David a Sancto Cajetano.

Am Hof (JR)

This square, on the site of the Roman military camp, is decorated by a bronze column to the Virgin Mary (Mariensäule, 1667). It was here that Franz II, on 6 August 1806, renounced the Imperial Crown, thus ending the Holy Roman Empire.

▶ *Take Bognergasse (16) to Graben.*

Peterskirche★ (JR)

🕐*daily 8am-6pm.*

This church is regarded as the most splendid among Vienna's Baroque churches and sports lavish frescoes and gilded stuccowork. It was built from 1702 to 1708 by Johann Lukas von Hildebrandt, among others, to replace a three-aisled Romanesque church, which was itself a replacement of Vienna's earliest place of worship, a 4C building in the camp of Vindobona. The oval cupola above the nave is ornamented with a fresco attributed to Michael Rottmayr (1714) and represents the Assumption. The **interior furnishings**★ are sumptuous down to the last detail. The magnificent high altar is by Antonio Galli-Bibiena, and the altar painting by Martin Altomonte.

Pestsäule★★ (JR)

The richly decorated Baroque plague column, dominating the elegant Graben, was erected in 1693 to fulfill an oath made by Emperor Leopold I during the disastrous plague epidemic of 1679. He is shown kneeling in prayer.

▶ *Turn right onto Spiegelgasse to the Donner fountain.*

Donnerbrunnen★ (JR X)

Neuer Markt (JR 87).

The 1739 fountain by Georg Raphaël Donner features a central statue representing Providence, which is surrounded by cherubs and fish spouting water. The statues orbiting the fountain personify the rivers Traun, Ybbs, Enns and Morava (March).

The Graben with the Plague Column, Vienna

H. Wiesenhofer/ÖSTERREICH WERBUNG

These are bronze copies of the lead originals now displayed in the museum of Baroque art in the Lower Belvedere.

▶ *Return to Stephansplatz via Kärntnerstraße.*

Kunsthistorisches Museum *(HS)*

🕐*Tue-Wed, Fri-Sun 10am-6pm, 10am-9pm Thu).* ♿ ⬤€10. ☎ 01/52 52 40. www.khm. at

The five collections of Vienna's prestigious **museum of fine arts** are among the most important and largest in the world, displayed over some 4km/2.5mi of galleries. The biggest crowd pleaser
is the Gemäldegalerie (Picture Gallery) with its truly princely collection of paintings. The other collections are the Ägyptisch-Orientalische Sammlung (Egyptian and Near Eastern Collection), the Antikensammlung (Collection of Greek and Roman Antiquities), the Münzkabinett (Coin Cabinet) and the Kunstkammer (Collection of Sculpture and Decorative Arts, closed until further notice).
Please note that not all works mentioned below are guaranteed to be on display as some may be on loan to other institutions or under restoration.

Egyptian and Near Eastern Collection★★

Mezzanine level, to the right, Galleries I-IX
Gallery I – Coffins, canopic jars, human mummies; sarcophagus of Nes-schu-tefnut (c 300 BC); papyrus bundle columns★ (18th dynasty)
Gallery II – Cult chamber of Ka-ni-nisut (c 2450 BC)
Gallery III – Ushabti statuettes, ushabti boxes, amulets, wooden stelas
Gallery IV – Statuettes of divinities: enthroned Isis suckling her child Horus; animal mummies, objects for cult and magic
Gallery V – Typology of burials from the 1st dynasty to Ptolemaic times; coffins, and stelas; papyri: Book of the Dead of Khons-mes
Gallery VI – Everyday life: clothing, cosmetic implements, jewelry, food, crafts, vessels of pottery and stone
Gallery VIA – Egyptian Writing, Book of the Dead of Khonsu-iu (3rd cent. BC); Cuneiform writing; monumental inscriptions, reliefs, bronzes from Yemen (3rd cent. BC – 2nd cent. AD)
Gallery VII – Statues and reliefs from Old Kingdom, Middle Kingdom, New Kingdom; statue of Khent with her son, painted limestone Statue of Tjanuna
Gallery VIII – Statues and reliefs from New Kingdom: statue group of Hamemhab and Horus; Late Period and Ptolemaic times: colossal heads of kings
Gallery IX – reserve head from Giza★★ (c 2600 BC), sphinx head of king Sesostris III (c 1840 BC), statue of king Thutmosis III★★★ (1504-1452 BC)

Collection of Greek and Roman Antiquities★★

Mezzanine level, to the right, Galleries X-XVIII
Gallery X – Greek sculpture: Doryphoros (Roman copy), *Portrait of Aristotle*★ (Roman copy).
Gallery XI – Greek and Roman sculpture: Amazon sarcophagus★ (4C BC), Grimani reliefs (1C AD).
Gallery XII – Roman Republic: Senatus Consultum (2C BC), Patera of Aquileia (1C BC).
Gallery XIII – Roman portraits: Roman emperors, Augustus (1C AD), Mummy portraits (2C AD)
Gallery XIV – Greek pottery: Brygos-Skyphos (5C BC), *Duris Bowl* ★(5C BC)

Gallery XV – Roman handicrafts: Bronze statuettes, Head of Zeus★ (1C AD)

Gallery XVI – Greek and Roman gems and cameos: Gemma Augustea (1C AD),

Ptolemaic cameo★ (3C BC)

Gallery XVII – Late Antique and Early Medieval period: Gold treasure of Nagyszentmiklós★ (6-8C AD)

Gallery XVIII – Early Christian art: Portrait of Eutropios (5C AD), textiles (4-6C AD)

Saliera (salt cellar) by Benvenuto Cellini

Kunsthistorisches Museum

Cabinet 1 – Cyprus: Bronze Age pottery, figurines, sculpture.
Cabinet 2 – Early Etruscan pottery (Bucchero).
Cabinet 3 – Etruscan: Athena Roccaspromonte (5C BC), Negau helmets (5C BC).
Cabinet 4 – Magna Graecia: pottery, Silver Centaur* (2C BC).
Cabinet 5 – Heroon of Trysa
Cabinet 6 – Roman Austria: Treasure from Mauer an der Url (1-3C AD).
Cabinet 7 – Roman Austria: Youth from the Magdalensberg★ (16C copy)

Collection of Sculpture and Decorative Arts★★

🔒 *Closed until further notice.*

Picture Gallery★★★

Rather than providing an exhaustive list of works, the following are particularly exceptional works which really are must-sees.

Gallery IX – Michael Coxcie: *Original Sin* and *The Expulsion from the Garden of Eden* (c 1550); works by Hans Vredeman de Vries and Frans Floris.

Room 14 – Jan van Eyck: *Cardinal Niccolò Albergati*★★ (c 1435) and The Goldsmith Jan de Leeuw; Jean Fouquet: *The Ferrara Court Jester Gonella*★ (c 1440); Hugo van der Goes: *Diptych with the Fall of Man and Salvation*★★ (c 1470); Rogier van der Weyden: *Crucifixion Triptych*★ (c 1440); Hieronymus Bosch: *Christ bearing the Cross*

Room 15 – Joos van Cleve: *Lucretia*a; Jan Gossaert: *St Luke painting the Madonna*

Gallery X – 14 of the total of 45 surviving paintings by **Pieter Bruegel the Elder.** These include: *Christ bearing the Cross*★ (1564), *The Tower of Babel*★★, *Children's Games*★★ (1560), *The Battle between Carnival and Lent*★★ (1559), *Peasant Dance*★ (1568-69), and *Peasant Wedding*★, *Hunters in the Snow*★★★ (1565).

Gallery XI – Jacob Jordaens: *The Bean King's Feast (Twelfth Night)* (c 1640-45); Frans Snyders: *The Fish Market* (c 1620-30).

Room 16 – Albrecht Dürer: *Young Venetian Woman* (1505), *The Martyrdom of the Ten Thousand Christians* (1508, with a self portrait of Dürer in the center of the painting), the *Adoration of the Holy Trinity*★★ (1511) and *Mary with the reclining Child* (1512).

Room 17 – Albrecht Dürer: portrait of *Emperor Maximilian I*★ (1519); Martin Schongauer: *The Holy Family*a (c 1480-90); Lucas Cranach the Elder: *Judith with the Head of Holofernes*★ (c 1530). Albrecht Altdorfer: *The Birth of Christ*★ (c 1520-25).

Room 18 – Hans Holbein the Younger: *Jane Seymour*★ (c 1536-37).

Room 19 – Giuseppe Arcimboldo: *Fire*★★ (1566); Georg Flegel: *Still Life of Dessert with a Bunch of Flowers*★ (1632).

Gallery XII – Anthony van Dyck:, *Nicolas Lanier*★★, *Venus in Vulcan's Forge*★.

Room 20 – Peter Paul Rubens: *Young Girl with Fan* (c 1612-14).

KUNSTHISTORISCHES MUSEUM (1st floor)

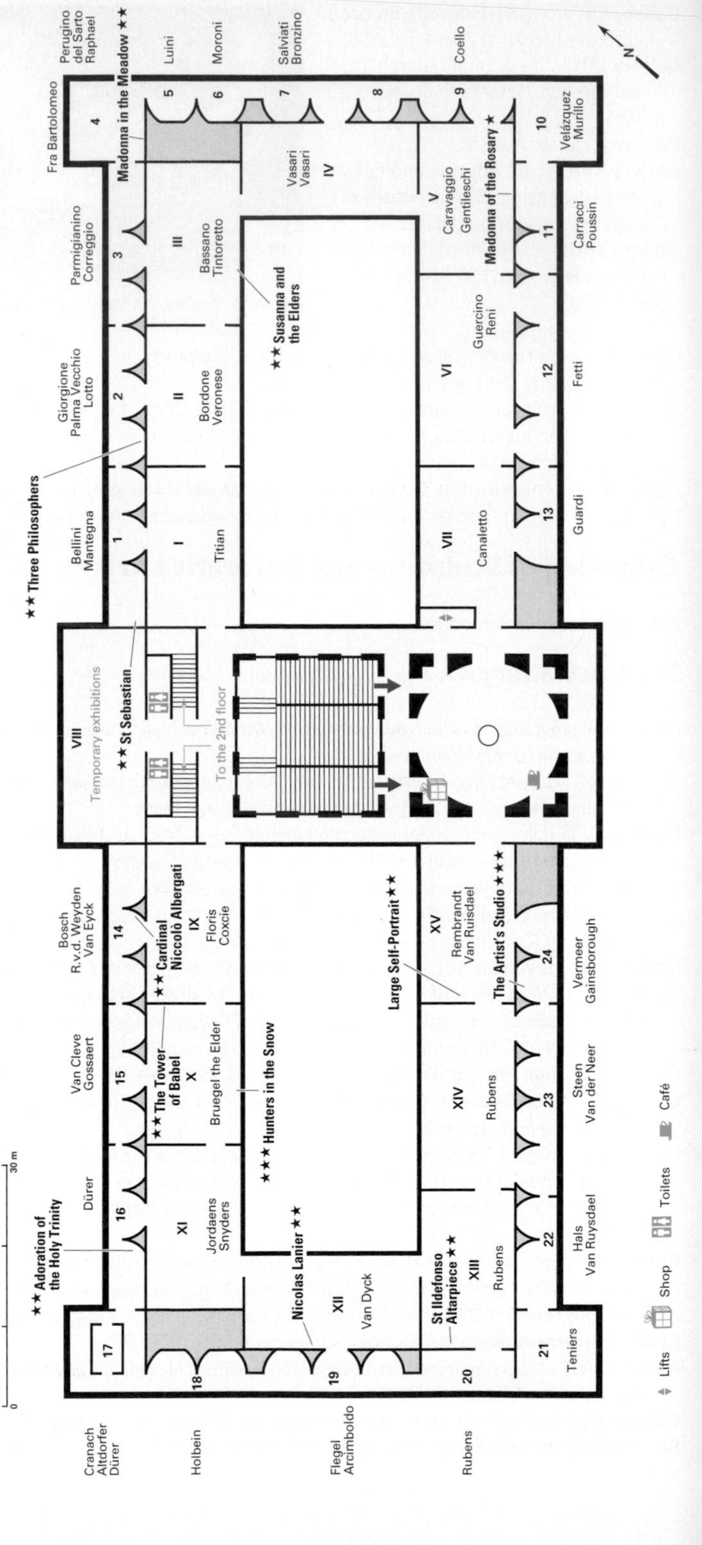

Kunsthistorisches Museum, Wien/ Bildagentur Buenos Dias

Archduke Leopold Wilhelm in his Picture Gallery in Brussels by David Teniers the Younger

Gallery XIII – *Self-portrait* (c 1638-40), *Hélène Fourment with Fur Cloak*★★ (c 1636-38), *St Ildefonso Altarpiece*★★ (c 1630-32).

Gallery XIV – *Vincenzo II, Gonzaga* (c 1604-05), *Medusa's Head* (c 1617-18).

Room 21 – David Teniers the Younger: *Archduke Leopold Wilhelm in his Picture Gallery in Brussels*★ (c 1651).

Room 22 – Salomon van Ruysdael: *Landscape with Wooden Fence and Cloudy Sky*

Room 23 – Aert van der Neer: *Riverscape with Boats by Moonlight* (c 1665-1709).

Room 24 – Thomas Gainsborough: *Suffolk Landscape* (c 1748); Jan Vermeer: *The Artist's Studio*★★★ (c 1665-66).

Gallery XV – Rembrandt: *The Artist's Mother as Hannah the Prophetess* and *The Artist's Son Titus van Rijn reading,* as well as the very interesting pair of paintings *Small Self-portrait*★ (c 1657) and *Large Self-portrait*★★ (1652).

Gallery I – Titian: *The Gipsy Madonna* (c 1510), *The Madonna with the Cherries* (c 1516-17), *Young Woman with a Fur*★ (c 1535) and *Ecce Homo*★ (1543).

Room 1 – Andrea Mantegna: *St Sebastian*★ (c 1457-59); Giovanni Bellini: *Young Woman at her Toilette* (1515).

Room 2 – Giorgione: *Laura* (1506) and the *Three Philosophers*★★ (c 1508-09); Lorenzo Lotto: *Portrait of a Young Boy in front of a White Curtain*★ (c 1508).

Gallery II – Veronese: *Adoration of the Magi* (c 1580-88).

Gallery III – Tintoretto: *Lorenzo Soranzo* (1553), *Susanna and the Elders*★★ (c 1555).

Room 3 – Correggio: *Abduction of Ganymede* (c 1530)

Room 4 – Perugino: *The Baptism of Christ* (c 1498-1500); Andrea del Sarto: *The Mourning of Christ* (c 1519-20); Raphael: the *Madonna in the Meadow*★★ (1505-06).

Room 5 – Bernardino Luini: *Salome with the Head of St John the Baptist* (c 1525-30).

Room 7 – Bronzino: *Holy Family with St Anne and St John the Baptist* (c 1540).

Room 10 – Velázquez: *Portraits of the Infanta*★. Murillo: *St Michael* (c 1665-68).

Room 11 – Annibale Carracci: *Pietà*★ (c 1603).

Gallery V – Caravaggio: *David with the Head of Goliath*★ (1606-07) and *Madonna of the Rosary*★ (c 1606-07).

Gallery VI – Guercino: *Return of the Prodigal Son*★ (c 1619); Giordano: *Archangel Michael and the Rebellious Angels*★ (c 1660-65).

Gallery VII – Hyacinthe Rigaud: *Count Ludwig Philipp Wenzel Sinzendorf* (1728); Canaletto: *Vienna from the Belvedere*★ (c 1758-61).

Coin Cabinet

Second floor, to the left.
This section of the museum holds a collection of some 700 000 items, making it one of the largest numismatic collections in the world. Besides medals, decorations and insignia, there is also an account of the evolution of money from coins to notes. The coin collection includes Ferdinand II of Tyrol's 16C portrait collection.

Museums Quartier (HS)

The former Imperial stables by Fischer von Erlach have been converted into a spectacular 60 000 sq meter/645 834 sq feet cultural complex that ranks among the world's ten largest. Blending Baroque and new architecture, it is a progressive beehive of activity that harbors the prestigious modern art-focused Leopold Museum and the Museum Moderner Kunst; the **Kunsthalle wien**, a contemporary exhibition space; the ZOOM Kindermuseum for kids; TanzQuartier, a center for dance; artist and architecture studios; new media production facilities and plenty of cafés, bars and shops. It is also an important festival location, hosting the Viennale film festival and the ImPulse dance festival, among others.

Leopold Museum

◐*Mon, Wed, Fri-Sun 10 am-6pm, Thu 10am-9pm.* ✎€9. ☎*01/52 57 00. www.leopoldmuseum.org.*
This museum presents a thorough survey of all major names and movements in modern Austrian art, including Viennese Secessionism, Viennese Modernism, and Austrian Expressionism. It is based on the private collection assembled by Rudolf and Elisabeth Leopold over five decades. Masterpieces by all the heavy-hitters are here, including the world's largest Egon Schiele collection and seminal works by Gustav Klimt, Oskar Kokoschka, Albin Egger-Lienz and Herbert Boeckl. A fine selection of Jugendstil objects by by Otto Wagner, Adolf Loos, Josef Hoffmann and others rounds off the presentation.

Museum Moderner Kunst (MUMOK)

◐*Tue-Wed, Fri-Sun 10am-6pm, Thu 10am-9pm.* ✎€9.☎*01/5 25 00. www.mumok.at*
Inside a radically angular building, this is the largest **collection of modern and contemporary art** in Austria, showcasing a comprehensive cross-section of international and Austrian 20C art. Works by Jawlensky and Kokoschka represent Expressionism; Fernand Léger, among others, stands for Cubism; Max Ernst and René Magritte for Surrealism; Arman for Nouveau Réalisme; and Robert Rauschenberg and Andy Warhol for Pop Art. Examples of international painting of the 1980s and 1990s include works by Georg Baselitz, Jörg Immendorf and Ernesto Tatafiore. There's also space devoted to "Wiener Aktionismus" (Hermann Nitsch, Günter Brus and Arnulf Rainer). Temporary exhibits add an extra dimenion to the permanent galleries.

ZOOM Kindermuseum

◐*Mon-Fri 8.30am-5pm, Sat-Sun 10am-5.30pm.* ✎€5. ☎*01/524 79 08. www.kindermuseum.at.*
Kids This children's museum is divided into two sections. Zoom Ozean is a multisensory experience designed to help kids under six develop motor and language skills. Older kids gravitate to the main exhibition, or the lab and studio where they can learn about art, science and culture in an interactive, playful environment. All sessions start at set times and reservations are recommended.

Prince Eugene of Savoy (1663-1736)

Eugene of Savoy joined the French army under Louis XIV but resigned his commission when he was refused the command of a regiment and entered into the service of Leopold I. At the age of 20, he joined the relief army commanded by the Polish king Jan Sobieski, which in 1683 freed Vienna from the Turkish siege.

The soldier once spurned by Louis XIV achieved great fame when the Austrian army under his command defeated the Turks in the Battle of Zenta (1697). Prince Eugene, the "saviour of Christendom" and a field marshal at the age of 25, became Joseph I's confidant and political adviser and senior minister under Charles VI. In 1714, he had the satisfaction of signing the Treaty of Rastatt with Louis XIV.

The Prince was showered with honors and money and had two magnificent residences, a town palace in the Himmelpfortgasse (now the Ministry of Finance), and his summer seat, the Belvedere.

Belvedere★★

🕐Tue-Sun 10am-6pm. ♿ ☕€9. ☎ 01/79 55 71 34. www.belvedere.at

The two palaces of the Belvedere were built by the architect Lukas von Hildebrandt for **Prince Eugene of Savoy** (1663-1736) and are seen as major works of Baroque architecture. The Unteres (Lower) Belvedere was built in 1716 as a summer residence, while the Oberes (Upper) Belvedere was completed in 1722 as a place for festivities. Both Belvedere palaces house collections from the **Österreichische Galerie Belvedere**. Collections of the 19C and 20C are in the Oberes Belvedere, while the Museum of Baroque Art and the Museum of Medieval Art are in the Unteres Belvedere.

Oberes Belvedere★★ (FV)

👁See Introduction: ABC of architecture.

The palace's main façade faces south and is distinguished by splendid doorways in the central section. The four figures of Atlas to the right of the vestibule, the **Sala Terrena**★, are by Lorenzo Mattielli, while Carlo Carlone was responsible for the frescoes. A grand staircase leads to the vast red **Marmorsaal** (Marble Hall) on the first floor. It was here on 15 May 1955 where the signing of the State Treaty took place, putting an end to the occupation of Austria by the Allied Powers.

Galerie des 19. und 20. Jahrhunderts★★ (M²⁵)

Ground floor
Special exhibitions.

1st floor
Crossing from the staircase to the Marmorsaal, the section on "Historicism, Realism and Symbolism" is on the left, while galleries on the right are dedicated to French Impressionism with works by Monet, Renoir as well as van Gogh's The Plein at Auvers. Works of Austrian artists will also claim your attention: Hans Makart (Lady at the Spinet★, The Five Senses★), Anton Romako (Empress Elisabeth★★, Mathilde Stern★), Gustav

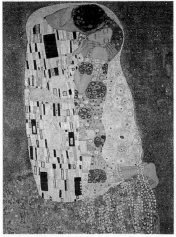

The Kiss by Gustav Klimt

BILDAGENTUR BUENOS DIAS

Klimt (*The Kiss*★★, *The Bride*★★) and Egon Schiele (*Death and the Maiden*★★, *Four Trees*★★).

2nd floor

From the top of the staircase, the sections "Classicism" and "Romanticism" are on the right and "Biedermeier" on the left. In addition to historical paintings, works by Moritz von Schwind (*Party Game*★), Ferdinand Georg Waldmüller, Caspar David Friedrich (*Rocky Landscape in the Elbsandsteingebirge*) and Friedrich von Amerling (*Girl in a Straw Hat*★) are displayed.

Belvedere Gardens

🕐*Apr-Oct daily 6am-sunset, Nov-Mar daily 6.30am-sunset.* ✍free . ☎ *01/7 98 41 20.*
The palace is surrounded by some of the grandest and most important Baroque gardens in Europe, laid out in the French style starting in 1697 by Lukas von Hildebrandt, Dominique Girard and Anton Zinner. The upper part represents Olympus, the central part Parnassus and the lower part the domain of the Four Elements. From the highest point there is a wonderful **view**★ over the garden and the city.

▶ *Descend to the Unteres Belvedere along the right-hand side of the gardens.*

Unteres Belvedere★ (KLS)

The Lower Belvedere is fronted by a court of honor entered through an impressive gateway bearing the cross of Savoy in its gable. The long building has a well-proportioned façade on the garden side and sumptuous apartments that make an ideal setting for the display of 18C Austrian painting and sculpture.

Barockmuseum★★

Paintings and sculptures from the late 17C and 18C Baroque period are displayed in various rooms, each of which is a work of art in its own right. The magnificent **Marble Room**★ features a ceiling fresco by Martin Altomonte depicting the *The Apotheosis of Prince Eugene*. You can also admire the original **Mehlmarkt fountain**★★ by **Georg Raphael Donner** (1693-1741), a copy of which stands on the Neuer Markt.

In the **Grotesque Room**★, named after the motifs of the stuccowork that adorns its walls, there are, besides the wonderfully luminous wall-paintings by Jonas Drentwett, the marvelous **character heads**★ sculpted by **Franz Xaver Messer-schmidt**, who also executed the figures of Maria Theresia and Francis of Lorraine in the marble gallery. This gallery is also home to the famous Herculanean Women. Nearby is the dazzling **Gold Room**★★ with its mirrors and gilded carved woodwork, in which **Balthasar Permoser**'s impressive marble sculpture of *The Apotheosis of Prince Eugene*★ is reflected many times over. The sculptor positioned a figure of himself at the feet of the prince.

Among the many paintings here, the following are stand-outs: *Christ on the Mount of Olives*★ by Paul Troger (c 1750), *Napoleon on the St Bernard Pass*★ by Jacques Louis David (1801) and *View of Laxenburg*★ by Johann Christian Brand (1758).

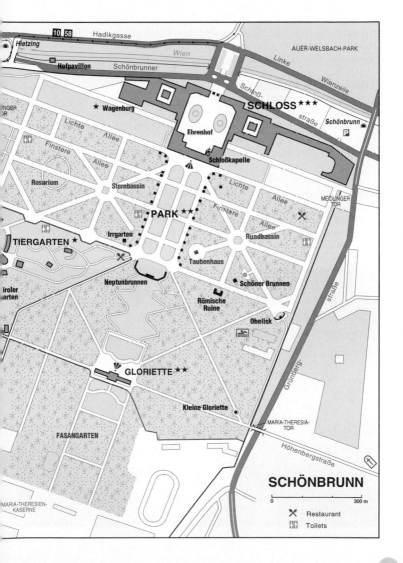

Museum mittelalterlicher Kunst★

The museum is housed in the Orangery adjoining the Unteres Belvedere. The works are mostly from the Gothic period from around 1400 until the early 16C. There are rare altar panel paintings and such impressive works as *Christ's Crucifixion*★ by Conrad Laib (1449); the *Mourning of Christ*★ by the Master of the Viennese Schottenaltar (c 1469); the *Legend of Susanna*★ by the Carinthian painter Urban Görtschacher; and several works by the Tyrolean painter and sculptor Michael Pacher.

Schloss Schönbrunn★★ (AZ)

U-Bahn – U-4 (green line): Schönbrunn or Hietzing stop.
A UNESCO World Heritage Site since 1996, the Imperial palace of Schönbrunn occupies what was once a favored hunting ground of the Habsburgs. Construction of the family's imposing summer residence began in 1695 and was originally based on the plans of Johann Bernhard Fischer von Erlach. The palace got its present form under Maria Theresia and reflects the vision of architect Nicolas Pacassi. The park was laid out by French landscape architect Jean Trehet and later modified by Johann Ferdinand Hetzendorf of Hohenberg, who also contributed the Neptune fountain, Roman ruin, Obelisk and Gloriette.

Tour of the Palace★★

🕒 *Jul-Aug daily 8.30am-6pm, Apr-Jun, Sep-Oct daily 8.30am-5pm, Nov-Mar daily 8.30am-4.30pm.* 👤 ∞€8.90 *(Imperial Tour), €11.50 (Grand Tour), includes audio-guide.* ☎ *01/81 11 32 39. www.schoenbrunn.at.*
The main building stretches for 180m/550ft in classically restrained Baroque style and is painted in a pleasing color known as Schönbrunn Yellow; green window frames provide additional accents.
Self-guided audio tours take in either 22 rooms (Imperial Tour) or 40 rooms (Grand Tour) out of a total of 1440, each of which seems to outdo the other in opulence. Elegant stuccowork, crystal chandeliers, richly ornamented faience stoves, and priceless tapestries and furniture give the apartments an exceptional air of magnificence.

Great Gallery

The **apartments of Emperor Franz Joseph and Empress Elisabeth** are followed by three **ceremonial rooms** decorated by the Austrian painter Josef Rosa and two **Chinese chambers**★, one adorned with lacquerwork, the other with porcelain. The **Maria Theresia apartments** are among the most luxurious in the palace. They include the **Blue Salon**, which is hung with Chinese tapestry and was where the negotiations took place that led to Karl I, last of the Habsburgs, abdication on 11 November 1918. Other stand-outs are the **Vieux-Lacque Room**★, with black oriental lacquered paneling framing intricate miniatures; the Napoleon Room, decorated with Flemish tapestry; and the lavish **Millionenzimmer**★ with its South American rosewood paneling framing Indo-Persian miniatures painted upon paper. Finally, the tour reaches the **Great Gallery**★★★, where the delegates to the 1814-15 Congress of Vienna danced and partied.

Schlosspark★★

Apr-Oct daily 6am-sunset, Nov-Mar daily 6.30am-sunset. free.

Kids The park gardens are a remarkable creation of Baroque art, mixed with a shot of Rococo and antiquity. Arbors and vast formal beds of flowers serve as backdrops for charming groups of allegorical statues and gracious fountains.

Shaded walks lead to the Neptune fountain (Neptunbrunnen), the Roman ruin (Römische Ruine) and the **Tiergarten**★ (*Apr-Sep daily 9am-6.30pm; Mar, Oct daily 9am-5.30pm; Feb daily 9am-5pm; Nov-Jan daily 9am-4.30pm;* €12; 01/8 77 92 94; www.zoovienna.at), the oldest zoological gardens in the world.

The **Palmenhaus**★ (*May-Sep daily 9.30am-6pm; Oct-Apr daily 9.30am-5pm.* €4. 01/8 77 50 87; www.bundesgaerten.at) is the European continent's largest glass and metal hothouse, completed in 1882. It shelters some 4 000 plants from all over the world, including Himalayan mountain plants and tropical rainforest vegetation.

Gloriette★★

Apr-Jun, Sep daily 9am-6pm, Jul-Aug daily 9am-7pm, Oct daily 9am-5pm. €2. 01/81 11 32 39.

This elegant colonnaded structure offers fine views of Schönbrunn and western Vienna from its roof terrace. It resembles a triumphal arch was built to commemorate Maria Theresa's victory over the Prussians in 1757 during the Seven Years War. The café is a nice spot for a break.

Wagenburg★

Apr-Oct daily 9am-6pm, Nov-Mar Tue-Sun 10am-4pm. €4.50. 01/8 77 32 44.

The **coach house** contains a great collection of Imperial coaches from the early 18C to the 20C. Worth keeping an eye out for are the **phaeton of the King of Rome**★ and the gilded and ornate **Imperial coach**★★ of Emperor Franz Stephan, Maria Theresa's husband, which was pulled by eight white horses.

Jugendstil Buildings

Rejecting the academic architecture of the Ring, the architects of the Vienna Secession designed several buildings that put their theories into practice, marking an important stage in the development of modern European architecture.

Wagner-Pavillons★ (JS)

Karlsplatz.

Otto Wagner's two highly original Viennese Jugendstil pavilions, designed in 1899, face each other to the north of the Karlskirche. The extraordinary combination of glass, white marble and green-painted metalwork, topped with a corrugated copper roof, was an innovative approach to architecture at the time. One building still serves as an entrance to the U-Bahn (subway, underground) and as an exhibition center, while the other houses a café in the summer months.

Secession★★ (JS)

⏱Tues, Wed, Fri-Sun 10am-6pm, Thu 10am-8pm. ♿ ⊚€6, includes Beethoven Frieze and current exhibit. €4.50 current exhibit only. ☎ 01/5 87 53 07.

The Secession building in Vienna has been run as an exhibition hall for contemporary by the artists' association of the same name since 1898. It is a Jugendstil masterpiece built by **Joseph Maria Olbrich**, a pupil of Wagner.

The undisputed highlight here is the 34m/111ft -long **Beethoven Frieze★★★**, a monumental 1902 work by **Gustav Klimt** on the theme of the Ninth Symphony.

Postsparkasse & Wagner:Werk★ (LR)

Georg-Koch-Platz 2. ⏱Mon-Wed, Fri 8am-3pm, Thu 8am-5.30pm, Sat 10am-5pm. ♿ ⊚€5. Main Hall free. ☎ 01/53 45 33 30 88. www.ottowagner.de.

Otto Wagner's seminal building, the postal savings banks was completed in 1912 using the time's most modern materials (aluminium, glass bricks) and construction methods. Still a bank today, its 'small lobby' recently opened as **Wagner:Werk**, a small exhibit about the architect containing some 200 historical photos, documents, newspaper articles, plans, innovative materials and a model of the building.

Wagner-Pavillon, Karlsplatz

Georg Mikes

Otto Wagner Kirche am Steinhof★★ (AS)

Baumgartnerhöhe 1. 👣Guided tour (45min) Sat 3pm by prior reservation. ⊚€4. ☎ 01/91 06 01 12 04.

Vienna's first modern church was completed by Wagner in 1907 for a mental institution, which it still serves today. Its interior is functional as well as aesthetic. The stoups containing holy water were designed to avoid contamination, the floor slopes towards the altar to create good sight lines for most worshippers, and all parts of the building are easily accessible for maintenance purposes. Such functionality is softened to some extent by the white-gold wall covering. The large side **stained-glass windows★** with their typically linear Jugendstil figures are an impressive sight.

Musical Memories

Staatsoper★★ (JS)

👣Guided tour (40min) Jul-Aug daily 11am, 1pm, 2pm and 3pm; May-Jun, Sep-Oct daily 1pm, 2pm and 3pm; Nov-Apr daily 2pm and 3pm. ⏱Good Fri, 24 Dec and during rehearsals (phone ahead for schedule). ♿⊚€5.50. ☎ 01/5 14 44 26 06.

Begun in 1861 and formally opened in 1869 by Emperor Franz Joseph II with a performance of Mozart's *Don Giovanni*, the opera house was the first of the great public edifices to be completed along the Ring. It has since been helmed by such outstanding directors as Gustav Mahler, Richard Strauss, Karl Böhm, Herbert von Karajan, Lorin Maazel and Claudio Abbado. Players in the famous **Vienna Philharmonic** (Wiener Philharmoniker) are recruited from the members of the Staatsoper orchestra.

Tours take in the stage and backstage, the **interval rooms** and the Gustav Mahler Room decorated with modern tapestries illustrating scenes from Mozart's *Magic*

Flute. Decor in the **foyer**★ is by the painter Moritz von Schwind. The **tea room** and the magnificent **grand staircase**★ were among the few sections of the building spared by a sweeping fire in 1945. Completing this sophisticated setting is the horseshoe-shaped main auditorium with its 2 280 seats.

Haydnhaus★ (EV M^{10})
Haydngasse 19. ⏰*Tue-Sun 10am-1pm, 2-6pm.* €2, Sun free. ☎ *01/5 96 13 07.*
The house where the composer wrote the oratorios *The Creation* (1798) and *The Seasons* (1801) is now a museum. Exhibits illustrate the context of the music and in particular the places that were important in Haydn's life.

Schubert Geburtshaus★ (ET M^5)
Nussdorfer Straße 54. ⏰*Tue-Sun 9am-1pm, 2-6pm.* €2, Sun free. ☎ *01/3 17 36 01.*
The house in which Schubert was born on 31 January 1797 and where he spent the first four years of his life (he later lived at Säulengasse 4) has been restored to its original modest state. There is a museum on the first floor.

Mozarthaus Vienna★ (KR) ♿ *see entry.*

Zentralfriedhof (CZ)
⏰*May-Aug 7am-7pm; Mar-Apr, Sep-Oct 7am-6pm; Nov-Feb 8am-5pm.* ♿ ☎ *01/7 60 41.*
Beethoven, Brahms, Gluck, Schubert and Hugo Wolf are all buried in the "Musicians' Corner" (Plot 32A) of this famous cemetery, alongside operetta and waltz masters Johann Strauss the Elder and the Younger, Josef Lanner, Karl Millöcker, Franz von Suppé. In Plot 32C lie Arnold Schoenberg and Franz Werfel Jürgens, while 14A has Theophil von Hansen and Hans Makart and 0 Antonio Salieri and Adolf Loos. *Cemetery plans are available at the second (main) entrance gateway.*

St. Marxer Friedhof (CZ)
Mozart was buried here on 6 December 1791 in a pauper's grave. His mortal remains have never been found.

Additional Sights

Within the Ring

Michaelerkirche (JR)
⏰*7am-10pm.* *Guided tours (30min) Mon-Fri 11am, 2pm, 3pm, Sat 3pm, 4pm.* €5. ☎ *01/533 8000. www.michaelerkirche.at.*
This Romanesque-Gothic church with its neo-Classical façade (1792) is famous for a group of rococo figures above the high altar (1781) representing the **Fall of the Angels**★. Tours lead down into the **crypt** where you can admire musty old coffins filled with bones and bodies in various states of decay.

Jüdisches Museum der Stadt Wien★ (JR)
⏰*Sun-Wed, Fri 10am-6pm, Thu 10am-8pm.* ♿ €5. ☎ *01/5 35 04 31. www.jmw.at.*
The Adelspalais Eskeles in Dorotheergasse 11 dates back to the 15C and since 1993 houses the city's **Jewish museum**. It displays religious and ceremonial objects, documents, paintings and drawings chronicling the history of Vienna's and Austria's large Jewish community.

Minoritenkirche (JR)
⏰*Apr-Oct daily 8am-6pm; Nov-Mar daily 9am-5pm.* ☎ *01/5 33 41 62.*

The early 14C Minorite church is easily recognized by its landmark octagonal tower. The huge mosaic on the north wall depicting Leonardo da Vinci's *Last Supper* was commissioned by Napeleon and executed by Roman artist Giacomo Raffaelli.

Beyond the Ring

Karlskirche★★ (KS)

Kreuzherrengasse. ○*Mon-Sat 9am-12.30pm, 1pm-6pm, Sun 12pm-5.45pm.* ⊛€6. ☎ *01/5 04 61 87. www.karlskirche. at.*

This massive domed church, which is dedicated to St Charles Borromeo, is an 18C work of Johann Bernhard Fischer von Erlach and a harmonious mix of styles and architectural features. It was built following a vow of Emperor Charles VI during the plague of 1713. Admission includes an elevator ride to a **viewing platform** at 32.5m/107ft inside the church. From up here you can get a sense of the building's dimensions, inspect Johann Michael Rottmayr's dome frescoes from close-up and enjoy sweeping city views. Several centuries' of church treasures can be admired at the new **Museum Borromeo**.

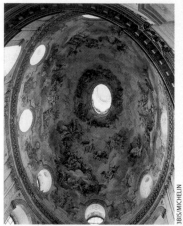

Dome of the Karlskirche, Vienna

Wienmuseum★ (KS)

Karlsplatz 8. ○*Tue-Sun 9am-6pm.* ⛦⊛€6. ☎ *01/50 58 74 70. www.wien-museum.at.*

The history of Vienna takes centerstage at this museum whose fine array of artefacts includes the **circular plan of Vienna**★ (1545) by Augustin Hirschvogel. Other noteworthy displays include excavations from the Roman military camp, medieval stained-glass windows and statues of royalty from the cathedral, booty taken from the Turks after the second siege of Vienna in 1683, porcelain and glassware from Viennese workshops and crafts from the Wiener Werkstätte. Added to these are the reconstructed interiors of the *Pompeian Room*★ (c 1800) from the Palais Caprara-Geymüller, author Franz Grillparzer's Biedermeier style living room, and Adolf Loos' dining room. Outstanding paintings include Baroque works by Maulbertsch, Rottmayr and Troger and various 19C masterpieces, including *Love*★ and *Emilie Flöge* by Gustav Klimt and *Self-portrait with Splayed fingers*★★ and *Blind Mother* by Egon Schiele.

Prater Giant Wheel

Prater★ (CY-GU)

Kids This immense green space, embraced by two arms of the Danube, was a hunting reserve under Emperor Maximilian II and opened to the public in 1766 under Joseph II. With its many cafés, the Prater was extremely popular during the heyday of the Viennese waltz. It won worldwide renown when it was featured in the film *The Third Man*; scenes for the James Bond film *The Living Daylights* were also shot here.

The most popular part of the Prater is the amusement park called "Wurstelprater," lorded over by the landmark 1897 **Riesenrad★★ (Giant Ferris Wheel)** (*May-Sep daily 9am-midnight; Mar-Apr, Oct daily 10am-10pm; Jan-Feb, Nov-Dec daily 10am-8pm.* €7.50. ☎ 01/7 29 54 30) which treats you to breathtaking **views**★ of the city.

Akademie der bildenden Künste – Gemäldegalerie★★(JS)

Enter from Makartgasse. *Tue-Sun 10am-6pm.* €7. ☎ 01/58 81 62 25. www.akademiegalerie.at.

This outstanding collection of paintings is housed in a neo-Renaissance building by Theophil Hansen. The single most important work is the extraordinary *Triptych of the Last Judgement*★★★ by **Hieronymus Bosch** (1460-1516), a terrifying work where monsters and phenomena symbolize the sins and suffering of humankind. There are plenty more highlights, including: *Lucretia*★★ by Lucas Cranach the Elder, *Boys playing Dice*★ by Bartolomé Esteban Murillo, a *Self-portrait*★ (c 1615) by Anthony van Dyck and *Portrait of a young Woman*★★ (1632) by Rembrandt. Top works from the 18C collection are the eight *Views of Venice*★ by Francesco Guardi and the famous *Still-life with Flowers and Fruit*★ (1703) by Rachel Ruysch.

Österreichisches Museum für Angewandte Kunst (MAK)★★ (LR)

Tue 10am-midnight, Wed-Sun 10am-6pm. €10. ☎ 01/71 13 60. www.mak.at.

The Austrian museum of applied arts takes up a neo-Renaissance building by Heinrich von Ferstel and has a remarkable **display concept**★★ where the layout of certain rooms was entrusted to artists: Baroque, Rococo and Classical furniture were set out by **Donald Judd**; the outstanding collection of lace and glassware by Franz Graf; Empire and Biedermeier exhibits by Jenny Holzer; 20C applied arts by Manfred Wakolbinger. A surprise is in store with the Historicism and Jugendstil display, which Barbara Bloom has reduced to Michael Thonet's seminal bentwood chairs.

The depth and range of the collection are truly astonishing. Highlights include **liturgical vestments**★ (c 1260) from the Benedictine monastery of Göss in Styria; a

Österreichisches Museum für Angewandte Kunst, Vienna

Museum für angewandte Kunst, Wien

tabletop★★ of painted cherrywood from late 15C Swabia; an amazing Biedermeier **cherrywood secretaire**★ made in Vienna in 1825; a superb collection of **oriental carpets and rugs**★★; **drawings**★★ prepared by Gustav Klimt for the Palais Stoclet in Brussels; and a sampling of items from the **Wiener Werkstätte**★★, the famous arts and crafts workshop.

Naturhistorisches Museum★ (HR)

Wed 9am-9pm , Thu-Sun 9am-6.30pm. €8. *01/52 17 70. www.nhm-wien. ac.at.*

The collections of Vienna's **natural history museum** are among the finest in the world and presented in a dynamic, contemporary fashion. Some of the biggest crowd magnets are in the Prehistory section (mezzanine level) and include the famous 25 000-year-old **Venus of Willendorf**★, remarkable finds from the **Hallstatt graves** and a dinosaur room**.** On the same floor, the **Mineralogy section**★★ has such rare and exquisite specimens as a 1m/3ft long piece of quartz crystal from Madagascar, a topaz from Brazil weighing 117kg/257lb and the famous "**bouquet of jewels**"★ (1760), a gift from Maria Theresa to her husband, Francis of Lorraine.

Upstairs, the Zoology section has an impressive collection of stuffed birds, including such extinct species as the moa and the dronte. There's also an extinct **Stellersche sea cow**★ and various other stuffed animals, including an Indian Ghavial, a fearsome river-dwelling crocodile endemic to India.

Naschmarkt (HJS)

Linke Wienzeile.

The market's produce stalls make a lively picture, full of local color. A **flea market** takes place Saturdays on Kettenbrückengasse, the extension of Naschmarkt.

Hundertwasserhaus (GU F)

Löwengasse/Kegelgasse.

The Viennese artist, **Friedensreich Hundertwasser**, used this 1984 apartment block to create a type of mass housing that marries human needs with the environment. His colorful, eccentric building makes ample use of arcaded loggias, galleries, statues and other design elements as well as an extraordinary range of materials (glass, brick, rendering etc). The terraced roof garden is also typical of his approach.

KunstHausWien (GU G)

Untere Weissgerberstraße 13. daily 10am-7pm. €9. 01/7 12 04 91. www. kunsthauswien.com.

This museum was designed by Hundertwasser and contains the world's only permanent exhibit about his work, philosophy and architecture. The other part of the building is used for temporary art exhibitions.

Heeresgeschichtliches Museum★ (GV)

Sat-Thu 9am-5pm. €5.10. *01/79 56 10. www.hgm.or.at.*

The exhaustive and excellent **army museum** inside a former munitions depot tells the history of Austria through

Hundertwasserhaus

Court furniture

The court furniture inspectors were entrusted with transporting furniture, carpets, tapestries etc to the various royal premises and to store and look after them. Until the early 19C only the Vienna Hofburg was permanently furnished, while the Imperial summer residences and hunting lodges were only furnished when any royals were in residence. For coronations and royal weddings (sometimes as far away as Frankfurt or Florence) furniture had to be transported for as many as 1 000 people. Up to 100 wagons would leave in advance of the royal party to outfit the living and function rooms. Only after Franz II took the reigns after 1808 were the less frequently used palaces and residences gradually left ready furnished.

its military exploits. All major conflicts since the Thirty Years' War are covered, including the Turkish threat, the Napoleonic era and the First World War. There are special rooms dedicated to Prince Eugen, the heroic general who dealt Turkish troops a decisive defeat; Maria Theresa and her feuds with Prussia; and Archduke Franz Ferdinand's assassination in Sarajevo, featuring the actual car in which he and his wife were shot.

Kaiserliches Hofmobiliendepot★ (EU M¹¹)
Andreasgasse 7. ⏱Tue-Sun 9am-5pm. ♿ ➿€6.90. ☎ 01/5 24 33 57. www.hofmobiliendepot.at.
This **collection of period furniture** - one of the world's largest - gives you a sense of what being "at home with the emperor" might have been like. Besides original furniture once used by the Habsburgs, interesting exhibits include the coffin in which Emperor Maximilian of Mexico was shipped back to Europe following his assassination; Prince Rudolf's cradle; and the wheelchair used by Maria Theresa's mother, Elisabeth Christine. On the second floor is the **Biedermeier** collection, which consists of bourgeois period rooms but also features bizarre spitoons and ingenious early toilets. The Modernist section has amazing furniture by Adolf Loos, Josef Hoffmann and Otto Wagner.

Technisches Museum (AZ M²)
⏱Mon-Fri 9am-6pm, Sat-Sun 10am-6pm. ➿€8.50. ☎ 01/89 99 80. www.tmw.at.
🧒Opposite Schloss Schönbrunn, the **technical museum** provides an interactive and comprehensive overview of technology and industry. The history of science, tool manufacturing, mining, process engineering, heavy industry and energy are among the themes explored here. Children especially will enjoy the hands-on experiments explaining various technical phenomena.

Excursions

Tour of the Kahlenberg Heights (AR)

Roundtrip of 33km/21mi. Leave Vienna via Heiligenstädter Straße (BX). At the Klosterneuburg-Kierling railway station turn left into the Stadtplatz and almost immediately left again. Cross the Kierlingbach creek and go uphill towards the abbey. Park in the Rathausplatz.

Klosterneuburg★ 👒 *See Klosterneuburg*

▶ *Follow Leopoldstraße south to the Weidlingbach Valley; cross Weidlinger Straße into Höhenstraße.*

Leopoldsberg★★

The most easterly spur of the Wienerwald, Leopoldsberg overlooks the Danube from 423m/1 388ft. Views are best from the Burgplatz opposite the Leopoldskirche.

▶ *Go back downhill, then turn left onto Höhenstraße.*

Kahlenberg★

There are attractive **views**★ over Vienna from the terrace next to the Kahlenberg restaurant (483m/1 585ft). In the foreground are the vineyards of Grinzing and to the right the rolling heights of the Wienerwald.

▶ *Continue on Höhenstraße as far as the Häuserl am Roan inn.*

From the parking lot, enjoy a fine view of Vienna and the Wienerwald.

▶ *Return towards the Kahlenberg; turn right into Cobenzlgasse (AR 21) down onto Grinzing.*

Grinzing★

Grinzing is the best known of Vienna's suburban wine villages. It is a pretty place with a friendly atmosphere best sampled in one of the many taverns, or Heurigen. It can get very busy here in the evenings.

Heiligenstadt

Beethoven devotees flock to Heiligenstadt's central square (Pfarrplatz) to see the little 17C house (no 2 – now a wine tavern), where the musician lived in 1817. In Probusgasse 6 stands the **Beethoven Testamenthaus** (🕐*Mar-Dec Tue, Thu, Sat-Sun 10am-noon,*

Grinzing

1-4.30pm; €1.20; *01/3 18 86 08), now a small museum, where the composer wrote his famous letter in 1802 called the *Testament of Heiligenstadt* when in despair over his deafness. The letter, addressed to his brother Carl, was never sent.

▶ *Return to Vienna along Hohe Warte* (BX 64) *and Döblinger Hauptstraße* (BXY 21).

Marchfeld Schlösser (Castles)

From Vienna to Marchegg – 58km/36mi.

The Marchfeld, a gravel plain to the east of Vienna, is a fertile region and popular hunting ground.

▶ *Leave Vienna heading east on B3, reaching Orth after about 24km/15mi/*

Orth an der Donau

This newly restored castle has a pedigree going back to the 12C, but most of the present building, including the four mighty corner towers, date from the 16C. The sleek Baroque annex was added in the 17C and used a hunting lodge by the Habsburgs. The castle now houses the visitors' center of the Nationalpark Donau-Auen.

▶ *Leave Orth on B 3 towards Wagram. Turn right in Pframa towards Eckartsau.*

Eckartsau

Guided tour (40min) Apr-Oct Sat-Sun 11am and 2pm. €8. 0 22 14/22 40
This former hunting castle went Baroque around 1730 courtesy of Joseph Emanuel Fischer von Erlach; Daniel Gran painted the frescoes. It served as the final residence on Austrian soil of the Habsburg family after Karl I's abdication on 11 November 1918. On 23 March 1919, the Imperial family left from here for exile in Switzerland.

▶ *From Eckartsau take the B3 back towards Kopfstetten to the junction with the B49. Turn left towards Marchegg, arriving at Schloss Niederweiden after 2km/1mi.*

SacherTorte

Frau Sacher, a leading personality in late 19C Vienna, fed the impoverished Austrian nobility in her famous restaurant long after they had ceased to pay. She was less generous with the recipe for her celebrated torte, but many have tried to equal her pastry prowess.

Preheat the oven to 165°C/325°F (thermostat 3). Grate 180g/5-6oz semi-sweet chocolate. Cream together until smooth 100g/half a cup sugar and 115g/half a cup butter. Beat in 6 yolks, one at a time, until the mixture is light and fluffy.

Add the chocolate and 115g/half a cup dry bread crumbs, 30g/quarter cup of finely ground blanched almonds and a pinch of salt. Beat the remaining egg whites until stiff but not dry, and fold them in gently.

Pour the mixture into an ungreased tin with a removable rim. Bake for 50min to 1hr.

When the torte is cool, slice it horizontally through the middle (you may turn the top layer over so that the finished cake is flat on top) and spread 225g/1 cup apricot jam or preserve between the layers. Cover with chocolate glaze. For the genuine Viennese touch, heap on the *Schlag!*

Niederweiden

Field Marshal Ernst Rüdiger von Starhemberg commissioned Johann Bernhard Fischer von Erlach to build this Baroque hunting lodge in 1693 (*Palm Sun-Oct Sat-Sun 10am-5pm; ☎ 0 22 14/28 03; www.schlosshof.at*). In 1726 it was acquired by Prince Eugen of Savoy before being taken over by Maria Theresa in 1755 who hired Nicolas Pacassi to made the alterations that gave the palace its present form. Beneath the slate mansard roof, only the oval **Great Hall**★ painted in the Chinese hints at the magnificence of the original decoration.

▶ *Leave B 49 and head towards Schlosshof.*

Schlosshof

In 1725 Prince Eugen had the estate of Hof with its fortified castle (*mid-Apr-Oct daily 10am-6pm; €8.50; ☎ 0 22 85/65 80*) converted by Lukas von Hildebrandt into a huge Baroque palace, while the French gardens were laid out with sculptures and fountains. Maria Theresa acquired Schlosshof together with Niederweiden, added a further storey and furnished it opulently. After 200 years of continuous neglect, Schlosshof has been restored to its original splendor, boasting fine stuccowork and paintings. The restoration of the **Sala terrena**★ deserves particular praise.

▶ *Return to B 49 via Groissenbrunn and drive on to Marchegg.*

Marchegg

Although rebuilt in the 17C and 18C in the Baroque style, the origins of Schloss Marchegg (*mid-Mar-Nov Tue-Sun 9am-noon, 1pm-5pm; ☎ 0 22 85/71 00 11*) are medieval. It now houses a hunting museum on the first floor, a local history museum in the basement and an Africa-themed exhibit in the former service tract.

The view from the corner room of the northeastern wing of the **stork colony**★★ in the water meadows behind the Schloss is unforgettable.

The white storks of Marchegg

White storks have been nesting in Marchegg for many years (always in the trees, rather than on roofs or towers like storks elsewhere), during which time a steady increase in the population has been recorded. They arrive here in spring after wintering in Africa, covering the 10 000km/6 200mi in their typical gliding flight. The female then lays three or four eggs in April, which the pair of storks take turns to incubate. The chicks are hatched after about a month and have gained sufficient strength by the end of August to undertake the long journey back to Africa. They stay there for two years, and only return to Europe in their third year, usually settling where they were born.

WIENER NEUSTADT

NIEDERÖSTERREICH
POPULATION 35 050 – ALT 265M/869FT

Wiener Neustadt was founded by Duke Leopold V of Babenberg in 1194 as a fortified border post against Hungary and allegedly built using part of the ransom paid for Richard the Lionheart. Under Friedrich III, between 1440 and 1493, the town was an Imperial residence. It was here where Maximilian I was born in 1459 and buried in 1519, far from his mammoth mausoleum in Innsbruck. In 1752, Maria Theresa founded a military academy here that is still going strong today. The historic town center, now an attractive pedestrian zone, has retained its medieval layout despite suffering heavy damage during the Second World War. ⓘ Hauptplatz 1-3, A-2700, ☏ 0 26 22/37 33 11. www.wiener-neustadt.at

▶ **Orient Yourself:** Wiener Neustadt is in eastern Austria, about 38mi/60km south of Vienna.
🅿 **Parking:** Central pay parking garages are on Ungargasse, at the beginning of the pedestrianized Herzog-Leopold-Straße and on Grazer Straße by the hospital. Parking is free from noon to 1.30pm in short-term spaces only.
🚫 **Don't Miss:** Burg
🕐 **Organizing Your Time:** Half a day may suffice to absorb the city's charms.
👁 **Also See:** Wienerwald

Sights

Burg
🎧Guided tour (20min) Mon-Fri 8am-4pm, Sat 8am-3pm, Sun noon-5pm. ⊙free.
☏ 0 26 22/3 8 10.
The core of the castle dates back to the 13C, but it was subject to numerous extensions and modifications. Since 1752, it has been home of the military academy founded by Maria Theresia, which at one point was commanded by General Rommel.
The main point of interest in the central courtyard is the **Wappenwand** (Heraldic Wall), which is festooned with 107 carved coats of arms from the House of Habsburg. These frame a statue of Friedrich III, the man behind the castle's Gothic **Georgs-kapelle**. The modest hall church is the burial place of Friedrich's son, Maximilian I, who was also born in the castle.

Neuklosterkirche
Ungargasse, near the Hauptplatz.
This Gothic abbey church has some magnificent Baroque altars. Behind the high altar is the beautiful **tomb**★ of Eleanor of Portugal, the wife of Friedrich III. It was carved by Nikolaus Gerhart of Leyden in 1467.

Hauptplatz
The main town square is presided over by the **Rathaus**, with origins in 1488 although converted to the neoclassical style in 1834. The Virgin Mary column

Türkensturz, Seebenstein

M. Hertlein/MICHELIN

dates to 1678. The beautiful arcaded houses on the square's north side are from the Gothic period.

▶ *Take the Böheimgasse to the Domplatz.*

Dom

The Late Romanesque cathedral had a Gothic transept and chancel added to it in the 14C, although the furnishings are mostly 18C Baroque. An attractive surviving Romanesque feature is the **Brauttor**★, a doorway decorated with bands of lozenge and zigzag motifs. The 12 larger-than-life-size figures of the Apostles adorning the pillars are by Lorenz Luchsperger. The **high altar**, with its six Corinthian columns made of red marble, is magnificent without being overdone. The red marble **pulpit** was created in 1609 by Johann Baptist Zelpi.

In the south tower is the **Turmmuseum** (*Apr-Oct 10am-5pm Tue-Wed, 10am-8pm Thu, 10am-noon Fri, 10am-4pm Sun; €2*). Explanatory panels about the role of the former fire watchmen accompany you on your way up to the viewing platform. Pick up keys at the **Stadtmuseum** (*Petersgasse 2a; same hours as Turmmuseum; €3; 0 26 22/37 39 50; www.stadtmuseum.wrn.at*), which provides a chronicle of town history.

Excursion

Seebenstein

17km/11mi south on A2 towards Graz. Park by the local administrative offices. Follow the path to the castle, heading south. This leads to a shaded footpath up to the Türkensturz. After about 10min walk, take the left fork to the castle.

Burg Seebenstein

Guided tour (50min) Easter-2nd Sun in Oct, Sat-Sun 10.30am, 2pm and 3pm. €4. 0 26 27/4 70 17.
This proud 11C fortress houses a private collection of medieval art, including a fine Madonna by Würzburg sculptor Tilman Riemenschneider (c 1460-1531).

▶ *Return to the fork and climb a well laid out forest path for about 45min.*

Türkensturz

This "ruined" folly was built in 1825-26 by Prince Johann I of Liechtenstein, and its name harks back to a legendary event during the Turkish invasions of the 16C. It is a wonderful look-out point, with views of the Raxalpe and Schneeberg range.

WIENERWALD★

NIEDERÖSTERREICH

The hilly Vienna Woods is a delightful green lung west of Austria's capital, a region of vine-covered hills and shady woods that offers a welcome escape from the summer heat. The name Wienerwald also conjures up the musical landscapes of Beethoven's Pastoral Symphony and, of course, that famous Strauss waltz, *Tales from the Vienna Woods.* Hauptplatz 11, A-3002 Purkersdorf, 0 22 31/6 21 76, www.wienerwald.info

▶ **Orient Yourself:** Wienerwald is just southwest of Vienna.
Don't Miss: Gumpoldskirchen, Hinterbrühl

🕐 **Organizing Your Time:** Touring the Wienerwald makes for a leisurely day trip.

Kids **Especially for Kids:** Naturpark Sparbach

Tour of the Wienerwald

Leave Vienna on the B 12 and follow the sign "Perchtoldsdorf Zentrum."

Perchtoldsdorf

In the center of the market place stands the fine Pestsäule (plague column) of 1713, the work of Johann Bernhard Fischer von Erlach. The **Türkenmuseum** in the Late

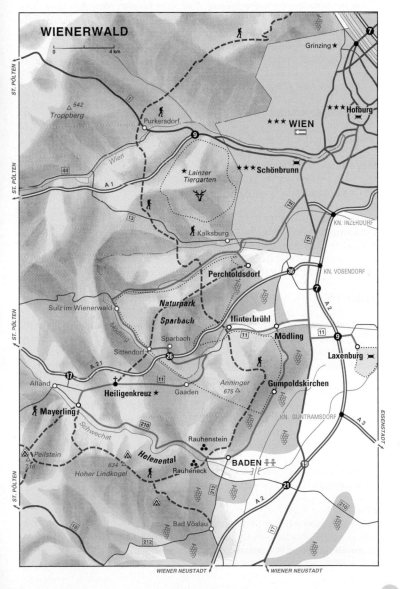

Gothic town hall keeps alive the memory of the Turkish incursions into Lower Austria. The porch of the parish church of St Augustine sports a multi-colored relief dating from 1449 portraying the **Marientod**✶ (Death of the Virgin Mary). The interior is dominated by a monumental Baroque high altar adorned with the patron saints of Styria, Carinthia, Upper Austria and Lower Austria.

To the west of the church are the remains of the Herzogsburg, a castle built between the 11C and the 15C.

▷ *In Perchtoldsdorf take the B 13 towards Vienna. After 1.3km/1mi turn onto the Kalten-leutgebnerstraße which becomes the Hauptstraße. After 11km/7mi turn left for Sulz im Wienerwald. Pass Sittendorf and follow the sign to "Naturpark Sparbach."*

Naturpark Sparbach

🕓*Apr-Oct daily 9am-6pm; Nov Sat-Sun 10am-3pm, Jan 10am-4pm, Feb 10am-5pm, Mar 10am-6pm.* ✎€3. ☎ *0 22 37/76 11.*

Kids Lower Austria's oldest nature reserve has rambling trails and game enclosures that are home to fallow deer, moufflons and other local creatures. There is also a children's zoo and a pretty lake with a watermill.

▷ *Cross the E 60/A 21 autobahn and turn right onto the B 11 direction Gaaden.*

Stift Heiligenkreuz★ ✆ *See Stift Heiligenkreuz.*

▷ *Continue on the B 11 direction Alland. After 4km/2.5mi turn left for Mayerling.*

Mayerling ✆ *See Mayerling.*

▷ *Turn left onto the B 210 direction Baden.*

Helenental

The Schwechat winds its way through this valley, which has been featured in tradi-tional songs numerous times. Some 60km/37mi of marked trails make this a good area for getting out and about. Just before reaching Baden, the ruins of the castles of Rauhenstein (12C, on the left) and Rauheneck (11C, on the right) come into view.

Baden✝✝ ✆ *See Baden.*

▷ *To get onto the Weinstraße (Wine Road) to Gumpoldskirchen and Mödling from the center of Baden, pass under the railway on the Kaiser-Franz-Joseph-Ring and then turn immediately left onto the B 212. Continue under another bridge, turn right at the stop sign and then immediately left for Gumpoldskirchen.*

Gumpoldskirchen

This charming place at the foot of the 674m/2 211ft high Anninger has achieved great fame for its superb white wines. An educational wine trail (*labeled Weinwan-derweg*) leads through the vineyards (here called "Rieden"). In town, the delightful Renaissance town hall in Kirchengasse catches the eye.

▷ *The road meanders through the vineyards, opening up wonderful views towards Mödling and Vienna .*

Mödling

This was a favorite haunt of three composers: Beethoven (*Hauptstraße 79, Ach-senaugasse 6*), Schönberg and Webern. In the **Pfarrkirche St. Othmar** of 1523 the vaulting is supported by a dozen columns representing the 12 Apostles. The circular

12C charnel house has a frescoed crypt. Mödling also boasts Austria's oldest war memorial in the shape of the Husarentempel (temple of the hussars).

▶ *Go west on Spitalmühlgasse, which joins Brühlerstraße, following signs for the "Seegrotte" and E6/A21. After the football stadium turn right onto the Hauptstraße, right again after the bridge and park.*

Hinterbrühl

The unique **Seegrotte**★ (lake grotto, ◑☎ *Guided tour (45min) Apr-Oct daily 9am-noon, 1-5pm; Nov-Mar Mon-Fri 9am-noon, 1-3pm, Sat-Sun 9am-noon, 1-3.30pm.* ✆€6. ☎ *0 22 36/2 63 64)* contains the largest underground lake in Europe, which can be explored on motor boat tours. The lake was created in 1912, when 20 million l/4.4 million gal of water poured into the lower gallery of this former mine.

▶ *Return to Mödling on the B 11. Pass through the town, and still on the B 11 proceed along the Triester Straße towards Schwechat. The road crosses the E 59/A 2 autobahn. Follow the signs for Laxenburg.*

Laxenburg

The **Blauer Hof** (Blue Court) in this former Imperial summer residence owes its name to its Dutch builder, Sebastian Bloe, rather than to its color. Crown Prince Rudolf was born here on 21 August 1858. It's on Schlossplatz, which is also home to the **Pfarrkirche** (parish church) of 1699 whose interior has an attractive pulpit in gilded wood and ceiling frescoes after a design by Johann Michael Rottmayr.

Laxenburg's park (*enter from Hofstraße*) was laid out in the English style by Emperor Joseph II. Franz I added a lake with an island topped by the Franzensburg, a faux neo-Gothic castle built by Michael Riedl in the early 19C. Near the park entrance is the **Altes Schloss** where Karl VI signed the "Pragmatic Sanction" in 1713, making it possible for his daughter Maria Theresa to ascend the throne.

▶ *Return to Vienna on the E 59/A 2 autobahn.*

STIFT WILHERING★★★

OBERÖSTERREICH

The Cistercian abbey of Wilhering hugs the south bank of the Danube upstream from Linz. Starting out as a Romanesque complex, the building was transformed into one of Austria's most striking examples of the Rococo style in the 18C. The most celebrated architects of the day, including Joseph Mathias Götz, Josef Munggenast and Johann Michael Prunner, hoped to snag the commission, but unexpectedly the job went to an unknown local craftsman called Johann Haslinger. ▯ *Linzer Straße 4, A-4073,* ☎ *07226/23110, www.stiftwilhering.at*

▶ **Orient Yourself:** The abbey is 8km/5mi west of Linz.
▶ **Don't Miss:** Abbey church
▶ **Organizing Your Time:** Budget an hour or two for a visit.
▶ **Also See:** Stift St. Florian, Schloss-Museum Hohenbrunn

Tour

Abbey courtyard

The Baroque pomp of the abbey's courtyard is mitigated by a characteristically Cistercian sense of measure and balance. The church façade, a white and pink confection, is subdivided by piers. The portal is the only visible remnant of the original Romanesque church.

Abbey church

Apr-Sep daily 7am-6pm; Oct-Mar daily 8am-4pm.
Wilhering's church is an outstanding example of the Rococo style in European architecture. It would be difficult to surpass this profusion of decoration, richness of color, ingenuity of painting and sculpture and delicacy of stuccowork. The whole decor of the church evokes a timeless joy.

High altar

The high altar centers on a painting of the *Assumption of the Virgin Mary* by **Martin Altomonte**, which epitomizes the church's entire decorative scheme. Altomonte also executed the paintings for the **side chapels**★★, which were his last compositions. When he learned about the huge program of frescoes planned for the ceilings, he successfully got his nephew Bartolemeo hired for the job.

Frescoes

Bartolomeo Altomonte, although less talented than his uncle, nonetheless did remarkable work at Wilhering, painting almost two-thirds of the church ceiling. The nave is decorated with an enormous painting of Mary as Queen of Heaven, surrounded by her court of saints and angels. Altomonte worked closely with stucco artists on this composition. The painted figures, gilt decoration and sculpted angels all contribute to an atmosphere of triumphant celebration.

Stucco

The stucco artist **Franz Joseph Holzinger** came from St. Florian with his students to spend three consecutive summers (1739-41) decorating the church. However, their style was considered too academic and all their work was destroyed. The abbot then hired young stucco workers trained in southern Germany who had eschewed the cumbersome, overbearing compositions of the Late Baroque period and adopted a more delicate style.

The **dome** above the transept crossing is the realm of *trompe-l'œil* and illusion. An erudite architectural composition, painted by the Italian Francesco Messenta, it opens at the top on a glimpse of sky; the men chained to the Earth by their sins are protected by the Virgin Mary from divine wrath.

To the right of the choir stalls, the imposing **pulpit** is decked out in black and white stucco and gold and nicely matches the elegant **choir organ** built in 1746 by Nicolas Rumel of Linz. The composer Anton Bruckner was especially fond of it.

Great Organ

The part of the nave accommodating the organ is itself a monumental work of art consisting of a magnificently worked iron gate and an elegant gallery that directs the gaze upward towards the pipes. Overhead, a clock marks the passing of time and a purple curtain in *trompe-l'œil* hangs from the vault, its heavy folds drawn back to reveal the theatrical scene.

Cloisters

The cloisters are reached through a door *(left)* from the narthex. A pre-Gothic 13C **doorway** leads into the old **chapter-house**; a series of fine 18C paintings depicts episodes in the life of St Bernard.

WÖRTHER SEE★

KÄRNTEN

The Wörther See, a lake stretching for some 17km/10mi between Velden and Klagenfurt, receives little water from mountain streams and is therefore pleasantly warm (24-28oC/75-82oF in summer). Velden and Pörtschach are among the clutch of popular resort towns along the lakeshore. A screen of low hills sometimes hides the Karawanken, but a short stroll is generally enough to bring back into view the magnificent splendor of this mountain barrier extending from Austria into Slovenia and Italy. ▪ *Villacher Straße 19, A-9220 Velden, ☎ 0810/977088, www.woerthersee.at*

▶ **Orient Yourself:** This late is in the far south of Austria, close to the Slovenian border, about 14km/9mi southeast of Klagenfurt.
🐾 **Don't Miss:** Velden, Maria Wörth
🕐 **Organizing Your Time:** Plan a full day to cover this route at leisure.
Especially for Kids: WIldpark Rosegg
Also See: Klagenfurt, Maria Saal

South Shore of the Lake★

From Villach to Klagenfurt *76km/47mi*

At first the route runs through the Drava Valley, within sight of the Karawanken. In Velden, follow the road along the south shore of the lake. Note the site of the Maria Wörth promontory and the panorama from the Pyramidenkogel.

Villach★ *See Villach.*

▶ *From Villach take road no 84 as far as the east bank of the Gail.*

Velden on the Wörther See

Maria Gail

The core of this pilgrimage church is Romanesque, although it was transformed to the Gothic style around 1450 and only sports a few remaining frescoes from the late Romanesque period. The focal point is a valuable Late Gothic **altarpiece**★★ (north wall) carved in the early 16C in a Villach workshop. Its central panel depicts the *Coronation of the Virgin*. Outside, on the south wall, are some interesting stone sculptures depicting a sort of Last Judgment scene and believed to date back to around 1300.

The road continues to climb, offering a wide general view of the Villach basin where the Gail and the Drava converge before embracing the beautiful **Faaker See** and the solitary Mittagskogel (alt 2 143m/7 031ft). The road descends to the Drava Valley.

Wildpark Rosegg

◷*Apr-June, Sep-Oct daily 9am-5pm; Jul-Aug daily 9am-6pm. ⊜€6.50. ☎ 0 42 74/5 23 57; www.rosegg.at/tierpark*

🄺🄸🄳🅂This wildlife park was laid out almost 200 years ago when the old castle at Rosegg was demolished. A great variety of animals make their home here, including lynx, monkeys, wolves, deer, mouflon sheep, bison, boar, eagles and falcons.

Next to the wildlife park is **Schloss Rosegg** (◷*May-8 Oct Tue-Sun 10am-6pm, July-Aug daily; ⊜€5.50. ☎ 0 42 74/30 09; www.rosegg.at),* home to a small museum of historical wax figures, including Empress Elisabeth (Sisi) and Napoleon.

Velden★★

The elegant, long-established spa resort lies at the west end of the Wörther See and is easily recognized by its yellow castle right by the river. This was built as a summer residence by the local ruler, Bartholomäus Khevenhüller, between 1590 and 1603. A reconstruction after a fire in 1893 retained the 17C plan. The main doorway is surmounted with obelisks and bears, on the pediment, the Khevenhüller family coat of arms. A lively promenade and grand villas lend Villach the typical character of a chic lakeside resort, further enhanced by its casino.

Maria Wörth★

The towers of the pilgrimage churches of Maria Wörth, in an idyllic setting on a promontory in the Wörther See, together with the round tower of the charnel house

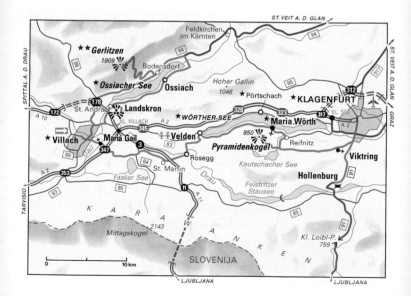

form a much photographed scene. Construction of the Gothic parish church went on from 1399 to 1540, although parts of the original Romanesque building were reused. The high altar of 1685 incorporates a *Virgin Mary and Child Enthroned* from the late 15C. The imposing Altar of the Holy Cross with its early-16C crucifix and the pulpit of 1761 complete the interior decor. The picture of the Madonna on the north wall of the chancel is a copy of the original gracing the church of Santa Maria del Popolo in Rome. The crypt is decorated with brightly painted floral motifs (17C).

In the chancel of the "**Winterkirche**" are **Romanesque murals**★ from the late 11C, the oldest in Carinthia and done in a style echoing Ottonian Romanesque.

Pyramidenkogel★

Turn right in Reifnitz, and drive 8km/5mi to the Pyramidenkogel.

A 54m/177ft high **viewing tower** (©*July-Aug daily 9am-9pm; June daily 9am-8pm; Apr, Oct daily 10am-6pm; May, Sep daily 9am-7pm.* €5.50. ☎ 0 42 73/24 43) crowns the summit (alt 850m/2 789ft). There is a fine **panoramic view**★★ over the great central valley of Carinthia, the Karawanken mountain barrier and, far to the west, the jagged Julian Alps. To the northeast lies the Ulrichsberg, looking like a sphinx emerging from the mass of hills. During the Celtic period this was one of the sacred mountains of Carinthia. In the foreground, the peninsula of Maria Wörth juts out into the waters of the lake.

Viktring

The abbey entrance is at the end of the village's main north-south street.

Viktring Abbey, founded by Bernard of Sponheim in 1142, is laid out around two vast courtyards with superimposed galleries. Its church was the only example east of the Rhine to be modeled on the abbey of Fontenay in Burgundy. The 14C saw the addition of Gothic ribbed vaulting and beautiful **stained-glass windows**, which are now partially obscured by the Early Baroque high altar of 1622. Restoration is underway on some remarkable 15C **ceiling frescoes**★.

▶ *Take road no 91 towards the Loibl pass. When it starts descending, turn left for the castle. Park a little before the fortified covered bridge.*

Schloss Hollenburg

The massive Hollenburg fortress, built during the 14C and 15C, commands the Drava Valley, here known as the Rosental. Although the castle exterior is relatively austere, the **interior courtyard**★ with its Renaissance arcades and outside staircase exudes an almost Italianate exuberance. There is a good **view**★ of the Karawanken from the balcony.

▶ *Return to road no 91 to enter Klagenfurt from the south.*

Klagenfurt★ ⬙ *See Klagenfurt.*

ZELL AM SEE★

SALZBURG
POPULATION 7 960 – ALT 757M/2 484FT

Zell am See enjoys a postcard-pretty location on the western shore of its name-sake lake and close to the Grossglocknerstraße mountain road and the beautiful Kapruner and Glemm valleys. The glacier-sheathed peaks of the Hohe Tauern, the rugged rocks of the Steinernes Meer and the soft Grasberge mountains define the landscape. The lively town has a beautifully laid-out pedestrian core and plenty of leisure facilities, including a swimming pool, ice-rink, golf course and riding center. In summer, Zell am See is the ideal starting point for hiking trips and excursions. *Brucker Bundesstraße 3, A-5710, ☎ 0 65 42/7 70, www.zellamsee.at*

▶ **Orient Yourself:** Zell am See is in western Austria, about 82km/51mi south of Salzburg.
Don't Miss: Pinzgauer Spaziergang
Also See: Großglockner Hochalpenstraße, Kaprunertal, Krimml Waterfalls

Ski area

In winter, the Schmittenhöhe massif provides a pleasant ski area with fairly gentle slopes at an altitude of between 760m/2 500ft and 2 000m/6 550ft. The upper sections can generally guarantee good snow cover from Christmas to April. Together with **Kaprun** (*see Kaprun*), Zell am See forms the **Europa-Sportregion,** which opens up a total of 150km/93mi of pistes on a combined ski pass.

Stadtpfarrkirche

Zell's 11C parish church has a beautiful façade in the Romanesque style. The interior bears the imprint of a number of periods, with a Romanesque nave, a narthex and

Zeller See

aisles in the Gothic style and Baroque ornamental elements. The 16C frescoes to the right of the altar are worth a closer look.

Schmittenhöhe★★

Alt 1 965m/6 447ft. *Schmittenhöhebahn cable-car* ⏱*20 May-9 June 9am-5pm; 10 June-22 Oct 8.30am-5pm; mid Nov-mid Apr 8.30am-5pm.* ☞*€19.90 roundtrip summer, one-day ski pass €37.50.* ☎ *0 65 42/78 90. www.schmitten.at*

Enjoy a splendid all-round view of the bold limestone massifs (Wilder Kaiser, Loferer and Leoganger Steinberge, Dachstein) and the sparkling glacial peaks of the Hohe Tauern (Grossvenediger, Sonnblick, Kitzsteinhorn, Grossglockner, Wiesbachhorn).

Pinzgauer Spaziergang (Pinzgau walk)★★

Allow about 6hr. Check with the tourist office about the schedule for the return bus from Saalbach. Take the Schmittenhöhe cable-car very early in the morning (purchase the ticket that includes the descent to Saalbach on the Schattberg-Xpress cable-car).

This hike is among the most famous in Austria. It starts from the Schmittenhöhebahn mountain station and runs at least 1 000m/3 300ft above the valley floor, crossing almost a dozen passes and often providing breathtaking **views**★★ of the surrounding mountains. Although it is not difficult, it is a rather long trek requiring a fair amount of stamina. Return is via the Schattberg X-press cable car down to Saalbach and from there by bus to Zell am See.

ZILLERTAL★★

TIROL

The Zillertal is among the most densely populated valleys and most important vacation destinations in the Tyrol. It covers a distance of about 60km/37mi from north to south, stretching from the Inn Valley to the Italian border. The upper, wide part of the valley lies in easily accessible low mountain countryside. After Mayrhofen, the most important resort in the region, it branches into four narrow valleys (Tuxertal, Zemmtal, Stilluppgrund and Zillergrund), which are hemmed in by the Zillertal Alps. This mountain chain, with mighty glaciers extending over almost 40km/25mi, is dominated by the **Hochfeller** (alt 3 510m/11 516ft) and the **Grosser Möseler** (alt 3 479m/11 414ft). *Schlitters, A-6262,* ☎ *0 52 88/8 71 87, www.zillertal.at*

▶ **Orient Yourself:** The valley is in western Austria, about 67km/42mi east of Innsbruck.

ⓖ **Don't Miss:** Gefrorene Wand, Hike to the Berliner Hütte

ⓒ **Also See:** Gerlos-Alpenstraße

Ski Area

The Zillertal Alps are primarily suitable for a more relaxed style of downhill skiing. There is no single integrated ski area but instead almost a dozen, rather scattered , massifs of modest size have been outfitted with ski lifts. The more interesting sections include the **Tux glacier** , **Mayrhofen-Finkenberg** , **Gerlos** and **Zell am Ziller.** A single ski pass is good for all areas, which are linked by buses. Good snow cover is not always guaranteed.

Major Resorts in the lower Valley

Zell am Ziller

Alt 575m/1 886ft. Zell am Ziller clusters round its **church**★, which was built in 1782 on an octagonal ground plan. The enormous, lantern-crowned dome was painted by Franz Anton Zeiller (1716-93) from Reutte with characters from the Old and New Testament grouped around the Trinity. In May, valley folks gather in Zell for the traditional "Gauderfest" festival which is celebrated with a procession, wrestling matches and the liberal consumption of the 20° proof Gauderbier, specially brewed for the occasion.

The town gives access to the family-friendly Zillertal Arena ski area with 115km/71mi of pistes and 47 ski lifts and is also a popular summer destination as the starting point for walking tours.

Mayrhofen 📨

Alt 630m/2 067ft. Mayrhofen lies 7km/4mi up the valley from Zell am Ziller and is the region's main tourist center with extensive lodging options, shopping opportunities and excellent sports facilities (including a swimming pool and ice rink). For over 100 years it has been highly reputed as a center for hikers and mountaineers. Skiing mainly takes place on the **Penken massif**, which soars as high as 2 250m/7 382ft (76km/47mi of pistes), and on the Ahorn massif.

Tuxertal★★★

From Mayrhofen to Hintertux *19km/12mi*

After Mayrhofen, the valley narrows noticeably and becomes increasingly steeper. The road passes through Finkenberg and Lanersbach at the foot of the Rastko-gel massif, beyond which the valley broadens out again level with Juns, providing an unobstructed view of the Tux glacier. The road ends in the small resort of **Hintertux** 📨 (alt 1 500m/4 921ft).

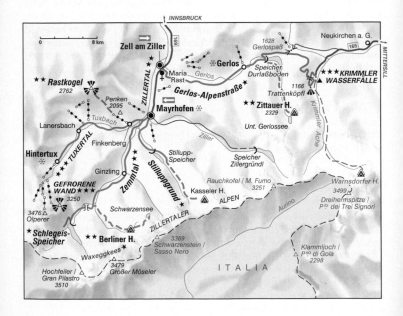

Ski slopes on the Tux glacier ⛷

By virtue of its good snow cover and large differences in altitude, this area is the most interesting for skiing in the entire Ziller Valley. Nineteen ski lifts lead to 86km/53mi of pistes at altitudes of between 1 500m/4 900ft and 3 250m/10 650ft. In winter, superb snow cover is found only above the first section (alt 2 100m/6 890ft), and in summer, only in the fourth section (alt 3 050-3 250m/10 000-10 650ft). The pistes at the Kaserer lifts are suitable for moderately good skiers, while the bumpy slopes on either side of the Lärmstange chair-lifts provide good opportunities for experienced skiers.

Gefrorene Wand★★★

Alt 3 250m/10 663ft. 3hr roundtrip. Ascent by two cable-cars and two chair-lifts. Thick-soled, water- and snowproof footwear, warm clothing and sunglasses are a must.

From the second section onwards, the eye roves over the vast ice formations of the Tux glacier and the rock face connecting Kleiner Kaserer and Armstange.

From the mountain station of the last chair-lift, the view is dominated by the pyramids of the **Olperer** (alt 3 476m/11 404ft) which towers above the gigantic Tux glacier. When visibility is good, it is possible to make out, to the north, the Kitzbühel Alps, the Karwendel mountains and the Zugspitzplatt. Walk 200m/220yd along the ski piste to a rocky peak in the shape of a bird's head.

There is a grand **panorama**★★★ over the Schlegeis-Stausee (a reservoir), which is dominated by the glacial cirque of the same name and flanked by the Hochfeiler and Grosser Möseler. Further to the left, you can see the glaciers of Waxeggkees and Hornkees at the foot of the Tuxerkamm ridge, and also the Schwarzenstein. In the background it is possible to make out the Dolomites (to the south) and also the Stubai and Ötztal Alps (to the west).

From the chair-lift, it is possible to climb up to the Gefrorene Wandspitze peak, from where there is a beautiful all-round view. Anyone wishing to go hiking on a glacier can walk down to the third section *(about 20min)*.

Hike up the Rastkogel★★

5hr roundtrip, difference in altitude of about 700m/2 300ft.

Travel up from Finkenberg (alt 840m/2 755ft), initially by cable-car, and then by chair-lift to the **Penken** (alt 2 095m/6 873ft) *(buy a return ticket)*. From the mountain station, a track leads gradually up to the Wanglalm. The route then continues upwards to the Wanglspitze peak and past the mountain station of the chair-lift from Vorderlanersbach to the Rastkogel. From the summit, there is a sweeping **panorama**★★ over the Zillertal Alps.

Zemmtal★★

From Mayrhofen to the Schlegeis-Speicher reservoir★

23km/14mi – toll after 15km/9mi. Allow a full day if including the hike to the Berliner Hütte (mountain lodge). The road is open from May to October. The journey can be made by bus from the station at Mayrhofen.

Drive up the valley from Mayrhofen towards Ginzling, cutting through a stretch of narrow, scenic **gorges**★. If you are traveling in anything larger than a passenger car or prefer to avoid this rather difficult section, you should go to the left through a long tunnel, although this robs the excursion of a large part of its charm.

After 8km/5mi you will reach **Ginzling**, a peaceful village at the fork of the Floitengrundtal and Gunggltal valleys. The journey continues to the Breitlahn parking lot, which is the start of the famous hike to the Berliner Hütte (mountain lodge). On the far side, the route continues on a single track **toll road**, on which traffic alternates through two long tunnels, as far as the Schlegeis-Speicher reservoir. The largest artificial lake in the area, it lies in a splendid **setting**★ at the foot of the Hochsteller massif and the Schlegeis glacial cirque. From the final bends in the road, there is an impressive **view**★ of the 131m/430ft high dam and of the Hochfeiler (alt 3 509m/11 512ft).

Hike to the Berliner Hütte★★

Park at the Breitlahn parking lot. Allow 5hr 15min roundtrip with a difference in altitude of 800m/2 625ft. The hike doesn't present technical difficulties but does require good stamina.

Large sections of the route are covered on a beautiful trail running alongside a mountain stream and leading through woods and over Alpine pastures. A good hour's walk brings you to the **Grawandhütte** (mountain lodge) (alt 1 636m/5 367ft), from where you can enjoy a **view**★ of the impressive rock walls of the Grosser Greiner and of the Schönbichl Horn with its small glacier, from which high waterfalls thunder.

On the climb up to the **Alpenrosenhütte**, vegetation thins out and the stream becomes ever more tempestuous. Immediately after the lodge, the magnificent Waxegg glacial cirque, or **Waxeggkees**★, suddenly comes into view. After a further 30min you will finally arrive, up a steep path, at the Berliner Hütte, an imposing mountain hut dating from 1898. It lies amid magnificent **Alpine scenery**★★ dominated by the Grosser Möseler, the Waxeggkees and the Hornkees.

Hikers with a particularly high level of stamina may like to carry on towards the **Schwarzensee Lake**. After only 30min, there is a beautiful **view**★ of the Schwarzenstein glacier, the Grosser Mörchner and the Zsigmondy peak.

Stilluppgrund★

From Mayrhofen to the Stillupptal waterfall inn

9km/6mi on a toll road. Journey by bus possible.

From Mayrhofen's Hauptstraße, turn left after a small bridge onto Ahornbahnstraße. A steeply rising road snakes its way uphill, passing through dense forest, small gorges and narrow Alpine pastures crammed in between mighty walls of rock.

The road leads to the far left end of the **Stilluppdamm** (alt 1 130m/3 707ft), from where there is a beautiful **view** across the lake, which lies in the middle of a rugged, unspoiled **natural landscape**★ and is framed on both sides by a waterfall. The road continues through a tunnel as far as a pretty inn, beyond which it is closed to traffic. It is possible to travel by bus to the **Grüne-Wand-Hütte** (alt 1 438m/4 718ft) and to hike from that point to the **Kasseler Hütte** (alt 2 177m/7 142ft) in about 2hr.

ZÜRS

VORARLBERG
POPULATION 130 – ALT 1 716M/5 630FT
LOCAL MAP SEE ARLBERGGEBIET

Zürs is a major winter sports resort that, along with Lech, Stuben and St. Anton, forms part of the Arlberg ski region. For centuries, the valley remained largely uninhabited in winter because of abundant snow fall, steep terrain and the associated risk of avalanches. All that changed in 1900 when the completion of the road over the Flexenpass brought a sudden influx of visitors. The first ski competitions were organized as early as 1906, the pioneers of modern skiing met here in the 1920s and Austria's first ski lifts were put into operation in 1937. Thanks to a deliberate effort to limit its growth, Zürs has remained a rather small if upscale resort with excellent leisure facilties, gourmet restaurants and nightclubs. 🏠 A-6763, ☎ 0 55 83/22 45, www.lech-zuers.at

▶ **Orient Yourself:** Zürs is in far western Austria about 112km/70mi west of Innsbruck and only 5km/3mi from Lech.
🅿 **Parking:** There's free parking by the Trittkopfbahn cable-car.
♿ **Also See:** Arlberggebiet

Ski Slopes

Although the ski area at Zürs is by no means vast, it is nevertheless of outstanding quality. The Rüfikopf, Family run and Muggengrat-Zürsersee pistes are suitable for beginners, while moderately skilled skiers might prefer the Palmen, Steinmännle and Madloch-Zürsersee pistes. More proficient skiers will be drawn to the magnificent **Muggengrat-Täli** piste and the unique run down from the Madlochjoch to Lech, which opens up magnificent **views**★★ over the Lechtal Alps. Besides this, there are wonderful opportunities for off-piste skiing alongside the Madloch and Muggengrat chair-lifts.

Zürs am Arlberg

Wiesenhofer/ Österreich Werbung

Zürs' location makes it the ideal starting point for excursions into the Arlberg area. The Lech snowfields are a perfect training ground for moderately good skiers, while experts prefer the steep pistes of the Valluga at St. Christoph or St. Anton (*bus service*). The only drawbacks of the Arlberg district are the lack of high-altitude peaks and of skiable links between the areas.

Viewpoints

Trittkopf★
Alt 2 423m/7 949ft. *Allow 20min roundtrip. Cable-car* ◷*Dec-Apr daily 8.30am-4pm.* ☜*€10.50 roundtrip.* ☎ *0 55 83/2 38 80.*
Enjoy a beautiful **view** of Zürs and the surrounding area, towering above which are the mighty crags of Hasenfluh, Flexenspitze and Wildgrubenspitze. Look south to the Arlberg pass road with the Verwall group, the Rätikon and the Swiss Alps.

Madlochjoch★
Alt 2 438m/7 999ft.(*Skiers only via the Seekopf and Madlochjoch chair-lifts*) offers views of the Schafberg from the mountain station, while **Muggengrat**★ (Alt 2 450m/8 038ft - *same conditions as above*) presents a scenic **Alpine landscape**★, from which the crags of Hasenfluh and Flexenspitze stand out in particular. The view stretches as far as the Verwall range to the south, and Lech and Oberlech at the foot of the Widderstein to the north.

STIFT ZWETTL

NIEDERÖSTERREICH

The great Cistercian abbey of Zwettl lies in a bend of the valley of the River Kamp, one of the most romantic in the Waldviertel. It was founded in 1137 by Hadmar I von Kuenring, whose dynasty ruled over the Waldviertel for centuries. The abbey flourished in the Middle Ages and again after the Counter Reformation. It even survived Joseph II's reforms and the Nazi period unscathed, so that today it is still a vigorous spiritual, cultural and economic hub of the region. ⚑ *Landstr. 10, A-3910,* ☎ *0 28 22/2 02 02 17, www.stift-zwettl.at*

▶ **Orient Yourself:** The abbey is in the Waldviertel in northern Austria, about 110km/62mi northeast of Linz and 122km/76mi northwest of Vienna.
⚐ **Also See:** Schloss Greillenstein, Schloss Rosenburg, Stift Altenburg

Tour

◷☞Guided tour (1hr) July-Sep Mon-Sat 10am, 11am, 2pm, 3pm and 4pm, Sun 11am, 2pm, 3pm and 4pm; May-June, Oct same schedule except no tours at 4pm. ☜€6.

Stiftskirche (Abbey church)★
The basic structure of the 14C church is Gothic but the requisite Baroque makeover in the 18C added the elegant **west front**★★ and slender tower topped with a curving roof and a lantern.
The **high altar**★ provides the majestic backdrop for a realistic representation of an oak tree, which recalls both the legend of the abbey's foundation (it is said to be built

Wiesenhofer/ÖSTERREICH WERBUNG

Zwettl Abbey

on the spot where an oak grew green leaves in winter) and also the Tree of Salvation. The **choir stalls**★ are richly inlaid and bear gilded vases and statues.

Kreuzgang★

The **cloisters**, completed in 1240, are a fine example of the transitional style between Romanesque and Gothic. In the hexagonal *lavatorium*, or washing place, you are surrounded by small columns with crocketed or plain vase capitals.

Kapitelsaal

The **chapter-house** is the oldest part of the abbey, dating from after 1175. Vaulting ribs radiate from a massive central pillar, dividing the room into four bays.

INDEX

INDEX

INDEX

ACCOMMODATIONS

RESTAURANTS

MAPS AND PLANS

LIST OF MAPS

MAPS AND PLANS

COMPANION PUBLICATIONS

MICHELIN MAP 730 AUSTRIA

A road map with tourist information, at a scale of 1:400 000, with an index of place names and maps of the Salzburg and Vienna conurbations.

... AND FOR GETTING TO AUSTRIA:

Michelin map 719 Germany, Austria, Benelux, Czech Republic

- a road map with tourist information, at a scale of 1: 1 000 000

Michelin map 970 Europe

- a road map with tourist information, at a scale of 1: 3 000 000, with an index of place names

Michelin Road Atlas Europe

- spiral-bound, with an index of place names, more than 40 states, 73 city and conurbation maps, including Salzburg and Vienna

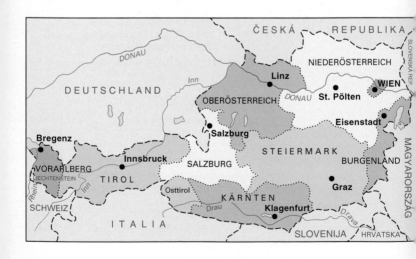

Legend

	Sight	Seaside Resort	Winter Sports Resort	Spa
Highly recommended	★★★	☼☼☼	❄❄❄	‡‡‡
Recommended	★★	☼☼	❄❄	‡‡
Interesting	★	☼	❄	‡

Tourism

◉ ▭	Sightseeing route with departure point indicated	AZ B	Map co-ordinates locating sights
🛉 🛉 🛉 🛉	Ecclesiastical building	🛈	Tourist information
⬙ ⬙	Synagogue – Mosque	⌒ ⁖	Historic house, castle – Ruins
▭	Building (with main entrance)	�” ✿	Dam – Factory or power station
▪	Statue, small building	☆ ⌒	Fort – Cave
⊥	Wayside cross	⊤	Prehistoric site
◎	Fountain	▼ W	Viewing table – View
●━━■━	Fortified walls – Tower – Gate	▲	Miscellaneous sight

Recreation

🏇	Racecourse	🚶	Waymarked footpath
⛸	Skating rink	◆	Outdoor leisure park/centre
≋ ▨	Outdoor, indoor swimming pool	🎢	Theme/Amusement park
⛵	Marina, moorings	⅄	Wildlife/Safari park, zoo
⌂	Mountain refuge hut	❀	Gardens, park, arboretum
□━■━□	Overhead cable-car	◎	Aviary, bird sanctuary
🚂	Tourist or steam railway		

Additional symbols

══ ══	Motorway (unclassified)	⊗ ⊙	Post office – Telephone centre
❶ ❶	Junction: complete, limited	⊠	Covered market
▭▭ ══	Pedestrian street	•✕•	Barracks
⋮⋮⋮⋮	Unsuitable for traffic, street subject to restrictions	△	Swing bridge
▦▦ ----	Steps – Footpath	⊍ ✕	Quarry – Mine
🚆 🚌	Railway – Coach station	B F	Ferry (river and lake crossings)
□⊦⊦⊦⊦	Funicular – Rack-railway	⛴	Ferry services: Passengers and cars
━━ ⬤	Tram – Metro, underground	⛵	Foot passengers only
Bert (R.)...	Main shopping street	③	Access route number common to MICHELIN maps and town plans

Abbreviations and special symbols

G	Police (Gendarmerie)	R	Town hall (Rathaus)
J	Law courts (Justizgebäude)	T	Theatre (Theater)
🅻	Provincial capital (Landeshauptstadt)	U	University (Universität)
L	Provincial government (Landhaus)	🅿	Park and Ride
M	Museum (Museum)	20	National road with right of way (Vorfahrtsberechtigte Bundesstraße)
POL.	Police (Polizei)	128	Other federal roads (Sonstige Bundesstraße)
		◙	Of special interest to children

NB: The German letter ß (eszett) has been used throughout this guide.

Michelin North America
One Parkway South – Greenville, SC 29615 USA
☎ 800-423-0485
www.MichelinTravel.com
michelin.guides@us.michelin.com

Manufacture française des pneumatiques Michelin

Société en commandite par actions au capital de 304 000 000 EUR
Place des Carmes-Déchaux – 63000 Clermont-Ferrand (France)
R.C.S. Clermont-Fd B 855 200 507

© Michelin, Propriétaires-éditeurs
Dépot légal février 2007 – ISSN 0763-1383
Printed in France: janvier 2007

Printing and Binding: IME